# POET'S MARKET 2017

includes a one-year online subscription to **Poet's Market** on

WritersMarket.com

*Where & How to Sell What You Write*

## THE ULTIMATE MARKET RESEARCH TOOL FOR WRITERS

To register your *Poet's Market 2017* book and **start your one-year online genre-only subscription**, scratch off the block below to reveal your activation code, then go to www.WritersMarket.com. Find the box that says "Purchased a Deluxe Edition?" then click on "Activate Your Account" and enter the activation code. It's that easy!

## UPDATED MARKET LISTINGS FOR YOUR INTEREST AREA
## EASY-TO-USE SEARCHABLE DATABASE • RECORD-KEEPING TOOLS
## PROFESSIONAL TIPS & ADVICE • INDUSTRY NEWS

Your purchase of *Poet's Market* gives you access to updated listings related to this genre of writing (valid through 12/31/17). For just $9.99, you can upgrade your subscription and get access to listings from all of our best-selling Market Books. Visit **www.WritersMarket.com** for more information.

# WritersMarket.com
*Where & How to Sell What You Write*

## Activate your WritersMarket.com subscription to get instant access to:

- **UPDATED LISTINGS IN YOUR WRITING GENRE:** Find additional listings that didn't make it into the book, updated contact information, and more. WritersMarket.com provides the most comprehensive database of verified markets available anywhere.

- **EASY-TO-USE SEARCHABLE DATABASE:** Looking for a specific magazine or book publisher? Just type in its name. Or widen your prospects with the Advanced Search. You can also search for listings that have been recently updated!

- **PERSONALIZED TOOLS:** Store your best-bet markets, and use our popular recording-keeping tools to track your submissions. Plus, get new and updated market listings, query reminders, and more every time you log in!

- **PROFESSIONAL TIPS & ADVICE:** From pay-rate charts to sample query letters, and from how-to articles to Q&As with literary agents, we have the resources writers need.

YOU'LL GET ALL OF THIS WITH YOUR INCLUDED SUBSCRIPTION TO

WritersMarket.com
*Where & How to Sell What You Write*

◀ 30ᵀᴴ ANNUAL EDITION ▶

# POET'S MARKET

## 2017

Robert Lee Brewer, Editor

WD
WRITER'S DIGEST
BOOKS
WritersDigest.com
Cincinnati, Ohio

Publisher: Phil Sexton

Writer's Market website: www.writersmarket.com
Writer's Digest website: www.writersdigest.com

Distributed in Canada by Fraser Direct
100 Armstrong Avenue
Georgetown, Ontario, Canada L7G 5S4
Tel: (905) 877-4411

Distributed in the U.K. and Europe by F&W Media International
Brunel House, Newton Abbot, Devon, TQ12 4PU, England
Tel: (+44) 1626-323200, Fax: (+44) 1626-323319
E-mail: postmaster@davidandcharles.co.uk

ISSN: 0883-5470
ISBN-13: 978-1-4403-4778-8
ISBN-10: 1-4403-4778-6

**Attention Booksellers:** This is an annual directory of F + W Media, Inc. Return deadline for this edition is December 31, 2017.

Edited by: Robert Lee Brewer
Designed by: Alexis Estoye
Production coordinated by: Debbie Thomas

# CONTENTS

**INDEXES**

# FROM THE EDITOR

Do you consider an audience when you write poetry? When I first started writing poems, I did so with an audience in mind. I wasn't selling out. In fact, I wasn't selling anything. But I did want to know if my poems were effective and affective.

Over the years, my writing technique has evolved, and I've found more success at figuring out what appeals most to publishers and readers. As a result, I receive more acceptances and fewer rejections than when I started submitting my writing.

The link between craft and publication success is precisely why this edition of *Poet's Market* includes articles covering the business, promotion, and craft of poetry. This edition includes advice on finishing poems, creating sonnets, homegrown promotions, keeping poetry alive, and so much more.

Of course, the real meat of this book has always been and will always be the hundreds of listings of publishers, publications, contests, and more. And we've got you covered with completely updated information and scores of listings that were not in the previous edition.

Plus, don't forget to take advantage of your free poetry-related webinar by heading to http://www.writersmarket.com/pm17-webinar.

Until next time, keep poeming!


Robert Lee Brewer

Senior Content Editor, *Poet's Market*
www.writersdigest.com/editor-blogs/poetic-asides
twitter.com/robertleebrewer

# HOW TO USE POET'S MARKET

Delving into the pages of *Poet's Market* implies a commitment—you've decided to take that big step and begin submitting your poems for publication. How do you *really* begin, though? Here are eight quick tips to help make sense of the marketing/submission process:

**1. BE AN AVID READER.** The best way to hone your writing skills (besides writing) is to immerse yourself in poetry of all kinds. It's essential to study the masters; however, from a marketing standpoint, it's equally vital to read what your contemporaries are writing and publishing. Read journals and magazines, chapbooks and collections, anthologies for a variety of voices; scope out the many poetry sites on the Internet. Develop an eye for quality, and then use that eye to assess your own work. Don't try to publish until you know you're writing the best poetry you're capable of producing.

**2. KNOW WHAT YOU LIKE TO WRITE—AND WHAT YOU WRITE BEST.** Ideally, you should be experimenting with all kinds of poetic forms, from free verse to villanelles. However, there's sure to be a certain style with which you feel most comfortable, that conveys your true "voice." Whether you favor more formal, traditional verse or avant-garde poetry that breaks all the rules, you should identify which markets publish work similar to yours. Those are the magazines and presses you should target to give your submissions the best chance of being read favorably—and accepted.

**3. LEARN THE "BUSINESS" OF POETRY PUBLISHING.** Poetry may not be a high-paying writing market, but there's still a right way to go about the "business" of submitting and publishing poems. Learn all you can by reading writing-related books and magazines. Read the articles in this book for plenty of helpful advice. Surf the Internet for a wealth of sites filled with writing advice, market news and informative links.

**4. RESEARCH THE MARKETS.** Study the listings in *Poet's Market* thoroughly; these present submission guidelines, editorial preferences and editors' comments as well as contact information (names, postal and e-mail addresses, and website URLs). In addition, the indexes in the back of this book provide insights into what an editor or publisher may be looking for.

However, studying market listings alone won't cut it. The best way to gauge the kinds of poetry a market publishes is to read several issues of a magazine/journal or several of a press's books to get a feel for the style and content of each. Websites may include poetry samples, reviews, archives of past issues, exclusive content, and especially submission guidelines. (If the market is an online publication, the current issue will be available in its entirety.) Submission guidelines are pure gold for the specific information they provide. However you acquire them—by SASE or e-mail, online, or in a magazine itself—make them an integral part of your market research.

**5. START SLOWLY.** It may be tempting to send your work directly to *The New Yorker* or *Poetry*, but try sending your work to less competitive markets as well. As you gain confidence and experience (and increased skill in your writing), you can move on to more recognized markets. Although it may tax your patience, slow and steady progress is a proven route to success.

**6. BE PROFESSIONAL.** Professionalism is not something you should "work up to." Make it show in your first submission, from the way you prepare your manuscript to the attitude you project in your communications with editors.

Follow those guidelines. Submit a polished manuscript. Choose poems carefully with the editor's needs in mind. Such practices show respect for the editor, the publication and the process; and they reflect *your* self-respect and the fact that you take your work seriously. Editors love that; and even if your work is rejected, you've made a good first impression that could help your chances with your next submission.

## KEY TO ICONS & ABBREVIATIONS

⊘ market does not accept unsolicited submissions

☼ Canadian market

➲ market located outside of the U.S. and Canada

⑤ market pays

⌘— tips to break into a specific market

○ market welcomes submissions from beginning poets

◑ market prefers submissions from skilled, experienced poets; will consider work from beginning poets

● market prefers submissions from poets with a high degree of skill and experience

◎ market has a specialized focus

**7. KEEP TRACK OF YOUR SUBMISSIONS.** First, do *not* send out the only copies of your work. There are no guarantees your submission won't get lost in the mail, misplaced in a busy editorial office, or vanish into a black hole if the publication or press closes down. Create a special file folder for poems you're submitting. Even if you use a word processing program and store your manuscripts digitally, keep a hard copy file as well (and be sure to back up your electronic files).

Second, establish a tracking system so you always know which poems are where. This can be extremely simple: index cards, a chart created with word processing or database software, or even a simple notebook used as a log. (You can enlarge and photocopy the Submission Tracker in this book or use it as a model to design your own version.) Note the titles of the poems submitted (or the title of the collection if you're submitting a book/chapbook manuscript); the name of the publication, press, or contest; date sent; estimated response time; and date returned *or* date accepted. Additional information you may want to log: the name of the editor/contact, date the accepted piece is published and/or issue number of the magazine, type/amount of pay received, rights acquired by the publication or press, and any pertinent comments.

Without a tracking system, you risk forgetting where and when manuscripts were submitted. This is even more problematic if you simultaneously send the same manuscripts to different magazines, presses or contests. And if you learn of an acceptance by one magazine or publisher, you *must* notify the others that the poem or collection you sent them is no longer available. You run a bigger chance of overlooking someone without an organized approach. This causes hard feelings among editors you may have inconvenienced, hurting your chances with these markets in the future.

**8. DON'T FEAR REJECTION. LEARN FROM IT.** No one enjoys rejection, but every writer faces it. The best way to turn a negative into a positive is to learn as much as you can from your rejections. Don't let them get you down. A rejection slip isn't a permission slip to doubt yourself, condemn your poetry or give up.

Look over the rejection. Did the editor provide any comments about your work or reasons why your poems were rejected? Probably he or she didn't. Editors are extremely busy and don't necessarily have time to comment on rejections. If that's the case, move on to the next magazine or publisher you've targeted and send your work out again.

If, however, the editor *has* commented on your work, pay attention. It counts for something that the editor took the time and trouble to say anything, however brief, good or bad. And consider any remark or suggestion with an open mind. You don't have to agree, but you shouldn't automatically disregard the feedback, either. Tell your ego to sit down and be quiet, then use the editor's comments to review your work from a new perspective. You might be surprised by how much you'll learn from a single scribbled word in the margin— or how encouraged you'll feel from a simple "Try again!" written on the rejection slip.

| Poem Title | Publication/Contest | Editor/Contact | Date Sent | Date Returned | Date Accepted | Date Published | Pay Recieved | Comments |
|---|---|---|---|---|---|---|---|---|
| | | | | | | | | |
| | | | | | | | | |
| | | | | | | | | |
| | | | | | | | | |
| | | | | | | | | |
| | | | | | | | | |
| | | | | | | | | |
| | | | | | | | | |
| | | | | | | | | |
| | | | | | | | | |
| | | | | | | | | |
| | | | | | | | | |
| | | | | | | | | |

## SUBMISSION TRACKER

# FREQUENTLY ASKED QUESTIONS

The following FAQ (Frequently Asked Questions) section provides the expert knowledge you need to submit your poetry in a professional manner. Answers to most basic questions, such as "How many poems should I send?," "How long should I wait for a reply?" and "Are simultaneous submissions okay?" can be found by simply reading the listings in the Magazines/Journals and Book/Chapbook Publishers sections. Also, see the Glossary of Listing terms.

## Can I submit handwritten poems?

Usually, no. Now and then a publisher or editor makes an exception and accepts handwritten manuscripts. However, check the preferences stated in each listing. If no mention is made, assume your poetry should be typed or computer-printed.

## How should I format my poems for online and print publications?

If you're submitting poems by regular mail (also referred to as *postal mail* or *snail mail*), follow this format:

Poems should be printed on white 8½×11 paper of at least 20 lb. weight. Left, right and bottom margins should be at least one inch. Starting ½ inch from the top of the page, type your name, address, telephone number, e-mail address and number of lines in the poem in the *upper right* corner, in individual lines, single-spaced. Space down about six lines and type the poem title, either centered or flush left. The title may appear in all caps or in upper and lower case. Space down another two lines (at least) and begin to type your poem. Poems are usually single-spaced, although some magazines may request double-spaced submissions. (Be alert to each market's preferences.) Double-space between stanzas. Type one poem to a page. For poems longer than one page, type your name in the *upper left* corner; on the next line, type a key word from the title of your poem, the page number, and indicate whether the stanza begins or is continued on the new page (i.e., MOTHMAN, Page 2, continue stanza *or* begin new stanza).

If you're submitting poems by e-mail:

In most cases, editors will request that poems be pasted within the body of your e-mail, *not* sent as attachments. Many editors prefer this format because of the danger of viruses, the possibility of software incompatibility, and other concerns associated with e mail attachments. Editors who consider e-mail attachments taboo may even delete the message without opening the attachment.

Of course, other editors do accept, and even prefer e-mail submissions as attachments. This information should be clearly stated in the market listing. If it's not, you're probably safer submitting your poems in the body of the e-mail.

Note, too, the number of poems the editor recommends including in the e-mail submission. If no quantity is given specifically for e-mails, go with the number of poems an editor recommends submitting in general. Identify your submission with a notation in the subject line. While some editors simply want the words "Poetry Submission," others want poem titles. Check the market listing for preferences. **Note:** Because of spam, filters and other concerns, some editors are strict about what must be printed in the subject line and how. If you're uncertain about any aspect of e-mail submission formats, double-check the website (if available) for information or contact the publication for directions.

Some publications may also accept submissions only via online submission forms, such as Submittable or Submishmash. These typically require setting up a log in and then either pasting the poems into a text box or attaching a digital file.

## What is a chapbook? How is it different from a regular poetry book?

A chapbook is a booklet, averaging 24-50 pages in length (some are shorter), usually digest-sized (5½×8½, although chapbooks can come in all sizes, even published within the pages of a magazine). Typically, a chapbook is saddle-stapled with a soft cover (card or special paper); chapbooks can also be produced with a plain paper cover the same weight as the pages, especially if the booklet is photocopied.

A chapbook is a much smaller collection of poetry than a full-length book (which runs anywhere from 50 pages to well over 100 pages, longer for "best of" collections and retrospectives). There are probably more poetry chapbooks being published than full-length books, and that's an important point to consider. Don't think of the chapbook as a poor relation to the full-length collection. While it's true a chapbook won't attract big reviews, qualify for major prizes or find national distribution through chain bookstores, it's a terrific way for a poet to build an audience (and reputation) in increments, while developing the kind of publishing history that may attract the attention of a book publisher one day.

Although some presses consider chapbooks through a regular submission process, many choose manuscripts through competitions. Check each publisher's listing for requirements, send for guidelines or visit the website (absolutely vital if a competition is involved), and check out some sample chapbooks the press has already produced (usually available from the press itself). Most chapbook publishers are as choosy as book publishers about the quality of work they accept. Submit your best poems in a professional manner.

## How do I format a collection of poems to submit to a book/chapbook publisher?

Before you send a manuscript to a book/chapbook publisher, request guidelines (or consult the publisher's website, if available). Requirements vary regarding formatting, query letters and samples, length, and other considerations. Usually you will use 8½×11, 20 lb. white paper; set left, right and bottom margins of at least one inch; put your name and title of your collection in the top left corner of every page; limit poems to one per page (although poems certainly may run longer than one page); and number pages consecutively. Individual publisher requirements might include a title page, table of contents, credits page (indicating where previously published poems originally appeared) and biographical note.

If you're submitting your poetry book or chapbook manuscript to a competition, you *must* read and follow the guidelines. Failure to do so could disqualify your manuscript. Guidelines for a competition might call for an official entry form to accompany the submission, a special title page, a minimum and maximum number of pages, and specific formatting instructions (such as paginating the manuscript and not putting the poet's name on any of the manuscript pages).

## What is a cover letter?

A cover letter is your introduction to the editor, telling him or her a little about yourself and your work. Most editors indicate their cover letter preferences in their listings. If an editor states a cover letter is "required," absolutely send one! It's also better to send one if a cover letter is "preferred." Experts disagree on the necessity and appropriateness of cover letters, so use your own judgment when preferences aren't clear in the listing.

A cover letter should be professional but also allow you to present your work in a personal manner. Keep your letter brief, no more than one page. Address your letter to the correct contact person. (Use "Poetry Editor" if no contact name appears in the listing.) Include your name, address, phone number and e-mail address (if available). If a biographical note is requested, include two to three lines about your background, interests, why you write poetry, etc. Avoid praising yourself or your poems in your letter (your submission should speak for itself). Include titles (or first lines) of the poems you're submitting. You may list a few of your most recent publishing credits, but no more than five; and keep in mind that some editors find publishing credits tiresome—they're more interested in the quality of the work you're submitting to *them*.

Show your familiarity with the magazine to which you're submitting: comment on a poem the magazine published, tell the editor why you chose to submit to her magazine, mention poets the magazine has published. Use a business-style format for a professional appearance and proofread carefully; typos, misspellings and other errors make a poor first impression. Remember that editors are people, too. Respect, professionalism and kindness go a long way in poet/editor relationships.

## What is an SASE?

An SASE is a self-addressed, stamped envelope—and you should never send a submission by regular mail without one. Also include a SASE if you send an inquiry to an editor. If your submission is too large for an envelope (for instance, a bulky book-length collection of poems), use a box and include a self-addressed mailing label with adequate return postage paper-clipped to it.

## What does it mean when an editor says "no previously published" poems?

If your poem appears *anywhere* in print for a public audience, it's considered "previously published." That includes magazines, anthologies, websites and online journals, and even printed programs (say for a church service, wedding, etc.). See the explanation for rights below, especially *second serial (reprint) rights* and *all rights* for additional concerns about previously published material.

One exception to the above guidelines is if your poem appears online in a *private* poetry forum, critique group, etc. As long as the site is private (i.e., a password is required to view and participate), your poem isn't considered "published." However, if your poem is printed on an online forum or bulletin board that's available for public viewing, even if you must use a password to post the poem or to comment, then your poem is considered "published" as far as rights are concerned.

## What rights should I offer for my poems?

Editors usually indicate in their listings what rights they acquire. Most journals and magazines license *first rights* (a.k.a. *first serial rights*), which means the poet offers the right to publish the poem for the first time in any periodical. All other rights to the material remain with the poet. (Note that some editors state that rights to poems "revert to poets upon publication" when first rights are acquired.) When poems are excerpted from a book prior to publication and printed in a magazine/journal, this is also called *first serial rights*. The addition of *North American* indicates the editor is the first to publish a poem in a U.S. or Canadian periodical. The poem may still be submitted to editors outside of North America or to those who acquire reprint rights.

When a magazine/journal licenses *one-time rights* to a poem (also known as *simultaneous rights*), the editor has *nonexclusive* rights to publish the poem once. The poet may submit that same poem to other publications at the same time (usually markets that don't have overlapping audiences).

Editors/publishers open to submission of work already published elsewhere seek *second serial (reprint) rights*. The poet is obliged to inform them where and when the poem previously appeared so they can give proper credit to the original publication. In essence, chapbook or book collections license reprint rights, listing the magazines in which poems previously appeared somewhere in the book (usually on the copyright page or separate credits page).

If a publisher or editor requires you to relinquish *all rights*, be aware that you're giving up ownership of that poem or group of poems. You cannot resubmit the work elsewhere, nor can you include it in a poetry collection without permission or by negotiating for reprint rights to be returned to you. It's highly recommended that poets refuse such an arrangement.

## What is a copyright? Should I have my poems copyrighted before I submit them for publication?

Copyright is a proprietary right that gives you the power to control your work's reproduction, distribution and public display or performance, as well as its adaptation to other forms. In other words, you have the legal right to the exclusive publication, sale or distribution of your poetry. What's more, your "original works of authorship" are protected as soon as they are "fixed in a tangible form of expression," i.e., written down or recorded. Since March 1989, copyright notices are no longer required to secure protection, so it's not necessary to include them on your poetry manuscript. Also, in many editors' minds, copyright notices signal the work of amateurs who are distrustful and paranoid about having work stolen.

If you still want to indicate copyright, use the © symbol or the word *copyright*, your name and the year. If you wish, you can register your copyright with the Copyright Office (directions and form available for download from www.copyright.gov). Since paying per poem is costly and impractical, you may prefer to copyright a group of unpublished poems for that single fee.

# HOW TO INCREASE YOUR ODDS OF PUBLICATION

*by Sage Cohen*

Writing poetry is an art, and so is the process of submitting your poems for publication. If you'd like to increase your odds of getting noticed and getting published, this article can help you align your best work with the right opportunities—so you can give your poems the chance they deserve.

## IDENTIFY THE RIGHT PUBLICATIONS FOR YOUR POETRY

You'll have the greatest odds of publication when you submit your poems to journals or contests that are most suited to your work—and therefore most likely to appreciate it. If you're not sure how to identify such possibilities, consider the following:

### Read the work of poets you love

A good way to get a feel for publishing possibilities is by reviewing the acknowledgments pages of the poetry collections you admire. If you connect to a particular poet's work, chances are good that your poetry could also be well suited to the journals where s/he has been published.

### Do your due diligence

Let's say you've collected a list of possible journals and contests based on the tip above. And let's say you've never sent out work for publication before. You can research here in *Poet's Market* to learn more about how your poetry and these opportunities might line up. For example, you'll want to submit only to journals that say they publish work by emerging as well as established poets. You'll want to confirm that contest submission fees and guidelines are in alignment with what you're willing to send and spend. And you may want to make sure your themes, poetic forms, and approach to language are compatible with the publication's description of what it is seeking. I also suggest learning what you can about the editors or contest judge(s)—and reading their poetry, if possible, so you get a feeling for their personal aesthetic.

## Always experience a journal before submitting

Before submitting your work to a publication, purchase its latest issue or view content online to get a sense of the poets and poems it features. Also consider how the publication's front cover, inside art, website design, production, paper quality, and font choice create a particular kind of experience. If you can imagine seeing your poetry in these pages, that's a good indication that the journal or site may be the right fit for you.

## Track what you learn to grow your knowledge base

I suggest creating a simple system—a document, binder, or folder—where you track what you've learned about each publication and record your thinking about how your poems align or do not align. This way, you'll have a growing knowledge base about the poetry market—and how various opportunities may be suited to your goals—as you investigate, submit and publish over time.

# CHOOSE THE RIGHT POEM/S

When you've chosen a publication or contest to which you'd like to submit, it's time to gather the poems for this opportunity. Consider running the poems you are considering through these filters of inquiry:

## Does something significant or resonant happen?

Poems get editors' attention when they introduce a new possibility, provide a palpable experience or revelation, and say something in a way it has never been spoken (or written) before. Ask yourself:

- What happens in this poem? (Or, if the poem is nonnarrative, do the language, sound, and/or imagery create the kind of experience or journey I intended?)
- If this poem is about or addressed to someone I know, does it also reveal something meaningful or relevant to people outside of the dynamic?
- What is discovered or transformed or revealed?

Because it can be tricky to experience your own, highly subjective material objectively, you may want to share your poems with a reader or two you trust and ask these questions of them. If you're not sure you are creating an experience that has impact or resonance, your poem may not yet be ready for publication.

## Have I found something fresh to say about a familiar theme?

If you're writing about a historical person or event or one that's been covered in the news in recent years, chances are good that most readers will have a good handle on the facts. To ensure that your poem makes an impact, ask yourself:

- What happens in this poem that is fresh, surprising, and different than the information already available on this topic?
- How is this poem departing from the work of "reporting" and moving into the territory of "illuminating"?
- How is this event or person serving as a leaping-off point for my own inquiry or discovery about myself, history, the natural world, or the human condition?

## IS MY WORK AS POLISHED AS POSSIBLE?

These 10 revision tips may help you identify opportunities to nip, tuck, and shine. Ask yourself:

1. Could I trim exposition at the beginning or summary information at the end that is not serving the poem?
2. Could I use a different voice to influence the experience of this poem? (For example, consider changing a third-person voice into the first person and see if this shift in intimacy is of benefit.)
3. Could my similes and metaphors be more distilled or powerful? If I've used an extended metaphor, does it hold up throughout the poem?
4. Where can I bring more energy to the language I've used? Can I use more active language to communicate similar ideas? Can modifiers be cut?
5. What if I changed past-tense verbs to the present tense (or vice versa)?
6. How might I shape the poem (line length, stanza breaks, white space) to more fully enact the emotion and rhythm of its content?
7. Are punctuation and capitalization and verb tense consistent? Would different choices (such as removing punctuation or capitalization) improve the experience?
8. Is there a music of repeating sounds throughout the poem? What words could I replace to create a more cohesive sound experience?
9. Are there opportunities to break lines in ways that give attention to important words or pace the momentum of the narrative more powerfully?
10. How might the title better encapsulate and add dimension to the experience of the poem? Could some of the exposition cut in step one be used to set the context of the poem in its title?

## ARRANGE YOUR POEMS INTENTIONALLY

The order of the poems you've submitted can make a difference in an editor's experience and opinion of your work—even if you're just submitting three to five poems. Think about the arrangement as a single composition that provides a coherent reading journey. Where do you want the reader to start—and finish? How do you want them to enter the realm of your poetry, and how are you intending to send them off?

## MAKE SUBMISSION GUIDELINES YOUR BIBLE

Every literary publication and contest will offer detailed guidelines about how and when they want to receive poems. Your job is to follow every single detail of those guidelines fanatically to ensure you don't rule yourself out with a simple oversight. Because it's easy to miss a detail when scanning instructions online, I recommend printing out the submission guidelines for any opportunity and then checking off each requirement as you meet it. Specifically:

- Follow simultaneous submission instructions. Some publications accept simultaneous submissions (meaning that you've sent the same poems to more than one publication for consideration at the same time), and others don't. Be careful to understand and honor each journal's parameters.
- Get your timing right. Publications have contest deadlines and specific reading windows. Send your work in advance of the specified deadline.
- Choose poems that fit. Ensure that you have chosen poems that match any specific requirements, such as: theme, form, length (number of lines or pages), number of poems allowed or required.
- Be deliberate about where you include your name. Some publications read and choose poems "blind," others don't. Be sure to understand whether the publication wants identifying information on the poems or not—and follow these guidelines carefully.
- Double-check the mailing address and editor names. No editor wants to see his or her name misspelled or receive mail addressed to his or her predecessor. It's also a good idea to confirm the gender of the person you are addressing if you have any doubt.
- Follow binding requirements. Publications often specify whether they want paper clips, staples or loose pages.
- Provide SASE (self-addressed, stamped envelope) if this is required or requested by the publication. Follow whatever process is requested.

- Include a check if you are submitting to a contest with a required reading fee. Make sure you make it out to the organization as requested in the amount required and specify the name of the contest to which you are submitting.

## FORMAT, PROOF, AND POLISH

First impressions are often the last impression. Think of your submission package as a gift that an editor or selection committee will enjoy opening and experiencing—whether you're submitting online or by mail:

- Use a standard font that is easy to read—such as Times New Roman, Garamond, or Calibri—using 12-point font, unless instructed otherwise. Your priority should be legibility and ease for the person(s) who will be considering your poem.
- Unless you are doing so for a very specific reason, think twice about bolding or italicizing fonts. Let your images, word choice, and line breaks do the work of creating emphasis.
- Print your poems on white, unrumpled, and unscented paper.
- Ensure your toner is working or that your photocopies are clear and crisp.

## WRITE A COVER LETTER THAT CONNECTS

Your cover letter should first and foremost provide whatever information is requested in the submission guidelines, if any. In the absence of specific instruction, write a concise note that covers the following:

- Explain you are submitting poems for [name of contest, issue, or general consideration].
- Describe in a sentence or two what you admire about the publication and why you chose to submit your work—if you have something authentic to say. Or, if you've had a previous communication with an editor (such as, they sent an encouraging rejection with a note inviting you to submit again in the future) you can mention that here.
- Lists the names of the poems being submitted. If this is a simultaneous submission, it is good form to mention this and confirm you intend to follow whatever process this publication has requested in its submission guidelines.
- Provide a brief biographical paragraph that describes key publishing or education highlights to reflect your literary experience and expertise. If you haven't published yet or don't have anything else relevant to report, no need to say anything here.
- Be polite and gracious.

Remember, this is a business communication. Some mistakes to avoid:

- Do not provide explanations about why you chose these poems for submission, why you wrote them, what they mean to you or your family, or how you have revised them.
- Do not advise editors about when you expect to hear back from them.
- Do not send a follow-up letter with a batch of poems that are edited versions of a previous submission.
- Do send a follow-up letter to withdraw any poems you have submitted as soon as they have been accepted elsewhere.

Over time, you'll get more efficient and adept with this process. Preparing your poems for submission will get faster, easier, and more automatic as you know what steps to take and mistakes to avoid. Your commitment to consistently putting your best work forward—and willingness to learn from the feedback you get along the way—will give you the very best odds of publication.

**SAGE COHEN** is the author of *Writing the Life Poetic* and *The Productive Writer*, both from Writer's Digest Books, and the poetry collection *Like the Heart, the World*. She holds an MFA in creative writing from New York University and a BA from Brown University. Sage has won first place in the Ghost Road Press poetry contest, been nominated for a Pushcart Prize and published a number of articles in *Writer's Digest* magazine. In 2011, she judged the Writer's Digest contest for non-rhyming poetry. To learn more about Sage, visit pathofpossibility.com.

# READY YOUR WORK FOR PUBLICATION

*by Lauren Camp*

Poetry is a sublime art form, but making it takes time. Breathtaking poems generally emerge from a slow, considered approach and a long gestation period.

Writing technical and magazine articles taught me structure, concision, and reporting strategies. Poetry teaches me to analyze the colors of each thought, and to look for ways to sculpt the statement. If every poem came out perfect right away, the experience would feel too clipped. I want the project to take a while, to "marinate" and evolve into language both exquisite and weirdly unexpected.

To ensure your poems get picked out from the editors' slush pile, take some time to prime your work for publication. Here are nine hands-on, critical techniques to help you assess your poems from different perspectives, and improve your writing.

## #1—LISTEN TO MILES DAVIS

On his 1959 album *Kind of Blue,* trumpeter and composer Miles Davis named a composition "So What." Ask that question of your poem. *So what* if you have a distinctive voice? *So what* if there's melody? Why should others care about your poem?

To create a poem with staying power, you have to be able to answer one tough question: is this worth saying? If you are writing the poem just to share an experience, the poem isn't done yet. Consider what the experience taught you. Would an audience be interested in that? Most experiences are universal in some way. Give readers an insight that they can connect to their lives.

## #2—EAT THE BANANA

Think hard about "the."

"The" means "the one and only." The ultimate. The whole enchilada. The all and everything of a subject.

Look at every single place you've used it. Is this what you're trying to infer? Did you really sit on "the" park bench? (I can think of a lot of benches—and a lot of parks). Did you really eat "the" banana? The one and only?

You see what I mean. It's easy to say it and write it, but when you start picking apart what you mean…well, maybe you shouldn't use "the." Try substituting "a"—a park bench, a banana, a trip to Peru—or see if the poem works without any articles at all.

## #3—STOP GOING AND DOING

Another easy fix is to shorten and tighten verbs. Why are you "going" when you could just "go"—or better yet, "fly" or "trudge"?

Gerunds ("ing" words) are so kind. They whisper over readers with a tinge of apology. They are almost always less effective than a lean verb—one without fat. Be insistent in your writing for a change. Make those verbs muscular. Ask them to really do something, to lift the line. Be more authoritative than you think you can; stop "ing-ing" around.

After you've made these changes, re-read your lines in a big, vigorous, and certain voice. How does the poem sound now?

Clearly, you can't cut all "ing" words all the time. Look for a balance of tensile strength with breathing space.

## #4—PULL YOURSELF OUT

We all write about ourselves in some way, but sometimes poems are just loaded with… well, us.

How many times do you have to say "I" for your readers to know the poem is happening to you? I bet you could safely eliminate some references to self, and readers would still be clued in. Try it. Take one "I" out, and see if it matters. Take out another. Don't forget to read out loud to make sure you haven't lost the flow—or the human quality of the poem.

Remove yourself just enough that you aren't ever-present, but be careful. If you take yourself completely out, the poem will seem choppy and abstract.

## #5—LOOK FOR SOFT SPOTS

My students step into soft spots all the time. So do I, and you will, too, because you must write first for you, and then, revise for someone else.

Where readers sink is the quicksand of the poem. The weight of messy language pulls them down. Sometimes our writing is thick and circular—especially if we are trying to say too much. Because we often write to figure something out for ourselves, rather than writing what we already know, we may be uncertain how to draw the map of what we're exploring. What a writer thinks is solid might not always be so to a reader.

How can you avoid these spots? Let the poem sit for a while. The irony of this technique is that the quick answer to finding your soft spots is time. Let the poem exist on your hard drive, unopened, until it becomes a little unfamiliar to you.

When sufficient time has passed, read it. Anything confusing or abstract will now be evident. You'll see where you've taken readers on a side journey, and forgotten to bring them back. Because the poem is again new to you, you'll know if you've complicated its map, and if there is a more direct route.

You want readers to get somewhere specific: your revelation. Take out references that send them to the wrong places.

## #6—WEAR THE STRONG SUIT OF SPECIFICITY

Be particular in your writing. Give details without drowning your readers in adjectives. Tell us which street, the hour it happened, the type of insect you heard in the air, the color of buttons on his shirt.

Israeli poet Yehuda Amichai once wrote that you must "put real things in your poems." Ask the poem every possible question you can. Is everything defined precisely? One of my students wrote about how, as a young child, she was instructed to put her small, cold hand inside the pocket of her mother's wool coat as a way for her mother to keep her close on dangerous urban streets. Holding fast to the pocket, the girl felt the nubbly texture. Because she described it, I could also feel the pocket lining, and the sense of security that came with it.

## #7—SMASH IT

Auguste Rodin advised young sculptors to stop gently picking at the clay and plaster of their sculpture when something wasn't going well. Instead, he encouraged them to "drop it on the floor and see what it looks like then."

It's easy to draw an analogy between this and poetry revising. Both creative acts sometimes require drastic changes to find the form your piece needs. Revision is all about seeing new options, but you might not be able to do this when you're trying to stay true to your initial intent.

If you are convinced that a poem isn't working and will never work, you are free to do anything at all to it. Construction workers often relish demolition work. Why not use their approach? Destruction frees the poem of the ghost of its earlier structure. Rather than remedying little parts, rebuild the whole.

Pick a line or phrase that seems strong. Let that chosen line become a new jumping off place, and jump in an unexpected direction.

Of course, if you're an archivist, and the idea of tossing big parts of the poem gives you hives, by all means, save the gems. (I collect the lines that I still like in a separate document.) But eviscerate them if they don't serve the poem you're revising.

# #8—INTERLACE

Have you ever tried splicing two poems together? In a way, it's like braiding hair. You pull a line from here and a line from there, again and again, until you have created a more complex structure, woven with new thoughts.

Take those good lines, and plait them into another poem. If they are on the same subject, aha! An easy fit. If not, well ... your job as poet becomes more challenging. How to match them together ... ?

In the mid-1960s, John Lennon wrote lyrics inspired by a news headline about a car accident and other events current at the time. His musical partner Paul McCartney had written a simple ditty about a man heading out late on a bus, and moving into a hazy dream. These were totally separate stories, neither quite complete in itself. Twined together, the lyrics became "A Day in the Life," on the *Sgt. Pepper's Lonely Hearts Club Band* album. Lennon said, "I had the bulk of the song and the words, but [Paul] contributed this little lick floating around in his head that he couldn't use for anything."

Isn't that how it is sometimes with a poem; a perfect phrase that needs a new home? Move it to another poem. Encourage it to be a strand in something larger, something with a separate music—maybe even one you didn't realize could exist. Take it from two lyrical masters; poetry interspersed with poetry can double the emotional impact.

# #9—CHANGE PACING

Revision is about taking innumerable steps to write the best possible poem. One technique worth trying is to change the speed of the poem.

If you're writing about something urgent or disturbing, and you want readers to keep moving through the poem—if, in fact, you believe readers should be nearly breathless when reading, try enjambment. In other words, don't let your lines end comfortably with commas or periods. Don't let anyone stop reading. Keep the thought in motion.

Think like a movie director for a thriller. When one of the characters is in danger, you want to design the scene to keep viewers on the edge of their seats, blood racing. How will you do this? Lighting, sound...whatever it takes to keep the suspense constant.

That's what you're after as a poet, too. Make your readers keep hurrying ahead to the next line, and the next. This doesn't mean you can't use punctuation. Instead, place those punctuation marks in the middle of lines, where periods are significantly less weighty and powerful.

For a different way to speed up, incorporate a full line of monosyllables. You'll get a ticker-tape effect from the rapid short words, hurtling readers through the line.

What if you want to move more slowly, and let readers revel in your images? Lines that are end-stopped (with periods) allow them to pause deeply. Stanza breaks take this even further—a maximum full stop. A complete resting place.

Switch the stride of your poem. As the writer, you know whether it should meander along or hurtle forth; now make your line decisions fit the mood of the piece, so readers know how to "hear" the poem.

It takes work to get a poem right, but this work can also be a joy. My students call this work "revisioning." Whatever techniques you employ, don't be too controlling. Allow spontaneity to guide the work.

**LAUREN CAMP** is the author of the collection *This Business of Wisdom* (West End Press), an interdisciplinary artist, and an educator. Her poems have appeared in *J Journal*, *Linebreak*, *Beloit Poetry Journal*, and you are here, among other journals. Her work gets accepted almost as frequently as it gets turned down, which she considers good odds. She has also guest edited special sections for *World Literature Today* (on international jazz poetry) and for *Malpaís Review* (on the poetry of Iraq). Lauren blogs about poetry at *Which Silk Shirt*. On Sundays, she hosts "Audio Saucepan," a weekly global music and poetry program on Santa Fe Public Radio. www.laurencamp.com

# THE ORGANIZED POET

*by Patricia Kennelly*

If you're like many poets I've talked with, it's not uncommon to have your poems everywhere. My desktop held overflowing notebooks, file folders and piles of random pieces of paper, scribbled with favorite words, lines, and poem starts. My computer's desktop wasn't any better. Although I knew most of my work was saved, my lack of organization made finding a particular poem time-consuming.

This wasn't too much of a problem until I started submitting my body of work. I struggled with getting my work to the right market. I missed good opportunities and important deadlines and created unnecessary stress by entering my poems at the last minute. Finding contests, markets and journals was the easy part; tracking down a poem or trying to read my illegible note about a "must enter" contest became challenging.

Most organizational experts agree that organizing any part of your life will save you time, money and help to eliminate stress. So why do so many poets have resistance to organizing their work? Some poets think that organization is the opposite of creativity and that being too businesslike will stifle their voices. I found the opposite to be true. Working on organization fueled my desire to write poetry and get my poems published.

When I decided to take ownership of my body of work and organize, I naturally approached the submission process in a professional manner. Doing the hard work ahead of time meant I had more time to find and research markets. The result? More published pieces and a clearer picture of where I wanted to go with my poetry.

Whatever system you choose (pen and paper, computer based, online or a combination of all) make sure it's one that will work for you. And if it doesn't work, consider trying another. The best organizational systems only function if you're ready to get organized and if they fit your personality. If any of these tips seem too daunting, consider asking a fellow poet to work with you in exchange for doing the same for them.

# 10 WAYS TO GET ORGANIZED

If you don't already have an uncluttered writing space, create one. It's difficult to work on organization if your space causes additional stress or distraction. These tips might help you become a more organized poet:

1. Find all of your publishable poems as well as your incomplete poems. This may take some time. Don't rush this process; finding, reading and organizing your forgotten words may inspire new work. Consider typing up your poem starts into one document so you know where to begin when you're stuck for inspiration.

2. Print hard copies of all work and separate publishable poems and poems that need revision into separate accordion files or three-ring binders. You can choose to file by title, subject/theme or type/form. Other poets include length of poem and tone.

3. Generate a virtual folder on your desktop. I titled mine "All Poetry" and created subfolders entitled "Publishable Poems," "Needs Work," and "Published Poems." Choose subfolder titles that make sense to you—you can use poem title, subject matter, form, or theme. Your goal is to be able to find your poems easily.

4. Create or find a submission tracker. If your goal is publication, having a system that tracks your submissions and that is easy to use and update will help create a sense of order.

5. Write or type up a list of goal markets for the year. I do this by going through *Poet's Market* and my favorite poetry newsletters and websites to find markets that seem to be a good fit. This document will grow every month as you discover more markets, contests and literary journals. Some poets find including the hyperlinks to be helpful.

6. Make an appointment with yourself. At least once every week I set aside some time to follow up with upcoming deadlines and to write a to-do list. More productive writers than myself do a to-do list every day, but with a full-time job I find that this weekly check-in is enough to keep me on task.

7. Subscribe to poetry newsletters and set Google alerts for specific contests you'd like to enter. Here is the challenging part—as soon as you receive the newsletter or alert, fill in your paper or virtual poetry calendar. And then delete the newsletter.

8. Keep office supplies including: envelopes, paper, file folders, printer ink and stamps stocked. While many magazines and journals are set up for e-mail submissions, there are still some journals that require a hard copy submission.

9. Organize your books by genre. I keep chapbooks, craft books, journals, and poetry magazines on one shelf for reference and inspiration. While the Internet makes it easy to access information, having all of your reference materials within easy reach could prevent you from getting distracted online.

10. Do set a date for completion of your new organizational system by choosing a realistic goal date and sticking to it. As Barbara Sher writes in *Wishcraft: How to Get What You Really Want,* "…your true goal, or target, has to be a concrete action or event, not only so you'll know for sure when you get there, but so that you can make that date with success in advance!"

## SET UP A POETRY CALENDAR

At the beginning of every year or starting today, consider purchasing a large spaced desk calendar specifically for poetry. Because I'm sitting at the desk every day it's easy to jot down poetry contests and submission deadlines I don't want to miss, especially the "no-entry fee" contests. If it's on my goal market list, I use different colored highlighters to show when the journal is open to submissions.

Writer Phyllis Kaelin also uses a similar paper-based calendar system but uses colorful sticky notes to chart her progress on a particular project. Her paper calendar system works hand in hand with her computer files. She says, "Within the project folder, I keep a running "notes document" where I put comments, plans, progress, word count etc. When I decide to submit I make a note there too."

If you don't already use an online calendar specifically for poetry set one up. If you're serious about poetry this can be used to track submissions, deadlines and markets but also helps keep you on track with readings, writing groups and poetry events. Popular online calendars include: Google Calendar (www.google.com/calendar), Convenient Calendar (www.convenientcalendar.com), and 30 Boxes (www.30boxes.com). I like using an online calendar that integrates with my smartphone so that I can send reminders to my phone, e-mail and/or virtual desktop.

## WHY USE A SUBMISSION TRACKER?

Even if you have a good memory, once you get in the habit of sending out your poems it's very easy to lose track of when and where your poems were sent. And there's nothing more frustrating than finding a good market for a particular poem and not remembering where or if it was sent out.

*Poet's Market* includes a basic submission tracker that you can enlarge and copy. Or if you're feeling creative, you can design your own paper submission tracker using headlines that make sense to you. Another option many poets use is index cards or a simple journal log. Alternatively you can convert *Poet's Market*'s submission tracker to a computer spreadsheet program such as Excel. If you're not comfortable setting up your own tracking spreadsheet on your computer, there are several free submission trackers available online.

The most popular submission trackers include: Duotrope (www.duotrope.com), Luminary Writer's Database (www.writersdb.com), and *Writer's Market* (www.writersmarket.com).

Rooze, an award-winning poet who is currently pursuing her MFA, says about Duotrope, "I like that they have a theme calendar and a deadline calendar. For each journal, they also list the average response time, percentage of submissions accepted, and the last time a response was received. This gives me a better context to know what to expect. Duotrope also specifies additional criteria, such as requirements around simultaneous submissions and previously printed poems."

The benefits of using a submission tracker far outweigh the time it will take to set one up. If you choose to include comments you can easily recognize when a poem needs a second look. If you use an online submission tracker your timely follow-up can also help other poets who use the database. Knowing that we're all in this submission process together, helping fellow poets just feels right.

If spreadsheets and submission trackers seem too left-brain, you might consider poet Jessy Randall's process. She says, "I write, with my hand and a pen, a poem. I mess around with, cross things out, rewrite lines, for a day or two. Then I set it aside for, if possible, at least a month, or even better, three months. Then I take a look at it again. If I think it's any good, I type it into a giant Word document that contains typed versions of all my poems, with the newest ones at the top. I fiddle around with it some more as I type it. I set it aside again for a while, maybe another month. If I still like it after all that, I submit it to a journal, bundling it together with other poems that somehow go with it. I keep track of where I've sent it, and when, in a Word document (to tell the truth, it's the same giant document). I also try to keep track of the general response time so I know when I should send a query. So I'll have something like:

"Name of Journal: Poem Title 1, Poem Title 2, Poem Title 3, sent January 2012, should respond in 6 months."

For the submission process Randall adds that the "submission information is in the top of my Word document, along with a list of the poems that aren't sent out anywhere at the moment. Then come all the typed poems. At the bottom of this giant document is where I keep track of rejections, in alphabetical order by journal name. If I need to, I can do a word search in the document to see if a particular journal has already seen a particular poem."

## YOU'RE PUBLISHED!

Unfortunately just being organized doesn't guarantee publication. But if you're committed to poetry and part of that commitment includes being organized and businesslike, with time and persistence, there's a very good chance that your work will be accepted.

When you do receive the letter or e-mail that your work is being accepted make sure to follow through. Update your submission tracker as well as your computer and/or paper files. It's very rewarding to move the poem (physically or virtually) from the publishable folder to the published folder and/or to write where and when your poem will be published. If the poem was a simultaneous submission be professional and notify the other publications that you are withdrawing your work.

Blogger and poet Sonya Fehér of Mama True (www.mamatrue.com) includes a Published Worksheet as part of her organizational system.

"The Published Worksheet includes the following fields:

- **MARKET**—Name of market in which the poem was published
- **DETAILS**—Volume # and other details from publication
- **LINK**—If the poem was published online, this gives me the location."

For poet Jessy Randall, being organized makes poetry more gratifying: "This may sound weird, but I particularly enjoy the housekeeping side of poetry, the keeping-track-of-submissions part. When I open up the file that shows me what's where, what's been rejected, what's forthcoming, I feel a real sense of accomplishment even if I didn't write anything that day. Because look at all the stuff that's percolating along without me doing anything!"

That's the favorite part for me too; once I set my organizational system in place I had more fun with the submission process. I missed fewer deadlines and felt more in control of my poetic career. Whether your body of work consists of five or 50 poems there's no time like today to start organizing. Taking the time to organize your work goes beyond the practical; it's a way to honor your time, work, and commitment to craft. It could very well be the inspiration you need to get published.

**PATRICIA KENNELLY** is a published poet, business owner and editor in Colorado Springs, Colorado. Her poems have most recently appeared in *Haibun Today*, *Messages from the Hidden Lake* and *The Denver Post*. She gently nags about writing daily and creativity at www.writingnag.com.

# THE HABITS OF HIGHLY PRODUCTIVE POETS

*by Scott Owens*

If they held a convention for all the people who have made a fortune off poetry, I'm not sure anyone would show up. The external rewards of writing poetry are relatively minimal. Writing poetry doesn't produce googobs of money. Any fame generated by the act is rather limited and usually accompanied by equal amounts of misunderstanding, suspicion, and other forms of notoriety. Even moral support is often lacking as family and friends may resent the time that poetry takes away from them, and readers and other poets may not support your particular aesthetic or the subjects you choose to write about.

Still, there are thousands of people who write poetry, some obsessively, some successfully, if productivity and a small following can be construed as success. The questions, then, are *Why do they do it?* and *How do they do it?* Ultimately, of course, the answers to both questions are as diverse as the people who write poetry, but some reasons and ways are common enough to merit general discussion.

W.S. Merwin claims that *poetry reconnects us to the world*. Gerald Stern gets a bit more specific when he writes that *poetry is a kind of religion, a way of seeking redemption, a way of understanding things so that they can be reconciled, explained, justified, redeemed*. Certainly these are wonderful reasons for why people write poetry, and they ring true to my own experience as both a writer and reader of poetry. They also relate to the first answer to the second question.

## HABIT #1: BELIEF

The first habit of productive poets is that they **believe** in poetry. They believe that it is more than a game with words, more even than just writing about the world (an admirable enough ambition in itself). They believe that it is, in fact, both an ontological and an epistemological act—both a way of being in the world, and a way of making meaning out of the world. They understand that the act of writing poetry helps them pay attention to, appreciate, and make meaning out of their existence, and they enjoy the way in which po-etry deepens their experience of people, moments, and things. They believe poetry, and their poetry more specifically, matters, and they will not be dissuaded from engaging with poetry and engaging with the world through poetry.

## HABIT #2: CONFIDENCE

This is, of course, intimately related to the second habit of productive poets in that it ne-cessitates that poets are **confident and courageous**. In other words, they believe in the significance of what they are doing no matter how many times and ways they are told by society, family, friends, even other poets that poetry, especially their poetry, doesn't matter or isn't right. Perhaps the best answer to why people write poetry is simply be-cause they have to or because they like doing it. If, as Merwin suggests, writing poetry makes you feel closer to the world, then you'll probably keep doing it no matter what anyone else says. And if, as Stern suggests, writing poetry helps you make meaning, sig-nificance, and value out of your perceptions and experiences, then it's likely you'll seek every opportunity to do it.

## HABIT #3: RECEPTIVE

Often, it is less a matter of seeking the opportunity than it is of being ready for it. The third habit of highly productive poets is that they are **ready to receive**. Ideas, images, lines for poetry are everywhere, every minute of every day, but our ability to remember the fine details of any particular event or perception is constantly eroded by the sheer mass of events and perceptions we encounter on a daily basis. Thus, highly productive poets are never without pen and paper so that they can jot down these observations when they occur. My writer's notebook goes with me everywhere. It's on the seat next to me when I drive; it's on my nightstand when I sleep; it's in my bookbag or binder when I go out; and on those rare occasions when I can't have it with me, I'm sure to have a folded up piece of paper in one pocket or another. And I don't use just any notebook ei-ther. I use a notebook that I like to spend time with, that I like the feel and heft of, that I want to open even when I don't think I have anything to write, and that I won't get con-fused with any other notebook. For me it's a Moleskine journal with about 200 unlined pages. Similarly, I keep one of my favorite pens with me at all times. For me that means a heavy, metallic-bodied, gel-type pen. Whatever your favorite is like, having it avail-able enhances the likelihood that you will write with relish rather than discomfort, and thus will do so longer and more frequently.

## HABIT #4: ATTENTION

Suitably armed for recording the significant details we encounter throughout every day, the fourth, and perhaps most important, habit of highly productive poets is referenced in Mary Oliver's unforgettable poem, "Summer Day," where she says, "I don't know exactly what a prayer is. / I do know how to **pay attention**." Paying attention consists of learning to notice the finer details, the significance of those details, and the connections between them that most people, caught up in the necessaries of daily existence, miss, or fail to remember for more than a moment. As simple as that sounds, this habit requires more development than any of the others. Perhaps the best method for developing it is to begin by doing it consciously. Set aside 30 minutes every day and pay close attention to something, somewhere. You might sit at a coffee shop and pay attention to people, or take a walk and pay attention to something in nature; you might practice yoga or meditation and learn to pay attention to more internal landscapes. After a while of doing this intentionally, you'll discover that you begin to pay closer attention to such details without having to make yourself do it. You'll notice more; you'll be conscious of the significance of things that most people take for granted; and you'll appreciate the connections between things that too often go unnoticed.

## HABIT #5: ATTUNED

Highly productive poets also **stay tuned in** to poetry. I am convinced, in fact, that most successful poets read a great deal more poetry than they ever undertake to write. They read poetry in books and magazines; they attend workshops, classes, and readings; they participate in critique and peer groups; they volunteer to edit journals and anthologies and judge contests; they read and write reviews; and they create opportunities for others to experience poetry, all of which keeps them thinking about poetry and honing their poetic skills and aesthetic. They do this because they love poetry; they do it because they believe that given the opportunity everyone will love and benefit from poetry; and in the process they make themselves better poets. My own hometown lacked a poetry reading series for local poets, so I partnered with a locally-owned coffee shop and created one that has been going on monthly for 7 years and has an average attendance of about 40 people. I also took on writing a semi-weekly poetry column, editing a quarterly online poetry journal, coordinating a quarterly ekphrastic reading series at the local art museum, and serving as an officer of the state poetry society. I think every state has such a society, and joining it is a great way to get tapped into the network of poets and poetry lovers, and to stay on top of opportunities to experience and participate in the world of poetry wherever you might be.

## HABIT #6: INIATIVE

Just as highly productive poets dive in to the world of poetry, they also **dive in** to the subjects they choose to write about. As the first habit suggests, whether they write about politics, personal experience, memory, perception, etc., they approach their subjects without letting fear occlude their vision or censor their words. They also dive in in the sense that they immerse themselves in the subject, not rushing to complete the poem, but luxuriating in it, granting it the time it deserves, writing way too much before beginning to whittle down the language and perceptions to the essentials that will form an effective final poem. Examining any act of creation will reveal that creation always involves waste, or "leftovers." Effectiveness comes through a process of sharpening, whittling away what is ineffective. Thus, most poets begin by overwriting, and then eliminate unneeded elements through the process of editing and shaping the poem. This is another one that takes a bit of practice in a world that encourages focusing on the end result and instant gratification rather than relaxing into and fully experiencing the process. Poets will use any number of techniques to help them expand upon the possibilities they venture into: clustering, free association, automatic writing, meditation, focused freewriting, etc. My suggestion is to use them all, sometimes on the same poem, and then make up your own as you discover what works. Driving long distances helps me; another poet friend of mine does his best work while mowing.

## HABIT #7: ENJOYMENT

Of course, the correlative habit is just as essential. A highly productive poet will also **enjoy the process**. I've encountered many people who claim to hate revising, but I can't think of a successful poet who has ever said so. Good poets tend to understand that the real craft of writing comes in the rewriting, and as difficult and sometimes painful as that process can be, it is the part of writing that they enjoy the most. It is, in fact, often a form of play for them. They work on a poem for weeks, months, sometimes years, trying out different perspectives, metaphors, arrangements of lines. They seek out criticism from others; they revise after poems are published, or after giving public readings. They see the poem as "finished" perhaps only after their own death has made it so. If Whitman could have at least 8 versions (some say as many as 19) of *Leaves of Grass*, then surely no lesser poet should doubt or fear the process of continual revision.

## HABIT #8: THICK-SKINNED

The eighth habit of productive poets, and for some the most difficult, is that they **grow thick skin**. They learn to distinguish between themselves and their work such that they can accept criticism of their work without internalizing it as criticism of themselves.

Often poetry is about personal experience, and some writers struggle to separate criticism of the poem from criticism of who they are, what they've been through, or how they view things. Productive poets, however, come to understand that once written and shared, any poem is an artifact, an object, something to be handled and shaped, and not a part of who they are. Thus they are able to consider the poem coldly and critically and ask of it what will make it more effective without taking such questions, regardless of the source, as a personal affront. From that perspective, productive poets strive to listen to criticism objectively. Even if they cannot manage that level of objectivity, however, knowing that ultimately all decisions regarding the poem rest with them, productive poets learn to accept commentary about the poem and move on with the writing they have undertaken.

Good habits are essential to prolonged success in virtually any endeavor. Inspiration is a nice idea, and a wonderful thing when it happens, but I think it unwise to count upon its striking very often without developing certain practices that increase the likelihood of its coming to be. This list of practices for those who wish to be productive poets is far from exhaustive, but it has been useful for me, and I hope that it will prove to be so for other poets as well.

**SCOTT OWENS** holds degrees from Ohio University, UNC Charlotte, and UNC Greensboro. He currently lives in Hickory, North Carolina, where he teaches at Catawba Valley Community College, edits *Wild Goose Poetry Review* and *234*, writes for the *Outlook Newspaper*, and serves as vice-president of the NC Poetry Society. His 11th book of poetry, *Eye of the Beholder*, was released by Main Street Rag. His work has received awards from the Academy of American Poets, the Pushcart Prize Anthology, the Next Generation/Indie Lit Awards, the NC Writers Network, the NC Poetry Society, and the Poetry Society of SC.

# ANATOMY OF A POETRY BOOK

.............................................

*by Amy Miller*

///////////////////////////////////////////////////////////////////////////////////

Congratulations! You just got the proofs for the poetry book you're about to publish with that dream press. You open the package, but all you see is a pile of loose papers—things have been added and moved around, and you're not sure what you're looking at. Or maybe you're self-publishing your book and you're juggling your Word files, trying to figure out what goes where. How much legalese do you need on the copyright page? Acknowledgments in the front or back? And what about the footnote for that poem with the lines in Turkish?

No matter who's publishing your book or what size it is—full-length or chapbook—making it look as professional as possible takes dozens of small decisions that you'll be better equipped to deal with if you know the basic conventions of book layout.

So here, from front to back, are the parts of a poetry book and some tips for polishing them.

## FRONT COVER

This one's a no-brainer, right? All it needs is the title and author, and a (hopefully) fabulous design.

But there's another element that appears on most poetry covers: the word "Poems" in small type below the title or above the author's name. While it's not mandatory, this makes it easy for readers and booksellers to distinguish your book from those of other genres, handy in today's crowded literary marketplace.

## FRONTMATTER

As the name implies, frontmatter is everything at the front of the book, before your poems begin. These pages are usually numbered with Roman numerals or have no page numbers.

- **Title page.** This right-hand page, usually the first in the book and always unnumbered, mimics the cover design: title, author, and maybe a black-and-white rendering of the cover graphics. Your publisher may place their logo at the bottom. "Poems" is optional here. The title page serves a crucial function: It's where you'll autograph the book, so make sure there's enough blank space on it to write your signature and an inscription. Some publishers also add a "half-title"—a right-hand page that precedes the title page, with just the book's title and perhaps the publisher's logo, followed by a blank left page.
- **Copyright page.** This is usually the left page following the full title page. It contains these elements: Copyright line, publisher's confact info, ISBN, LCCN, Library of Congress data, printing history, country of origin, design/printing credits and colophon, and contractual language. More on these in Copyright Page sidebar.

## COPYRIGHT PAGE

- **Copyright line.** A brief statement legally proclaiming this book as your writing is a publishing convention found in nearly every book. The least you'll need is "Copyright © 2017 by Joe Smith"; the year is when the book is first published, regardless of when the poems were written, and the name is yours. (For an anthology with many authors, it's the publisher's or editor's name; the individual authors retain rights to their poems through a contract with the publisher.) Some publishers spell out copyright protection more explicitly by adding something like, "All rights reserved. Except for brief quotations in critical articles or reviews, no part of this book may be reproduced in any manner without prior written permission from the publisher." There are myriad ways to word this. If you're self-publishing, look at similar books and choose language that's clear but not too complicated; overkill can look amateurish here. **Tip:** Your copyright line (the year the book was originally published) will stay the same no matter which printing it is.
- **Publisher's contact info.** This will be your publisher's address, or, if you're self-publishing, your own website, e-mail address, or P.O. Box (maybe not your street address). If somebody likes your book, make sure they can reach you.
- **ISBN, LCCN, and Library of Congress Data.** If your book has an ISBN (International Standard Book Number, used by retailers to identify and order the book), list it on the copyright page: "ISBN: XXX-X-XXXXXXXXX." Similarly, if your publisher decides your book needs an LCCN (Library of Congress Control Number, used by librarians for ordering and cataloging), it goes here too, as does Library of Congress Cataloging-in-Publication Data, the small-print description and cryptic numbers you see in many books. If you're working through a publisher, they will handle all this. If you're

self-publishing, you may decide to get an ISBN; self-publishing platforms like CreateSpace or Blurb can provide one for you. LCCNs and LOC Cataloging Data are usually unnecessary for self-published poetry books.

- **Printing history.** This line states when that individual copy of the book was printed. In the old days of film and plates, it was denoted by a long line of numbers ("1 2 3 4 5   21 20 19 18 17," for example); the outer numbers indicated which printing it was and the year printed. Some publishers still follow this convention, but with digital technology now the norm, this line is often rendered in plain English—"First printing, 2017"—and changed in the digital file with each subsequent printing. But if you're self-publishing through an on-demand service, "first printing" has no real meaning since there is no "first batch" of books—each copy is printed when the buyer orders it. Instead, many print-on-demand authors use a line like "First printed in 2017" on the copyright page; then, on the last page of the book, the printer will automatically insert the date that particular copy was printed.

- **Country of origin.** The country where the book was printed should be listed on the copyright page (e.g., "Printed in the United States of America"). If you're using a print-on-demand service and don't know where it will be printed, you can omit this line; most of these services will automatically print the country of origin on the last page of the book.

- **Design/printing credits and colophon.** If you're using someone else's photos or art in the book, or if you employed a book designer, this is where to acknowledge them. (To credit a longer list of people, see "Acknowledgments page" in "Backmatter.") Some publishers also include a colophon—a note on the fonts used—or mention the printer or paper, especially if it's recycled or otherwise noteworthy.

- **Contractual language.** If the book's writing or publication was supported by a grant, sponsor, or residency, you or the publisher may be obligated to acknowledge that on the copyright page.

- **Table of contents.** Most full-length poetry collections have a table of contents (TOC), if the poems have titles. In a chapbook, it's optional but a nice touch. The TOC should always start on a right-hand page. If it runs an odd number of pages, the left-hand page that follows should be blank; if the TOC is two pages (i.e., it ends on a left page), the following right-hand page should be a half-title (see "Title Page" above), a dedication or book epigraph, or, if your book is divided into sections, a page with the title of your first section. The last page of the frontmatter should be a blank left.

- **Acknowledgments.** If some of the poems appeared previously in literary journals, you're obligated to mention it somewhere in the book. If it's just a few, you can list them on the copyright page: "Grateful acknowledgment is made to *Literary Annual* and *The Big Poetry Review*, in which some of these poems appeared." If the list is longer, put them on their own page. (See "Acknowledgments page" under "Backmatter.")

- **Dedication line.** If you want a short dedication thanking your spouse, your dog, or someone else, you can place this somewhere on the copyright page. Or your publisher may decide to give it a page to itself, usually a right-hand page followed by a blank left just before the table of contents or first poem.

## THE POEMS

The first poem should start on a right-hand page. If your book is in sections, each section title should be all by itself on a right-hand page, followed by a blank left, with the first poem of each section starting on the next right page.

Epigraphs and footnotes. An epigraph—a quote, news snippet, etc., that inspired or informs the poem—is printed below the poem's title, often in italics. A footnote, on the other hand, is text separate from the poem that provides something the reader needs to know, such as an explanation of a foreign phrase or unfamiliar term. Footnotes can clutter up a poetry book, so if you have any, consider putting them on a separate Notes page in the back (see "Backmatter").

**Tip:** In most poetry books, page 1 is either the first poem or the first section-head page. (Again, the frontmatter is either unnumbered or numbered with Roman numerals.) And right-hand pages are always odd-numbered; left pages are always even.

## BACKMATTER

Backmatter is everything after the poems. While frontmatter follows very specific industry conventions, backmatter is more of a free-for-all; you may have some of the following elements, or none.

- **Acknowledgments page.** If more poems appeared in journals than will fit on the copyright page, list those credits on a page by themselves, alphabetically by poem or journal. You can also use this page to thank people who helped you with the book.
- **Notes page.** Footnotes or any information that would enhance a reader's understanding of a poem—say, a dedication or the inspiration behind it—can be listed by page number and poem title on a Notes page. Notes pages are uncommon but can be illuminating, the kind of insider info that you might hear at a reading.
- **Author bio.** Some books have two bios, one in the back of the book and another on the back cover; some only have one on the back cover. If you have two, make them different; the back-cover one should be brief, while the (inside) bio page can be more expansive.

- **Blank pages.** Some books have a few blank sheets at the back of the book, or even at the front before the title page. Here's an industry secret: Sometimes publishers have to add blank pages because books are printed in signatures, large sheets on which several pages (4, 8, 16, etc.) are printed at once. If the number of pages in the book doesn't come out to a multiple of (4, 8, 16, whatever), the publisher may solve the equation by adding a half-title page and/or putting a few blank sheets at the very back or very front of the book.

**Tip:** Pages that are blank on both sides should only go at the very front or back, where they serve as decoration, because of a cardinal rule of publishing: "No blank right-hand pages." A blank right anywhere else is considered a design gaffe.

## BACK COVER

The back cover has several important elements.

- **Shelving category.** At one time, most books had a shelving category on the back—in our case, "Poetry"—to help bookstore staff know where to put it. Some books still do, usually in the upper or lower left-hand corner, but it's less common now that books are often sold online.
- **Blurbs.** If you have blurbs—testimonials from other writers praising your book—the usual number is three; you rarely see fewer or more than that.
- **Author bio and photo.** Again, your bio can go here and/or on a page of its own at the back of the book. If you're doing two bios, put a photo with only one, preferably the back cover.
- **Barcode.** This electronic rendering of the ISBN number simplifies book handling for stores and online retailers. It should appear in the lower right-hand corner of the back cover, with the ISBN printed above it. Your publisher or print-on-demand service will insert this, but if you're designing your own cover, make sure to leave a space for it.
- **Cover price.** This usually is listed near the barcode, or in an easy-to-spot corner of the back cover. If you're self-publishing, you have the option of not printing a price on it at all, leaving you free to change the price at any time without having to do a reprint.

**AMY MILLER'S** writing has appeared in journals ranging from *Nimrod*, *Rattle*, and *ZYZZYVA* to *Fine Gardening* and *Asimov's Science Fiction*. She has worked in publishing for more than three decades, including 15 years as a managing editor, during which she has ushered some 80 books from the manuscript stage through the printed product. She blogs at writers-island. blogspot.com.

# THE INS AND OUTS OF POETIC TRANSLATION

*by Lawrence Schimel*

There are many reasons, both personal and artistic, why a poet might want to translate a poem into English; translating poetry can help you learn another language, offer you a chance to slip into another writer's voice, or jump-start your own creativity. And the good news is that anyone is free to translate any poem—for their own individual use. But in order to publish your translation in any way, even if it is only on a personal blog, you first need to make sure you have or acquire the permission to do so.

While lots of other books and articles address the art of translating, this article aims to cover the practical side of publishing translations.

## UNDERSTANDING COPYRIGHT AND TRANSLATIONS

When you translate a poem, you are creating a literary work with its own copyright. Your translation is unique to you and no one can publish it without your permission.

But a translation is also a subsidiary copyright, because it is based on a pre-existing work. If the original work is now in the public domain, then you're free to publish your translation without any restrictions. (A good source for information on whether or not a work is in the public domain in the US can be found here: http://copyright.cornell.edu/resources/publicdomain.cfm)

But if the original work is still protected by copyright, the permission of the copyright holder (whether the poet herself, her publisher, her agent or her estate) is also needed in order for the translation to be published. This means that any magazine or publisher who wishes to publish the translation in any way needs to clear permission from both the original author (or their representative) and also from the translator.

This works in both directions: just as a translator cannot authorize publication for anything without permission, the author (or their representative) cannot publish or republish the translated work without the translator's permission.

While the copyright to your translation is unique to you, that doesn't mean that translations of the same original work can't be made by others—for personal use, by anyone, or with permission of the copyright holder, if for publication. It's important for the translator to know whether a work has already been published in English translation, even if by another translator, since many journals seek to be the first to publish a work. You may as a translator find yourself in a position of translating a book and seeking publication, even though portions of it may have already been translated by others and published in journals. You could not offer those poems to journals in your own translation as work that has never been previously published in English before, even though your own translation is, at that point, both original and unpublished. (You could, however, query an editor to explain why you have felt it necessary to re-translate this author, in which case they may make an exception—especially since your translation of the work is unpublished.)

Most journals don't want to have to deal with the hassle of negotiating for the rights to publish the work, possibly requiring communicating in another language they may not speak, and require the translator to clear those rights before even submitting the work.

So usually translators act as a bridge, securing on the one hand permission to publish the work in translation from the author or their publisher or agent, and also entering into agreements with periodicals or publishers to publish the work on behalf of both the original author and themselves.

## CLEARING PERMISSIONS: DIRECT CONTACT WITH AUTHORS

So how does one go about securing those rights and acquiring permission to publish your translation of a poet's work? And at what stage should you do so?

The easiest way is to try and contact the poet directly—to express an interest in translating their work, and to make sure others are not already engaged in the process of translating and trying to publish the same work you're interested in. If you're interested in publishing the translations you undertake, you should verify that the rights are available early in the process—although it is often helpful to have some sample translations to show the poet or their publisher or agent, especially if you do not already have an established publication history as a translator and/or poet.

Treat contacting the author as you would the writing of any submission cover letter. You are auditioning for a job—to become the poet's "voice" in English, whether for a single poem or their entire oeuvre—and want to make as good an impression as ever.

Literary translation involves a lot of investment (and faith) on the part of the translator, even before submitting the work, all without any guarantee of acceptance: the translator must find the work, secure the permission to publish it, translate it into English, submit it for publication and keep their fingers crossed that it appeals to an editor's tastes and needs. The process of establishing a name for the translated poet works very similarly to the path undertaken by a poet for untranslated work: placing poems in journals to eventually have enough published poems to interest a publisher in bringing out a book.

Therefore, each new poet that one translates becomes, in a way, an additional career. The translator becomes "responsible" for building the translated poet's reputation, trying to place the work in journals that are receptive to their aesthetic, etc. If the submission process seems overwhelming for a poet trying to place their own poems, that workload is in effect repeated for each additional poet you translate, and who you must advocate for, to editors as well as readers.

Yvette Siegert, who has translated the work of cult Argentine poet Alejandra Pizarnik, notes "It's intriguing to see how a colossally important writer can be ignored for the longest time and suddenly be the author everyone is eager to read. Being able to participate in shepherding the writing into publication at that moment is incredibly—artistically—rewarding for me."

Since promoting the author whose work you've translated often requires as much effort as promoting your own work, that's another reason it's often useful for the translator to have a direct contact with the poet, when possible.

Living poets often control the translation rights to their own work, or will be able to put the translator in touch with their publisher or agent to get permission from them if need be.

When it comes to publication in periodicals or anthologies, quite often a simple, signed statement from the poet is sufficient—or even an e-mail granting the translator permission.

While many magazine guidelines stipulate that it is the responsibility for the translator to acquire the rights to publish the translation before submitting same for publication, how that permission is offered and even at what stage of the submission process varies greatly. According to Curtis Bauer, translations editor for the journal *Waxwing*, "That permission can be as simple as inclusion in the query letter the information that they have received permission by the rights holder, or a scan of a letter from the publisher granting the translator permission. We don't have a set form."

Quite often, translators are asked to submit both the translation and the original work—even if only the translation will be published. And many journals, even if they don't explicitly state that they are looking for work in translation, are in fact open to submissions of the same; if in doubt, you can always query the editors.

---

**SAMPLE PERMISSION FORMS:**

Here are two sample permission forms used by translators working directly with the poets whose work they are translating and seeking to publish:

I, [Author], give [Translator] my authorization to translate and seek publication for [Title]. If desired, I give her permission to publish my original work alongside the translation.

I, [Author], own the rights to the book [Title] ([Publisher]), and grant [Translator] the rights to translate this book and submit it for publication to the publishers of his choice.

Each publisher will usually have their own form or style in granting permissions. Here is a sample form from an Italian publisher:

[Translator Address]

[Date]

re. : English-language rights

Dear _____[Translator]_____,

We are pleased to inform you that the translation rights to _____[Book Title]_____ by _____Author_____are held by [Publisher] and that the English-language rights are available.

We hereby grant you, _____[Translator]_____, the non-exclusive permission to translate the above mentioned book into the English language and to submit the translation to magazines, publishing houses and literary reviews for possible publication.

You will quote, the name of the Author and the copyright notice   as follows:

_____[Author]_____, _____[Book Title]_____

(c) [Date] [Publisher]. All rights reserved.

All rights not specifically mentioned in this letter shall be deemed to be fully reserved by [Publisher].

This letter has been forwarded in duplicate copy: please return a copy, duly countersigned, to our offices for our files.

Best regards,

(Rights & Acquisitions Department, [Publisher])

---

# CLEARING PERMISSIONS: PUBLISHERS OR ESTATES

Sometimes, it is necessary for a more formal agreement to be entered into.

The instructions for applying for a translation grant from the National Endowment for the Arts specifies, "Simply stating the availability of English-language rights to a work does not demonstrate that you have been granted permission to translate a work. Although the NEA does not require applicants to secure publishing rights, it will not fund work that is not authorized by the rights holder(s) and therefore would not have a chance of eventual publication. You must demonstrate, in writing, that the author/rights holder(s) will allow you to undertake a translation of the work specified in your application."

Likewise, while the right to publish individual poems is often something that the poet herself can grant to the translator, should an English-language publisher then be interested in bringing out a book (usually after a number of translations have been placed in journals, or if the project wins a grant), it may then become necessary for negotiations to take place with the publisher or agent. This is often something that can be handled directly between the US publisher and the foreign publisher, although depending on the languages involved, the translator may need to assist with translating communication back-and-forth and otherwise helping smooth the process along.

Tracking down a poet is often easier in today's electronic world with so many social media networks, but if you can't manage to establish a direct contact, your next step would be to contact the rights department of their publisher. Explain your interest and ask them to forward your communication to the author, if appropriate, or they may be able to grant you the necessary permissions themselves.

In the case of authors who are deceased, control may lie with the publisher or it may be necessary to track down the author's heirs or estate and once again state your case.

When Yvette Siegert read translations of Pizarnik's work, she felt a strong connection to the poetry but knew she wanted to try a different angle. "I approached the Pizarnik estate to inquire if the rights were available. It was my first time doing this, and my e-mail was more of an impassioned pitch. In Spanish, I explained how I read the poet's work and what insights I could contribute as a new translator, and I outlined my ideas for reaching out to publishers. I also shared personal details about how I discovered Pizarnik and why I loved her writing so much."

Siegert's passion for Pizarnik's work has resulted in not just numerous book publications but also grants from the National Endowment from the Arts and PEN, among other institutions.

## HOW THE MONEY IS SPLIT

Since a translation is a separate (if subsidiary) copyright, ideally both the original poet and the translator will each be paid for any publication.

Very often, however, journals don't differentiate between translated work and poems written originally in English, and for the sake of simplicity tend to deal only with the translator—as a result, how payments (if any) get split is usually handled by a private agreement between the translator and the poet.

Most of the translators I know who work directly with authors offer to split any income evenly with the authors—although in many cases the poets tell the translators to keep any money received. This is what happened to Meg Matich, an award-winning translator from the Icelandic, who adds, "In my experience, poets tend to think of their translators as the ones doing the work—the poems have already been written, and presumably published in their country. And so they're less interested in the small monetary gains—more excited by sharing their work."

In the case of book publication, generally there will be contracts signed with both the translator and the poet (or their publisher or representative), which will spell out what advance payments (if any) are to be made, to the poet and/or the translator, and how royalties are to be divided between the two parties.

Depending on where the poet is from, there may be funding available (often covering part or all of the translation costs) that can be applied for from national bodies, such as NORLA (http://norla.no/en/subsidies/for-translators) for translations from the Norwegian or the French Embassy (http://frenchculture.org/books/grants-and-programs/publishing-grants-prizes/publishers) for translations of Francophone literature. Often it is the publisher who needs to apply for this funding, although for some languages or countries translators can apply directly. It is often helpful for translators to investigate what funding resources are available, to include as part of their "pitch" when presenting translation projects to publishers, as the editors may not be familiar with everything that is available. And especially for poetry projects, any additional support can be a big help.

---

## RESOURCES

**The American Literary Translators Association (ALTA)** provides community, support, and resources for literary translators, including translators of poetry. ALTA offers between four and six $1,000 fellowships to new and emerging translators to attend their annual conference. Membership is open to both translators and others who wish to support literary translation. http://www.literarytranslators.org/

**The National Endowment for the Arts (NEA)** offers grants of $12,500 or $25,000 for translation projects of fiction, poetry, or drama from other languages into English. Applications are reviewed annually. https://www.arts.gov/grants-individuals/translation-projects

**The PEN/Heim Translation Grants Fund** offers grants for between $2,000-4,000 direct to translators " to support the translation of book-length works of fiction, creative nonfiction, poetry, or drama that have not previously appeared in English in print or have appeared only in an outdated or otherwise flawed translation." Projects do not need to be under contract with a publisher, but applicants must supply "a letter from the copyright holder stating that English-language rights to the book are available."http://www.pen.org/content/penheim-translation-fund-grants-2000-4000

**LAWRENCE SCHIMEL** has publlished 10 books of poetry in translation from the Spanish, in both bilingual and monolingual editions, as well as many poems in translation for journals around the world, including Modern Poetry in Translation (UK), Pleiades (US), So to Speak (US), and Shearsman (UK). In addition to his poetry press, A Midsummer Night's Press, Schimel has an imprint devoted to poetry in translation by women writers called Periscope. Learn more at http://amidsummernightspress.com.

# KEEPING POETRY ALIVE

## How and Why We Should Write Reviews

...............................................

*by Stacey Balkun*

As an MFA student, I tried to read as many new books as I could. I loved making connections between books and seeing how emerging poets were growing, especially because I felt I could learn from reading diverse contemporary writers. I was lucky enough to have lunch with a visiting poet who said that being well-read wasn't enough; that all writers must contribute to the larger conversation. She urged me to enter the community by writing reviews of these books and to share what I've read with a larger audience. Having never written a review before, I set out to do it with very little guidance.

I've been continuing to review ever since, despite the question of their value: Are reviews important to the potential reader? The poet? The press? Other critics have argued about this value and I don't wish to enter that argument. I do, however, agree with Kevin Prufer's belief that "[t]he purpose of poetry reviewing is to keep the art of poetry alive." Reviews are invaluable to the poetry community as a whole and instrumental to the review writer.

## ENGAGING WITH POETRY

In simplest terms, a review is a reader engaging with a book through prose. Like a good essay, a good review is self-aware; it shows the writer's thinking on the page. It seeks understanding rather than dismissal. A great review explores a book rather than assesses worth. It's engaging and opens doors for the reader rather than slamming them shut and, ideally, a review writer will glean as much from the process of writing as the audience will from reading it.

In a post on the Poetic Asides blog in August 2014, Jeannine Hall Gailey wrote that reviewing "encourages you to slow down and pay attention to the poetry world around you." In a world of seemingly endless poetry publications, it's easy to dismiss a daunting book with the promise of another ahead. Reading with the intent to review forces us to forgo that option and consider the book in our hands more seriously.

Advice for writing reviews generally fall within three categories: positive, neutral, and negative. "Negative" may feel like an odd word, since reviewing implies criticism, which is by nature, not completely praise. In a 2009 article published in *Poetry*, Jason Guriel calls for us to "retire the adjective 'negative' in favor of something far more accurate, if a little awkward, like 'necessarily skeptical.'" This new phrase may help us reshape our thinking about criticism and open up a new way to be critical without being disproving. As readers, we each have different aesthetics and pleasures and peeves, and it may be difficult to feel we have the authority to review a book, especially if we feel negatively about it. However, we need not let our tastes stop us from entering the conversation; rather, we should all review books as they come out.

Although the review guidelines I've generated are structured for writing a longer, in-depth review, there are more ways to be a part of the community by sharing our experience with books. For example, websites like Goodreads and Amazon are two markets for concise reviews that can be a single sentence. We can use these platforms to respond to new titles and stimulate conversation, quickly and efficiently.

## WRITING REVIEWS

Reviews are not formulaic, necessarily, but here are some prompts to help new reviewers understand the form. The obvious first step is to read. Read a book multiple times. Write all over it and take notes—try to see it as a whole thing. Does it add up to more than the sum of its parts? Once you've dug around inside its pages, tease out some major points. Consider its form, moving outside in.

First, look at the big picture: Is the book divided into sections? Are there epigraphs? Next, look at the form of the poems. Are they all free verse? Does the poet write in sonnets, ghazals, or other forms? If so, is there a pattern? Some books are tightly knit by theme, imagery, or form and some are organized by time. Examine the subject matter and the narrative arc and focus on what interests you the most: What discoveries have you made within the text?

Think of your writing as stimulating a conversation. Reviews are for readers, so tell them what they need to know about the book. Even if your initial reaction is negative, reconsider the previously listed elements and free write about what solicited such a negative reaction. Try to look at the book as a student of poetry would—what could it teach you about making your own manuscript? How is it contributing to the overall conversation of contemporary poetry?

If you love a book, the whole review may come easily, but what if you have tried everything yet still don't want to write about a book? Sometimes I solicit a title and I just don't connect with it. Some reviewers will return a book, but as an emerging writer who is eternally grateful to the small presses who send me books, I'm personally not comfortable doing so. Instead, I go through the list of questions mentioned earlier and try to approach the collection through content or craft. Is the book on an important topic? Can a writer learn from its form? I've decided I'm not personally comfortable writing entirely negative reviews and yet I don't believe in false praise, so if I find myself stuck, I try to do an interview or offer the title to another reviewer on our team.

If you want to go ahead with a "necessarily skeptical" review, keep in mind what Timothy Donnelly once said in an interview with Craig Teicher: "When a reviewer manages to point out a book's shortcomings evenhandedly, with care and dignity, and with an eye to raising the bar a little higher for readers and for writers, too—that's another story. I'd love to see more reviews like that."

Our job is to raise the bar, not our egos. Write with care and dignity, and remember, this review is not about you. There's no reason to tear a book apart; instead, explain your reaction rationally. It's ultimately more important to focus on camaraderie and openness than ownership and gatekeeping. I don't believe this means reviewers should censor themselves, but rather consider balance: show us what isn't working, but weigh it against what is. There may be one small image in a book that touches you deeply, even if the writing as a whole doesn't impress you. Show us that image as honestly as you can, and let the reader make up his or her own mind.

Not all reviewers agree. However, I feel strongly about evening the playing field of poetry and I believe that reviewing titles by and interviewing underrepresented authors has a big impact on the literary landscape by stimulating conversation and creating web presence for some authors and their books. Many print journals have an online presence for features, interviews, and reviews, therefore such articles can be easily accessed in the classroom. Imagine the possibilities if students of writing could be exposed to a diversity of new books with the quick click of an instructor's mouse. In this way, reviews could be a gateway to entering the literary culture: new readers are able find poets, and poets find exposure.

## CONNECTING WITH THE POETIC COMMUNITY

Our community of poets is small. We need to support each other and stay aware of trends in poetry while giving each new book the respect, time, and patience it deserves, and we need to get these reviews out there to be read. Some options for publishing reviews are *American Poetry Review*, *Bone Bouquet* (books by women-identified poets published in the last four years), *Boxcar Poetry Review* (first books of poetry), *Poetry Northwest*, *Prairie Schooner* (a single book or two or three books together), *Sycamore Review* (forthcoming titles), *Third Coast* (prefers reviews of first or second books, or books from smaller presses).

Several journals accept queries for reviews, including *Moon City Press* (new and up-coming titles), *The Chattahoochee Review*, and *Kenyon Review*. The Rumpus accepts pitches or complete reviews. *Poets & Writers* has a comprehensive list of review outlets listed online (http://www.pw.org/review_outlets?perpage=*). If you have a specific title in mind, however, look at the book's acknowledgements page: That list of journals is a great starting point. Most journals love to support their contributors. Be sure to include the connection in your query; but first, do your homework and check to see if they've already reviewed that title.

How do you write that query? Short, simple, sweet. In your pitch, include the date of the book's release, why this particular title would be a good fit for that particular market, and what's struck you the most about the book. Let your voice and skills come through. Show that you care about this community enough to contribute your thoughts, and show gratitude to the journal for supporting the community.

Remember, this is your chance to share something you love with the world and that something is not necessarily limited to the book itself. Book reviews can kindle conversation around new books and trends as well as garner new audiences for underrepresented authors whose voices we absolutely do need. Yes, we need poetry and yes, we need reviews to celebrate our work and keep poetry alive.

**STACEY BALKUN** is the author of two chapbooks, *Jackalope-Girl Learns to Speak* (Dancing Girl Press) and *Lost City Museum* (ELJ Publications). She received her MFA from Fresno State, and her work has appeared or will appear in *Gargoyle, Muzzle, THRUSH, Bodega,* and other publications. A 2015 Hambridge Fellow, Balkun served as Artist-in-Residence at the Great Smoky Mountains National Park in 2013..

# GET THE MOST OUT OF YOUR WRITING RESIDENCY

*by Jeannine Hall Gailey*

A residency can provide much-needed time to you to focus and create, for inspiration and collaboration—or become an exercise in frustration. Here's how to maximize your valuable poetry retreat time.

You researched a bunch of residency opportunities, wrote your application, sent it in, waited months to hear back, and now you have the good news—you've been accepted to a writing residency. The first time you go to a writing residency, you might not know what to expect or quite how to prepare.

First, do some basic research. You should read up on your chosen destination, getting the basics: Do they provide meals? Will you need to bring a car? Do they allow visitors? What will the weather be like in that part of the country in that time of year? Will there be Wi-Fi? How about a fridge? Every residency is different, so don't be afraid to ask questions of the people running the residency or friends who have attended it before. You'll want to know, for instance, if a certain residency has private bathrooms or communal, if you'll have a roommate or private quarters, or, if you have allergies or a disability that requires handicapped-accessibility, whether they can make accommodations. Most residency program runners are very friendly and want you to have the best possible experiences.

Whether you'll be there for a month during the summertime or just a week in the winter, whether you'll be in a beach-side cabin on the West Coast or deep-in-the-woods lodge in the far Northeast, here are a few tips to make the most of your time at a writing residency:

## 1. SET A FEW ACHIEVABLE GOALS

Have a specific goal you want to achieve, but don't beat yourself up if you don't get to everything. On my most recent residency, I had too many disparate things I wanted to get done on the trip, and I didn't quite have the physical fortitude to be as efficient as I am at home. I did my "have-to" work first, and my "want-to" work second. I think it's okay to have an adventure and new experiences at a residency, because even if you don't achieve everything, you'll still have devoted yourself for a bit of dedicated time to your art, and that is great. My latest residency resulted in a book review, some pages on my PR for Poets book, and a handful of new poems. But during the residency before that, I barely wrote anything at all, despite having more time, and spent most of my time trying to do water-colors. And that was okay. No one was harmed, except my sketch pad…The point is, if you go with a goal—"I want to put together my first book manuscript from this bunch of sixty poems," or "I want to edit this set of poems," or "I want to generate new work"—you are more likely to accomplish it if it's specific and reasonably sized for the amount of time you're going to have.

Aimee Nezhukumatathil, award-winning author of *Lucky Fish*, recommends putting physical reminders of your goals around you. "Before each residency, I wrote out some goals—both lofty and small, like 'Finish draft of three Niagara Falls poems,' 'read article on toucans,' 'get 7 hours of solid sleep.' I found my writing goals easier to manage when I could see them in front of me, taped up on a wall."

If you go to a residency with something specific to work on, even if you change your mind once you get there or start writing something different mid-stream, you're more likely to leave the residency feeling good about your time there.

## 2. ENJOY THE CHANGE OF SCENERY

Take advantage of the specific area you're in for your residency. On my last residency at The Helen Riaboff Whiteley Center on San Juan Island, I noticed some of the scholars barely left the campus—which was indeed beautiful and had a water view—but, after a few hours of reading and writing each morning, and before a few hours reading and writing after dark, I needed a couple of hours to get out and about and experience the amazing sights and sounds on offer. Seeing whales, foxes, eagles, otters, seals…they may not have directly impacted what I wrote, but I'm sure seeing the different vistas—Lime Kiln Point's rocky outcropping with a 360-degree view of the ocean, American Camp's drift-wood beaches and meadows—helped stimulate my mind more than just staying in the (admittedly pretty sweet) little cabin. If you're a food person, this extends to going out and getting a coffee and scone at the local coffee shop, or trying the local seafood the cute little organic restaurant that only the locals know about that someone recommended to you when you checked in. Residencies aren't just for reading, studying and writing—they're also about getting you out of your routine and having adventures. Many residencies are in gorgeous settings—and it's up to you to experience your unique surrounding.

## 3. PLAN AHEAD FOR WELL-BEING

Prepare in advance for your health and well-being. Bring the things from home you need to sleep—white noise machine, your pillow, special pajamas—because if you're anything like me, you'll have trouble sleeping in a new weird bed that's not your own, so do what you can to make yourself comfortable. Sleep is important for mental power. This may seem like a no-brainer, but be sure to pack all the medicine you might need, because you don't you don't want to be scrambling around an unfamiliar town after hours trying desperately to find a Benadryl or a special kind of asthma inhaler. Be sure to bring any prescriptions you might need, because the chances of finding a decent Urgent Care center in walking distance of a writing residency is pretty low.

## 4. BE OPEN TO INSPIRATION

Be social and aware of any special opportunities your residency offers. Some residencies have open studio sessions where you can interact with other residents, some have weekly get-togethers, some involve no interaction at all. My short conversations with the other residents and the staff were always rewarding and interesting. There is a lot of silence on a residency—a lot of them have no phones, no televisions, and no internet service. This can get to you if you're an extrovert who's used to a lot of background noise while they work and lots of socializing, so sometimes these small meaningful interactions can help get you inspired and remind you you're still part of humanity. And always check out any resources your particular residency has—my last one had a working marine biology laboratory, boats, and a great library—because inspiration might hit while observing bioluminescent sea creatures or looking through old science periodicals. You never know.

## 5. PACK FOR THE UNFORESEEN

Don't worry about how you look, but be prepared for multiple weather situations and "the unforeseen." I know it might be hard to let go of all the little things we end up doing to look good for people, but at a residency, the wildlife won't care what you look like, and if you wear yoga pants and Ugg boots every day, and never put on a lick of mascara, no one is going to start a scandalous whisper. You want to be comfortable, too, so be sure you pack for the weather. In the Northwest autumn, for example, it can be so changeable, I was glad I brought sunscreen, a warm coat, a raincoat, boots appropriate for mud, and multiple kinds of scarves. On the ferry on the way home, I had to wrap myself in a blanket I packed, because it was so cold and wet and windy, so yes, take that extra blanket. Pack for all emergencies, too—a flashlight or candles (did I mention I was unprepared when the power went out on the whole island my residency was on?) and a first aid kit. So, bottom line—less makeup, more Emergen-C and sunscreen.

## 6. PACK YOUR OWN "BRAIN FOOD"

Bring a variety of reading materials, because you never know what will inspire you or when you will have down time on your hands. Some days I was in the mood to read difficult fiction or poetry, and other days I just wanted to read magazines. Aimee Nezhukumatathil had this advice: "Depending on your residency, books might not be readily available, so I'd recommend bringing books both related to your project and those that you have been meaning to read just for reading's sake. That was one of the biggest surprises for me: how much I was able to read out there, so plan ahead and bring a backpack full of reading pleasure!"

A Kindle was useful on my boat ride and ferry wait, and if you have an airplane ride, a Kindle saves a lot of packing space (as long as you can charge it…) Don't forget chargers for your laptop, reading device, and cell. And if you write by hand, be sure to have a little notebook and pen you can carry that are not too heavy on days you might want to hike and write outside.

If you're lucky enough to have Wi-Fi or internet service on your residency, beware of getting distracted from your work. This wasn't a problem for me, but Kelli Russell Agodon, author of Hourglass Museum and co-founder and editor of Two Sylvias Press, gives this advice: "Stay disconnected. Stay off of Facebook and all social media. Do not check the news and if you need to do online research, make a list of things you want to look up and give yourself no more than three minutes to look up each item (if you have five things to research, that gives you 15 minutes of online time later in the day). If you connect with your family, do so by text, otherwise it's too easy to lose that sacred writing space and be drawn back into the world. Bring your favorite books to refer to. The goal of a writing residency is to go deep. Allow yourself the time, solitude, and space to disappear from your regular life into the world of writing."

## BONUS TIP: BE KIND AND CONSIDERATE

One last tip: Remember to be a gracious guest wherever you are staying. This can mean everything from not leaving your personal residency area a shambles, putting a note of thanks to them in your next book, and treating everyone from the other residents to the person who checks you in with warmth and gratitude. A residency is, yes, supposed to be alone time, but you want to leave the best possible memories for everyone involved when you go, and ideally, you want them to invite you back. And you never know when you'll make a friend.

Now you're prepped and ready to go enjoy—and be productive during—your residency!

**JEANNINE HALL GAILEY** served as the second Poet Laureate of Redmond, Washington. She is the author of five books of poetry: *Becoming the Villainess, She Returns to the Floating World, Unexplained Fevers, The Robot Scientist's Daughter*, and winner of the Moon City Press book award, *Field Guide to the End of the World*. Her website is www.webbish6.com and you can follow her on Twitter @webbish6.

# MISTAKES POETS MAKE

In putting together listings for *Poet's Market*, we ask editors for any words of advice they want to share with our readers. Often the editors' responses include comments about what poets should and shouldn't do when submitting work—the same comments, over and over. That means a lot of poets are repeating similar mistakes when they send out their poems for consideration.

The following list includes the most common of those mistakes—the ones poets should work hardest to avoid.

## NOT READING A PUBLICATION BEFORE SUBMITTING WORK

Researching a publication is essential before submitting your poetry. Try to buy a sample copy of a magazine (by mail, if necessary) or at least see if an issue is available at the library. It may not be economically feasible for poets to purchase a copy of every magazine they target, especially if they send out a lot of poems. However, there are additional ways to familiarize yourself with a publication.

Read the market listing thoroughly. If guidelines are available, send for them by e-mail or regular mail, or check for them online. A publication's website often presents valuable information, including sample poems, magazine covers, and guidelines.

## SUBMITTING INAPPROPRIATE WORK

Make good use of your research so you're sure you understand what a magazine publishes. Don't rationalize that a journal favoring free verse might jump at the chance to consider your long epic poem in heroic couplets. Don't convince yourself your experimental style will be a good fit for the traditional journal filled with rhyming poetry. Don't go into denial about whether a certain journal and your poetry are made for each other. It's counterproductive and ultimately wastes postage (not to mention time—yours and the editor's).

## SUBMITTING AN UNREASONABLE NUMBER OF POEMS

If an editor recommends sending three to five poems (a typical range), don't send six. Don't send a dozen poems and tell the editor to pick the five she wants to consider. If the editor doesn't specify a number (or the listing says "no limit"), don't take that as an invitation to mail off 20 poems. The editors and staff of literary magazines are busy enough as it is, and they may decide they don't have time to cope with you. (When submitting book or chapbook manuscripts to publishers, make sure your page count falls within the range they state.)

Don't go to the other extreme and send only one poem, unless an editor says it's okay (which is rare). One poem doesn't give an editor much of a perspective on your work, and it doesn't give you very good odds on getting the piece accepted.

## IGNORING THE EDITOR'S PREFERENCES REGARDING FORMATS

If an editor makes a point of describing a preferred manuscript format, follow it, even if that format seems to contradict the standard. (Standard format includes using 8½ × 11 white paper and conventional typeface and point size; avoid special graphics, colors or type flourishes; put your name and address on every page.) Don't devise your own format to make your submission stand out. Keep everything clean, crisp and easy to read (and professional).

Be alert to e-mail submission formats. Follow directions regarding what the editor wants printed in the subject line, how many poems to include in a single e-mail, whether to use attachments or paste work in the body of the message, and other elements. Editors have good reasons for outlining their preferences; ignoring them could mean having your e-mail deleted before your poems are even read.

## OMITTING A SELF-ADDRESSED STAMPED ENVELOPE (SASE)

Why do editors continuously say "include an SASE with your submission?" Because so many poets don't do it. Here's a simple rule: Unless the editor gives alternate instructions, include a #10 SASE, whether submitting poems or sending an inquiry.

## WRITING BAD COVER LETTERS (OR OMITTING THEM COMPLETELY)

Cover letters have become an established part of the submission process. There are editors who remain indifferent about the necessity of a cover letter, but many consider it rude to be sent a submission without any other communication from the poet.

Unless the editor says otherwise, send a cover letter. Keep it short and direct, a polite introduction of you and your work. (See "Frequently Asked Questions" for more tips on cover letters, and an example.)

Here are a few important don'ts:

- **DON'T** list all the magazines where your work has appeared; limit yourself to five magazine titles. The work you're submitting has to stand on its own.
- **DON'T** tell the editor what a good poet you are—or how good someone else thinks you are.
- **DON'T** tell the editor how to edit, lay out or print your poem. Some of those decisions are up to the editor, assuming she decides to accept your poem in the first place.
- **DON'T** point out the poem is copyrighted in your name or include the copyright symbol. All poems are automatically copyrighted in the poet's name as soon as they're "fixed" (i.e., written down), and editors know this.

## NOT MAINTAINING GOOD EDITOR/POET RELATIONS

Most editors are hard-working poetry lovers dedicated to finding and promoting good work. They aspire to turn submissions around as quickly as possible and to treat all poets with respect. They don't want to steal your work. Often they aren't paid for their labor and may even have to dip into their own pockets just to keep their magazines going.

Poets should finesse their communications with editors regarding problems, especially in initial letters and e-mail. Editors (and their magazines and presses) aren't service-oriented businesses, like the phone company. Getting huffy with an editor as if arguing with your cable provider about an overcharge is inappropriate. Attitude isn't going to get you anywhere; in fact, it could create additional obstacles.

That's not to say poets shouldn't feel exasperated when they're inconvenienced or ill-treated. None of us likes to see our creations vanish, or to pay good money for something we're never going to receive (like a subscription or sample copy). However, exasperated is one thing; outraged is another. Too often poets go on the offensive with editors and make matters worse. Experts on how to complain effectively recommend you keep your cool and stay professional, no matter what kind of problem you're trying to work out.

*For additional advice on editor/poet relations, see "Dealing With Problem Editors."*

# DEALING WITH PROBLEM EDITORS

There *are* problem editors out there. Some rip people off, prey on poets' desires to be published, or treat poets and their work with flagrant disregard. Fortunately, such editors are in the minority.

Now and then you may discover the disorganized editor or the overwhelmed editor; these two cause heartache (and heartburn) by closing up shop without returning manuscripts or failing to honor paid requests for subscriptions and sample copies. More often than not, their transgressions are rooted in chaos and irresponsibility, not malicious intent. Frustrating as such editors are, they're not out to get you.

There are many instances, too, where larger circumstances are beyond an editor's control. For example, a college-oriented journal may be student-staffed, with editors changing each academic year. Funds for the journal may be cut unexpectedly by administration belt-tightening, or a grant could be cancelled. The editorial office may be moved to another part of the university. An exam schedule could impact a publishing schedule. All of these things cause problems and delays.

Then again, a literary journal may be a one-person, home-based operation. The editor may get sick or have an illness in the family. Her regular job may suddenly demand lots of overtime. There may be divorce or death with which the editor has to cope. A computer could crash. Or the editor may need to scramble for money before the magazine can go to the printer. Emergencies happen, and they take their toll on deadlines. The last thing the editor wants is to inconvenience poets and readers, but sometimes life gets in the way.

Usually, difficulties with these kinds of "problem" editors can be resolved satisfactorily through communication and patience. There are always exceptions, though. Here are a few typical situations with problem editors and how to handle them.

## AN EDITOR IS RUDE.

If it's a matter of bad attitude, take it with a grain of salt. Maybe he's having a rotten day. If there's abusive language and excessive profanity involved, let us know about it. (See the complaint procedure.)

## AN EDITOR HARSHLY CRITICIZES YOUR POEM.

If an editor takes time to comment on your poetry, even if the feedback seems overly critical, consider the suggestions with an open mind and try to find something valid and useful in them. If, after you've given the matter fair consideration, you think the editor was out of line, don't rush to defend your poetry or wave your bruised ego in the editor's face. Allow that the editor has a right to her opinion (which you're not obligated to take as the final word on the quality of your work), forget about it and move on.

## AN EDITOR IS SLOW TO RESPOND TO A SUBMISSION.

As explained above, there may be many reasons why an editor's response takes longer than the time stated in the market listing or guidelines. Allow a few more weeks to pass beyond the deadline, then write a polite inquiry to the editor about the status of your manuscript. (Include an SASE if sending by regular mail.) Understand an editor may not be able to read your letter right away if deadlines are pressing or if he's embroiled in a personal crisis. Try to be patient. If you haven't received a reply to your inquiry after a month or so, however, it's time for further action.

## AN EDITOR WON'T RETURN YOUR MANUSCRIPT.

Decide whether you want to invest any more time in this journal or publisher. If you conclude you've been patient long enough, write a firm but professional letter to the editor withdrawing your manuscript from consideration. Request that the manuscript be returned; but know, too, a truly indifferent editor probably won't bother to send it back or reply in any way. Keep a copy of your withdrawal letter for your files, make a new copy of your manuscript and look for a better market.

Also, contact *Poet's Market* by letter or e-mail with details of your experience. We always look into problems with editors, although we don't withdraw a listing on the basis of a single complaint unless we discover evidence of consistent misbehavior. We do, however, keep complaints on file and watch for patterns of unacceptable behavior from any specific market.

# AN EDITOR TAKES YOUR MONEY.

If you sent a check for a subscription or sample copy and you haven't received anything, review your bank statement to see if the check has been cashed. If it has, send the editor a query. Politely point out the editor has cashed your check, but you haven't yet received the material you were expecting. Give the editor the benefit of the doubt: An upcoming issue of a magazine could be running late, your subscription could have been overlooked by mistake, or your copy could have been lost in transit or sent in error to the wrong address.

If your check has *not* been cashed, query the editor to see if your order was ever received. It may have been lost (in the mail or on the editor's desk), the editor may be holding several checks to cash at one time, or the editor may be waiting to cash checks until a tardy issue is finally published.

If you get an unsatisfactory response from the editor (or no response at all), wait a few weeks and try again. If the matter still isn't resolved, let us know about it. We're especially interested in publishers who take money from poets but don't deliver the goods. Be sure to send us all the details of the transaction, plus copies of any correspondence (yours and the editor's). We can't pursue your situation in any legal way or act as mediator, but we can ban an unscrupulous publisher from *Poet's Market* and keep the information as a resource in case we get later complaints.

Should you continue trying to get your money back from such editors? That's your decision. If your loss is under $10 (say, for a subscription or sample copy), it might cost you less in the long run to let the matter go. And the fee for a "stop payment" order on a check can be hefty—possibly more than the amount you sent the editor in the first place. Yes, it's infuriating to be cheated, but sometimes fighting on principle costs more than it's worth.

If your monetary loss is significant (for instance, you shelled out a couple hundred dollars in a subsidy publishing agreement), consider contacting your state attorney general's office for advice about small claims court, filing a complaint and other actions you can take.

# IS IT A CON?

What is a "con?" Con is short for "confidence," an adjective defined by *Webster's* as "of, relating to, or adept at swindling by false promise," as in "confidence man" or "confidence game." While the publishing world is full of legitimate opportunities for poets to gain honor and exposure for their work, there are also plenty of "cons." How can you tell the difference? The following are some of the most common situations that cost poets disappointment, frustration—and cash. Learn to spot them before submitting your work, and don't let your vanity be your guide.

## ANTHOLOGIES

Has this happened to you? You see an ad in a perfectly respectable publication announcing a poetry contest with big cash prizes. You enter, and later you receive a glowing letter congratulating you on your exceptional poem, which the contest sponsor wants to include in his deluxe hardbound anthology of the best poetry submitted to the contest. The anthology costs only, say, $65. You don't have to buy it—they'll still publish your poem—but wouldn't you be proud to own one? And wouldn't it be nice to buy additional copies to give to family and friends? And for an extra charge you can include a biographical note. And so on.

Of course, when the anthology arrives, the quality of the poetry may not be what you were expecting, with several poems crammed unattractively onto a page. Apparently everyone who entered the contest was invited to be published; you basically paid cash to see your poem appear in a phone-book-like volume with no literary merit whatsoever.

Were you conned? Depends on how you look at it. If you bought into the flattery and believed you were being published in an exclusive, high-quality publication, no doubt you feel duped. On the other hand, if all you were after was seeing your poem in print, even knowing you'd have to pay for the privilege, then you got what you wanted. (Unless you've deceived yourself into believing you've truly won an honor and now have a worthy publishing credit; you don't.)

If you don't want to add insult to injury, resist additional spiels, like having your poem printed on coffee mugs and T-shirts (you can do this yourself through print shops or online services like www.cafepress.com) or spending large sums on awards banquets and conferences. And, before you submit a single line of poetry, find out what rights the contest sponsor acquires. You may be relinquishing all rights to your poem simply by mailing it in or submitting it through a website. If the poem no longer belongs to you, the publisher can do whatever he wishes with it. Don't let your vanity propel you into a situation you'll always regret.

---

### HELPFUL WEBSITES

The following websites include specific information about questionable poetry publishers and awards. For more websites of value to poets, see Additional Resources.

- An Incomplete Guide to Print On Demand Publishers offers articles on POD publishing, comparisons of POD publishers (contracts, distribution, fees, etc.) and an online forum: http://booksandtales.com/pod/index.php
- Answers to frequently asked questions about poetry awards from the Academy of American Poets: www.poets.org/page.php/prmID/116
- Poets will find warnings and other valuable publishing information on the Preditors & Editors website: www.anotherealm.com/prededitors/
- Writer Beware tracks contests, publishers and literary agents: www.sfwa.org/beware
- Literary Contest Caution at http://windpub.com/literary.scams

---

## READING AND CONTEST FEES

Suppose you notice a promising market for your poetry, but the editor requires a set fee just to consider your work. Or you see a contest that interests you, but you have to pay the sponsor a fee just to enter. Are you being conned?

In the case of reading fees, keep these points in mind: Is the market so exceptional that you feel it's worth risking the cost of the reading fee to have your work considered? What makes it so much better than markets that do not charge fees? Has the market been around awhile, with an established publishing schedule? What are you paid if your work is accepted? Are reasonably priced samples available so you can judge the production values and quality of the writing?

Reading fees don't necessarily signal a suspicious market. In fact, they're increasingly popular as editors struggle with the costs of publishing books and magazines, including the man-hours required to read loads of (often bad) submissions. However, fees represent an additional financial burden on poets, who often don't receive any monetary reward for their poems to begin with. It's really up to individual poets to decide whether paying a fee is beneficial to their publishing efforts. Think long and hard about fee-charging markets that are new and untried, don't pay poets for their work (at the very least a print publication should offer a contributor's copy), charge high prices for sample copies or set fees that seem unreasonable.

Entry fees for contests often fund prizes, judges' fees, honorariums and expenses of running and promoting the contest (including publishing a "prize" collection or issue of a magazine). Other kinds of contests charge entry fees, from Irish dancing competitions to bake-offs at a county fair. Why not poetry contests?

That's not to say you shouldn't be cautious. Watch out for contests that charge higher-than-average fees, especially if the fees are out of proportion to the amount of prize money being given. (Look through the Contests & Awards section to get a sense of what most competitions charge.) Find out how long the contest has been around, and verify whether prizes have been awarded each year and to whom. In the case of book and chapbook contests, send for one of the winning publications to confirm that the publisher puts out a quality product. Regard with skepticism any contest that tells you you've won something, then demands payment for an anthology, trophy or other item. (It's okay if a group offers an anthology for a modest price without providing winners with free copies. Most state poetry societies have to do this; but they also present cash awards in each category of the contest, and their entry fees are low.)

## SUBSIDY PUBLISHERS, PRINT-ON-DEMAND

Poetry books are a hard sell to the book-buying public. Few of the big publishers handle these books, and those that do feature the "name" poets (i.e., the major prize winners and contemporary masters with breathtaking reputations). Even the small presses publish only so many books per year—far less than the number of poets writing.

No wonder so many poets decide to pay to have their poetry collections published. While some may self-publish (i.e., take full control of their book, working directly with a printer), others turn to subsidy publishers (also called "vanity publishers") and print-on-demand (POD) publishers.

There are many differences between subsidy publishing and POD publishing, as well as similarities (having to pay to get published is a big one). Whether or not you get conned is entirely up to you. You have to take responsibility for asking questions, doing research on presses, and reading the fine print on the contract to make sure you know exactly what you're paying for. There are landmines in dealing with subsidy and POD publishers, and you have to investigate thoroughly and intelligently to avoid damage.

Some questions to keep in mind: Are fees inflated compared to the product and services you'll be receiving? Will you still own the rights to your book? Does the publisher put out a quality product that's attractive and cleanly printed? (Get a sample copy and find out.) How many copies of the book will you receive? How much will you have to pay for additional copies? How will your book be sold and distributed? (Don't count on seeing your volume in bookstores.)

Will you receive royalties? How much? Does the publisher offer any kind of promotional assistance or is it all up to you? Will those promotion efforts be realistic and results-oriented? (Sometimes "promotion" means sending out review copies, which is a waste—such volumes are rarely reviewed.) Don't wait until *after* you've signed a contract (and a check) to raise these issues. Do your homework first.

Obviously, poets who don't stay on their toes may find themselves preyed upon. And a questionable publishing opportunity doesn't have to be an out-and-out rip-off for you to feel cheated. In every situation, you have a choice *not* to participate. Exercise that choice, or at least develop a healthy sense of skepticism before you fling yourself and your poetry at the first smooth talker who compliments your work. Poets get burned because they're much too impatient to see their work in print. Calm your ego, slow down and devote that time, energy and money toward reading other poets and improving your own writing. You'll find that getting published will eventually take care of itself.

# BLOGGING BASICS

*by Robert Lee Brewer*

In these days of publishing and media change, writers have to build platforms and learn how to connect to audiences if they want to improve their chances of publication and overall success. There are many methods of audience connection available to writers, but one of the most important is through blogging.

Since I've spent several years successfully blogging—both personally and professionally—I figure I've got a few nuggets of wisdom to pass on to writers who are curious about blogging or who already are.

Here's my quick list of tips:

1. **START BLOGGING TODAY.** If you don't have a blog, use Blogger, WordPress, or some other blogging software to start your blog today. It's free, and you can start off with your very personal "Here I am, world" post.

2. **START SMALL.** Blogs are essentially simple, but they can get complicated (for people who like complications). However, I advise bloggers start small and evolve over time.

3. **USE YOUR NAME IN YOUR URL.** This will make it easier for search engines to find you when your audience eventually starts seeking you out by name. For instance, my url is http://robertleebrewer.blogspot.com. If you try Googling "Robert Lee Brewer," you'll notice that My Name Is Not Bob is one of the top five search results (behind my other blog: Poetic Asides).

4. **UNLESS YOU HAVE A REASON, USE YOUR NAME AS THE TITLE OF YOUR BLOG.** Again, this helps with search engine results. My Poetic Asides blog includes my name in the title, and it ranks higher than My Name Is Not Bob. However, I felt the play on my name was worth the trade off.

5. **FIGURE OUT YOUR BLOGGING GOALS.** You should return to this step every couple months, because it's natural for your blogging goals to evolve over time. Initially,

your blogging goals may be to make a post a week about what you have written, submitted, etc. Over time, you may incorporate guests posts, contests, tips, etc.

6. **BE YOURSELF.** I'm a big supporter of the idea that your image should match your identity. It gets too confusing trying to maintain a million personas. Know who you are and be that on your blog, whether that means you're sincere, funny, sarcastic, etc.

7. **POST AT LEAST ONCE A WEEK.** This is for starters. Eventually, you may find it better to post once a day or multiple times per day. But remember: Start small and evolve over time.

8. **POST RELEVANT CONTENT.** This means that you post things that your readers might actually care to know.

9. **USEFUL AND HELPFUL POSTS WILL ATTRACT MORE VISITORS.** Talking about yourself is all fine and great. I do it myself. But if you share truly helpful advice, your readers will share it with others, and visitors will find you on search engines.

10. **TITLE YOUR POSTS IN A WAY THAT GETS YOU FOUND IN SEARCH ENGINES.** The more specific you can get the better. For instance, the title "Blogging Tips" will most likely get lost in search results. However, the title "Blogging Tips for Writers" specifies which audience I'm targeting and increases the chances of being found on the first page of search results.

11. **LINK TO POSTS IN OTHER MEDIA.** If you have an e-mail newsletter, link to your blog posts in your newsletter. If you have social media accounts, link to your blog posts there. If you have a helpful post, link to it in relevant forums and on message boards.

12. **WRITE WELL, BUT BE CONCISE.** At the end of the day, you're writing blog posts, not literary manifestos. Don't spend a week writing each post. Try to keep it to an hour or two tops and then post. Make sure your spelling and grammar are good, but don't stress yourself out too much.

13. **FIND LIKE-MINDED BLOGGERS.** Comment on their blogs regularly and link to them from yours. Eventually, they may do the same. Keep in mind that blogging is a form of social media, so the more you communicate with your peers the more you'll get out of the process.

14. **RESPOND TO COMMENTS ON YOUR BLOG.** Even if it's just a simple "Thanks," respond to your readers if they comment on your blog. After all, you want your readers to be engaged with your blog, and you want them to know that you care they took time to comment.

15. **EXPERIMENT.** Start small, but don't get complacent. Every so often, try something new. For instance, the biggest draw to my Poetic Asides blog are the poetry prompts and challenges I issue to poets. Initially, that was an experiment—one that worked very well. I've tried other experiments that haven't panned out, and that's fine. It's all part of a process.

# SEO TIPS FOR WRITERS

Most writers may already know what SEO is. If not, SEO stands for *search engine optimization*. Basically, a site or blog that practices good SEO habits should improve its rankings in search engines, such as Google and Bing. Most huge corporations have realized the importance of SEO and spend enormous sums of time, energy and money on perfecting their SEO practices. However, writers can improve their SEO without going to those same extremes.

In this section, I will use the terms of *site pages* and *blog posts* interchangeably. In both cases, you should be practicing the same SEO strategies (when it makes sense).

Here are my top tips on ways to improve your SEO starting today:

1. **USE APPROPRIATE KEYWORDS.** Make sure that your page displays your main keyword(s) in the page title, content, URL, title tags, page header, image names and tags (if you're including images). All of this is easy to do, but if you feel overwhelmed, just remember to use your keyword(s) in your page title and content (especially in the first and last 50 words of your page).

2. **USE KEYWORDS NATURALLY.** Don't kill your content and make yourself look like a spammer to search engines by overloading your page with your keyword(s). You don't get SEO points for quantity but for quality. Plus, one of the main ways to improve your page rankings is when you...

3. **DELIVER QUALITY CONTENT.** The best way to improve your SEO is by providing content that readers want to share with others by linking to your pages. Some of the top results in search engines can be years old, because the content is so good that people keep coming back. So, incorporate your keywords in a smart way, but make sure it works organically with your content.

4. **UPDATE CONTENT REGULARLY.** If your site looks dead to visitors, then it'll appear that way to search engines too. So update your content regularly. This should be very easy for writers who have blogs. For writers who have sites, incorporate your blog into your site. This will make it easier for visitors to find your blog to discover more about you on your site (through your site navigation tools).

5. **LINK BACK TO YOUR OWN CONTENT.** If I have a post on Blogging Tips for Writers, for instance, I'll link back to it if I have a Platform Building post, because the two complement each other. This also helps clicks on my blog, which helps SEO. The one caveat is that you don't go crazy with your linking and that you make sure your links are relevant. Otherwise, you'll kill your traffic, which is not good for your page rankings.

6. **LINK TO OTHERS YOU CONSIDER HELPFUL.** Back in 2000, I remember being ordered by my boss at the time (who didn't last too much longer afterward) to ignore any competitive or complementary websites—no matter how helpful their content—because they were our competitors. You can try basing your online strategy on these

principles, but I'm nearly 100 percent confident you'll fail. It's helpful for other sites and your own to link to other great resources. I shine a light on others to help them out (if I find their content truly helpful) in the hopes that they'll do the same if ever they find my content truly helpful for their audience.

7. **GET SPECIFIC WITH YOUR HEADLINES.** If you interview someone on your blog, don't title your post with an interesting quotation. While that strategy may help get readers in the print world, it doesn't help with SEO at all. Instead, title your post as "Interview With (insert name here)." If you have a way to identify the person further, include that in the title too. For instance, when I interview poets on my Poetic Asides blog, I'll title those posts like this: Interview With Poet Erika Meitner. Erika's name is a keyword, but so are the terms *poet* and *interview*.

8. **USE IMAGES.** Many expert sources state that the use of images can improve SEO, because it shows search engines that the person creating the page is spending a little extra time and effort on the page than a common spammer. However, I'd caution anyone using images to make sure those images are somehow complementary to the content. Don't just throw up a lot of images that have no relevance to anything. At the same time...

9. **OPTIMIZE IMAGES THROUGH STRATEGIC LABELING.** Writers can do this by making sure the image file is labeled using your keyword(s) for the post. Using the Erika Meitner example above (which does include images), I would label the file "Erika Meitner headshot.jpg"—or whatever the image file type happens to be. Writers can also improve image SEO through the use of captions and ALT tagging. Of course, at the same time, writers should always ask themselves if it's worth going through all that trouble for each image or not. Each writer has to answer that question for him (or her) self.

10. **USE YOUR SOCIAL MEDIA PLATFORM TO SPREAD THE WORD.** Whenever you do something new on your site or blog, you should share that information on your other social media sites, such as Twitter, Facebook, LinkedIn, online forums, etc. This lets your social media connections know that something new is on your site/blog. If it's relevant and/or valuable, they'll let others know. And that's a great way to build your SEO.

Programmers and marketers could get even more involved in the dynamics of SEO optimization, but I think these tips will help most writers out immediately and effectively while still allowing plenty of time and energy for the actual work of writing.

## BLOG DESIGN TIPS FOR WRITERS

Design is an important element to any blog's success. But how can you improve your blog's design if you're not a designer? I'm just an editor with an English Lit degree and no formal training in design. However, I've worked in media for more than a decade now and can share some very fundamental and easy tricks to improve the design of your blog.

Here are my seven blog design tips for writers:

1. **USE LISTS.** Whether they're numbered or bullet points, use lists when possible. Lists break up the text and make it easy for readers to follow what you're blogging.
2. **BOLD MAIN POINTS IN LISTS.** Again, this helps break up the text while also highlighting the important points of your post.
3. **USE HEADINGS.** If your posts are longer than 300 words and you don't use lists, then please break up the text by using basic headings.
4. **USE A READABLE FONT.** Avoid using fonts that are too large or too small. Avoid using cursive or weird fonts. Times New Roman or Arial works, but if you want to get "creative," use something similar to those.
5. **LEFT ALIGN.** English-speaking readers are trained to read left to right. If you want to make your blog easier to read, avoid centering or right aligning your text (unless you're purposefully calling out the text).
6. **USE SMALL PARAGRAPHS.** A good rule of thumb is to try and avoid paragraphs that drone on longer than five sentences. I usually try to keep paragraphs to around three sentences myself.
7. **ADD RELEVANT IMAGES.** Personally, I shy away from using too many images. My reason is that I only like to use them if they're relevant. However, images are very powerful on blogs, so please use them—just make sure they're relevant to your blog post.

If you're already doing everything on my list, keep it up! If you're not, then you might want to re-think your design strategy on your blog. Simply adding a header here and a list there can easily improve the design of a blog post.

## GUEST POSTING TIPS FOR WRITERS

Recently, I've broken into guest posting as both a guest poster and as a host of guest posts (over at my Poetic Asides blog). So far, I'm pretty pleased with both sides of the guest posting process. As a writer, it gives me access to an engaged audience I may not usually reach. As a blogger, it provides me with fresh and valuable content I don't have to create. Guest blogging is a rare win-win scenario.

That said, writers could benefit from a few tips on the process of guest posting:

1. **PITCH GUEST POSTS LIKE ONE WOULD PITCH ARTICLES TO A MAGAZINE.** Include what your hook is for the post, what you plan to cover, and a little about who you are. Remember: Your post should somehow benefit the audience of the blog you'd like to guest post.

2. **OFFER PROMOTIONAL COPY OF YOUR BOOK (OR OTHER GIVEAWAYS) AS PART OF YOUR GUEST POST.** Having a random giveaway for people who comment on a blog post can help spur conversation and interest in your guest post, which is a great way to get the most mileage out of your guest appearance.

3. **CATER POSTS TO AUDIENCE.** As the editor of *Writer's Market* and *Poet's Market*, I have great range in the topics I can cover. However, if I'm writing a guest post for a fiction blog, I'll write about things of interest to a novelist—not a poet.

4. **MAKE IT PERSONAL, BUT PROVIDE NUGGET.** Guest posts are a great opportunity for you to really show your stuff to a new audience. You could write a very helpful and impersonal post, but that won't connect with readers the same way as if you write a very helpful and personal post that makes them want to learn more about you (and your blog, your book, your Twitter account, etc.). Speaking of which...

5. **SHARE LINKS TO YOUR WEBSITE, BLOG, SOCIAL NETWORKS, ETC.** After all, you need to make it easy for readers who enjoyed your guest post to learn more about you and your projects. Start the conversation in your guest post and keep it going on your own sites, profiles, etc. And related to that...

6. **PROMOTE YOUR GUEST POST THROUGH YOUR NORMAL CHANNELS ONCE THE POST GOES LIVE.** Your normal audience will want to know where you've been and what you've been doing. Plus, guest posts lend a little extra "street cred" to your projects. But don't stop there...

7. **CHECK FOR COMMENTS ON YOUR GUEST POST AND RESPOND IN A TIMELY MAN- NER.** Sometimes the comments are the most interesting part of a guest post (no of- fense). This is where readers can ask more in-depth or related questions, and it's also where you can show your expertise on the subject by being as helpful as possible. And guiding all seven of these tips is this one:

8. **PUT SOME EFFORT INTO YOUR GUEST POST.** Part of the benefit to guest posting is the opportunity to connect with a new audience. Make sure you bring your A-game, because you need to make a good impression if you want this exposure to actually help grow your audience. Don't stress yourself out, but put a little thought into what you submit.

**ONE ADDITIONAL TIP:** Have fun with it. Passion is what really drives the popularity of blogs. Share your passion and enthusiasm, and readers are sure to be impressed.

---

**ROBERT LEE BREWER** is an editor with the Writer's Digest Writing Community and author of *Solving the World's Problems* (Press 53). Follow him on Twitter @robertleebrewer.

# 6 WAYS TO PROMOTE YOUR NEW BOOK

......................................................

*by Jeannine Hall Gailey*

When your new book arrives, you naturally want to shout the news from the rooftops, run and put a copy in everyone's hand, proudly take a selfie with your box of books and put it on Facebook. But what else can you do to promote your book that won't leave your online reputation in shambles?

In an ideal world, all you'd have to do is write the book, and everyone else—your publisher, your readers, your friends and family—would get word out about your book for you. Sadly, no matter who your publisher is you will be your book's best publicist. You can keep a social media presence with Tumblr, Twitter, Facebook, a blog, etc. But you know those annoying spammy tweets from authors clogging up your feeds with yet another glowing blurb or Amazon rank? You don't want to be that person.

My personal two "golden rules" of promotion—one of which looks a lot like the actual golden rule—are:

1. Do unto others as you would have them do unto you. Whether it's reviews, retweets, or just kind mentions on blogs, remember that you don't live in a vacuum, and you can hardly expect others to enthusiastically support your book if you haven't done much for your peer's books. Show up to your friends' book parties and debut readings, and you'll have a higher likelihood of a full house at your own.
2. Don't do anything online you wouldn't do in real life. If you wouldn't knock on your best friend's doorstep and tell them three days in a row to buy your book, don't do it in e-mail or Facebook messages, either.

Now, here are six ways to create positive buzz about your new title in a seemingly endless sea of new titles, and do it without alienating people. These tips will make the whole process as simple and painless for everyone as possible.

## START CLOSE TO HOME

Because you have been working as a positive force for poetry in your immediate community the last few years (right??) you should have some friends and well-wishers who will be happy to help "boost your signal." The greater your involvement in building up your local poetry community and the more people you positively impact, the better.

For instance, I frequently write poetry book reviews for different outlets and write blurbs for writers I like, because I see it as "giving back" to the literary community. I also do it because someone once said to me when I was a young poet: "How can you hope for others to read and review your book if you don't read and review other people's books?" But reviewing isn't the only way to give back. You can run a reading series, edit a literary magazine, or even start your own press. Now that you have a book out, you'll realize that seemingly small gestures such as "liking" a post on Facebook, retweeting a book announcement, or reviewing a great book on Amazon or Goodreads, count more than you thought.

Also remember that it's much easier to sell your book of poetry in your hometown, at a reading full of friends and family, than it will be to sell it to strangers and students you've never met before. Remember, they're already cheering you on.

Similarly, you can reach out to people who have been kind to you in the past—reviewers who liked your previous work, mentors who have offered you help, your writing group—although this can only work if you're keeping either a list of people (with contact information, be it an e-mail address or a physical address) who might be interested in more of your work in the future. So keep up a list that I call it my "literary Christmas card list," and I actually use it to send Christmas cards, not just literary announcements. Again, being genuine friends with a lot of people will only help you in your efforts, so it pays to be generous. Karma, etc.

## HELP PROMOTE OTHERS

This ties in with the previous tip. It makes sense that if you are kind and generous to others, helping spread the word about their good news, they are more likely to be kind and generous when you need help. When you think about sharing news about your book, think about the ways that news can help others—your publishers, editors, and others who have supported you along the way.

Award-winning poet Aimee Nezhukumatathil, a Professor of English at SUNY-Fredonia says: "I'm a big fan of using social media to post someone's poem that catches my breath, with a link to his/her recent book, or even better, to share my 'discovery' of an up-and-coming writer. On Twitter, even reading a line or two is enough to prick my curiosity. I've looked up poets and bought books from other people's postings. As for my own work, I share the occasional notice about where a recent poem or essay was published to help spread the word about the editors and magazines who believed in my work in the first place."

Being involved in helping other people succeed is a great way to build your literary community, so give others a boost when you can.

## BOOK ANNOUNCEMENTS

A well-written, non-spammy (and spell-checked!) e-mail announcement to send to your friends, family, and colleagues is an easy thing a new author can do to let people know their book is available. Be friendly, respectful, and direct, and be sure to include, perhaps at the end, a direct link to buy your new book. If you want to include a few people who might have sent you kind notes in the past, or indicated interest in hearing about your new work, don't feel bad—do it. Remember that this can be a great way to get back in touch with old friends; I often have childhood friends, teachers, or students who write back after years of being out of contact. But please don't buy one of those prefabricated mailing list or send your news to every business acquaintance.

Marie Gauthier, Director of Sales & Marketing for Tupelo Press, reminds us to "remember to treat friends as allies, not customers. They want to help you spread the word; it's your job to make it as easy for them to help as you can, sending them the cover image of your book or a jpeg of a beautiful publicity release, items with visual appeal that are simple to share." She also advises writers to "include something personal or quirky or extra in your email that can help elevate it in the receiver's mind from 'spam.'"

Jericho Brown, award-winning poet, professor, and editor, has a few pieces of practical advice, warning writers to think hard about when and how they announce their book. "It makes sense to pay attention to the world in which we live and to be a real part of it. Don't post that you've won a big award or send an e-mail about your book the same day Zimmerman is declared not guilty. If you do send an e-mail to a group, make sure it's just once a year and that you include a link to the message or site you're promoting. Finally, if you want 4,000 people to know your good news at once, know also that you want to thank 4,000 people individually for congratulating you."

Be unique, be yourself, and be socially aware of timing when you send out your announcement.

## SOCIAL MEDIA

Yes, it's probably a good idea to have a presence on social media—an author page on Facebook that allows people the option of learning news about your work, for instance, or a good basic website, and maybe a Twitter, Instagram, Pinterest, or Tumblr account.

The good news about this kind of promotion is that you can do it in your pajamas! The bad news is that it's easy to overdo it and become unintentionally obnoxious. The other downside? Most people aren't constantly reading their Twitter or Facebook feeds, or checking your blog, so it's hard to know when those messages are being missed by a particular audience.

So, be smart about the way you promote your new book on social media.

Catherine Trestini, Digital Marketing and Social Media Strategist, suggests: "One author kept sending me messages on LinkedIn about his book IN ALL CAPS for weeks. It became so irritating that I eventually removed him from my network. So my first rule of thumb is to leave your spam at the front door. Readers need a reason to want your book. Make a good impression. But let him set the example of what not to do on social media. Similarly, remember to post different and new things about your book. Every day, we're zombie-scrolling through our Facebook feeds, subconsciously looking for great things to 'like' or comment on. Use your wit, empathy, and brainy attitude to engage me. My second piece of advice is: Do something awesome that speaks about who 'you' are on your Facebook page, and do it often (at least once a day). It will collect "likes" and comments and woo your readers. Only write what you would want to read, including talking about your book online."

Make your posts authentic, and only talk about your own book part of the time—again, be sure to post other people's news, interesting relevant articles (whether that's on Buffy the Vampire Slayer's impact on pop culture or the latest news on Fukushima) and try to give your followers more than just advertising.

## POSTCARDS, BOOKMARKS, AND OTHER "SWAG"

I know it's a new media world, but don't discount the power and pleasure of real mail and the physical object. In my own experience, sending out postcards is one of the best ways to give people a tactile reminder that your book is out—as well as show off a brilliant cover design. You should include a direct link to purchase the book on the postcard somewhere, as well as a way to contact you to get a signed copy, so it will be as easy as possible for them to purchase it. And a personal note on the postcard never hurts.

I've seen fascinating "swag" at readings, from intricate mini-books the size of a business card to elaborate bookmarks, magnets and stickers. The idea is to leave an audience member at a reading or conference-goer a physical memento that will perhaps lead them later to think about your book and purchase it.

## READINGS

With a new book coming out, of course you're planning a few readings, maybe around your own town, maybe a more ambitious tour across several states. This one you cannot do in your pajamas, but there are a lot of ways you can make readings more fun for your audience and give your friends a real reason to come out and cheer you on.

Don't just plan a reading—plan a book release party, where you can celebrate and spend time with your friends and family afterward. If your friends are so inclined, they could even host a poetry salon, an informal gathering with cocktails or snacks where you might read a few poems, offer to sell and sign books, but mostly, give writers an excuse to socialize with you and with each other.

For example, when you go to a reading out of town, make sure you're paired up with a popular local writer as well, and try to do something fun to connect—set up a workshop beforehand, or an informal reception afterwards.

Kelly Davio, former editor of *LA Review* and author of *Burn This House*, gives this advice from her recent first book tour: "Anytime I give a reading, I make sure to stay and listen attentively to every other poet, whether that's another featured reader or someone who has just come for the open mic. Listening to others is an important way that we poets can show respect for our readership; if we're asking others to listen to our poems or buy our books, we need to give our attention to their work as well."

In the end, you really want to be able to share your excitement about your book without being pushy or disrespectful, and a lot of that comes down to being genuine and self-aware.

**JEANNINE HALL GAILEY** served as the second Poet Laureate of Redmond, Washington and is the author of three books of poetry, *Becoming the Villainess, She Returns to the Floating World,* and *Unexplained Fevers.* Her website is www.webbish6.com and you can follow her on Twitter @webbish6.

# POETRY ON STAGE

## Practical Advice for Live Performance

........................................

*by Daniel Ari*

/////////////////////////////////////////////////////////////////////////////////

Butterflies. Cottonmouth. Sweaty palms and the sound of your own heart beating. Knowing that these are natural reactions to entering the spotlight—even for seasoned speakers—might make them only slightly easier to endure. But preparation and practice can boost your confidence, so you can enjoy the rewards that come with performing your poetry for an audience.

## FACING THE FEAR

If you're not someone who intrinsically loves being on stage, you may decide never to go there. But there are benefits of public reading that can make it worthwhile to work through stage fright.

**YOUR POETRY IMPROVES.** Going through the process of presenting can help clarify your poetic voice and give you the perspective to catch words or phrases that make you stumble or that cloud your meaning. You might also receive constructive input from friends and supportive audience members.

**YOUR AUDIENCE GROWS.** Getting on stage can help you build your following. People who like what you do will want to read what you've written and become advocates of your work. Having a venue gives you the opportunity to sell books, plug your blog, add to your mailing list, and so on.

**YOUR SPEAKING ABILITY IMPROVES.** Becoming a more confident speaker can benefit other areas of your life. If you regularly address groups or run meetings, then café poetry readings are a good place to practice in a situation with lower stakes.

**IT CAN BE EXCITING.** Connecting with an audience can be truly exhilarating, and the chance to feel proud of your work can be the biggest reward.

**AUDIENCES WANT TO HEAR YOU.** Audiences at readings have made the decision to be there, and they are ready to receive you. Rise to the occasion with good material that's well prepared, and enjoy their appreciation.

## PREPARE TO PERFORM

Attend enough readings, and you're likely to encounter a few brilliant writers—who have no sense of delivery. As you listen, you might notice their richness of language and deft handling of thematic subtleties. But their monotone voice and apparent lack of sensitivity to the audience will have you involuntarily glancing toward the exit.

Though any poet can simply walk up to a microphone and start reading, it's better to think of your reading as a theatrical performance and to devote time and attention to the project. A reading that satisfies both you and your audience takes preparation.

**CHOOSE POEMS THAT WORK WELL IN YOUR VOICE.** Gather more than enough poetry, too much for the stage time you will be given. Read each piece you are considering out loud a few times, and narrow down your selection to those poems that you can recite most fluidly and sincerely.

**PREPARE FOR PRACTICE.** Double-check the pronunciation of any difficult or unusual words. Listen carefully to what you are saying in the poem and think how you might emphasize and intone the words appropriately. Would the poem benefit from a brief introduction? If so, consider scripting and practicing that part as well so you can keep it to the point.

**THINK LIKE A DIRECTOR.** As you start to practice, consider how you want the poem to sound. Formal or conversational? Energetically quick or suspensefully slow? How loud do you want to speak? Will your tone, tempo or volume change? Consider your options, and look for what most naturally supports the poem in your voice.

**TAKE NOTES.** Many performers mark up practice copies of their poems to remind themselves how they want the reading to sound. You can highlight words you want to emphasize and make notes about when to speed up or slow down. Some poets I know who have studied music use musical notations to indicate crescendos, accents, pauses and so on.

**MEMORIZE.** The subject of an entire article in its own right, memorization doesn't come naturally to everyone; however, getting off paper can make a huge difference in performance. When you speak from memory, your hands are free to gesture more naturally. Your eyes can engage the audience, and the audience will clearly sense your commitment to the poem when you have committed it to memory.

Here are two techniques I use to memorize poems: 1) Recite the first two lines of your poem until you can speak them from memory; then add lines three and four. Keep adding lines as you recite the whole poem from the beginning, until you've assimilated the whole piece. 2) Record the poem and play it for yourself. Speak along with the recording of your voice. Repeat until you can recite along with yourself without pausing or mistakes.

These techniques can take hours or extend over days. Both are possible to do while you're doing something else like washing dishes, commuting to work, gardening, etc.

Once you have your poems in your memory, be sure to keep them there. Practice at least once a day until your reading date and a couple times a month afterward so the poems stay ready for the next time.

**SLOW DOWN AND RELAX.** When you're on stage, your tendency will be to speak more quickly than when you rehearse. This will be less of an issue if, when you rehearse, you consciously slow yourself down. Doing so will help offset your natural acceleration in the spotlight.

**PRACTICE MORE.** It's nearly impossible to over-rehearse. Instead, you're likely to discover new meanings and interpretations in your poems the more your practice them.

**VIDEOTAPE YOURSELF.** As you critique your performance, seeing yourself as an audience will see you can give you useful insights. Some readers pace as they read; others repeat a gesture or stand unnaturally still. With video, you'll see any unconscious habits you have—and then you can let go of them or consciously change them. Remember to be gentle with yourself. As you watch, focus on what you can improve, but also focus on how cool you are for preparing a performance. Make a point of feeling proud of yourself.

**DO A PRE-SHOW.** Gather a couple of close friends, a spouse, a supportive sibling or neighbor and recite for them. This is like easing into a hot tub. Reciting for a couple of friendly faces is your warm up to getting on stage in front of strangers. If you'd like feedback from your pre-show audience, ask them direct and specific questions such as:

- Was my voice loud enough?
- Did you understand each word?
- Did you understand and enjoy the poem?

## FIND YOUR VENUE

An Internet search for "Poetry Readings" in your area will turn up cafes, bookstores, clubs, bars, theaters, galleries, speakeasies, or other venues. Contact them online or by phone to find out what's going on and how you can participate.

It's a good idea to visit the venue to check out the scene before you go to read, especially if you're new to public reading. By watching other performers and talking to event hosts, you can find out how much time performers get and any other parameters you need to know. You'll also get a sense of what the audience appreciates.

Poetry Slams, for example, usually keep readers to a strict limit of three minutes of high-energy recitation—from memory—before penalties apply in the form of docked points from the volunteer judges. Yes, judges. Delivering a poem significantly different from the usual style at a poetry slam increases the chance of audience heckling, which is not meant to be hurtful, but is a traditional part of some poetry slams. Café open mics, on the other hand, are typically laid back with looser time limits in a wider range of styles. The main thing is to know in advance what you can expect from the venue and its audience.

Many organizers of ongoing events select featured readers whom they've come to know. If you want to be a featured reader at a regular event, a good way to get there is to keep showing up. Introduce yourself to the organizers, and when it seems right, let your interest be known. They'll let you know how you can earn a featured slot.

If performing for strangers worries you, consider arranging your own reading at a private residence. You can decide who to invite, how to decorate, when to start and end, what to charge, what food or beverages to serve, who else will perform, and so on. Though it takes more effort and leadership on your part, setting up your own reading lets you create exactly the event you want.

When you know where and when you're performing, spread the word. If it's your first time and you could use some moral support, invite close friends to be there or to go with you. If you're a seasoned performer doing a featured reading or a one-person show, be sure to advertise. Use Facebook and Evite to get on your desired audiences' calendars. You can also send a quick press release to your local arts weekly, radio station and online calendar sites.

Note that people respond more consistently to personal phone calls, e-mails or texts. If there are people you really want to be there, take the extra time to contact them directly.

## BEFORE YOU PERFORM

The poems you choose to recite should be ones that move you and that you're enthusiastic to share. As you practice, you claim the words; they enter your mind and soul. So when it comes time to read, trust the words. Draw confidence from the excellence of the poetry and the time you've put into your performance. On the day or evening of your performance, these steps can support your sense of confidence and help your reading go just right:

**DRESS FOR THE VENUE.** Attractive, clean and hip are always appropriate. You can do something flashy, but don't let your clothes distract from your words. Dress like Lady Gaga, and your clothing will overshadow your poetry.

**EAT LIGHT.** If you're feeling nervous, don't eat for a couple of hours before your performance, but stay hydrated.

**SET UP YOUR CAMERA.** If you're recording or having someone record you, be sure to get connected early and test your equipment before the show starts.

**WARM UP.** Try to find some time backstage or outside to warm up your voice. It will help you relax and improve your projection, pacing, breathing and enunciation. Here are some easy warm ups:

1. Yawn or sigh deeply a couple of times. Make the natural yawning sounds to relax your throat and vocal chords.
2. Recite a few tongue twisters. Red leather, yellow leather. She sells sea shells by the sea shore. You know New York; you need New York; you know you need unique New York.
3. Recite one or two lines of your poem while grotesquely over-enunciating each word. This will loosen your tongue, lips, jaw and nasal passages.
4. Blow air through your lips with and without engaging your vocal chords.
5. With your fingertips, massage your jaw, lips, cheeks and chin.
6. Make exaggerated chewing motions as though you are chomping twenty pieces of gum at once. Make the sounds that would go with the motions.
7. Finish by taking three slow, deep breaths. This is especially good to do before you go on stage. If an emcee introduces you, take that time to breathe consciously, deeply and slowly. And then...

You're on!

## DO IT.

Once you're on, you're on. Go with the words of the poem and the performance you prepared. When you practice, it will help to develop these good habits so they come naturally when you're on stage:

- Stand up straight so your lungs and throat are fully open.
- Put your breath behind your voice and project your words to the far end of the room.
- Speak slowly and let the words take their resonance in sound and meaning.
- Let yourself pause between stanzas or thoughts.

Your voice when performing shouldn't sound exactly like your everyday conversational voice, even if you're reciting in a conversational tone. Your words will be somewhat slower, more distinct, more fully enunciated. It may sound funny to you until you're used to it, but an audience depends on the enhanced clarity and resonance to get the full effect of what you're saying.

When you're on stage, strive to make eye contact with the audience. I find it helps to imagine that everyone there is an old friend of mine, even the person dourly glaring up at me from the fourth row.

If there's a microphone, simply project into it with your mouth positioned about a foot away. Many novice performers get distracted trying to adjust the mic stand or cord. The less of that you can do the better—you don't even have to touch the microphone. And if there are any issues with the microphone or sound system, politely ask if you can get some help before you start your recitation.

If you lose your place in the poem or stumble over a word, simply take a breath and start the line or stanza again. It's okay for you to take a moment in quiet to find your place and to look at the audience. You'll see that they are ready for you to continue, and they want you to succeed. Remember: You own the poem. Trust the words and let them come through you.

At the end of your reading, I suggest doing what feels right to you in terms of acknowledging your applause and thanking your emcee or host; but usually a bow of the head is polite and sufficient.

When I get off stage, I try to take a few deep, calming breaths before I talk to anyone. It's good to let your endorphins settle before you start meeting and greeting. But do let yourself receive kudos from your audience.

If you want feedback on your performance, watch the video if you have one and look for ways to inflect words differently or improve your delivery. Don't be overly critical. Focus only on your words and your delivery. Consider asking friends and other performers you trust for honest and constructive input. It's also good to watch other poets perform so you can see what styles and behaviors you want to model and make your own.

For the long term, keep doing it. Keep building your confidence, your repertoire, and your audience. Be sure to practice a few times a month to keep poems ready for opportunities to share. You might find your recitations welcome in your place of worship, among wedding toasts, or at informal social gatherings. When the moment's right, you'll be ready to make the gentle offer, "Would you like to hear a poem?"

**DANIEL ARI**'s book, *One Way to Ask*, pairs poems in an original form called queron with imagery by more than 60 artists. Besides being a professional copywriter, he writes and publishes poetry and organizes poetry performances and events throughout the Pacific Northwest. He blogs at fightswithpoems.blogspot.com.

# HOMEGROWN PROMOTIONS

## 10 Places to Promote Your Poetry

*by Hunter Liguore*

Creating a homegrown presence for your poetry begins right in your own neighborhood and town, giving you immediate opportunities to connect with readers. When I think "homegrown," I think local, and local, for me, means accessible and reachable. Those are the benefits I tout when I'm marketing myself to local businesses.

Most towns come fully equipped with a variety of venues where poets can showcase their work. The amount of people that I reach varies from place to place, but I've found the numbers encouraging and often competitive to online markets. I started promoting my work as "homegrown" as a means to combat the long wait times that occur with online journals and publishing. It's not necessarily a substitute, but the benefits include things like: immediate applause; a steady, reachable fan base; face-to-face discussions about my work; loyalty; word of mouth; and most of all, a deeper sense of community.

## GETTING STARTED

Where can you start to look for venues to support your homegrown poetry? I initially started on my own street by dropping off a weekly poem and invite, in my neighbors' mailboxes, that led to a summer barbecue on my front lawn that everyone was invited to. Come to find out, I wasn't the only poet on the street. Although the barbecue didn't spawn instant fame or a year's worth of chapbook sales, it did start the beginning of a small group of readers interested in my work.

A few months later, when I self-published a chapbook, one made by hand, I had people to tell about it, and sold several. It was then I realized that readers were a lot closer than the Internet led me to believe—I had a whole town of people who might be interested in my work, and what made me different than my online competitors was being homegrown.

# PLACES FOR HOMEGROWN PROMOTION

The following is a list of places I began calling, visiting, and arranging poetry readings. While many of these places, to start, will give you space and time for free, and without monetary payment, the end result has so many other benefits. What began as "free readings," turned into return "paid visits." The goal with homegrown promotion is to encourage and build a devoted fan base, one you can sell your products to, or arrange for future paid performances, just like a musician would.

## 1. The Farmer's Market

The farmer's market was the first place I sought out to give poetry readings to showcase my work. They usually occur in the center of town, weekly, and over the course of the summer. A poet can build an immense following, just by showing up every week. There is usually some kind of entertainment, like a band, and if there isn't, you can suggest it to the people organizing it, by asking if they wouldn't mind if you read some poetry to people shopping. Most organizers are more than happy to have you. You'll need a small amp and mic, which can be acquired pretty inexpensively from a local music store. (You might use it at some of these other places too.)

## 2. Historical Societies

Historical societies come in all shapes and sizes. They range from really tiny (as in you might even drive past it it's so small) to being quite big, with a huge following. In either case, historical societies are usually equipped to offer events, and have a ready membership and mailing list. If you can locate a historical society for an author, even better. In New England, for instance, author houses are plentiful, and they host readings, book clubs, and workshops. If your historical society doesn't offer readings, ask to organize one specifically for local poets, yourself included.

## 3. The Library

The library is the town's hub for readers. Get in touch with those in charge of buying books and make sure to let them know poetry is important to acquire, including your own homegrown collections. Once your books are in stock, talk to the special events coordinator about arranging a poetry reading or poetry writing workshop. Both can go a long way in promoting your work as a poet. Be consistent and schedule events regularly to build readership and visibility.

## 4. Local Races

Depending on where you live, your town, or those nearby, should offer marathons or races on a regular basis. Races attract a regular group of runners who often go town to town to compete. Most events also include vendors that give away product samples and information. Because the races are public, you can show up with your mic and poems and share them to a ready audience, one usually milling around between the start and finish of the race. (Check to see if you need a permit from the town first). At the least, you can hand out business cards and poetry samples (see below for more ideas).

## 5. Religious Institutions

Churches have become a source for entertainment and often have musicians, speakers, and authors—including poets—come to visit. Often a paying opportunity, check your local newspaper for area events at local churches or temples to see which ones might be interested in a performance reading—if you have friends who are also poets, you might establish a group of "homegrown poets" to showcase. Equally, your local occult shop or coven might also have reading opportunities. For instance, around Halloween, I bring out all my holiday poetry and give a reading at my local Wiccan shop, and reach new readers; the store will usually carry your chapbooks for the month of October, leading to the event.

## 6. Natural Foods Stores

Most towns have a natural foods market that caters to local products and farms. I approach the owner/manager with my story of how great it would be to carry some homegrown poetry on consignment. I also ask if I can "demo" or "sample" my product right alongside the local honey company, and usually get a yes. If the store has a café of any kind, I will do a giveaway for all those who attend—usually a sample of my work bound up in a one-of-a-kind chapbook and a free coffee.

## 7. Restaurants/Bars

Restaurants and bars are always looking for entertainment. If your local restaurant is booking musicians on Friday and Saturday nights, then ask if they'd be willing to showcase poetry on a Monday or Tuesday night. I often solicit restaurant/bars early in the year and try to schedule gigs around President's Day, Martin Luther King Day or Valentine's Day; the work I showcase is themed to the holiday. If I'm doing the event by myself or with another poet, we usually read from the work of published authors and our own work—like a band that plays originals and covers!

## 8. Nature Centers/Animal Shelters

Nature centers and animal shelters cater to a clientele with interests in the environment, animals, preservation, nature, walking, and recreation. They also usually have an education department that offers a variety of events or classes to the public. For animal shelters, you'll find adoption days that you can arrange to be at and volunteer for, while putting aside some time to be the performance for the day via your mic and poems. For nature centers, you might arrange a walking tour centered around nature poetry, or a writing class on the same theme, which culminates in a poetry reading for students.

## 9. Bus

If you love traveling, then you might find a haven of readers on your local bus route. I started out by taking the same bus at the same time everyday, and took notes on what people were reading. Then one week I showed up with free books that I had put aside for donation; I passed them out and started making friends. After that, I brought samples of my own work to share to anyone interested. People usually perk up when someone's getting something free. With every sample, I'm sure to include my contact information. I let them know if they have an upcoming birthday party or anniversary and need a performer, they can count on me. I've done a few readings on buses—but it takes timing to pick the right poem to fit in-between stops.

## 10. Colleges, High Schools

If you're looking to engage locally, no better place to begin with but your local college or high school. You can start with the English department, which usually sponsors readings throughout the semester. I suggest sending a letter to those instructors teaching poetry (writing or literature), to see if they would be interested in a local poet coming into the class to speak about the life of the poet; it will usually include a reading as well. Some schools will offer a stipend for your visit.

# WHAT TO BRING TO YOUR HOMEGROWN PERFORMANCE

Once you've scheduled your first homegrown performance, the next step is to build your marketing kit to bring with you. Every poet should have with them the essentials: a business card or postcard with links to your website and books. (If you don't have a book yet, include links to journals.) Bring along a tip-jar for donations, and a mailing list sign up sheet, which you'll later use to send out event reminders. Additionally, you might bring the following:

## 1. Samples

Published or unpublished, you'll want to bring something that has your work in it. It might be copies of a literary journal that published one of your poems, or a published/ self-published book, or you might create a DIY one-of-a-kind collection to sell. I also print postcards, sample booklets, or other artistic creations, like painted pottery and t-shirts with my poems on them. I always emphasize that they are unique, and not available online, which fosters greater interest.

## 2. Sign

While it's important to say your name when you're reading, it can often go unheard. To alleviate any confusion of who's reading, make a sign with your name on it, so everyone can get in touch with you. If they take pictures, it will automatically have your name included.

## 3. List of Services

Building a fan base includes awareness to what services you provide. I have a service list that includes performance readings for weddings, anniversaries, parties, book clubs, and other events. I also include fees for editing and writing classes. I recently added a poetry-related field trip to an author's house.

## 4. Giveaways

Part of what makes homegrown promotions so exciting is engaging with an audience—everyone likes to participate. Giveaways are a great way of promoting interest, and giving back to those listening. What you give away is up to you—once I gave away ears of corn, attached with a poem, at a farmer's market.

## 5. Calendar of Events

It goes without saying, the more events you book locally, the more stars you'll have on a calendar—and because you're local, it's easier to convince people to come see you. Make sure to have a calendar to hand out with your upcoming appearances—include your social media links, with incentives to join.

# BE CREATIVE

Being homegrown means interacting and getting to know your neighbors. People will start to recognize you, especially if you have given them something to remember. Sometimes I wear a funky colored wig, or a very bright t-shirt with a picture of my state and the words, "Homegrown Poet." Anything that's easy for folks to remember. So be creative and create a brand that works for you. Before long, you'll have people coming up to you asking, "Hey, aren't you that local poet?" Then you know you're on your way!

**HUNTER LIGUORE** is an American writer with degrees in history and writing. A two-time Push-cart Prize nominee, her work has appeared in various publications, including *Bellevue Literary Review*, *Irish Times*, and *DESCANT*. She was the 2015 Writer-in-Residence at the Edwin Way Teale Nature Preserve, and the first place recipient of the 2015 Ethnographic Fiction competition sponsored by the American Anthropological Association. Her forthcoming novel, *Next Breath*, is represented by Regal Hoffman & Associates..

# SOCIAL MEDIA PRIMER FOR POETS

......................................................

*by Robert Lee Brewer*

Beyond the actual writing, the most important thing writers can do for their writing careers is to build a writer platform. This writer platform can consist of any number of quantifiable information about your reach to your target audience, and one hot spot is social media.

**HERE'S THE THING:** It's more important to chase quality connections than quantity connections on social media.

Social media is one way to quantify your reach to your target audience. If you write poetry, your target audience is people who read poetry (often other folks who write poetry). If you write cookbooks, your target audience is people who like to cook.

In both cases, you can drill down into more specifics. Maybe the target audience for the poetry book is actually people who read sonnets. For the cookbook, maybe it's directed at people who like to cook desserts.

## 4 SOCIAL MEDIA TIPS

Anyway, social media is one way to connect with your target audience and influencers (like agents, editors, book reviewers, other writers) who connect to your target audience. Sites like Facebook, Twitter, LinkedIn, YouTube, Pinterest, Goodreads, Red Room, and so many more—they're all sites dedicated to helping people (and in some cases specifically writers) make connections.

Here are my four social media tips for writers:

1. **START SMALL.** The worst thing writers can do with social media is jump on every social media site ever created immediately, post a bunch of stuff, and then quit because they're overwhelmed on the time commitment and underwhelmed by the lack of re-

sponse. Instead, pick one site, complete all the information about yourself, and start browsing around in that one neighborhood for a while.

2. **LOOK FOR CONNECTIONS.** Notice that I did not advise looking for leads or followers or whatever. Don't approach strangers online like a used car salesman. Be a potential friend and/or source of information. One meaningful connection is worth more than 5,000 disengaged "followers." Seriously.

3. **COMMUNICATE.** There are two ways to make a mistake here. One, never post or share anything on your social media account. Potential new connections will skip over your ghost town profile assuming your account is no longer active. Plus, you're missing an opportunity to really connect with others. The other mistake is to post a million (hopefully an exaggeration) things a day and never communicate with your connections. It's social media, after all; be social.

4. **GIVE MORE THAN YOU TAKE.** So don't post a million things a day, but be sure to share calls for submissions, helpful information (for your target audience), fun quotes, great updates from your connections (which will endear you to them further). Share updates from your end of the world, but don't treat your social media accounts as a place to sell things nonstop. Remember: Don't be a used car salesman.

**ONE FINAL TIP: Focus.** Part of effective platform building is knowing your target audience and reaching them. So with every post, every status update, every tweet, every connection, etc., keep focused on how you are bringing value to your target audience.

## POPULAR SOCIAL NETWORKING SITES

The social media landscape is constantly shifting, but here are some that are currently popular:

- Bebo (http://bebo.com)
- Digg (http://digg.com)
- Facebook (http://facebook.com)
- Flickr (http://flickr.com)
- Google+ (http://plus.google.com)
- Habbo (http://habbo.com)
- Hi5 (http://hi5.com)
- Instagram (http://instagram.com)
- LinkedIn (http://linkedin.com)
- MeetUp (http://meetup.com)
- Ning (http://ning.com)
- Orkut (http://orkut.com)
- Pinterest (http://pinterest.com)

- Reddit (http://reddit.com)
- StumbleUpon (http://stumbleupon.com)
- Twitter (http://twitter.com)
- Yelp (http://yelp.com)
- YouTube (http://youtube.com)
- Zorpia (htttp://zorpia.com)

# 9 THINGS TO DO ON ANY SOCIAL MEDIA SITE

Not all social media sites are created the same. However, there are some things poets can do on any site to improve the quantity and quality of the connections they make online.

1. **USE YOUR REAL NAME.** If the point of social media is to increase your visibility, then don't make the mistake of cloaking your identity behind some weird handle or nickname. Use your real name—or that is, use your real byline as it appears (or would appear) when published.

2. **USE YOUR HEADSHOT FOR AN AVATAR.** Again, avoid concealing your identity as a cartoon image or picture of a celebrity or pet. The rules of online networking are the same as face-to-face networking. Imagine how silly it would be to see someone holding up a picture of a pet cat while talking to you in person.

3. **COMPLETE YOUR PROFILE.** Each site has different ways to complete this information. You don't have to include religious or political views, but you do want to make your site personal while still communicating your interest and experience in poetry. One tip: Give people a way to contact you that doesn't involve using the social networking site. For instance, an e-mail address.

4. **LINK TO WEBSITES.** If you have a blog and/or author website, link to these in your profile on all social media sites. After all, you want to make it as easy as possible for people to learn more about you. If applicable, link to your previously published books at points of purchase too.

5. **MAKE EVERYTHING PUBLIC.** As a poet, you are a public figure. Embrace that state of mind and make everything you do public on social media. This means you may have to sacrifice some privacy, but there are pre-Facebook ways of communicating private matters with friends and family.

6. **UPDATE REGULARLY.** Whether it's a status update or a tweet, regular updates accomplish two things: One, they keep you in the conversation; and two, they let people you know (and people you don't know) see that you're actively using your account. Activity promotes more connections and conversations, which is what poets want on social media sites.

7. **JOIN AND PARTICIPATE IN RELEVANT GROUPS.** One key to this tip is relevancy. There are lots of random groups out there, but the ones that will benefit you the most are ones relevant to your interests and goals. Another key is participation. Participate in your group when possible.

8. **BE SELECTIVE.** Piggybacking on the previous tip, be selective about who you friend, who you follow, which groups you join, etc. Don't let people bully you into following them either. Only connect with and follow people or groups you think might bring you value—if not immediately, then eventually.

9. **EVOLVE.** When I started social media, MySpace was the top hangout. Eventually, I moved on to Facebook and Twitter (at the urging of other connections). Who knows which sites I'll prefer in five months, let alone five years, from now. Evolve as the landscape evolves. In fact, even my usage of specific sites has had to evolve as user behavior changes and the sites themselves change.

## FINAL THOUGHT

If you have a blog, be sure to use it to feed your social media site profiles. Each new post should be a status update or tweet. This will serve the dual purpose of bringing traffic to your blog and providing value to your social media connections.

# POETIC FORMS

...................................................

*by Robert Lee Brewer*

///////////////////////////////////////////////////////////////////////

Not every poet likes the idea of writing in poetic forms, but for many poets—including myself—poetic forms are a sort of fun challenge. Whether playing with a sestina or working haiku, I find that attempting poetic forms often forces me into corners that make me think differently than if I'm just writing in free verse.

If you don't have any—or much—experience with poetic forms, I encourage you to peruse the following list and try them. If you are very familiar with poetic forms, I hope the following list can act as a reference for when you're unsure of the rhyme scheme for a triolet versus a kyrielle—or shadorma.

Have fun poeming!

## ABSTRACT POETRY

Apparently, *abstract* was a term used by Dame Edith Sitwell to describe poems in her book *Facade*. Abstract (or sound) poetry is more about how sounds, rhythms, and textures evoke emotions than about the actual meanings of words.

## ACROSTIC POETRY

Acrostic poetry is very easy and fun. The most basic form spells words out on the left-hand side of the page using the first letter of each line. For instance,

> I like to write
> Acrostic poems
> Mostly because
> Reading them
> Out loud is
> Bound to be fun.

If you notice, the first letter of every line makes the simple sentence, "I am Rob." It's very simple, and you can make it as difficult as you want—where the fun part begins.

The brave at heart can even try double acrostics—that is, spelling things out using the first and last letter of each line.

## ALPHABET POETRY

There are many different ways to write an alphabet poem. You can write a poem in which the first letter of each word is a different letter of the alphabet. A tactic for writing this poem is to write out the alphabet ahead of time so that you can pay attention to which letters have been used and which letters are still up for grabs. Of course, you can also do this consecutively through the alphabet.

Another method for alphabet poems is to go through the alphabet using the first letter of the first word for each line.

Poets can always flip the alphabet, too. That is, instead of going A to Z, write alphabet poems from Z to A. It's all about having fun and stretching your mind, kind of like school.

## ANAGRAMMATIC POETRY

In Christian Bok's comments about his poem "Vowels" in *The Best American Poetry 2007*, he writes, "'Vowels' is an anagrammatic text, permuting the fixed array of letters found only in the title. 'Vowels' appears in my book *Eunoia*, a lipogrammatic suite of stories, in which each vowel appears by itself in its own chapter." So an anagrammatic poem uses only the letters used in the title.

For instance, if I titled a poem "Spread," it could use only words like red, dresses, drape, spare, pear, pressed, etc.

The real challenge with this kind of poem is first picking a word that has at least a couple vowels and a good mix of consonants. Then, brainstorm all the words you can think of using only those letters (as many times as you wish, of course).

## THE BLITZ POEM

The blitz poem was created by Robert Keim and is a 50-line poem of short phrases and images. Here are the rules:

- Line 1 should be one short phrase or image (like "build a boat")
- Line 2 should be another short phrase or image using the same first word as the first word in Line 1 (something like "build a house")
- Lines 3 and 4 should be short phrases or images using the last word of Line 2 as their first words (so Line 3 might be "house for sale" and Line 4 might be "house for rent")

- Lines 5 and 6 should be short phrases or images using the last word of Line 4 as their first words, and so on until you've made it through 48 lines
- Line 49 should be the last word of Line 48
- Line 50 should be the last word of Line 47
- The title of the poem should be three words long and follow this format: (first word of Line 3) (preposition or conjunction) (first word of line 47)
- There should be no punctuation

There are a lot of rules, but it's a pretty simple and fun poem to write once you get the hang of it.

## THE BOP

The Bop is a poetic form that was developed by poet Afaa Michael Weaver at a Cave Canem summer retreat. Here are the basic rules:

- 3 stanzas
- Each stanza is followed by a refrain
- First stanza is 6 lines long and presents a problem
- Second stanza is 8 lines long and explores or expands the problem
- Third stanza is 6 lines long and either presents a solution or documents the failed attempt to resolve the problem

## CASCADE POEM

The cascade poem was a form invented by Udit Bhatia. For the cascade poem, a poet takes each line from the first stanza of a poem and makes those the final lines of each stanza afterward. Beyond that, there are no additional rules for rhyming, meter, etc.

So to help this make sense, here's what a cascade poem with a tercet would look like:

A
B
C

a
b
A

c
d
B

e
f
C

A quatrain cascade would look so:

A
B
C
D

a
b
c
A

d
e
f
B

g
h
i
C

j
k
l
D

And, of course, you can make this even more involved if you want.

## CONCRETE POETRY

Concrete poetry is one of the more experimental poetic forms available to poets. Concrete poems use space and sound to communicate the meanings of the words. Words can cover other words; and the poem has trouble standing without the structure. Concrete poetry is more visual than other poetic forms.

Of course, concrete poetry has plenty of detractors because of the weight structure has on the words, but as much thought goes into concrete poetry as any other form.

## ELEGY

An elegy is a song of sorrow or mourning—often for someone who has died. However, poets being an especially creative and contrary group have also written elegies for the ends of things, whether a life, a love affair, a great era, a football season, etc.

While there are such things as elegiac couplets and elegiac stanzas, form does not rule an elegy; content *is* king (or queen) when writing elegies.

## EPITAPHS

The epitaph is a note meant to appear on a tombstone. From the Greek, epitaph means "upon a tomb." Since it has to fit on a tombstone, this note is usually brief and often rhymes. Some epitaphs are funny; most are serious. Most try to get the reader thinking about the subject of the tombstone.

## THE FIB

Fibonacci poetry was founded by Gregory K. Pincus as a 6-line poem that follows the Fibonacci sequence for syllable count per line.

For the 6-line poem that means:

- 1 syllable for first line
- 1 syllable for second line
- 2 syllables for third
- 3 syllables for fourth
- 5 syllables for fifth
- 8 syllables for sixth

There are variations where the Fibonacci expands even further with each line, but to understand how to accomplish this, you need to understand the Fibonacci math sequence of starting with 0 and 1 and then adding the last two numbers together to add to infinity.

$0+1=1$
$1+1=2$
$1+2=3$
$2+3=5$
$3+5=8$
$5+8=13$
$8+13=21$
$13+21=34$
and so on and so forth...

Anyway, those lines can easily get more and more unwieldy the more you let them expand. So, there's another variation that has taken flight in making Fibonacci poems that ascend and descend in syllables. For poets who also like mathematics, this is definitely an interesting form to get your mind working.

# FOUND POEMS

Found poetry is all about taking words not originally meant to be a poem (as they originally appeared) and turning those words into a poem anyway. You can use newspaper articles, bits of conversation, instructions, recipes, letters, e-mails, direct mail and even spam e-mail.

With found poetry, you do not alter the original words, but you can make line breaks and cut out excess before and/or after the poem you've "found." The power of found poetry is how words not intended as poetry can take on new and profound meanings as found poems.

## Ghazal

The ghazal (pronounced "guzzle") is a Persian poetic form. The original form was very simple: five to 15 couplets using the same rhyme with the poet's name in the final couplet. The main themes were usually love or drinking wine.

Contemporary ghazals have abandoned the rhymes and insertion of the poet's name in the final couplet. In fact, even the themes of love and drinking wine are no longer mandatory—as the poem now just needs the couplets which are complete thoughts on their own but also all work together to explore a common theme (whatever that might be).

If you wish to stay traditional though, here's the rhyme scheme you would follow:

a
a

b
a

c
a

and so on to the final stanza (depending upon how many you include).

Many traditional ghazals will also incorporate a refrain at the end of each couplet that could be one word or a phrase.

# HAIKU

Haiku is descended from the Japanese *renga* form, which was often a collaborative poem comprised of many short stanzas. The opening stanza of the renga was called *hokku*. Eventually, haiku evolved from the leftover and most interesting hokku that were not used in renga.

Most haiku deal with natural topics. They avoid metaphor and simile. While most poets agree that haiku have three short lines, there is some disagreement on how long those lines are. For instance, some traditional haiku poets insist on 17 syllables in lines of 5/7/5. Other contemporary haiku poets feel that the first and third lines can be any length as long as they're shorter than the middle line.

Haiku do not have to include complete sentences or thoughts. They do not have titles. The best haiku contain some shift in the final line.

## HAY(NA)KU

Hay(na)ku is a very simple poetic form created in 2003 by poet Eileen Tabios. Hay(na)ku is a 3-line poem with one word in the first line, two words in the second, and three in the third. There are no restrictions beyond this.

There are already some variations of this new poetic form. For instance, a reverse hay(na)ku has lines of three, two, and one word(s) for lines one, two, and three respectively. Also, multiple hay(na)ku can be chained together to form longer poems.

## INSULT POETRY

There are no hard and fast rules to the insult poem, but it's usually done in a joking (all in good fun) fashion as opposed to seriously trying to annoy anyone. Many insult poems also have a repetitive form or recurring method of delivering the insults. The insult poem is a good way to show just how clever you are (or think you are). But beware writing them! Once you attack someone (even in jest), you are suddenly fair game to receive an insult poem in retaliation.

## KYRIELLE

The kyrielle is a French four-line stanza form—with 8 syllables per line—that has a refrain in the fourth line. Often, there is a rhyme scheme in the poem consisting of the following possibilities:

- aabb
- abab
- aaab
- abcb

The poem can be as long as you wish and as short as two stanzas (otherwise, the refrain is not really a refrain, is it?), and, as with many French forms, it is very nice for stretching your poetic muscles.

# LIMERICKS

The origin of the limerick is shrouded in some mystery, but most sources seem to point to the early 18th century—one theory being that soldiers returning from France to the Irish town of Limerick started the form, the other theory pointing to the 1719 publication of *Mother Goose Melodies for Children*. Either way, Edward Lear popularized the form in the mid-19th century.

Basically, the limerick is a five-line poem consisting of a tercet split by a couplet. That is, lines 1, 2, and 5 are a bit longer and rhyme, while the shorter lines of 3 and 4 rhyme. After studying many effective limericks, there is not a precise syllable count per line, but the norm is about 8-10 syllables in the longer lines and around 6 syllables in the shorter lines.

# LIST POEMS

A list poem (also known as a catalog poem) is a poem that lists things, whether names, places, actions, thoughts, images, etc. Even a grocery list could turn into a poem with this form.

# LUNE

The lune is also known as the American Haiku. It was first created by the poet Robert Kelly and was a result of Kelly's frustration with English haiku. After much experimentation, he settled on a 13-syllable, self-contained poem that has 5 syllables in the first line, 3 syllables in the second line and 5 syllables in the final line.

Unlike haiku, there are no other rules. No need for a cutting word. Rhymes are fine; subject matter is open. While there are fewer syllables to use, this form has a little more freedom.

There is also a variant lune created by the poet Jack Collom. His form is also a self-contained tercet, but it's word-based (not syllable-based) and has the structure of 3 words in the first line, 5 words in the second line and 3 words in the final line.

# MONOTETRA

The monotetra is a poetic form developed by Michael Walker. Here are the basic rules:

- Comprised of quatrains (four-line stanzas) in tetrameter (four metrical feet) for a total of 8 syllables per line
- Each quatrain consists of mono-rhymed lines (so each line in the first stanza has the same type of rhyme, as does each line in the second stanza, etc.)
- The final line of each stanza repeats the same four syllables
- This poem can be as short as one quatrain and as long as a poet wishes

Personally, I like the rhyme scheme and the repetitive final line of each stanza.

# OCCASIONAL POEMS

There are no specific guidelines for occasional poems except that they mark a specific occasion. The poems can be long or short, serious or humorous, good or bad—just as long as they mark the occasion. Good occasions for poems include birthdays, weddings and holidays.

# ODES

The ode is a poetic form formed for flattery. There are three types of odes: the Horation; the Pindaric; and the Irregular.

The Horation ode (named for the Latin poet, Horace) contains one stanza pattern that repeats throughout the poem—usually 2 or 4 lines in length.

The Pindaric ode (named for the Greek poet, Pindar) is made up of a pattern of three stanzas called triads. This type of ode can be composed of several triads, but the first (the strophe) and the second (antistrophe) should be identical metrically with the third (epode) wandering off on its own metrical path.

The irregular ode (named for no one in particular) does away with formalities and focuses on the praising aspect of the ode.

# PALINDROME POETRY

The palindrome seems like a simple enough form—until you actually try to write a good one. The rules are simple enough:

1. You must use the same words in the first half of the poem as the second half, but
2. Reverse the order for the second half, and
3. Use a word in the middle as a bridge from the first half to the second half of the poem.

At first, the simplicity of the rules made me feel like this would be easy enough to do, but I ran into problems almost immediately. For instance, you can't start the poem with the word "the" unless you plan to end the poem on the word "the." And just because something makes sense in the first half doesn't guarantee it'll pass the same test on the way back.

# PANTOUM

The pantoum is a poetic form originating in Malay where poets write quatrains (4-line stanzas) with an *abab* rhyme scheme and repeat lines 2 and 4 in the previous stanza as lines 1 and 3 in the next stanza.

Poets differ on how to treat the final quatrain: Some poets repeat lines 1 and 3 of the original quatrain as lines 2 and 4 in the final quatrain; other poets invert lines 1 and 3 so that the beginning line of the poem is also the final line of the poem.

Also, the pantoum can be as long or as short as you wish it to be, though mathematically it does require at least 4 lines.

## PARADELLE

The paradelle is a poetic form that Billy Collins originally introduced as "one of the more demanding French forms," though eventually Collins fessed up that he created it as a joke.

However, Collins was not kidding about the demanding rules of the paradelle. Here they are:

- The paradelle is a 4-stanza poem.
- Each stanza consists of 6 lines.
- For the first 3 stanzas, the 1st and 2nd lines should be the same; the 3rd and 4th lines should also be the same; and the 5th and 6th lines should be composed of all the words from the 1st and 3rd lines and only the words from the 1st and 3rd lines.
- The final stanza should be composed of all the words in the 5th and 6th lines of the first three stanzas and only the words from the 5th and 6th lines of the first three stanzas.

## PARODY POEMS

A parody poem is one that pokes fun at another poem or poet. The best parodies are those that are easily recognizable—and funny, of course.

## RONDEAU

The rondeau is a form that has a refrain and rhymes. The traditional rondeau is a poem consisting of 3 stanzas, 13 original lines, and 2 refrains (of the first line of the poem) with 8 to 10 syllables per line and an A/B rhyme scheme. The skeleton of the traditional rondeau looks like this:

A(R)
A
B
B
A

A
A
B
A(R)

A
A

B

B

A

A(R)

There are variations of the rondeau, including the rondeau redouble, rondel, rondel double, rondelet, roundel, and roundelay. Of course, poets tend to break the rules on each of these as well, which is what poets like to do.

## SESTINA

The sestina is one of my favorite forms. You pick 6 words, rotate them as the end words in 6 stanzas and then include 2 of the end words per line in your final stanza.

Let's pick 6 random words: bears, carving, dynamite, hunters, mothers, blessing.

Here's how the end words would go:

*Stanza 1*

Line 1-bears (A)

Line 2-carving (B)

Line 3-dynamite (C)

Line 4-hunters (D)

Line 5-mothers (E)

Line 6-blessing (F)

*Stanza 2*

Line 7-blessing (F)

Line 8-bears (A)

Line 9-mothers (E)

Line 10-carving (B)

Line 11-hunters (D)

Line 12-dynamite (C)

*Stanza 3*

Line 13-dynamite (C)

Line 14-blessing (F)

Line 15-hunters (D)

Line 16-bears (A)

Line 17-carving (B)

Line 18-mothers (E)

*Stanza 4*

Line 19-mothers (E)
Line 20-dynamite (C)
Line 21-carving (B)
Line 22-blessing (F)
Line 23-bears (A)
Line 24-hunters (D)

*Stanza 5*

Line 25-hunters (D)
Line 26-mothers (E)
Line 27-bears (A)
Line 28-dynamite (C)
Line 29-blessing (F)
Line 30-carving (B)

*Stanza 6*

Line 31-carving (B)
Line 32-hunters (D)
Line 33-blessing (F)
Line 34-mothers (E)
Line 35-dynamite (C)
Line 36-bears (A)

*Stanza 7*

Line 37-bears (A), carving (B)
Line 38-dynamite (C), hunters (D)
Line 39-mothers (E), blessing (F)

While many poets try to write sestinas in iambic pentameter, that is not a requirement. Also, when choosing your six end words, it does help to choose words that can be altered if needed to help keep the flow of the poem going.

# SEVENLING

The sevenling was created by Roddy Lumsden. Here are the rules:

- The sevenling is a 7-line poem (clever, huh?) split into three stanzas.
- The first three lines should contain an element of three. It could be three connected or contrasting statements, a list of three details or names, or something else

along these lines. The three things can take up all three lines or be contained any-
where within the stanza.
- The second three lines should also contain an element of three. Same deal as the first
stanza, but the two stanzas do not need to relate to each other directly.
- The final line/stanza should act as either narrative summary, punchline, or unusual
juxtaposition.
- Titles are not required. But when titles are present, they should be titled Sevenling
followed by the first few words in parentheses.
- Tone should be mysterious, offbeat or disturbing.
- Poem should have ambience which invites guesswork from the reader.

## SHADORMA

Shadorma is a Spanish 6-line syllabic poem of 3/5/3/3/7/5 syllable lines respectively.

## SKELTONIC POETRY

Skeltonic verse is named after the poet John Skelton (1460-1529), who wrote short rhyming lines that just sort of go on from one rhyme to the next for however long a poet wishes
to take it. Most skeltonic poems average less than six words a line, but keeping the short
rhymes moving down the page is the real key to this form.

## SONNET

The sonnet is a 14-line poem that usually rhymes and is often written in iambic pentameter, though not always. Over time, this Italian poem has been pushed to its limits and
some contemporary sonnets abandon many of the general guidelines.

The two most famous forms of the sonnet are the *Shakespearean Sonnet* (named after William Shakespeare) and the *Petrarcan Sonnet* (named after Francesco Petrarca). The
rhyme scheme for a Shakespearean Sonnet is:

a
b
a
b

c
d
c
d

e
f
e
f

g
g

The rhyme scheme for the Petrarcan Sonnet is a little more complicated. The first eight lines (or octave) are always rhymed abbaabba. But the final six lines (or sestet) can be rhymed any number of ways: cdcdcd, cdedce, ccdccd, cdecde, or cddcee. Of course, this offers a little more flexibility near the end of the poem.

But sonnets don't necessarily need to be Shakespearean or Petrarcan to be considered sonnets. In fact, there are any number of other sonnet varieties.

A few extra notes about the sonnet:

- A crown of sonnets is made by seven sonnets. The last line of each sonnet must be used as the first line of the next until the seventh sonnet. The last line of that seventh sonnet must be the first line of the first sonnet.
- A sonnet redouble is a sequence of 15 sonnets. Each line from the first sonnet is used (in order) as the the last line of the following 14 sonnets.

## TANKA

If a haiku is usually (mistakenly) thought of as a 3-line, 5-7-5 syllable poem, then the tanka would be a 5-line, 5-7-5-7-7 syllable poem. However, as with haiku, it's better to think of a tanka as a 5-line poem with 3 short lines (lines 2, 4, 5) and 2 very short lines (lines 1 and 3).

While imagery is still important in tanka, the form is a little more conversational than haiku at times. It also allows for the use of poetic devices such as metaphor and personification (2 big haiku no-no's).

## TRIOLET

The triolet (TREE-o-LAY) has 13th-century French roots linked to the rondeau or "round" poem. Like other French forms, the triolet is great for repetition, because the first line of the poem is used three times and the second line is used twice. If you do the math on this 8-line poem, you'll realize there are only three other lines to write: two of those lines rhyme with the first line, the other rhymes with the second line.

A diagram of the triolet would look like this:

A (first line)
B (second line)
a (rhymes with first line)
A (repeat first line)
a (rhymes with first line)
b (rhymes with second line)
A (repeat first line)
B (repeat second line)

# VILLANELLE

The villanelle, like the other French forms, incorporates rhyme and repetition. This French form was actually adapted from Italian folk songs (villanella) about rural life. One of the more famous contemporary villanelles is "Do Not Go Gentle Into That Good Night," by Dylan Thomas.

The villanelle consists of five tercets and a quatrain with line lengths of 8-10 syllables. The first and third lines of the first stanza become refrains that repeat throughout the poem. It looks like this:

A(1)
b
A(2)

a
b
A(1)

a
b
A(2)

a
b
A(1)

a
b
A(2)

a
b
A(1)
A(2)

# POETS AND COLLABORATION

## The Benefits and Trials of Collaborating

*by Jeannine Hall Gailey*

What is collaboration? For a poet, it is the act of working with another artist (or several artists) to create and produce a new piece of art. It could be a collage that incorporates lines of your poems, a piece of music interpreting your work, an interactive art exhibit, even a play.

Many people think of poets as being solitary types, but there are advantages to stepping away from the laptop and into conversation with other types of artists. Interaction and conversation with artists in a variety of media and genres can spark new ideas and build unexpected connections. The rewards of working in multiple art forms include reaching larger (and new) audiences as well as challenging yourself to think about your work in a new mediuam and way.

While poetry often lacks a visual or auditory component, I think including all the senses in an experience helps people connect with a piece more fully. For instance, listening to the Star Wars score by itself is pretty stirring, but the John Williams piece is even more moving when accompanied by the sound effects, imagery, and dialogue of the movie.

Collaboration can be a one-way response, or a conversation where artists respond to each other. You may be familiar with book cover art or ekphrastic poems, which are composed in response to a work of art, such as Auden's "Musée des Beaux Arts" that describes the painting "Landscape with the Fall of Icarus." Those are examples of one-way responses. But collaboration can also be two-way, like a conversation between friends, in which there is an exchange of ideas and art over time. Collaborations can happen between poets and sculptors, neon or glass artists, painters, musicians, and filmmakers.

## ADVANTAGES TO COLLABORATIONS

What are the advantages of working with other types of artists? It can be hard for poets to get outside of our little "boxes of words" and be vulnerable enough to share our work with others. The rewards include things like: seeing our work brought to life in a way we never imagined, making friends in our community, building support between different artistic communities, increasing opportunities to be inspired by other works of art and the fascinating conversations to be had with other types of artists (my personal favorite), and also increasing the audiences for your work. One of my bestselling readings was when an artist friend invited me along to one of her gallery openings to read poems to accompany the visuals of her work. Almost everyone there, mostly art patrons, bought a book!

I brought collaboration into much of my work as Redmond, Washington's second Poet Laureate, because I thought it was important to incorporate and introduce multiple points-of-view and media types, and because, in a town known for its techie, rather than literary, population, it would be a way to introduce the unknownwn poetry with the more familiar say, art and music. I wanted to enrich our community's experiences with a wider variety of art forms and show how poetry could be relevant to them. It was also a chance to show the often startling beauty of works emerging from cooperation between artists and art forms.

Similar opportunities can come to you through arts organizations, festivals, and art galleries at any time, so it's good to consider with what type of artist you think you would most like to work.

## COLLABORATIONS WITH VISUAL ARTISTS

When you think about poets working with visual artists, you might automatically think about cover art. I had a great time working with the cover artist of my first and third books, Michaela Eaves. She took the time to read early versions of my books and create concepts and hire artist's models to pose for the scenes that eventually became the covers of *Becoming the Villainess* and *Unexplained Fevers*. We went on to collaborate on a series of images and poems interpreting Japanese folk tales for one of my Redmond Poet Laureate projects that were later used inside the second edition of my second book, *She Returns to the Floating World*.

Michaela Eaves talks about her experience with poet-artist collaboration: "The expected rules and boundaries are much looser when it comes collaborating with a poet. If you illustrate a straight-up prose story, the publisher, reader, and author expect a certain level of illustrative representation. Here's a story about a girl that likes to wear glass slippers, so you create a piece about a girl making the best of her bad footwear choices. Poetry allows you to loosen the reins and explore symbolism and intent, not just act out what's on the page. The poet may mention slippers, but you are illustrating the feel of it rather than the facts. Working directly with the poet is great because you can get to the heart of what she's trying to say by asking questions rather than just relying on guesswork."

Visual artist collaborations can include more than just book covers or illustrations; it can include poetry used to accompany a visual art exhibition. Mary Coss of METHOD Gallery in Seattle paired poets with visual artists of different media for the 2015 show, TEXTure. Carol Milne, a talented glass artist recently featured in the *Boston Globe*, worked with my poems for the show, which also featured Northwest poets Sherman Alexie (paired with neon artists Lia Yaranon Hall and Cedar Mannan) and Daemond Arrindell (paired with fabric artist Maura Donegan.) Carol picked out two poems from my book *The Robot Scientist's Daughter* and created a uranium-glass snowman with words like "Cesium" and "Uranium" woven into the pattern of the glass representing radioactive snow, and then I wrote a poem in response to her work.

Carol Milne, when asked to describe how the project came together: "Well, frankly, I've never been too fond of poetry. Most of it is too brooding and esoteric, where I lean towards the ironic, amusing and down-to-earth. However, I think it's good to challenge one's preconceptions, and I thought it sounded like a fun project. I browsed the meager Northwest poetry section of the library, and then, while surfing the Internet for Northwest poets, I ended up on the Jack Straw website where I found Jeannine's poem, 'Cesium Burns Blue.' It struck me with its visual beauty and dark message. I found a kindred spirit working in another medium. It was refreshing to come back to ironic work, making a political/environmental statement, through discovering similar work in written form. Jeannine's work explores innocence and daily life with horrific undertones of environmental hazards. The contrast personalizes and drives home the horror of nuclear contamination. The power of the arts: to get you personally engaged without spewing statistics."

Kelly Davio, the editor of *The Tahoma Literary Review* who collaborated with Redmond, Washington-area visual artists (and me) for the "Voices in the Corridor" project for VALA arts center offers another perspective on collaboration: "Collaborating with the visual artists in the 'Voices in the Corridor' project was a wonderful chance to shake up my own artistic process. While I tend to be measured and exact when I write, the visual artists seemed to work intuitively, feeling the ways in which their pieces fit in and adapted to the gallery space. Riffing off their works and making my own process more flexible allowed me to write work I never would have produced otherwise." And Jessica F. Kravitz Lambert, the founder of VALA and one of the two artists who came up with the idea for our collaborative project, said: "Working with writers allows visual artists another opportunity to share the themes in their work with another set of artists that can interpret and dialogue with the artwork created, allowing the audience to have yet another way of 'seeing' the artwork."

## COLLABORATIONS WITH PERFORMANCE ARTISTS—THEATER GROUPS, FILMMAKERS, AND CHOREOGRAPHERS

One of the first collaborations I was even involved with was when I was contacted by a theater group called "The Alley Cat Players." They had a copy of my first book, *Becoming the Villainess*, and wanted to use it as the basis for a series of one-act plays they would perform in Florida. I wish I had lived closer to Florida so I could have seen one of the performances!

Other types of collaborations include "videopoems," in which filmmakers might collaborate with a poet to create a video that choreographs with a poem while it is being read, creating an effect similar to a music video.

Dance teams and choreographers can work to interpret poems as well.

## COLLABORATIONS WITH MUSICIANS

Of course, you may have thought of poets working with lyrics (such as Wyn Cooper's poem, "Fun," that became Sheryl Crow's pop hit "All I Wanna Do"), but have you ever thought of writing with a musician and songwriter? Bushwick Book Club is a group of collaborative musicians in Seattle. They interpret writings from Shakespeare, the Bible, and contemporary poetry and turn them into songs that they perform in a spirited venue with much joy and riotous musician-like behavior. (I've been to a few of these performances, and let me say, hanging out with a musician crowd, you can definitely tell which are the poets and which are the musicians—rowdier, more attractive, and better dressed.) Geoff Larson, the executive director of Bushwick Seattle, describes the process of collaboration: "The Bushwick Book Club Seattle process of writing original music inspired by others' writings is a unique exercise that allows songwriters to chase any idea or thread the author's work may spark. Like any writing process, it can be a pretty solitary endeavor, and emerging at the end of it to share the result with an audience is a gratifying and interactive moment. When that audience includes the creator of the 'source material,' that interaction is all the more magical when two creative forces feed off of one another in a moment of mutual appreciation, each having generated something and then let it go into the world for others to receive."

Joy Mills, who collaborated with me on one poem/song ("Sleeping Beauty Loves the Needle") for a Bushwick Book Club project, describes her experience working with poets: "Working with Jeannine and other poets in the past has been such a gratifying experience as a musician because I consider poetry to be a foundation for so many creative forms. Poetry is music. The meter, rhythm, word play, rhyme and structure all lend themselves openly to being placed into song. With Jeannine, I much preferred to put her poem to music, rather than interpret it with my own lyrics. To use an already-existing piece and try to wrap the music around it allowed me to broaden my craft through collaborative approach. Poetry and music come from the same motherland in so many ways, allowing us to distill the vast world around us, if only for a fleeting spell." It was truly surreal and a real treat to get up on stage and read my poem, and then hear Joy perform with her guitar the song she interpreted and created from my poem.

Several famous poets, including Yusef Komunyakaa, Margaret Atwood and Dana Goia, have collaborated with classically trained composers to create operas from their work, in a practice of collaboration that dates back to the seventeenth century.

## COLLABORATIONS WITH OTHER WRITERS

This could be the subject of its own article! Collaborating with other poets can result in wonderful work that yields often work that highlights the strong points of both writers. Denise Duhamel, a frequent and generous collaborator with other poets, highlights this: "I love throwing in with another poet and see where the imagination is ignited by the other. The poem becomes less a force of the will of one writer and a magic revelation full of surprises for the collaborators."

For the previously mentioned "Voices in the Corridor" project for the city of Redmond, not only did Kelly Davio and I respond to the projects for four visual artists, but we also wrote haikus responding to both the Redmond landscape and did a kind of "call and response" to each other's work.

## REAP THE REWARDS OF REACHING OUT

In any collaboration, the conversation between poet and artist can enlarge and enlighten.

The risks are worth it, because the chance to include, improvise and bring a larger scope to your work is worth the occasional hiccup and increases your chances of reaching a greater and more diverse audience with your work. Branch out and take advantage of opportunities to exchange ideas and to collaborate. Watch a theater group transform your work with their acting abilities, or a musician take your work to a new level with the addition of a score. With inspiration and a little hard work, the results may take you far beyond what you might have achieved alone.

**JEANNINE HALL GAILEY** recently served as the second Poet Laureate of Redmond, Washington. She is the author of four books of poetry, *Becoming the Villainess*, *She Returns to the Floating World*, *Unexplained Fevers*, and *The Robot Scientist's Daughter*. Her website is www.webbish6.com.

# WRITING POEMS FROM PROMPTS

*by Amorak Huey*

The prompt is a thoroughly entrenched part of the pedagogy in creative writing courses from kindergarten to college. "Here's a topic," the teacher will say, "here's a challenge, an idea, a form to try." In return, students dutifully respond with a piece of writing that conforms to the instructions as best as they can manage. Perhaps because these kinds of exercises are so associated with "school writing," prompts may for some writers carry a stigma as something "real writers" don't use, as a trick or gimmick, as a crutch for beginners.

It need not be so.

For many poets, the prompt can be an essential component of an active writing life. The first step to using a prompt successfully is not to think of it as a school assignment that must be followed to the letter. A prompt should be a launching pad for your poems, not a leash that ties them down. The best prompt gives you a quick shove off the edge of a cliff you might not have even known was there—and then disappears as you negotiate the fall yourself.

## DEFEATING WRITER'S BLOCK

One of the best things a prompt can do for a poet is to eliminate that most difficult of questions: What do I write about? Much of the world has this notion that poems are mystical gifts from the muses, words bestowed from on high to the poet who waits patiently for inspiration. That sounds nice, and while there's certainly something mysterious and intangible in the creative process, sitting around and hoping for some external inspiration is not a recipe for getting much writing done. Perhaps it worked for Wordsworth or Byron, but my guess is that even the poets we study in literature classes got more accomplished by sitting down with quill in hand than by waiting to be granted some divine gift.

Writer's block is usually some blend of anxiety and self-doubt combined with the many things that demand time in our daily lives. An excuse, in other words. A writing prompt can be just the trick to get past that excuse. It frees you up to write without waiting for inspiration; it also removes some of the pressure we all place on ourselves. If the piece of writing doesn't live up to your hopes, you can always blame the prompt.

T.S. Eliot famously said: "When forced to work within a strict framework, the imagination is taxed to its utmost, and will produce its richest ideas. Given total freedom, the work is likely to sprawl." Think of the blank page (or these days, the blank Word document). It's intimidating, that scary expanse of whiteness, all the emptiness, infinite possibilities. Where to start? How does anyone ever write anything? The answer is in the Eliot quote: You need constraint. A framework. Some limitation: steel against which you can strike the flint of your imagination. That's what the prompt is for. Poet and professor Dean Rader says, "Novice poets tend to rely on abstractions and bigness, so I try to give exercises and prompts that force them to be concrete and specific." The prompt, in other words, shrinks the world, narrows the infinite down to the possible.

## SETTING CHALLENGES FOR YOURSELF

For student writers, the prompts given by their instructors might feel restrictive, frustrating, a burden weighing down their creativity. Yet once you're writing outside of the classroom context, all that freedom can be a little dizzying: you can write what you want, when you want, *if* you want. One of the most common things former students say to me is that they miss having writing prompts. I've had students e-mail me years after graduation asking for some new prompt to kickstart their writing again. Here's a secret, one of the tricks of the poetry trade: Poets have to invent prompts for themselves. As Diane Thiel says, "All writers learn by reading and by setting themselves exercises."

We all, we writers and poets, set ourselves language challenges every time we sit down with our (metaphorical) quill in hand. Write a five-line poem about X. Use this newspaper headline or that Facebook status in a poem. Write a poem in which the letter *I* does not appear. Write a sonnet. Write a sestina. Write a villanelle. The entire concept of formal poetry is itself a kind of prompt, an artificial constraint in the sense Eliot referred to: Write down your feelings about love, only do it in 14 lines of iambic pentameter following a particular rhyme scheme. Even the very choice to write a poem is a prompt. Why not write a short story, a novel, a journal entry, a blog post? A poem makes a particular kind of demand on your creativity, suggests certain things about form and focus in the same way a prompt suggests things about subject matter or approach. Poet and professor W. Todd Kaneko says, "Often the prompt has less to do with topic and more to do with restraint—do something specific with time or rhyming action or sound—anything to help me get something moving on the page. … I think writing prompts are most useful when they are based around an element of craft."

Even if you don't have a teacher to spark your writing with a ready-made syllabus full of assignments, you can always come up with them on your own. Invent whatever restrictions you like. Think of it as a game. (And if you want outside assistance, check out the many prompts provided in the sources at the end of this article.)

## BEGINNING AND BEGINNING AGAIN

Here's another secret about poetry: Every poet is, in some sense, a beginning poet. Every poem is a fresh start. Sure, some aspects of the craft might grow easier over time, with years of experience in reading and writing, but each new poem offers a new opportunity for discovery, for experimentation—and for failure. Yes, some (much? most?) writing fails. But of course failure is an essential part of writing; as Samuel Beckett said, "Fail again. Fail better." It's easy for a writer to focus too much on product and not enough on process, to see failure as an endpoint instead of a necessary detour on the writing journey.

The best way to think about prompts, then, is to see them as more about process than about product. They are intended to provoke you, to put you into situations that you have to find your way out of, like one of those reality shows where you're dropped on a desert island and have to figure out how to build a hut before it rains. A prompt offers both a challenge and a learning opportunity. Cindy Hunter Morgan says prompts offer a writer "framework and focus." Chris Haven says, "I think poets should think of our writing as responding to an implied assignment. We report on news from worlds that resemble ours or don't, real ones or imagined ones. A prompt allows us to get outside of our own requirements and widen our scope of what readers might require."

## MOVING FROM PROMPT TO POEM

But of course, process is not the only thing that matters. In the end, we do want to create meaningful poems—work that appears to have been hand-delivered by the muses even if it wasn't. It might seem that prompts are an artificial way to achieve this kind of writing; that is, writing from a prompt might feel more contrived than natural. And it's probably true that most published poems probably don't come directly from prompts in the sense of the prompts you were given in your writing classes: What did *you* do on your summer vacation?

The key to getting beyond any sort of artificiality goes back to the idea that a prompt should not limit but inspire your work. The prompt is a starting place, not the destination. Robin Behn and Chase Twichell, in the introduction to *The Practice of Poetry*, an excellent book full of exercises and prompts, write:

> A good exercise serves as a scaffold—it eventually falls away, leaving behind something new in the language, language that now belongs to the writer. ... Exer-

cises can result in a new understanding of the relation of image to meaning, or a way into the unconscious, perhaps a way of marrying autobiography with invention, or a sense of the possibility of different kinds of structures, ways to bring a dead poem to life, a new sense of rhythm, or a slight sharpening of the ear. Exercises can help you think about, articulate, and solve specific creative problems. Or they can undermine certain assumptions you might have, forcing you to think—and write—beyond the old limitations.

A scaffold that eventually falls away—it's the perfect metaphor. Here's another: A writing prompt is not a box that your poem must fit into, but a pot that the poem grows out of. Start in the direction your prompt suggests, but if the poem seems to lead somewhere else, follow. If writing about your most recent summer vacation leads to a memory of some youthful July week spent at your grandmother's lake cabin which in turn leads to a memory of your first crush and you wind up writing more about the crush, so be it. Even if those early lines about last summer disappear entirely from the final piece, they have served a purpose.

Not every prompt will lead you to your favorite poem. Some prompts will be easy. Some will seem hard. Often it's the hard ones you should look at more carefully. Ask yourself: What makes this hard? What in particular am I struggling with here? If you really, really hate a particular prompt, try to figure out why. Try to learn something from the difficulty. One of my goals in every creative writing class I teach and with every prompt I assign is to push students outside their comfort zones and away from their assumptions about themselves and their limitations. Writing should be challenging, every time.

Here are five tips for using prompts effectively:

1. Take the prompt seriously. Work at figuring out what it's asking you do to.
2. Imagine all the different poems that might emerge from a single prompt. Then ask yourself which of those poems you'd like to write.
3. If one prompt is falling flat, combine it with another. The creative process benefits immensely from the friction of two disparate forces.
4. Use the prompt as an excuse to play. Writing poetry should be a playful act most of the time anyway. (That does not mean it's not also serious work. It's both.)
5. Abandon the prompt as soon as it's no longer serving the poem that has emerged on the page.

In the end, to paraphrase Richard Hugo, you owe a prompt nothing and the poem you're writing everything. A poem will never be measured by how well the poet grappled with the prompt that started it. A poem must be measured by its own internal standards, by its music and language and the way it both creates and reflects the world we live in. You won't get to walk around with your poem explaining how the prompt influenced this line or that image. The scaffolding, necessary though it may have been in the composing process, must fall away. Your poem must stand alone.

---

## SIX STELLAR SOURCES OF POETRY PROMPTS

There is no shortage of prompts in the world. A Google search for "poetry writing prompts" yields more than 180,000 hits. If you'd prefer a more curated list, here are six sources of thoughtful, helpful prompts:

- The previously mentioned book *The Practice of Poetry: Writing Exercises from Poets Who Teach* by Robin Behn and Chase Twichell offers a wide range of carefully designed and classroom-tested prompts.
- Natalie Goldberg's classic book *Writing Down the Bones: Freeing the Writer Within* has a Zen approach to writing, with many exercises and activities intended to free you from the self-censor that lurks inside you.
- *Wingbeats: Exercises and Practice in Poetry*, edited by Scott Wiggerman and David Meischen, offers an impressive array of prompts from some of America's preeminent contemporary poets.
- Robert Lee Brewer's "Poetic Asides" blog offers a steady stream of weekly prompts throughout the year and daily prompts for Poem-A-Day challenges in November and April, in addition to poetic form challenges, poet interviews, and more.
- *The Daily Poet: Day-By-Day Prompts for Your Writing Practice* is a fairly new book by Kelli Russell Agodon and Martha Silano designed to lead through a very productive year of writing poems.
- *The Crafty Poet: A Portable Workshop* by Diane Lockward offers model poems and interviews with poets in addition to detailed writing exercises.

---

**AMORAK HUEY**, a former newspaper editor and reporter, teaches professional and creative writing at Grand Valley State University, where he assigns all kinds of writing prompts to his students. He is author of the chapbook *The Insomniac Circus* (Hyacinth Girl), and his poems appear in *The Best American Poetry 2012, Poet's Market 2014, The Southern Review, Hayden's Ferry Review, Rattle,* and many other journals.

# THE ART OF FINISHING A POEM

...........................................

*by Sage Cohen*

Every poet's process for ideating, generating, and finishing poems is unique. This can be quite liberating—and also tricky. With no Gold Standard against which to measure a poem, it's not always obvious when a poem is complete, or what needs to happen to get it there.

I believe each poem is striving to fulfill its own destiny. And we must attune ourselves to understand when it has arrived. The better you know yourself and the more robust your toolbox, the more practiced you will become at helping each poem reach its potential. So you can cross the finish line with confidence.

## THE THREE STAGES OF CREATION

Knowing how to finish a poem depends on knowing how and when to write, incubate, and revise throughout the creation process.

- **Write.** In first draft mode, be as receptive to the poem as possible. Focus on generating only, without editing. Let it all come through without judgment and get it down in all of its messy, unpotentiated glory. Write and keep writing until you have exhausted all possibilities.
- **Incubate.** Many poems are well served by an incubation period after the first or early drafts. When you are at an impasse, try simply letting the poem rest—for as many nights, weeks, or years as necessary. Be intentional about your desire to complete it, but tread lightly. Read the poem before sleep and write down what it reveals to you the following morning. Keep it folded in your pocket or taped to your bathroom mirror. Consider it a friend you are getting to know. Invite it to reveal itself to you when it is ready.

- **Revise.** There are endless ways to approach revision, and different poems may thrive under different revision conditions. I'm gong to cover a wide swath of possibilities so you can experiment and see what's right for you. The more you practice, the better you'll know which strategies to apply, and when.

Some poems feel cut from whole cloth; they come through us nearly fully formed. Others may go through any number of iterations of incubation and revision. There's no right order for the three steps above, and you can't do it wrong. Just keep exploring until you feel you've made it to the next landmark.

## 13 WAYS OF LOOKING AT A POEM

A poet and a poem are one. A poet and a poem and the delete key are one. I'm leaning heavily on a Wallace Stevens reference here, from his poem "13 Ways of Looking at a Blackbird." What I love about this poem is that it instructs me in the epic range of seeing, interpreting, and giving voice to what we see. A close study of blackbirds can endlessly inform our human experience. And a close study of your poem can reveal multiple paths to its destiny. When revising, consider these 13 poetic concerns.

1. **Exposition.** Does your poem have introductory information that helped you get started but is not serving the poem now? Trimming unnecessary lines from the beginning and end of a poem can often make a big difference in the poem's energy and impact.
2. **Language.** Does every word in your poem have the nuance you are seeking? Could modifiers be removed, flimsy adjectives be fortified, action verbs made more active, or passive? How would your poem change if "surprised" became "shocked" or "blindsided"?
3. **Imagery.** Are there places where you could increase specificity and even bring in the visceral by showing instead of telling? (Consider the difference between "She was weak" and "She could barely lift the spoon to her mouth.") What do you want the reader to know, see and feel? Could your images be working harder to take them there?
4. **Sound.** When you read it out loud, does your poem's sound augment its gestalt? Is there a music of repeating sounds? Should there be? Could the sounds be more harsh or soft to reflect the emotion and energy of the poem?
5. **Line breaks.** Line breaks control the reader's momentum. Do yours have the energy you're striving for? Is there a quick staccato of short lines, or an unspooling momentum of longer lines? Is the last word of each line the one you want the reader's eye to linger on a moment longer? Could the line break modulate the idea or image in a more engaging way?

6. **Stanzas.** Stanzas give visual shape to a poem, defined by the white space around them. Like lines, stanzas also moderate a poem's pacing by shaping the trajectory of language. Should you change a solid block of even lines to jagged and uneven ones instead to reflect the speaker's struggle? If your poem is a single stanza now, could it benefit from the spaciousness of couplets?

7. **Point of view.** What kind of insights or information could be revealed if you chose a different speaker? Would this serve the poem better? For example, let's say a mother is the speaker and the poem is about her daughter's dead bird. What would happen if the poem were rewritten from the daughter's point of view? Or the bird's?

8. **Titles.** A poem's title is like a moon, absorbing and reflecting back its light. The way it illuminates the journey of the poem is up to you. Is yours working as hard as it could to bring the reader into the poem, and to reveal something fresh about the poem's truth? Is the title that worked well at your first draft still the right fit at draft 15?

9. **Voice and syntax.** The poem's voice and syntax should reflect the person speaking, place, and time period that the reader is entering—or diverge purposefully. The language you use should convey the context and viscerally bring the reader into that moment in time. For example, how would a conflict voiced in a Victorian parlor differ from a conflict at a 1960s protest march, or in a contemporary doctor's office?

10. **Grammar.** Capitalization, punctuation, and grammar choices give important cues to the reader about the speaker, tone, and formality or informality. Are your choices serving the poem best?

11. **Pivot.** Some shift must happen in the poem that leaves the reader somewhere other than where he or she started. How can your poem more effectively pivot to reveal a truth, change the speaker, or land the reader in unexpected terrain?

12. **Emotion.** What is the emotional tone of the poem? Anguished? Content? Tense? Remorseful? How do all of the craft concerns above work in concert to make this tone undeniable?

13. **Shiver factor.** Poems pack a lot of punch when they have a je ne sais quoi resonance that I call "shiver factor". If your poem evokes a physical response (in you, and eventually in your readers), you've arrived. There's no specific way to edit for this; the shiver is more of an outcome of all of your other apt revision choices.

## SEEK MEANINGFUL FEEDBACK

Once you've put your poem through your own revision filters, it's a good time to request feedback from others. The input you get will help you better understand the experience others are having of your work—so you can evaluate if you are reaching your intended goal. Here are some ideas for making the feedback you get most useful.

- Friends and family. Think of friends and family as a sample of your future readers. When you ask the people you care about to weigh in on your poems, be specific about what you're looking for. If you want to know what's working well, say so. If you're looking for places where they get stuck or confused, make that clear.
- Writing groups. Writing groups are a great way to get specific, constructive feedback from people who are practiced in the craft of poetry. You're likely to get a wide range of opinions about the successes and opportunities in your work. Your job is to learn which readers are most useful to you in discovering fresh ways forward.
- Editors. If you send out poems for publication and they are not accepted, this suggests that either you haven't found the right home for your work, or your poems could use more refinement. If a poem has been rejected by three or more publications, consider further revision.
- Audiences. When reading in front of a live audience, notice where they laugh, gasp, lean forward, make eye contact. Notice also when they seem tuned out and disengaged. These are important clues about how your poems will land with other readers experiencing your work in print. Proceed accordingly.

Remember that you are your best expert. Other people's opinions are a training ground for refining your own opinions and honing of your craft. You get to decide what feedback serves you best, then use it to advance your work.

## GET A HANDLE ON PROCRASTINATION AND PERFECTIONISM

Two of the most insidious rivals to finishing poems are procrastination and perfectionism. And I believe both are expressions of fear. Scared that a poem doesn't measure up, we either avoid returning to it at all or we obsessively rewrite it until we've lost the golden thread that led us to the poem in the first place. The best way to relax their grip is to identify procrastination and perfectionism when they come up—then make a game plan for how to work with yourself. Here are two of my best ideas for doing so.

If you find yourself on Facebook for hours when you'd planned to write or revise, I suggest giving yourself a time limit: 10 minutes on Facebook, then 10 minutes at your desk. No pressure to write anything fantastic, just a commitment to sit and write. This gives you an escape valve for your habit of distraction and a simple step to take toward following through on your writing goal.

Or, if you have the tendency to endlessly revise and never finish your poems, try setting a cutoff limit. You could start by allowing only seven drafts per poem, then wean yourself down to three drafts total. Again, you're honoring your tendencies, but also setting a clear limit. This can create a path through your resistance toward your poem's greatest potential.

## COMPLETION IS A PRACTICE THROUGH WHICH WE INHERIT OURSELVES

I consider the poems I complete to be "finished for now". This takes the hard-edged finality of "finished" off the table and gives my poems and me more breathing room. (Some I revisit and revise years or decades later. Most simply stay finished.) The distance between drafting a poem and completing a poem is crossed with courage. When we decide to trust our instincts, we discover who we are. When we make choices and stand by them, we refine our craft. Each poem we complete seasons us as people and poets. Nothing is ever lost in the great ache to say something, to reach someone, to bring meaning through the small universe of a poem. Each finished poem takes us closer to the poet we were meant to be.

**SAGE COHEN** is the author of the poetry collection *Like the Heart, the World* (Queen of Wands Press) and nonfiction books *Writing the Life Poetic*; *The Productive Writer*; and *Fierce on the Page* (all from Writer's Digest Books). Cohen holds an MFA from New York University and a BA from Brown University. She offers strategies and support for writers at pathofpossibility.com and for divorcing parents at radicaldivorce.com.

# CREATING A SONNET

*by Tasha Cotter*

This sonnet came about in a workshop I attended in September at the Kentucky Women Writers Conference. The guest lecturer was the lovely, awe-inspiring poet Molly Peacock who led about 12 of us on a two-day quest to create, polish, and perfect a sonnet. My sonnet got away from me, taking me down one wrong path, watching as I broke end-rhymes and grappled with syllabics. But I spun and wove the metaphorical fabric until I was basically happy with what I had by the end of the conference. I don't typically write in form, so completing a sonnet in a couple of days was pretty unexpected.

On the first draft you'll see the beginning of the poem—and me grappling with the Shakespearean sonnet form, which I've always been partial to. And you can see my own marginalia—a book recommendation Peacock mentioned, *The Young Romantics*, scrawled at the bottom of the page. In the classroom we talked about—and read—some of the great sonnets like "Love is Not All," by Edna St. Vincent Millay, "Design," by Robert Frost, and "Ozymandias," by Percy Byshee Shelley. It was "Ozymandias" that I couldn't get out of my head, though I was more than a little hypnotized by the lushness of Millay. After rereading Shelley I knew there was something in that poem that touched on what my own poem had to say. Then it hit me: that image of the broken statue—that shattered face of a king….and the vast landscape. It was that image that jumpstarted my own poem.

By the second draft I had settled on a title and worked to incorporate all the corrections and ideas from my first draft—I was basically trying to tidy up the house and tighten my syllabics and rhyme. But still, changes were still taking place within the poem: words were turned over, logic was tightened, and whole lines were altered completely. I fretted over the end-rhyme. And I was still grappling with the images of the landscape, which I wanted to use to its full potential. I sat there, late that same night staring at the poem in my notebook—did I like those three words dream to follow? Were they earning their keep in the poem? I had to rewrite the poem to find out.

By the last draft I was still mentally grappling with the spine of the poem (just like I was in the second draft), but I did like the parameters the form asked me to work in. By the third draft I tried to focus on getting the meaning of the poem right—to finish the thinking on it, above all else. With a sonnet it's tempting to go for the easy answers, the hard work being finding those rhymes which are unexpected, serve the world of the poem, and (almost imperceptibly) reimagine and awaken it. That said, by the third draft I was still guarding the syllabics and making sure the poem didn't get unwieldy. I liked abiding by my nine to eleven beats per line that I felt served the poem well. Typing out the final draft I read the poem aloud several times and made a few small changes. I hadn't written a sonnet in over a year and it hadn't been easy to play by all its rules, but I felt like I'd followed through with what the poem asked of me, which is the ultimate test of the poem in its final form, I think.

**I Left a Girl in the Mountains**, by Tasha Cotter

The dripping sink, a chipped table, and you
to do what I needed to do. I turned
from you and left life a cracked statue
to rust on the roadside. What remained?
An antelope rushed to the ditch for shelter
as if it, too, knew I'd try to come back
blazing and wild. But back then I was sure
I understood what I needed. The fact
we were failing built a hungry shadow
and each night I worked to keep it alive.
Without you there were no landmarks to follow.
The blank face of freedom. The plains, wide
as a canyon echo. And so I began
the wrong turn, but I told you, I won't return.

**TASHA COTTER** is the author of *Some Churches* (Gold Wake Press) and *Red Carpet Day Job* (BookFish Books). Twice nominated for the Pushcart Prize, her work has appeared in journals such as *Contrary Magazine, NANO fiction*, and *Booth*. Find her online at www.tashacotter.com or follow her on Twitter at @TashCotter.

8 and 6
The magic
proportion

broken statue in the mountain

I + the boys
Mountains  to the

we put that year into the ground

I left the Girl in the Mountain

|      |  | dripping sink | chipped | |  |
|------|--|---------------|---------|--|--|
| 10   | the ~~household things~~, a table, ~~not you.~~ | | | | a |
| 10   | To do what I needed to do. I said | | | | b |
| 10   | Thank you and left it a ~~my~~ broken statue | | | | a |
| 10   | to rest on the roadside. The mountains ~~~~ shook, | | | | b |
| 11   | ~~gap, but not you,~~ an antelope rushed the roadside for shelter | | | | c |
| 10 ∧ | as if ~~they~~ H, too, knew I'd return a flame | | | | d |
| 9 sure? | blazing and will. Wrong. But? I'm not ~~are you~~ sure. | | | | c |
| 10   | ~~Because~~ I knew nothing would stay the same | | | | d |
| 11   | ~~~~ we were falling, sinking under a shadow | | | | e |
| 11   | ~~~~ as we cleared our path to light | | | | f |
| But we were determined to survive the night | | | | | |
| fought and | | | | | |
| 11   | But when I left there was no dream to follow | | | | e |
| wide side 10 | just freedom. A blank face. And the plains, wide | | | | f |
| 11   | overwhelming echoes. An introduction | | | | g |
|      | ~~no one can know you if you don't know yourself~~ | | | | g |
|      | ~~to whoever were us, under construction.~~ | | | | |
|      | to a wrong turn, will I ever return? ~~but will I know~~ but I promised I won't return | | | | |
|      | ~~to what came next~~ | | | | |

to ~~reality~~
a wrong turn

percussion

instruction

junction

construction

to read
"The Young Romantics"

Draft 1

I kept the Owl in the Mountains

The dripping sink, a chipped table, and you. (a)
To do what I needed to do. I ~~wired~~ forced (b)
~~from~~ you and left life a ~~cracked~~ cracked statue (a)
to rest on the roadside. In the quiet that remained ~~remained~~ (c)
An antelope rushed the roadside for shelter (d)
as if it, too, suspected ~~I'd return~~ I'd return (e)
blurry and wild, ~~Because back they~~ Because back they was sup (f)
~~........................~~ (g) I understood
what I needed to save (h)
We were falling. Sinking under ~~her~~ Shadow
and ~~......~~ each night I ~~worked~~ to keep her alive.

When I left there was no dream to follow.
The blank
face of freedom (Just freedom, the blank face) ~~........~~ The plains, wide
as a canyon ~~.............~~ celise. An introduction (g)
to a wrong turn, but I ~~promised~~ I must return. (g)
told her

# I Left a Girl in the Mountains

The dripping sink, a chipped table, and you.    ⑩ ⓐ
To do what I needed to do, I turned    ⑩ ⓑ
from you and left life a cracked statue    ⑦ ⓐ
to rust on the roadside. ~~what~~ remained?    ⑨ ⓑ
an antelope rushed the roadside for shelter    ⑪ ⓓ
as if it, too, suspected I'd ~~~~ come back    ⑨ ⓓ
blazing and wild. ~~But back~~ then I was sure    ⑩ ⓒ
I understood what I needed, ~~but the fact~~    ⑩ ⓓ
We were faili~~ng~~ Sinking under her shadow    ⑩ ⓔ
as ~~~~ each night I raced to keep her alive.    ⑩ Ⓕ
when I left there was no dream to follow.    ⑩ ⓔ
The blank face of freedom. The plains, wide,    ⑨ Ⓕ
as a canyon echos, An introduction,    ⑩ ⓖ
~~~~ a wrong turn, but I told her, I won't return.    ⑪ ⓖ

return

# SLANTS ON RHYME

.......................................

*by Daniel Ari*

If you grew up in an English-speaking country, you know that it didn't go well for Jack and Jill. They went up the hill to fetch a pail of water. Jack fell down—and broke his crown—and Jill came tumbling *after*, which doesn't quite rhyme with *water*.

Nursery rhymes may be where we first develop our love for words that share sounds, though in *Goatfoot Milktongue Twinbird: Interviews, Essays, and Notes on Poetry*, Donald Hall suggests that it may develop even before that. He suggests that repetitive and slightly varied sounds mimic what we hear in utero from mother's heartbeat, breath and digestion. Hall also notes how rhymes make the tongue move in repetitive motions, proto-consciously reminding us of the comfort of nursing. Regardless of why, there's no denying that rhyme is a sensory effect that humans enjoy.

It's one of the elements that makes blues music so appealing, for example. In a form traditionally used to air grievances, the rhyme built into the standard blues lyric provides a sonic silver lining. That the singer has no shoes on his feet, and no food to eat is given a smidgen of salve through the comforting sound of rhyme.

For many people, the taste for rhyme remains where it begins, with that lovely return of words to the tonic sound as in *gently down the stream, life is but a dream*. Perfect rhymes comfort and satisfy the mind. But I believe poets should want to cultivate a more sophisticated ear, even if we choose to return to the types of rhymes we heard from Mother Goose. And even Mother Goose wasn't a purist, as we know from *after, water*.

Excuse the soapbox, but poets are the foodies of language. You wouldn't think much of an epicure who ate only cheddar and Swiss and blanched at the fragrance of Pont l'Eveque. As poets, even if our tested preference is for perfect rhyme or free verse, we ought, I think, to be able to recognize and appreciate a broad range of aural, visual and intellectual effects—and know when to use them.

# WHY RHYME?

Rhymes can give poems a musical, harmonious, symmetrical, balanced sound. They can make a poem feel comforting, familiar and welcome, regardless of the subject of the poem. The auditory effect—present in the brain even when a reader reads silently off the page—is a main reason poets choose to rhyme. But there are at least three other reasons to consider rhyme, especially when we think of it in its general sense.

1. **Tradition.** Some poetic forms span ages and cultures. If you want to participate in the 800-year-old tradition of writing sonnets, for example, you'll need to be conscious of how rhyme has been used in the form. Rhyme is not just part of the practice, but also a signal to your readers that you are participating. Readers who know the tradition will recognize your sonnet as such and be able to read it in light of that form's long, varied history.

2. **Memorization.** A key reason for rhyme's stickiness is that it's a mnemonic device. From poetry's oldest roots in the oral tradition, rhymes have helped poets remember and repeat their works. Rhyme remains prevalent in today's spoken-word poetry because it not only helps the poet remember her flow, but also enhances an audience's comprehension. An audience hearing a poem can't pore over the words as in page reading, but rhyme helps hearers anticipate words and linger on them a bit longer. If you're a poet of the stage as well as the page, rhyming is an option you don't want to overlook.

3. **Process.** Rhyme can augment a poet's writing process itself. Being required to complete a rhyme forces a poet to seek words more carefully and opens the poet to receiving words she might not have otherwise encountered. These new, surprising words bring meanings and gravities of their own and can drive the poem in directions that surprise the poet. In using rhyme as a writing tool, poets broaden and deepen their interface with the language, which can be helpful whether or not rhyme remains detectable to a reader.

Some poets who seek a conversational or prosy sound to their work eschew rhyme altogether. But for poets who want to experiment with rhyme, there are many ways to use it that are subtle enough to evade the notice of all but the most deliberate of readers. Yet the resonance of even the subtlest rhyme may still create echoes of sound and meaning in the minds of the poet and the reader.

# WAYS TO RHYME

There's a huge range of choices when it comes to rhyme (and some good books on the subject such as *The Sounds of Poetry*, by Robert Pinsky). We'll start in familiar territory and journey outward to where the word *rhyme* applies only in its most inclusive sense.

## Sounds of rhymes

> I'm nobody! Who are you?
> Are you nobody, too?
> —Emily Dickinson

> We were very tired, we were very merry—
> We had gone back and forth all night on the ferry.
> —Edna St. Vincent Millay

What many people call rhyme, skilled poets know more accurately as *perfect*, *true* or *pure* rhyme. Two words form this kind of rhyme when they start with different sounds and end with the same stressed vowel plus any sounds that follow it.

*You* and *too* make a perfect rhyme because /y/ and /t/ start the words differently and the accented vowel /oo/ ends both words with the same sound. In the Millay sample, *merry* and *ferry* share the accented vowel sound /air/ and the long /e/ that follows it. Millay's is a *double perfect rhyme* because the rhyming part of the words comprises two syllables. *Antelope, cantaloupe* is a triple (or *dactylic*) perfect rhyme. *Appreciation, depreciation* is a quadruple, though at that point, the rhyme's harmony weakens considerably.

> Like one in danger, Cautious,
> I offered him a Crumb,
> And he unrolled his feathers,
> And rowed him softer Home –

> Than Oars divide the Ocean,
> Too silver for a seam,
> Or Butterflies, off Banks of Noon,
> Leap, plashless as they swim.
> —Emily Dickinson

One step away from perfect rhyme, the territory broadens immensely. The general definition of rhyme—and the definition of general rhyme—applies to words that share any phonetic similarity, like *crumb* and *home*, an example of consonance.

In consonance, consonant sounds match. *Tumble* and *timing* demonstrate double consonance. Consonance gets subtler when only one sound matches, perhaps one in an unaccented syllable or one that occurs in different places within different words. Examples with increasing subtlety:

> *him, home*
> *than, noon*
> *danger, offered*
> *silver, votive*

In this last example, only the internal /v/ is shared, and if these words weren't adjacent or at the ends of sequential lines, the rhyme could go undetected.

Pararhyme describes words in which vowel sounds differ within the same consonant pattern as in *seam, swim* and *crumb, cream*.

Alliteration refers to consonance that begins a sequence of words. My favorite example is this deliberately ham-fisted couplet from Shakespeare's *Midsummer Night's Dream*:

> "Whereat, with blade, with bloody blameful blade,
>    he bravely broached his boiling bloody breast."

Assonance refers to matched vowel sounds as in *rowed* and *home* from the passage above. As with other types of rhyme, assonance has many possibilities. The number of assonant sounds can be doubled as in *plashless, ashen* (short /a/, short /e/) or tripled as in *butterflies, summertime* (short /u/, /er/, long /i/). The positions of assonant sounds can also vary like the long /o/ shared by *ocean* and *sailboat*.

Uneven or wrenched rhyme describes words that share a vowel and all following sounds, but unlike perfect rhyme, the accents do not match. You can hear the unevenness in rhymes like *deferred, offered* or *riding, wing*. While we're discussing accented syllables, weak rhyme describes words that share end assonance or consonance in unaccented syllables. Jack and Jill's *water, after* is a good example of weak rhyme.

Near or forced rhymes have similar but non-identical phonetics. You hear these in a lot of nursery rhymes such as "Baa Baa Black Sheep," which pairs *dame* with *lane*. The /m/ and /n/ sounds are phonetic relatives, so the near rhyme is harmonious to the ear though it falls outside of what would be called perfect.

Identical rhyme is the rhyming of a word with itself or an exact homophone. It's similar to musical unison, in which two instruments or voices meet on the same note, in that the ear's longing for harmony isn't quite satisfied by identical rhyme.

Eye rhyme pairs words that look like they should rhyme but don't such as *daughter* and *laughter*. Aurally, there is no rhyme at all, but when reading these words on a page, especially if they end two subsequent lines, the mind can pick up on the visual resonance.

Taken together, non-perfect rhymes are often lumped under the label slant rhyme. *Orange* is infamously unrhymable, but with slant rhyme on your palette, you can pair it with *grange, garage, hinged, foraging, ranger, anger, orangutan*, and so on. As you play with words with a broader understanding of what rhyme can be, you will develop a more sophisticated ear and eye. And that can increase your ability to give your readers the experience you want them to have.

## POSITIONS OF RHYMES

> … America, land of opportunity, mirages and camouflages, more than usually speaking loudly, saying nothing. You confusing me; you losing me. Your game is twisted, want me enlisted in your usury. Foolishly, most men join the ranks cluelessly, buffoonishly accept the deception, believe the perception, reflection rarely seen across the surface of the looking glass...
> —Mos Def

Poets needn't accept that rhymes should always appear at the ends of lines. Besides sound, the placement of rhyming words in relation to each other offers a huge field for exploration and experimentation. Hip-hop lyrics like the passage above show how versatile and effective internal and repeating rhymes can be. Marvel at the septuple repetition of the double-assonance rhyme created with *opportunity, usually, confusing me, losing me, usury, foolishly, buffoonishly*.

In hip-hop, sets like this are called *multi-syllable rhymes* or *multis*. Beyond the complexity of their double and triple rhymes—perfect or slant—is their liberal use of internal rhyme, rhymes embedded within lines. Internal rhyme is not uncommon in canonical poetry. Theodore Roethke's poem "I Knew a Woman" offers this example wherein *those*, rhyming *repose* and *nose*, is placed back into the line:?

> Her several parts could keep a pure repose,
> Or one hip quiver with a mobile nose
> (She moved in circles, and those circles moved).

The frequent, often adjacent use of rhyming words is called chiming. In the Mos Def passage above, you experience chiming in "accept the deception, believe the perception, reflection."

Broken, split or enjambed rhyme hyphenates a word across a line break in order to form an end rhyme as in Gerard Manley Hopkins' "The Windhover":

> I caught this morning morning's minion, king-
>   dom of daylight's dauphin, dapple-dawn-drawn Falcon, in his riding
>   Of the rolling level underneath him steady air, and striding
> High there, how he rung upon the rein of a wimpling wing
> In his ecstasy!...

Of course, you make rhymes obvious to a reader by repeating them, placing them beside one another, or putting them at the ends lines. To make them subtler, move rhyming words away from one another and place them in the middles or beginnings of lines.

# BEYOND RHYME

> There once was a farmer who took a young miss
> In back of the barn where he gave her a
> Lecture on horses and chickens and eggs,
> And told her that she had such beautiful Manners...
>    —from the song "Sweet Violets"

Beyond the sounds and positions of rhyme is a wilder world of word play, techniques that may be called rhyme only its widest sense. The song "Sweet Violets" simply doesn't rhyme, yet as you read or hear the verse, your mind fills in the missing rhymes automatically. In fact, this is called mind rhyme, and I proclaim (from my perennial soapbox) that it requires just as much craft as more overt styles of rhymes. It's my opinion that word play has a place among the techniques a poet can use to develop the sound, look and process of their poetry.

Here are some wordplay techniques I've encountered or used as, or in lieu of, rhyme. Note that this catalog is no more than a starting point.

In echo verse, the last one or more sounds of a line repeat as the next complete line as in George Herbert's "Heaven":

> But are there cares and business with the pleasure?
> Leisure.
> Light, joy and leisure; but shall they persever?
> Ever.

In a poem, I "rhymed" this set of words: *slate, steal, tales* and *least*. Call that anagrammatic rhyme.

In another formal poem that required rhymed sets of four words each, I used the old game of word ladders and rhymed *honey-hones-bones-boxes* and *home-come-comb-womb*. As you can see, one and only one letter changes between each word.

Do you notice anything interesting about the first three letters of these first four lines of Willard Espy's 12 line poem?

> Janet was quite ill one day.
> Febrile troubles came her way.
> Martyr-like, she lay in bed:
> Aproned nurses softly sped.

Espy wrote *An Almanac of Words at Play*, a book my family devoured together when I was a boy. (That book has a lot of good ideas, and I think it helped set my course for life.) His were the only calendar acrostics I'd seen before trying the form myself decades later.

The days of the week don't work as well as an acrostic as no words besides Tuesday start with tues-, but maybe there's an other opportunity here. The question for poet word players is what linguistic patterns might a poem use as a spontaneous form or rhyme-like requirement? The periodic table, state names, titles of *Harry Potter* books... many possibilities exist. What might you do with a catalog of phrases, words, or abbreviations from a subject you're interested in?

Let's go even father afield. Words might "rhyme" based on meaning instead of sound like *red, scarlet, flushed, stop*. I know synonyms are not the same as rhymes, but I could imagine someone building or following a poetry form based on reiterated-yet-varied ideas instead of reiterated-yet-varied phonics.

Associative harmony is a term I came up with to describe what remains when rhyme has been edited out over revisions. There could be associative harmony between *azure* and *truth*, for example. Perhaps in the first draft of a poem *blue* and *true* were rhymed; but in revision azure seemed more accurate than blue, and the noun truth delivered more impact than the adjective true. Associative harmony is like a palimpsest of rhyme; it's all but undetectable to a reader, but it could still be an integral part of the poet's creative process.

I believe many more possibilities exist for poets to explore and invent. Though not a polyglot, I sense a lot of possibility in techniques and linguistics adapted from other languages. Poets might borrow language patterns, rules or understandings from Cantonese, Hebrew, Miwok, Hindi or Klingon. Poets might also adapt ideas from the languages of mathematics, chemistry or quantum physics.

Bringing out my soapbox one last time, I would encourage poets who haven't done so already to venture out of the comfort zone of perfect rhyme. And I'd encourage free-verse poets to try different flavors of rhyme that support the sound they want to achieve. We have the opportunity to explore how words relate to one another in countless ways and to discover new connections heretofore untapped. It excites me to think of all the ways we can broaden and deepen the appreciation of our expressive art for ourselves and for those who may find inspiration here.

**DANIEL ARI** met poetry in 1986 and has had a tumultuous but ultimately rewarding relationship with it ever since. He still strives to define poetry for himself, and by writing essays on poetry for *Poet's Market*, guest lecturing on E. E. Cummings, leading writing sessions at his home in Richmond, CA, and continuing to write, publish and perform, he feels he's getting ever closer. In his book *One Way to Ask* from Norfolk Press, Daniel introduces a new poetry form called queron and pairs each poem with illustrations by 67 artists including Roz Chast, R. Crumb, Bill Griffith, Wayne White and Henrik Drescher. Order the book at norfolkpress.com.

# FRESHEN YOUR POETRY

............................................................

*by Nancy Susanna Breen*

///////////////////////////////////////////////////////////////////

During a recent stint of poetry judging, I decided to keep a running list of the words and phrases that turned up again and again in entries. What I discovered is that too many poets, especially new or developing poets, depend on clichés in their writing. Others simply don't stretch enough for originality when crafting their lines. Instead, they invoke wording and images that have become exhausted with use.

You can freshen your poetry and increase your individuality by targeting stale language during the revising process. Like mold on bread, instances of exhausted images and overused words act as alerts once you know what you're looking for.

## CLICHÉS

A cliché is any trite phrase or expression; that is, a phrase or expression that has been run into the ground. Avoid clichés like the plague. (See how easy it is to work clichés into your writing? There are two in those two sentences.) Because of their familiarity, clichés are comfortable and seemingly add a conversational touch to a line of poetry. They seem to guarantee clarity as well, because readers know what the clichés mean.

However, when poets turn to the same tired phrases and overused words, their poems all sound alike. Cliché-ridden lines have a cookie cutter effect. They result in poems that seem prefabricated, assembled of standard parts.

Here's a brief list of clichés that turned up more than three times in the batch of poems I was judging:

lips are/were sealed
blood, sweat, and tears
into thin air
heart and soul
thick and thin

> bitter end
> on a silver platter
> life is precious
> time stands still
> as far as the eye can see
> tore like a knife
> sands in an hourglass
> sun, moon, and stars

If you need help recognizing clichés, the Internet offers some valuable sites. For example, ClicheList.net provides an alphabetized list of clichés, each example linked to an explanation of its meaning. Cliché Finder (www.westegg.com/cliche) allows you to search its 3,000-plus cliché bank by keyword; "cat" turned up over 50 examples, such as "cat has your tongue," "cat's meow," and "raining cats and dogs." There's also a cliché generator that provides 10 random clichés at a time. Make a practice of reading through those 10 random clichés daily for a month and you'll find it much easier to spot clichés in your poems.

# OH, NO! NOT ANOTHER [BLANK] POEM

Clichés include dull, stereotypical ideas and situations. Consequently, entire poems can be clichés. Gather a large enough sample of poems, such as entries in a poetry contest or submissions to a magazine, and you'll see several examples of the same clichéd poem, sometimes with surprisingly little variation. Below are types of poems poets can't seem to resist writing. Exercise heightened originality if attempting these poems.

## Butterflies

I have nothing against butterflies, and I appreciate how symbolic they are. However, they turn up constantly as poem subjects, accompanied by all the typical verbs: flit, flutter, and so on. Describing or referring to butterflies emerging from cocoons is also popular. Understand how commonplace butterflies are before writing an entire poem about them if you really want to set your work apart. For that matter, restrain yourself from using them as images or symbols without plenty of careful thought.

## Sea and sand

Poets simply must write about the ocean. (I certainly have.) They stroll through the tide, meditate on the coming and going of the tide, study what the tide leaves behind, and compare life to the movements of the tide.

There's nothing wrong with writing about strolling on the beach, watching the waves, or examining the shells and driftwood at low tide. However, because they're so popular with poets, the ocean and beach are hard to write about in an original way, especially if the physical descriptions basically make up the poem.

Poets consistently choose the same words to describe the sea and shore, and the ring of familiarity isn't a virtue. Even a touching account of a dying person visiting the sea- side for the last time or a broken-hearted lover examining a ruined relationship fades into sameness when the speakers' actions are similar and they seem to be viewing the scene through the same pair of eyes.

## Seasonal

The most uninspired, and uninspiring, poetry I see usually focuses on one of the seasons or on all four at once. This is primarily because poets pull out all the standard images, as if putting up those colored cardboard cutouts in a classroom: colored leaves and pump- kins for fall, snowflakes for winter, buds and robins for spring, a big, smiling sun for sum- mer. Such images are beloved and iconic; and because of this, you need to move past them when writing about a season. Read enough poems that cite "the golden leaves drift lazily to ground" and you'll wince at the mere thought of autumn.

I'm going to go a step farther and suggest that freshening the seasonal imagery you use isn't enough—you should avoid the seasons as the sole subjects of poems. Instead, use the season as a background. That way your poem develops into sometime more than a laundry list of the same old spring showers, hot July noons, and shimmering blankets of snow on a rolling landscape.

## Love

It's a shame so many love poems come across as time-creased valentines. I've rarely read a clichéd love poem that made me doubt the sincerity of the writer's feelings. When such verse seems cribbed from the most mundane greeting card, though, especially when ex- pressed in *oo-aa* rhymes, the poem appears mass-produced rather than the true expres- sion of an individual. Poems about unrequited love or rejection are especially painful, not because of the sadness involved but because a kind of injured, righteous indignation overrides the poet's artistic common sense. And, of course, the same images are evoked and the same flowery language applied as though squeezed out of a tube of frosting.

When writing a poem that addresses a romantic partner or someone who has cast you aside, consider sending it only to the intended recipient or keeping it strictly to yourself. Otherwise, be sure you can treat the work as a piece of literary art, not a love letter. Even then, make it your own. Don't resort to gooey Valentine verses or resentful poison notes.

A subset of the love poem is the "love is" poem. If you insist on defining love, have something new to say. "Love is" poems range from a list of clichéd comparisons, both positive and negative (a delicate rose, a knife to the heart, a blanket against the cold) to a series of unsurprising adjectives (kind, understanding, forgiving, harsh, demoralizing, etc.). Throw out the cookie-cutter images and the threadbare language or don't bother at all, at least not if you're writing for a general readership. The same goes for "my love is like" poems.

# OTHER CLICHÉ PITFALLS

## Hearts

In poetry, hearts aren't mere organs that pump blood. Poets have them doing more tricks than a trained poodle in a one-ring circus: pounding, shrieking, weeping, dancing, swelling, bleeding, exploding, freezing, or stopping dead (without killing the poet). Poets assist their hearts in hyperactivity by opening them, shutting them, writing on them, exploring them, hiding things in them, and nursing them. Other people do things to poets' hearts as well: stomp on them, warm them, break them, steal them, stab them, fill them with joy or sadness, play with them, heal them, and reawaken them when they're dead (figuratively speaking).

"Heart" is one of those words you have to handle carefully, if at all. Despite its versatility, in most cases you can leave "heart" out of your poem. It's a cliché that can do more harm than good; and the more animated the heart is in your poem, the more danger of giving the reader a mental image that resembles a Wile E. Coyote cartoon.

Obviously, if you're writing about someone's cardiac event, *heart* is a necessary clinical term, not a cliché. Where emotions are concerned, though, don't go breaking, teasing, or exposing anyone's heart in your poems.

## Despair

It's astonishing how many poets "plunge into the abyss" or "descend into oblivion" at some point in their poetry. Sometimes they hurtle their entire beings into the black pit of nothingness; in other instances, their minds or hearts take the dive of despair.

Sadly, it's hard for readers to take you seriously when you're melodramatic. Write with even more finesse when addressing such intense emotional conditions as grief and depression. Imagine an over-the-top actor in 19th-century theater wailing to the balcony, writhing on the stage, or whirling his cape around him like a shroud. This shouldn't be the effect you want your lines to convey.

Read the confessional poetry of Sylvia Plath, Robert Lowell, Anne Sexton, John Berryman, and others to learn how to calibrate your language so you express the most emotion with the least hyperbole.

## Tears

Too many poets turn the human face into a Niagara Falls of tears. These tears run, cascade, course, drip, trickle, and flow. Or poets turn to clichés to describe weeping, such as "cried like a baby," "cried a river," or "cried her eyes out."

When you write skillfully, showing rather than telling, you can convey sorrow without using tears at all. Uncontrolled waterworks are just overkill; they don't make the scene more convincing. Think of a movie where an actor cries. It's usually an extreme situation when a character dissolves into heaving sobs; otherwise, the viewers don't buy it. Often a character struggling *not* to cry is more affecting than drenched cheeks. Remember that the next time you're inclined to flood someone's face with tears in your poem.

## Colors

Although simply putting "green," "blue," or "red" into your descriptions is pretty mundane, it's almost worse to employ clichéd colors. If you notice "ruby red," "golden yellow," "baby pink," "sky blue," and similar color clichés in your poems, revise them to more specific colors or create original similes—in other words, don't just substitute "red as a ruby" or "blue as a summer sky." Come up with something vivid and new. If your color phrase turns up in the lyrics of pop songs or standards, it's too worn-out to use in your poetry. For inspiration, review some paint company websites for the creative ways they name various colors, then work on original examples of your own.

While I'm discussing colors, I want to mention red, white, and blue. This combination is a favorite of poets writing about the military, patriotism, or the United States in general. Unfortunately, those colors used together have become cliché, detracting from verse that may otherwise make valid statements. There's plenty to say about a soldier's sacrifice, love of one's country, or the esteem for U.S. liberty and democracy without tying everything up in red, white, and blue bunting. Make your poem stirring enough and readers will see the stars and stripes without a specific reference.

## ABOUT DEAD METAPHORS

When people repeat a metaphor so often its original imagery gives way to a new, literal meaning, the result is a *dead metaphor*. I once heard the poet Donald Hall cite the use of dead metaphors as one of the most common reasons he rejects poems. One of his examples was *sea of wheat*, which now means an expanse of wheat rather than an ocean-like view of the grain field.

Determining what constitutes a dead metaphor and when to delete it can be confusing. For instance, *eye of the needle* is considered a dead metaphor, yet it's also what we call that opening in the top of a needle. On the other hand, in the phrase *he plowed through the stacks of paper*, "plowed" at first glance seems a vigorous verb choice rather than a dead metaphor. However, consider how many times you hear this metaphor in televised news reports. "The robbery suspect plowed through the festival crowd." "The car plowed into the front porch of the home." *Plow* doesn't conjure up its original imagery of a blade digging through dirt; it's taken on a meaning of its own through heavy repetition as a popular term.

If you're unsure about dead metaphors, apply the yardstick of frequency: If the term in question gets repeated a lot, especially in the media, revise the term whether it's a dead metaphor or not.

## BE ALERT, NOT OBSESSIVE

Don't inhibit your writing by being overly conscious about stale language as you're putting the words down. First or even second and third drafts aren't a time for self-editing. When you revise, watch carefully for overused words and tired imagery. They're tricky little devils to catch because we're so used to them. Reread this article and I'm sure you'll target some clichés or dead metaphors that slipped right by me. The point is to be aware of them as you hone your skills. Over time you'll become more astute about when you need to cast them aside to freshen up the lines of your poems.

**NANCY SUSANNA BREEN** is a poet, freelance writer, and editor. Her poetry is available in e-chapbook form at www.Smashwords.com as is an e-book of writing prompts, *Nudged by Quotes—20 Writing Prompts Inspired by The World's Great Poetry, Volume 10: Poetical Quotations*. She's the former editor of *Poet's Market* and judges poetry contests at the state and national levels.

# MAGAZINES/ JOURNALS

/////////////////////////////////////////////////////////////////////////////////////////////////

Literary magazines and journals usually provide a poet's first publishing success. In fact, you shouldn't be thinking about book/chapbook publication until your poems have appeared in a variety of magazines, journals and zines (both print and online). This is the preferred way to develop an audience, build publishing credits and learn the ins and outs of the publishing process.

In this section you'll find hundreds of magazines and journals that publish poetry. They range from small black-and-white booklets produced on home computers to major periodicals with high production values and important reputations. To help you sort through these markets and direct your submissions most effectively, we've organized information in each listing according to a basic format that includes contact information, magazine needs, how to submit, and more.

## GETTING STARTED, FINDING MARKETS

If you don't have a certain magazine or journal in mind, read randomly through the listings, making notes as you go. (Don't hesitate to write in the margins, underline, use highlighters; it also helps to flag markets that interest you with Post-It Notes). Browsing the listings is an effective way to familiarize yourself with the kind of information presented and the publishing opportunities that are available at various skill levels.

If you have a specific market in mind, however, begin with the General Index. Here all the book's listings are alphabetized along with additional references that may be buried within a listing (such as a press name or competition title).

### 2RIVER VIEW

7474 Drexel Dr., University City MO 63130. **E-mail:** 1ong@2River.org. **E-mail:** su3m1t@2river.org. **Website:** www.2river.org. **Contact:** Richard Long. *2River View*, published quarterly online, is a site of poetry, art, and theory. Considers unpublished poetry only. Claims first electronic rights and first North American rights, "meaning that publications here at *2River* must be the first publication to feature the work online and/or in print." Publishes ms 3 months after acceptance. Guidelines online.

**MAGAZINES NEEDS** Submit up to 5 poems once per reading period (see website for dates), pasted in body of e-mail. Prefers poems with these qualities: image, subtlety, and point of view; a surface of worldly exactitude, as well as a depth of semantic ambiguity; and a voice that negotiates with its body of predecessors. Publishes 10 poets/issue.

### 30 N

(formerly *North Central Review*), North Central College, CM #235, 30 N. Brainard St., Naperville IL 60540. (630)637-5291. **E-mail:** nccreview@noctrl.edu. **Website:** 30northblog.wordpress.com. *30 N*, published semiannually, considers work in all literary genres, including occasional interviews, from undergraduate writers globally. The journal's goal is for college-level, emerging creative writers to share their work publicly and create a conversation with each other. All styles and forms are welcome as submissions. The readers tend to value attention to form (but not necessarily fixed form), voice, and detail. Very long poems or sequences (running more than 4 or 5 pages) may require particular excellence because of the journal's space and budget constraints. Does not want overly sentimental language and hackneyed imagery. These are all-too-common weaknesses that readers see in submissions; recommends revision and polishing before sending work. Considers poetry by teens (undergraduate writers only). Acquires first rights. Publishes ms 1-4 months after acceptance. Responds in 1-4 months. Guidelines for SASE, by e-mail, online and in magazine.

○ *30 N* is 120 pages, digest-sized, perfect-bound, with cardstock cover with 4-color design. Press run is about 750, distributed free to contributors and publication reception attendees. Single copy: $5; subscription: $10. Make checks payable to North Central College.

**MAGAZINES NEEDS** Accepts e-mail submissions (as Word attachments only); no fax submissions. Cover letter is preferred. Include name, postal address, phone number, and e-mail address (.edu address as proof of student status). If necessary (i.e., .edu address not available), include a photocopy of student ID with number marked out as proof of undergraduate status. Reads submissions September-March, with deadlines in February and October. Poems are circulated to an editorial board. All submissions are read by at least 3 staff members, including an editor. Rarely comments on rejected poems. No line limit. Pays 2 contributor copies.

**TIPS** "Don't send anything you just finished moments ago—rethink, revise, and polish. Avoid sentimentality and abstraction. That said, the *30 N* publishes beginners, so don't hesitate to submit and, if rejected, submit again."

### 34THPARALLEL MAGAZINE

Paris, France. **E-mail:** 34thparallel@gmail.com. **Website:** www.34thparallel.net. **Contact:** Martin Chipperfield. *34thParallel Magazine*, published quarterly in digital and print editions, promotes and publishes the exceptional writing of new and emerging writers, writing that experiments with and tests boundaries, that communicates a sense of wonder, reality, tragedy, fantasy, and brilliance. Guidelines on website.

○ "Milan Kundera wrote that fiction is like a parallel reality (okay, so he didn't say that exactly). But reality and fiction mix up, don't you think? Our lives exist in words; it's how we make our reality. But maybe the fiction is truer? What if in our writing we reach out beyond the parallels of reality and fiction? Question life, challenge the boundaries, confront our perceptions and misconceptions. Welcome to the *34thParallel*."

**TIPS** "We want it all, but we don't want everything. Take a look at the mag to get a feel for our style."

### 580 SPLIT, A JOURNAL OF ARTS & LETTERS

Mills College, Graduate English Department, 5000 MacArthur Blvd., Oakland CA 94613-0982. **E-mail:** five80split@gmail.com. **Website:** www.mills.cdu/academics/graduate/eng/about/580_split.php. "*580 Split* is an annual journal of arts and literature published by graduate students of the English Department at Mills College. This national literary journal includes innovative and risk-taking fiction, creative nonfiction, poetry, and art and is one of the few literary journals carried by the Oakland Public Library. *580 Split* is also distributed in well-known Bay Area bookstores." Publishes ms 4-6 months after acceptance. Responds in 3 months. Guidelines online.

**MAGAZINES NEEDS** Submit via online submissions manager. Pays 1 contributor copy.

**TIPS** "Get a hold of a past issue, read through it, find out what we are about. Check the website for most recent information."

## ABLE MUSE

467 Saratoga Ave., #602, San Jose CA 95129-1326. **Website:** www.ablemuse.com. **Contact:** Alex Pepple, editor. *"Able Muse: A Review of Poetry, Prose & Art* published twice/year, predominantly publishes metrical poetry complemented by art and photography, fiction, and nonfiction, including essays, book reviews, and interviews with a focus on metrical and formal poetry. We are looking for well-crafted poems of any length or subject that employ skillful and imaginative use of meter and rhyme, executed in a contemporary idiom, that reads as naturally as your free-verse poems." Acquires first rights. Time between acceptance and publication is 3 months. Sometimes comments on rejected poems. Responds in 4 months. Sometimes sends prepublication galleys. Subscription: $24 for 1 year.

Considers poetry by teens. "High levels of craft still required even for teen writers." Also sponsors 2 annual contests: The Able Muse Write Prize for Poetry & Fiction and The Able Muse Book Award for Poetry (in collaboration with Able Muse Press at www.ablemusepress.com). See website for details.

**MAGAZINES NEEDS** Has published poetry by Mark Jarman, A.E. Stallings, Annie Finch, Rhina P. Espaillat, Rachel Hadas, and R.S. Gwynn. Receives about 1,500 poems/year, accepts about 5%. Submit 1-5 poems and short bio. Electronic submissions only through the online form at www.ablemuse.com/submit, or by e-mail to editor@ablemuse.com. "The e-mail submission method is being phased out. We strongly encourage using the online submission method." Will not accept postal submissions. Reviews books of poetry. Send materials for review consideration.

## ABRAXAS

P.O. Box 260113, Madison WI 53726-0113. **E-mail:** abraxaspress@hotmail.com. **Website:** www.abraxaspressinc.com/welcome.html. **Contact:** Ingrid Swanberg, editor in chief; Warren Woessner, senior editor. *ABRAXAS*, published irregularly (nine- to twelve-month intervals or much longer) is interested in contemporary lyric poetry, experimental poetry, and poetry in translation. When submitting translations, please include poems in the original language. *ABRAXAS'* new format features longer selections of fewer contributors. Does not want political posing or academic regurgitations. Has published poetry by Ivan Argüelles, Denise Levertov, César Vallejo, d.a. levy, T.L. Kryss, and Andrea Moorhead. Sample copy: $4 USD plus $1.90 s&h (or $9 international s&h). Subscription: $32 for 4 issues; $52 international for 4 issues. Guidelines online. Unsolicited submissions are considered only during specified reading periods (announced online).

*ABRAXAS* is up to 80 pages, digest-sized, litho-offset-printed, flat-spined, with matte or glossy card cover with original art and photography. Press run is 700.

**MAGAZINES NEEDS** Submit 7-10 poems with SASE. No electronic submissions. Pays 1 contributor copy and offers 40% discount on additional copies.

## ABZ

P.O. Box 2746, Huntington WV 25727. (304)638-5701. **E-mail:** editor@abzpress.onmicrosoft.com. **E-mail:** abzpress@gmail.com. **Website:** abzpress.sharepoint.com/pages/default.aspx. *ABZ*, published every other year, wants poetry using interesting and exciting language. Reads submissions May 1-August 1. Sample copy: $8. Guidelines online.

**MAGAZINES NEEDS** Submit poems by mail with SASE. Does not consider e-mail submissions. Pays 2 contributor copies and small stipend.

**TIPS** "We want to read your best poems."

## ACM (ANOTHER CHICAGO MAGAZINE)

**E-mail:** editors@anotherchicagomagazine.net. **Website:** www.anotherchicagomagazine.net. **Contact:** Caroline Eick Kasner, managing editor; Matt Rowan, fiction editor; David Welch, poetry editor; Colleen O'Connor, nonfiction editor. *"Another Chicago Magazine* is a biannual literary magazine that publishes work by both new and established writers. We look for work that goes beyond the artistic and academic to include and address the larger world. The editors read submissions in fiction, poetry, and creative nonfiction year round. The best way to know what we publish is to read what we publish. If you haven't read *ACM* before, order a sample copy to know if your work is appropriate." Sends prepublication galleys. Acquires first serial rights. Responds in 3 months to queries; in 6 months to mss. Guidelines online.

○ Work published in *ACM* has been included frequently in *The Best American Poetry* and *The Pushcart Prize*. **Charges $3 submissions fee.**

**MAGAZINES NEEDS** Submit poems via online submissions manager in 1 document.

**TIPS** "Support literary publishing by subscribing to at least 1 literary journal—if not ours, another. Get used to rejection slips, and don't get discouraged. Keep introductory letters short. Make sure ms has name and address on every page, and that it is clean, neat, and proofread. We are looking for stories with freshness and originality in subject angle and style, and work that encounters the world."

## ACORN

Spare Poems Press, 115 Conifer Lane, Walnut Creek CA 94598. **Website:** www.acornhaiku.com. **Contact:** Susan Antolin, editor. "Biannual magazine dedicated to publishing the best of contemporary English-language haiku and in particular to showcasing individual poems that reveal the extraordinary moments found in everyday life." Buys first rights, one-time rights. Publishes ms an average of 1-3 months after acceptance. Responds in 3 weeks to mss. Guidelines and sample poems online at www.acornhaiku.com.

○ Reads submissions January through February and July through August only.

**MAGAZINES NEEDS** "Decisions made by editor on a rolling basis. Poems judged purely on merit." Sometimes acceptance conditional on minor edits. Often comments on rejected poems. Accepts submissions via mail or e-mail, however e-mail is preferred. "Does *not* want epigrams, musings, and overt emotion poured into 17 syllables; surreal, science fiction, or political commentary 'ku; strong puns or raunchy humor. A 5-7-5 syllable count is not necessary or encouraged." Length: 1-5 lines; 17 or fewer syllables.

**TIPS** "This is primarily a journal for those with a focused interest in *haiku*. It is a much richer genre than one might surmise from many of the recreational websites that claim to promote '*haiku*.'"

## ACUMEN MAGAZINE

**E-mail:** patriciaoxley6@gmail.com. **Website:** www.acumen-poetry.co.uk. **Contact:** Patricia Oxley, general editor. *Acumen*, published 3 times/year in January,

May, and September, is "a general literary magazine with emphasis on good poetry." Wants "well-crafted, high-quality, imaginative poems showing a sense of form." Does not want "experimental verse of an obscene type." Has published poetry by Ruth Padel, William Oxley, Hugo Williams, Peter Porter, Danielle Hope, and Leah Fritz. Responds in 3 months. Submission guidelines online.

○ *Acumen* is 120 pages, A5, perfect-bound.

**MAGAZINES NEEDS** Submit 5-6 poems at a time. All submissions should be accompanied by SASE. Include name and address on each separate sheet. Accepts e-mail submissions, but see guidelines on the website. Will send rejections, acceptances, proofs, and other communications via e-mail overseas to dispense with IRCs and other international postage. Any poem that may have chance of publication is shortlisted, and from list final poems are chosen. All other poems returned within 2 months. "If a reply is required, please send IRCs. One IRC for a decision, 3 IRCs if work is to be returned." Willing to reply by e-mail to save IRCs. Unwanted poetry returned if postage or e-mail address attached. Pays "by negotiation" and 1 contributor copy.

**TIPS** "Read *Acumen* carefully to see what kind of poetry we publish. Also, read widely in many poetry magazines, and don't forget the poets of the past—they can still teach us a great deal."

## THE ADIRONDACK REVIEW

Stanhope St., Brooklyn NY 11237, United States. **E-mail:** editors@theadirondackreview.com. **E-mail:** www.theadirondackreview.submittable.com. **Website:** www.theadirondackreview.com. **Contact:** Angela Leroux-Lindsey, editor in chief; Megan Nolan, fiction editor; Nicholas Samaras, poetry editor; Giovanni Appruzzese, translations editor; Alex Guarco, associate editor. *The Adirondack Review* is an online quarterly literary magazine featuring poetry, fiction, art, photography, and translations. Responds to queries in 2-4 months.

**MAGAZINES NEEDS** Submit 2-5 poems at a time via online submissions manager; include brief bio.

**TIPS** "*The Adirondack Review* accepts submissions all year long, so send us your poetry, fiction, nonfiction, translation, reviews, interviews, and art and photography."

## THE ADROIT JOURNAL

**E-mail:** editors@theadroitjournal.org. **Website:** theadroitjournal.org. **Contact:** Peter LaBerge, editor-in-chief. At its foundation, the journal has its eyes focused ahead, seeking to showcase what its global staff of emerging writers sees as the future of poetry, prose, and art. The journal is currently published on a quarterly online basis. Guidelines online.

**MAGAZINES NEEDS** Submit up to 8 poems at a time, no legth limits.

**TIPS** "We're ready for your best work. Please note that all submissions should be accompanied by a cover letter and brief third-person biography statement."

## ⬤ ADVOCATE, PKA'S PUBLICATION

1881 Little Westkill Rd., Prattsville NY 12468. (518)299-3103. **Website:** advocatepka.weebly.com; www.facebook.com/Advocate/PKAPublications; www.facebook.com/GaitedHorseAssociation. **Contact:** Patricia Keller, publisher. *Advocate, PKA's Publication*, published bimonthly, is an advertiser-supported tabloid using "original, previously unpublished works, such as feature stories, essays, 'think' pieces, letters to the editor, profiles, humor, fiction, poetry, puzzles, cartoons, or line drawings. Advocates for good writers and quality writings. We publish art, fiction, photos and poetry. *Advocate*'s submitters are talented people of all ages who do not earn their livings as writers. We wish to promote the arts and to give those we publish the opportunity to be published." Acquires first rights for mss, artwork, and photographs. Pays on publication with contributor copies. Publishes ms 2-18 months after acceptance. Responds to queries in 6 weeks; mss in 2 months. Sample copy: $5 (includes guidelines). Subscription: $18.50 (6 issues). Previous 6 issues are on our website. Advocate publishes only original, previously unpublished works by writers who do not yet earn their living by writing. Sample copy available for $5.00 or $18.50 for a year (6 issues).

⬤ "This publication has a strong horse orientation." Includes Gaited Horse Association newsletter. Horse-oriented stories, poetry, art and photos are currently needed.

**MAGAZINES NEEDS** "Poetry ought to speak to people and not be so oblique as to have meaning only to the poet. If I had to be there to understand the poem, don't send it. Also looking for horse-related poems, stories, drawings, and photos." Considers poetry by children and teens (when included with release form signed by adult). Accepts about 25% of poems received. Wants "nearly any kind of poetry, any length." Occasionally comments on rejected poems. Submit any number of poems at a time. No religious or pornographic poetry. Pays contributor copies.

**HOW TO CONTACT** "Contact either through our website or send with an SASE via mail."

**TIPS** "Please, no simultaneous submissions, work that has appeared on the Internet, pornography, overt religiousity, anti-environmentalism, or gratuitous violence. Artists and photographers should keep in mind that we are a b&w paper. Please do not send postcards. Use envelope with SASE."

## AFRICAN VOICES

African Voices Communications, Inc., 270 W. 96th St., New York NY 10025. (212)865-2982. **E-mail:** africanvoicesart@gmail.com. **Website:** www.african-voices.com. **Contact:** Maitefa Angaza, managing editor; Mariahadessa Ekere Tallie, poetry editor. *African Voices*, published quarterly, is an "art and literary magazine that highlights the work of people of color. We publish ethnic literature and poetry on any subject. We also consider all themes and styles: avantgarde, free verse, haiku, light verse, and traditional. We do not wish to limit the reader or author." Buys first North American serial rights. Pays on publication. Publishes ms an average of 3-6 months after acceptance. Responds in 3 months to queries. Editorial lead time 3 months. Sample copy: $6. Subscription: $20.

⬤ *African Voices* is about 48 pages, magazine-sized, professionally printed, saddle-stapled, with paper cover. Receives about 100 submissions/year, accepts about 30%. Press run is 20,000.

**MAGAZINES NEEDS** Submit no more than 2 poems at a time. Accepts submissions by postal mail. Cover letter and SASE required. Seldom comments on rejected poems. Has published poetry by Reg E. Gaines, Maya Angelou, Jessica Care Moore, Asha Bandele, Tony Medina, and Louis Reyes Rivera. Length: 5-100 lines/poem. Pays contributor copies.

**ALSO OFFERS** Reviews books of poetry in 500-1,000 words. Send materials for review consideration to Ekere Tallie. Considers poetry written by children. Offers periodic poetry contests and readings. Send SASE for details.

**TIPS** "A ms stands out if it is neatly typed with a well-written and interesting storyline or plot. Originality is encouraged. We are interested in more horror, erotic, and drama pieces. *AV* wants to highlight the diversity in our culture. Stories must touch the humanity in us all. We strongly encourage new writers/poets to send in their work. Accepted contributors are encouraged to subscribe."

## AFTER THE PAUSE

**E-mail:** afterthepause@gmail.com. **Website:** afterthepause.com. Founding Editor: Michael Prihoda.. "We are open to reading/viewing anything. Give us the wildest pieces of your imagination! Literary ephemera of all kinds welcome. We feature experimental poetry, flash fiction, visual poetry, and visual art from new, emerging, and veteran writers." Guidelines online.

**MAGAZINES NEEDS** Send up to 5 poems of any format, length, style in an attached Word document.

**TIPS** "If we receive something too close to publication of an issue it is automatically considered for the following issue."

## 🕏 AGNI

Boston University, 236 Bay State Rd., Boston MA 02215. (617)353-7135. **E-mail:** agni@bu.edu. **Website:** www.agnimagazine.org. **Contact:** Sven Birkerts, editor. Eclectic literary magazine publishing first-rate poems, essays, translations, and stories. Buys serial rights, rights to reprint in *AGNI* anthology (with author's consent). Pays on publication. Publishes ms an average of 6 months after acceptance. Responds in 4 months to mss. No queries please. Sample copy: $10 or online. Guidelines online.

💬 Reading period is September 1-May 31 only. Online magazine carries original content not found in print edition. All submissions are considered for both. Founding editor Askold Melnyczuk won the 2001 Nora Magid Award for Magazine Editing. Work from *AGNI* has been included and cited regularly in the *Pushcart Prize*, O. Henry, and *Best American* anthologies.

**MAGAZINES NEEDS** Submit online or by regular mail, no more than 5 poems at a time. E-mailed submissions will not be considered. Include a stamped addressed envelope or your e-mail address if sending by mail. Pays $20/page up to $150 (higher some years with grant support), plus a one-year subscription, and, for print publication, 2 contributor copies and 4 gift copies.

**TIPS** "We're also looking for extraordinary translations from little-translated languages. It is important to read work published in *AGNI* before submitting, to see if your own might be compatible."

## 🕏 AGNIESZKA'S DOWRY (AGD)

A Small Garlic Press (ASGP), 5445 N. Sheridan Rd., #3003, Chicago IL 60640. **E-mail:** marek@aspg.com. **Website:** asgp.org. **Contact:** Marek Lugowski and Katrina Grace Craig Valvis, co-editors. *"Agnieszka's Dowry (AgD)* is an innovative installation of mostly contemporary and mostly not-yet-famous literary texts (poems, letters to Agnieszka, occasional short short stories), computer and freehand art, photography, and more. The magazine is published both in print and online. The print version consists of professionally crafted chapbooks. The online version comprises fast-loading pages employing an intuitive, if uncanny, navigation in an interesting space, all conducive to fast and comfortable reading. No restrictions on form or type. We use contextual and juxtapositional tie-ins with other material in making choices, so visiting the online *AgD* or reading a chapbook of an *AgD* issue is required of anyone making a submission." Acquires one-time rights where applicable. Responds in 2 months. Single copy: $2 plus $8 s&h. Make checks payable to A Small Garlic Press.

💬 *Agnieszka's Dowry* is 5.5x8.5, stapled, 20-60 pages, heavy opaque white laser paper, cardstock cover, saddle-stitched (stapled), with cover art and often with internal art, in grayscale.

**MAGAZINES NEEDS** Submit 5-10 poems at a time. Accepts e-mail submissions only (pasted into body of message in plain text, sent to both editors simultaneously; no attachments). "We ask you to read well into *Agnieszka's Dowry* and to fit your submissions to the partially filled content of its open issues." Pays 1 contributor copy.

## 🕏 ALASKA QUARTERLY REVIEW

University of Alaska Anchorage, 3211 Providence Dr. (ESH 208), Anchorage AK 99508. **Fax:** (907)786-6916. **E-mail:** uaa_aqr@uaa.alaska.edu. **Website:** www.uaa.alaska.edu/aqr. **Contact:** Ronald Spatz, editor in chief. *"Alaska Quarterly Review* is a literary journal devoted to contemporary literary art, publishing fiction, short plays, poetry, photo essays, and literary nonfiction in traditional and experimental styles. The editors encourage new and emerging writers, while continuing to publish award-winning and established writers." Buys first North American serial rights. Upon request, rights will be transferred back to author after publication. Publishes ms an average of 6 months after acceptance. Responds in 4 months to queries; in 6 weeks-4 months to mss. Sample copy: $6. Guidelines online.

○ Magazine: 6×9; 232-300 pages; 60 lb. Glatfelter paper; 12 pt. C15 black ink or 4-color; varnish cover stock; photos on cover and photo essays. Reads mss August 15-May 15.

**MAGAZINES NEEDS** Submit poetry by postal mail. Include cover letter with contact information and SASE for return of ms. No light verse. Length: up to 20 pages. Pays contributor copies and honoraria when funding is available.

**ALSO OFFERS** Guest poetry editors have included Stuart Dybek, Jane Hirshfield, Stuart Dischell, Maxine Kumin, Pattiann Rogers, Dorianne Laux, Peggy Shumaker, Olena Kalytiak Davis, Nancy Eimers, Michael Ryan, and Billy Collins.

**TIPS** "Although we respond to e-mail queries, we cannot review electronic submissions."

### ◑ ALBATROSS

The Anabiosis Press, 2 South New St., Bradford MA 01835. (978)469-7085. **E-mail:** rsmyth@anabiosispress.org. **Website:** www.anabiosispress.org. **Contact:** Richard Smyth, editor. *Albatross*, published "as soon as we have accepted enough quality poems to publish an issue—about 1 per year," considers the albatross "to be a metaphor for the environment. The journal's title is drawn from Coleridge's *The Rime of the Ancient Mariner* and is intended to invoke the allegorical implications of that poem. This is not to say that we publish only environmental or nature poetry but that we are biased toward such subject matter. We publish mostly free verse, and we prefer a narrative style." Acquires all rights. Returns rights provided that "previous publication in *Albatross* is mentioned in all subsequent reprintings." Time between acceptance and publication is 6 months to a year. Responds in 2-3 months to poems. Sample copy for $5. Subscription: $8 for 2 issues. Guidelines online.

○ *Albatross* is 28 pages, digest-sized, laser-typeset, with linen cover.

**MAGAZINES NEEDS** Submit 3-5 poems at a time. Accepts e-mail submissions if included in body of message (but is "sometimes quicker at returning mailed submissions"). Name and address must accompany e-mail submissions. Cover letter is not required. "We do, however, need bio notes and SASE for return or response. Poems should be typed single-spaced, with name, address, and phone number in upper left corner." Has published poetry by Richard Brobst, Carol Hamilton, Adam Penna, Susan Richardson, and Lenny Dellarocca. Wants "poetry written in a strong, mature voice that conveys a deeply felt experience or makes a powerful statement." Does not want "rhyming poetry, prose poetry, or haiku." Length: up to 100 lines/poem. Pays 1 contributor copy.

### ◒ ALBERTA VIEWS

Alberta Views, Ltd., Suite 208, 320 23rd Ave. SW, Calgary AB T2S 0J2, Canada. (403)243-5334; (877)212-5334. **Fax:** (403)243-8599. **E-mail:** queries@albertaviews.ab.ca. **Website:** www.albertaviews.ab.ca. **Contact:** Evan Osenton, editor. "We are a regional magazine providing thoughtful commentary and background information on issues of concern to Albertans. Most of our writers are Albertans." Buys first North American serial rights, electronic rights. Pays on publication. Publishes ms an average of 3 months after acceptance. Responds in 6 weeks to queries; 2 months to mss. Editorial lead time 4 months. Sample copy free. "If you are a writer, illustrator, or photographer interested in contributing to *Alberta Views*, please see our contributor's guidelines online."

○ No phone queries.

**MAGAZINES NEEDS** Accepts unsolicited poetry. Submit complete ms.

### THE ALEMBIC

Providence College, English Dept., Attn: The Alembic Editors, 1 Cunningham Square, Providence RI 02918-0001. **Website:** www.pcc.edu/about/literary-magazines/alembic. **Contact:** Magazine has revolving editor. Editorial term: 1 year. "*The Alembic* is an international literary journal featuring the work of both established and student writers and photographers. It is published each April by Providence College in Providence, Rhode Island." Acquires first rights. Publication is not copyrighted. Responds in 1 month to queries; in 8 months to mss. Sample: $15. Subscription: $25/2years.

○ Magazine: 6×9, 80 pages. Contains illustrations, photographs.

**MAGAZINES NEEDS** Submit up to 5 poems. Does not accept online submissions. Has published poems by Tara McLaughlin, Melanie Souchet, Jackleen Holton, Peter Mishler, Dennis Rhodes, Donna Pucciani, and Sarah O'Brien.

**TIPS** "We're looking for stories that are wise, memorable, grammatical, economical, poetic in the right places, and end strongly. Take Heraclitus' claim that 'character is fate' to heart and study the strategies, styles, and craft of such masters as Anton Chekov, J. Cheever, Flannery O'Connor, John Updike, Rick Bass, Phillip Roth, Joyce Carol Oates, William Treavor, Lorrie Moore, and Ethan Canin."

### ALIMENTUM, THE LITERATURE OF FOOD

P.O. Box 210028, Nashville TN 37221. **E-mail:** editor@ alimentumjournal.com. **Website:** www.alimentum-journal.com. **Contact:** Peter Selgin, fiction and nonfiction editor; Esther Cohen, poetry editor. "*Alimentum* celebrates the literature and art of food. We welcome work from like-minded writers, musicians, and artists." Acquires first North American serial rights. Rights revert to authors upon publication. Pays on publication. Manuscript published 1-2 years after acceptance. Responds in 3 months to mss. Sample copy: $10. Guidelines online. "We do not read year round. Check website for reading periods."

○ Semiannual. *Alimentum* is 128 pages, perfect-bound, with matte-coated cover with 4-color art, interior b&w illustration; includes ads. Contains illustrations. Essays appearing in *Alimentium* have appeared in *Best American Essays* and *Best Food Writing*.

**MAGAZINES NEEDS** Send up to 5 poems by mail. Please include SASE. Has published poetry by Dick Allen, Stephen Gibson, Carly Sachs, Jen Karetnik, and Virginia Chase Sutton. Pays 1 contributor copy.

**ALSO OFFERS** Publishes an annual broadside of "menupoems" for restaurants during National Poetry Month in April.

**TIPS** "No e-mail submissions, only snail mail. Mark outside envelope to the attention of Poetry, Fiction, or Nonfiction Editor."

### ⊙ ALIVE NOW

1908 Grand Ave., P.O. Box 340004, Nashville TN 37203. (615)340-7254. **E-mail:** alivenow@upperroom.org. **Website:** www.alivenow.org; alivenow. upperroom.org. **Contact:** Beth A. Richardson, editor. *Alive Now*, published bimonthly, is a devotional magazine that invites readers to enter an ever-deepening relationship with God. "*Alive Now* seeks to nourish people who are hungry for a sacred way of living. Submissions should invite readers to see God in the midst of daily life by exploring how contemporary issues impact their faith lives. Each word must be vivid and dynamic and contribute to the whole. We make selections based on a list of upcoming themes. Mss which do not fit a theme will be returned." Pays on acceptance. Subscription: $17.95/year (6 issues); $26.95 for 2 years (12 issues). Additional subscription information, including foreign rates, available on website. Guidelines online.

**MAGAZINES NEEDS** Prefers electronic submissions attached as Word document. Postal submissions should include SASE. Include name, address, theme on each sheet. Pays $35 minimum.

### ALLIGATOR JUNIPER

(928)350-2012. **Website:** alligatorjuniper.wordpress. com. "*Alligator Juniper* features contemporary poetry, fiction, creative nonfiction, and b&w photography. We encourage submissions from writers and photographers at all levels: emerging, early career, and established." Annual magazine comprised of the winners and finalists of national contests. "All entrants pay an $18 submission fee and receive a complementary copy of that year's issue in the spring. First-place winning writers in each genre receive a $1,000 prize. The first-place winner in photography receives a $500 award. Finalists in writing and images are published and paid in contributor copies. There is currently no avenue for submissions other than the annual contest." Usually responds in January to mss. Always comments on mss. Sample copy: $5. Guidelines online.

**MAGAZINES NEEDS** Accepts submissions only through annual contest. If submitting by regular mail, include $18 entry fee payable to *Alligator Juniper* for each set of up to 5 poems. Include cover letter with name, address, phone number, and e-mail. Include author's name on first page. "Double-sided submissions are encouraged." No e-mail submissions. Length: open.

### ⊙⊙ AMBIT

Staithe House, Main Rd., Brancaster Staithe, Norfolk PE31 8PB, United Kingdom. **E-mail:** info@ambitmagazine.co.uk. **Website:** www.ambitmagazine.co.uk. **Contact:** Briony Bax, editor; Liz Berry and Declan Ryan, poetry editors. *Ambit* magazine is a literary and artwork quarterly published in the U.K. and read internationally. *Ambit* is put together entirely from unsolicited, previously unpublished poetry and short fiction submissions. Responds in 2-3 months. Sample copy: £9. Submit using Submittable portal on website on www.ambitmagazine.co.uk. There are 2 windows for submissions: February 1-April 1 and September 1-November 1. Please only submit during these windows. No e-mail submissions. Guidelines available in magazine or online.

**MAGAZINES NEEDS** Submit 3-6 poems via Submittable. No previously published poems (including on websites or blogs). Poems should be typed, double-spaced. Never comments on rejected poems. Does not want "indiscriminately centre-justified poems, jazzy fonts, or poems all in italics for the sake of it." Payment details on website.

**TIPS** "Read a copy of the magazine before submitting!"

### AMERICA

106 W. 56th St., New York NY 10019. **E-mail:** zdavis@americamedia.org. **Website:** www.americamagazine.org. **Contact:** Zac Davis, editorial assistant. "Published weekly for adult, educated, largely Roman Catholic audience. Founded by the Jesuit order and directed today by Jesuits and lay colleagues, *America* is a resource for spiritual renewal and social analysis guided by the spirit of charity. The print and Web editions of *America* feature timely and thought-provoking articles written by prestigious writers and theologians, and incisive book, film, and art reviews." Buys all rights. Pays on acceptance. Guidelines online.

**MAGAZINES NEEDS** "Many poems we publish address matters of faith and spirituality, but this is not a requirement for publication. We are looking for authentic, truthful, good poetry." Submit via online submissions manager. Length: up to 30 lines/poem. Pays competitive rate.

### ◑ THE AMERICAN DISSIDENT: A JOURNAL OF LITERATURE, DEMOCRACY & DISSIDENCE

217 Commerce Rd., Barnstable MA 02630. **E-mail:** todslone@hotmail.com. **Website:** www.theamericandissident.org. **Contact:** G. Tod Slone, editor. *The American Dissident*, published 2 times/year, provides "a forum for, amongst other things, criticism of the academic/literary established order, which clearly discourages vigorous debate, cornerstone of democracy, to the evident detriment of American Literature. The journal seeks rare poets daring to risk going against that established-order grain." Wants "poetry, reviews, artwork, and short (1,000 words) essays in English, French, or Spanish, written on the edge with a dash of personal risk and stemming from personal experience, conflict with power, and/or involvement." Submissions should be "iconoclastic and parrhesiastic in nature." Acquires first North American serial rights. Publishes ms 2-6 months after acceptance. Responds in 1 month. Almost always comments on rejected poems. Single copy: $9; subscriptions: individuals, $18; institutions $20. Guidelines available for SASE.

◑ Magazine: 56-64 pages, digest-sized, offset-printed, perfect-bound, with card cover. Press run is 200.

**MAGAZINES NEEDS** Submit 3 poems at a time. E-mail submissions from subscribers only. "Far too many poets submit without even reading the guidelines. Include SASE and cover letter containing not credits, but rather personal dissident information, as well as incidents that provoked you to 'go upright and vital, and speak the rude truth in all ways' (Emerson)." Pays 1 contributor copy.

**TIPS** "Every poet knows what he or she should not write about to avoid upsetting those in positions of literary, cultural, and/or academic power. *The American Dissident* seeks to publish those poets who now and then will break those taboos and thus raise truth-telling above getting published, funded, invited, tenured, nominated, and/or anointed. *The American Dissident* is one of the very few literary journals encouraging and publishing in each issue hardcore criticism with its own regard."

### AMERICAN LITERARY REVIEW

University of North Texas, P.O. Box 311307, Denton TX 76203-1307. (940)565-2755. **E-mail:** americanliteraryreview@gmail.com. **Website:** www.americanliteraryreview.com. **Contact:** Bonnie Friedman, editor in chief. "The *American Literary Review* publishes "excellent poetry, fiction, and nonfiction by writers at all stages of their careers." Beginning in fall 2013, *ALR* became an online publication. Publishes ms within 2 years of acceptance. Responds in 3-5 months to mss. Guidelines online.

◑ Reading period is from October 1-May 1.

**MAGAZINES NEEDS** "Poetry selections are made by a widely read group with eclectic tastes who look for the best poems, regardless of form or subject matter." Has published poetry by Kathleen Pierce,

Mark Irwin, Stephen Dunn, William Olsen, David St. John, and Cate Marvin. Submit up to 5 poems online through submission manager for a fee of $3. Does not accept submissions via e-mail or postal mail.

**TIPS** "We encourage writers and artists to examine our journal."

## THE AMERICAN POETRY REVIEW

The University of the Arts, 320 S. Broad St., Hamilton #313, Philadelphia PA 19102. **E-mail:** dbonanno@aprweb.org; escanlon@aprweb.org. **Website:** www.aprweb.org. **Contact:** David Bonanno and Elizabeth Scanlon, editors. "*The American Poetry Review* is dedicated to reaching a worldwide audience with a diverse array of the best contemporary poetry and literary prose. *APR* also aims to expand the audience interested in poetry and literature, and to provide authors, especially poets, with a far-reaching forum in which to present their work." Acquires first serial rights. Responds in 6 months. Sample: $4.50. Guidelines online.

- *APR* has included the work of over 1,500 writers, among whom there are 9 Nobel Prize laureates and 33 Pulitzer Prize winners.

**MAGAZINES NEEDS** Submit up to 5 poems via online submissions manager. Has published poetry by D.A. Powell, James Franco, Dean Faulwell, and Caroline Pittman.

## THE AMERICAN READER

**E-mail:** poetry@theamericanreader.com. **E-mail:** fiction@theamericanreader.com. **Website:** theamericanreader.com. **Contact:** Uzoamaka Maduka, editor-in-chief. *The American Reader* is a bimonthly print literary journal. The magazine is committed to inspiring literary and critical conversation among a new generation of readers, and restoring literature to its proper place in American cultural discourse. Guidelines online.

**MAGAZINES NEEDS** Interested in submissions of portfolios only (approximately 4-7 poems).

## AMERICAN TANKA

**E-mail:** editor@americantanka.com. **Website:** www.americantanka.com. "*American Tanka* seeks to present the best and most well-crafted English-language tanka being written today, in a visually calm space that allows the reader's eye to focus on the single poem and linger in the moment it evokes." Wants "concise and vivid language, good crafting, and echo

of the original Japanese form but with unique and contemporary content." Does not want "anything that's not tanka. No sequences or titled groupings." Acquires first North American serial rights. Responds in 2 months. See www.americantanka.com/submit for submission guidelines.

**MAGAZINES NEEDS** Submit up to 5 poems. Accepts submissions by online submission form found on website or by e-mail (pasted into body). Welcomes submissions from anyone who has been writing tanka: experienced tanka poets, experienced poets in other forms, and novices. Seeks concise, well-crafted, 5-line tanka that evoke a specific moment in time. Has published poetry by Sanford Goldstein, Marianne Bluger, Jeanne Emrich, Michael Dylan Welch, Tom Hartman, Larry Kimmel, Pamela Miller Ness, George Swede, and many others. Length: up to 5 lines/poem.

## AMPERSAND

Nicholas Building, 915/37 Swanston St., Melbourne VIC 3000, Australia. **E-mail:** alice@ampersandmagazine.com.au. **Website:** ampersandmagazine.com.au. **Contact:** Alice Gage, editor. *Ampersand* is an art and culture journal that explores creativity, societal change and the human condition through multi-disciplines. "We are interested in the discussion of any subject matter, particularly that which is unfashionable, unorthodox, illuminating or rare." Guidelines online.

**MAGAZINES NEEDS** *Ampersand* publishes the work of 1 poet in each issue. Submit your work as a Word document, accompanied by an introductory e-mail giving a brief explanation of what you are sending, its word count, and which section you think it would suit.

## ANALOG SCIENCE FICTION & FACT

Dell Magazines, 44 Wall St., Suite 904, New York NY 10005-2401. **E-mail:** analog@dellmagazines.com. **Website:** www.analogsf.com. **Contact:** Trevor Quachri, editor. *Analog* seeks "solidly entertaining stories exploring solidly thought-out speculative ideas. But the ideas, and consequently the stories, are always new. Real science and technology have always been important in *ASF*, not only as the foundation of its fiction but as the subject of articles about real research with big implications for the future." Buys first North American serial rights, buys nonexclusive foreign serial rights. Pays on acceptance. Publishes ms an average of 10 months after acceptance. Responds in

2-3 months to mss. Sample copy: $5 and SASE. Guidelines online.

🜂 Fiction published in *Analog* has won numerous Nebula and Hugo Awards.

**MAGAZINES NEEDS** Send poems via online submissions manager (preferred) or postal mail. Does not accept e-mail submissions. Length: up to 40 lines/poem. Pays $1/line.

**TIPS** "I'm looking for irresistibly entertaining stories that make me think about things in ways I've never done before. Read several issues to get a broad feel for our tastes, but don't try to imitate what you read."

## 🜂🜂🜁 ANCIENT PATHS

E-mail: skylarburris@yahoo.com. **Website:** www.editorskylar.com/magazine/table.html. **Contact:** Skylar H. Burris, editor. *Ancient Paths* provides "a forum for quality spiritual poetry and short fiction. We consider works from writers of all religions, but poets and authors should be comfortable appearing in a predominantly Christian publication. Works published in *Ancient Paths* explore themes such as redemption, sin, forgiveness, doubt, faith, gratitude for the ordinary blessings of life, spiritual struggle, and spiritual growth. Please, no overly didactic works. Subtlety is preferred." Acquires electronic rights. Author is free to republish work elsewhere. Pays on publication. Time between acceptance and publication 1-4 months. Responds in 8 weeks, usually sooner. Sample copy of a past printed issue: $9. Purchase online. Guidelines available on website.

🜂 New issues of *Ancient Paths* are no longer being produced in print. *Ancient Paths Online* is published as a regularly updated Facebook page with a new poem or piece of flash fiction featured at least once per week. Please send seasonally themed works for Lent and Advent at least one month prior to the start of each season. Works on other themes may be sent at any time.

**MAGAZINES NEEDS** E-mail all submissions. Paste poems in e-mail message. Use the subject heading "AP Online Submission (title of your work)." Include your name and e-mail address at the top of your e-mail. Poems may be rhymed, unrhymed, free verse, or formal and should have a spiritual theme, which may be explicit or implicit, but which should not be overly didactic. No "preachy" poetry; avoid inconsistent meter and forced rhyme; no stream-of-consciousness or avant-garde work; no esoteric academic poetry; no concrete (shape) poetry; no use of the lowercase "i" for the personal pronoun; do not center poetry. Length: 8-60 lines. Pays $1.25 per poem. Published poets also receive discount code for $3 off 2 past printed issues.

**TIPS** "Read the great religious poets: John Donne, George Herbert, T.S. Eliot, Lord Tennyson. Remember not to preach. This is a literary magazine, not a pulpit. This does not mean you do not communicate morals or celebrate God. It means you are not overbearing or simplistic when you do so."

## 🜂 ANDERBO.COM

E-mail: rrofihe@yahoo.com. E-mail: editors@anderbo.com. **Website:** www.anderbo.com. **Contact:** Rick Rofihe, edito in chief. Online literary magazine/journal. "Quality fiction, poetry, 'fact,' and photography on a website with 'print-feel' design." Member CLMP. Acquires first rights, first North American serial rights, one-time rights, electronic rights. Publication is copyrighted. Publishes ms 1 month after acceptance. Responds in 2 weeks to queries; in 1 month to mss. Editorial lead time 1-2 months. Guidelines available on website.

🜂 Received the Best New Online Magazine or Journal, *storySouth* Million Writers Award in 2005.

**MAGAZINES NEEDS** "We are looking for serious, affecting work." Publishes 40 poems/year. Send up to 6 poems in the body of e-mail or as attachment in DOC or RTF format. "We prefer your poems to be in the e-mail or together as a single attachment."

**TIPS** "We are looking for fiction that is unique, urgent, accessible, and involving. Look at our site and read what we've already published."

## 🜂🜁 THE ANTIGONISH REVIEW

St. Francis Xavier University, P.O. Box 5000, Antigonish NS B2G 2W5, Canada. (902)867-3962. **Fax:** (902)867-5563. **E-mail:** tar@stfx.ca. **Website:** www.antigonishreview.com. **Contact:** Bonnie McIsaac, office manager. *The Antigonish Review*, published quarterly, tries "to produce the kind of literary and visual mosaic that the modern sensibility requires or would respond to." After publication, rights retained by author. Pays on publication. Publishes ms an average of 8 months after acceptance. Responds in 1 month to queries; in 6 months to mss. Editorial lead time 4 months. Sample copy: $7. Guidelines for #10 SASE or online.

**MAGAZINES NEEDS** Open to poetry on any subject written from any point of view and in any form. However, writers should expect their work to be considered within the full context of old and new poetry in English and other languages. Has published poetry by Andy Wainwright, W.J. Keith, Michael Hulse, Jean McNeil, M. Travis Lane, and Douglas Lochhead. Submit 6-8 poems at a time. A preferable submission would be 3-4 poems. Lines/poem: not over 80, i.e., 2 pages. Pays $10/page to a maximum of $50 and 2 contributor copies.

**TIPS** "Send for guidelines and/or sample copy. Send ms with cover letter and SASE with submission."

## ⑤ ANTIOCH REVIEW

P.O. Box 148, Yellow Springs OH 45387-0148. (937)769-1365. **E-mail:** ccheck@antiochreview.org. **Website:** www.antiochreview.org. **Contact:** Robert S. Fogarty, editor; Judith Hall, poetry editor. Literary and cultural review of contemporary issues and literature for general readership. *The Antioch Review* "is an independent quarterly of critical and creative thought. For well over 70 years, creative authors, poets, and thinkers have found a friendly reception—regardless of formal reputation. We get far more poetry than we can possibly accept, and the competition is keen. Here, where form and content are so inseparable and reaction is so personal, it is difficult to state requirements or limitations. Studying recent issues of *The Antioch Review* should be helpful." Pays on publication. Publishes ms an average of 10 months after acceptance. Responds in 3-6 months to mss. Sample copy: $7. Guidelines online.

**MAGAZINES NEEDS** Has published poetry by Richard Howard, Jacqueline Osherow, Alice Fulton, Richard Kenney, and others. Receives about 3,000 submissions/year. Submit 3-6 poems at a time. No previously published poems or simultaneous submissions. Include SASE with all submissions. No light or inspirational verse. Poetry submissions are not accepted between between May 1-September 1. Pays $20/printed page, plus 2 contributor copies.

## APALACHEE REVIEW

Apalachee Press, P.O. Box 10469, Tallahassee FL 32302. (850) 644-9114. **E-mail:** arsubmissions@gmail.com (for queries outside the U.S.). **Website:** apalacheereview.org. **Contact:** Michael Trammell, editor; Kathleen Laufenberg, nonfiction editor; Mary Jane Ryals, fiction editor; Jay Snodgrass and Chris Hayes, poetry editors. "At *Apalachee Review*, we are interested in outstanding literary fiction, but we especially like poetry, fiction, and nonfiction that addresses intercultural issues in a domestic or international setting/context." Annual. Acquires one-time rights, electronic rights. Publication is copyrighted. Pays on publication. Publishes mss 1 year after acceptance. Responds to queries in 4-6 weeks; mss in 3-14 months. Sometimes comments on/critiques rejected mss. Sample copy: $8 for current issue; $5 for back issue. Subscription: $15 for 2 issues ($30 foreign). Guidelines online.

○ *Apalachee Review* is 90 pages, digest-sized, professionally printed, perfect-bound, with card cover. Press run is 300-400. Includes photographs. Member CLMP.

**MAGAZINES NEEDS** Submit 3-5 poems at a time. Accepts submissions by postal mail only. "Submit clear copies, with name and address on each." SASE required. Reads submissions year round. Staff reviews books of poetry. Send materials for review consideration. Has published poetry by Rita Mae Reese and Charles Harper Webb. Pays 2 contributor copies.

## APPALACHIAN HERITAGE

CPO 2166, Berea KY 40404. (859)985-3699. **Fax:** (859)985-3903. **E-mail:** appalachianheritage@berea.edu. **Website:** appalachianheritage.net. **Contact:** Jason Howard, editor. "We are seeking poetry, short fiction, literary criticism and biography, book reviews, and creative nonfiction, including memoirs, opinion pieces, and historical sketches. Unless you request not to be considered, all poems, stories, and articles published in *Appalachian Heritage* are eligible for our annual Plattner Award. All honorees are rewarded with a sliding bookrack with an attached commemorative plaque from Berea College Crafts, and First Place winners receive an additional stipend of $200." Acquires first print and electronic rights. Responds in 1 month to queries; 3-5 months to mss. Guidelines online.

○ Submission period: August 15-March 15.

**MAGAZINES NEEDS** Length: up to 42 lines. "One-page poems cannot exceed 42 lines, and two-page poems cannot exceed 84 lines." Pays 3 contributor copies.

**TIPS** "Sure, we are *Appalachian Heritage* and we do appreciate the past, but we are a forward-looking contemporary literary quarterly, and, frankly, we receive too many nostalgic submissions. Please spare us the

'Papaw Was Perfect' poetry and the 'Mamaw Moved Mountains' manuscripts and give us some hard-hitting prose, some innovative poetry, some inventive photography, and some original art. Help us be the ground-breaking, stimulating kind of quarterly we aspire to be."

## ◐◑ APPLE VALLEY REVIEW: A JOURNAL OF CONTEMPORARY LITERATURE

88 South 3rd St., Suite 336, San Jose CA 95113. E-mail: editor@leahbrowning.net. **Website:** www.applevalleyreview.com. **Contact:** Leah Browning, editor. *Apple Valley Review: A Journal of Contemporary Literature,* published semiannually online, features "beautifully crafted poetry, short fiction, and essays." Acquires first rights and first serial rights, and retains the right to archive the work online for an indefinite period of time. "As appropriate, we may also choose to nominate published work for awards or recognition. Author retains all other rights." Time between acceptance and publication is 1-6 months. Sometimes comments on rejected poems and mss. Responds to mss in 1 week-2 months. Guidelines online.

**MAGAZINES NEEDS** Wants "work that has both mainstream and literary appeal. All work must be original, previously unpublished, and in English. Translations are welcome if permission has been granted. Preference is given to short (under 2 pages), nonrhyming poetry." Considers poetry by children and teens: "Our audience includes teens and adults of all ages." Has published poetry by Laura Lee Beasley, Cameron Conaway, Robert Lavett Smith, Sharlene Teo, Donna Vorreyer, Do-hyeon Ahn, and Susan Johnson. Receives about 5,000+ poems/year, accepts less than 1%. Accepts e-mail submissions (pasted into body of message, with "poetry" in subject line); no disk submissions. Reads submissions year round. Does not want "erotica, work containing explicit language or violence, or work that is scholarly, critical, inspirational, or intended for children." Length: "No line limit, though we prefer short poems (under 2 pages)."

**CONTEST/AWARD OFFERINGS** Offers the annual *Apple Valley Review* Editor's Prize. Award is $100 and a gift of a book. Submit 1-6 poems. **Entry fee:** none. **Deadline:** rolling; all submissions to the *Apple Valley Review* and all work published during a given calendar year will be considered for the prize.

## ◑◉ ARC POETRY MAGAZINE

P.O. Box 81060, Ottawa ON K1P 1B1, Canada. **E-mail:** managingeditor@arcpoetry.ca. **Website:** www.arcpoetry.ca. **Contact:** Monty Reid, managing editor. *Arc Poetry Magazine* has been publishing the best in contemporary Canadian and international poetry and criticism for over 30 years. *Arc* is published 3 times/year, including an annual themed issue each fall. Canada's poetry magazine publishes poetry, poetry-related articles, interviews, and book reviews, and also publishes on its website; *Arc* also runs a Poet-in-Residence program. Acquires first Canadian serial rights. Responds in 4-6 months. Subscriptions: 1 year: $35 CDN; 2 years: $60 CND (in Canada). U.S. subscriptions: 1 year: $45 CAD; 2 years: $80 CAD. International subscriptions: 1 year: $55 CDN; 2 year: $90 CDN. Online ordering available for subscriptions and single copies (with occasional promotions). Guidelines online.

◖ *Arc* is 130-160 pages, perfect-bound, printed on matte white stock with a crisp, engaging design and a striking visual art portfolio in each issue. Receives over 2,500 submissions/year; accepts about 40-50 poems. Press run is 1,500.

**MAGAZINES NEEDS** *Arc* accepts unsolicited submissions of previously unpublished poems from September 1-May 31; maximum of 3 poems, 1 submission per year per person. Use online submissions manager. Has published poetry by Don Coles, Karen Solie, Nicole Brossard, Christian Bok, Elizabeth Bachinsky, George Elliott Clarke, Ken Babstock, Michael Ondaatje, Stephanie Bolster, and Don Domanski. Pays $40 CAD/page, plus contributor copy.

**CONTEST/AWARD OFFERINGS** Poem of the Year Contest—**Deadline:** February 1; $5,000 grand prize; entry fee includes one-year subscription. Confederation Poets Prize and Critic's Desk Award for best poem and reviews published in *Arc* in the preceding year. Other awards include the Archibald Lampman Award and the Diana Brebner Prize.

## ARDENT!

Poetry in the Arts, Inc., 1301 Ridgeview Lane, Bismarck ND 50501. **E-mail:** rimer777@gmail.com. **Website:** www.poetryinarts.org/publishing/ardent.html. **Contact:** Dillon McKinsey, executive editor. *Ardent!*, published annually, is a journal of poetry and art. All forms and styles are considered. *Ardent!* is perfect-bound.

**MAGAZINES NEEDS** Submit up to 3 poems by e-mail (pasted in body) or postal mail. "Include a statement giving Poetry in the Arts, Inc. your permission to use your work." Provide brief bio.

## ● ARKANSAS REVIEW: A JOURNAL OF DELTA STUDIES

Department of English and Philosophy, P.O. Box 1890, Office: Humanities and Social Sciences, State University AR 72467-1890. (870) 972-3043; (870) 972-2210. **Fax:** (870)972-3045. **E-mail:** mtribbet@astate. edu. **E-mail:** jcollins@astate.edu; arkansasreview@ astate.edu. **Website:** altweb.astate.edu/arkreview. **Contact:** Dr. Marcus Tribbett, general editor. "All material, creative and scholarly, published in the *Arkansas Review* must evoke or respond to the natural and/or cultural experience of the Mississippi River Delta region." Buys first North American serial rights. Time between acceptance and publication is about 6-18 months. Occasionally publishes theme issues. Responds in 2 weeks to queries; in 4 months to mss. Editorial lead time 4 months. Sample copy for $7.50. Subscription: $20. Make checks payable to ASU Foundation. Guidelines online.

○ *Arkansas Review* is 92 pages, magazine-sized, photo offset-printed, saddle-stapled, with 4-color cover. Press run is 600; 50 distributed free to contributors.

**MAGAZINES NEEDS** Receives about 500 poems/year; accepts about 5%. Accepts e-mail and disk submissions. Cover letter is preferred. Include SASE. Has published poetry by Greg Fraser, Jo McDougall, and Catherine Savage Brosman. Length: 1-100 lines. Pays 3 contributor copies.

**ALSO OFFERS** Staff reviews books/chapbooks of poetry "that are relevant to the Delta" in 500 words, single- and multibook format. Send materials for review consideration to Janelle Collins ("inquire in advance").

**TIPS** "Immerse yourself in the literature of the Delta, but provide us with a fresh and original take on its land, its people, its culture. Surprise us. Amuse us. Recognize what makes this region particular as well as universal, and take risks. Help us shape a new Delta literature."

## ARSENIC LOBSTER

**E-mail:** lobster@magere.com. **Website:** arseniclobster.magere.com. **Contact:** Susan Yount, poetry editor. Guidelines online.

**MAGAZINES NEEDS** Submit 3-5 poems by e-mail. "Poems should be timeless, rich in imagery, and edgy; seeking elegant emotion, articulate experiment. Be compelled to write." "We do not want political rants or Hallmark poetry."

**TIPS** "All works must be previously unpublished. Include a lively, short biography. Poetry topics, reviews and criticism, and art/photographs (.pdf or .jpg attachment only) are also welcome."

## ● ARTS & LETTERS JOURNAL OF CONTEMPORARY CULTURE

Georgia College & State University, Milledgeville GA 31061. (478)445-1289. **Website:** al.gcsu.edu. **Contact:** Laura Newbern, editor. *Arts & Letters Journal of Contemporary Culture*, published semiannually, is devoted to contemporary arts and literature, featuring ongoing series such as The World Poetry Translation Series and The Mentors Interview Series. Wants work that is of the highest literary and artistic quality. Acquires one-time rights. Pays on publication. Responds in 1-2 months to mss. Guidelines online at artsandletters.gcsu.edu/submit.

○ Work published in *Arts & Letters Journal* has received the Pushcart Prize.

**MAGAZINES NEEDS** Submit via online submissions manager. Include cover letter. "Poems are screened, discussed by group of readers. If approved by group, poems are submitted to poetry editor for final approval." Has published poetry by Margaret Gibson, Marilyn Nelson, Stuart Lishan, R.T. Smith, Laurie Lamon, and Miller Williams. No light verse. Pays $10 per printed page (minimum payment: $50) and 1 contributor copy.

**ALSO OFFERS** Offers the annual Arts & Letters/Rumi Prize for Poets.

## ● ART TIMES

P.O. Box 730, Mount Marion NY 12456. (845)246-6944. **Fax:** (845)246-6944. **E-mail:** info@arttimesjournal.com. **Website:** www.arttimesjournal.com. **Contact:** Raymond J. Steiner, editor. "Art Times est. 1984, covers the arts fields with essays about music, dance, theater, film, art, and includes short fiction and poetry as well as editorials is now, after 32 years, exclusively online. Our readers are mostly over 40, affluent, art-conscious and sophisticated. (Italy, France, Germany, Greece, Russia, etc.)." Buys first North American serial rights, buys first rights. Pays upon publication for short fiction and essays only.

Publishes within a year of submission. Responds in 6 months Poetry 20 line limit; short fiction and essays 1,500 words.

**MAGAZINES NEEDS** Wants "poetry that strives to express genuine observation in unique language. All topics, all forms. We prefer well-crafted 'literary' poems. No excessively sentimental poetry." Publishes 2-3 poems each month "Nothing violent, sexist, erotic, juvenile, racist, romantic, political, off-beat, or related to sports or juvenile fiction." Length: no more than 20 lines. Byline and permanently online.

**HOW TO CONTACT** Submission with SASE via mail or e-mail.

**TIPS** "Competition is greater (more submissions received), but keep trying. We publish new as well as published writers. Be familiar with *Art Times* and its special audience."

## ⊙⊙ ASCENT ASPIRATIONS

1560 Arbutus Dr., Nanoose Bay BC C9P 9C8, Canada. **E-mail:** ascentaspirations@shaw.ca. **Website:** www.ascentaspirations.ca. **Contact:** David Fraser, editor. "*Ascent Aspirations* magazine publishes monthly online and once in print. The print issues are operated as contests. Please refer to current guidelines before submitting. *Ascent Aspirations* is a quality electronic publication dedicated to the promotion and encouragement of aspiring writers of any genre. The focus, however, is toward interesting experimental writing in dark mainstream, literary, science fiction, fantasy, and horror. Poetry can be on any theme. Essays need to be unique, current, and have social, philosophical commentary." Rights remain with author. Responds in 1 week to queries; 3 months to mss. Sometimes comments on rejected mss. Guidelines by e-mail or on website. Accepts multiple submissions and reprints.

○ Magazine: 40 electronic pages; illustrations; photos. Receives 100-200 unsolicited mss/month. Accepts 40 mss/issue; 240 mss/year. Publishes ms 3 months after acceptance. Publishes 10-50 new writers/year. Has published work by Taylor Graham, Janet Buck, Jim Manton, Steve Cartwright, Don Stockard, Penn Kemp, Sam Vargo, Vernon Waring, Margaret Karmazin, Bill Hughes, and recently spoken-word artists Sheri-D Wilson, Missy Peters, Ian Ferrier, Cathy Petch, and Bob Holdman.

**MAGAZINES NEEDS** Submit 1-5 poems at a time. Prefers e-mail submissions (pasted into body of message or as attachment in Word); no disk submissions. "If you must submit by postal mail because it is your only avenue, provide a SASE with IRCs or Canadian stamps." Reads submissions on a regular basis year round. "We accept all forms of poetry on any theme. Poetry needs to be unique and touch the reader emotionally with relevant human, social, and philosophical imagery." Considers poetry by children and teens. Does not want poetry "that focuses on mainstream, overtly religious verse." "No payment at this time."

**TIPS** "Short fiction should first of all tell a good story, take the reader to new and interesting imaginary or real places. Short fiction should use language lyrically and effectively, be experimental in either form or content, and take the reader into realms where they can analyze and think about the human condition. Write with passion for your material, be concise and economical, and let the reader work to unravel your story. In terms of editing, always proofread to the point where what you submit is the best it possibly can be. Never be discouraged if your work is not accepted; it may just not be the right fit for a current publication."

## ASHEVILLE POETRY REVIEW

P.O. Box 7086, Asheville NC 28802. (828)450-0357. **E-mail:** editor@ashevillereview.com. **Website:** www.ashevillereview.com. **Contact:** Keith Flynn, founder/managing editor. *Asheville Poetry Review*, published annually, prints "the best regional, national, and international poems we can find. We publish translations, interviews, essays, historical perspectives, and book reviews as well." Wants "quality work with well-crafted ideas married to a dynamic style. Any subject matter is fit to be considered so long as the language is vivid with a clear sense of rhythm. We subscribe to the Borges dictum that great poetry is a combination of 'algebra and fire.'" Rights revert back to author upon publication. Up to 1 year from acceptance to publishing time. Responds in up to 4 months. Sample: $13. "We prefer poets purchase a sample copy prior to submitting." Guidelines available for SASE or on website.

○ *Asheville Poetry Review* is 160-300 pages, digest-sized, perfect-bound, laminated, with full-color cover. Receives about 8,000 submissions/year, accepts about 5%. Press run is 3,000. Subscription: $22.50 for 2 years, $43.50 for 4 years. Occasionally publishes theme issues. Reviews books/chapbooks of poetry. Send materials for review consideration. Has published poetry by Sherman Alexie, Eavan Boland, Gary Snyder, Colette Inez, Robert Bly, and Fred Chappell.

**MAGAZINES NEEDS** Submit 3-5 poems at a time. No e-mail submissions. Cover letter is required. Include comprehensive bio, recent publishing credits, and SASE. Reads submissions January 15-July 15. Poems are circulated to an editorial board. Seldom comments on rejected poems. Pays 1 contributor copy.

**CONTEST/AWARD OFFERINGS** Sponsors the William Matthews Poetry Prize: $1,000 awarded for a single poem, reads submissions September 15-January 15. See website for complete guidelines.

## ASININE POETRY

**E-mail:** editor@asininepoetry.com. **Website:** www.asininepoetry.com. **Contact:** Shay Tasaday, editor. Humorous poetry and prose, published quarterly online, "features 8-9 new works each issue. We specialize in poetry that does not take itself seriously." Wants "any form of poetry, but for us the poetry must be in a humorous, parodic, or satirical style. We prefer well-crafted poems that may contain serious elements or cover serious subjects—but which are also amusing, absurd, or hilarious."

**MAGAZINES NEEDS** Does not want serious, straightforward poems. Has published poetry by Hal Sirowitz, William Trowbridge, Elizabeth Swados, Daniel Thomas Moran, and Colonel Drunky Bob. Receives about 800 poems/year, accepts about 2%. Submit 3-4 poems at a time. Considers previously published poems and simultaneous submissions. Accepts e-mail (pasted into body of message). Do not snail mail. Length: up to 50 lines/poem.

**CONTEST/AWARD OFFERINGS** Guidelines available on website.

## ASSARACUS

Sibling Rivalry Press, P.O. Box 26147, Little Rock AR 72221. **E-mail:** info@siblingrivalrypress.com. **Website:** siblingrivalrypress.com/assaracus. **Contact:** Bryan Borland, publisher; Seth Pennington, editor. *Assaracus* is a literary journal featuring poetry by self-identified gay men. Named for the earth-bound brother of Ganymede, the youth swooped up by Zeus' eagle to serve the god, *Assaracus* is published four times a year. Guidelines online.

**MAGAZINES NEEDS** Submit up to 10 poems in 1 document along with a 75-max-word bio.

**TIPS** "Poems do not have to be gay-themed or include gay content. We do ask that poets published in *Assaracus* self-identify as gay males, although we do not police identity."

## ATLANTA REVIEW

P.O. Box 8248, Atlanta GA 31106. **E-mail:** atlanta.review@yahoo.com. **Website:** www.atlantareview.com. **Contact:** Dan Veach, editor/publisher. *Atlanta Review*, published semiannually, is devoted primarily to poetry but occasionally features interviews and b&w artwork. Publishes ms 6 months after acceptance. Responds in 1 month. Sample copy: $5. Single copy: $10; subscription: $15. Guidelines online.

Work published in *Atlanta Review* has been included in *The Best American Poetry* and *The Pushcart Prize*. *Atlanta Review* is 128 pages, digest-sized, professionally printed on acid-free paper, flat-spined, with glossy color cover. Receives about 10,000 poems/year, accepts about 1%. Press run is 1,000.

**MAGAZINES NEEDS** Wants "quality poetry of genuine human appeal." Submit up to 5 poems at a time. No e-mail submissions from within the U.S.; postal submissions only. Include SASE for reply. Authors living outside the U.S. and Canada may submit work via e-mail. Cover letter is preferred. Include brief bio. Put name and address on each poem. Reads submissions according to the following deadlines: June 1 for Fall; December 1 for Spring. Has published poetry by Seamus Heaney, Billy Collins, Derek Walcott, Maxine Kumin, Alicia Stallings, Gunter Grass, Eugenio Montale, and Thomas Lux. Pays in contributor copies.

**CONTEST/AWARD OFFERINGS** International Poetry Competition has a Grand Prize of $1,000. At least twenty entrants are published each year. Deadline March 1; entry details on website.

## THE ATLANTIC MONTHLY

The Watergate, 600 New Hampshire Ave., NW, Washington DC 20037. (202)266-6000. **Fax:** (202)266-6001. **E-mail:** submissions@theatlantic.com; pitches@theatlantic.com. **Website:** www.theatlantic.com. **Contact:** Scott Stossel, magazine editor; Ann Hulbert, literary editor. General magazine for an educated readership with broad cultural and public-affairs interests. "*The Atlantic* considers unsolicited mss, either fiction or nonfiction. A general familiarity with what we have published in the past is the best guide to our needs and preferences." Buys first North American serial rights. Pays on acceptance. Responds in 4-6 weeks to mss. Guidelines online.

**MAGAZINES NEEDS** "Interest is in the broadest possible range of work: traditional forms and free verse, the meditative lyric and the 'light' or comic poem, the work of the famous and the work of the unknown. We have long been committed to the discovery of new poets. Our 1 limitation is length; we are unable to publish very long poems." *The Atlantic Monthly* publishes some of the most distinguished poetry in American literature. "We read with interest and attention every poem submitted to the magazine and, quite simply, we publish those that seem to us to be the best." Has published poetry by Maxine Kumin, Stanley Plumly, Linda Gregerson, Philip Levine, Ellen Bryant Voigt, and W.S. Merwin. Receives about 60,000 poems/year. Submit 2-6 poems by e-mail or mail.

**TIPS** "Writers should be aware that this is not a market for beginner's work (nonfiction and fiction), nor is it truly for intermediate work. Study this magazine before sending only your best, most professional work. When making first contact, cover letters are sometimes helpful, particularly if they cite prior publications or involvement in writing programs. Common mistakes: melodrama, inconclusiveness, lack of development, unpersuasive characters and/or dialogue."

## AUTUMN SKY POETRY DAILY

**E-mail:** autumnskypoetryeditor@gmail.com. **E-mail:** autumnskypoetryeditor@gmail.com. **Website:** autumnskypoetrydaily.com. **Contact:** Christine Klocek-Lim, editor. "*Autumn Sky Poetry Daily* publishes 1 poem every weekday and occasionally on weekends. The editor reserves the right to skip a day here and there, depending on the poems received, the weather, vacation time, and/or electrical interference with her brain." Acquires first electronic rights upon acceptance. Rights returned to author upon publication. Reserves right to archive poem indefinitely online, but will remove at request of author. Time between acceptance and publication is 1 week. Responds in 1 week. "If your poem isn't published within 1 week, consider it rejected. No formal response (e-mail, owl, aural hallucination) will be sent."

**MAGAZINES NEEDS** Send 1 poem in the body of an e-mail to autumnskypoetryeditor@gmail.com with "SUBMISSION" in subject heading (no cover letter). Include links to your website, Facebook, Twitter, etc. (please, no bio). If submitting a formal poem, please feel free to include the name of the form (sestina, quatina, prose poem, etc.). Does not want "nonthoughtful line breaks, tortured meter, clichés, bad sonics, and all the other things that make poetry unpleasant to read."

## THE AVALON LITERARY REVIEW

CCI Publishing, P.O. Box 780696, Orlando FL 32878. (407)574-7355. **E-mail:** submissions@avalonliteraryreview.com. **Website:** www.avalonliteraryreview.com. **Contact:** Valerie Rubino, managing editor. "*The Avalon Literary Review* welcomes work from both published and unpublished writers and poets. We accept submissions of poetry, short fiction, and personal essays. While we appreciate the genres of fantasy, historical romance, science fiction, and horror, our magazine is not the forum for such work." Quarterly magazine. Buys one-time rights. Pays on publication. Publishes ms an average of 6 months after acceptance. Editorial lead time is 3-6 months. Sample copy: $10, by e-mail or on website. Writer's guidelines online at website or by e-mail.

**MAGAZINES NEEDS** Accepts 40-60 poems/year. Electronic submissions only. No rhyming verse. Length: no more than 50 lines. Pays 5 contributor copies.

**TIPS** "The author's voice and point of view should be unique and clear. We seek pieces which spring from the author's life and experiences. Fiction submissions which explore both the sweet and bitter of life, with a touch of humor, and poetry with vivid imagery, are a good fit for our review."

## THE AVOCET, A JOURNAL OF NATURE POETRY

P.O. Box 19186, Fountain Hills AZ 85269. **E-mail:** cportolano@hotmail.com. **E-mail:** angeldec24@hotmail.com (For The Weekly Avocet). **Website:** www.avocetreview.com. **Contact:** Charles Portolano, editor. *The Avocet, a Journal of Nature Poetry*, published quarterly, is "looking for poetry that moves the reader through the beauty, the peace, and the fury of nature in all its glory. We want poems that have people interacting with nature, animals in their element, poems that have a message on the importance of Mother Nature and our life on this magical planet. Think of the season when sending your submission." Time between acceptance and publication is up to 3 months.

Responds to submissions in 2 months. Single copy: $7.50. Subscription: $24. Make checks payable to *The Avocet*. Read a copy of an issue to get a feel of what we are looking for in Nature poetry, please.

**MAGAZINES NEEDS** Submit up to 4 poems at a time. Considers previously published poems, if acknowledged. Include cover letter with e-mail. No SASE if you have an e-mail address; mss will not be returned.

### THE AWAKENINGS REVIEW

Awakenings Project, The, P.O. Box 177, Wheaton IL 60187. (630)606-8732. **E-mail:** ar@awakeningsproject.org. **Website:** www.awakeningsproject.org. Irene O'Neill, associate editor. **Contact:** Robert Lundin, editor. *The Awakenings Review* is published by the Awakenings Project. Begun in cooperation with the University of Chicago Center for Psychiatric Rehabilitation in 2000, *The Awakenings Review* has been acclaimed internationally and draws writers from all over the United States and from several other countries including Israel, South Africa, Australia, Finland, Switzerland, the United Kingdom, and Canada. Acquires first rights. Publishes ms 8 months after acceptance. Responds in 1 month. Guidelines available in magazine, for SASE, by e-mail, or on website.

**MAGAZINES NEEDS** Submit 5 poems at a time. No e-mail submissions. Cover letter is preferred. Include SASE and short bio. Poems are read by a board of editors. Often comments on rejected poems. Occasionally publishes theme issue. Length: 61 characters. Pays 1 contributor copy, plus discount on additional copies.

### THE AWL

**E-mail:** notes@theawl.com. **E-mail:** poems@theawl.com. **Website:** theawl.com. **Contact:** Mark Bibbins, poetry editor.

### ○ BABYSUE®

babysue: ATTN: LMNOP aka dONW7, P.O. Box 15749, Chattanooga TN 37415. **E-mail:** lmnop@babysue.com. **Website:** www.babysue.com; www.lmnop.com; www.donw7.com. **Contact:** Don W. Seven, editor/publisher. *babysue* is an ongoing online magazine featuring continually updated cartoons, poems, literature, and reviews. It is also published twice/year and offers obtuse humor for the extremely open-minded. Responds "immediately, if we are interested." Seldom

comments on rejected poems. Sample: $7; cash only (no checks or money orders).

**MAGAZINES NEEDS** "We are open to all styles but prefer short poems." No restrictions. "We print prose, poems, and cartoons. We usually accept about 5% of what we receive." Has published poetry by Edward Mycue, Susan Andrews, and Barry Bishop. Pays 1 contributor copy.

**TIPS** "We do occasionally review other magazines."

### THE BAFFLER

P.O. Box 390049, Cambridge MA 2139. (212)390-1569. **Website:** thebaffler.com. **Contact:** Nicole Terez Dutton, poetry editor. *The Baffler* is a printed and digital magazine of art and criticism, now published quarterly. Guidelines online.

**MAGAZINES NEEDS** Poetry with grace is most welcome; anything that sounds like an academic "workshop" or writers' "colony" will be printed out and lit on fire.

**TIPS** "Do you have the negative capability to contribute to *The Baffler*? Muckraking, stem-winding, take-downing, doomsaying, and howling with indescribable pain are all to be expected and duly considered—so long as they don't lack humor."

### THE BALTIMORE REVIEW

**E-mail:** editor@baltimorereview.org. **Website:** www.baltimorereview.org. **Contact:** Barbara Westwood Diehl, senior editor. *The Baltimore Review* publishes poetry, fiction, and creative nonfiction from Baltimore and beyond. Submission periods are August 1-November 30 and February 1-May 31. Buys first North American serial rights. Pays $40 on publication. Publishes ms an average of 6 months after acceptance. Responds in 3 months or less. Guidelines online.

**MAGAZINES NEEDS** Submit 1-3 poems. See editor preferences on submission guidelines on website. Pays $40.

**CONTEST/AWARD OFFERINGS** Sponsors 2 theme contests per year, $500, $200, and $100 prizes; all entries considered for publication. See website for themes and guidelines.

**TIPS** "See editor preferences on staff page of website."

### ● BARKING SYCAMORES

**E-mail:** barkingsycamores@gmail.com. **Website:** barkingsycamores.wordpress.com. **Contact:** N.I. Nicholson, editor in chief; V. Solomon Maday, assistant editor in chief. *Barking Sycamores* is a literary journal whose mission is to publish poetry, short fiction (1,000 words or less), creative nonfiction (beginning in Issue 8), and artwork by neurodivergent writers. We also seek to add positively to the public discussion about neurodivergence as a whole in the form of essays on literature and the interrelationship between neurodivergence and the creative process. Acquires perpetual electronic rights, and exclusive rights for 60 days from date of publication. Publishes ms 2 weeks after acceptance. Responds in 3 weeks to queries and mss. Sample copy online. Guidelines online.

**MAGAZINES NEEDS** Does not want polemic, preachy, or rant-like poetry.

## BARN OWL REVIEW

**Website:** www.barnowlreview.com. **Contact:** Mary Biddinger and Jay Robinson, editors in chief; Sarah Dravec, Susan Grimm, Matthew Guenette, Nathan Kemp, and Amy Bracken Sparks, poetry editors. A handsomely designed print journal looking for work that takes risks while still connecting with readers. Aims to publish the highest-quality poetry from both emerging and established writers.

○ Uses online submissions manager for submissions and questions. Open annually for submissions June 1-November 1.

**MAGAZINES NEEDS** *Barn Owl Review* favors no particular poetic school or style; "however, we look for innovation and risk-taking in the poems that we publish." Submit 3-5 poems (in single attachment) via Submittable. Pays 2 contributor copies.

## BARRELHOUSE

**E-mail:** yobarrelhouse@gmail.com. **Website:** www.barrelhousemag.com. **Contact:** Dave Housley, Mike Ingram, and Joe Killiany, fiction editors; Tom McAllister, nonfiction editor; Dan Brady, poetry editor. "*Barrelhouse* is a biannual print journal featuring fiction, poetry, interviews, and essays about music, art, and the detritus of popular culture." Responds in 2-3 months to mss.

○ Stories originally published in *Barrelhouse* have been featured in the *Best American Nonrequired Reading*, *Best American Science Fiction and Fantasy*, and the Million Writer's Award.

**MAGAZINES NEEDS** Submit up to 5 poems via online submissions manager. DOC or RTF files only. Pays $50 and 2 contributor copies.

## BARROW STREET

71 First Ave., Suite 12, New York NY 10003. **E-mail:** inquiry@barrowstreet.org. **Website:** www.barrowstreet.org. **Contact:** Lorna Blake, Patricia Carlin, Peter Covino, and Melissa Hotchkiss, editors. *Barrow Street*, published annually, "is dedicated to publishing new and established poets." Wants "poetry of the highest quality; open to all styles and forms." Has published poetry by Molly Peacock, Lyn Hejinian, Carl Phillips, Marie Ponsot, Charles Bernstein, and Stephen Burt. Acquires first rights. Responds in 1 week-4 months. Sample copy: $10. Subscription: $18 for 2 years, $25 for 3 years. Guidelines online.

○ Poetry published in *Barrow Street* is often selected for *The Best American Poetry*. *Barrow Street* is 96-120 pages, digest-sized, professionally printed, perfect-bound, with glossy cardstock cover with color or b&w photography. Receives about 3,000 poems/year, accepts about 3%. Press run is 1,000. Reading period: December 1-March 15.

**MAGAZINES NEEDS** Submit poems via online submissions manager. "Please always check our website to confirm submission guidelines." Does not accept hard copy submissions. Cover letter is preferred. Include brief bio. Must have name, address, e-mail, and phone on each page submitted or submission will not be considered. Length: up to 8 pages/submission. Pays 2 contributor copies.

## BATEAU

P.O. Box 1584, Northampton MA 01061. (413)586-2494. **E-mail:** dmahoney@coa.edu. **E-mail:** bateaupress@gmail.com. **Website:** www.bateaupress.org. **Contact:** Daniel Mahoney, editor in chief. "*Bateau*, published annually, subscribes to no trend but serves to represent as wide a cross-section of contemporary writing as possible. For this reason, readers will most likely love and hate at least something in each issue. We consider this a good thing. To us, it means *Bateau* is eclectic, open-ended, and not mired in a particular strain." Acquires first North American serial rights, electronic rights. Publishes ms 3-8 months after acceptance. Responds in 1-6 months. Single copy: $15. Make checks payable to Bateau Press. Guidelines for SASE or on website. Submissions closed June-August.

○ *Bateau* is around 80 pages, digest-sized, offset print, perfect-bound, with a 100% recycled letterpress cover. Press run is 250.

**MAGAZINES NEEDS** Submit via e-mail (bateau-press@gmail.com). Include "SUBMISSION" and the genre in subject heading. Brief bio is encouraged but not required. Has published poetry by Tomaz Salamun, John Olsen, Michael Burkhardt, Joshua Marie Wilkinson, Allison Titus, Allan Peterson, and Dean Young. Receives about 5,000 poems/year, accepts about 60. Length: up to 5 pages. Pays contributor copies.

**TIPS** "Send us your best work. Send us funny work, quirky work, outstanding work, work that is well punctuated or lacks punctuation. Fearless work. Work that wants to crash on our sofa."

## BAYOU

Department of English, University of New Orleans, 2000 Lakeshore Dr., New Orleans LA 70148. **E-mail:** bayou@uno.edu. **Website:** bayoumagazine.org. **Contact:** Joanna Leake, editor in chief. "A nonprofit journal for the arts, each issue of *Bayou* contains beautiful fiction, nonfiction, and poetry. From quirky shorts to more traditional stories, we are committed to publishing solid work, regardless of style. At *Bayou* we are always interested first in a well-told tale. Our poetry and prose are filled with memorable characters observing their world, acknowledging both the mundane and the sublime, often at once, and always with an eye toward beauty. *Bayou* is packed with a range of material from established, award-winning authors as well as new voices on the rise. Recent contributors include Eric Trethewey, Virgil Suarez, Marilyn Hacker, Sean Beaudoin, Tom Whalen, Mark Doty, Philip Cioffari, Lyn Lifshin, Timothy Liu, and Gaylord Brewer. In 1 issue every year, *Bayou* features the winner of the annual Tennessee Williams/New Orleans Literary Festival One-Act Play Competition." Responds in 3-5 months to mss. Guidelines online at website.

◯   Does not accept e-mail submissions. Reads submissions August 1-May 1.

**MAGAZINES NEEDS** Submit via online submission system or postal mail. Length: "We have no strict length restrictions, though obviously it is harder to fit in very long poems." Pays 2 contributor copies.

**TIPS** "Do not submit in more than 1 genre at a time. Don't send a second submission until you receive a response to the first."

◐   **BEAR CREEK HAIKU**
P.O. Box 596, Longmont CO 80502, USA. **E-mail:** darylayaz@me.com; darylayaz@gmail.com. **Website:** bearcreekhaiku.blogspot.com. **Contact:** Ayaz Daryl Nielsen, editor; Frosty and Tama, assistant editors. Time between acceptance and publication 2 months. Sample copy for SASE. Guidelines online.

**MAGAZINES NEEDS** Submit 1-20 poems via postal mail. Send SASE with submission; SASE is used to mail contributor copy. If no poetry is accepted, submission is returned; if some poems are accepted, the remainder are shredded (with dignity). E-mail submissions welcomed from countries other than the US. Length: approximately 15 lines. Pays 1 contributor copy for SASE.

◐   **THE BEAR DELUXE MAGAZINE**
Orlo, 240 N. Broadway, #112, Portland OR 97227. **E-mail:** bear@orlo.org. **Website:** www.orlo.org. **Contact:** Tom Webb, editor-in-chief; Kristin Rogers Brown, art director. "*The Bear Deluxe Magazine* is a national independent environmental arts magazine publishing significant works of reporting, creative nonfiction, literature, visual art, and design. Based in the Pacific Northwest, it reaches across cultural and political divides to engage readers on vital issues effecting the environment. Published twice per year, *The Bear Deluxe* includes a wider array and a higher percentage of visual artwork and design than many other publications. Artwork is included both as editorial support and as standalone or independent art. It has included nationally recognized artists as well as emerging artists. As with any publication, artists are encouraged to review a sample copy for a clearer understanding of the magazine's approach. Unsolicited submissions and samples are accepted and encouraged." Buys first rights, buys one-time rights. Pays on publication. Publishes ms an average of 6 months after acceptance. Responds in 3-6 months to mail queries. Only responds to e-mail queries if interested. Editorial lead time 6 months. Sample copy: $5. Guidelines online.

**MAGAZINES NEEDS** Submit 3-5 poems at a time. Poems are reviewed by a committee of 3-5 people. Publishes 1 theme issue per year. Length: up to 50 lines/poem. Pays $20, subscription, and contributor copies.

**TIPS** "Offer to be a stringer for future ideas. Get a copy of the magazine and guidelines, and query us with specific nonfiction ideas and clips. We're looking for original, magazine-style stories, not fluff or PR. Fiction, essay, and poetry writers should know we have an open and blind review policy and they should keep sending their best work even if rejected once. Be as specific as possible in queries."

## 🌀 THE BEATNIK COWBOY

3410 Corral Drive, Apt. 208, Rapid City SD 57702. **E-mail:** submissions@thebeatnikcowboy.com. **Contact:** Dr. Randall Rogers and Chris Butler, editors. *"The Beatnik Cowboy* seeks the best poetry from all poets around the world. We do not want poetry that slaps us open-hand across the face, but instead gives us a swift kick in the yarbles." Acquires one-time rights. Responds in 1 month. Sometimes critiques poems. Guidelines online.

**MAGAZINES NEEDS** Submit 3 poems by e-mail.

## BELLEVUE LITERARY REVIEW

NYU Langone Medical Center, Department of Medicine, 550 First Ave., OBV-A612, New York NY 10016. (212)263-3973. **E-mail:** info@blreview.org. **Website:** www.blreview.org. **Contact:** Stacy Bodziak, managing editor. *Bellevue Literary Review,* published semiannually, prints "works of fiction, nonfiction, and poetry that touch upon relationships to the human body, illness, health, and healing." Acquires first North American serial rights. Publishes ms 3-6 months after acceptance. Responds in 3-6 months to mss. Sends galleys to author. Sample copy: $7. Single copy: $12; subscription: $20 for 1 year, $35 for 2 years; $48 for 3 years (plus $5/year postage to Canada, $8/year postage foreign). Make checks payable to *Bellevue Literary Review.* Guidelines for SASE or on website.

> Work published in *Bellevue Literary Review* has appeared in *The Pushcart Prize* and *Best American Short Stories.* Recently published work by Linda Pastan, Rachel Hadas, and Tom Sleigh. Closed to submissions in July and August.

**MAGAZINES NEEDS** Submit via online submissions manager. Pays 2 contributor copies, one-year subscription, and one-year gift subscription.

## BELOIT POETRY JOURNAL

Beloit Poetry Journal, P.O. 1450, Windham ME 04062. **E-mail:** bpj@bpj.org. **Website:** www.bpj.org. **Contact:** Rachel Contreni Flynn and Melissa Crowe, editors. *Beloit Poetry Journal,* published quarterly, prints "the most outstanding poems we receive, without bias as to length, school, subject, or form. For more than 65 years of continuous publication, we have been distinguished for the extraordinary range of our poetry and our discovery of strong new poets." Wants "visions broader than the merely personal; language that makes us laugh and weep, recoil, resist—and pay attention. We're drawn to poetry that grabs hold of the whole body, not just the head." Responds in 4 months to mss. Sample copy: $7. Guidelines available on website.

> Has published poetry by Sherman Alexie, Eduardo Corral, Jenny Johnson, Albert Goldbarth, Sonia Sanchez, A.E. Stallings, Douglas Kearney, Susan Tichy, and Ocean Vuong.

**MAGAZINES NEEDS** Submit via online submission manager or postal mail. Limit submissions to 5 pages or a single long poem. Pays 3 contributor copies.

**ALSO OFFERS** "The Chad Walsh Poetry Prize ($3,000) is awarded to the author of the poem or group of poems that the editorial board judges to be outstanding among those we published in the previous year."

**TIPS** "We seek only unpublished poems or translations of poems not already available in English. Poems may be submitted electronically on our website submission manager. Before submitting, please buy a sample issue or browse our website archive."

## 🌀💲 BELTWAY POETRY QUARTERLY

**E-mail:** info@beltwaypoetry.com. **Website:** www.beltwaypoetry.com. **Contact:** Kim Roberts and Gowri Koneswaran, editors. *Beltway Poetry Quarterly,* published online, "features poets who live or work in the greater Washington, D.C., metro region. *Beltway* showcases the richness and diversity of Washington, D.C., authors, with poets from different backgrounds, races, ethnicities, ages, and sexual orientations represented. We have included Pulitzer Prize winners and those who have never previously published. We publish academic, spoken word, and experimental authors—and those whose work defies categorization." Most issues are curated, but at least 1 issue per year is open to submissions from regional authors. Those issues are themed; submissions must address the announced theme. Reading periods and themes change annually; check website for details. Responds in 2 months to mss.

**MAGAZINES NEEDS** "Other than 1 annual themed issue, we are a curated journal and consider poems by invitation only. Themed issues and their open reading periods change each year; check website for guidelines. Themed issues have included prose poems, poems about working for the Federal government, and poems celebrating immigrant roots. Two issues per year feature portfolios, a larger group of poems than most journals generally include, up to 8 poems each by 5-7 authors from the greater-D.C. region, and these issues are open only by invitation. Most featured authors are found through earlier participation in themed issues; featured authors are paid a stipend."

### ◑⑤ BEYOND CENTAURI

White Cat Publications, LLC, 33080 Industrial Rd., Suite 101, Livonia MI 48150. (734)237-8522. **Fax:** (313)557-5162. **E-mail:** beyondcentauri@whitecatpublications.com. **Website:** www.whitecatpublications.com/guidelines/beyond-centauri. *Beyond Centauri*, published quarterly, contains fantasy, science fiction, sword and sorcery, very mild horror short stories, poetry, and illustrations for readers ages 10 and up. Publishes ms 1-2 months after acceptance. Responds in 2-3 months. Single copy: $7.

○ *Beyond Centauri* is 44 pages, magazine-sized, offset printed, perfect-bound, with paper cover for color art, includes ads. Press run is 100; 5 distributed free to reviewers.

**MAGAZINES NEEDS** Wants fantasy, science fiction, spooky horror, and speculative poetry for younger readers. Considers poetry by children and teens. Has published poetry by Bruce Boston, Bobbi Sinha-Morey, Debbie Feo, Dorothy Imm, Cythera, and Terrie Leigh Relf. Looks for themes of science fiction and fantasy. Poetry should be submitted in the body of an e-mail, or as an RTF attachment. Does not want horror with excessive blood and gore. Length: up to 50 lines/poem. Pays $2/original poem, $1/reprints, $1/scifaiku and related form, plus 1 contributor copy.

### ◑⑤ BIBLE ADVOCATE

Church of God (Seventh Day), P.O. Box 33677, Denver CO 80233. (303)452-7973. **E-mail:** bibleadvocate@cog7.org. **Website:** baonline.org. **Contact:** Sherri Langton, associate editor. "Our purpose is to advocate the Bible and represent the Church of God (Seventh Day) to a Christian audience." Buys first rights, second serial (reprint) rights, electronic rights. Pays on publication. Publishes ms an average of 3-9 months after acceptance. Responds in 2 months to queries. Editorial lead time 3 months. Sample copy

for SAE with 9x12 envelope and 3 first-class stamps. Guidelines online.

○ "Though the Church of God (Seventh Day) believes in the virgin birth and resurrection of Christ, we do not publish articles or poetry on celebrating a traditional Christmas or Easter. Please become familiar with our doctrines."

**MAGAZINES NEEDS** Seldom comments on rejected poems. No avant-garde. Length: 5-20 lines. Pays $20 and 2 contributor copies.

**TIPS** "Be fresh, not preachy! Articles must be in keeping with the doctrinal understanding of the Church of God (Seventh Day). Therefore, the writer should become familiar with what the Church generally accepts as truth as set forth in its doctrinal beliefs. We reserve the right to edit mss to fit our space requirements, doctrinal stands, and church terminology. Significant changes are referred to writers for approval. No fax or handwritten submissions, please."

### BIG BRIDGE

**E-mail:** walterblue@bigbridge.org. **Website:** www.bigbridge.org. **Contact:** Michael Rothenberg and Terri Carrion, editors. "*Big Bridge* is a webzine of poetry and everything else. If we like it, we'll publish it. We're interested in poetry, fiction, nonfiction essays, journalism, and art (photos, line drawings, performance, installations, siteworks, comics, graphics)." Guidelines online.

**MAGAZINES NEEDS** Only accepts electronic submissions. Submit via e-mail.

**TIPS** "We are guided by whimsy and passion and urgency. Each issue will feature an online chapbook."

### ◐ BIG MUDDY: A JOURNAL OF THE MISSISSIPPI RIVER VALLEY

Southeast Missouri State University Press, One University Plaza, MS 2650, Cape Girardeau MO 63701. (573) 651-2044. **E-mail:** upress@semo.edu. **Website:** www.semopress.com/bigmuddy/. **Contact:** Susan Swartwout, publisher/editor. "*Big Muddy* explores multidisciplinary, multicultural issues, people, and events mainly concerning, but not limited to, the 10-state area that borders the Mississippi River. We publish fiction, poetry, historical essays, creative nonfiction, environmental essays, biography, regional events, photography, art, etc." Acquires first North American serial rights. Usually publishes ms 6-12 months after acceptance. Responds in 12 weeks to mss. Send SASE for return of ms or send a disposable copy of ms and #10 SASE for reply only. Sample copy: $6. Guidelines online.

**MAGAZINES NEEDS** Receives 50 unsolicited mss/month. Accepts 20-25 mss/issue. Accepts multiple submissions. Pays 2 contributor copies; additional copies $5.

**TIPS** "We look for clear language, avoidance of clichés except in necessary dialogue, a fresh vision of the theme or issue. Find some excellent and honest readers to comment on your work-in-progress and final draft. Consider their viewpoints carefully. Revise if needed."

### 🟢 BIG PULP

**E-mail:** editors@bigpulp.com. **Website:** www.bigpulp.com. **Contact:** Bill Olver, editor. *Big Pulp* defines "pulp fiction" very broadly: It's lively, challenging, thought-provoking, thrilling, and fun, regardless of how many or how few genre elements are packed in. Doesn't subscribe to the theory that genre fiction is disposable; a great deal of literary fiction could easily fall under one of their general categories. Places a higher value on character and story than genre elements. Acquires one-time and electronic rights. Pays on publication. Publishes ms 1 year after acceptance. Responds in 2 months to mss. Sample copy: $10; excerpts online at no cost. Guidelines online.

○ "Submissions are only accepted during certain reading periods. Our website is updated to reflect when we are and are not reading, and what we are looking for."

**MAGAZINES NEEDS** All types of poetry are considered, but poems should have a genre connection. Length: up to 100 lines/poem. Pays $5/poem.

**TIPS** "We like to be surprised, and we have few boundaries. Fantasy writers may focus on the mundane aspects of a fantastical creature's life or the magic that can happen in everyday life. Romances do not have to be requited or have happy endings, and the object of one's obsession may not be a person. Mysteries need not focus on 'whodunit?' We're always interested in science or speculative fiction focusing on societal issues, but writers should avoid being partisan or shrill. We also like fiction that crosses genre; for example, a science fiction romance or a fantasy crime story. We have an online archive for fiction and poetry and encourage writers to check it out. That said, *Big Pulp* has a strong editorial bias in favor of stories with monkeys. Especially talking monkeys."

### BILINGUAL REVIEW

Arizona State University, Hispanic Research Center, P.O. Box 875303, Tempe AZ 85287-5303. (480)965-3867. **Fax:** (480)965-0315. **E-mail:** brp@asu.edu. **Website:** www.asu.edu/brp/submit. **Contact:** Gary Francisco Keller, publisher. *Bilingual Review* is "committed to publishing high-quality writing by both established and emerging writers." Acquires all rights (50% of reprint permission fees given to author as matter of policy). Publishes ms 1 year after acceptance. Responds in 2-3 months. Often comments on rejected mss.

**MAGAZINES NEEDS** Submit via postal mail. Send 2 copies of poetry with SAE and loose stamps. Does not usually accept e-mail submissions except through special circumstance/prior arrangement.

### THE BITTER OLEANDER

4983 Tall Oaks Dr., Fayetteville NY 13066. **E-mail:** info@bitteroleander.com. **Website:** www.bitteroleander.com. **Contact:** Paul B. Roth, editor and publisher. "We're reading to find a language uncommitted to the commonplace and more integrated with the natural world. A language that helps define the same particulars in nature that exist in us and have not been socialized out of us." Publishes ms an average of 1-6 months after acceptance. Responds in 1 month. Editorial lead time is 6 months. Sample copy: $10. Guidelines online.

**MAGAZINES NEEDS** Seeks "highly imaginative poetry whose language is serious. Particularly interested in translations." Has published poetry by Alberto Blanco (Mexico), José-Flore Tappy (Switzerland), Ana Minga (Ecuador), Károly Bari (Hungary), Astrid Cabral (Brazil), and numerous well-known and not-so-well-known U.S. poets. Does not want rhyming, strict metered poetry; confessional or love poetry; profanity. Length: 1-50 lines. Pays 1 contributor copy.

**CONTEST/AWARD OFFERINGS** Hosts the Bitter Oleander Press Library of Poetry Award (BOPLOPA). Guidelines online.

**TIPS** "If you are writing poems or short fiction in the tradition of 98% of all journals publishing in this country, then your work will usually not fit for us. If within the first 400 words my mind drifts, the rest rarely makes it. Be yourself, and listen to no one but yourself."

### BLACKBIRD

Virginia Commonwealth University Department of English, P.O. Box 843082, Richmond VA 23284. (804)827-4729. **E-mail:** blackbird@vcu.edu. **Web-**

site: www.blackbird.vcu.edu. *Blackbird* is published twice a year. Responds in 6 months. Guidelines online at website.

**MAGAZINES NEEDS** Submit 2-6 poems at a time. "If submitting online, put all poems into 1 document."

**TIPS** "We like a story that invites us into its world, that engages our senses, soul, and mind. We are able to publish long works in all genres, but query *Blackbird* before you send a prose piece over 8,000 words or a poem exceeding 10 pages."

## BLACKBOX MANIFOLD

Pembroke College, Cambridge CB2 1RF, United Kingdom. **E-mail:** ah217@cam.ac.uk. **Website:** manifold. group.shef.ac.uk. **Contact:** Dr. Alex Houen. *Blackbox Manifold* is an online forum with a slant towards innovative poetry that has prose, narrative, or sequences in its sights. "That said, we don't hold allegiance to any one poetry school or group, and we're happy to receive submissions from established and emerging poets alike." Responds in 6 weeks. Sample copies online. Guidelines online.

**MAGAZINES NEEDS** We welcome submissions of previously unpublished reviews, short essays, and poems (particularly poems with prose, narrative, or sequences in their sights)." Submit up to 4 poems with a brief biographical statement.

## BLACK LACE

P.O. Box 83912, Los Angeles CA 90083. (310)410-0808. **Fax:** (310)410-9250. **E-mail:** newsroom@blk.com. **Website:** www.blacklace.org. "*Black Lace* seeks stories, articles, photography, models, illustration, and a very limited amount of poetry all related to black women unclothed or in erotic situations." Acquires first North American rights, anthology rights. Responds in 1 month. Guidelines online.

**MAGAZINES NEEDS** Submit by postal mail (include SASE if you want your work returned), fax, or e-mail.

**TIPS** "*Black Lace* seeks erotic material of the highest quality, but it need not be written by professional writers. The most important thing is that the work be erotic and that it feature black women in the life or ITL themes. We are not interested in stories that demean black women or place them in stereotypical situations."

## BLACK WARRIOR REVIEW

P.O. Box 862936, Tuscaloosa AL 35486. (205)348-4518. **E-mail:** interns.bwr@gmail.com. **Website:** www.bwr. ua.edu. **Contact:** Bronwyn Valentine, editor. "We publish contemporary fiction, poetry, reviews, essays, and art for a literary audience. We publish the freshest work we can find." Buys first rights. Pays on publication. Publishes ms 6 months after acceptance. Responds in 3-6 months. Sample copy: $10. Guidelines online.

Work that appeared in the *Black Warrior Review* has been included in the *Pushcart Prize* anthology, *Harper's Magazine, Best American Short Stories, Best American Poetry,* and *New Stories from the South.*

**MAGAZINES NEEDS** "We welcome most styles and forms, and we favor poems that take risks—whether they be quiet or audacious." Submit poems in 1 document. Length: up to 10 pages. Pays one-year subscription and nominal lump-sum fee.

**TIPS** "We look for attention to language, freshness, honesty, a convincing and sharp voice. Send us a clean, well-printed, proofread ms. Become familiar with the magazine prior to submission."

## BLUE COLLAR REVIEW

Partisan Press, P.O. Box 11417, Norfolk VA 23517. **E-mail:** red-ink@earthlink.net. **Website:** www.partisanpress.org. **Contact:** A. Markowitz, editor; Mary Franke, co-editor. *Blue Collar Review (Journal of Progressive Working Class Literature)*, published quarterly, contains poetry, short stories, and illustrations "reflecting the working-class experience—a broad range from the personal to the societal. Our purpose is to promote and expand working-class literature and an awareness of the connections between workers of all occupations and the social context in which we live. Also to inspire the creativity and latent talent in 'common' working people." Sample copy: $7. Subscription: $20 for 1 year; $35 for 2 years. Make checks payable to Partisan Press. Guidelines online. Work not meeting guidelines may be returned or discarded.

*Blue Collar Review* is 60 pages, digest-sized, offset-printed, saddle-stapled, with colored card cover, includes ads. Receives hundreds of poems/year, accepts about 15%. Press run is 500.

**MAGAZINES NEEDS** Send up to 5 poems. Include name and address on each page. Cover letter is helpful but not required. Size 10 SASE is required for response. Has published poetry by Simon Perchik, Jim Daniels, Mary McAnally, Marge Piercy, Alan Catlin, and Rob Whitbeck. Pays contributor copies.

**CONTEST/AWARD OFFERINGS** Sponsors Working People's Poetry Contest. **Entry fee:** $15/poem. **Deadline:** May 15. Prize: $100, one-year subscription to *Blue Collar Review* and 1 year online posting of poem.

**ALSO OFFERS** Partisan Press looks for "poetry of power that reflects a working-class consciousness and moves us forward as a society. Must be good writing reflecting social realism including but not limited to political issues." Publishes about 3 chapbooks/year; not presently open to unsolicited submissions. "Submissions are requested from among the poets published in the *Blue Collar Review*." Has published *A Possible Explanation* by Peggy Safire and *American Sounds* by Robert Edwards. Chapbooks are usually 20-60 pages, digest-sized, offset-printed, saddle-stapled or flat-spined, with card or glossy covers. Sample chapbooks are $7 and listed on website.

## Ⓓ BLUELINE

120 Morey Hall, Dept. of English and Communication, Postdam NY 13676. (315)267-2044. **Fax:** (315) 267-3256. **E-mail:** blueline@potsdam.edu. **Website:** bluelinemagadk.com. **Contact:** Donald McNutt, editor; Caroline Downing, art editor; Donald McNutt, nonfiction editor; Stephanie Coyne-Deghett, fiction editor; Rebecca Lehmann, poetry editor. "*Blueline* seeks poems, stories, and essays relating to the Adirondacks and regions similar in geography and spirit, or focusing on the shaping influence of nature. Submission period is July-November. *Blueline* welcomes electronic submissions as Word document (.doc or .docx) attachments. Please identify genre in subject line. Please avoid using compression software." Acquires first North American serial rights. Publishes ms 3-6 months after acceptance. Responds in up to 3 months to mss. "Decisions in early February." Occasionally comments on rejected mss. Sample copy: $9. Guidelines available on our website, SASE, or by e-mail.

Ⓠ   "Proofread all submissions. It is difficult for our editors to get excited about work containing typographical and syntactic errors."

**MAGAZINES NEEDS** Submit 3-5 poems at a time. Submit July 1-November 30 only. Include short bio. Poems are circulated to an editorial board. Has pub-

lished poetry by M.J. Iuppa, Alice Wolf Gilborn, Lyn Lifshin, Todd Davis, Maurice Kenny, Richard Levine, and Lee Slonimsky. Reviews books of poetry in 500-750 words, single- or multibook format. "We are interested in both beginning and established poets whose poems evoke universal themes in nature and show human interaction with the natural world. We look for thoughtful craftsmanship rather than stylistic trickery." Does not want "sentimental or extremely experimental poetry." Lines/poem: 75 maximum; "occasionally we publish longer poems." Pays 1 contributor copy.

**TIPS** "We look for concise, clear, concrete prose that tells a story and touches upon a universal theme or situation. We prefer realism to romanticism but will consider nostalgia if well done. Pay attention to grammar and syntax. Avoid murky language, sentimentality, cuteness, or folksiness. We would like to see more good, creative nonfiction centered on the literature and/or culture of the Adirondacks, Northern New York, New England, or Eastern Canada. If ms has potential, we work with author to improve and reconsider for publication. Our readers prefer fiction to poetry (in general) or reviews. Write from your own experience, be specific and factual (within the bounds of your story), and if you write about universal features such as love, death, change, etc., write about them in a fresh way. You'll catch our attention if your writing is interesting, vigorous, and polished."

## BLUE MESA REVIEW

700 Lomas NE, Suite 108, Albuquerque NM 87102. **E-mail:** bmreditr@unm.edu. **Website:** bluemesareview.org. **Contact:** Has rotating editorial board; see website for current masthead. "Originally founded by Rudolfo Anaya, Gene Frumkin, David Johnson, Patricia Clark Smith, and Lee Bartlette in 1989, the *Blue Mesa Review* emerged as a source of innovative writing produced in the Southwest. Over the years the magazine's nuance has changed, sometimes shifting towards more craft-oriented work, other times realigning with its original roots." Requests first North American serial rights for print and nonexclusive electronic rights for website. Responds in 2-6 months.

Ⓠ   Open for submissions from September 30-March 31. Contest: June 1-August 31. Only accepts submissions through online submissions manager.

**MAGAZINES NEEDS** Submit 3-5 poems via online submissions manager.

**TIPS** "In general, we are seeking strong voices and lively, compelling narrative with a fine eye for craft. We look forward to reading your best work!"

## BLUESTEM

**Website:** www.bluestemmagazine.com. **Contact:** Charlotte Pence, editor. *Bluestem*, formerly known as *Karamu*, produces a quarterly online issue (December, March, June, September) and an annual print issue. Submissions are accepted September 1-May 1. There is no compensation for online contributors but we will promote your work enthusiastically and widely. Past issues have included themes such as: The Humor Issue, The Music Issue, The Millennium. Produced by the English Department at Eastern Illinois University. Responds in 6-8 weeks. "Sample back issues of *Bluestem (Karamu)* are available for $5 for each issue you would like."

 ⬭ Only accepts submissions through online submissions manager.

**MAGAZINES NEEDS** Submit using online submissions manager. Include bio (less than 100 words) with submission. Pays 1 contributor copy and discount for additional copies.

## BLUE UNICORN, A TRI-QUARTERLY OF POETRY

22 Avon Rd., Kensington CA 94707. **E-mail:** staff@ blueunicorn.com. **Website:** www.blueunicorn.org.

**MAGAZINES NEEDS** *Blue Unicorn, A Tri-Quarterly of Poetry*, published in October, February, and June, is "distinguished by its fastidious editing, both with regard to contents and format." Wants "well-crafted poetry of all kinds, in form or free verse, as well as expert translations on any subject matter. We shun the trite or inane, the soft-centered, the contrived poem. Shorter poems have more chance with us because of limited space." Has published poetry by James Applewhite, Kim Cushman, Patrick Worth Gray, Joan LaBombard, James Schevill, and Gail White. *Blue Unicorn* is 56 pages, narrow digest-sized, finely printed, saddle-stapled. Receives more than 2,000 submissions/year, accepts about 150. Single copy: $7 (foreign add $3); subscription: $18 for 3 issues (foreign add $6).

**HOW TO CONTACT** Submit 3-5 poems at a time. No previously published poems or simultaneous submissions. Cover letter is "OK, but will not affect our selection." Sometimes comments on rejected poems. Guidelines available for SASE. Responds in up to 3 months (generally within 6 weeks). Pays one contributor copy.

**CONTEST/AWARD OFFERINGS** Sponsors an annual (spring) contest with prizes of $150, $75, $50, and sometimes special awards; distinguished poets as judges; publication of top 3 poems and 6 honorable mentions in the magazine. Guidelines available for SASE. Entry fee: $6 for first poem, $3 for each additional poem.

## BODY LITERATURE

**Website:** bodyliterature.com. *B O D Y* is an international online literary journal. "We publish the highest quality poetry and prose from emerging and established writers. Sample copies online. Guidelines online.

**MAGAZINES NEEDS** Submit up to 5 poems in 1 document; each poem should start a new page.

## BOMBAY GIN

Writing and Poetics Dept., Jack Kerouac School, Naropa University, 2130 Arapahoe Ave., Boulder CO 80302. (303)245-4669. **Fax:** (303)546-5297. **E-mail:** bgin@naropa.edu. **Website:** www.bombayginjournal. com. **Contact:** Jade Lascelles, editor-in-chief. *Bombay Gin*, published annually, is the literary journal of the Jack Kerouac School of Disembodied Poetics at Naropa University. Produced and edited by MFA students, *Bombay Gin* publishes established writers alongside unpublished and emerging writers. We have a special interest in works that push conventional literary boundaries. Submissions of poetry, prose, visual art, translation, and works involving hybrid forms and cross-genre exploration are encouraged. Translations are also considered. Guidelines are the same as for original work. Translators are responsible for obtaining any necessary permissions." One-year subscription: $10 + $3 shipping.

 ⬭ *Bombay Gin* is 150-200 pages, digest-sized, professionally printed, perfect-bound, with color card cover. Has published work by Amiri Baraka, Lisa Robertson, CA Conrad, Sapphire, Fred Moten, Anne Waldman, Diane di Prima and bell hooks, among others.

**MAGAZINES NEEDS** Please see website for current details on submission time frames and guidelines. Pays 1 contributor copies.

## ⑤ BOMB MAGAZINE

New Arts Publications, 80 Hanson Place, Suite 703, Brooklyn NY 11217. (718)636-9100. **Fax:** (718)636-9200. **Website:** www.bombmagazine.com. **Contact:** Mónica de la Torre, senior editor. "Written, edited, and produced by industry professionals and funded by those interested in the arts, *BOMB Magazine* publishes work which is unconventional and contains an edge, whether it be in style or subject matter." Buys first rights, buys one-time rights. Pays on publication. Publishes ms an average of 3-6 months after acceptance. Responds in 3-5 months to mss. Editorial lead time 3-4 months. Sample copy: $10. Guidelines by e-mail.

**MAGAZINES NEEDS** *BOMB Magazine* accepts unsolicited poetry and prose submissions for our literary supplement *First Proof* by online submission manager in January and August. Submissions sent outside these months will not be read. Submit 4-6 poems via online submission manager. E-mailed submissions will not be considered. Pays $100 and contributor copies.

**TIPS** "Manuscripts should be typed, double-spaced, and proofread, and should be final drafts. Purchase a sample issue before submitting work."

## BORDERLANDS: TEXAS POETRY REVIEW

P.O. Box 40876, Austin TX 78704. **E-mail:** borderlandspoetry@gmail.com. **Website:** www.borderlands.org. *Borderlands: Texas Poetry Review*, published semiannually, prints high-quality, outward-looking poetry by new and established poets, as well as brief reviews of poetry books and critical essays. Cosmopolitan in content, but particularly welcomes Texas and Southwest writers. Wants poems that exhibit social, political, geographical, historical, feminist, or spiritual awareness coupled with concise artistry. Does not want introspective work about the speaker's psyche, childhood, or intimate relationships. Has published poetry by Walter McDonald, Naomi Shihab Nye, Mario Susko, Wendy Barker, Larry D. Thomas, Reza Shirazi, and Scott Hightower. Sample copy: $12. Guidelines online.

○ *Borderlands* is 100-150 pages, digest-sized, offset-printed, perfect-bound, with 4-color cover. Receives about 2,000 poems/year, accepts about 120. Press run is 1,000.

**MAGAZINES NEEDS** Submit 5 typed poems at a time. Include cover letter. Include SASE with sufficient return postage. Open to traditional and experimental forms.

**TIPS** "Editors read year-round in 2 cycles. Submissions postmarked March 15-June 15 will be considered for the Fall/Winter issue, and submissions postmarked September 15-December 15 will be considered for the Spring/Summer issue. Occasionally, work may be held for publication in the following issue. Note that response times may be slower for work received immediately after a deadline. Do not submit work while we are considering a previous submission."

## BOSTON COLLEGE MAGAZINE

140 Commonwealth Ave., Chestnut Hill MA 2467. (617)552-4820. **Fax:** (617)552-2441. **E-mail:** bcm@bc.edu. **Website:** bcm.bc.edu. **Contact:** Ben Birnbaum, editor.

## ⑤ BOSTON REVIEW

P.O. Box 425786, Cambridge MA 02142. (617)324-1360. **Fax:** (617)452-3356. **Website:** www.bostonreview.net. Editors: Deborah Chasman and Joshua Cohen.. "The editors are committed to a society and culture that foster human diversity and a democracy in which we seek common grounds of principle amidst our many differences. In the hope of advancing these ideals, the *Review* acts as a forum that seeks to enrich the language of public debate." Buys first North American serial rights, buys first rights. Publishes ms an average of 4 months after acceptance. Responds in 4 months to queries. Sample copy for $6.95 plus shipping or online. Guidelines online.

○ *Boston Review* is a recipient of the Pushcart Prize in Poetry.

**MAGAZINES NEEDS** "We are open to both traditional and experimental forms. What we value most is originality and a strong sense of voice." Send materials for review consideration. Reads poetry between September 15 and May 15 each year. Payment varies.

**TIPS** "The best way to get a sense of the kind of material *Boston Review* is looking for is to read the magazine. "

## ⑤ BOULEVARD

Opojaz, Inc., 6614 Clayton Rd., Box 325, Richmond Heights MO 63117. **E-mail:** richardburgin@netzero.com; jessicarogen@boulevardmagazine.org. **Website:** www.boulevardmagazine.org; boulevard.submittable.com/submit. **Contact:** Jessica Rogen, editor. "*Boulevard* is a diverse literary magazine presenting original creative work by well-known authors, as well as by writers of exciting promise." Triannual magazine featuring fiction, poetry, and essays. Sometimes comments on rejected mss. *Boulevard* has been called 'one of the half-dozen best literary journals' by Poet Laureate Daniel Hoffman in *The Philadelphia Inquirer*. We strive to publish the finest in poetry, fiction, and nonfiction. We frequently publish writers with previous credits, and we are very interested in publishing less experienced or unpublished writers with exceptional promise. We've published everything from John Ashbery to Donald Hall to a wide variety of styles from new or lesser known poets. We're eclectic. We are interested in original, moving poetry written from the head as well as the heart. It can be about any topic." Buys first North American serial rights. Rights revert to author upon publication. Pays on publication. Publishes ms an average of 9 months after acceptance. Responds in 2 weeks to queries; in 4-5 months to mss. Sample copy: $10. Subscription: $15 for 3 issues, $27 for 6 issues, $30 for 9 issues. Foreign subscribers, please add $10. Make checks payable to Opojaz, Inc. Subscriptions are online at www.boulevardmagazine.org/subscribe.html. Guidelines online.

○    *Boulevard* is 175-250 pages, digest-sized, flat-spined, with glossy card cover. Receives over 600 unsolicited mss/month. Accepts about 10 mss/issue. Publishes 10 new writers/year. Recently published work by Joyce Carol Oates, Floyd Skloot, John Barth, Stephen Dixon, David Guterson, Albert Goldbarth, Molly Peacock, Bob Hicok, Alice Friman, Dick Allen, and Tom Disch.

**MAGAZINES NEEDS** Submit by mail or via Submittable. Accepts multiple submissions. Does not accept poems May 1-October 1. SASE for reply. Does not consider book reviews. "Do not send us light verse." Does not want "poetry that is uninspired, formulaic, self-conscious, unoriginal, insipid." Length: up to 200 lines/poem. Pays $25-250.

**ALSO OFFERS** The Poetry Contest for Emerging Writers: $1,000 and publication in *Boulevard*, awarded to the winning group of 3 poems. Postmark deadline is June 1. Entry fee is $15 for each group of three poems, with no limit per author. It includes a one-year subscription to *Boulevard*. For contests, make check payable to *Boulevard* or submit online at https://boulevard.submittable.com/submit.

**TIPS** "Read the magazine first. The work *Boulevard* publishes is generally recognized as among the finest in the country. We continue to seek more good literary or cultural essays. Send only your best work."

## THE BREAKTHROUGH INTERCESSOR

Breakthrough, Inc., P.O. Box 121, Lincoln VA 20160. **Fax:** (540)338-1934. **E-mail:** breakthrough@intercessors.org. **Website:** intercessors.org. *The Breakthrough Intercessor*, published quarterly, focuses on "encouraging people in prayer and faith; preparing and equipping those who pray." Accepts multiple articles per issue: 300- to 1,000-word true stories on prayer, or poems on prayer. Time between acceptance and publication varies. Subscription: $18. Make checks payable to Breakthrough, Inc. Guidelines available on website.

○    *The Breakthrough Intercessor* is 36 pages, magazine-sized, professionally printed, saddle-stapled with self-cover, includes art/graphics. Press run is 4,000.

**MAGAZINES NEEDS** Send poem, along with title, author's name, address, phone number, and e-mail. Accepts fax, e-mail (pasted into body of message or attachment), and mailed hard copy. Length: 12 lines/poem minimum.

## THE BRIAR CLIFF REVIEW

3303 Rebecca St., Sioux City IA 51104. (712)279-5477. **E-mail:** tricia.currans-sheehan@briarcliff.edu; jeanne.emmons@briarcliff.edu. **Website:** bcreview.org. **Contact:** Tricia Currans-Sheehan, Jeanne Emmons, Phil Hey, Paul Weber, editors. *The Briar Cliff Review*, published annually in April, is "an attractive, eclectic literary/art magazine." It focuses on, but is not limited to, "Siouxland writers and subjects. We are happy to proclaim ourselves a regional publication. It doesn't diminish us; it enhances us." Acquires first serial rights. Time between acceptance and publication is up to 6 months. Responds in 4-5 months to mss; in 6-8 months to poems. Sample copy: $15, plus 9x12 SAE. Guidelines available on website or for #10 SASE.

○    Member: CLMP, Humanities International Complete. Reads submissions August 1-November 1 only.

**MAGAZINES NEEDS** Wants quality poetry with strong imagery and tight, well-wrought language. Especially interested in, but not limited to, regional, Midwestern content. Receives about 1,000 poems/year; accepts about 30. Considers simultaneous submissions but expects prompt notification of acceptance elsewhere. Submit by postal mail (send SASE for return of ms) or via Submittable. No e-mail submissions, unless from overseas. Cover letter is required. "Include short bio. Submissions should be typewritten or letter quality, with author's name and address on each page. No mss returned without SASE." Seldom comments on rejected poems. Pays 2 contributor copies; additional copies available for $12.

**TIPS** "So many stories are just telling. We want some action. It has to move. We prefer stories in which there is no gimmick, no mechanical turn of events, no moral except the one we would draw privately."

## BRILLIANT CORNERS: A JOURNAL OF JAZZ & LITERATURE

Lycoming College, 700 College Place, Williamsport PA 17701. (570)321-4279. **Fax:** (570)321-4090. **E-mail:** feinstein@lycoming.edu. **Website:** www.lycoming.edu/brilliantcorners. **Contact:** Sascha Feinstein. "We publish jazz-related literature—fiction, poetry, and nonfiction. We are open as to length and form." Semiannual. Acquires first North American serial rights. Publishes ms 4-12 months after acceptance. Responds in 2 weeks to queries; in 1-2 months to mss. Rarely comments on rejected mss. Sample copy: $7. Guidelines online.

Does not read mss May 15-September 1.

**MAGAZINES NEEDS** Submit 3-5 poems at a time. No e-mail or fax submissions. Cover letter is preferred. Staff reviews books of poetry. Send materials for review consideration. Wants "work that is both passionate and well crafted—work worthy of our recent contributors." Has published poetry by Amiri Baraka, Jayne Cortez, Yusef Komunyakaa, Philip Levine, Sonia Sanchez, and Al Young. Does not want "sloppy hipster jargon or improvisatory nonsense."

**TIPS** "We look for clear, moving prose that demostrates a love of both writing and jazz. We primarily publish established writers, but we read all submissions carefully and welcome work by outstanding young writers."

## BUENOS AIRES REVIEW

**E-mail:** editors@buenosairesreview.org. **Website:** buenosairesreview.org. *The Buenos Aires Review* presents the best and latest work by emerging and established writers from the Americas, in both Spanish and English. "We value translation and conversation. We're bilingual. And we're passionate about the art and craft that allows us to be, so we provide a

dedicated space for translators to discuss their recent projects." Guidelines online.

**MAGAZINES NEEDS** Submit 3-6 poems through online portal.

## BURNSIDE REVIEW

**Website:** www.burnsidereview.org. **Contact:** Sid Miller, founder and editor; Dan Kaplan, managing editor. *Burnside Review*, published every 9 months, prints "the best poetry and short fiction we can get our hands on." Each issue includes 1 featured poet with an interview and new poems. "We tend to publish writing that finds beauty in truly unexpected places; that combines urban and natural imagery; that breaks the heart." Acquires first rights. Pays on publication. Publishes ms 9 months after acceptance. Responds in 1-6 months. Submit seasonal material 3-6 months in advance. Single copy: $8; subscription: $13.

**MAGAZINES NEEDS** "We like lyric. We like narrative. We like when the 2 merge. We like whiskey. We like hourglass figures. We like to be surprised. Surprise us." Has published poetry by Linda Bierds, Dorianne Laux, Ed Skoog, Campbell McGrath, Paul Guest, and Larissa Szporluk. Reads submissions year round. "Editors read all work submitted." Seldom comments on rejected work. Submit 3-5 poems via online submissions manager. Pays $25 and 1 contributor copy.

## BY&BY POETRY

**Website:** byandbylit.org. **Contact:** Jason Sears, editor. *By&By Poetry* aims to provide an eclectic online showcase for both established and up-and-coming poets. "We aspire to shape *By&By* into a celebration of poetry, a place where poets can congregate, read, and be heard. Join us." Sample copies online. Guidelines online.

**MAGAZINES NEEDS** Submit up to 5 poems with a cover letter and short bio.

**TIPS** "We welcome poems of any form, length, or style. Quite simply, we want your best."

## CAHABA RIVER LITERARY JOURNAL

Rivercity Today / X-Press, 2413 Bethel Rd., Logansport LA 71049. (318)564-6031. **E-mail:** cahabariverliteraryjournal@gmail.com. **Website:** cahabariverliteraryjournal.wordpress.com. **Contact:** Marcella Simmons, editor. *Cahaba River Literary Journal* publishes quality fiction, poetry, and photography in every genre. Purchases simultaneous rights; rights revert back to author at time of publication. Publishes 1 month after accepting ms. Responds in 1 week to queries; in 1 month to mss. Editorial lead time 1 month. Sample copy: $5.50. Guidelines available for SASE or via e-mail.

○ All mss should be submitted with a cover letter, brief bio, and name and address.

**MAGAZINES NEEDS** Length: up to 25 lines/poem.

**TIPS** "Present to me your best works: I want to laugh, cry, be sad, or get angry at the story or poem."

## CALIFORNIA QUARTERLY

California State Poetry Society, P.O. Box 7126, Orange CA 92863. **Website:** www.californiastatepoetrysociety.org. **Contact:** John Forrest Harrell, president. The California State Poetry Society is dedicated to the advancement of poetry and its dissemination. Although located in California, its members are from all over the U.S. and abroad. Levels of membership/dues: $35/year for an individual, $39/year for a family or library, $51/year foreign. Benefits include membership in the National Federation of State Poetry Societies (NFSPS); 4 issues of *California Quarterly*, *Newsbriefs*, and *The Poetry Letter*. Sponsors monthly and annual contests. Additional information available for SASE or on the website. Acquires first rights. Rights revert to poet after publication. Sample copy: $10. See *CQ*'s tab of website or mail request with $10 to CSPS VP/Membership, 2560 Calabria Ct., Dublin CA 94568.

**MAGAZINES NEEDS** Submit 3-5 poems by postal mail with SASE or on website.Submit original poems only; no previously published poems. Foreign poems with translations welcome. Pays 1 contributor copy.

## CALLALOO: A JOURNAL OF AFRICAN DIASPORA ARTS & LETTERS

Texas A&M University, 249 Blocker Hall, College Station TX 77843-4212, United States. (979)458-3108. **Fax:** (979)458-3275. **E-mail:** callaloo@tamu.edu. **Website:** callaloo.tamu.edu. *Callaloo: A Journal of African Diaspora Arts & Letters*, published quarterly, is devoted to poetry dealing with the African Diaspora, including North America, Europe, Africa, Latin and Central America, South America, and the Caribbean. Features about 15-20 poems (all forms and styles) in each issue along with short fiction, interviews, literary criticism, and concise critical book reviews. Responds in 6 months to mss. Sample online: muse.jhu.edu/journals/callaloo/toc/cal.36.1.html. Submission guidelines online.

**MAGAZINES NEEDS** Submit no more than 5 poems at a time; no more than 10 per calendar year. Submit using online submissions manager only: callaloo.expressacademic.org/login.php. Has published poetry by Aimeé Ceésaire, Lucille Clifton, Rita Dove, Yusef Komunyakaa, Natasha Tretheway, and Carl Phillips.

**TIPS** "We look for freshness of both writing and plot, strength of characterization, plausibility of plot. Read what's being written and published, especially in journals such as *Callaloo*."

## ⦿ CALYX

P.O. Box B, Corvallis OR 97339. (541)753-9384. **Fax:** (541)753-0515. **E-mail:** info@calyxpress.org; editor@calyxpress.org. **Website:** www.calyxpress.org. **Contact:** Brenna Crotty, senior editor. "*CALYX* exists to publish fine literature and art by women and is dedicated to publishing the work of all women, including women of color, older women, working-class women and other voices that need to be heard. We are committed to discovering and nurturing developing writers." Publishes ms an average of 6-12 months after acceptance. Responds in 4-8 months to mss. Sample copy: $10 plus $4 postage and handling.

○ Annual open submission period is October 1-December 31.

**MAGAZINES NEEDS** "When submitting through our online submissions manager, please put all poems in the same document." Wants "excellently crafted poetry that also has excellent content." Pays in contributor copies and one-volume subscription.

**TIPS** "A forum for women's creative work—including work by women of color, lesbian and queer women, young women, old women—*CALYX* breaks new ground. Each issue is packed with new poetry, short stories, full-color artwork, photography, essays, and reviews."

## CAMAS: THE NATURE OF THE WEST

The University of Montana, Environmental Studies Program, Rankin Hall 1O16, Missoula MT 59812. (406)243-6273. **Fax:** (406)243-6090. **E-mail:** camas@mso.umt.edu. **Website:** www.camasmagazine.org. **Contact:** Co-editor. Published bi-annually in Winter and Summer. "*Camas* seeks to create an evocative space that celebrates, explores, and acknowledges the complex relationship of people and land and environment in the American West." Buys one-time rights. Copyrighted publication. Publishes mss 2 months after acceptance. Responds in 1 month to queries. Sample copy: $8.50, online at website and by e-mail. Writer's guidelines online and by e-mail.

○ "Please check our website or Facebook page for theme and submission periods."

**MAGAZINES NEEDS** "Poetry or other written work of intrigue is accepted. Word count varies. Length: 3-100 lines/poem.

**TIPS** "Submit work that speaks to contemporary social issues associated with environmental concerns of the American West. The link to the region can be tenuous or subtle."

## ○○⑤ THE CAPILANO REVIEW

281 Industrial Ave., Vancouver BC V6A 2P2, Canada. (604)984-1712. **E-mail:** contact@thecapilanoreview.ca. **Website:** www.thecapilanoreview.ca. **Contact:** Todd Nickel, managing editor. Triannual visual and literary arts magazine that "publishes only what the editors consider to be the very best fiction, poetry, drama, or visual art being produced. *TCR* editors are interested in fresh, original work that stimulates and challenges readers. Over the years, the magazine has developed a reputation for pushing beyond the boundaries of traditional art and writing. We are interested in work that is new in concept and in execution." Buys first North American serial rights. Pays on publication. Publishes ms an average of within 1 year after acceptance. Responds in 4-6 months to mss. Sample copy: $10 (outside of Canada, USD). Guidelines with #10 SASE with IRC or Canadian stamps.

**MAGAZINES NEEDS** Submit up to 8 pages of poetry. Pays $50-300.

## ○ THE CARIBBEAN WRITER

University of the Virgin Islands, RR 1, P.O. Box 10,000, Kingshill, St. Croix USVI 00850. (340)692-4152. **Fax:** (340)692-4026. **E-mail:** info@thecaribbeanwriter.org. **E-mail:** submit@thecaribbeanwriter.org. **Website:** www.thecaribbeanwriter.org. **Contact:** Alscess Lewis-Brown, editor. "*The Caribbean Writer* features new and exciting voices from the region and beyond that explore the diverse and multi-ethnic culture in poetry, short fiction, personal essays, creative nonfiction, and plays. Social, cultural, economic, and sometimes controversial issues are also explored, employing a wide array of literary devices." Acquires first North American serial rights. Single copy: $20; subscription: $25 for 2 years. Guidelines available by e-mail or on website.

○ Poetry published in *The Caribbean Writer* has appeared in *The Pushcart Prize. The Caribbean Writer* is 300+ pages, digest-sized, handsomely printed on heavy stock, perfect-bound, with glossy card cover. Press run is 1,200.

**MAGAZINES NEEDS** Reviews books of poetry and fiction in 1,000 words. Send materials for review consideration. Submit up to 6 poems at a time. E-mail as attachment; no fax submissions. Name, address, phone number, e-mail address, and title of ms should appear in cover letter along with brief bio. Title only on ms. Has published poetry by Edwidge Danticat, Geoffrey Philp, and Thomas Reiter. Pays 1 contributor copy.

**ALSO OFFERS** All submissions are eligible for the Daily News Prize ($300) for poetry, Also holds the Marguerite Cobb McKay Prize to a Virgin Island author ($200), the David Hough Literary Prize to a Caribbean author ($500), the Canute A. Brodhurst Prize for Fiction ($400), the Cecile Dejongh Literary Prize to an author whose work best expresses the spirit of the Caribbean ($500), and the Marvin Williams Literary Prize for first-time publication in the Caribbean ($500).

## THE CAROLINA QUARTERLY

CB #3520 Greenlaw Hall, University of North Carolina, Chapel Hill NC 27599-3520. (919)408-7786. **E-mail:** carolina.quarterly@gmail.com. **Website:** www.thecarolinaquarterly.com. *The Carolina Quarterly*, published 3 times/year, prints fiction, poetry, reviews, nonfiction, and visual art. No specifications regarding form, length, subject matter, or style. Considers translations of work originally written in languages other than English. Acquires first rights. Responds in 4-6 months. Sample copy: $9.

○ *The Carolina Quarterly* is about 100 pages, digest-sized, professionally printed, perfect-bound, with glossy cover, includes ads. Press run is 1,000. Accepts submissions September through May. Subscription: $24 for individuals, $30 for institutions.

**MAGAZINES NEEDS** Submit up to 6 poems via online submissions manager or postal mail (address submissions to Poetry Editor). Has published poetry by Denise Levertov, Richard Wilbur, Robert Morgan, Ha Jin, and Charles Wright. Receives about 6,000 poems/year, accepts about 1%.

## CARUS PUBLISHING COMPANY

30 Grove St., Suite C, Peterborough NH 03458. **Website:** www.cricketmag.com. See listings for *Babybug, Cicada, Click, Cricket, Ladybug, Muse, Spider,* and *Ask.* Carus Publishing owns Cobblestone Publishing, publisher of *AppleSeeds, Calliope, Cobblestone, Dig, Faces,* and *Odyssey.*

## CAVEAT LECTOR

400 Hyde St., #606, San Francisco CA 94109. (415)928-7431. **Fax:** (415)928-7431. **E-mail:** editors@caveat-lector.org. **E-mail:** caveatlectormagazine@gmail.com. **Website:** www.caveat-lector.org. **Contact:** Christopher Bernard, co-editor. *Caveat Lector*, published 2 times/year, is devoted to the arts and cultural and philosophical commentary. As well as literary work, they publish art, photography, music, streaming audio of selected literary pieces, and short films. Poetry, fiction, artwork, music, and short films are posted on website. "Don't let those examples limit your submissions. Send what you feel is your strongest work, in any style and on any subject." Acquires first rights.

- All submissions should be sent with a brief bio and SASE, or submitted electronically (poetry submissions only accepted through postal mail). Reads poetry submissions February 1-June 30; reads all other submissions year round.

**MAGAZINES NEEDS** Wants poetry on any subject, in any style, as long as the work is authentic in feeling and appropriately crafted. Looking for accomplished poems, something that resonates in the mind long after the reader has laid the poem aside. Wants work that has authenticity of emotion and high craft; poems that, whether raw or polished, ring true; and if humorous, are actually funny, or at least witty. Classical to experimental. Note: Sometimes request authors for audio of work to post on website. Has published poetry by Joanne Lowery, Simon Perchik, Les Murray, Alfred Robinson, and Ernest Hilbert. **Submit poetry through postal mail only.** Send brief bio and SASE with submission. Pays contributor copies.

## CAVE WALL

Cave Wall Press, LLC, P.O. Box 29546, Greensboro NC 27429-9546. **E-mail:** editor@cavewallpress.com. **Website:** www.cavewallpress.com. "*Cave Wall,* published twice a year, is a national literary magazine dedicated to publishing the best in contemporary poetry. We are interested in poems of any length and style from both established and emerging poets. Each issue includes b&w art. Poems first published in *Cave Wall* have been featured on *Poetry Daily, Verse Daily, The Writer's Almanac,* and in the *Best New Poets* awards anthology." Buys first North American serial rights. Responds in 1-5 months to mss. Guidelines on website.

**MAGAZINES NEEDS** Submit poems by mail with SASE. *Cave Wall* reads unsolicited poetry submissions twice a year. Check the website for our reading periods. Pays 2 contributor copies.

**TIPS** "We encourage you to read an issue of *Cave Wall* before you submit. Find out what kind of poetry we like. Please note that we read blind. Your name should not appear on your poems."

## ○ CC&D: CHILDREN, CHURCHES & DADDIES: THE UNRELIGIOUS, NON-FAMILY-ORIENTED LITERARY AND ART MAGAZINE

Scars Publications and Design, **E-mail:** ccandd96@scars.tv. **Website:** scars.tv/ccd. **Contact:** Janet Kuypers. "Our biases are works that relate to issues such as politics, sexism, society, and the like, but are definitely not limited to such. We publish good work that makes you think, that makes you feel like you've lived through a scene instead of merely reading it. If it relates to how the world fits into a person's life (political story, a day in the life, coping with issues people face), it will probably win us over faster. We have received comments from readers and other editors saying that they thought some of our stories really happened. They didn't, but it was nice to know they were so concrete, so believable that people thought they were nonfiction. Do that to our readers." Publishes every other month online and in print; issues sold via Amazon.com throughout the U.S., U.K., and continental Europe. Publishes short shorts, essays, and stories. Also publishes poetry. Always comments on/critiques rejected mss if asked. Publishes ms 1 year after acceptance. Responds in 2 weeks to queries and mss. "Responds much faster to e-mail submissions and queries." Sample copy: $6 for issues published before 2010. Guidelines available for SASE, via e-mail, or on website.

- Has published Mel Waldman, Kenneth DiMaggio, Linda Webb Aceto, Brian Looney, Joseph Hart, Fritz Hamilton, G.A. Scheinoha, and Ken Dean.

**MAGAZINES NEEDS** If you do not have e-mail and want to snail-mail a poetry submission, we do not accept poetry snail-mail submissions longer than 10 lines.

## CELLPOEMS

**E-mail:** submissions@cellpoems.org. **Website:** cellpoems.org. **Contact:** Eric Smith, editor emeritus. *Cellpoems* is a poetry journal distributed via text message. In the tradition of great, short poems, we hope to present work that has undergone the duress of revision and come out hard-boiled and striking. Guidelines online.

**MAGAZINES NEEDS** Submit "strange, profound, weird, and memorable language condensed in 140 characters or less (including title and author's first initial + last name; previously unpublished work only, please)."

## THE CHAFFIN JOURNAL

English Department, Eastern Kentucky University, Richmond KY 40475-3102. (859)622-3080. **E-mail:** robert.witt@eku.edu. **Website:** www.english.eku.edu/chaffin_journal. **Contact:** Robert Witt, editor. *The Chaffin Journal*, published annually in December, prints quality short fiction and poetry by new and established writers/poets. "We publish fiction on any subject; our only consideration is the quality." Acquires one-time rights. Pays on publication. Publishes 6 months after acceptance. Send SASE for return of ms. Responds in 1 week to queries; in 3 months to mss. Sample copy: $6.

Receives 20 unsolicited mss/month. Accepts 6-8 mss/year. Does not read mss October 1-May 31. Publishes 2-3 new writers/year. Has published work by Meridith Sue Willis, Marie Manilla, Raymond Abbott, Marjorie Bixler, and Chris Helvey.

**MAGAZINES NEEDS** Submit 5 poems per submission period. Considers simultaneous submissions (although not preferred); no previously published poems. No e-mail or disk submissions. Cover letter is preferred. "Submit typed pages with only 1 poem per page. Enclose SASE." Wants any form, subject matter, or style of poetry. Has published poetry by Taylor Graham, Diane Glancy, Judith Montgomery, Simon Perchik, Philip St. Clair, and Virgil Suárez. Does not want "poor quality." Pays 1 contributor copy.

**TIPS** "All mss submitted are considered."

## CHANTARELLE'S NOTEBOOK

**E-mail:** chantarellesnotebook@yahoo.com. **Website:** www.chantarellesnotebook.com. **Contact:** Kendall A. Bell and Christinia Bell, editors. *Chantarelle's Notebook*, published quarterly online, seeks "quality work from undiscovered poets. We enjoy poems that speak to us—poems with great sonics and visuals." Acquires one-time rights. Rights revert to poet upon publication. Responds in 10 weeks. Never comments on rejected poems. Sample copy online. Guidelines available on website. "Please follow the guidelines—all the information is there!"

**MAGAZINES NEEDS** Receives about 500 poems/year, accepts about 20%. Submit 3-5 poems at a time. Accepts e-mail submissions (pasted into body of message; "we will not open any attachments—they will be deleted"). Cover letter is required. "Please include a short bio of no more than 75 words, should we decide to accept your work." Reads submissions year round. "The editors will review all submissions and make a decision within a week's time." Has published poetry by Emily Brogan, Heather Cadenhead, Taylor Emily Copeland, Amber Decker, Raina Masters, and Donna Vorreyer. Does not want "infantile rants, juvenile confessionals, greeting card-styled verse, political posturing, or religious outpourings." Considers poetry by children and teens. "There are no age restrictions, but submissions from younger people will be held to the same guidelines and standards as those from adults." Length: "shorter poems have a better chance, but long poems are fine."

## THE CHARITON REVIEW

Truman State University Press, 100 E Normal Ave., Kirksville MO 63501. (660)785-8336. **E-mail:** chariton@truman.edu. **Website:** http://tsup.truman.edu/product/chariton-review/. *The Chariton Review* is an international literary journal publishing the best in short fiction, essays, poetry, and translations in 2 issues each year. Guidelines available on website. Send a printout of the submission via snail mail; overseas authors may send submissions as email attachments. See also *The Chariton Review* Short Fiction Prize at http://tsup.truman.edu/prizes.asp.

**MAGAZINES NEEDS** Poetry collections are published through TSUP's annual T.S. Eliot Prize for Poetry. Deadline is October 31 of each year. See competition guidelines at http://tsup.truman.edu/prizes.asp.

## ⑨ THE CHATTAHOOCHEE REVIEW

555 N. Indian Creek Dr., Clarkston GA 30021. E-mail: gpccr@gpc.edu. **Website:** thechattahoocheereview.gpc.edu. **Contact:** Lydia Ship, managing editor. *The Chattahoochee Review*, published quarterly, prints poetry, short fiction, essays, reviews, and interviews. "We publish a number of Southern writers, but *The Chattahoochee Review* is not by design a regional magazine. All themes, forms, and styles are considered as long as they impact the whole person: heart, mind, intuition, and imagination." Acquires first rights. Publishes ms 6 months after acceptance. Responds in 1 week-6 months. Sample copy: $6. Subscription: $20/year. Guidelines for SASE or on website.

💬 Has recently published work by George Garrett, Jim Daniels, Jack Pendarvis, Ignacio Padilla, and Kevin Canty. *The Chattahoochee Review* is 160 pages, digest-sized, professionally printed, flat-spined, with four-color silk-matte card cover. Press run is 1,250; 300 are complimentary copies sent to editors and "miscellaneous VIPs." No e-mail submissions.

**MAGAZINES NEEDS** "*TCR* publishes excellent poetry of all types, including informal personal narratives, prose poems, and formal poems." Submit 3-5 poems via online submissions manager. Pays 2 contributor copies.

## CHAUTAUQUA LITERARY JOURNAL

Chautauqua Institution, P.O. Box 28, 1 Ames Ave., Chautauqua NY 14722. **E-mail:** clj@uncw.edu. **Website:** ciweb.org. **Contact:** Jill Gerard and Philip Gerard, editors. *Chautauqua*, published annually in June, prints poetry, short fiction, and creative nonfiction. The editors actively solicit writing that expresses the values of Chautauqua Institution broadly construed: a sense of inquiry into questions of personal, social, political, spiritual, and aesthetic importance, regardless of genre. Considers the work of any writer, whether or not affiliated with Chautauqua Institution. Looking for a mastery of craft, attention to vivid and accurate language, a true lyric "ear," an original and compelling vision, and strong narrative instinct. Above all, it values work that is intensely personal, yet somehow implicitly comments on larger public concerns, like work that answers every reader's most urgent question: Why are you telling me this? Acquires first rights plus one-time nonexclusive rights to reprint accepted work in an anniversary issue. Publishes ms 1 year after acceptance. Responds in 3-6 months. Guidelines online.

💬 Reads submissions February 15-April 15 and August 15-November 15. Work published in *Chautauqua* has been included in *The Pushcart Prize* anthology.

**MAGAZINES NEEDS** "A *Chautauqua* poem is not just a pretty exercise in language. It exhibits the writer's craft and attention to language, employs striking images and metaphors, and engages the mind. It emerges from the poet's deep reading and knowledge of poetic tradition, reacts to that tradition to reveal a definite aesthetic approach, opening insights into the larger world of human concerns. This may include traditional or experimental work, but each poem should be meaningful to a serious reader beyond the writer's private code of expression." Submit up to 3 poems through online submissions manager. Pays 2 contributor copies.

**TIPS** "*Chautauqua* has added a new section, which celebrates young writers, ages 12-18. Work should be submitted by a teacher, mentor, or parent. Please confirm on the entry that the piece can be classified as a Young Voices entry. We ask that young writers consider the theme. Essays and stories should remain under 1,500 words. For poetry, please submit no more than 3 poems and/or no more than 6 pages."

## CHEST

CHEST Global Headquarters, 2595 Patriot Blvd., Glenview IL 60026. (800)343-2222. **E-mail:** poetrychest@aol.com. **Website:** www.chestjournal.org. **Contact:** Michael Zack, M.D., poetry editor. *CHEST*, published monthly, "is the official medical journal of the American College of Chest Physicians, the world's largest medical journal for pulmonologists, sleep, and critical care specialists, with over 30,000 subscribers." Wants "poetry with themes of medical relevance." Retains all rights. Responds in 2 months; always sends prepublication galleys. Subscription: $276. Make checks payable to American College Chest Physicians.

💬 *CHEST* is approximately 300 pages, magazine-sized, perfect-bound, with a glossy cover, and includes ads. Press run is 22,000. Number of unique visitors: 400,000 to website.

**MAGAZINES NEEDS** Only accepts e-mail submissions (as attachment or in body of e-mail); no fax or disk submissions. Brief cover letter preferred. Reads submissions year round. Poems are circulated to an editorial board. Sometimes comments on rejected poems. Never publishes theme issues. Guidelines available in magazine and on website. Length: up to 350 words.

## CHICAGO QUARTERLY REVIEW

**Website:** www.chicagoquarterlyreview.com. **Contact:** S. Afzal Haider and Elizabeth McKenzie, senior editors. "The *Chicago Quarterly Review* is a nonprofit, independent literary journal publishing the finest short stories, poems, translations, and essays by both emerging and established writers. We hope to stimulate, entertain, and inspire." Acquires one-time rights. Publishes ms 6 months-1 year after acceptance. Responds in 6-8 months to mss. Sometimes comments on rejected mss. Sample copy: $15. Guidelines online.

**MAGAZINES NEEDS** Submit 3-5 poems through online submissions manager only. Pays 2 contributor copies.

**TIPS** "The writer's voice ought to be clear and unique and should explain something of what it means to be human. We want well-written stories that reflect an appreciation for the rhythm and music of language, work that shows passion and commitment to the art of writing."

## CHICAGO REVIEW

Taft House, 935 E. 60th St., Chicago IL 60637. **E-mail:** chicago-review@uchicago.edu. **Website:** chicagoreview.org. **Contact:** Eric Powell, managing editor. "Since 1946, *Chicago Review* has published a range of contemporary poetry, fiction, and criticism. Each year typically includes 2 single issues and a double issue with a special feature section." Guidelines available on website.

**MAGAZINES NEEDS** Submit via online submission form, Submittable. Include cover letter. Length: no strict length requirements, but the poetry editors prefer to read at least 3 pages of work. Pays contributor copies.

**TIPS** "We strongly recommend that authors familiarize themselves with recent issues of *Chicago Review* before submitting. Submissions that demonstrate familiarity with the journal tend to receive more attention than those that appear to be part of a carpet-bombing campaign."

## CHICKEN SOUP FOR THE SOUL PUBLISHING, LLC

Chicken Soup for the Soul Publishing, LLC, P.O. Box 700, Cos Cob CT 06807. **E-mail:** webmaster@chickensoupforthesoul.com (for all inquires). **Website:** www.chickensoup.com. Buys one-time rights. Pays on publication. Responds upon consideration. Guidelines online.

"Stories must be written in the first person."

**MAGAZINES NEEDS** No controversial poetry.

**TIPS** "We no longer accept submissions by mail or fax. Stories and poems can only be submitted on our website. Select the 'submit Your Story' tab on the left toolbar. The submission form can be found there."

## CHIRON REVIEW

Chiron, Inc., 522 E. South Ave., St. John KS 67576-2212. **E-mail:** editor@chironreview.com. **Website:** www.chironreview.com. **Contact:** Michael Hathaway, publisher. *Chiron Review*, published quarterly, presents the widest possible range of contemporary creative writing—fiction and nonfiction, traditional and off-beat—in an attractive, perfect-bound digest, including artwork and photographs. No taboos. Acquires first-time rights. Pays on publication. Publishes ms 3-12 months after acceptance. Responds in 2-8 weeks. Subscription: $60, ppd/year (4 issues) and $80 ppd overseas. Single issue: $20 ppd and $34 ppd overseas. Guidelines available for SASE or on website.

**MAGAZINES NEEDS** Submit up to 3 poems by postal mail with SASE, or by e-mail as DOC attachment. Has published poetry by Charles Bukowski, Charles Harper Webb, Edward Field, Wanda Coleman, Thich Nhat Hanh, and Marge Piercy. Pays 1 contributor copy.

**TIPS** "Please check our website to see if we are open to submissions. When you do send submissions, please have mercy on the editors and follow the guidelines noted here and on our website."

## THE CHRISTIAN CENTURY

104 S. Michigan Ave., Suite 1100, Chicago IL 60603-5901. (312)263-7510. **Fax:** (312)263-7540. **E-mail:** main@christiancentury.org. **E-mail:** submissions@christiancentury.org; poetry@christiancentury.org. **Website:** www.christiancentury.org. **Contact:** Jill Peláez Baumgaertner, poetry editor. "We seek mss that articulate the public meaning of faith, bringing the resources of religious tradition to bear on such topics as poverty, human rights, economic justice, in-

ternational relations, national priorities, and popular culture. We are also interested in pieces that examine or critique the theology and ethos of individual religious communities. We welcome articles that find fresh meaning in old traditions and that adapt or apply religious traditions to new circumstances. Authors should assume that readers are familiar with main themes in Christian history and theology, are accustomed to the historical-critical study of the Bible and are already engaged in relating faith to social and political issues. Many of our readers are ministers or teachers of religion at the college level. Book reviews are solicited by our books editor. Please note that submissions via e-mail will not be considered. If you are interested in becoming a reviewer for *The Christian Century*, please send your résumé and a list of subjects of interest to "Attn: Book reviews." Authors must have a critical and analytical perspective on the church and be familiar with contemporary theological discussion." Buys all rights. Pays on publication. Responds in 4-6 weeks to queries; in 2 months to mss. Editorial lead time 1 month. Sample copy: $3.50. Guidelines online.

**MAGAZINES NEEDS** Wants "poems that are not statements but experiences, that do not talk about the world but show it. We want to publish poems that are grounded in images and that reveal an awareness of the sounds of language and the forms of poetry even when the poems are written in free verse."

**ALSO OFFERS** Reviews books of poetry in 300-400 words for single-book format; 400-500 words for multibook format.

**TIPS** "We suggest reading the poems in the past several issues to gain a clearer idea of the kinds of poetry we are seeking. We publish shorter poems that are grounded in images and that reveal an awareness of the sounds of language and the forms of poetry even when the poems are written in free verse."

## ⊖ CHRISTIAN COMMUNICATOR

American Christian Writers, 9118 W. Elmwood Dr., Suite 1G, Niles IL 60714-5820. (847)296-3964. **Fax:** (847)296-0754. **E-mail:** ljohnson@wordprocommunications.com. **Website:** acwriters.com. **Contact:** Lin Johnson, managing editor; Sally Miller, poetry editor (sallymiller@ameritech.net). Buys first rights, buys second serial (reprint) rights. Pays on publication. Publishes ms an average of 6-12 months after acceptance. Responds in 6-8 weeks to queries; in 8-12 weeks

to mss. Editorial lead time 3 months. Sample copy for SAE and 4 first-class stamps. Writers guidelines by e-mail or on website.

**MAGAZINES NEEDS** Length: 4-20 lines. Pays $5.

**TIPS** "We primarily use how-to articles and profiles of editors. However, we're willing to look at any other pieces geared to the writing life."

## CHRISTIANITY AND LITERATURE

Pepperdine University, Humanities Division, 24255 Pacific Coast Hwy., Malibu CA 90263-7232. **E-mail:** christianityandliterature@pepperdine.edu. **Website:** christianityandliterature.com/journal. Poetry submissions: Tulane University, Dept. of English, Norman Mayer 122, New Orleans LA 70118. **Contact:** Mark Eaton, editor; Prof. Peter Cooley, poetry editor. "*Christianity & Literature* is devoted to the scholarly exploration of how literature engages Christian thought, experience, and practice. The journal presupposes no particular theological orientation but respects an orthodox understanding of Christianity as a historically defined faith. Contributions appropriate for submission should demonstrate a keen awareness of the author's own critical assumptions in addressing significant issues of literary history, interpretation, and theory." Rights to republish revert to poets upon written request. Time between acceptance and publication is 6-12 months. "Poems are chosen by our poetry editor." Responds within 4 months. Sample copy: $10 (back issue) .Subscription: $25 for 1 year; $45 for 2 years. Guidelines available on website.

**MAGAZINES NEEDS** Submit up to 6 poems. Accepts submissions by surface mail only. Cover letter is required. Submissions must be accompanied by SASE. Reviews collections of literary, Christian poetry occasionally in some issues (no chapbooks). Pays 1 contributor copy and 5 offprints of poem.

**TIPS** "We look for poems that are clear and surprising. They should have a compelling sense of voice, formal sophistication (though not necessarily rhyme and meter), and the ability to reveal the spiritual through concrete images. We cannot return submissions that are not accompanied by SASE."

## ⊖ CHRISTIAN LIVING IN THE MATURE YEARS

The United Methodist Publishing House, 2222 Rosa L. Parks Blvd., P.O. Box 17890, Nashville TN 37228-7890. (615)749-6474. **Fax:** (615)749-6512. **E-mail:** matureyears@umpublishing.org. Buys first North American serial rights. Pays on acceptance. Publishes ms an average of 1 year after acceptance. Responds in 6-7 months to mss. Sample copy: $6, plus 9x12 SAE. Writer's guidelines for #10 SASE or by e-mail.

**MAGAZINES NEEDS** Wants upbeat poetry. Must express hope; strong imagery preferred. Length: 3-16 lines; up to 50 characters maximum. Pays $5-20/poem.

**TIPS** "Practice writing dialogue! Listen to people talk; take notes; master dialogue writing! Not easy but well worth it! Most inquiry letters are far too long. If you can't sell me an idea in a brief paragraph, you're not going to sell the reader on reading your finished article or story."

## THE CHRISTIAN SCIENCE MONITOR

210 Massachussetts Ave., Boston MA 02115. **E-mail:** homeforum@csmonitor.com. **Website:** www.csmonitor.com. **Contact:** Editor, The Home Forum. *The Christian Science Monitor*, a Web-first publication that also publishes a weekly print magazine, regularly features personal nonfiction essays and, occasionally, poetry in its Home Forum section. "We're looking for upbeat essays of 600-800 words and short (20 lines maximum) poems that explore and celebrate daily life." Buys 90 days' exclusive rights, nonexclusive thereafter. Pays on publication. Publishes ms 1-8 months after acceptance. Responds in 3 weeks to mss; only responds to accepted mss. Editorial lead time 6-8 weeks. Sample copy online. Guidelines online or by e-mail.

**MAGAZINES NEEDS** Accepts submissions via online form. Does not want "work that presents people in helpless or hopeless states; poetry about death, aging, or illness; or dark, violent, sensual poems. No poems that are overtly religious or falsely sweet." Length: up to 20 lines/poem. Pays $25/haiku; $50/poem.

## CIDER PRESS REVIEW

P.O. Box 33384, San Diego CA 92163. **Website:** ciderpressreview.com. **Contact:** Caron Andregg, publisher/editor in chief; Ruth Foley, managing editor. *Cider Press Review*, published quarterly online and annually in print, features "the best new work from contemporary poets." It was founded by co-publishers/editors Caron Andregg and Robert Wynne. Since its inception, *CPR* has published thousands of poems by over 500 authors. "Our reading period is from January 1-May 31 each year, and full mss (in conjunction with the *CPR* Annual Book Award) between Septem-

ber 1-November 30 and again between April 1 and June 30 each calendar year." Acquires first North American serial rights. Publishes ms 3-12 months after acceptance. Responds in 1-6 months. Single copy: $14.95; subscription: $24 for 2 issues (1 journal, 1 book from the *Cider Press Review* Book Award). Sample: $12 (journal). Guidelines online.

○ *Cider Press Review* is 128 pages, digest-sized, offset-printed, perfect-bound, with 4-color coated card cover. Receives about 2,500 poems/year, accepts about 3%. Press run for print edition is 500.

**MAGAZINES NEEDS** Wants "thoughtful, well-crafted poems with vivid language and strong images. We prefer poems that have something to say. We would like to see more well-written humor. We also encourage translations." Does not want "didactic, inspirational, greeting card verse, empty word play, therapy, or religious doggerel." Always sends prepublication galleys. Has published poetry by Robert Arroyo, Jr., Virgil Suárez, Linda Pastan, Kathleen Flenniken, Tim Seibles, Joanne Lowery, Thomas Lux, and Mark Cox. Submit up to 5 poems at a time. Strongly prefers submissions through online submissions manager, but accepts postal mail submissions. Cover letter is preferred. Include short bio (25 words maximum). SASE or valid e-mail address required for reply. Poems are circulated to an editorial board. Pays 1 contributor copy.

**ALSO OFFERS** Also welcomes reviews under 500 words of current full-length books of poetry.

**TIPS** Each year, Cider Press publishes an annual journal of poetry and the winning mss from the *Cider Press Review* Book Award and the Editors' Prize for a first or second book. Mss entries must be accompanied by a required entry fee. Prize is $1,000 or $1,500 and publication for a full-length book of poetry and 25 copies.

## CIMARRON REVIEW

205 Morrill Hall, English Department, Oklahoma State University, Stillwater OK 74078. **E-mail:** cimarronreview@okstate.edu. **Website:** cimarronreview.com. **Contact:** Toni Graham, editor; Lisa Lewis, poetry editor. "One of the oldest quarterlies in the nation, *Cimarron Review* publishes work by writers at all stages of their careers, including Pulitzer prize winners, writers appearing in the Best American Series and the Pushcart anthologies, and winners of national

book contests. Since 1967, *Cimarron* has showcased poetry, fiction, and nonfiction with a wide-ranging aesthetic. Our editors seek the bold and the ruminative, the sensitive and the shocking, but above all they seek imagination and truth-telling, the finest stories, poems, and essays from working writers across the country and around the world." Buys first North American serial rights. Publishes ms 2-6 months after acceptance. Responds in 3-6 months to mss. Sample copy: $9. Guidelines available on website.

○  *Cimarron Review* is 6.5×8.5; 110 pages. Accepts 3-5 mss/issue; 12-15 mss/year. Publishes 2-4 new writers/year. Eager to receive mss from both established and less experienced writers "who intrigue us with their unusual perspective, language, imagery, and character." Has published work by Molly Giles, Gary Fincke, David Galef, Nona Caspers, Robin Beeman, Edward J. Delaney, William Stafford, John Ashbery, Grace Schulman, Barbara Hamby, Patricia Fargnoli, Phillip Dacey, Holly Prado, and Kim Addonizio.

**MAGAZINES NEEDS** Submit 3-6 poems at a time with SASE, or submit online through submission manager; include cover letter. No restrictions as to subject matter. Wants "poems whose surfaces and structures risk uncertainty and which display energy, texture, intelligence, and intense investment." Pays 2 contributor copies.

**TIPS** "All postal submissions must come with SASE. A cover letter is encouraged. No e-mail submissions from authors living in North America. Query first and follow guidelines. In order to get a feel for the kind of work we publish, please read an issue or two before submitting."

## THE CINCINNATI REVIEW

P.O. Box 210069, Cincinnati OH 45221-0069. (513)556-3954. **E-mail:** editors@cincinnatireview. com. **Website:** www.cincinnatireview.com. **Contact:** Michael Griffith, fiction editor; Don Bogen, poetry editor. A journal devoted to publishing the best new literary fiction, creative nonfiction, and poetry, as well as book reviews, essays, and interviews. Buys first North American serial rights, electronic rights. All rights revert to author/poet upon publication. Pays on publication. Publishes ms an average of 6 months after acceptance. Responds in 4 months to mss. Always sends prepublication galleys. Sample copy: $7

(back issue). Single copy: $9 (current issue). Subscription: $15. Guidelines available on website.

○  *The Cincinnati Review* is 180-200 pages, digest-sized, perfect-bound, with matte paperback cover with full-color art. Press run is 1,000. Reads submissions August 15-March 15.

**MAGAZINES NEEDS** Submit up to 10 pages of poetry at a time via submission manager only. Pays $30/page.

**TIPS** "Each issue includes a translation feature. For more information on translations, please see our website."

## THE CLAREMONT REVIEW

Suite 101, 1581-H Hillside Ave., Victoria BC V8T 2C1, Canada. **Website:** www.theclaremontreview.ca. **Contact:** Jody Carrow, editor in chief. The editors of *The Claremont Review* publish first-class poetry, short stories, short plays, visual art, and photography by young adults, aged 13-19, from anywhere in the English speaking world. Responds in 10-12 weeks to mss. Guidelines available on website.

○  "We publish anything from traditional to postmodern but with a preference for works that reveal something of the human condition. By this we mean stories that explore real characters in modern settings. Who are we, what are we doing to the planet, what is our relationship to one another, the earth, or God? Also, reading samples on the website or from past issues will give you a clearer indication of what we are looking for."

**MAGAZINES NEEDS** Submit complete, double-spaced ms by postal mail. Include cover letter with name, age, mailing address, e-mail address, school, and brief bio. Allows up to 6 items in each submission. Does not want rhyming poetry. Only accepts submissions from writers aged 13-19.

**TIPS** "Read guidelines before submitting."

## CLARK STREET REVIEW

P.O. Box 1377, Berthoud CO 80513. **E-mail:** clarkreview@earthlink.net. **Contact:** Ray Foreman, editor. *Clark Street Review*, published 6 times/year, uses narrative poetry and short shorts. Tries "to give writers and poets cause to keep writing by publishing their best work." Press run is 200. Acquires one-time rights. Publishes ms 2 months after acceptance. Responds in 3 weeks. Single copy: $2; subscription: $6 for 6 issues postpaid for writers only. Make checks payable to R. Foreman. Guidelines for SASE or by e-mail.

○ "Editor reads everything with a critical eye of 30 years experience in writing and publishing small-press work."

**MAGAZINES NEEDS** Wants "narrative poetry under 100 lines that reaches readers who are mostly published poets and writers. Subjects are open." Does not want "obscure or formalist work." Has published poetry by Alan Catlin, Charles Porto Lano, David Ochs, Rex Sexton, Jennifer Lagier, Cathy Porter, Charles Ries, Anselm Brocki, Ed Galling, Ellaraine Lockie, and J. Glenn Evans. Receives about 1,000 poems/year, accepts about 10%. Submit narrative poems (human condition poetry only). Send disposable sharp hard copies. Include SASE for reply. No cover letter. No limit on submissions. Length: up to 55 characters in width, flush left.

### CLOUDBANK: JOURNAL OF CONTEMPORARY WRITING

P.O. Box 610, Corvallis OR 97339. (541)752-0075. **E-mail:** michael@cloudbankbooks.com. **Website:** www.cloudbankbooks.com. **Contact:** Michael Malan, editor. *Cloudbank* publishes poetry, short prose, and book reviews. Acquires one-time rights. Rights revert to poets upon publication. Responds in 4 months to poems. Single copy: $8; subscription: $15. Make checks payable to *Cloudbank*. Guidelines available in magazine, for SASE, by e-mail, or on website.

○ *Cloudbank* is digest-sized, 92 pages of print, perfect-bound; color artwork on cover, includes ads. Press run is 400. Subscribers: 300; shelf sales: 100 distributed free.

**MAGAZINES NEEDS** Submit 5 poems or less at a time by mail with SASE. Cover letter is preferred. Does not accept fax, e-mail, or disk submissions from USA; overseas e-mail submissions accepted. Reads year round. Rarely sends prepublication galleys. Receives 1,600 poems/year; accepts about 8%. Has published poetry by Dennis Schmitz, Christopher Buckley, Stuart Friebert, Dore Kiesselbach, Karen Holmberg, and Vern Rutsala. Pays $200 prize for 1 poem or flash fiction piece per issue.

**ALSO OFFERS** *Cloudbank* Contest for $200 prize. $15 entry fee. See website for guidelines.

**TIPS** "Please consider reading a copy of *Cloudbank* before submitting."

### CLOUD RODEO

**E-mail:** editors@cloudrodeo.org; submit@cloudrodeo.org. **Website:** cloudrodeo.org. "We want your problems deploying a term liek nonelen. We want your isolated photographs of immense locomotives slogged down by the delirium of drunken yet pristine jungles. We want the one eye you caught on fire doing alchemy. The world you collapsed playing architect. We want what you think is too. We want you to anesthetize this aesthetic. Your Enfer, your Ciel, your Qu'importe. We want all your to to sound out." Acquires first electronic publishing rights. Guidelines online.

**MAGAZINES NEEDS** Submit up to 5 poems via e-mail as a .doc or .docx attachment.

**TIPS** "Let's get weird."

### ○ COAL CITY REVIEW

Coal City Press, English Department, University of Kansas, Lawrence KS 66045. **E-mail:** briandal@ku.edu. **Website:** coalcitypress.wordpress.com. **Contact:** Brian Daldorph, editor. *"Coal City Review*, published annually, usually late in the year, publishes poetry, short stories, reviews: "the best material I can find." Publishes ms 6 months after acceptance. Responds in 3 months. Guidelines on website.

**MAGAZINES NEEDS** "Check out a copy to see what we like." Pays contributor copies.

### COLD MOUNTAIN REVIEW

Department of English, Appalachian State University, ASU Box 32052, Boone NC 28608. **E-mail:** coldmountain@appstate.edu. **Website:** www.coldmountain.appstate.edu. *Cold Mountain Review*, published twice/year (Spring and Fall), features poetry, interviews with poets, poetry book reviews, and b&w graphic art. Has published poetry by Sarah Kennedy, Robert Morgan, Susan Ludvigson, Aleida Rodriíguez, R.T. Smith, and Virgil Suaárez. Responds in 3 months. Guidelines for SASE.

○ *Cold Mountain Review* is about 72 pages, digest-sized, neatly printed with 1 poem/page (or 2-page spread), perfect-bound, with light cardstock cover. Publishes only 10-12 poems/issue; "hence, we are extremely competitive: send only your best." Reading period is August-May.

**MAGAZINES NEEDS** Include short bio and SASE. "Please include name, address, phone number, and (if available) e-mail address on each poem. Poems should be single-spaced on 1 side of the page." Pays in contributor copies.

## THE COLLAGIST

Dzanc Books, **E-mail:** bookreviews@thecollagist. com. **Website:** thecollagist.com. **Contact:** Matthew Olzmann and Gabriel Blackwell, editors-in-chief. *The Collagist* is a monthly journal published on the 15th of each month, containing short fiction, poetry, essays, book reviews, and one of more excerpts from novels forthcoming from (mostly) indpendent presses. Guidelines online.

**MAGAZINES NEEDS** Submit through online submission manager. Check site for reading periods.

## 🟢 COLORADO REVIEW

Center for Literary Publishing, Colorado State University, 9105 Campus Delivery, Fort Collins CO 80523. (970)491-5449. **E-mail:** creview@colostate.edu. **Website:** coloradoreview.colostate.edu. **Contact:** Stephanie G'schwind, editor in chief and nonfiction editor; Steven Schwartz, fiction editor; Don Revell, Sasha Steensen, and Matthew Cooperman, poetry editors; Dan Beachy-Quick, book review editor. Literary magazine published 3 times/year. Buys first North American serial rights. Rights revert to author upon publication. Pays on publication. Publishes ms an average of 6 months after acceptance. Responds in 2 months to mss. Editorial lead time 1 year. Sample copy: $10. Guidelines online.

    Work published in *Colorado Review* has been included in *Best American Poetry*, *Best New American Voices*, *Best Travel Writing*, *Best Food Writing*, and the *Pushcart Prize Anthology*.

**MAGAZINES NEEDS** Considers poetry of any style. Poetry mss are read August 1-April 30. Mss received May 1-July 31 will be returned unread. Has published poetry by Sherman Alexie, Laynie Browne, John Gallaher, Mathias Svalina, Craig Morgan Teicher, Pam Rehm, Elizabeth Robinson, Elizabeth Willis, and Rosmarie Waldrop. Pays minimum of $30 or $10/page for poetry.

## COLUMBIA: A JOURNAL OF LITERATURE AND ART

Columbia University, New York NY 10027. **E-mail:** info@columbiajournal.org. **Website:** columbiajournal.org. **Contact:** Raluca Albu, managing editor. "*Columbia: A Journal of Literature and Art* is an annual publication that features the very best in poetry, fiction, nonfiction, and art. We were founded in 1977

and continue to be one of the few national literary journals entirely edited, designed, and produced by students. You'll find that our minds are open, our interests diverse. We solicit mss from writers we love and select the most exciting finds from our virtual submission box. Above all, our commitment is to our readers—to producing a collection that informs, surprises, challenges, and inspires."

    Reads submissions March 1-September 15.

**MAGAZINES NEEDS** Submit poetry via online submissions manager.

## COMMON GROUND REVIEW

Western New England University, H-5132, Western New England University, 1215 Wilbraham Rd., Springfield MA 01119. **E-mail:** editors@cgreview.org. **Website:** cgreview.org. **Contact:** Janet Bowdan, editor. *Common Ground Review*, published semiannually (Spring/Summer, Fall/Winter), prints poetry and 1 short nonfiction piece in the Fall issue and 1 short fiction piece in the Spring issue. "This is the official literary journal of Western New England." Acquires one-time rights. Publishes ms 4-6 months after acceptance. Responds in 2 months to mss. Submit seasonal poems 6 months in advance. Guidelines and Submittable link available on submissions page of website.

**MAGAZINES NEEDS** Cover letter and biography are required. Submit via postal mail or online submissions manager. "Poems should be single-spaced indicating stanza breaks; include name, address, phone number, e-mail address, brief bio, and, for postal mail submissions, SASE (submissions without SASE will not be notified)." Reads submissions year round, but deadlines for noncontest submissions are August 31 and March 1. "Editor reads and culls submissions. Final decisions made by editorial board." Seldom comments on rejected poems. Has published poetry by James Doyle, B.Z. Niditch, Ann Lauinger, Kathryn Howd Machan, and Sheryl L. Nelms. Does not want "greeting card verse, overly sentimental, or stridently political poetry." Length: up to 60 lines/poem. Pays 1 contributor copy.

**ALSO OFFERS** Sponsors an annual poetry contest, open Jan. 1st-March 15th. Offers 1st Prize: $500; 2nd Prize: $200; 3rd Prize: $100; Honorable Mentions. **Entry fee:** $15 for 1-3 unpublished poems. **Deadline:** March 1 for contest submissions only. All contest submissions are considered for publication in *Common Ground Review*.

**TIPS** "For poems, use a few good images to convey ideas. Poems should be condensed and concise, free from words that do not contribute. The subject matter should be worthy of the reader's time and should appeal to a wide range of readers. Sometimes the editors may suggest possible revisions."

## COMMON THREADS

6519 Crab Apple Dr., Canal Winchester OH 43110. (614)829-5040. **E-mail:** team@ohiopoetryassn.org. **Website:** www.ohiopoetryassn.org. **Contact:** Chuck Salmons, OPA president. *Common Threads*, published annually in autumn, is the Ohio Poetry Association's member journal. **Submissions limited to OPA members and student contest winners.** "We accept poems from both beginners and accomplished writers. We like poems to make us think as well as feel. We are uninterested in work that is highly sentimental, overly morbid, religiously coercive, or pornographic. Poetry by students will also be considered and prioritized if student is an OPA high school contest winner." While devoted primarily to members' poetry, *Common Threads* can include book reviews, essays on craft, interviews, and other articles related to poetry as an art. All rights revert to poet upon publication. Single copy: $5. Subscription ($20; $15 for seniors 65+) in the form of annual OPA membership dues includes annual issue of *Common Threads*. Visit www.ohiopoetryassn.org for membership applications and additional information on submissions.

**MAGAZINES NEEDS** Previously published poems are considered if first publisher is noted on submission. Submit up to 3 poems at a time to editor@ohiopoetryassociation.org (preferred) or as hard copies c/o 91 E. Duncan St., Columbus OH 43202 (w/SASE or e-mail address) throughout the year, with August 31 deadline for consideration. Length: up to 50 lines/poem.

## COMMONWEAL

Commonweal Foundation, 475 Riverside Dr., Room 405, New York NY 10115. (212)662-4200. **Fax:** (212)662-4183. **E-mail:** editors@commonwealmagazine.org. **Website:** www.commonwealmagazine.org. **Contact:** Paul Baumann, editor; Tiina Aleman, production editor. Buys all rights. Pays on publication. Responds in 2 months to queries. Sample copy free. Guidelines online.

**MAGAZINES NEEDS** *Commonweal*, published every 2 weeks, is a Catholic general interest magazine for college-educated readers. Does not publish inspirational poems. Length: no more than 75 lines. Pays 75¢/line plus 2 contributor copies. Acquires all rights. Returns rights when requested by the author.

**TIPS** "Articles should be written for a general but well-educated audience. While religious articles are always topical, we are less interested in devotional and churchy pieces than in articles which examine the links between 'worldly' concerns and religious beliefs."

## COMPOSE

**E-mail:** editor@composejournal.com. **Website:** composejournal.com. *Compose: A Journal of Simply Good Writing* is a biannual, online publication that features work by both established and emerging writers of fiction, poetry, and nonfiction. Guidelines online.

**MAGAZINES NEEDS** Submit up to 6 poems in 1 document.

## THE COMSTOCK REVIEW

4956 St. John Dr., Syracuse NY 13215. **Website:** www.comstockreview.org. *The Comstock Review* accepts "poetry strictly on the basis of quality, not reputation. We publish both noted and mid-career poets as well as those who are new to publishing. It is the quality of the poem that is the decisive factor. We do not accept overly sexual material, sentimental or "greeting card" verse, and very few haiku." Responds in 3 months.

*The Comstock Review* is 5.25x8.35, perfect-bound.

**MAGAZINES NEEDS** "We look for well-crafted poetry, either free or formal verse, with attention paid to the beauty of language, exceptional metaphor, unique voice, and fresh, vivid imagery. Poems may reflect any subject, although we have a slight bias toward poems dealing with the human condition in all its poignancy and humor." Accepts submissions of 4-5 poems, with SASE, for the Open Reading Period postmarked from January 1-March 31. Length: up to 38 lines/poem.

## CONCEIT MAGAZINE

P.O. Box 884223, San Francisco CA 94188-4223. **E-mail:** conceitmagazine2007@yahoo.com. **Website:** conceitmagazine.weebly.com. Also on Facebook, Twitter, LinkedIn, Goodreads, and Grouply.. **Con-**

tact: Perry Terrell, editor. crochet Acquires one-time rights. Publication is copyrighted. Responds in 3 weeks to queries; in 6 months to mss. Send either SASE (or IRC) for return of ms or disposable copy of ms and #10 SASE for reply only. Sample copy free with 2 first-class stamps. Guidelines available for SASE, via e-mail, or on website.

 Magazine publishing poetry, short stories, articles, and essays. "Very few guidelines—let me see your creative work."

**MAGAZINES NEEDS** Query first or send poems with cover letter. Accepts submissions by e-mail and snail mail. Include estimated word count, brief bio, list of publications. Pays 1 contributor copy. Additional copies $4.50. Pay via PayPal to conceitmagazine@yahoo.com.

**TIPS** "We are a 'literary sharing' organization. Uniqueness and creativity make a ms stand out. Be brave and confident. Let me see what you created."

### CONCHO RIVER REVIEW

Angelo State University, ASU Station #10894, San Angelo TX 76909. (325)486-6137. **E-mail:** crr@angelo.edu. **Website:** conchoriverreview.org. **Contact:** R. Mark Jackson, general editor. *"CRR* aims to provide its readers with escape, insight, laughter, and inspiration for many years to come. We urge authors to submit to the journal and readers to subscribe to our publication." Requests first print and electronic rights. Responds in 1-2 months for poetry and in 2-6 months for fiction and nonfiction. Guidelines online.

**MAGAZINES NEEDS** Welcomes original poetry submissions from all poets, established or emerging. Submit 3-5 poems at a time. Electronic submissions preferred. See website for appropriate section editor. "Length and form are open, but shorter poems (1 page or less) are preferred."

### CONDUIT

788 Osceola Ave., St. Paul MN 55105. **E-mail:** waltz@conduit.org. **Website:** conduit.org. **Contact:** William D. Waltz, editor-in-chief. *Conduit* is looking for previously unpublished poetry and prose that demonstrates orginality, intelligence, courage, irreverence, and humanity. Responds in 9 months. Guidelines online.

**MAGAZINES NEEDS** Submmit 3-5 poems by mail. Pays in copies.

**TIPS** "If you haven't seen or read *Conduit* before, we recommend you sample our mad concoction before submitting."

### CONFRONTATION

English Department, LIU Post, Brookville NY 11548. (516)299-2963. **E-mail:** confrontationmag@gmail.com. **Website:** www.confrontationmagazine.org. Terry Kattleman, publicity director/production editor. **Contact:** Jonna Semeiks, editor in chief; Belinda Kremer, poetry editor. *"Confrontation* has been in continuous publication since 1968. Our taste and our magazine is eclectic, but we always look for excellence in style, an important theme, a memorable voice. We enjoy discovering and fostering new talent. Each issue contains work by both well-established and new writers. We read August 16-April 15. Do not send mss or e-mail submissions between April 16 and August 15." Buys first North American serial rights, electronic rights, first rights, one-time rights, all rights. Pays on publication. Publishes work in the first or second issue after acceptance. Responds in 10 weeks to mss. "We prefer single submissions. Clear copy. **No e-mail submissions unless writer resides outside the U.S.** Mail submissions with a SASE."

 *Confrontation* has garnered a long list of awards and honors, including the Editor's Award for Distinguished Achievement from CLMP (given to Martin Tucker, the founding editor of the magazine) and NEA grants. Work from the magazine has appeared in numerous anthologies, including the *Pushcart Prize, Best Short Stories,* and *The O. Henry Prize Stories.*

**MAGAZINES NEEDS** *"Confrontation* is interested in all poetic forms. Our only criterion is high literary merit. We think of our audience as an educated, lay group of intelligent readers." Has published poetry by David Ray, T. Alan Broughton, David Ignatow, Philip Appleman, Jane Mayhall, and Joseph Brodsky. Submit no more than 12 pages at a time (up to 6 poems). *Confrontation* also offers the annual Confrontation Poetry Prize. No sentimental verse. No previously published poems. Length: up to 2 pages. Pays $75-100; more for commissioned work.

**CONTEST/AWARD OFFERINGS** Offers Confrontation Poetry Prize. See website for details.

**TIPS** "We look for literary merit. Keep honing your skills, and keep trying."

## CONGRUENT SPACES

820 Taylor St. #5, Medford OR 97504. **E-mail:** congruentspacesmag@gmail.com. **Website:** www.congruentspaces.com. **Contact:** Michael Camarata, editor. *"Congruent Spaces* was developed as a common ground for a diverse variety of voices and writing styles within the writing community. In keeping with this sense of community, all submissions are posted directly to the slush pile in our Writer's Lair, where our community of writers and readers come together to read and rate these submissions. For each issue we then select from the top-rated submissions which stories and poems appear within the pages of our magazine. Our magazine covers fantasy, horror, literary/mainstream fiction, poetry, and science fiction." Purchases one-time rights. Submissions are currently accepted online only. For current guidelines, visit congruentspaces.com/home/submission.

**MAGAZINES NEEDS** Submit 1 poem at a time on website. No erotic or pornographic poetry. Length: up to 120 lines/poem. Pays 1 contributor copy and one-month membership.

**TIPS** "Don't submit your work unless you truly believe it is ready for publication. Be sure to proof your formatting for readability before posting the ms for our ratings process. The most common error is failing to adequately separate paragraphs after copying and pasting the submission in the submission form. The easier it is to read your ms, the better your chances of receiving a quality rating and being published."

## THE CONNECTICUT RIVER REVIEW

P.O. Box 516, Cheshire CT 06410. **E-mail:** patriciamottola@yahoo.com. **Website:** www.ctpoetry.net. **Contact:** Pat Mottola, editor. *Connecticut River Review*, published annually in July or August by the Connecticut Poetry Society, prints original, honest, diverse, vital, well-crafted poetry. Wants any form, any subject. Has published poetry by Marge Piercy, Rhina P. Espaillat, Wally Swist, Charles Rafferty, Maria Mazziotti Gillan, and Vivian Shipley. Poet retains copyright. Responds in 2-12 weeks. Guidelines available for SASE or on website.

Accepts submissions from January 1-April 15. *Connecticut River Review* is digest-sized, attractively printed, perfect-bound. Receives about 2,000 submissions/year, accepts about 100. Press run is about 300. Membership in the Connecticut Poetry Society is $30 per year and includes *Connecticut River Review* and *Long River Run*, a members-only magazine.

**MAGAZINES NEEDS** Submit no more than 3-5 poems at a time. Considers simultaneous submissions if notified of acceptance elsewhere; no previously published poems. Cover letter is preferred. Include bio. Complete contact information typed in upper right corner; SASE required. Pays 1 contributor copy.

## CONNOTATION PRESS

**Website:** connotationpress.com. **Contact:** Ken Robidoux, publisher. *Connotation Press* accepts submissions in poetry, fiction, creative nonfiction, playwriting, screenplay, interview, book review, music review, etc. "Basically, we're looking at virtually every genre or crossover genre you can create." Guidelines online.

**MAGAZINES NEEDS** Submit 3-5 poems via online form.

## ⓢ CONTEMPORARY HAIBUN

P.O. Box 2461, Winchester VA 22604-1661. (540)722-2156. **E-mail:** boblucky01@yahoo.com; ray@raysweb.net. **Website:** www.contemporaryhaibunonline.com; www.redmoonpress.com. Ray Rasmussen, technical editor. **Contact:** Bob Lucky, editor/publisher. *Contemporary Haibun Online* is a quarterly journal published in January, April, July and October. Considers poetry by children and teens. Acquires first North American serial rights. Time between acceptance and publication varies according to time of submission. Sample available for SASE or by e-mail.

*contemporary haibun* is 128 pages, digest-sized, offset-printed on quality paper, with 4-color heavy-stock cover. Receives several hundred submissions/year, accepts about 5%. Print run is 1,000. Subscription: $17 plus $5 p&h. Has published poetry by J. Zimmerman, Chen-ou Liu, Renée Owen, and Matthew Caretti.

**MAGAZINES NEEDS** Submit up to 3 haibun at a time. Accepts e-mail submissions. Include SASE for postal submissions. Poems are circulated to an editorial board.

## ⓞⓢ CONTRARY

**E-mail:** chicago@contrarymagazine.com. **Website:** www.contrarymagazine.com. **Contact:** Jeff McMahon, editor; Frances Badgett, fiction editor; Shaindel Beers, poetry editor. *Contrary* publishes fiction, poetry, and literary commentary, and prefers work that combines the virtues of all those categories. Founded at the University of Chicago, it now operates independently and not-for-profit on the South Side of Chicago. "We like work that is not only contrary in content, but contrary in its evasion of the expectations established by its genre. Our fiction defies traditional story form. For example, a story may bring us to closure without ever delivering an ending. We don't insist on the ending, but we do insist on the closure. And we value fiction as poetic as any poem." Quarterly. Member CLMP. Acquires first rights and perpetual archive and anthology rights. Publication is copyrighted. Pays on publication and receipt of invoice. Mss published 21 days after acceptance. Responds to queries in 2 weeks; in 3 months to mss. Rarely comments on/critiques rejected mss. Editorial lead time 3 months. Guidelines online.

**MAGAZINES NEEDS** Accepts submissions through website only: www.contrarymagazine.com/Contrary/Submissions.html. Include estimated word count, brief bio, list of publications.Often comments on rejected poems. Pays $20 per byline, $60 for featured work.

**TIPS** "Beautiful writing catches our eye first. If we realize we're in the presence of unanticipated meaning, that's what clinches the deal. Also, we're not fond of expository fiction. We prefer to be seduced by beauty, profundity, and mystery than to be presented with the obvious. We look for fiction that entrances, that stays the reader's finger above the mouse button. That is, in part, why we favor microfiction, flash fiction, and short shorts. Also, we hope writers will remember that most editors are looking for very particular species of work. We try to describe our particular species in our mission statement and our submission guidelines, but those descriptions don't always convey nuance. That's why many editors urge writers to read the publication itself, in the hope that they will intuit an understanding of its particularities. If you happen to write that particular species of work we favor, your submission may find a happy home with us. If you don't, it does not necessarily reflect on your quality or your ability. It usually just means that your work has a happier home somewhere else."

## CONVERGENCE: AN ONLINE JOURNAL OF POETRY AND ART

**E-mail:** clinville@csus.edu. **Website:** www.convergence-journal.com. **Contact:** Cynthia Linville, managing editor. "We look for well-crafted work with fresh images and a strong voice. Work from a series or with a common theme has a greater chance of being accepted. Seasonally-themed work is appreciated (spring and summer for the January deadline, fall and winter for the June deadline). Please include a 75-word bio with your work (bios may be edited for length and clarity). A cover letter is not needed. Absolutely no simultaneous or previously published submissions."

Deadlines are January 5 and June 5.

**MAGAZINES NEEDS** New interpretations of the written word by pairing poems and flash fiction with complementary art. "We are open to many different styles, but we do not often publish formal verse. Read a couple of issues to get a sense of what we like; namely, well-crafted work with fresh images and a strong voice." Convergence is published quarterly online, Has published poetry by Oliver Rice, Simon Perchik, Mary Ocher. Receives about 800 poems/year, accepts about 10 per issue plus monthly selections for "Editor's Choice." Has about 200 online subscribers. Guidelines available on website. Does not often publish formal verse. Does not want "poetry with trite, unoriginal language or unfinished work." Length: 50 max. No payment.

**HOW TO CONTACT** No simultaneous or previously published submissions. Accepts e-mail submissions only. Reads submissions year round. Time between acceptance and publication is 1-2 months. Poems are circulated to an editorial board. Responds in 6 months. Acquires first rights.

**TIPS** "We look for freshness and originality and a mastery of the craft of flash fiction. Working with a common theme has a greater chance of being accepted."

## COPPER NICKEL

**Website:** copper-nickel.org. **Contact:** Brian Barker and Nicky Beer, editors. Work published in Copper Nickel has appeared in Best American Poetry, Best American Short Stories, and Pushcart Prize anthologies. Responds in 2 months. Guidelines online.

**MAGAZINES NEEDS** Submit 4-6 poems between August 1 and May 1. Pays 2 contributor copies.

## COTTONWOOD

Room 400 Kansas Union, 1301 Jayhawk Blvd., University of Kansas, Lawrence KS 66045. **E-mail:** tlorenz@ku.edu. **Website:** www2.ku.edu/~englishmfa/cottonwood. **Contact:** Tom Lorenz, fiction editor. "Established in the 1960s, *Cottonwood* is the nationally circulated literary review of the University of Kansas. We publish high-quality literary work in poetry, fiction, and creative nonfiction. Over the years authors such as William Stafford, Rita Dove, Connie May Fowler, Virgil Suarez, and Cris Mazza have appeared in the pages of *Cottonwood*, and recent issues have featured the work of Kim Chinquee, Quinn Dalton, Carol Lee Lorenzo, Jesse Kercheval, Joanne Lowery, and Oliver Rice. We welcome submissions from new and established writers. New issues appear once yearly, in the fall." Acquires one-time rights. Responds in 6 months. Guidelines online.

**MAGAZINES NEEDS** Wants poems "on daily experience, perception; strong narrative or sensory impact, nonderivative." Submit with SASE. Pays contributor copies.

**TIPS** "We're looking for depth and originality of subject matter, engaging voice and style, emotional honesty, command of the material and the structure. *Cottonwood* publishes high-quality literary fiction, but we are very open to the work of talented new writers. Write something honest and that you care about, and write it as well as you can. Don't hesitate to keep trying us. We sometimes take a piece from a writer we've rejected a number of times. We generally don't like clever, gimmicky writing. The style should be engaging but not claim all the the attention itself."

## CRAB CREEK REVIEW

7315 34th Ave. NW, Seattle WA 98117. **E-mail:** crabcreekreview@gmail.com. **Website:** www.crabcreekreview.org. **Contact:** Jenifer Lawrence, editor-in-chief; Martha Silano, poetry editor. *Crab Creek Review* is an 80- to 120-page, perfect-bound paperback. "We are an international journal based in the Pacific Northwest that is looking for poems, stories, and essays that pay attention to craft while still surprising us in positive ways with detail and content. We publish well-known and emerging writers." Buys first North American rights. Responds in 2-4 months to mss. Sample copy: $6. Subscription: $15/year, $28/2 year. Accepts submissions via Submittable only. Guidelines online.

Nominates for the Pushcart Prize and offers annual *Crab Creek Review* Editors' Prize of $100 for the best poem, essay, or short story published in the previous year. Annual *Crab Creek Review* poetry prize: $500.

**MAGAZINES NEEDS** Submit via online submission form. Has published poetry by Oliver de la Paz, Dorianne Laux, Denise Duhamel, and translations by Ilya Kaminsky and Matthew Zapruder. Pays 1 contributor copy.

## CRAB ORCHARD REVIEW

Dept. of English, Southern Illinois University Carbondale, Faner Hall 2380, Mail Code 4503, 1000 Faner Dr., Carbondale IL 62901. (618)453-6833. **Fax:** (618)453-8224. **E-mail:** jtribble@siu.edu. **Website:** www.craborchardreview.siu.edu. **Contact:** Jon Tribble, managing editor. "We are a general-interest literary journal published twice/year. We strive to be a journal that writers admire and readers enjoy. We publish fiction, poetry, creative nonfiction, fiction translations, interviews, and reviews." Buys first North American serial rights. Publishes ms an average of 9-12 months after acceptance. Responds in 3 weeks to queries; 9 months to mss. Sample copy for $12. Guidelines online.

**MAGAZINES NEEDS** Wants all styles and forms from traditional to experimental. Does not want greeting card verse; literary poetry only. Has published poetry by Luisa A. Igloria, Erinn Batykefer, Jim Daniels, and Bryan Tso Jones. Postal submissions only. Cover letter is preferred. "Indicate stanza breaks on poems of more than 1 page. Poems that are under serious consideration are discussed and decided on by the managing editor and poetry editor." Pays $25/published magazine page, $50 minimum, 2 contributor copies and 1-year subscription.

## CRAZYHORSE

College of Charleston, Department of English, 66 George St., Charleston SC 29424. (843)953-4470. **E-mail:** crazyhorse@cofc.edu. **Website:** http://crazyhorse.cofc.edu. **Contact:** Jonathan Bohr Heinen, managing editor; Emily Rosko, poetry editor; Anthony Varallo, fiction editor; Bret Lott, nonfiction editor. "We like to print a mix of writing regardless of its form, genre, school, or politics. We're especially on the lookout for original writing that doesn't fit the categories and that engages in the work of honest communication." Buys first North American serial rights. Publishes ms an average of 6-12 months after acceptance. Responds in 1 week to queries. Responds in 3-4 months to mss. Sample copy for $5. Guidelines for SASE or by e-mail.

Reads submissions September 1-May 31.

**MAGAZINES NEEDS** Submit 3-5 poems at a time. No fax, e-mail or disk submissions. Cover letter is preferred. Pays $20 per page ($200 maximum) and 2 contributor copies.

**TIPS** "Write to explore subjects you care about. The subject should be one in which something is at stake. Before sending, ask, 'What's reckoned with that's important for other people to read?'"

## CREAM CITY REVIEW

c/o UWM Department of English, P.O. Box 413, Milwaukee WI 53201. **E-mail:** info@creamcityreview.org. **Website:** www.creamcityreview.org. **Contact:** Loretta McCormick, editor in chief; Mollie Boutell, managing editor. *Cream City Review* publishes "memorable and energetic fiction, poetry, and creative nonfiction. Features reviews of contemporary literature and criticism as well as author interviews and artwork. We are interested in camera-ready art depicting themes appropriate to each issue." Responds in 8 months to mss. Sample back issue: $7. Guidelines online at www.creamcityreview.org/submit. Check for regular updates at www.facebook.com/creamcityreview. Submit using online submissions manager only.

**MAGAZINES NEEDS** Submit poems via online submissions manager only.

**TIPS** "Please include a few lines about your publication history. *CCR* seeks to publish a broad range of writings and a broad range of writers with diverse backgrounds. We accept submissions from August 1-November 1 and December 1-April 1. No e-mail submissions, please."

## CREATIVE WITH WORDS PUBLICATIONS

P.O. Box 223226, Carmel CA 93922. **Fax:** (831)655-8627. **E-mail:** geltrich@mbay.net. **Website:** creativewithwords.tripod.com. **Contact:** Brigitta Gisella Geltrich-Ludgate, publisher and editor. *Creative With Words* publishes "poetry, prose, illustrations, photos by all ages." Publishes ms 1-2 months after acceptance. Responds in 2-4 weeks. Guideline online.

**MAGAZINES NEEDS** Submit up to 5 poems by mail or e-mail. Always include SASE and legitimate address with postal submissions. Cover letter preferred.

**TIPS** "We offer a great variety of themes. We look for clean family-type fiction/poetry. Also, we ask the writer to look at the world from a different perspective, research topic thoroughly, be creative, apply brevity, tell the story from a character's viewpoint, tighten

dialogue, be less descriptive, proofread before submitting, and be patient. We will not publish every ms we receive. It has to be in standard English, well written, proofread. We do not appreciate receiving mss where we have to do the proofreading and correct the grammar."

## CRUCIBLE

Barton College, P.O. Box 5000, Wilson NC 27893. **E-mail:** crucible@barton.edu. **Website:** www.barton.edu/crucible. *Crucible*, published annually in the fall, publishes poetry and fiction as part of its Poetry and Fiction Contest run each year. Deadline for submissions: May 1. Acquires first rights. Notifies winners by October each year. Sample: $8. Guidelines online.

 *Crucible* is under 100 pages, digest-sized, professionally printed on high-quality paper, with matte card cover. Press run is 500.

**MAGAZINES NEEDS** Submit "poetry that demonstrates originality and integrity of craftsmanship as well as thought. Traditional metrical and rhyming poems are difficult to bring off in modern poetry. The best poetry is written out of deeply felt experience which has been crafted into pleasing form." Wants "free verse with attention paid particularly to image, line, stanza, and voice." Does not want "very long narratives, poetry that is forced." Has published poetry by Robert Grey, R.T. Smith, and Anthony S. Abbott. Submit up to 5 poems by e-mail. Ms accepted only through May 1. Do not include name on poems. Include separate bio. Pays $150 for 1st prize, $100 for 2nd prize, contributor copies.

## CUMBERLAND RIVER REVIEW

333 Murfreesboro Rd., Nashville TN 37210. **E-mail:** crr@trevecca.edu. **Website:** crr.trevecca.edu. **Contact:** Graham Hillard, editor. *The Cumberland River Review* is a quarterly online publication of new poetry, fiction, essays, and art. The journal is produced by the department of English at Trevecca Nazarene University and welcomes submissions from both national and international writers and artists. Responds in 3 months. Guidelines online.

**MAGAZINES NEEDS** Submit 3-5 poems in a single document between September and April.

## CURA: A LITERARY MAGAZINE OF ART AND ACTION

441 E. Fordham Rd., English Department, Dealy 541W, Bronx NY 10548. **E-mail:** curamag@fordham.edu. **Website:** www.curamag.com. **Contact:** Sarah

Gambito, editor. *CURA: A Literary Magazine of Art and Action* is a multimedia initiative based at Fordham University committed to integrating the arts and social justice. Featuring creative writing, visual art, new media, and video in response to current news, we seek to enable an artistic process that is rigorously engaged with the world at the present moment. *CURA* is taken from the Ignatian educational principle of "cura personalis," care for the whole person. On its own, the word *cura* is defined as guardianship, solicitude, and significantly, written work. Acquires first rights. Publishes ms 5 months after acceptance. Editorial lead time is 5 months. Sample copy online. Guidelines online.

○ Reading period: October 15 - March 15.

**MAGAZINES NEEDS** Pays 1 contributor copy.

## CURRENT ACCOUNTS

Current Accounts, Apt. 2D, Bradshaw Hall, Hardcastle Gardens, Bolton BL2 4NZ, UK. **E-mail:** bswscribe@gmail.com. **E-mail:** fjameshartnell@aol.com. **Website:** sites.google.com/site/bankstreetwriters. **Contact:** Rod Riesco. *Current Accounts*, an online publication, prints poetry, drama, fiction, and nonfiction by members of Bank Street Writers, and other contributors. Acquires first rights. Uploads ms 6 months after acceptance. Responds ASAP. Guidelines available for SASE, by fax, by e-mail, or on website.

○ Receives about 200 poems and stories/plays per year; accepts about 5%.

**MAGAZINES NEEDS** Open to all types of poetry. No requirements, although some space is reserved for members. Considers poetry by children and teens. Has published poetry by Pat Winslow, M.R. Peacocke, and Gerald England. E-mail submissions only. Doesn't mind rhyming poetry. Travel or tourist poetry needs to be more than just exotic names and places. Titles need care. Poetry should be poetic in some form. Experimental work is welcome. Length: up to 40 lines/poem. Pays 1 contributor copy.

**TIPS** Bank Street Writers meets once/month and offers workshops, guest speakers, and other activities. E-mail for details."We like originality of ideas, images, and use of language. No inspirational or religious verse unless it's also good in poetic terms."

## CUTTHROAT, A JOURNAL OF THE ARTS

P.O. Box 2414, Durango CO 81302. (970)903-7914. **E-mail:** cutthroatmag@gmail.com. **Website:** www.cutthroatmag.com. **Contact:** Beth Alvarado, fiction editor; William Luvaas, online fiction editor; William Pitt Root, poetry editor. "We publish only high-quality fiction, creative nonfiction, and poetry. We are looking for the cutting edge, the endangered word, fiction with wit, heart, soul, and meaning." *CUTTHROAT* is a literary magazine/journal and "one separate online edition of poetry, translations, short fiction, essays, and book reviews yearly." Acquires first North American serial rights. Sends galleys to author. Publication is copyrighted. Responds in 1-2 weeks to queries; in 6-8 months to mss. Sometimes comments on/critiques rejected mss. Sample copy: $10. Guidelines available for SASE or on website.

○ Member CCLMP.

**MAGAZINES NEEDS** Submit 3-5 poems. Reading periods for online editions are March 15-June 1; for print editions, July 15-October 10. "We prefer online submissions through our submission manager! If submitting by mail, please include cover letter and SASE for response only; mss are recycled." Has published Joy Harjo, Linda Hogan, Patricia Smith, Wendell Berry, Naomi Shihab Nye, Marvin Bell, Richard Jackson, Sean Thomas Dougherty, Doug Anderson, Dan Vera, Martin Espada, TR Hummer, Daniel Nathan Terry, and many more.

**TIPS** "Read our magazine, and see what types of work we've published. The piece must have heart and soul, excellence in craft. "

## THE DALHOUSIE REVIEW

Dalhousie University, Halifax NS B3H 4R2, Canada. **E-mail:** dalhousie.review@dal.ca. **Website:** dalhousiereview.dal.ca. **Contact:** Carrie Dawson, editor. *Dalhousie Review*, published 3 times/year, is a journal of criticism publishing poetry and fiction. Considers works from both new and established writers. Responds in 3-9 months. Subscription: $30 US for 1 year.

○ *Dalhousie Review* is 144 pages, digest-sized. Press run is 500.

**MAGAZINES NEEDS** Submit via postal mail only. Reads year round. Length: up to 40 lines/poem. Pays 2 contributor copies and 10 offprints.

## DARKLING MAGAZINE

Darkling Publications, 28780 318th Ave., Colome SD 57528. **E-mail:** darkling@mitchelltelecom.net; jvanoort@darklingpublications.com. **Website:** darklingpublications.com. **Contact:** James C. Van Oort, editor in chief. *Darkling Magazine*, published annually in late summer, is "primarily interested in poetry.

All submissions should be dark in nature and should help expose the darker side of man. Dark nature does not mean whiny or overly murderous, and being depressed does not make an artist's work dark." Has published poems by Robert Cooperman, Kenneth DiMaggio, Arthur Gottlieb, Simon Perchik, Cathy Porter, and Susanna Rich, among others.

Reading period: October 1-May 15.

**MAGAZINES NEEDS** Submit by postal mail (with SASE) or e-mail (pasted into the body of message or as attachment). "Profanity should be used with extreme caution, and should be inherently necessary to the piece in order to be considered. Pornography of any sort will not be considered and will merit no response whatsoever." Length: any length is acceptable, but epic length poetry must be of exceptional quality and content to be considered.

**TIPS** "Darkling Publications considers serious work from serious artists, and publishes only the best of the best alongside work from artists we feel show great promise but are early in their writing careers. Please submit only what you feel is your best work; darkness has many veins, sinews, and bloodlines, so show us the best of your dark art."

## THE DEAD MULE SCHOOL OF SOUTHERN LITERATURE

**E-mail:** deadmule@gmail.com; submit.mule@gmail.com. **Website:** www.deadmule.com. Robert MacEwan, technical and design. **Contact:** Valerie MacEwan, publisher and editor. "No good southern fiction is complete without a dead mule." *The Dead Mule* is one of the oldest, if not *the* oldest, continuously published online literary journals alive today. Publisher and editor Valerie MacEwan welcomes submissions. *The Dead Mule School of Southern Literature* wants flash fiction, visual poetry, essays, and creative nonfiction. Twenty Years Online. 1996-2016. Celebrate With a Dead Mule. Acquires first electronic rights and indefinite archival rights. All other rights revert to author upon publication. Publishes ms less than 6 months after acceptance. Responds in 6 weeks. "Submissions handled through the website, not via e-mail. We use Submittable. Go to deadmule.com/submissions for the link. Please do not query the editor directly."

"*The Dead Mule School of Southern Literature* Institutional Alumni Association recruits year round. We love reading what you wrote."

**MAGAZINES NEEDS** Check the *Mule* for poetry information.

**TIPS** "Read the site to get a feel for what we're looking to publish. Read the guidelines. We look forward to hearing from you. We are nothing if not for our writers. *The Dead Mule* strives to deliver quality writing in every issue. It is in this way that we pay tribute to our authors. Send us something original."

## DENVER QUARTERLY

University of Denver, 2000 E. Asbury, Denver CO 80208. (303)871-2892. **E-mail:** denverquarterly@gmail.com. **Website:** www.du.edu/denverquarterly. **Contact:** Laird Hunt, editor. Publishes fiction, articles, and poetry for a generally well-educated audience, primarily interested in literature and the literary experience. Audience reads *DQ* to find something a little different from a strictly academic quarterly or a creative writing outlet. Quarterly. Reads September 15-May 15. Acquires first North American serial rights. Publishes ms 1 year after acceptance. Responds in 3 months. Sample copy: $10.

*Denver Quarterly* received an Honorable Mention for Content from the American Literary Magazine Awards, and selections have been anthologized in the *Pushcart Prize* anthologies.

**MAGAZINES NEEDS** Submit 3-5 poems by postal mail or online submissions manager. Pays $5/page and 2 contributor copies.

**TIPS** "We look for serious, realistic, and experimental fiction: stories which appeal to intelligent, demanding readers who are not themselves fiction writers. Nothing so quickly disqualifies a ms as sloppy proofreading and mechanics. Read the magazine before submitting to it. We try to remain eclectic, but the odds for beginners are bound to be small considering the fact that we receive nearly 10,000 mss per year and publish only about 10 short stories."

## THE DERONDA REVIEW

**E-mail:** derondareview@att.net. **Website:** www.derondareview.org; www.pointandcircumference.com. Mindy Aber Barad, co-editor for Israel, P.O. Box 1299, Efrat 90435, Israel. **E-mail:** maber4kids@yahoo.com.. **Contact:** Esther Cameron, editor in chief; Mindy Aber Barad (Israel only), co-editor. Annual literary journal publishing poetry and seeking to "promote a literature of introspection, dialogue, and social concern." Acquires first rights. Publishes ms 1 year after acceptance. Responds in 4 months; "if longer, please query by e-mail." "Please read an online issue before submitting."

🔾 Now mainly a digital publication, with print copies for libraries.

**MAGAZINES NEEDS** Cover letter is unnecessary. E-mail submissions preferred. "Do include SASE with sufficient postage to return all mss or with 'reply Only' clearly indicated. Poets whose work is accepted will be asked for URLs and titles of books available to be published in the online contributors exchange."

**TIPS** "Longer selections of poets frequently published in the magazine are posted on www.pointandcircumference.com."

### ◑ DESCANT: FORT WORTH'S JOURNAL OF POETRY AND FICTION

TCU Department of English, Box 297270, Ft. Worth TX 76129. (817)257-5907. **Fax:** (817)257-6239. **E-mail:** descant@tcu.edu; m.pitt@tcu.edu. **Website:** www.descant.tcu.edu. **Contact:** Matthew Pitt, editor in chief and fiction editor; Alex Lemon, poetry editor. "*descant* seeks high-quality poems and stories in both traditional and innovative form." Member CLMP. Acquires one-time rights. Pays on publication. Responds in 5 months to mss. Sample copy: $15 by SASE, e-mail, or fax.

🔾 Reading period: Septmeber 1-April 1. Offers 4 annual cash awards for work already accepted for publication in the journal: The $500 Frank O'Connor Award for the best story in an issue; the $250 Gary Wilson Award for an outstanding story in an issue; the $500 Betsy Colquitt Award for the best poem in an issue; and the $250 Baskerville Publishers Award for outstanding poem in an issue. Several stories first published by *descant* have appeared in *Best American Short Stories*.

**MAGAZINES NEEDS** Length: up to 60 lines/poem. Pays 2 contributor copies; additional copies $6.

**TIPS** "We look for character and quality of prose. Send your best short work."

### DEVIL'S LAKE

600 N. Park St., Suite 6195, Madison WI 53706. E-mail: devilslake.editor@gmail.com. **Website:** english.wisc.edu/devilslake. Responds in 5 months. Guidelines online.

**MAGAZINES NEEDS** Submit 3-5 poems in a single document.

### ⑤ DEVOZINE

1908 Grand Ave., P.O. Box 340004, Nashville TN 37203-0004. **E-mail:** devozine@upperroom.org. **Website:** www.devozine.org. **Contact:** Sandy Miller, editor. *devozine*, published bimonthly, is a 64-page devotional magazine for youth (ages 14-19) and adults who care about youth. Offers meditations, scripture, prayers, poems, stories, songs, and feature articles to "aid youth in their prayer life, introduce them to spiritual disciplines, help them shape their concept of God, and encourage them in the life of discipleship."

**MAGAZINES NEEDS** Considers poetry by teens. Submit by postal mail with SASE, or by e-mail. Include name, age/birth date (if younger than 25), mailing address, e-mail address, phone number, and fax number (if available). Always publishes theme issues (available for SASE or online). Indicate theme you are writing for. Length: 10-20 lines/poem. Pays $25.

### ◐ DIAGRAM

Department of English, University of Arizona, P.O. Box 210067, Tucson AZ 85721-0067. **E-mail:** editor@thediagram.com. **Website:** www.thediagram.com. **Contact:** Ander Monson, editor; T. Fleischmann and Nicole Walker, nonfiction editors; Sarah Blackman and Lauren Slaughter, fiction editors; Heidi Gotz and E.A. Ramey, poetry editors. "*DIAGRAM* is an electronic journal of text and art, found and created. We're interested in representations, naming, indicating, schematics, labeling and taxonomy of things; in poems that masquerade as stories; in stories that disguise themselves as indices or obituaries. We specialize in work that pushes the boundaries of traditional genre or work that is in some way schematic. We do publish traditional fiction and poetry, too, but hybrid forms (short stories, prose poems, indexes, tables of contents, etc.) are particularly welcome! We also publish diagrams and schematics (original and found)." Buys first North American serial rights. Publishes ms 6-9 months after acceptance. Responds in 2 weeks to queries; in 2 months to mss. Often comments on rejected mss. Sample copy: $12. Writer's guidelines online.

🔾 Publishes 6 new writers/year. Bimonthly. Member CLMP. "We sponsor yearly contests for unpublished hybrid essays and innovative fiction. Guidelines on website."

**MAGAZINES NEEDS** Submit 3-6 poems. Electronic submissions accepted through submissions manager; no e-mail, disk, or fax submissions. Electronic submissions much preferred; print submissions must include SASE if response is expected. Cover letter is preferred. Reads submissions year round. Poems are circulated to an editorial board. Sometimes comments on rejected poems. Sometimes publishes theme issues. Receives about 1,000 poems/year, accepts about 5%. Does not want light verse. No length limit.

**ADDITIONAL INFORMATION** *DIAGRAM* also publishes periodic, perfect-bound print anthologies.

**TIPS** "Submit interesting text, images, sound, and new media. We value the insides of things, vivisection, urgency, risk, elegance, flamboyance, work that moves us, language that does something new, or does something old—well. We like iteration and reiteration. Ruins and ghosts. Mechanical, moving parts, balloons, and frenzy. We want art and writing that demonstrates interaction; the processes of things; how functions are accomplished; how things become or expire, move or stand. We'll consider anything."

## DIODE POETRY JOURNAL

**E-mail:** submit@diodepoetry.com. **Website:** www.diodepoetry.com. **Contact:** Patty Paine, editor. "*Diode* is looking for poetry that excites and energizes, and that uses language that crackles and sparks. We're looking for poetry from all points on the arc, from formal to experimental." Acquires one-time rights. Rights revert to poet upon publication. Time between acceptance and publication varies. Responds in 1-2 months. Always sends prepublication galleys. Guidelines available on website.

○ Does not want "light verse, erotic." Receives about 6,000 poems/year; accepts about 2%.

**MAGAZINES NEEDS** Submit 3-5 poems at a time. Accepts submissions by e-mail; attach document as DOC or RTF. Cover letter is required. Reads submissions year round. Sometimes comments on rejected poems. Has published poetry by Bob Hicok, Beckian Fritz Golberg, G.C. Waldrep, Dorianne Laux, David Wojahn, and Rae Armantrout.

## DMQ REVIEW

**E-mail:** editors@dmqreview.com. **Website:** www.dmqreview.com. **Contact:** Sally Ashton, editor in chief. *DMQ Review* seeks work that represents the diversity of contemporary poetry and demonstrates literary excellence, whether it be lyric, free verse, prose, or experimental form. Buys first North American se-

rial rights. Publishes ms 1-3 months after acceptance. Responds in 3 months. Guidelines online.

**MAGAZINES NEEDS** Submit up to 5 poems via online submissions manager. Has published poetry by David Lehman, Ellen Bass, Amy Gerstler, Bob Hicok, Ilya Kaminsky, and Jane Hirshfield. Receives about 3,000-5,000 poems/year, accepts about 1%.

**ALSO OFFERS** Nominates for the Pushcart Prize. Also considers submissions of visual art, which is published with the poems in the magazine with links to the artists' websites.

**TIPS** "Check our current and past issues, and read and follow submission guidelines closely."

## THE DOS PASSOS REVIEW

Briery Creek Press, Longwood University, Department of English and Modern Languages, 201 High St., Farmville VA 23909. **E-mail:** brierycreek@gmail.com. **E-mail:** dospassosreview@gmail.com. **Website:** brierycreekpress.wordpress.com/the-dos-passos-review. **Contact:** Managing Editor. "We are looking for writing that demonstrates characteristics found in the work of John Dos Passos, such as an intense and original exploration of specifically American themes; an innovative quality; and a range of literary forms, especially in the genres of fiction and creative nonfiction. We are not interested in genre fiction, or prose that is experiment for the sake of experiment. We are also not interested in nonfiction that is scholarly or critical in nature. Send us your best unpublished literary prose or poetry." Responds to mss in 2-12 weeks. Guidelines are available by e-mail, SASE, or on the website.

○ Reading periods: April 1-July 31 for Fall issue; February 1-May 31 for Spring issue.

**MAGAZINES NEEDS** Submit 3-5 poems ms by e-mail as attachment. Include cover letter and brief bio. Pays 2 contributor copies.

## DOWN IN THE DIRT

**E-mail:** dirt@scars.tv. **Website:** www.scars.tv/dirt. **Contact:** Janet Kuypers, editor. *Down in the Dirt*, published every other month online and in print issues sold via Amazon.com throughout the U.S., U.K., and continental Europe, prints "good work that makes you think, that makes you feel like you've lived through a scene instead of merely read it." Also considers poems. *Down in the Dirt* is published "electronically as well as in print, either as printed magazines sold through our printer over the Internet, on the Web, or sold through our printer." Publishes ms within 1 year after acceptance. Responds in 1 month to queries; in 1 month to mss. If asked, always comments on rejected mss. Sample copy: $6 for issues before 2010. Samples from 2010 and beyond do not exist; you can just directly purchase the issues online any time. Guidelines for SASE, e-mail, or on website.

○ Has published work by Mel Waldman, Ken Dean, Jon Brunette, John Ragusa, and Liam Spencer.

**MAGAZINES NEEDS** Accepts e-mail submissions (vastly preferred to snail mail; pasted into body of message or as Microsoft Word DOC file attachment) and disk submissions (formatted for Macintosh). "If you do not have e-mail and want to snail-mail a poetry submission, we do not accept poetry snail-mail submissions longer than 10 lines. Currently, accepted writings get their own Web page in the 'writings' section at scars.tv/dirt, and samples of accepted writings are placed into an annual collection book that Scars Publications produces." Has published work by I.B. Rad, Pat Dixon, Mel Waldman, and Brian Looney. Does not want smut, rhyming poetry, or religious writing. Any length is appreciated.

**ALSO OFFERS** Scars Publications sponsors a contest "where accepted writing appears in a collection book. Write or e-mail (dirt@scars.tv) for information." Also able to publish electronic chapbooks. Write for more information.

### DRESSING ROOM POETRY JOURNAL

**E-mail:** dressingroompoetryjournal@gmail.com. **Website:** dressingroompoetryjournal.com. **Contact:** Meg Johnson, editor. Guidelines online.

**MAGAZINES NEEDS** Send 3-7 poems in an attachment.

### ○ DRUNKEN BOAT

119 Main St., Chester CT 06412. **E-mail:** editor@drunkenboat.com. **Website:** www.drunkenboat.com. *Drunken Boat*, published 2 times/year online, is a multimedia publication reaching an international audience with an extremely broad aesthetic. "*Drunken Boat* is committed to actively seeking out and promoting the work of marginalized and underrepresented artists, including especially people of color, women, queer, differently abled, and gender nonconforming artists." To cover operational costs, charges a $3 fee for each submission. Responds in 3 months to mss. Guidelines online.

**MAGAZINES NEEDS** "Submit no more than 3 poems, in a single document. Our aesthetic is very broad. We welcome work ranging from received form to the cutting edge avant-garde, from one line to the multipage, from collaborations to hybridizations and cut-ups as well as works that use other media in their composition, originality and in translation (with the writer's permission), American and from around the globe." Has published more than 500 poets, including Heather McHugh, Jane Hirshfield, Alfred Corn, Alice Fulton, Ron Silliman, and Roseanna Warren. Receives about 3,000 poems/year, accepts about 5%.

**TIPS** "Submissions should be submitted in Word and RTF format only. (This does not apply to audio, visual, and Web work.) Accepts chapbooks. See our submissions manager system."

### DUCTS

**E-mail:** vents@ducts.org. **Website:** www.ducts.org. **Contact:** Mary Cool, editor in chief; Tim Tomlinson, fiction editor; Lisa Kirchner, memoir editor; Amy Lemmon, poetry editor; Jacqueline Bishop, art editor. *Ducts* is a semiannual webzine of personal stories, fiction, essays, memoirs, poetry, humor, profiles, reviews, and art. "*Ducts* was founded in 1999 with the intent of giving emerging writers a venue to regularly publish their compelling, personal stories. The site has been expanded to include art and creative works of all genres. We believe that these genres must and do overlap. *Ducts* publishes the best, most compelling stories, and we hope to attract readers who are drawn to work that rises above." Pays on publication. Responds in 1-6 months. Guidelines available on website.

**MAGAZINES NEEDS** Submit 3-5 poems to poetry@ducts.org. Reads poetry January 1-August 31. Pays $20.

**TIPS** "We prefer writing that tells a compelling story with a strong narrative drive."

### ○ EARTHSHINE

P.O. Box 245, Hummelstown PA 17036. **E-mail:** poetry@earthshinepoetry.org. **Website:** www.earthshinepoetry.org. **Contact:** Sally Zaino and Julie Moffitt, poetry editors. *Earthshine*, published irregularly in print and constantly online, features poetry and 1-2 pieces of cover art per volume. "When the online journal is full, a printed volume is produced and offered for sale. Subscriptions will be available as the publication becomes regular. The voice of *Earthshine* is one of illumination, compassion, humanity, and reason. Please see the submission guidelines webpage for updated information. Poems are the ultimate rumination, and if the world is to be saved, the poets will be needed; they are who see the connections between all things, and the patterns shared. We seek poetry of high literary quality, which will generate its own light for our readers." Acquires first rights and requests ongoing electronic rights. Time between acceptance and publication is "almost immediate" for online publication and "TBD" for printed publication. Responds in 1-2 months. Sample: $8. Guidelines available in magazine, for SASE, and on website.

🖝 Has published poetry by Richard Schiffman, Anne Pierson Wiese, Steven Keletar, Mario Susko, and Daniel J. Langton.

**MAGAZINES NEEDS** Accepts e-mail submissions (pasted into body of message); no fax or disk submissions. Cover letter is preferred. "Please let us know where you heard about *Earthshine*. If submitting by mail, please include an SASE for reply only. Please do not send the only copy of your work." Reads submissions year round. Sometimes comments on rejected poems. Never publishes theme issues. Pays 2 contributor copies.

## ECLECTICA

**E-mail:** editors@eclectica.org. **Website:** www.eclectica.org. **Contact:** Tom Dooley, managing editor. "A sterling-quality literary magazine on the World Wide Web. Not bound by formula or genre, harnessing technology to further the reading experience and dynamic, and interesting in content. *Eclectica* is a quarterly online journal devoted to showcasing the best writing on the Web, regardless of genre. 'Literary' and 'genre' work appear side-by-side in each issue, along with pieces that blur the distinctions between such categories. Pushcart Prize, National Poetry Series, and Pulitzer Prize winners, as well as Nebula Award nominees, have shared issues with previously unpublished authors." Buys first world electronic (online/Internet) rights. All rights revert to author upon publication, except for anthology rights. Guidelines online.

🖝 Submission deadlines: December 1 for January/February issue, and March 1 for April/May issue.

**MAGAZINES NEEDS** Seeks "outstanding poetry." Submit using online submissions manager.

**TIPS** "We pride ourselves on giving everyone (high schoolers, convicts, movie executives, etc.) an equal shot at publication, based solely on the quality of their work. Because we like eclecticism, we tend to favor the varied perspectives that often characterize the work of international authors, people of color, women, alternative lifestylists—but others who don't fit into these categories often surprise us."

## ECOTONE

Department of Creative Writing, University of North Carolina Wilmington, 601 S. College Rd., Wilmington NC 28403. (910)962-2547. **Fax:** (910)962-7461. **E-mail:** info@ecotonejournal.com. **Website:** www.ecotonejournal.com. **Contact:** Kate O'reilly, managing editor; Cathe Shubert, nonfiction editor; Ryan Kaune, fiction editor; Stephanie Trott, poetry editor. "*Ecotone* is a literary journal of place that seeks to publish creative works about the environment and the natural world while avoiding the hushed tones and clichés of much of so-called nature writing." Responds in 6 months to mss.

🖝 Reading period is August 15-April 15.

**MAGAZINES NEEDS** Send poems via postal mail or online submissions manager.

## EKPHRASIS

Frith Press, P.O. Box 161236, Sacramento CA 95816-1236. **E-mail:** frithpress@aol.com. **Website:** ekphrasisjournal.com. **Contact:** Laverne Frith and Carol Frith, editors. *Ekphrasis*, published semiannually in March and September, is an "outlet for the growing body of poetry focusing on individual works from any artistic genre. Poetry should transcend mere description. Open to all forms." Acquires first North American serial rights, one-time rights. Publishes ms 1 year after acceptance. Responds in 4 months. Seldom comments on rejected poems. Sample: $6. Subscription: $12/year. Make checks payable, in U.S. funds, to Laverne Frith. Guidelines available for SASE or on website.

🖝 *Ekphrasis* is 32-50 pages, digest-sized, photocopied, saddle-stapled. Poems from *Ekphrasis* have been featured on *Poetry Daily*. Nominates for the Pushcart Prize.

**MAGAZINES NEEDS** Submit 3-5 poems at a time. Considers previously published poems "infrequently; must be credited." Cover letter is required, including short bio with representative credits and phone number. Include SASE. Until further notice, Frith Press will publish **occasional chapbooks by invitation only**. Has published poetry by Jeffrey Levine, Peter Meinke,

David Hamilton, Barbara Lefcowitz, Molly McQuade, Alice Friman, and Annie Boutelle. Does not want "poetry without ekphrastic focus. No poorly crafted work. No archaic language." Pays 1 contributor copy.

## 🜚 ELLIPSIS

Westminster College, 1840 S. 1300 E., Salt Lake City UT 84105. (801)832-2321. **E-mail:** ellipsis@westminstercollege.edu. **Website:** www.westminstercollege.edu/ellipsis. *Ellipsis*, published annually in April, needs good literary poetry, fiction, essays, plays, and visual art. Buys first North American serial rights. Pays on publication. Publishes ms an average of 3 months after acceptance. Responds in 6 months to mss. Sample copy: $7.50. Guidelines online.

○ Reads submissions August 1-January 1. Staff changes from year to year. Check website for an updated list of editors. *Ellipsis* is 120 pages, digest-sized, perfect-bound, with color cover. Accepts about 5% of submissions received. Press run is 2,000; most distributed free through college.

**MAGAZINES NEEDS** Submit poems via online submissions manager. Include cover letter. Has published poetry by Allison Joseph, Molly McQuade, Virgil Suárez, Maurice Kilwein-Guevara, Richard Cecil, and Ron Carlson. Pays $10/poem and 2 contributor copies.

## EMRYS JOURNAL

P.O. Box 8813, Greenville SC 29604. (864)409-3679. **E-mail:** emrys.info@gmail.com. **Website:** www.emrys.org. **Contact:** Lindsey DeLoach Jones, editor. *Emrys Journal* publishes fiction, poetry, and creative nonfiction. "We are pleased to have published works of the highest quality from both emerging and established writers." Responds 10 weeks after submission period ends. Sample copy: $3. Guidelines online.

○ Reading period: August 1-November 1.

**MAGAZINES NEEDS** Submit poetry via online submissions manager.

**TIPS** "Before submitting, please familiarize yourself with our magazine by reading past contributions to the *Emrys Journal*."

## 🜚 ENGLYN

**E-mail:** englynjournal@outlook.com. **Website:** englynjournal.blogspot.co.uk. *Englyn* accepts only submissions of short poetry consisting of exactly four lines. This can include, but is not restricted to, free quatrains, rhyming quatrains, ryuka, four-line haiku, dodoitsu, four-line tanka, englynion and rubaiyat. "Regardless of name, we are looking for four-line poems that perfectly capture their subject matter. In short, if the poem consists of no fewer or no more than four lines, we'll consider publishing it. (Please note, poems must be in English.)" Sample copy online. Guidelines online.

**MAGAZINES NEEDS** Submit no more than 10 4-line poems via e-mail.

## EPOCH

251 Goldwin Smith Hall, Cornell University, Ithaca NY 14853-3201. (607)255-3385. **Website:** english.arts.cornell.edu/publications/epoch. **Contact:** Michael Koch, editor; Heidi E. Marschner, managing editor. Looking for well-written literary fiction, poetry, personal essays. Newcomers welcome. Open to mainstream and avant-garde writing. Buys first North American serial rights. Pays on publication. Publishes ms an average of 6 months after acceptance. Responds in 2 weeks to queries; in 6 weeks to mss. Sometimes comments on rejected mss. Editorial lead time 6 months. Sample copy: $5. Guidelines online and for #10 SASE.

**MAGAZINES NEEDS** Mss not accompanied by SASE will be discarded unread. Occasionally provides criticism on poems. Considers poetry in all forms. Pay varies; pays $50 minimum/poem.

**TIPS** "Tell your story, speak your poem, straight from the heart. We are attracted to language and to good writing, but we are most interested in what the good writing leads us to, or where."

## 🜚 EUROPEAN JUDAISM

Leo Baeck College, The Sternberg Centre for Judaism, 80 East End Rd., London N3 2SY, England. **E-mail:** european.judaism@lbc.ac.uk. **Website:** www.journals.berghahnbooks.com/ej. **Contact:** Managing Editor. "For over 40 years, *European Judaism* has provided a voice for the postwar Jewish world in Europe. It has reflected the different realities of each country and helped rebuild Jewish consciousness after the Holocaust. It is a peer-reviewed journal with emphasis on European Jewish theology, philosophy, literature, and history. Each issue includes a poetry and book reviews section." *European Judaism* is online. Individual Rate (Online Only): $34.95/£21.95/€24.95. Student Rate (Online Only): $19.95/ £12.95/ €14.95. Please visit the website for institutional pricing. Guidelines online.

**MAGAZINES NEEDS** Submit by e-mail, accompanied by 1 double-spaced copy and a brief biographical note on the author. Please visit the website for further details.

### EVANSVILLE REVIEW

University of Evansville Creative Writing Department, 1800 Lincoln Ave., Evansville IN 47722. (812)488-1042. **E-mail:** evansvillereview@evansville.edu. **Website:** evansvillereview.evansville.edu. **Contact:** Rachel Wyatt, editor in chief; Kelly Danahy, nonfiction editor; Tia Balmer, fiction editor; Joy Grace Chen, poetry editor. "*The Evansville Review* is an annual literary journal published at the University of Evansville. Our award-winning journal includes poetry, fiction, nonfiction, plays, and interviews by a wide range of authors, from emerging writers to Nobel Prize recipients. Past issues have included work by Joyce Carol Oates, Arthur Miller, John Updike, Joseph Brodsky, Elia Kazan, Edward Albee, Willis Barnstone, Shirley Ann Grau, and X.J. Kennedy." Acquires one-time rights. Pays on publication. Responds in 3 months. Sample: $5. Guidelines online.

◯   Reading period: September 1-December 1.

**MAGAZINES NEEDS** No fax or e-mail submissions; postal submissions only. Cover letter is required. Include brief bio. Pays contributor copies.

### EVENING STREET REVIEW

Evening Street Press, Inc., 2701 Corabel LN #27, Sacramento CA 95821. **E-mail:** editor@eveningstreetpress.com. **Website:** www.eveningstreetpress.com. "Intended for a general audience, *Evening Street Press* is centered on Elizabeth Cady Stanton's 1848 revision of the Declaration of Independence: 'that all men and women are created equal,' with equal rights to 'life, liberty, and the pursuit of happiness.' It focuses on the realities of experience, personal and historical, from the most gritty to the most dreamlike, including awareness of the personal and social forces that block or develop the possibilities of this new culture." Rights revert to author upon publication. Publishes ms an average of 8 months after acceptance. Responds in 2-6 months to mss. Editorial lead time 6 months. Sample copy: $12. Guidelines online or for #10 SASE.

**MAGAZINES NEEDS** Submit 3-6 poems. E-mail submissions preferred. Does not want "the incoherent kind" of poetry. Pays 1 contributor copy.

**TIPS** "Does not want to see male chauvinism. Mss are read year round. See website for chapbook and book competitions."

### EXIT 13 MAGAZINE

P.O. Box 423, Fanwood NJ 07023-1162. (908)889-5298. **E-mail:** exit13magazine@yahoo.com. **Website:** www.facebook.com/exit13magazine. **Contact:** Tom Plante, editor. "*Exit 13*, published annually, uses poetry that is short, to the point, with a sense of geography. It features poets of all ages, writing styles, and degrees of experience, focusing on where and how we live and what's going on around us. The emphasis is on geography, travel, adventure, and the fertile ground of the imagination. It's a travelogue in poetry, a reflection of the world we see, and a chronicle of the people we meet along the way." Acquires one-time and possible anthology rights. Responds in 4 months. Sample copy: $10. Guidelines available in magazine or for SASE.

◯   *Exit 13* is about 76 pages. Press run is 300.

**MAGAZINES NEEDS** Submit through postal mail or e-mail. Paste in body of e-mail. Has published poetry by Carole Stone, Wanda Praisner, Nancy Scott, Sander Zulauf, Paul Sohar, and Charles Rammelkamp. Pays 1 contributor copy.

### ◐◑  FAILBETTER.COM

2022 Grove Ave., Richmond VA 23221. **E-mail:** submissions@failbetter.com. **Website:** www.failbetter.com. **Contact:** Thom Didato, editor. "We are a quarterly online magazine published in the spirit of a traditional literary journal—dedicated to publishing quality fiction, poetry, and artwork. While the Web plays host to hundreds, if not thousands, of genre-related sites (many of which have merit), we are not one of them." Acquires exclusive first Internet rights. Responds to e-mails in 2-3 months; to postal mail in 3-6 months. Guidelines online.

◯   Member CLMP.

**MAGAZINES NEEDS** Submit work by pasting it into the body of an e-mail. Must put "Submission" in e-mail's subject line. Do not send attachments. Also accepts postal mail submissions.

**TIPS** "Read an issue. Read our guidelines! We place a high degree of importance on originality, believing that even in this age of trends it is still possible. We are not looking for what is current or momentary. We are not concerned with length: One good sentence may find a home here, as the bulk of mediocrity will not. Most importantly, know that what you are saying could only come from you. When you are sure of this, please feel free to submit."

## FAULTLINE

University of California at Irvine, Dept. of English, 435 Humanities Instructional Building, Irvine CA 92697. (949)824-1573. **E-mail:** faultline@uci.edu. **Website:** faultline.sites.uci.edu. Poetry Editor: Walker Pfost. Fiction Editor: Jennifer Milton.. Buys first North American serial rights. Publishes ms an average of 5 months after acceptance. Responds in 4 weeks to queries; in 4 months to mss. Editorial lead time 4 months. Sample copy: $5 or online. Writer's guidelines online.

Reading period is August 15-January 15. Submissions sent at any other time will not be read. Editors change in September of each year.

**MAGAZINES NEEDS** Submit up to 5 poems via online submissions manager or postal mail. Pays contributor copies.

**TIPS** "Our commitment is to publish the best work possible from well-known and emerging authors with vivid and varied voices."

## FEELINGS OF THE HEART

c/o Feelings of the Heart, 3637 SE Sixth St. N6, Topeka KS 66607. **E-mail:** aliceharnisch@yahoo.com. **Website:** www.freewebs.com/feelingsoftheheartliteraryjournal. **Contact:** Alice M. Harnisch, editor/publisher/poet/writer. *"Feelings of the Heart* is seeking poetry, writings, and any other work that you wish to submit for publication in a small print journal. *FOTH* accepts all types of works as long as they are in good taste." Sample: $6. Subscription: $20/year (4 issues); $40/2 years (8 issues). Please make checks/money orders out to Ms. Alice M. Harnisch and send to address above.

**MAGAZINES NEEDS** Submit by mail (please send SASE for reply) or e-mail. Considers all lengths; no word count limits.

**TIPS** "Check out our Facebook page: www.facebook.com/feelingsoftheheartliteraryjournal."

## FICKLE MUSES

**E-mail:** publisher@ficklemuses.com. **Website:** ficklemuses.com. **Contact:** Sari Krosinsky, publisher and art editor; Jennifer Cunningham and Sherre Vernon, fiction editors; Jennifer Lynn Krohn, poetry editor. *"Fickle Muses* is an online journal of poetry, fiction, and art engaged with myth and legend. We feature a poet or fiction writer each week, accompanied by fea-

tured artwork. New features are posted on Sundays." Acquires one-time, nonexclusive electronic rights. Publishes ms 1-3 months after acceptance. Responds in 2-4 months. Guidelines online at ficklemuses.com/submission-guidelines.

Fiction and poetry submissions should creatively incorporate myth or legend, for example by retelling ancient myths in the context of the contemporary world, reimagining characters and events within earlier contexts, evoking mythologies underlying speculative genres, or otherwise cultivating new growth from our mythic roots. Art submissions are open to any theme or style.

## THE FIDDLEHEAD

University of New Brunswick, Campus House, 11 Garland Court, Box 4400, Fredericton NB E3B 5A3, Canada. (506)453-3501. **Fax:** (506)453-5069. **E-mail:** fiddlehd@unb.ca. **Website:** www.thefiddlehead.ca. **Contact:** Kathryn Taglia, managing editor; Ross Leckie, editor; Mark Anthony Jarman and Gerard Beirne, fiction editors; Phillip Crymble, Ian LeTourneau, and Rebecca Salazar, poetry editors; Sabine Campbell and Ross Leckie, reviews editors. "Canada's longest living literary journal, *The Fiddlehead* is published 4 times/year at the University of New Brunswick, with the generous assistance of the University of New Brunswick, the Canada Council for the Arts, and the Province of New Brunswick. It is experienced, wise enough to recognize excellence, and always looking for freshness and surprise. *The Fiddlehead* publishes short stories, poems, book reviews, and a small number of personal essays. Our full-color covers have become collectors' items and feature work by New Brunswick artists and from New Brunswick museums and art galleries. The journal is open to good writing in English from all over the world, looking always for freshness and surprise. Our editors are always happy to see new unsolicited works in fiction and poetry. Work is read on an ongoing basis; the acceptance rate is around 1-2%. Apart from our annual contest, we have no deadlines for submissions." Purchases first serial rights for unsolicited stories, poems, and creative nonfiction. All other rights remain with the author. Pays on publication. Responds in 3-9 months to mss. Occasionally comments on rejected mss. Sample copy: $15 U.S. Writer's guidelines online at www.thefiddlehead.ca/submissions.html.

"No criteria for publication except quality. For a general audience, including many poets and writers." Has published work by George Elliott Clarke, Kayla Czaga, Daniel Woodrell, and Clea Young. *The Fiddlehead* also sponsors an annual writing contest.

**MAGAZINES NEEDS** Send SASE and *Canadian* stamps or IRCs for return of mss. No e-mail, fax, or disc submissions. Simultaneous submissions only if stated on cover letter; must contact immediately if accepted elsewhere. Pays up to $40 (Canadian)/published page and 2 contributor copies.

**CONTEST/AWARD OFFERINGS** Sponsors poetry contest.

**TIPS** "If you are serious about submitting to *The Fiddlehead*, you should subscribe or read several issues to get a sense of the journal. Contact us if you would like to order sample back issues ($10-15 plus postage)."

## FIELD: CONTEMPORARY POETRY & POETICS

Oberlin College Press, 50 N. Professor St., Oberlin OH 44074-1095. (440)775-8408. **Fax:** (440)775-8124. **E-mail:** oc.press@oberlin.edu. **Website:** www.oberlin.edu/ocpress. **Contact:** Marco Wilkinson, managing editor. *FIELD: Contemporary Poetry and Poetics*, published semiannually in April and October, is a literary journal with "emphasis on poetry, translations, and essays by poets. See electronic submission guidelines." Buys first rights. Pays on publication. Responds in 6-8 weeks to mss. Editorial lead time 4 months. Sample copy for $8. Guidelines online and for #10 SASE.

*FIELD* is 100 pages, digest-sized, printed on rag stock, flat-spined, with glossy color card cover. Subscription: $16/year, $28 for 2 years. Sample: $8 postpaid. Has published poetry by Michelle Glazer, Tom Lux, Carl Phillips, Betsy Sholl, Charles Simic, Jean Valentine and translations by Marilyn Hacker and Stuart Friebert.

**MAGAZINES NEEDS** Submissions are read August 1 through May 31. Submit 2-6 of your best poems. No e-mail submissions. Include cover letter and SASE. Submit using submission manager. Pays $15/page and 2 contributor copies.

**TIPS** "Keep trying!"

## FILLING STATION

P.O. Box 22135, Bankers Hall, Calgary AB T2P 4J5, Canada. **E-mail:** mgmt@fillingstation.ca; poetry@fillingstation.ca; fiction@fillingstation.ca; nonfiction@fillingstation.ca; art@fillingstation.ca. **Website:** www.fillingstation.ca. **Contact:** Paul Zits, managing editor. *filling Station*, published 3 times/year, prints contemporary poetry, fiction, visual art, interviews, reviews, and articles. "We are looking for all forms of contemporary writing, but especially that which is innovative and/or experimental." Publishes ms 3-4 months after acceptance. Responds in 3-4 months. "After your work is reviewed by our Collective, you will receive an e-mail from an editor to let you know if your work has been selected for publication. If selected, you will later receive a second e-mail to let you know which issue your piece has been selected to appear in. Note that during the design phase, we sometimes discover the need to shuffle a piece to a future issue instead. In the event your piece is pushed back, we will inform you." Sample: $8. Subscription: $24/3 issues; $42 for 6 issues. Newsstand: $10. Writer's guidelines online at www.fillingstation.ca/submit.

**MAGAZINES NEEDS** Up to 6 pages of poetry may be sent to poetry@fillingstation.ca. A submission lacking mailing address and/or bio will be considered incomplete.

**TIPS** "*filling Station* accepts singular or simultaneous submissions of previously unpublished poetry, fiction, creative nonfiction, nonfiction, or art. We are always on the hunt for great writing!"

## FLINT HILLS REVIEW

Department of English, Modern Languages, and Journalist (Box 4019), Emporia State University, 1 Kellogg Circle, Emporia KS 66801. **E-mail:** bluestem@emporia.edu. **E-mail:** bluestem@emporia.edu. **Website:** www.emporia.edu/fhr. **Contact:** Kevin Rabas. *Flint Hills Review*, published annually, is "a regionally focused journal presenting writers of national distinction alongside new authors. *FHR* seeks work informed by a strong sense of place or region, especially Kansas and the Great Plains region. We seek to provide a publishing venue for writers of the Great Plains and Kansas while also publishing authors whose work evidences a strong sense of place, writing of literary quality, and accomplished use of language and depth of character development." Acquires one-time rights. Publishes ms 4-12 months after acceptance. Responds in 3-9 months to mss. Sample: $5.50. Guidelines online at www.emporia.edu/fhr/submit.html.

**MAGAZINES NEEDS** Wants all forms of poetry except rhyming. Does not want sentimental or gratuitous verse. Has published poetry by E. Ethelbert Miller, Elizabeth Dodd, Walt McDonald, and Gwendolyn Brooks. Include short bio. Reads submissions November-March. Pays 2 contributor copies; additional copies at discounted price.

**TIPS** "Submit writing that has strong imagery and voice, writing that is informed by place or region, writing of literary quality with depth of character development. Hone the language down to the most literary depiction possible in the shortest space that still provides depth of development without excess length."

## THE FLORIDA REVIEW

Department of English, University of Central Florida, P.O. Box 161346, Orlando FL 32816-1346. **E-mail:** flreview@ucf.edu. **Website:** floridareview.cah.ucf.edu. **Contact:** Lisa Roney, editor. "We publish fiction and essays of high literary quality—stories that delight, instruct, and take risks. Our audience consists of avid readers of fiction, poetry, graphic narrative, and creative nonfiction." Responds in 2-4 weeks to queries; in 3-8 months to mss. Sample copy: $10. Writer's guidelines online.

O Recently published work by Gerald Vizenor, Billy Collins, Sherwin Bitsui, Kelly Clancy, Denise Duhamel, Tony Hoagland, Baron Wormser, Marcia Aldrich, and Patricia Foster. As of November 2015, *The Florida Review* no longer accepts mailed submissions.

**MAGAZINES NEEDS** "We look for clear, strong poems, filled with real people, emotions, and objects. Any style will be considered." Submit via online submissions manager.

**TIPS** "We're looking for writers with fresh voices and original stories. We like risk."

## FLOYD COUNTY MOONSHINE

720 Christiansburg Pike, Floyd VA 24091. (540)745-5150. **E-mail:** floydshine@gmail.com. **Website:** www.floydcountymoonshine.org. **Contact:** Aaron Lee Moore, editor in chief. *Floyd County Moonshine*, published biannually, is a "literary and arts magazine in Floyd, Virginia, and the New River Valley. We accept poetry, short stories, and essays addressing all manner of themes; however, preference is given to those works of a rural or Appalachian nature. *Floyd County*

*Moonshine* publishes a variety of home-grown Appalachian writers in addition to writers from across the country. The mission of *Floyd County Moonshine* is to publish thought-provoking, well-crafted, free-thinking, uncensored prose and poetry. Our literature explores the dark and Gothic as well as the bright and pleasant in order to give an honest portrayal of the human condition. We aspire to publish quality literature in the local color genre, specifically writing that relates to Floyd, Virginia, and the New River Valley. Floyd and local Appalachian authors are given priority consideration; however, to stay versatile we also aspire to publish some writers from all around the country in every issue. We publish both well-established and beginning writers." Single copy: $10. Subscription: $20 for 1 year, $38 for 2 years. Writer's guidelines online.

O Wants "literature addressing rural or Appalachian themes." Has published poetry by Steve Kistulentz, Louis Gallo, Ernie Wormwood, R.T. Smith, Chelsea Adams, and Justin Askins.

**MAGAZINES NEEDS** Accepts e-mail (preferred). Submit a Word document as attachment. Accepts previously published works and simultaneous submissions on occasion. Cover letter is unnecessary. Include brief bio. Reads submissions year round. Pays 1 contributor copy.

**TIPS** "If we favor your work, it may appear in several issues, so prior contributors are also encouraged to resubmit. Every year we choose at least 1 featured author for an issue. We also nominate for Pushcart prizes, and we will do book reviews if you mail us the book."

## FLUENT MAGAZINE

245 Timber Lane, Harpers Ferry WV 25425. **E-mail:** info@fluent-magazine.com. **Website:** www.fluent-magazine.com. **Contact:** Nancy McKeithen. *FLUENT Magazine*, headquartered in West Virginia's Eastern Panhandle, is a free-subscription quarterly online magazine covering arts and culture in West Virginia, Pennsylvania, Maryland, Virginia, and the Washington DC area. "We reach an audience in four states plus other subscribers around the world. Each issue features a two-page spread by an individual poet. *FLUENT*'s broader arts and culture coverage emphasizes visual arts, and includes fiction, music, personal essays, humor and interviews drawn from the four-state region."

**MAGAZINES NEEDS** "We prefer material that has never been published. We will consider poems excerpted from previously published books and chapbooks. Explicitly sexual or violent material will likely not work for us. We feature four poets a year, devoting a two-page spread to each. We'll need your home address and phone. Brief biographical material if you care to provide it. We read all poetry with names covered-up."

## FLYWAY

Department of English, 206 Ross Hall, Iowa State University, Ames IA 50011-1201. **E-mail:** flywayjournal@gmail.com; flyway@iastate.edu. **Website:** www.flyway.org. **Contact:** Elizabeth A. Giorgi, managing editor. Based out of Iowa State University, *Flyway: Journal of Writing and Environment* publishes poetry, fiction, nonfiction, and visual art exploring the many complicated facets of the word environment—at once rural, urban, and suburban—and its social and political implications. Also open to all different interpretations of environment. Acquires first North American serial rights, electronic rights, and future anthology rights. Publishes ms 4 months after acceptance. Often comments on rejected mss. Sample copy and guidelines on website.

O    Reading period is September 15-May 15. Has published work by Rick Bass, Jacob M. Appel, Madison Smartt Bell, Jane Smiley. Also sponsors the annual fall "Notes from the Field" nonfiction contest, and the spring "Sweet Corn Prize in Fiction" short story contest. Details on website.

**MAGAZINES NEEDS** Submit up to 5 poems (combined in 1 document) only via online submission manager. Pays one-year subscription to *Flyway*.

**TIPS** "For *Flyway*, there should be tension between the environment or setting of the story and the characters in it. A well-known place should appear new, even alien and strange through the eyes and actions of the characters. We want to see an active environment, too—a setting that influences actions, triggers it's one events."

## ⊘⑤ FOGGED CLARITY

(231)670-7033. **E-mail:** editor@foggedclarity.com; submissions@foggedclarity.com. **Website:** www.foggedclarity.com. **Contact:** Editors. "*Fogged Clarity* is an arts review that accepts submissions of poetry, fiction, nonfiction, music, visual art, and reviews of work in all mediums. We seek art that is stabbingly eloquent. Our print edition is released once every year, while new issues of our online journal come out at the beginning of every month. Artists maintain the copyrights to their work until they are monetarily compensated for said work. If your work is selected for our print edition and you consent to its publication, you will be compensated." Acquires first North American serial rights. Rights revert to author upon publication. Averages 1-2 months from acceptance to publishing. Responds in 3 months to mss. Accepts queries by e-mail only. Sample copy online. Guidelines available at www.foggedclarity.com/submissions.

O    "By incorporating music and the visual arts and releasing a new issue monthly, *Fogged Clarity* aims to transcend the conventions of a typical literary journal. Our network is extensive, and our scope is as broad as thought itself; we are, you are, unconstrained. With that spirit in mind, *Fogged Clarity* examines the work of authors, artists, scholars, and musicians, providing a home for exceptional art and thought that warrants exposure."

**MAGAZINES NEEDS** Submit up to 5 poems by e-mail (submissions@foggedclarity.com) as attached .DOC or .DOCX file. Subject line should be formatted as: "Last Name: Medium of Submission." For example, "Evans: Poetry." Include brief cover letter, complete contact information, and a third-person bio.

**TIPS** "The editors appreciate artists communicating the intention of their submitted work and the influences behind it in a brief cover letter. Any artists with proposals for features or special projects should feel free to contact Ben Evans directly at editor@foggedclarity.com."

## FOLIATE OAK LITERARY MAGAZINE

University of Arkansas-Monticello, Arts & Humanities, 562 University Dr., Monticello AR 71656. **E-mail:** foliateoak@gmail.com. **Website:** www.foliateoak.com. **Contact:** Diane Payne, faculty advisor. "The *Foliate Oak Literary Magazine* is a student-run magazine accepting hybrid prose, poetry, fiction, flash, creative nonfiction and artwork." Acquires one-time, nonexclusive rights. Publishes ms an average of 1 month after acceptance. Responds in 1 week to queries; in 2 month to mss. Editorial lead time 1 month. Guidelines online.

"After you receive a rejection/acceptance notice, please wait 1 month before submitting new work. **Submission Period: August 1-April 24**. We do not read submissions during summer break. If you need to contact us for anything other than submitting your work, please write to foliateoak@gmail.com." No e-mail submissions.

**MAGAZINES NEEDS** Submit poems via online submission manager. "We enjoy poems that we understand, preferably not rhyming poems, unless you make the rhyme so fascinating we'll wonder why we ever said anything about avoiding rhymes. Give us something fresh, unexpected, and that will make us say, 'Wow!'" "No homophobic, religious rants, or pornographic, violent poems. Please avoid using offensive language." We tend to shy away from poems that rhyme.

**ALSO OFFERS** "At the end of the year, we'll use selected works from our website for the annual print anthology."

**TIPS** "Please submit all material via our online submission manager. Read our guidelines before submitting. We are eager to include multimedia submissions of videos, music, and collages. Submit your best work."

## FOLIO, A LITERARY JOURNAL AT AMERICAN UNIVERSITY

Department of Literature, American University, Washington DC 20016. (202)885-2971. **Fax:** (202)885-2938. **E-mail:** folio.editors@gmail.com. **Website:** www.american.edu/cas/literature/folio. **Contact:** Editor in chief and managing editor. "*Folio* is a nationally recognized literary journal sponsored by the College of Arts and Sciences at American University in Washington, DC. Since 1984, we have published original creative work by both new and established authors. Past issues have included work by Michael Reid Busk, Billy Collins, William Stafford, and Bruce Weigl, and interviews with Michael Cunningham, Charles Baxter, Amy Bloom, Ann Beattie, and Walter Kirn. We look for well-crafted poetry and prose that is bold and memorable." Acquires first North American serial rights. Copies available for purchase: foliolitjournal.submittable.com/submit or at Politics & Prose, Upshur Street Books, and The Potter's House. Guidelines available on website: foliolitjournal.submittable.com/submit.

Poems and prose are reviewed by editorial staff and senior editors. Press run is 250; 50-60 distributed free to the American University community and contributors. Reads submissions September 1-January 1.

**MAGAZINES NEEDS** Submit via the online submission form at foliolitjournal.submittable.com/submit. Considers simultaneous submissions "with notice." No fax, e-mail, or disk submissions. Cover letter is preferred. Include name, address, e-mail address, brief bio, and phone number. Receives about 1,000 poems/year, accepts about 25.

## FOOTHILL: A JOURNAL OF POETRY

165 E. 10th St., Claremont CA 91711. (909)607-3962. **Fax:** (909)621-8029. **E-mail:** foothill@cgu.edu. **Website:** www.cgu.edu/foothill. **Contact:** Kevin Riel; editor in chief. Directed by students at Claremont Graduate University, *Foothill: a journal of poetry*, a biannual journal, is the only literary journal devoted exclusively to poetry written by graduate students who are based in the United States. *Foothill* acquires electronic rights as well as right to print poem in year-end print journal. Rights revert to poets upon publication. Responds in 5 weeks. Sometimes comments on rejected poems. Single copy: $15. Subscription: $25. Make checks payable to CGU. Guidelines available in magazine, by e-mail, and on website.

Published online quarterly, with 1 print edition each year. Digest-sized, 72 pages, digital press, perfect bound. Press run is 500. No ads. Never publishes theme issues.

**MAGAZINES NEEDS** Accepts any poetry by graduate students (currently enrolled or recently graduated) from anywhere in the world. Students do not need to be enrolled in an MFA or writing program. Welcomes poetry submissions from those in other disciplines. Submit via e-mail. Include document as attachment in e-mail. Cover letter preferred. Poems are circulated to an editorial board. Accepts submissions year round. Welcomes submissions from beginning poets. Does not consider poetry by children or teens. No limit for poem length.

## FOURTEEN HILLS

Department of Creative Writing, San Francisco State University, 1600 Holloway Ave., San Francisco CA 94132. **Website:** www.14hills.net. "*Fourteen Hills* publishes the highest-quality innovative fiction and poetry for a literary audience." Editors change each year. Always sends prepublication galleys. Acquires one-time rights. Responds in 4-9 months to mss. Sometimes comments on rejected mss. SASE for return of ms. Sample: $10. Guidelines online.

**MAGAZINES NEEDS** Submit up to 3 poems via online submissions manager. Length: up to 70 lines/poem; ideally 30-35 lines/poem. Pays 2 contributor copies and offers discount on additional copies.

**TIPS** "Please read an issue of *Fourteen Hills* before submitting."

### THE FOURTH RIVER

Chatham University, Woodland Rd., Pittsburgh PA 15232. **E-mail:** 4thriver@gmail.com. **Website:** thefourthriver.com. *The Fourth River*, an annual publication of Chatham University's MFA in Creative Writing Programs, features literature that engages and explores the relationship between humans and their environments. Wants writings that are richly situated at the confluence of place, space, and identity, or that reflect upon or make use of landscape and place in new ways. Buys first North American serial rights. Pays with contributor copies only. Publishes mss in 5-8 months after acceptance. Responds in 3-5 months to mss. Sample copy: $5 (back issue). Single copy: $10; subscription: $16 for 2 years. Guidelines online.

**MAGAZINES NEEDS** Submit 3-5 poems via online submissions manager.

### ❶❸ FREEFALL MAGAZINE

Freefall Literary Society of Calgary, 922 Ninth Ave. SE, Calgary AB T2G 0S4, Canada. **E-mail:** editors@freefallmagazine.ca. **Website:** www.freefallmagazine.ca. **Contact:** Ryan Stromquist, managing editor. "Magazine published triannually containing fiction, poetry, creative nonfiction, essays on writing, interviews, and reviews. We are looking for exquisite writing with a strong narrative." Buys first North American serial rights (ownership reverts to author after one-time publication). Pays on publication. Guidelines and submission forms on website.

**MAGAZINES NEEDS** Submit 2-5 poems via website. Attach submission file (file name format is lastname_firstname_storytitle.doc or .docx or .pdf). Accepts any style of poetry. Length: up to 6 pages. Pays $25/poem and 1 contributor copy.

**TIPS** "Our mission is to encourage the voices of new, emerging, and experienced Canadian writers and provide a platform for their quality work."

### ❺ FREEXPRESSION

P.O. Box 4, West Hoxton NSW 2171, Australia. (02)96075559. **E-mail:** editor@freexpression.com.au. **Website:** www.freexpression.com.au. **Contact:** Peter F. Pike, managing editor. *FreeXpresSion*, published monthly, contains "creative writing, how-to articles, short stories, and poetry, including cinquain, haiku, etc., and bush verse." Open to all forms. "Christian themes OK. Humorous material welcome. No gratuitous sex; bad language OK. We don't want to see anything degrading." Purchases first Australian rights. Publishes ms 2 months after acceptance. Responds in 1 month. Subscription: $15 AUS for 3 months, $32 AUS for 6 months, $60 AUS for 1 year. Guidelines available in magazine, for SAE and IRC, or by fax or e-mail.

⬤ *FreeXpresSion* also publishes books up to 200 pages **through subsidy arrangements with authors.** Some poems published throughout the year are used in *Yearbooks* (annual anthologies). *FreeXpresSion* is 32 pages, magazine-sized, offset-printed, saddle-stapled, full color. Receives about 3,500 poems/year, accepts about 30%.

**MAGAZINES NEEDS** Submit 3-4 poems at a time. Accepts e-mail (pasted into body of message) and disk submissions. Cover letter is preferred. Has published poetry by many prize-winning poets like Ron Stevens, Ellis Campbell, Brenda Joy, David Campbell, and Max and Jacqui Merckenschlager. Length: "Very long poems are not desired but would be considered."

**ALSO OFFERS** Sponsors an annual contest with 3 categories for poetry: blank verse (up to 120 lines); traditional verse (up to 120 lines), and haiku. 1st Prize in blank verse: $250 AUS; 2nd Prize: $100 AUS; 1st Prize in traditional rhyming poetry: $250 AUS; 2nd Prize: $100 AUS. Haiku, 1st Prize $120 AUS; 2nd Prize $80 AUS; 3rd Prize $50 AUS. Guidelines and entry form available by e-mail or download from website.

### ❺ THE FRIEND

The Friend Publications Ltd, 173 Euston Rd., London England NW1 2BJ, United Kingdom. (44)(207)663-1010. **Fax:** (44)(207)663-1182. **E-mail:** editorial@thefriend.org. **Website:** www.thefriend.org. Completely independent, *The Friend* brings readers news and views from a Quaker perspective, as well as from a wide range of authors whose writings are of interest to Quakers and non-Quakers alike. There are articles on issues such as peace, spirituality, Quaker belief, and ecumenism, as well as news of Friends from Britain and abroad. Guidelines online.

○ Prefers queries, but sometimes accepts unsolicited mss.

**MAGAZINES NEEDS** There are no rules regarding poetry, but doesn't want particularly long poems.

## THE FRIEND MAGAZINE

The Church of Jesus Christ of Latter-day Saints, 50 E. North Temple St., Salt Lake City UT 84150. **E-mail:** friend@ldschurch.org. **Website:** www.lds.org/friend. **Contact:** Paul B. Pieper, editor; Mark W. Robison, art director. "The *Friend* is published by The Church of Jesus Christ of Latter-day Saints for boys and girls up to 3-12 years of age." Online.

**MAGAZINES NEEDS** Pays $30 for poems.

## ☕ THE FROGMORE PAPERS

21 Mildmay Rd., Lewes, East Sussex BN7 1PJ, England. **Website:** www.frogmorepress.co.uk. **Contact:** Jeremy Page, editor. *The Frogmore Papers*, published semiannually, is a literary magazine with emphasis on new poetry and short stories. Responds in 6 months. Subscription: £10 for 1 year (2 issues); £15 for 2 years (4 issues). Guidelines online.

○ *The Frogmore Papers* is 46 pages, photocopied in photo-reduced typescript, saddle-stapled, with matte card cover. Accepts 2% of poetry received. Press run is 500. Reading periods: October 1-31 for March issue and April 1-30 for September issue.

**MAGAZINES NEEDS** "Poems where the form drives the meaning are unlikely to find favour. Poems written by people who clearly haven't read any poetry since Wordsworth will not find favour. Prose may be experimental or traditional, but is unlikely to be accepted if it's either very experimental or very traditional." Has published poetry by Marita Over, Brian Aldiss, Carole Satyamurti, John Mole, Linda France, and Tobias Hill. Submit 4-6 poems by e-mail or mail (postal submissions only accepted from within the UK). Length: 20-80 lines/poem. Pays 1 contributor copy.

**ALSO OFFERS** Sponsors the annual Frogmore Poetry Prize. Write for information.

## FROGPOND: JOURNAL OF THE HAIKU SOCIETY OF AMERICA

Haiku Society of America, P.O. Box 26347, Knoxville TN 37912. **E-mail:** frogpondhsa@gmail.com. **Website:** www.hsa-haiku.org/frogpond. **Contact:** Aubrie Cox, editor. *Frogpond*, published triannually, is the international journal of the Haiku Society of America, an affiliate of the American Literature Association. Its primary function is to "publish the best in contemporary English-language haiku and senryu, linked forms including sequences, renku, rengay, and haibun, essays and articles on these forms, and book reviews." Responds at the end of each submission period (June 1-August 1; September 15-November 15; February 15-April 15). Single issue: $14. Subscription: USA, $35/year; Canada/Mexico, $37/year; for seniors and students in North America, $30; elsewhere, $47/year. Guidelines available for SASE or on website. Detailed instructions on website.

**MAGAZINES NEEDS** Submissions to *Frogpond* by e-mail are preferred. "Postal submissions should be accompanied by SASE with sufficient U.S. postage to reach your location. Submit to fnbanwarth@yahoo.com or 985 S. Grandview, Dubuque, IA."

**ALSO OFFERS** The "Best of Issue" prize is awarded to a poem from each issue of *Frogpond* through a gift from the Museum of Haiku Literature, located in Tokyo. The Haiku Society of America also sponsors a number of other contests, most of which have cash prizes: The Harold G. Henderson Haiku Award Contest, the Gerald Brady Senryu Award Contest, the Bernard Lionel Einbond Memorial Renku Contest, the HSA Haibun Contest, the Nicholas A. Virgilio Memorial Haiku Competition for High School Students, the Mildred Kanterman Merit Book Awards for outstanding books in the haiku field. Guidelines available on website.

## ⑤ FUGUE LITERARY MAGAZINE

200 Brink Hall, University of Idaho, P.O. Box 44110, Moscow ID 83844. **E-mail:** fugue@uidaho.edu. **Website:** www.fuguejournal.com. **Contact:** Alexandra Teague, faculty advisor. Biannual literary magazine. "Submissions are accepted online only. Poetry, fiction, and nonfiction submissions are accepted September 1-April 1. All material received outside of this period will not be read." $3 submission fee per entry. See website for submission instructions. Responds in 3-6 months to mss. Sample copy: $8. Guidelines online.

Work published in *Fugue* has won the Pushcart Prize and has been cited in *Best American Essays*.

**MAGAZINES NEEDS** Submit up to 3 poems using online submissions manager. Pays 2 contributor copies and additional payment.

**ALSO OFFERS** "For information regarding our annual prose and poetry contest, please visit our website."

**TIPS** "The best way, of course, to determine what we're looking for is to read the journal. As the name *Fugue* indicates, our goal is to present a wide range of literary perspectives. We like stories that satisfy us both intellectually and emotionally, with fresh language and characters so captivating that they stick with us and invite a second reading. We are also seeking creative literary criticism which illuminates a piece of literature or a specific writer by examining that writer's personal experience."

## GARGOYLE

Paycock Press, 3819 13th St. N, Arlington VA 22201. (703)525-9296. **E-mail:** rchrdpeabody9@gmail.com. **Website:** www.gargoylemagazine.com. **Contact:** Richard Peabody, editor; Lucinda Ebersole, co-editor. "*Gargoyle* has always been a scallywag magazine, a maverick magazine, a bit too academic for the underground and way too underground for the academics. We are a writer's magazine in that we are read by other writers and have never worried about reaching the masses." Annual. Acquires first North American rights, which revert to the authors upon publication. "We do retain the right to load work onto our website or to collect in a 'best of' anthology down the road." Publishes ms 1 year after acceptance. Responds in 1 month to queries, proposals, and mss. Sample copy: $12.95. Catalog online at FAQ link. "We don't have guidelines; we have never believed in them." Query in an e-mail. "We prefer electronic submissions. Please use submission engine online." For snail mail, send SASE for reply and return of ms, or send a disposable copy of ms.

**MAGAZINES NEEDS** Pays 1 contributor copy and offers 50% discount on additional copies.

**TIPS** "We have to fall in love with a particular fiction."

## A GATHERING OF THE TRIBES

P.O. Box 20693, Tompkins Square Station, New York NY 10009. (212)777-2038. **E-mail:** gatheringofthetribes@gmail.com. **E-mail:** tribes.editor@gmail.com.

**Website:** www.tribes.org. **Contact:** Steve Cannon. *A Gathering of the Tribes* is a multicultural and multigenerational publication featuring poetry, fiction, interviews, essays, visual art, and musical scores. Audience is anyone interested in the arts from a diverse perspective." Publishes ms 3-6 months after acceptance. "Due to the massive number of submissions we receive, we do not guarantee responses or return work that is not accepted for publication." Sample copy: $15. Guidelines on website.

**MAGAZINES NEEDS** Submit up to 5 poems by postal mail or e-mail. No metrical or rhyming poetry, "unless it is exceedingly contemporary/experimental." Pays 1 contributor copy.

**TIPS** "Make sure your work has substance."

## THE GEORGIA REVIEW

The University of Georgia, Main Library, Room 706A, 320 S. Jackson St., Athens GA 30602. (706)542-3481. **Fax:** (706)542-0047. **E-mail:** garev@uga.edu. **Website:** thegeorgiareview.com. **Contact:** Stephen Corey, editor. "Our readers are inquisitive people and avid consumers of art and literature. All work submitted should be marked by singularity of vision, exceptional skillfulness of craft, and thoughtful engagement with the contemporary world." Electronic submissions available for $3 fee. Reading period: August 15-May 15. Buys first North American serial rights. Pays on publication. Publishes ms an average of 6 months after acceptance. Responds in 2 weeks to queries; in 2-3 months to mss. Sample copy: $10. Guidelines online.

**MAGAZINES NEEDS** "We seek original, excellent poetry." Submit 3-5 poems at a time. Pays $4/line.

## GERTRUDE

P.O. Box 28281, Portland OR 97228. **E-mail:** editor@gertrudepress.org. *Gertrude*, the annual literary arts journal of Gertrude Press, is a "publication featuring the voices and visions of the gay, lesbian, bisexual, transgender, and supportive community." Responds in 9-12 months to mss. Sample copy: $8. Subscription: $18 for 1 year, $32 for 2 years.

**MAGAZINES NEEDS** Has published poetry by Judith Barrington, Deanna Kern Ludwin, Casey Charles, Michael Montlack, Megan Kruse, and Noah Tysick. Submit up to 6 poems via online submissions manager. Length: open, but "poems less than 60 lines are preferable."

**TIPS** "We look for strong characterization and imagery, and new, unique ways of writing about universal experiences. Follow the construction of your work until the ending. Many stories start out with zest, then flipper and die. Show us, don't tell us."

## THE GETTYSBURG REVIEW

Gettysburg College, Gettysburg College, 300 N. Washington St., Gettysburg PA 17325. (717)337-6770. **Fax:** (717)337-6775. **E-mail:** mdrew@gettysburg.edu. **Website:** www.gettysburgreview.com. **Contact:** Mark Drew, editor; Ellen Hathaway, managing editor. Published quarterly, *The Gettysburg Review* considers unsolicited submissions of poetry, fiction, and essays. "Our concern is quality. Mss submitted here should be extremely well written." Reading period September 1-May 31. Buys first North American serial rights. Pays on publication. Publishes ms an average of 6 months after acceptance. Responds in 1 month to queries; in 3-5 months to mss. Editorial lead time 1 year. Sample: $15. Guidelines online.

**MAGAZINES NEEDS** Considers "well-written poems of all kinds on all subjects." Has published poetry by Rita Dove, Alice Friman, Philip Schultz, Michelle Boisseau, Bob Hicok, Linda Pastan, and G.C. Waldrep. Does not want sentimental, clichéd verse. Pays $2/line, a one-year subscription, and 1 contributor copy.

## GINOSKO LITERARY JOURNAL

73 Sais Ave., San Anselmo CA 94960. (415)785-3160. **E-mail:** editorginosko@aol.com. **Website:** www.ginoskoliteraryjournal.com. **Contact:** Robert Paul Cesaretti, editor. "*Ginosko* (ghin-océ-koe): To perceive, understand, realize, come to know; knowledge that has an inception, a progress, an attainment. The recognition of truth by experience." Accepting short fiction and poetry, creative nonfiction, interviews, social justice concerns, and literary insights for www.ginoskoliteraryjournal.com. Copyright reverts to author. Editorial lead time 1-2 months. Guidelines online.

Reads year round. Length of articles flexible; accepts excerpts. Publishing as semiannual e-zine. Print anthology every 2 years. Check downloadable issues on website for tone and style. Downloads free; accepts donations. Member CLMP.

**MAGAZINES NEEDS** Submit via postal mail, e-mail (prefers attachments: WPS, DOC, or RTF), or online submissions manager (ginosko.submittable.com/submit).

## GRAIN

P.O. Box 3986, Regina SK S4P 3R9, Canada. (306)791-7749. **Fax:** (306)565-8554. **E-mail:** grainmag@skwriter.com. **Website:** www.grainmagazine.ca. "*Grain, The Journal of Eclectic Writing* is a literary quarterly that publishes engaging, diverse, and challenging writing and art by some of the best Canadian and international writers and artists. Every issue features superb new writing from both developing and established writers. Each issue also highlights the unique artwork of a different visual artist. *Grain* has garnered national and international recognition for its distinctive, cutting-edge content and design." Acquires first Canadian serial rights. Pays on publication. Responds in 6 months to mss. Sample: $13 CAD. Subscription: $35 CAD/year, $55 CAD for 2 years. (See website for U.S. and foreign postage fees.) Guidelines online.

*Grain* is 112-128 pages, digest-sized, professionally printed. Press run is 1,100. Receives about 3,000 submissions/year. **Submissions are read September 1-May 31 only.** Mss postmarked June 1-August 31 will not be read.

**MAGAZINES NEEDS** Wants "high-quality, imaginative, well-crafted poetry." Postal submissions only. Send typed, unpublished material only (considers work published online to be previously published). Has published poetry by Lorna Crozier, Don Domanski, Cornelia Haeussler, Patrick Lane, Karen Solie, and Monty Reid. Length: up to 6 pages. Pays $50/page ($250 maximum) and 3 contributor copies.

**TIPS** "Only work of the highest literary quality is accepted. Read several back issues."

## GRASSLIMB

P.O. Box 420816, San Diego CA 92142. **E-mail:** editor@grasslimb.com. **Website:** www.grasslimb.com. **Contact:** Valerie Polichar, editor. "*Grasslimb* publishes literary prose, poetry, and art. Fiction is best when it is short and avant-garde or otherwise experimental." Acquires first print publication serial rights. Responds in 4 months to mss. Rarely comments on rejected mss. Sample copy: $3. Guidelines for SASE, e-mail, or on website.

**MAGAZINES NEEDS** Submit poems via e-mail or postal mail with SASE. Pays $5-20/poem.

**TIPS** "We publish brief fiction work that can be read in a single sitting over a cup of coffee. Work is generally 'literary' in nature rather than mainstream. Experimental work welcome. Remember to have your work proofread and to send short work. We cannot read over 3,000 words and prefer under 2,000 words. Include word count."

## THE GREAT AMERICAN POETRY SHOW

Eavesdropping on the Cosmos, LLC, P.O. Box 691197, West Hollywood California 90069. (310)935-8417. E-mail: larry@tgaps.com. E-mail: larry@tgaps.com. Website: www.tgaps.net. Contact: Larry Ziman, editor/publisher. *The Great American Poetry Show* is a hardcover, serial, poetry anthology. "Volume 1, published in 2005 with 150 pages, featured 113 poems from 83 poets. Volume 2, published in 2010 with 176 pages, featured 134 poems from 92 poets. And Volume 3, published in 2015 with 181 pages, featured 135 poems from 73 poets." Press run for each volume was 1,000. Print and reprint rights specified by contract; poets keep copyrights to their poems. Responds usually within 1-4 weeks ("depends on how busy we are"). Single copy: $35 (print), $.99 (pdf download only). Submit whatever poems whenever in the body of an e-mail or submit your poems in just one e-mail attachment. No stamped-mail submissions.

◌ *The Great American Poetry Show* is sheet-fed offset-printed, perfect-bound, with cloth cover and art/graphics.

**MAGAZINES NEEDS** Submit any number and length of poems at a time. Accepts e-mail submissions in body of e-mail or as one attachment. Cover letter is optional. No stamped-mail submissions. "If we reject a submission of your work, please send us another group to go through." Has published poetry by Brad Johnson, Carol Carpenter, Philip Wexler, Fredrick Zydek, Patricia Polak, Steve De France, Lois Swann, Alan Catlin, Sarah Brown Weitzman, Kevin Pilkington, Susan Sonde, Doug Ramspeck, Leonard Orr, and Julie M. Tate. Wants poems on any subject, in any style, of any length. Pays 2 contributor copies.

**TIPS** "Please visit our website with over 10,000 links to articles, essays, interviews, reviews, magazines, publishers, and blogs."

## ◒ GREEN HILLS LITERARY LANTERN

Truman State University, Department of English, Truman State University, Kirksville MO 63501. E-mail: adavis@truman.edu. Website: ghll.truman.edu. Contact: Adam Brooke Davis, managing editor; Joe Benevento, poetry editor. *Green Hills Literary Lantern* is published annually, in June, by Truman State University. Historically, the print publication ran

between 200-300 pages, consisting of poetry, fiction, reviews, and interviews. The digital magazine is of similar proportions and artistic standards. Open to the work of new writers, as well as more established writers. Holds all rights, but returns rights to author on request. Does not provide payment. Publishes ms an average of 6 months after acceptance. Responds in 2 months to mss and queries. Sample copies online. Guidelines online.

**MAGAZINES NEEDS** "We prefer poetry written by poets who are more interested in communicating something that seems important, beautiful, funny, or interesting to them than they are in making themselves seem erudite, clever, or in the know. We pay attention to all the usual things—command of line; attention to the sound, rhythm, and imagery; arresting figurative language—but we also seek poetry that has some investment of real feeling rather than bloodless exhibitions of technical talent." Length: up to 60 lines/poem.

## GREEN MOUNTAINS REVIEW

Johnson State College, 337 College Hill, Johnson VT 05656. (802)635-1350. E-mail: gmr@jsc.edu. Website: greenmountainsreview.com. Contact: Elizabeth Powell, editor; Jessica Hendry Nelson, nonfiction editor; Jacob White, fiction editor; Ben Aleshire, assistant poetry editor. Semiannual magazine covering poems, stories, and creative nonfiction by both well-known authors and promising newcomers. Acquires first North American serial rights. Rights revert to author upon request. Publishes ms 6-12 months after acceptance. Responds in 1 month to queries; in 6 months to mss. Sample copy: $7. Guidelines available free.

◌ The editors are open to a wide range of styles and subject matter. Open reading period: September 1-March 1.

**MAGAZINES NEEDS** Submit poems via online submissions manager. Has published poetry by Carol Frost, Sharon Olds, Carl Phillips, David St. John, and David Wojahn.

**TIPS** "We encourage you to order some of our back issues to acquaint yourself with what has been accepted in the past."

## GREENPRINTS

P.O. Box 1355, Fairview NC 28730. (828)628-1902. E-mail: pat@greenprints.com. Website: www.greenprints.com. Contact: Pat Stone, managing editor. "*GreenPrints* is the 'Weeder's Digest.' We share the human—*not* how-to—side of gardening. We publish true personal gardening stories and essays: humorous, heartfelt, insightful, inspiring." Buys first North American serial rights. Responds in 3 months to mss. No editorial lead time. Sample: $5. Guidelines online.

○ "We love good, true, well-told personal *stories*— all must be about gardening!"

**MAGAZINES NEEDS** "If it's not hands-on and gardening based, please don't send it." Pays $25.

**TIPS** Wants "a great, true, *unique* personal *story* with dialogue, a narrative, and something special that happens to make it truly stand out."

### ● THE GREENSBORO REVIEW

MFA Writing Program, 3302 HHRA Building, UNC-Greensboro, Greensboro NC 27402. (336)334-5459. **E-mail:** jlclark@uncg.edu. **Website:** greensbororeview. submittable.com/submit. **Contact:** Jim Clark, editor. "A local lit mag with an international reputation. We've been 'old school' since 1965." Acquires first North American serial rights. Responds in about 4 months. Sample copy: $8. Guidelines online.

○ Stories for *The Greensboro Review* have been included in *Best American Short Stories, The O. Henry Awards Prize Stories, New Stories from The South* and *Pushcart Prize.* Does not accept e-mail submissions.

**MAGAZINES NEEDS** Submit via online submission form. Include cover letter. Length: no length limit. Pays contributor copies.

**TIPS** "We want to see the best being written regardless of theme, subject, or style."

### THE GRIFFIN

Gwynedd Mercy College, 1325 Sumneytown Pike, P.O. Box 901, Gwynedd Valley PA 19437-0901. (215)641-5518. **Fax:** (215)641-5552. **E-mail:** allego.d@gmercyu. edu. **Website:** www.gmercyu.edu/about-gwynedd-mercy/publications/griffin. **Contact:** Dr. Donna M. Allego, editor. Published by Gwynedd Mercy University, *The Griffin* is a literary journal for the creative writer—subscribing to the belief that improving the human condition requires dedication to and respect for the individual and the community. Seeks works which explore universal qualities—truth, justice, integrity, compassion, mercy. Publishes poetry, short stories, short plays, and reflections. Does not buy rights. Publishes an average of 12 months after acceptance. Responds in 9 months to ms. Sample copy available on website. Guidelines available on website.

**MAGAZINES NEEDS** Any style of well-crafted verse considered. Submit complete poems via e-mail or on disk with a hard copy. Include short author bio. Length: up to 30 lines/poem.

**TIPS** "Pay attention to the word length requirements, the mission of the magazine, and how to submit ms as set forth. These constitute the writer's guidelines listed online."

### GUERNICA MAGAZINE

112 W. 27th St., Suite 600, New York NY 10001. **E-mail:** editors@guernicamag.com; art@guernicamag. com; publisher@guernicamag.com. **Website:** www. guernicamag.com. **Contact:** See masthead online for specific editors. "*Guernica* is called a 'great online literary magazine' by *Esquire. Guernica* contributors come from dozens of countries and write in nearly as many languages." Publishes mss 3-4 months from acceptance. Responds in 2 months. Guidelines online.

○ Received Caine Prize for African Writing, Best of the Net.

**MAGAZINES NEEDS** Submit 3-5 poems via online submissions manager. Accepts 15-20 poems/year. Has published James Galvin, Barbara Hamby, Terrance Hayes, Richard Howard.

**TIPS** "Please read the magazine first before submitting. Most stories that are rejected simply do not fit our approach. Submission guidelines online."

### GULF COAST: A JOURNAL OF LITERATURE AND FINE ARTS

4800 Calhoun Rd., Houston TX 77204-3013. (713)743-3223. **E-mail:** editors@gulfcoastmag.org. **Website:** www.gulfcoastmag.org. **Contact:** Adrienne Perry, editor; Martin Rock, managing editor; Carlos Hernandez, digital editor; Henk Rossouw, Luisa Muradyan, and Erika Jo Brown, poetry editors; Jennifer McFarland, Dino Piacentini, and Joshua Foster, fiction editors; Georgia Pearle and Nathan Stabenfeldt, nonfiction editors; Matthew Salesses, online fiction editor; Christopher Murray, online poetry editor; Melanie Brkich, online nonfiction editor. Buys first North American serial rights. Publishes ms 6 months-1 year after acceptance. Responds in 4-6 months to mss. Sometimes comments on rejected mss. Back issue: $8, plus 7x10 SASE with 4 first-class stamps. Writer's guidelines for #10 SASE or on website.

**MAGAZINES NEEDS** Submit up to 5 poems at a time. Considers simultaneous submissions with notification; no previously published poems. Cover letter is required. List previous publications and include a brief bio. Reads submissions September-April. Pays $50/page.

**TIPS** "Submit only previously unpublished works. Include a cover letter. Online submissions are strongly preferred. Stories or essays should be typed, double-spaced, and paginated with your name, address, and phone number on the first page and the title on subsequent pages. Poems should have your name, address, and phone number on the first page of each." The Annual Gulf Coast Prizes award publication and $1,500 each in poetry, fiction, and nonfiction; opens in December of each year. Honorable mentions in each category will receive a $250 second prize. Postmark/online entry deadline: March 22 of each year. Winners and honorable mentions will be announced in May. **Entry fee:** $23 (includes one-year subscription). Make checks payable to *Gulf Coast*. Guidelines available on website.

## GULF STREAM MAGAZINE

English Department, FIU, Biscayne Bay Campus, 3000 NE 151 St., AC1-335, North Miami FL 33181. **E-mail:** gulfstreamlitmag@gmail.com. **Website:** www.gulfstreamlitmag.com. **Contact:** Miguel Pichardo, editor-in-chief. "*Gulf Stream Magazine* has been publishing emerging and established writers of exceptional fiction, nonfiction, and poetry since 1989. We also publish interviews and book reviews. Past contributors include Sherman Alexie, Steve Almond, Jan Beatty, Lee Martin, Robert Wrigley, Dennis Lehane, Liz Robbins, Stuart Dybek, David Kirby, Ann Hood, Ha Jin, B.H. Fairchild, Naomi Shihab Nye, F. Daniel Rzicznek, and Connie May Fowler. *Gulf Stream Magazine* is supported by the Creative Writing Program at Florida International University in Miami, Florida. Each year we publish 2 online issues." Acquires first serial rights. Responds in 6 months. Guidelines online.

**MAGAZINES NEEDS** "Submit online only. Please read guidelines on website in full. Submissions that do not conform to our guidelines will be discarded. We do not accept e-mailed or mailed submissions. We read from September 1-November 1 and January 1-March 1." Cover letter is required. Wants "poetry of any style and subject matter as long as it's of high literary quality." Has published poetry by Robert Wrigley, Jan Beatty, Jill Bialosky, and Catherine Bowman.

**TIPS** "Looks for fresh, original writing—well-plotted stories with unforgettable characters, fresh po-

etry, and experimental writing. Usually longer stories do not get accepted. There are exceptions, however."

## HAIGHT ASHBURY LITERARY JOURNAL

558 Joost Ave., San Francisco CA 94127. (415)584-8264. **E-mail:** haljeditor@gmail.com. **Website:** haightashburyliteraryjournal.wordpress.com; www.facebook.com/pages/Haight-Ashbury-Literary-Journal/365542018331. **Contact:** Alice Rogoff and Cesar Love, editors. *Haight Ashbury Literary Journal*, publishes "well-written poetry and fiction. *HALJ*'s voices are often of people who have been marginalized, oppressed, or abused. *HALJ* strives to bring literary arts to the general public, to the San Francisco community of writers, to the Haight Ashbury neighborhood, and to people of varying ages, genders, ethnic groups, and sexual preferences. The journal is produced as a tabloid to maintain an accessible price for low-income people." Rights revert to author. Responds in 4 months. Sample: $6. Subscription: $14 for 2 issues, $28 for 4 issues; $75 for back issues and future issues. Guidelines available for SASE.

**MAGAZINES NEEDS** Submit up to 6 poems at a time. Submit only once every 6 months. No e-mail submissions (unless overseas); postal submissions only. "Please type 1 poem to a page, put name and address on every page, and include SASE. No bio." Sometimes publishes theme issues (each issue changes its theme and emphasis). Has published poetry by Dan O'Connell, Diane Frank, Dancing Bear, Lee Herrick, Al Young, and Laura Beausoleil.

## 🜚 HANGING LOOSE

Hanging Loose Press, 231 Wyckoff St., Brooklyn NY 11217. **E-mail:** print225@aol.com. **Website:** www.hanginloosepress.com. **Contact:** Robert Hershon and Mark Pawlak, editors. *Hanging Loose*, published in April and October, concentrates on the work of new writers. Wants excellent, energetic poems and short stories. Responds in 3 months. Sample copy: $14. Guidelines online.

> *Hanging Loose* is 120 pages, offset-printed on heavy stock, flat-spined, with 4-color glossy card cover.

**MAGAZINES NEEDS** Submit up to 6 poems at a time by postal mail with SASE. "Would-be contributors should read the magazine first." Has published poetry by Sherman Alexie, Paul Violi, Donna Brook, Kimiko Hahn, Harvey Shapiro, and Ha Jin. Considers poetry by teens (1 section contains poems by high-school-age poets). Pays small fee and 2 contributor copies.

**ALSO OFFERS** Hanging Loose Press does not consider unsolicited book mss or artwork.

### HARPUR PALATE

English Department, Binghamton University, P.O. Box 6000, Binghamton NY 13902-6000. **E-mail:** harpur.palate@gmail.com. **Website:** harpurpalate. blogspot.com. **Contact:** Sri Siddhi N. Upadhyay, editor in chief; Liam Meilleur, editor in chief and fiction editor; Carolyn Keller, managing editor and nonfiction editor; Brian Kelly, poetry editor; Roberta Borger, fiction editor. *Harpur Palate*, published biannually, is "dedicated to publishing the best poetry and prose, regardless of style, form, or genre. We have no restrictions on subject matter or form. Quite simply, send us your highest-quality fiction and poetry." Buys first North American serial rights, electronic rights. Publishes ms an average of 1-2 months after acceptance. Responds in 1-3 week to queries; in 2-4 months to mss. No response without SASE. Sometimes comments on rejected mss. Accepts simultaneous submissions if stated in the cover letter. Sample copy: $8. Current issue: $12. Subscription: $18/year (2 issues). Make checks payable to *Harpur Palate*. Guidelines online.

○ Submission periods are September 1-November 15 for the Winter issue and February 1-April 15 for the Summer issue.

**MAGAZINES NEEDS** Prefers submissions through online submissions manager, or send poems by postal mail with SASE. No more than 1 submission per envelope. Reads submissions during open submission period only. Poems are circulated to an editorial board. Seldom comments on rejected poems. Has published poetry by Sherman Alexie, Tess Gallagher, Alex Lemon, Marvin Bell, Ryan G. Van Cleave, Sascha Feinstein, Allison Joseph, Neil Shepard, and Ruth Stone. Length: up to 10 pages total. Pays 2 contributor copies.

**TIPS** "We are interested in high-quality writing of all genres but especially literary poetry and fiction. We also sponsor a fiction contest for the Summer issue and a poetry and nonfiction contest for the Winter issue with $500 prizes."

### HARTWORKS

D.C. Creative Writing Workshop, 601 Mississippi Ave. SE, Washington DC 20032. (202)297-1957. **Fax:** (202)645-3426. **E-mail:** info@dccww.org. **Website:**

www.dccww.org. **Contact:** Nancy Schwalb, artistic director. *hArtworks* appears 3 times/year. "We publish the poetry of Hart Middle School students (as far as we know, Hart may be the only public middle school in the U.S. with its own poetry magazine) and the writing of guest writers such as Nikki Giovanni, Alan Cheuse, Arnost Lustig, Henry Taylor, Mark Craver, and Cornelius Eady, along with interviews between the kids and the grown-up pros. We also publish work by our writers-in-residence, who teach workshops at Hart, and provide trips to readings, slams, museums, and plays." Wants "vivid, precise, imaginative language that communicates from the heart as well as the head." Does not want "poetry that only 'sounds' good; it also needs to say something meaningful." Has published poetry by Maryum Abdullah, Myron Jones, Nichell Kee, Kiana Murphy, James Tindle, and Sequan Wilson. Single copy: $12; subscription: $30. Make checks payable to D.C. Creative Writing Workshop.

○ Although this journal doesn't accept submissions from the general public, it's included here as an outstanding example of what a literary journal can be (for anyone of any age). *hArtworks* is 92 pages, magazine-sized, professionally printed, perfect bound, with card cover. Receives about 1,000 poems/year, accepts about 20%. Press run is 500; 100 distributed free to writers, teachers.

**MAGAZINES NEEDS** "Writers-in-residence solicit most submissions from their classes, and then a committee of student editors makes the final selections. Each year, our second issue is devoted to responses to the Holocaust."

### HARVARD REVIEW

Lamont Library, Harvard University, Cambridge MA 02138. (617)495-9775. **E-mail:** info@harvardreview. org. **Website:** harvardreview.fas.harvard.edu. **Contact:** Christina Thompson, editor; Suzanne Berne, fiction editor; Major Jackson, poetry editor. Semiannual magazine covering poetry, fiction, essays, drama, graphics, and reviews in the spring and fall by an eclectic range of international writers. "Previous contributors include John Updike, Alice Hoffman, Joyce Carol Oates, Miranda July, and Jim Crace. We also publish the work of emerging and previously unpublished writers." Responds in 6 months to mss. Guidelines online.

○ Does not accept e-mail submissions. Reading period: November 1-May 31.

**MAGAZINES NEEDS** Submit up to 5 poems via online submissions manager or postal mail.

**TIPS** "Writers at all stages of their careers are invited to apply; however, we can only publish a very small fraction of the material we receive. We recommend that you familiarize yourself with *Harvard Review* before you submit your work."

## HAWAI'I PACIFIC REVIEW

**Website:** hawaiipacificreview.org. **Contact:** Tyler Mc-Mahon, editor; Christa Cushon and Jordana Dintruff, managing editors. "*Hawai'i Pacific Review* is the on-line literary magazine of Hawai'i Pacific University. It features poetry and prose by authors from Hawai'i, the mainland, and around the world. *HPR* was started as a print annual in 1987. In 2013, it began to publish exclusively online. *HPR* publishes work on a rolling basis. Poems, stories, and essays are posted 1 piece at a time, several times a month. All contents are archived on the site." Acquires online rights. All other rights remain with the author.

**MAGAZINES NEEDS** Submit up to 3 poems at a time via online submissions manager (each poem should be a separate submission). "Because we try to be readable on all sorts of screens and devices, we can't do justice to poems with unorthodox spacing. For this reason, we strongly prefer poetry that sticks to the left margin."

**TIPS** "We look for the unusual or original plot, and prose with the texture and nuance of poetry. Character development or portrayal must be unusual/original; humanity shown in an original insightful way (or characters); sense of humor where applicable. Be sure it's a draft that has gone through substantial changes, with supervision from a more experienced writer, if you're a beginner. Write about intense emotion and feeling, not just about someone's divorce or shaky relationship. No soap-opera-like fiction."

## HAWAI'I REVIEW

University of Hawaii Board of Publications, 2445 Campus Rd., Hemenway Hall 107, Honolulu HI 96822. (808)956-3030. **Fax:** (808)956-3083. **E-mail:** hawaiireview@gmail.com. **Website:** www.kaleo.org/hawaii_review. *Hawai'i Review* is a student-run biannual literary and visual arts print journal featuring national

and international writing and visual art, as well as regional literature and visual art of Hawai'i and the Pacific. Buys first North American serial rights, archive rights. Publishes ms an average of 3 months after acceptance. Responds in 3 months to mss. Sample copy: free, plus $5 shipping (back issue). Single copy: $12.50. Guidelines online.

○ Accepts submissions online through Submittable only. Offers yearly award with $500 prizes in poetry and fiction.

**MAGAZINES NEEDS** Submit up to 6 poems via online submission manager. Length: up to 500 lines/poem (though space limitations are taken into account for longer poems).

**TIPS** "Make it new."

## ◐⑤ HAYDEN'S FERRY REVIEW

c/o Dept. of English,, Arizona State University, P.O. Box 870302, Tempe AZ 85287. **Website:** haydensferryreview.com. **Contact:** Editorial staff changes every year; see website for current masthead. "*Hayden's Ferry Review* publishes the best-quality fiction, poetry, and creative nonfiction from new, emerging, and established writers." Buys first North American serial rights. Publishes ms an average of 6 months after acceptance. Responds in 6 months to mss. Editorial lead time 5 months. Sample copy: $13. Guidelines online.

○ Work from *Hayden's Ferry Review* has been selected for inclusion in *Pushcart Prize* anthologies and *Best Creative Nonfiction*. No longer accepts postal mail or e-mail submissions.

**MAGAZINES NEEDS** Submit up to 6 poems via online submissions manager. Pays 2 contributor copies and one-year subscription.

## HELIOTROPE

**E-mail:** heliotropeditor@gmail.com. **Website:** www.heliotropemag.com. *Heliotrope* is a quarterly e-zine that publishes fiction, articles, and poetry. Buys first world electronic rights with 120-day exclusivity, first print rights for series of chapbooks, nonexclusive anthology rights. Pays on publication. Responds in 1 month to mss. Guidelines online.

**MAGAZINES NEEDS** Submit via e-mail. Pays $50.

## ❤️⊘ THE HELIX

**E-mail:** helixmagazine@gmail.com. **Website:** helix-magazine.org. **Contact:** See masthead online for current editorial staff. "*The Helix* is a Central Connecticut State University publication, and it puts out an issue every semester. It accepts submissions from all over the globe. The magazine features writing from CCSU students, writing from the Hartford County community, and an array of submissions from all over the world. The magazine publishes multiple genres of literature and art, including poetry, fiction, drama, nonfiction, paintings, photography, watercolor, collage, stencil, and computer-generated artwork. It is a student-run publication and is funded by the university." Acquires first North American serial rights. All rights revert to author upon publication. Guidelines online.

**MAGAZINES NEEDS** Submit by online submissions manager.

**TIPS** "Please see our website for specific deadlines, as it changes every semester based on a variety of factors, but we typically leave the submission manager open sometime starting in the summer to around the end of October for the Fall issue, and during the winter to late February or mid-March for the Spring issue. Contributions are invited from all members of the campus community, as well as the literary community at large."

## HELLOHORROR

Houston TX **E-mail:** info@hellohorror.com. **E-mail:** submissions@hellohorror.com. **Website:** www.hellohorror.com. **Contact:** Brent Armour, editor in chief. "*HelloHorror* is an online literary magazine. We are currently in search of literary pieces, photography, and visual art, including film from writers and artists that have a special knack for inducing goose bumps and raised hairs. This genre has become, especially in film, noticeably saturated in gore and high shockvalue aspects as a crutch to avoid the true challenge of bringing about real, psychological fear to an audience that's persistently more and more numb to its tactics. While we are not opposed to the extreme, blood and guts need bones and cartilage. Otherwise it's just a sloppy mess." Buys first serial rights. Publishes ms 3-12 months after acceptance. Responds in 1-6 months to queries and mss. Sample copy and guidelines online at website. See hellohorror.com/submit for full submission guidelines and recommendations.

"Specifically, we are looking for pieces grounded in psychological fear rather than gore. We will not automatically pass on a gore drenched story, but it needs to have its foundations in psychological horror."

**MAGAZINES NEEDS** Submit poems via e-mail. "All types are accepted so long as they are of the horror genre."

**TIPS** "We like authors that show consideration for their readers. A great horror story leaves an impression on the reader long after it is finished. Consider your reader and consider yourself. What really scares you as opposed to what's stereotypically supposed to scare you? Bring us and our readers into that place of fear with you."

## HIGHLIGHTS FOR CHILDREN

803 Church St., Honesdale PA 18431. (570)253-1080. **Fax:** (570)251-7847. **E-mail:** customerservice@highlights.com. **Website:** www.highlights.com. **Contact:** Christine French Cully, editor-in-chief. "This book of wholesome fun is dedicated to helping children grow in basic skills and knowledge, in creativeness, in ability to think and reason, in sensitivity to others, in high ideals, and worthy ways of living—for children are the world's most important people. We publish stories for beginning and advanced readers. Up to 500 words for beginning readers, up to 800 words for advanced readers." Buys all rights. Pays on acceptance. Responds in 2 months to queries. Sample copy free. Guidelines on website in "Company" area.

**MAGAZINES NEEDS** Lines/poem: 16 maximum ("most poems are shorter"). Considers simultaneous submissions ("please indicate"); no previously published poetry. No e-mail submissions. "Submit typed manuscript with very brief cover letter." Occasionally comments on submissions "if manuscript has merit or author seems to have potential for our market." Guidelines available for SASE. Responds "generally within 2 months." Always sends prepublication galleys. Pays 2 contributor copies; "money varies." Acquires all rights.

**TIPS** "Know the magazine's style before submitting. Send for guidelines and sample issue if necessary." Writers: "At *Highlights* we're paying closer attention to acquiring more nonfiction for young readers than we have in the past." Illustrators: "Fresh, imaginative work encouraged. Flexibility in working relationships a plus. Illustrators presenting their work need not confine themselves to just children's illustrations as long as work can translate to our needs. We also use animal illustrations, real and imaginary. We need crafts, puzzles and any activity that will stimulate children mentally and creatively. Know our publication's standards and content by reading sample issues, not just the guidelines. Avoid tired themes, or put a fresh twist on an old theme so that its style is fun and lively. Write what inspires you, not what you think the market needs. We are pleased that many authors of children's literature report that their first published work was in the pages of *Highlights*. It is not our policy to consider fiction on the strength of the reputation of the author. We judge each submission on its own merits. Query with simple letter to establish whether the nonfiction subject is likely to be of interest. Expert reviews and complete bibliography required for nonfiction. A beginning writer should first become familiar with the type of material that *Highlights* publishes. Include special qualifications, if any, of author. Write for the child, not the editor. Write in a voice that children understand and relate to. Speak to today's kids, avoiding didactic, overt messages. Even though our general principles haven't changed over the years, we are contemporary in our approach to issues. Avoid worn themes."

## HIRAM POETRY REVIEW

P.O. Box 162, Hiram OH 44234. **E-mail:** poetryreview@hiram.edu. **Website:** hirampoetryreview. wordpress.com. **Contact:** Willard Greenwood, poetry editor. *Hiram Poetry Review*, published annually in spring, features distinctive, beautiful, and heroic poetry. Wants works of high and low art. Tends to favor poems that are pockets of resistance in the undeclared war against plain speech, but interested in any work of high quality. Acquires first North American serial rights. Rights return to poets upon publication. Responds in 6 months. Subscription: $9/year; $23/3 years.

○ Press run is 400 (300 subscribers, 150 libraries). **MAGAZINES NEEDS** Send 3-5 poems at a time. Considers simultaneous submissions. No e-mail submissions unless international. Cover letter is required. Include brief bio. Reads submissions year round. Length: up to 50 lines/poem. Pays 2 contributor copies.

## THE HOLLINS CRITIC

P.O. Box 9538, Hollins University, Roanoke VA 24020-1538. **Website:** www.hollins.edu/who-we-are/news-media/hollins-critic. *The Hollins Critic*, published 5 times a year, presents the first serious surveys of the whole bodies of contemporary writers' work, with complete checklists. In past issues, you'll find essays on such writers as John Engels (by David Huddle), James McCourt (by David Rollow), Jane Hirshfield (by Jeanne Larsen), Edwidge Danticat (by Denise Shaw), Vern Rutsala (by Lewis Turco), Sarah Arvio (by Lisa Williams), and Milton Kessler (by Liz Rosenberg). Buys first North American serial rights. Pays on publication. Publishes ms an average of 1 year after acceptance. Responds in 2 months to mss. Sample copy for $3. Guidelines for #10 SASE.

○ Uses a few short poems in each issue, interesting in form, content, or both. *The Hollins Critic* is 24 pages, magazine-sized. Press run is 500. Subscription: $12/year ($17 outside US). No postal or e-mail submissions. Has published poetry by Natasha Trethewey, Carol Moldaw, David Huddle, Margaret Gibson, and Julia Johnson.

**MAGAZINES NEEDS** Submit up to 5 poems at a time using the online submission form at www. hollinscriticsubmissions.com, available September 15-December 1. Submissions received at other times will be returned unread. Reading period: September 15-December 15. Publishes 16-20 poems/year. Pays $25/poem plus 5 contributor copies.

**TIPS** "We accept unsolicited poetry submissions; all other content is by prearrangement."

## ○ HOME PLANET NEWS

P.O. Box 455, High Falls NY 12440. (845)687-4084. **E-mail:** homeplanetnews@gmail.com. **Website:** www. homeplanetnews.org. **Contact:** Donald Lev, editor. Triannual. *Home Planet News* publishes mainly poetry along with some fiction, as well as reviews (books, theater, and art) and articles of literary interest. Acquires one-time rights. Publishes ms 1 year after acceptance. Responds in 6 months to mss. Sample: $4. Guidelines available for SASE or on website. Usually best to just send work.

○ *HPN* has received a small grant from the Puffin Foundation for its focus on AIDS issues. Receives 12 unsolicited mss/month. Accepts 1 mss/issue; 3 mss/year. Has published work by Hugh Fox, Walter Jackman, and Jim Story. "Our spin-off publication, *Home Planet News Online*, can be found at homeplanetnews.org/aonline.html. We urge everyone to check it out."

**MAGAZINES NEEDS** Submit 3-6 poems at a time. Cover letter is preferred. Send SASE. Seldom comments on rejected poems. Occasionally publishes theme issues. Upcoming themes available in magazine. Reviews books/chapbooks of poetry and other magazines in 1,200 words, single- and multibook format. Send materials for review consideration to Donald Lev. "Note: We do have guidelines for book reviewers; please write for them or check website. Magazines are reviewed by a staff member." Length: no limit, but shorter poems (under 30 lines) stand a better chance. Pays one-year gift subscription plus 3 contributor copies.

**TIPS** "We use very little fiction, and a story we accept just has to grab us. We need short pieces of some complexity, stories about complex people facing situations which resist simple resolutions."

## ❸ HOOT

A postcard review of {mini} poetry and prose, 4234 Chestnut St., Apt. 1 R, Philadelphia PA 19104. **E-mail:** info@hootreview.com. **E-mail:** onlinesubmissions@hootreview.com. **Website:** www.hootreview.com. **Contact:** Amanda Vacharat and Dorian Geisler, editors/co-founders. *HOOT* publishes 1 piece of writing, designed with original art/photographs, on the front of a postcard every month, as well as 2-3 pieces online. The postcards are intended for sharing, to be hung on the wall, etc. Therefore, *HOOT* looks for very brief, surprising-yet-gimmick-free writing that can stand on its own, that also follows "The Refrigerator Rule"—something that you would hang on your refrigerator and would want to read and look at for a whole month. This rule applies to online content as well. Buys first North American serial rights and electronic rights. Pays on publication. Publishes ms 2 months after acceptance. Sample copy: $2. Writer's guidelines available on website.

○ Costs $2 to submit up to 2 pieces of work. Submit through online submissions manager.

**MAGAZINES NEEDS** Length: up to 10 lines. Pays $10-100 for print publication.

**TIPS** "We look for writing with audacity and zest from authors who are not afraid to take risks. We ap-

preciate work that is able to go beyond mere description in its 150 words. We offer free online workshops every otherWednesday for authors who would like feedback on their work from the *HOOT* editors. We also often give feedback with our rejections. We publish roughly 6-10 new writers each year."

## HORIZONS

100 Witherspoon St., Louisville KY 40202. (844)797-2872. **E-mail:** yvonne.hileman@pcusa.org. **Website:** www.pwpcusahorizons.com. **Contact:** Yvonne Hileman, assistant editor. *Horizons* magazine provides information, inspiration, and education from the perspectives of women who are committed to Christ, the church and faithful discipleship. *Horizons* brings current issues dealing with family life, the mission of the church and the challenges of culture and society to its readers. Interviews, feature articles, Bible study resources, and departments offer help and insight for up-to-date, day-to-day concerns of the church and individual Christians. Buys all rights. Pays on publication. Publishes ms an average of 4 months after acceptance. Sample copy for $4 and 9x12 SAE. Guidelines for writers are on the *Horizons* website.

**MAGAZINES NEEDS** Accepts poems of varying themes and topics.

## HOTEL AMERIKA

Columbia College, English Department, 600 S. Michigan Ave., Chicago IL 60605. (312)369-8175. **Website:** www.hotelamerika.net. **Contact:** David Lazar, editor; Lisa Wagner, managing editor. *Hotel Amerika* is a venue for both well-known and emerging writers. Publishes exceptional writing in all forms. Strives to house the most unique and provocative poetry, fiction, and nonfiction available. Guidelines online.

○ Mss will be considered between September 1 and May 1. Materials received after May 1 and before September 1 will be returned unread. Send submissions only via mail, with SASE. Work published in *Hotel Amerika* has been included in *The Pushcart Prize* and *The Best American Poetry* and featured on *Poetry Daily*.

**MAGAZINES NEEDS** Welcomes submissions in all genres.

## HUBBUB

5344 SE 38th Ave., Portland OR 97202. (503)775-0370. **E-mail:** lisa.steinman@reed.edu. **Website:** www.reed.edu/hubbub. J. Shugrue and Lisa M. Steinman, co-editors. *Hubbub*, published once/year, is designed "to feature a multitude of voices from interesting, contemporary American poets." Wants "poems that are well crafted, with something to say. We have no single style, subject, or length requirement and in particular will consider long poems." Acquires first North American serial rights. Pays on publication. Publishes poems 1-12 months (usually) after acceptance. Responds in 4 months. Sample: $3.35 (back issues), $7 (current issue). Subscription: $7/year. Guidelines available for SASE or online.

○ *Hubbub* is 50-70 pages, digest-sized, offset-printed, perfect-bound, with cover art. Receives about 1,200 submissions/year, accepts up to 2%. Press run is 350.

**MAGAZINES NEEDS** Submit 3-6 typed poems at a time. Include SASE. "We review 2-4 poetry books/year in short (three-page) reviews; all reviews are solicited. We do, however, list books received/recommended." Send materials for review consideration. Has published poetry by Madeline DeFrees, Cecil Giscombe, Carolyn Kizer, Primus St. John, Shara McCallum, and Alice Fulton. Does not want light verse. No length requirements. Pays $20/poem.

**CONTEST/AWARD OFFERINGS** Offers 4 prizes/issue: the Vern Rutsala Award ($1,000), the Vi Gale Award ($500), the Kenneth O. Hanson Award ($100), and the Stout Award ($75). No applications; no submission fees.

### THE HUDSON REVIEW

The Hudson Review, Inc., 33 W. 67th St., New York NY 10023. (212)650-0020. **Website:** hudsonreview.com. **Contact:** Paula Deitz, editor. Pays on publication. Publishes ms an average of 6 months after acceptance. Responds in 6 months to mss. Editorial lead time 3 months. Sample copy: $11. Guidelines online.

○ Send with SASE. Mss sent outside accepted reading period will be returned unread if SASE contains sufficient postage.

**MAGAZINES NEEDS** Submit up to 7 poems by postal mail between **April 1-June 30** only.

**TIPS** "We do not specialize in publishing any particular 'type' of writing; our sole criterion for accepting unsolicited work is literary quality. The best way for you to get an idea of the range of work we publish is to read a current issue. Unsolicited mss submitted outside of specified reading times will be returned unread. Do not send submissions via e-mail."

### HUNGER MOUNTAIN

Vermont College of Fine Arts, 36 College St., Montpelier VT 05602. (802)828-8517. **E-mail:** hungermtn@vcfa.edu. **Website:** www.hungermtn.org. **Contact:** Samantha Kolber, managing editor. Accepts high-quality work from unknown, emerging, or successful writers. Publishing fiction, creative nonfiction, poetry, and young adult & children's writing. Four writing contests annually. Buys first worldwide serial rights. Pays on publication. Publishes ms an average of 1 year after acceptance. Responds in 4 months to mss.

**MAGAZINES NEEDS** Submit 1-5 poems at a time. "We are looking for truly original poems that run the aesthetic gamut: lively engagement with language in the act of pursuit. Some poems remind us in a fresh way of our own best thoughts; some poems bring us to a place beyond language for which there aren't quite words; some poems take us on a complicated language ride that is, itself, its own aim. Complex poem-architectures thrill us and still-points in the turning world do, too. Send us the best of what you have." Submit using online submissions manager. No light verse, humor/quirky/catchy verse, greeting card verse. $25 for poetry up to two poems (plus $5 per poem for additional poems); $25 for poetry up to two poems (plus $5 per poem for additional poems).

**ALSO OFFERS** Annual contests: Ruth Stone Poetry Prize; The Howard Frank Mosher Short Fiction Prize; the Katherine Paterson Prize for Young Adult and Children's Writing; The Hunger Mountain Creative Nonfiction Prize. Visit www.hungermtn.org for information about prizes.

**TIPS** "Mss must be typed, prose double-spaced. Poets submit poems as one document. No multiple genre submissions. Fresh viewpoints and human interest are very important, as is originality and diversity. We are committed to publishing an outstanding journal of the arts. Do not send entire novels, mss, or short story collections. Do not send previously published work."

### HYDE PARK LIVING

Community Publications, Inc., 179 Fairfield Ave., Bellevue KY 41073. (859)291-1412. **E-mail:** hydepark@livingmagazines.com. **Website:** www.livingmagazines.com. **Contact:** Grace DeGregorio. Buys all rights. Pays on publication. Editorial lead time 2 months. Guidelines by e-mail.

**MAGAZINES NEEDS** Please query.

## I-70 REVIEW

Writing from the Middle and Beyond, 913 Joseph Dr., Lawrence KS 66049. **E-mail:** i70review@gmail.com. **Website:** www.fieldinfoserv.com. **Contact:** Gary Lechliter, Maryfrances Wagner, Greg Field, and Jan Duncan-O'Neal, editors. *I-70 Review* is an annual literary magazine. "Our interests lie in writing grounded in fresh language, imagery, and metaphor. We prefer free verse in which the writer pays attention to the sound and rhythm of the language. We appreciate poetry with individual voice and a good lyric or a strong narrative. In fiction, we like short pieces that are surprising and uncommon. We want writing that captures the human spirit with unusual topics or familiar topics with different perspective or approaches. We reject stereotypical and clichéd writing, as well as sentimental work or writing that summarizes and tells instead of shows. We look for writing that pays attention to words, sentences, and style. We publish literary writing. We do not publish anything erotic, religious, or political." Buys one-time, first North American serial rights. Pays with contributor copies only. Publishes annually in September. Responds in 4-6 weeks, sometime sooner, on queries. Sample poetry online. Sample copy available for SASE and $13.50 (issue plus postage/handling). Guidelines online or by e-mail.

Open submission period is July 1-December 31.

**MAGAZINES NEEDS** "We publish a variety of literary styles but prefer lyric and narrative. We want nothing sentimental, nothing with sing-songy rhyme, nothing abstract or clichéd or predictable. Nothing political, religious, didactic, or erotic. We accept some experimental as long as it is well-crafted and accessible. We reject writing that makes no sense or provides no meaning for the reader, and we rarely publish work difficult to format." Length: 3-40 lines/poem. Pays contributor copies.

## IBBETSON ST. PRESS

25 School St., Somerville MA 02143-1721. **E-mail:** dougholder@post.harvard.edu. **Website:** ibbetsonpress.com. **Contact:** Doug Holder, editor; Rene Schwiesow and Lawrence Kessenich, managing editors; Harris Gardner, poetry editor. *Ibbetson St. Press*, published semiannually in June and November, prints "down-to-earth" poetry that is well written and has clean, crisp images with a sense of irony and humor. Wants mostly free verse but is open to rhyme. Does not want maudlin, trite, overly political, vulgar-for-vulgar's-sake work. Acquires one-time rights. Time between acceptance and publication is up to 8 months. Responds in 2 months. Single copy: $10. Subscription: $19. Make checks payable to *Ibbetson St. Press*. Guidelines available for SASE.

*Ibbetson St. Press* is 50 pages, magazine-sized, desktop-published, with glossy white cover; includes ads. Receives about 1,000 poems/year, accepts up to 10%. Press run is 200. Also archived at Harvard, Brown, University of Wisconsin, Poets House-NYC, Endicott College, and Buffalo University Libraries.

**MAGAZINES NEEDS** Submit 3-5 poems at a time. E-mail submissions only. Cover letter is required. Three editors comment on submissions. Has published poetry by Marge Piercy, X.J. Kennedy, Ted Kooser, Elizabeth Swados, Teisha Twomey, Gloria Mindock, Harris Gardner, Diana-der Hovanessian, Michael Todd Steffan, and Gary Metras. Does not accept unsolicited chapbook mss. Has published *Dead Beats* by Sam Cornish, *On the Wings of Song* by Molly Lynn Watt, *Fairytales and Misdemeanors* by Jennifer Matthews, *Steerage* by Bert Stern, *From the Paris of New England* by Doug Holder, *Blood Soaked Dresses* by Gloria Mindock; *East of the Moon* by Ruth Kramer Baden, and *Lousia Solano: The Grolier Poetry Book Shop* edited by Steve Glines and Doug Holder. Pays 1 contributor copy.

**ALSO OFFERS** Reviews books/chapbooks of poetry and other magazines in 250-500 words. Send materials for review consideration.

## ICONOCLAST

1675 Amazon Rd., Mohegan Lake NY 10547-1804. **Website:** www.iconoclastliterarymagazine.com. **Contact:** Phil Wagner, editor and publisher. *Iconoclast* seeks and chooses the best new writing and poetry available—of all genres and styles and entertainment levels. Its mission is to provide a serious publishing opportunity for unheralded, unknown, but deserving creators, whose work is often overlooked or trampled in the commercial, university, or Internet marketplace. Buys first North American serial rights. Pays on publication. Responds in 6 weeks to mss. Sample copy: $4. Subscription: $20 for 6 issues.

**MAGAZINES NEEDS** "Try for originality; if not in thought than expression. No greeting card verse or noble religious sentiments. Look for the unusual in the usual, parallels in opposites, the capturing of what is unique or often unnoticed in an ordinary or extraordinary moment. What makes us human—and the resultant glories and agonies. The universal usually wins out over the personal. Rhyme isn't as easy as it looks—especially for those unversed in its study." Submit by postal mail; include SASE. Cover letter not necessary. Length: up to 2 pages. Pays $2-6/poem and 1 contributor copy per page or work. Contributors get 40% discount on extra copies.

**TIPS** "Please don't send preliminary drafts—rewriting is half the job. If you're not sure about the story, don't truly believe in it, or are unenthusiastic about the subject (we will not recycle your term papers or thesis), then don't send it. This is not a lottery (luck has nothing to do with it)."

## ❶❸ THE IDAHO REVIEW

Boise State University, 1910 University Dr., Boise ID 83725. **E-mail:** mwieland@boisestate.edu. **Website:** idahoreview.org. **Contact:** Mitch Wieland, editor. *The Idaho Review* is the literary journal of Boise State University. Acquires one-time rights. Pays on publication. Publishes ms 1 year after acceptance. Responds in 3-5 months. Guidelines online.

⬭ Recent stories appearing in *The Idaho Review* have been reprinted in *The Best American Short Stories, The O. Henry Prize Stories, The Pushcart Prize*, and *New Stories from the South*.

**MAGAZINES NEEDS** Submit up to 5 poems. Prefers submissions using online submissions manager, but will accept submissions by postal mail.

**TIPS** "We look for strongly crafted work that tells a story that needs to be told. We demand vision and intelligence and mystery in the fiction we publish."

## ❷❍ IDIOM 23

Central Queensland University, Rockhampton QLD 4702, Australia. **E-mail:** idiom@cqu.edu.au. **Website:** www.cqu.edu.au/idiom23. *Idiom 23*, published annually, is "named for the Tropic of Capricorn and is dedicated to developing the literary arts throughout the Central Queensland region. Submissions of original short stories, poems, articles, and b&w drawings and photographs are welcomed by the editorial collective. *Idiom 23* is not limited to a particular viewpoint but, on the contrary, hopes to encourage and publish a broad spectrum of writing. The collective seeks out creative work from community groups with as varied

backgrounds as possible." Single copy: $20, available at bookshop.cqu.edu.au. Guidelines online.

**MAGAZINES NEEDS** Submit poetry via online submissions manager. Length: 1 page/poem.

## ILLUMEN

Alban Lake Publishing, P.O. Box 782, Cedar Rapids IA 52406-0782. **E-mail:** illumensdp@yahoo.com. **Website:** albanlake.com. **Contact:** Terrie Leigh Relf, editor. "*Illumen* is a print magazine of speculative poetry. It is published biannually on 1 April and 1 October in perfect-bound digest format. It contains speculative poetry, illustrations, articles, and reviews." Buys first North American serial rights, one-time rights, buys second serial (reprint) rights. Responds in 4 months. Guidelines online.

**MAGAZINES NEEDS** "Speculative poetry is 1 result of the application of imagination to reality. In speculative poetry, one's 'vision' often is taken from a different angle, from another perspective, perhaps even from another time and place. Speculative poetry is usually tinged with 1 or more of the genres. Thus, in speculative poetry you find hints of science fiction, fantasy, folklore, myth, the surreal ... and yes, even horror. Good speculative poetry will awaken a sense of adventure in the reader. That's what we're looking for: good, original speculative poetry." Submit poetry by e-mail. "Speculative horror poetry evokes moods, often dark and spooky ones. It should not make you upchuck. Remember: twisted is an attitude, not an action." Length: up to 100 lines/poem. Pays 2¢/word, minimum $3.

**TIPS** "*Illumen* publishes beginning writers as well as seasoned veterans. Be sure to read and follow the guidelines before submitting your work. The best advice for beginning writers is to send your best effort, not your first draft."

## ILLUMINATIONS

Department of English, College of Charleston, 66 George St., Charleston SC 29424-0001. **E-mail:** illuminations@cofc.edu. **Website:** illuminations.cofc. edu. **Contact:** Simon Lewis, editor. "Over these many years, *Illuminations* has remained consistently true to its mission statement to publish new writers alongside some of the world's finest, including Nadine Gordimer, James Merrill, Carol Ann Duffy, Dennis Brutus, Allen Tate, interviews with Tim O'Brien, and letters from Flannery O'Connor and Ezra Pound. A number of new poets whose early work appeared in *Illumina-*

*tions* have gone on to win prizes and accolades, and we at *Illuminations* sincerely value the chance to promote the work of emerging writers." Returns rights on request. Sample copy: $10.

○ "As a magazine devoted primarily to poetry, we publish only 1-2 pieces of short fiction and/or nonfiction in any given year, and sometimes publish none at all. "

**MAGAZINES NEEDS** Open to any form and style, and to translations. Does not want to see anything "bland or formally clunky." Has published poetry by Brenda Marie Osbey, Geri Doran, Dennis Brutus, and Carole Satyamurti. Submit up to 6 poems by postal mail or online submissions manager. Pays 2 contributor copies of current issue; 1 of subsequent issue.

### ILLYA'S HONEY

**E-mail:** dpcer09@gmail.com. **Website:** www.illyas-honey.com. Melanie Pruit-Helsem. **Contact:** Ann Howells and Melanie Pruit, editors. *Illya's Honey* is the online literary journal of the Dallas Poet's Community. Its main purpose has always been to publish well-crafted poetry using the best electronic means available. Acquires first rights and anthology rights. less than three months, frequently much less than three months usually under one month, occasionally as long as three months Sample copy online. Guidelines online.

○ Online magazine published in January, April, July, and October.

**MAGAZINES NEEDS** "The editorial philosophy is simple: Poetry which strikes a truth, which artfully conveys the human condition, is most likely to be selected. Vulgarity and coarseness just for the sake of the exercise will not be considered." Submit via online submissions manager; no postal submissions. "We eschew the overly didactic, porn, overtly religious, hate mongering any none."

**HOW TO CONTACT** Through submission form.

**CONTEST/AWARD OFFERINGS** "We nominate for Pushcart prizes."

**TIPS** "Please read the journal before submitting. It's free!"

### ⑤ IMAGE

3307 Third Ave. W., Seattle WA 98119. (206)281-2988. **Fax:** (206)281-2979. **E-mail:** image@imagejournal.org. **Website:** www.imagejournal.org. **Contact:** Gregory Wolfe, publisher and editor. "*Image* is a unique forum for the best writing and artwork that is informed by—or grapples with—religious faith. We have never been interested in art that merely regurgitates dogma or falls back on easy answers or didacticism. Instead, our focus has been on writing and visual artwork that embody a spiritual struggle, that seek to strike a balance between tradition and a profound openness to the world. Each issue explores this relationship through outstanding fiction, poetry, painting, sculpture, architecture, film, music, interviews, and dance. *Image* also features 4-color reproductions of visual art." Buys first North American serial rights. Pays on acceptance. Publishes ms an average of 8 months after acceptance. Responds in 1 month to queries; in 5 months to mss. Sample copy: $16 or online. Guidelines online.

**MAGAZINES NEEDS** Wants poems that grapple with religious faith, usually Judeo-Christian. Send up to 5 poems by postal mail (with SASE for reply or return of ms) or online submissions manager. Does not accept e-mail submissions. Length: up to 10 pages. Pays $2/line ($150 maximum) and 4 contributor copies.

**TIPS** "Fiction must grapple with religious faith, though subjects need not be overtly religious."

### INDEFINITE SPACE

P.O. Box 40101, Pasadena CA 91114. **E-mail:** indefinitespace@yahoo.com. **Website:** www.indefinitespace.net. "Published annually. From minimalist to avant garde, *Indefinite Space* is open to innovative, imagistic, philosophical, experimental creations: poetry, drawings, collage, photography. Reads year round." Poet retains copyright. Responds in 3 months. Seldom comments on rejected poems. Single copy: $10; subscription: $18 for 2 issues. Make checks payable to Marcia Arrieta.

○ *Indefinite Space* is 48 pages, digest-sized.

**MAGAZINES NEEDS** No rhyming poetry. Has published poetry by Andrea Moorhead, Rob Cook, Linda King, Bob Heman, Khat Xiong, and Guy R. Beining. Pays 1 contributor copy.

### ⑤⑤ INDIANA REVIEW

Ballantine Hall 529, 1020 E. Kirkwood Ave., Indiana University, Bloomington IN 47405. **E-mail:** inreview@indiana.edu. **Website:** indianareview.org. **Contact:** See masthead for current editorial staff. "*Indiana Review*, a nonprofit organization run by IU graduate students, is a journal of innovative fiction, nonfiction, and poetry. We're interested in energy, originality, and careful attention to craft. While we publish many well-known writers, we also welcome new and emerging poets and fiction writers." Buys first North American serial rights. Pays on publication. Publishes ms an average of 3-6 months after acceptance. Responds in 4 or more months to mss. Sample copy: $12. Guidelines online. "We no longer accept hard-copy submissions. All submissions must be made online."

See website for open reading periods.

**MAGAZINES NEEDS** "We look for poems that are skillful and bold, exhibiting an inventiveness of language with attention to voice and sonics." Wants experimental, free verse, prose poem, traditional form, lyrical, narrative. Submit poetry via online submissions manager. Pays $5/page ($10 minimum), plus 2 contributor copies.

**CONTEST/AWARD OFFERINGS** Holds yearly poetry and prose poem contests.

**TIPS** "We're always looking for nonfiction essays that go beyond merely autobiographical revelation and utilize sophisticated organization and slightly radical narrative strategies. We want essays that are both lyrical and analytical where confession does not mean nostalgia. Read us before you submit. Often reading is slower in summer and holiday months. Only submit work to journals you would proudly subscribe to, then subscribe to a few. Take care to read the latest 2 issues and specifically mention work you identify with and why. Submit work that 'stacks up' with the work we've published. Offers annual poetry, fiction, and short short/prose poem prizes. See website for full guidelines."

## INDIA-USA PUNJABI ENGLISH MAGAZINE

22619 97th Ave. S., Kent WA 98031. **E-mail:** aasra@q. com. **Contact:** Sarab Singh, editor. *India-USA Punjabi English Magazine*, published bimonthly, features current events mainly Indian, but has featured others, too, of interest. Also features interviews, yoga, and other articles, and poetry. Acquires one-time rights. Rights revert to poet upon publication. Time between acceptance and publication is 2 months. Sometimes comments on rejected poems. Single copy: $3 (postage); subscription: $20/year. "The magazine is distributed free in the Seattle area and available through other libraries. We charge $3/copy for p&h or $2/copy if you purchase more than 10 copies. Back issue: $2."

Guidelines in magazine. "We will print 1 poem per issue. We usually charge $4 to print a small poem and more for long poems. (Please note we do not send a free copy in which your poem is printed. The money usually goes to cover p&h.)"

Magazine: measures approximately 8.5x11, press printed, staple bound, includes ads. Page count varies.

**MAGAZINES NEEDS** Submit 1-2 small poems at a time. Cover letter is required. Include SASE, name, address, telephone number, and e-mail address with age and gender on cover letter. Include a short bio. "If interested we can print 'About the Poet' along with the poem." Reads submissions year round. Sometimes publishes theme issues. Has published poetry by Tripat Singh, Elizabeth Tallmadge, and Carmen Arhiveleta.

**CONTEST/AWARD OFFERINGS** Best Poem of the Year is awarded one-year free subscription.

## INNISFREE POETRY JOURNAL

**E-mail:** editor@innisfreepoetry.org. **Website:** www. innisfreepoetry.org. **Contact:** Greg McBride, editor. *Innisfree Poetry Journal* "welcomes original, previously unpublished poems year round. We accept poems only via e-mail from both established and new writers whose work is excellent. We publish well-crafted poems, poems grounded in the specific which speak in fresh language and telling images. And we admire musicality. We welcome those who, like the late Lorenzo Thomas, 'write poems because I can't sing.'" Acquires first North American serial rights. "Acquires first publication rights, including the right to publish it online and maintain it there as part of the issue in which it appears, to make it available in a printer-friendly format, to make the issue of *Innisfree* in which it appears downloadable as a PDF document and available as a printed volume. All other rights revert to the poet after online publication of the poem in *The Innisfree Poetry Journal*." Guidelines available on website.

**MAGAZINES NEEDS** Submit up to 5 poems by e-mail; single Word attachment. "Include your name as you would like it to appear in *Innisfree* in the subject line of your submission. Format all poems flush with the left margin—no indents other than any within the poem itself. Simultaneous submissions are welcome. If a poem is accepted elsewhere, however, please be sure to notify us immediately."

## INTERPRETER'S HOUSE

36 College Bounds, Old Aberdeen Aberdeen AB24 3DS, England. **E-mail:** theinterpretershouse@aol.com. **Website:** www.theinterpretershouse.com. **Contact:** Martin Malone, editor. *The Interpreter's House*, published 3 times/year in February, June, and October, prints short stories and poetry. Responds in 3 months. Sample copy: £5 plus £1.20 postage. Guidelines online.

Submission windows: October for the Spring issue, February for the Summer issue, June for the Autumn issue.

**MAGAZINES NEEDS** Submit up to 5 poems by mail (with SASE) or e-mail. Wants "good poetry, not too long." Has published poetry by Dannie Abse, Tony Curtis, Pauline Stainer, Alan Brownjohn, Peter Redgrove, and R.S. Thomas. "All work is dealt with swiftly. Usually no more than 1 poem is accepted, and writers who have already appeared in the magazine are asked to wait for at least 3 issues before submitting again." Does not want "Christmas-card verse or incomprehensible poetry." Pays in contributor copies.

## IOTA

Templar Poetry, Fenelon House, 58 Dale Rd., Matlock, Derbyshire DE4 3NB, England. (44)01629 582500. **E-mail:** info@templarpoetry.com. **E-mail:** submissions@templarpoetry.co.uk. **Website:** www.templarpoetry.com. **Contact:** Alex McMillen. *Iota* considers "any style and subject; no specific limitations as to length." Has published poetry by Jane Kinninmont, John Robinson, Tony Petch, Chris Kinsey, Christopher James, and Michael Kriesel. Responds in 3 months (unless production of the next issue takes precedence).

**MAGAZINES NEEDS** Submit up to 6 poems at a time. No previously published poems. Cover letter is required with name and address. No name and address on each poem. Online submissions accepted; see details at www.templarpoetry.com Reviews books of poetry. Send materials for review consideration. There is a £1.50 administration fee for submitting poetry online. Pays 1 contributor copy.

**ADDITIONAL INFORMATION** The editors also publish Templar Poetry (www.templarpoetry.com), sponsor the annual Derwent Poetry Festival, and host an online poetry bookshop of their titles at www.templarpoetry.com. "Templar Poetry is a major UK poetry publisher and publishes poetry collections, non-fiction, and an annual anthology of poetry linked to international pamphlet and collection awards. Details at www.templarpoetry.com

**CONTEST/AWARD OFFERINGS** Sponsors an annual poetry Pamphlet/Chapbook-Iota Shot Award, offering 2-3 awards of £100, plus publication of *ishot* chapbook. Submission fee: £15.50 online. Worldwide submissions in English welcome. **Deadline:** November 19.

## THE IOWA REVIEW

308 EPB, The University of Iowa, Iowa City IA 52242. (319)335-0462. **E-mail:** iowa-review@uiowa.edu. **Website:** www.iowareview.org. Lynne Nugent, managing editor. **Contact:** Harilaos Stecopoulos. *The Iowa Review*, published 3 times/year, prints fiction, poetry, essays, reviews, and, occasionally, interviews. Receives about 5,000 submissions/year, accepts up to 100. Press run is 2,900; 1,500 distributed to stores. Buys first North American serial rights; buys nonexclusive anthology, classroom, and online serial rights. Pays on publication. Publishes ms an average of 12-18 months after acceptance. Responds to mss in 4 months. Sample: $8.95 and online. Subscription: $20. Guidelines online.

This magazine uses the help of colleagues and graduate assistants. Its reading period for unsolicited work is September 1-December 1. From January through April, the editors read entries to the annual Iowa Review Awards competition. Check the website for further information.

**MAGAZINES NEEDS** Submit up to 8 pages at a time. Online submissions accepted, but no e-mail submissions. Cover letter (with title of work and genre) is encouraged. SASE required. Reads submissions "only during the fall semester, September through November, and then contest entries in the spring." Occasionally comments on rejected poems or offers suggestions on accepted poems. "We simply look for poems that, at the time we read and choose, we find we admire. No specifications as to form, length, style, subject matter, or purpose. Though we print work from established writers, we're always delighted when we discover new talent." Pays $1.50/line, $40 minimum.

**TIPS** "We publish essays, reviews, novel excerpts, stories, poems, and photography. We have no set guidelines regarding content but strongly recommend that writers read a sample issue before submitting."

## IRIS

**E-mail:** submissions@creatingiris.org; editorial@creatingiris.org. **Website:** www.creatingiris.org. "*Iris* seeks works of fiction and poetry that speak to LGBT young adults and their allies. We are interested in creative, thoughtful, original work that engages our young readers. We seek writing that challenges them and makes them think. We're looking for stories that capture their imaginations and characters that are relatable. We think there's a need in the young adult literary market for writing that speaks to the everyday experiences of LGBT adolescents: Themes of identity, friendship, coming out, families, etc., are especially welcome. The protagonist need not identify as LGBT, but we do ask that there be some kind of LGBT angle to your story. We welcome all genres of fiction and poetry!" Acquires first digital rights. Sample copy online. Guidelines online.

○ "Because we publish for a young demographic, work submitted to *Iris* may not include depictions of sex, drug use, and violence. They can certainly be discussed and referenced, but not directly portrayed."

**MAGAZINES NEEDS** Submit poems via e-mail as attachment. Include cover letter in text of e-mail.

## ISLAND

P.O. Box 4703, Hobart Tasmania 7000, Australia. **E-mail:** admin@islandmag.com. **Website:** www.islandmag.com. **Contact:** Geordie Williamson, editor at large. *Island* seeks quality fiction, poetry, and essays. It is "one of Australia's leading literary magazines, tracing the contours of our national, and international, culture while still retaining a uniquely Tasmanian perspective." Buys one-time rights. Subscriptions and sample copies available for purchase online. Guidelines online.

○ Only publishes the work of subscribers; you can submit if you are not currently a subscriber, but if your piece is chosen, the subscription will be taken from the fee paid for the piece.

**MAGAZINES NEEDS** Submit via online submissions manager. Pay varies.

## JABBERWOCK REVIEW

Department of English, Mississippi State University, Drawer E, Mississippi State MS 39762. **E-mail:** jabberwockreview@english.msstate.edu. **Website:** www.jabberwockreview.org.msstate.edu. **Contact:** Becky Hagenston, editor. "*Jabberwock Review* is a literary journal published semi-annually by students and faculty of Mississippi State University. The journal consists of poetry, fiction, and nonfiction from around the world. Funding is provided by the Office of the Provost, the College of Arts & Sciences, the Shackouls Honors College, the Department of English, fundraisers, and subscriptions." Rights revert to author upon publication. Responds in 3-5 months. "If you have not heard from us in 5 months, feel free to contact us about the status of your submission." Guidelines online.

○ Submissions accepted August 15-October 20 and January 15-March 15.

**MAGAZINES NEEDS** "Poems of multiple pages should indicate whether or not stanza breaks accompany page breaks." Pays contributor copies.

**CONTEST/AWARD OFFERINGS** Submissions to the Nancy Hargrove Editors' Prizes in Fiction and Poetry accepted January 15-March 15.

**TIPS** "It might take a few months to get a response from us, but your ms will be read with care. Our editors enjoy reading submissions (really!) and will remember writers who are persistent and committed to getting a story 'right' through revision."

## JACK AND JILL

U.S. Kids, P.O. Box 567, Indianapolis IN 46206. (317)634-1100. **E-mail:** jackandjill@saturdayeveningpost.org. **Website:** www.uskidsmags.com. "*Jack and Jill* is an award-winning magazine for children ages 6-12. It promotes the healthy educational and creative growth of children through interactive activities and articles. The pages are designed to spark a child's curiosity in a wide range of topics through articles, games, and activities. Inside you will find: current real-world topics in articles in stories; challenging puzzles and games; and interactive entertainment through experimental crafts and recipes." Buys all rights. Pays on publication. Publishes ms an average of 8 months after acceptance. Responds to mss in 3 months. Guidelines online.

○ "Please do not send artwork. We prefer to work with professional illustrators of our own choosing."

**MAGAZINES NEEDS** Submit via postal mail; no e-mail submissions. Wants light-hearted poetry appropriate for the age group. Mss must be typewritten with poet's contact information in upper-right corner of each poem's page. SASE required. Length: up to 30 lines/poem. Pays $25-50.

**TIPS** "We are constantly looking for new writers who can tell good stories with interesting slants—stories that are not full of outdated and time-worn expressions. We like to see stories about kids who are smart and capable but not sarcastic or smug. Problem-solving skills, personal responsibility, and integrity are good topics for us. Obtain current issues of the magazine and study them to determine our present needs and editorial style."

## JERRY JAZZ MUSICIAN

**Website:** www.jerryjazzmusician.com. "*Jerry Jazz Musician*'s mission is to explore the culture of 20th-century America with, as noted jazz critic Nat Hentoff wrote, 'jazz as the centerpiece.' We focus on publishing content geared toward readers with interests in jazz music, its rich history, and the culture it influenced—and was influenced by. We regularly publish original interviews, poetry, literature, and art, and encourage readers to share their own perspectives."

**MAGAZINES NEEDS** Submit 1-2 poems at a time. Length: 6-100 lines/poem.

## JEWISH CURRENTS

P.O. Box 111, Accord NY 12404. (845)626-2427. **E-mail:** editor@jewishcurrents.org. **E-mail:** submissions@jewishcurrents.org. **Website:** www.jewishcurrents.org. **Contact:** Lawrence Bush, editor. *Jewish Currents*, published 4 times/year, is a progressive Jewish bimonthly magazine that carries on the insurgent tradition of the Jewish left through independent journalism, political commentary, and a 'countercultural' approach to Jewish arts and literature. Publishes mss 6-9 months after acceptance. Responds in 3 months. Subscription: $30/year.

- *Jewish Currents* is 80 pages, magazine-sized, offset-printed, saddle-stapled with a full-color arts section, "Jcultcha & Funny Pages." The Winter issue is a 12-month arts calendar.

**MAGAZINES NEEDS** Submit 4 poems at a time with a cover letter. "Writers should include brief biographical information." Poems should be typed, double-spaced; include SASE. Pays contributor copies.

**ALSO OFFERS** "We also run a national poetry contest October 15-January 15."

## J JOURNAL: NEW WRITING ON JUSTICE

524 W. 59th St., Seventh Floor, New York NY 10019. (212)237-8697. **E-mail:** jjournal@jjay.cuny.edu. **Website:** www.jjournal.org. **Contact:** Adam Berlin and Jeffrey Heiman, editors. "*J Journal* publishes literary fiction, creative nonfiction, and poetry on the justice theme—social, political, criminal, gender, racial, religious, economic. While the justice theme is specific, it need not dominate the work. We're interested in innovative writing that examines justice from all creative perspectives. Tangential connections to justice are often better than direct." Acquires first rights. Publication is copyrighted. Contributor copies on publication. Publishes ms 6 months after acceptance. Responds in 1 month to queries; in 3 months to mss. Sometimes comments on/critiques rejected mss. Sample copy: $10. Guidelines online.

- Several stories in *J Journal* have been recognized in the Pushcart anthology.

**MAGAZINES NEEDS** Submit up to 3 poems. Include brief bio and list of publications. Pays 2 contributor copies. Additional copies $10.

**TIPS** "We're looking for literary fiction, memoir, personal narrative, or poetry with a connection, direct or tangential, to the theme of justice."

## JOSEPHINE QUARTERLY

**Website:** www.josephinequarterly.com. **Contact:** Jenny Sadre-Orafai and Komal Patel Mathew, co-founders/editors. *Josephine Quarterly* is a quarterly online literary journal accepting only unpublished poetry and art. "Our tastes tend to run wild, from Mary Ruefle to Anne Sexton to Bob Hicok to Olena Kalytiak Davis to Zachary Schomburg to Lucille Clifton to Louise Gluck. A good poem is a good poem. We know what we want when we see it." The editors are interested in work from both established and new voices. Acquires one-time and nonexclusive journal rights to publish an author's work online. Responds in 7-10 weeks. Guidelines online.

**MAGAZINES NEEDS** Submit up to 5 poems of any length via online submissions manager.

## THE JOURNAL

The Ohio State University, 164 Annie and John Glenn Ave., Columbus OH 43210. (614)292-6065. **Fax:** (614)292-7816. **E-mail:** managingeditor@thejournalmag.org. **Website:** thejournalmag.org. "We are interested in quality fiction, poetry, nonfiction, art, and reviews of new books of poetry, fiction, and non-fiction. We impose no restrictions on category, type, or length of submission for fiction, poetry, and non-fiction. We are happy to consider long stories and self-contained excerpts of novels. Please double-space all prose submissions. Please send 3-5 poems in 1 submission. We only accept online submissions and will not respond to mailed submissions." Buys first North American serial rights. Publishes ms an average of 1 year after acceptance. Responds in 4-6 months to mss. Sample copy: $8 on Submittable or free online spring and fall issues. Guidelines online: thejournalmag.org/submit. Submit online only at thejournal.submittable.com/submit.

O "We're open to all forms; we tend to favor work that gives evidence of a mature and sophisticated sense of the language."

**MAGAZINES NEEDS** "However else poets train or educate themselves, they must do what they can to know our language. Too much of the writing we see indicates poets do not, in many cases, develop a feel for the possibilities of language and do not pay attention to craft. Poets should not be in a rush to publish—until they are ready." Publishes about 100 poems/year. Pays 2 contributor copies and a one-year subscription.

### THE JOURNAL

Original Plus Press, 38 Pwllcarn Terrace, Blaengarw Wales CF32 8AS, United Kingdom. **E-mail:** smithsssj@aol.com. **Website:** thesamsmith.webs.com. *The Journal*, published 3 times/year, features English poetry/translations, reviews, and articles. Wants "new poetry howsoever it comes; translations and original English-language poems." Does not want "staid, generalized, all form/no content." Buys all rights. Pays on publication. Publishes ms an average of 6 months after acceptance. Responds in 4 weeks to queries. Often comments on rejected poems. Editorial lead time 6 months.

O Since 1997, Original Plus Press has been publishing collections of poetry. Has recently published books by Grahaeme Barrasford Young, Dina Kafiris, Alfred Todd, Fiona Sinclair, Neil Leadbeater, Janette Ayachi, Paul Lee, Kate Ruse, and Chris Deakins. "From now on we will be publishing mainly chapbooks. Send SASE (or SAE and IRC) or e-mail for details."

**MAGAZINES NEEDS** Submit up to 6 poems at a time. Accepts e-mail submissions. Cover letter is preferred. "Please send 2 IRCs with hard-copy submissions." Always sends prepublication galleys. Pays 1 contributor copy "only to U.K. contributors. Contributors outside the U.K. receive PDF copy of that issue."

**TIPS** "Send 6 poems; I'll soon let you know if it's not *Journal* or Original Plus material."

### JOURNAL OF NEW JERSEY POETS

County College of Morris CH 300, 214 Center Grove Rd., Randolph NJ 07869-2086. **Fax:** (973)328-5425. **E-mail:** journalofnjpoets@ccm.edu. **Website:** www.journalofnjpoets.com. **Contact:** Emily Birx, editor. *Journal of New Jersey Poets*, published annually in April, is "not necessarily about New Jersey—but of, by, and for poets from New Jersey." Wants "serious work that conveys the essential, real, whole emotional moment of the poem to the reader without sentimentality." Acquires first North American serial rights. Publishes ms 1 year after acceptance. Responds in up to 1 year. Sample: $10 (includes postage and handling). Subscription: $16 for 2 issues ($16/issue for institutions). Guidelines available for SASE or by e-mail.

O *Journal of New Jersey Poets* is about 90 pages, perfect-bound, offset-printed on recycled stock. Press run is 500.

**MAGAZINES NEEDS** All reviews are solicited. Send 2 copies of books for review consideration. Poets who live or work in New Jersey (or who formerly lived or worked here) are invited to submit up to 3 poems with their New Jersey bio data mentioned in the cover letter. Accepts e-mail submissions, "but they will not be acknowledged nor returned. Include SASE with sufficient postage for return of ms, or provide instructions to recycle." Annual deadline for submissions: October 1. Has published poetry by X.J. Kennedy, Allen Ginsberg, Amiri Baraka, Gerald Stern, Kenneth Burke, Stephen Dobyns, Thomas Edison, Ruth Moon Kempher, Joe Weil, Joe Salerno, and Catherine Doty. Pays 2 contributor copies and a one-year subscription.

**ALSO OFFERS** Offers New Jersey Poets Prize. Deadline: November 1.

### JOURNAL OF THE AMERICAN MEDICAL ASSOCIATION (JAMA)

330 N. Wabash Ave., Chicago IL 60611-5885. (312)464-4444 or (312)464-2402. **E-mail:** jamams@jamanetwork.org. **Website:** www.jama.com. **Contact:** Howard Bauchner, editor-in-chief; Phil B. Fontanarosa, executive editor. *JAMA* is an international peer-reviewed general medical journal published 48 times/

year. It is the most widely circulated journal in the world. *JAMA* publishes Original Investigations, Reviews, Brief Reports, Special Communications, Viewpoints, and other categories of articles. Publishes mss 1 month after acceptance. Guidelines online.

○ Receives about 6,000 mss annually. Publishes 9% of mss.

**MAGAZINES NEEDS** *JAMA* includes a poetry and medicine column, and publishes poetry in some way related to a medical experience, whether from the point of view of a health care worker or patient, or simply an observer. Has published poetry by Jack Coulehan, Floyd Skloot, and Walt McDonald. Length: up to 50 lines/poem.

### KAIMANA: LITERARY ARTS HAWAI'I

Hawai'i Literary Arts Council, P.O. Box 11213, Honolulu HI 96828. **E-mail:** reimersa001@hawaii.rr.com. **Website:** www.hawaii.edu/hlac. *Kaimana: Literary Arts Hawai'i*, published annually, is the magazine of the Hawai'i Literary Arts Council. Wants submissions with "some Pacific reference—Asia, Polynesia, Hawai'i—but not exclusively." Responds with "reasonable dispatch." Subscription: $15, includes membership in HLAC. Sample: $10.

○ *Kaimana* is 64-76 pages, 7.5x10, saddle-stapled, with high-quality printing. Press run is 1,000. "Poets published in *Kaimana* have received the Pushcart Prize, the Hawaii Award for Literature, the Stefan Baciu Award, the Cades Award, and the John Unterecker Award."

**MAGAZINES NEEDS** Submit poems with SASE. No e-mail submissions. Cover letter is preferred. Sometimes comments on rejected poems. Has published poetry by Kathryn Takara, Howard Nemerov, Anne Waldman, Reuel Denney, Haunani-Kay Trask, and Simon Perchik. Pays 2 contributor copies.

**TIPS** "Hawai'i gets a lot of 'travelling regionalists,' visiting writers with inevitably superficial observations. We also get superb visiting observers who are careful craftsmen anywhere. *Kaimana* is interested in the latter, to complement our own best Hawai'i writers."

### ❶❸ KALEIDOSCOPE

701 S. Main St., Akron OH 44311-1019. (330)762-9755. **Fax:** (330)762-0912. **E-mail:** kaleidoscope@udsakron. org. **Website:** www.kaleidoscopeonline.org. **Contact:** Gail Willmott, editor in chief. "*Kaleidoscope* magazine creatively focuses on the experiences of disability through literature and the fine arts. Unique to the field of disability studies, this award-winning publication expresses the diversity of the disability experience from a variety of perspectives including: individuals, families, friends, caregivers, educators, and healthcare professionals, among others." Buys first rights. Rights revert to author upon publication. Pays on publication. Responds in 6-9 months. Guidelines online. Submissions and queries electronically via website and e-mail.

○ *Kaleidoscope* has received awards from the Great Lakes Awards Competition and Ohio Public Images; received the Ohioana Award of Editorial Excellence.

**MAGAZINES NEEDS** Wants poems that have strong imagery, evocative language. Submit up to 5 poems by website or e-mail. Include cover letter. "Do not get caught up in rhyme scheme. We want high quality with strong imagery and evocative language." Reviews any style.

**TIPS** "The material chosen for *Kaleidoscope* challenges and overcomes stereotypical, patronizing, and sentimental attitudes about disability. We accept the work of writers with and without disabilities; however the work of a writer without a disability must focus on some aspect of disability. The criteria for good writing apply: effective technique, thought-provoking subject matter, and, in general, a mature grasp of the art of storytelling. Writers should avoid using offensive language and always put the person before the disability."

### KANSAS CITY VOICES

Whispering Prairie Press, P.O. Box 410661, Kansas City MO 64141. **E-mail:** info@wppress.org. **Website:** www.wppress.org/kansas-city-voices. **Contact:** Jessica Conoley, managing editor. *Kansas City Voices*, published annually, features an eclectic mix of fiction, poetry, and art. "We seek exceptional written and visual creations from established and emerging voices." Buys first North American serial rights. Pays on publication. Publishes ms an average of 6 months after acceptance. Sample copy online. Guidelines online.

○ Submission period: December 15-March 15.

**MAGAZINES NEEDS** Length: up to 35 lines/poem. Pays small honorarium and 1 contributor copy.

**TIPS** "There is no 'type' of work we are looking for, and while we would love for you to read through our previous issues, it is not an indicator of what kind of work we actively seek. Our editors rotate, our tastes evolve, and good work is just *good work*. We want to feel something when we encounter a piece. We want to be excited, surprised, thoughtful, and interested. We want to have a reaction. We want to share the best voices we find. Send us that one."

## THE KELSEY REVIEW

**E-mail:** kelsey.review@mccc.edu. **Website:** www.mccc.edu/community_kelsey-review.shtml. **Contact:** Ed Carmien, co-editor. *The Kelsey Review*, published annually online in September by Mercer County Community College, serves as "an outlet for literary talent of people living and working in Mercer County, New Jersey." Rights revert to author on publication. Responds no later than August 15 to mss. Sample copy online. Guidelines online.

Submission deadline: May 31.

**MAGAZINES NEEDS** Submit up to 6 pages of poetry via online submissions manager. Submissions are limited to people who live, work, or give literary readings in the Mercer County, New Jersey area. Has published poetry by Vida Chu, Dan O'Brien, and Carolina Morales. Does not want to see poetry "about kittens and puppies."

**TIPS** "See *The Kelsey Review* website for current guidelines. Note: We only accept submissions from the Mercer County, New Jersey area."

## THE KENYON REVIEW

Finn House, 102 W. Wiggin, Gambier OH 43022. (740)427-5208. **Fax:** (740)427-5417. **E-mail:** kenyonreview@kenyon.edu. **Website:** www.kenyonreview.org. **Contact:** Alicia Misarti. "An international journal of literature, culture, and the arts, dedicated to an inclusive representation of the best in new writing (fiction, poetry, essays, interviews, criticism) from established and emerging writers." Buys first rights. Pays on publication. Publishes ms an average of 1 year after acceptance. Responds in 4 months to mss. Editorial lead time 1 year. Sample copy: $10; includes postage and handling. Call or e-mail to order. Guidelines online.

The *Kenyon Review* receives about 8,000 submissions/year. Also publishes *KR Online*, a separate and complementary online literary magazine.

**MAGAZINES NEEDS** Features all styles, forms, lengths, and subject matters. Considers translations. Has published poetry by Billy Collins, D.A. Powell, Jamaal May, Rachel Zucker, Diane di Prima, and Sea-

mus Heaney. Submit up to 6 poems at a time. No previously published poems. Only accepts mss via online submissions program; visit website for instructions. Do not submit via e-mail or snail mail. Accepts submissions September 15-December 15. Pays 16¢/published word of poetry (minimum payment $40; maximum payment $200); word count does not include title, notes, or citations.

**TIPS** "We no longer accept mailed or e-mailed submissions. Work will only be read if it is submitted through our online program on our website. Reading period is September 15 through December 15. We look for strong voice, unusual perspective, and power in the writing."

## LADY CHURCHILL'S ROSEBUD WRISTLET

150 Pleasant St., #306, Easthampton MA 01027. **E-mail:** smallbeerpress@gmail.com. **Website:** www.smallbeerpress.com/lcrw. **Contact:** Gavin Grant, editor. *Lady Churchill's Rosebud Wristlet* accepts fiction, nonfiction, poetry, and b&w art. "The fiction we publish tends toward, but is not limited to, the speculative. This does not mean only quietly desperate stories. We will consider items that fall out with regular categories. We do not accept multiple submissions." First serial, nonexclusive anthology, and nonexclusive electronic rights. Pays on publication. Publishes ms 6-12 months after acceptance. Responds in 6 months to mss. Sometimes comments on rejected mss. Sample copy: $5. Guidelines online.

**MAGAZINES NEEDS** Send complete ms with a cover letter. Include estimated word count. Send SASE (or IRC) for return of ms, or send a disposable copy of ms and #10 SASE for reply only. Pays $5/poem.

**TIPS** "We recommend you read *Lady Churchill's Rosebud Wristlet* before submitting. You can pick up a copy from our website or from assorted book shops."

## LA FOVEA

**E-mail:** editors@lafovea.org. **Website:** www.lafovea.org. **Contact:** Frank Giampietro, creator; Virginia McLure, editor. Published 20 times/year online. "Each nerve editor (found on the main page of website) is in charge of a nerve. The nerves are made up of poets who are invited to submit to *La Fovea*. Click on the editor's name to see all the poets and poems in his or her nerve. The nerve editor asks a poet to submit 2 poems. After that poet has had his or her poems on *La Fovea*, he or she will ask another poet to submit poems. If the last poet on the nerve does not find a poet to submit poems for whatever reason, the nerve is dead. It's okay to have a dead nerve. The most important thing is for the nerve editor to notice a nerve has died and begin a new nerve from their first page of poems."

**MAGAZINES NEEDS** Wants any poetry. "If a poet wants to submit to *La Fovea* but has not been invited, he or she may submit to *La Fovea* and choose the editor whom the poet believes most matches his or her family of aesthetic style. The editor of the nerve may choose to send these poems to the current nerve editor and ask if he or she wishes to publish the poet's work. If the poet does not wish to publish the work, than the work will be returned to the submitter." Has published poetry by Denise Duhamel, Campbell McGrath, and Julianna Baggott. Submit only 3 poems at a time by e-mail, along with short bio.

## LAKE EFFECT: A JOURNAL OF THE LITERARY ARTS

School of Humanities & Social Sciences, Penn State Erie, The Behrend College, 4951 College Dr., Erie PA 16563-1501. (814)898-6281. **Fax:** (814)898-6032. **E-mail:** gol1@psu.edu. **Website:** www.pserie.psu.edu/lakeeffect. **Contact:** George Looney, editor in chief. *Lake Effect* is a publication of the School of Humanities and Social Sciences at Penn State Erie, The Behrend College. Sample copy: $6. Guidelines online at website.

**MAGAZINES NEEDS** *"Lake Effect* is looking for poems that demonstrate an original voice and that use multilayered, evocative images presented in a language shaped by an awareness of how words sound and what they mean. Each line should help to carry the poem. *Lake Effect* seeks poems from both established poets and from new and emerging voices." Submit up to 4 poems by mail with SASE. Length: open.

## LANDFALL: NEW ZEALAND ARTS AND LETTERS

Otago University Press, P.O. Box 56, Dunedin 9054, New Zealand. (64)(3)479-4155. **E-mail:** landfall.press@otago.ac.nz. **Website:** www.otago.ac.nz/press/landfall. **Contact:** Editor. *Landfall: New Zealand Arts and Letters* contains literary fiction and essays, poetry, extracts from work in progress, commentary on New Zealand arts and culture, work by visual artists including photographers and reviews of local books.

(*Landfall* does not accept unsolicited reviews.) Guidelines for SASE or on website.

Deadlines for submissions: January 10 for the May issue, June 10 for the November issue. "*Landfall* is open to work by New Zealand and Pacific writers or by writers whose work has a connection to the region in subject matter or location. Work from Australian writers is occasionally included as a special feature."

**MAGAZINES NEEDS** Prefers e-mail submissions. Accepts postal mail submissions, but must include SASE. Include contact information and brief bio.

## LEADING EDGE MAGAZINE

4087 JKB, Provo UT 84602. **E-mail:** editor@leadingedgemagazine.com; fiction@leadingedgemagazine.com; art@leadingedgemagazine.com; poetry@leadingedgemagazine.com; nonfiction@leadingedgemagazine.com. **Website:** www.leadingedgemagazine.com. **Contact:** Leah Welker, editor in chief. "*Leading Edge* is a magazine dedicated to new and upcoming talent in the fields of science fiction and fantasy. We strive to encourage developing and established talent and provide high-quality speculative fiction to our readers." Does not accept mss with sex, excessive violence, or profanity. Buys first North American serial rights. Pays on publication. Publishes ms an average of 2-4 months after acceptance. Responds within 12 months to mss. Single copy: $5.95. "We no longer provide subscriptions, but *Leading Edge* is now available on Amazon Kindle, as well as print-on-demand." Guidelines online.

Accepts unsolicited submissions.

**MAGAZINES NEEDS** Publishes 2-4 poems per issue. "Poetry should reflect both literary value and popular appeal and should deal with science fiction- or fantasy-related themes." No e-mail submissions. Cover letter is preferred. Include name, address, phone number, length of poem, title, and type of poem at the top of each page. Please include SASE with every submission." Pays $10 for first 4 pages; $1.50/each subsequent page.

**TIPS** "Buy a sample issue to know what is currently selling in our magazine. Also, make sure to follow the writer's guidelines when submitting."

## LILITH MAGAZINE: INDEPENDENT, JEWISH & FRANKLY FEMINIST

250 W. 57th St., Suite 2432, New York NY 10107. (212)757-0818. **Fax:** (212)757-5705. **E-mail:** info@lilith.org. **Website:** www.lilith.org. **Contact:** Susan Weidman Schneider, editor in chief; Naomi Danis, managing editor. *Lilith Magazine: Independent, Jewish & Frankly Feminist*, published quarterly, welcomes submissions of high-quality, lively writing: reportage, opinion pieces, memoirs, fiction, and poetry on subjects of interest to Jewish women. Responds in 3 months. Sample copy: $7. Guidelines online.

◐ *Lilith Magazine* is 48 pages, magazine-sized, with glossy color cover. Press run is about 10,000 (about 6,000 subscribers). Subscription: $26/year. For all submissions: Make sure name and contact information appear on each page of mss. Include a short bio (1-2 sentences), written in third person. Accepts submissions year round.

**MAGAZINES NEEDS** Has published poetry by Irena Klepfisz, Lyn Lifshin, Marcia Falk, Adrienne Rich, and Muriel Rukeyser. Send up to 3 poems at a time via online submissions form or mail; no e-mail submissions. Copy should be neatly typed and proofread for typos and spelling errors.

**TIPS** "Read a copy of the publication before you submit your work. Please be patient."

## LILLIPUT REVIEW

282 Main St., Pittsburgh PA 15201-2807. **E-mail:** lilliputreview@gmail.com. **Website:** sites.google.com/site/lilliputreview/home; lilliputreview.blogspot.com. *Lilliput Review*, published irregularly, is "shipped 2 issues at a time, every fourth issue being a broadside that features the work of a single poet." Wants poems in any style or form, no longer than 10 lines. Has published poetry by Roberta Beary, Albert Huffstickler, Charlie Mehrhoff, and John Martone. Acquires first rights. Publishes poems 1 year after acceptance. Responds in 6 months. Sample: $1 or SASE. Subscription: $5 for 6 issues, $10 for 15 issues; $12 for institutions (12 issues). Make checks payable to Don Wentworth, or make a payment to Paypal on the blog. Guidelines available for SASE or on website.

**MAGAZINES NEEDS** Submit up to 3 poems at a time, 10 lines or less. SASE required. Considers previously published poems if noted as such. Editor comments on submissions "occasionally; I always try to

establish human contact." Does not want any poetry over 10 lines. Length: up to 10 lines/poem. Pays 2 contributor copies/poem.

**ALSO OFFERS** The Modest Proposal Chapbook Series began in 1994, publishing 1 chapbook/year, 18-24 pages in length. Has published *Now Now* by Cid Corman. **Chapbook submissions are by invitation only.** Query with standard SASE. Sample chapbook: $3.

## LINEBREAK

333 Kimpel Hall, University of Arkansas, Fayetteville AR 72701. **E-mail:** editors@linebreak.org. **Website:** linebreak.org. **Contact:** Johnathon Williams, founding editor; Ash Bowen. "*Linebreak* is a weekly online magazine of original poetry. Each poem we publish is read and recorded by another working poet selected by the editors." Has published Dorianne Laux, Bob Hicok, D.A. Powell, C. Dale Young, Richard Siken, Sandra Beasley. Publishes ms 4 months after acceptance. Responds in 6 weeks. Guidelines available on website.

◐ Poems published on *Linebreak* have been selected for the Best New Poets anthology and nominated for the Pushcart Prize.

**MAGAZINES NEEDS** Submit up to 5 poems at a time through upload form on website. Considers simultaneous submissions. Reads submissions year round. Poems are circulated to an editorial board. Sometimes comments on rejected poems. Guidelines available on website. Sometimes sends prepublication galleys. Acquires electronic rights: "We require the rights to publish and archive the work indefinitely on our website, and the right to create an audio recording of each poem, which is also archived indefinitely. Copyright remains with the author."

## LIPS

P.O. Box 616, Florham Park NJ 07392. (201)724-8500. **E-mail:** LBoss79270@aol.com. **Contact:** Laura Boss, poetry editor. *Lips*, published twice/year, takes pleasure "in publishing previously unpublished poets as well as the most established voices in contemporary poetry. We look for quality work: the strongest work of a poet; work that moves the reader; poems that take risks that work. We prefer clarity in the work rather than the abstract. Poems longer than 6 pages present a space problem." Acquires first rights. Responds in 1 month (but has gotten backlogged at times). Sometimes sends prepublication galleys. Sample: $10, plus $2.50 for postage. Guidelines available for SASE.

*Lips* is about 150 pages, digest-sized, flat-spined. Has published poetry by Robert Bly, Allen Ginsberg, Michael Benedikt, Ruth Stone, Maria Mazziotti Gillan, Stanley Barkan, Lyn Lifshin, and Ishmael Reed.

**MAGAZINES NEEDS** Submit 6 pages maximum at a time. Poems should be typed. Reads submissions September through March only. Receives about 16,000 submissions/year, accepts about 1%. Pays 1 contributor copy.

## THE LISTENING EYE

Kent State University Geauga Campus, 14111 Claridon-Troy Rd., Burton OH 44021. (440)286-3840. **E-mail:** grace_butcher@msn.com. **E-mail:** Only from other countries. **Contact:** Grace Butcher, editor. "We look for powerful, unusual imagery, content, and plot in our short stories. In poetry, we look for tight lines that don't sound like prose, unexpected images or juxtapositions, the unusual use of language, noticeable relationships of sounds, a twist in viewpoint, an ordinary idea in extraordinary language, an amazing and complex idea simply stated, play on words and with words, an obvious love of language. Poets need to read the 'Big Three'—Cummings, Thomas, Hopkins—to see the limits to which language can be taken. Then read the 'Big Two'—Dickinson to see how simultaneously tight, terse, and universal a poem can be, and Whitman to see how sprawling, cosmic, and personal. Then read everything you can find that's being published in literary magazines today, and see how your work compares to all of the above." Acquires first or one-time rights. Time between acceptance and publication is up to 6 months. Responds in 4 weeks to queries; 4 months to mss. Sample copy: $4, plus $1 postage. Writer's guidelines for SASE.

**MAGAZINES NEEDS** Submit up to 4 poems at a time. Accepts previously published poems "occasionally"; no simultaneous submissions. No e-mail submissions "unless from overseas." Cover letter is required. Poems should be typed, single-spaced, with 1 poem/page—name, address, phone number, and e-mail address on each page with SASE for return of work. Poems are circulated to the editor and 2 assistant editors who read and evaluate work separately, then meet for final decisions. Length: Prefers shorter poems (less than 2 pages), but will consider longer if space allows. Pays 2 contributor copies.

**ALSO OFFERS** Awards $30 to the best sports poem in each issue.

## LITERAL LATTÉ

200 E. Tenth St., Suite 240, New York NY 10003. (212)260-5532. **E-mail:** litlatte@aol.com. **Website:** www.literal-latte.com. **Contact:** Jenine Gordon Bockman and Jeffrey Michael Bockman, editors and publishers. Bimonthly online publication. Print anthologies featuring the best of the website. "We want great writing in all styles and subjects. A feast is made of a variety of flavors." Buys first rights and requests permission for use in anthology. On publication for contests. Publishes an average of 6 months after acceptance. Responds in 6 months to mss. Editorial lead time 3 months. Writer's guidelines online, via e-mail, or for #10 SASE.

**MAGAZINES NEEDS** "We want any poem that captures the magic of the form." Length: up to 4,000 words.

**ADDITIONAL INFORMATION** "We will publish an anthology in book form featuring the best of our Web magazine."

**CONTEST/AWARD OFFERINGS** The Literal Latté Poetry Award: $1,000 first prize.

**TIPS** "Keeping free thought free and challenging entertainment are not mutually exclusive. Words make a ms stand out, words beautifully woven together in striking and memorable patterns."

## LITERARY JUICE

Issaquah WA 98027. **E-mail:** info@literaryjuice.com. **Website:** www.literaryjuice.com. **Contact:** Sara Rajan, editor in chief; Andrea O'Connor and Dinesh Rajan, managing editors. Bimonthly online literary magazine that publishes original, unpublished works of fiction, poetry, art, and photography. Does not publish works of nonfiction, essays, or interviews. Acquires electronic rights. Responds in 4 months to mss. Guidelines available on website.

**MAGAZINES NEEDS** Submit via online submissions manager. Length: 2-20 lines.

**TIPS** Looking for works that are not only thought-provoking, but venture into unconventional territory as well. Avoid submitting mainstream stories and poems (stories about zombies or politics fall into this category). Instead, take the reader to a new realm that has yet to be explored.

## LITERARY MAMA

**E-mail:** lminfo@literarymama.com. **Website:** www. literarymama.com. **Contact:** Maria Scala, editor in chief. "Online monthly magazine that features writing about the complexities and many faces of motherhood. Departments include columns, creative nonfiction, fiction, literary reflections, poetry, profiles, and book reviews. We prefer previously unpublished work and are interested in work that offers a fresh perspective." Responds in 3 weeks-3 months to mss. "We correspond via e-mail only." Guidelines online.

 "*Literary Mama* is not currently a paying market. We are all volunteers here: editors, writers, and editorial assistants. With the publication of each issue, we make a concerted effort to promote the work of our contributors via Facebook, Twitter, and our e-zine."

**TIPS** "We seek top-notch creative writing. We also look for quality literary criticism about mother-centric literature and profiles of mother writers. We publish writing with fresh voices, superior craft, and vivid imagery. Please send submission (copied into e-mail) to appropriate departmental editors. Include a brief cover letter. We tend to like stark revelation (pathos, humor, and joy); clarity; concrete details; strong narrative development; ambiguity; thoughtfulness; delicacy; irreverence; lyricism; sincerity; the elegant."

## THE LITERARY REVIEW: AN INTERNATIONAL JOURNAL OF CONTEMPORARY WRITING

Fairleigh Dickinson University, 285 Madison Ave., Madison NJ 07940. (973)443-8564. **Fax:** (973)443-8364. **E-mail:** info@theliteraryreview.org. **Website:** www.theliteraryreview.org. **Contact:** Minna Proctor, editor. *The Literary Review*, published quarterly, is "interested in innovative writing, good stories, and work that feels as if it had to be written. In other words, we like writing that has the courage of its convictions." Acquires first rights. Responds in 8-12 months. Sample copy: $10 domestic, $10 + $5 shipping outside U.S.; request a "general issue."

 *TLR Online*, available on the website, features original work not published in the print edition. *The Literary Review* is about 200 pages, digest-sized, professionally printed, flat-spined, with glossy color cover. Receives about 1,200 submissions/year, accepts 100-150. Press run is 2,000 (800 subscribers, one-third are overseas).

**MAGAZINES NEEDS** Submit via online submissions manager. Has published poetry by Albert Goldbarth, Mary Jo Bang, David Citino, Rick Mulkey, Virgil Suárez, and Gary Fincke. Pays 2 contributor copies and one-year subscription.

## THE LITERARY REVIEW

285 Madison Ave., Madison NJ 07940. (973)443-8564. **Fax:** (973)443-8364. **E-mail:** info@theliteraryreview.org. **Website:** www.theliteraryreview.org. **Contact:** Minna Proctor, editor. Acquires first rights. Responds in 6-12 months. Sample copy: $10. Guidelines online.

 Work published in *The Literary Review* has been included in *Editor's Choice*, *Best American Short Stories*, and *Pushcart Prize* anthologies. Uses online submissions manager.

**MAGAZINES NEEDS** Pays 2 contributor copies and one-year subscription.

**TIPS** "We want original dramatic situations with complex moral and intellectual resonance and vivid prose. We don't want versions of familiar plots and relationships. Too much of what we are seeing today is openly derivative in subject, plot, and prose style. We pride ourselves on spotting new writers with fresh insight and approach."

## LITTLE PATUXENT REVIEW

P.O. Box 6084, Columbia MD 21045. **E-mail:** editor@littlepatuxentreview.org. **Website:** www.littlepatuxentreview.org. **Contact:** Steven Leyva, editor. "*Little Patuxent Review (LPR)* is a community-based, biannual print journal devoted to literature and the arts, primarily in the Mid-Atlantic region. We profile the work of a major poet or fiction writer and a visual artist in each issue. We celebrate the launch of each issue with a series of readings and broadcast highlights on *LPR*'s YouTube channel. All forms and styles considered. Please see our website for the current theme." Buys first rights. Responds in 3-5 months to mss. Sample copy: $10. Guidelines available in magazine and on website.

 *LPR* is about 120 pages; digest-sized; 100# finch cover; artwork (varies depending on featured artist). Has published poetry by Lucille Clifton, Martín Espada, Donald Hall, Joy Harjo, Marie Howe, Myra Sklarew, Clarinda Harriss, and Alan King. 2011 Pushcart Prize for "Patronized" by Tara Hart.

**MAGAZINES NEEDS** Submit up to 3 poems by on-line submissions manager; no mail or e-mail submissions. Include word count and 75-word bio. Length: up to 100 lines/poem. Pays 1 contributor copy.

**ALSO OFFERS** "*LPR* co-sponsors monthly arts Salon Series events in conjunction with the Columbia Art Center, featuring literary readings, art presentations, and musical performances. Events are free and open to the public. Contributors are invited to participate in reading series and literary festivals, such as the Baltimore Book Festival. As part of our outreach effort, the *LPR* in the Classroom Program provides *LPR* issues to high schools and colleges at a discounted rate."

**TIPS** "Please see our website for the current theme. Poetry and prose must exhibit the highest quality to be considered. Please read a sample issue before submitting."

### ◑❸ THE LONDON MAGAZINE

11 Queen's Gate, London SW7 5EL, United Kingdom. (44)(0)20 7584 5977. **E-mail:** admin@thelondonmagazine.org. **Website:** www.thelondonmagazine.org. **Contact:** Steven O'Brien, editor. "We publish literary writing of the highest quality. We look for poetry and short fiction that startles and entertains us. Reviews, essays, memoir pieces, and features should be erudite, lucid, and incisive. We are obviously interested in writing that has a London focus, but not exclusively so, since London is a world city with international concerns." Buys first rights. Pays on publication. Published ms an average of 4 months after acceptance. Responds in 1 month to queries; 3 months to mss. Editorial lead time 3 months. Sample copy: £6.95. Guidelines online.

**MAGAZINES NEEDS** "Abstraction is the enemy of good poetry. Poetry should display a commitment to the ultra specificities of language and show a refined sense of simile and metaphor. The structure should be tight and exact." Submit up to 6 poems via online submissions manager, e-mail (as an attachment), or postal mail (enclose SASE). "We do not publish long, loose poems." Length: up to 40 lines/poem.

**TIPS** "Please look at *The London Magazine* before you submit work so that you can see the type of material we publish."

### LONE STARS MAGAZINE

4219 Flint Hill St., San Antonio Texas 78230-1619. **E-mail:** lonestarsmagazine@yahoo.com. **Website:** www.lonestarsmagazine.net. **Contact:** Milo Rosebud, editor/publisher. *Lone Stars*, published 3 times/year, features contemporary poetry and artwork. Acquires one-time publication rights. Authors retain all rights. Time between acceptance and publication is 3-6 months. Responds within 3 months. Sample (past issues): $5.50. Single copy: $7. Subscription: $20 for 3 issues. Guidelines available for SASE.

◐    *Lone Stars* is 25+ pages, magazine-sized, photocopied, saddle-stapled, bound with tape. Press run is 200+.

**MAGAZINES NEEDS** Wants poetry "that holds a continuous line of thought." Does not want profanity. Considers poetry by children and teens. Submit 3-5 poems at a time. Cover letter is preferred. Submit poems on any subject, formatted and "typed the way you want them in print." **Charges reading fee of $1 per poem.** Has published poetry by Terry Lee, Eve J. Blohm, Linda Amos, and many more.

**ALSO OFFERS** Sponsors Annual Songbook Lyric Poetry Contest, Annual Light of the Stars Poetry Contest, The Write Idea Interactive Poetry Contests, and Great "One-Liner" Contributions. Details available with e-mail or SASE.

**TIPS** "Submit poetry that expresses a reasonable train of thought."

### LONG LIFE

Longevity through Technology, The Immortalist Society, 24355 Sorrentino Ct., Clinton Township MI 48035. **E-mail:** info@cryonics.org. **Website:** www.cryonics.org/resources/long-life-magazine. "*Long Life* magazine is a publication for people who are particularly interested in cryonic suspension: the theory, practice, legal problems, etc. associated with being frozen when you die in the hope of eventual restoration to life and health. Many people who receive the publication have relatives who have undergone cryonic preparation or have made such arrangements for themselves or are seriously considering this option. Readers are also interested in other aspects of life extension such as anti-aging research and food supplements that may slow aging. Articles we publish include speculation on what the future will be like; problems of living in a future world, and science in general, particularly as it may apply to cryonics and life extension." Publication is copyrighted. Responds in 1 month to queries and mss. Sample copy is free for SASE.

**MAGAZINES NEEDS** "Poems are welcomed, especially short, humorous poems with a cryonics or life-extension theme." Pays 1 contributor copy.

**TIPS** "We are a small magazine but with a highly intelligent and educated readership which is socially and economically diverse. We currently don't pay for material but are seeking new authors and provide contributors with copies of the magazine with the contributor's published works. Look over a copy of *Long Life*, or talk with the editor to get the tone of the publication. There is an excellent chance that your ms will be accepted if it is well written and 'on theme.' Pictures to accompany the article are always welcome, and we like to publish photos of the authors with their first ms."

### LONG STORY SHORT, AN E-ZINE FOR WRITERS

P.O. Box 475, Lewistown MT 59457. **E-mail:** alongstory_short@aol.com. **Website:** www.alongstoryshort. net. **Contact:** Anisa Claire, Kim Bussey, editors. *Long Story Short, An E-zine for Writers* publishes "the best fiction and poetry from both emerging and established writers. Acquires nonexclusive world electronic and print rights, nonexclusive archival Web rights. Publishes ms up to 6 months after acceptance, depending on theme. Guidelines available on website. "Read them!"

○ Free newsletter with poetry of the month chosen by poetry editor; includes author's bio and web page listed in the e-zine. Offers light critique of submissions upon request and a free writing forum.

**MAGAZINES NEEDS** Submit by e-mail; no attachments. Considers poetry by children (ages 10 and up) and teens. Has published poetry by Michael Lee Johnson, Maria Ercilla, Shonda Buchanan, Patricia Wellingham-Jones, Floriana Hall, and Russell Bittner. Length: up to 32 lines/poem. Pays 1 contributor copy.

### THE LOS ANGELES REVIEW

P.O. Box 2458, Redmond WA 98073. (626)356-4760. **Fax:** (626)356-9974. **E-mail:** lareviededitor@gmail. com. **Website:** losangelesreview.org. **Contact:** Alisa Trager, managing editor. Acquires one-time rights. Pays on publication. Publishes ms 2-5 months after

acceptance. Responds in 1-2 months to mss. Sample copy: $15. Guidelines available on website.

**MAGAZINES NEEDS** Submit 3-4 poems at a time. Wants poems that "will surprise us, wow us, and make us wish we'd written them ourselves. We are open to form, free verse, prose poems, and experimental styles. Our only criterion is quality."

**TIPS** "Read a few recent issues to see what we're about. Pay close attention to the submission guidelines. We like cover letters, but please keep them brief."

### LOST LAKE FOLK OPERA

Shipwreckt Books Publishing Company, 309 W. Stevens Ave., Rushford MN 55971. **E-mail:** contact@ shipwrecktbooks.com. **Website:** www.shipwreckt-books.com. **Contact:** Tom Driscoll, managing editor. *Lost Lake Folk Opera* magazine accepts submissions of critical journalism, short fiction, poetry, and graphic art. Published twice annually. Retains one-time rights. Pays on acceptance; offers contributor copies, and discount contributor copy price. Publishes ms 6-9 months after acceptance. Responds in 6 weeks on queries; 3 months on mss. Editorial lead time: 3 monthsminimum. Sample copy available for cover price with SASE. Guidelines available by e-mail.

**MAGAZINES NEEDS** Length: 1-250 lines. Does not offer payment.

**TIPS** " When in doubt, edit and cut. Please remember to read your submission. Don't expect LLFO to wash your car and detail it. Send clean copies of your work."

### LOUISIANA LITERATURE

SLU Box 10792, Hammond LA 70402. **E-mail:** lalit@ selu.edu. **Website:** www.louisianaliterature.org. **Contact:** Jack B. Bedell, editor. "Since 1984, *Louisiana Literature* has featured some of the finest writing published in America. The journal has always striven to spotlight local talent alongside nationally recognized authors. Whether it's work from established writers or from first-time publishers, *Louisiana Literature* is always looking to print the finest poetry and fiction available." Acquires one-time rights. Publishes ms 6-12 after acceptance. Responds in 1-3 months to mss. Sometimes comments on rejected mss. Sample copy: $8. Guidelines for SASE or online.

**MAGAZINES NEEDS** Submit 3-5 poems at a time via online submissions manager. Reads submissions year round, "although we work more slowly in summer." Sometimes sends prepublication galleys. Send materials for review consideration; include cover letter. Pays 2 contributor copies.

**TIPS** "Cut out everything that is not a functioning part of the story. Make sure your ms is professionally presented. Use relevant, specific detail in every scene. We love detail, local color, voice, and craft. Any professional ms stands out."

## THE LOUISIANA REVIEW

Division of Liberal Arts, Louisiana State University Eunice, P.O. Box 1129, Eunice LA 70535. (337)550-1315. **E-mail:** bfonteno@lsue.edu. **Website:** web.lsue.edu/la-review. **Contact:** Dr. Billy Fontenot, fiction editor; Dr. Jude Meche, poetry editor; Dr. Diane Langlois, art editor. *The Louisiana Review*, published annually during the fall or spring semester, offers "Louisiana poets, writers, and artists a place to showcase their most beautiful pieces. Others may submit Louisiana- or Southern-related poetry, stories, and art. Publishes photographs. Sometimes publishes nonfiction." Wants "strong imagery, metaphor, and evidence of craft." Acquires one-time rights. Not copyrighted, but has an ISSN number. Pays on publication. Publishes ms 6-12 months after acceptance. Single copy: $5.

○ *The Louisiana Review* is 100 pages, digest-sized, professionally printed, perfect-bound. Press run is 300-600.

**MAGAZINES NEEDS** Submit up to 5 poems at a time. No previously published poems. No fax or e-mail submissions. "Include cover letter indicating your association with Louisiana, if any. Has published poetry by Gary Snyder, Antler, and David Cope. Receives up to 2,000 poems/year, accepts 30-50. Does not want "sing-song rhymes, abstract, religious, or overly sentimental work." Pays 1 contributor copy.

**TIPS** "We do like to have fiction play out visually as a film would, rather than be static and undramatized. Louisiana or Gulf Coast settings and themes preferred."

## THE LOUISVILLE REVIEW

Spalding University, 851 S. Fourth St., Louisville KY 40203. (502)873-4398. **Fax:** (502)992-2409. **E-mail:** louisvillereview@spalding.edu. **Website:** www.louisvillereview.org. **Contact:** Ellyn Lichvar, managing editor. *The Louisville Review*, published twice/year, prints poetry, fiction, nonfiction, and drama. Has a section devoted to poetry by writers under age 18 (grades K-12) called The Children's Corner. Sample:

$5. Single copy: $8. Subscription: $14/year, $27/2 years, $40/3 years (foreign subscribers add $6/year for s&h). Guidelines online.

○ *The Louisville Review* is 150 pages, digest-sized, flat-spined. Receives about 700 submissions/year, accepts about 10%.

**MAGAZINES NEEDS** Accepts submissions via online manager; please see website for more information. "Poetry by children must include permission of parent to publish if accepted. Address those submissions to The Children's Corner." Reads submissions year round. Has published poetry by Wendy Bishop, Gary Fincke, Michael Burkard, and Sandra Kohler. Pays in contributor copies.

## LULLWATER REVIEW

P.O. Box 122036, Atlanta GA 30322. **E-mail:** emorylullwaterreview@gmail.com. **Website:** www.lullwaterreview.wordpress.com. **Contact:** Aneyn M. O'Grady, editor-in-chief; Gabriel Unger, managing editor. "We're a small, student-run literary magazine published out of Emory University in Atlanta, Georgia with 2 issues yearly—once in the fall and once in the spring. You can find us in the *Index of American Periodical Verse*, the *American Humanities Index* and as a member of the Council of Literary Magazines and Presses. We welcome work that brings a fresh perspective, whether through language or the visual arts." Buys first North American serial rights. Pays on publication. Publishes ms an average of 1-2 months after acceptance. Responds in 1-3 months to queries; 3-6 months to mss. Sample copy for $5. Guidelines with #10 SASE.

**MAGAZINES NEEDS** *Lullwater Review*, published in May and December, prints poetry, short fiction, and artwork. Wants poetry of any genre with strong imagery, original voice, on any subject. Has published poetry by Amy Greenfield, Peter Serchuk, Katherine McCord, and Ha Jin. Submit 6 or fewer poems at a time. Considers simultaneous submissions; no previously published poems. Cover letter is preferred. Prefers poems single-spaced with name and contact info on each page. "Poems longer than 1 page should include page numbers. We must have a SASE with which to reply." Reads submissions September 1-May 15 only. Poems are circulated to an editorial board. Seldom comments on rejected poems. No profanity or pornographic material. Pays 3 contributor copies.

**TIPS** "We at the *Lullwater Review* look for clear co-gent writing, strong character development and an engaging approach to the story in our fiction submissions. Stories with particularly strong voices and well-developed central themes are especially encouraged. Be sure that your manuscript is ready before mailing it off to us. Revise, revise, revise! Be original, honest, and of course, keep trying."

## LUMINA

Sarah Lawrence College, **E-mail:** lumina@gm.slc.edu. **Website:** luminajournal.com. **Contact:** Sarah Dean, editor in chief; Steven Wolf, fiction editor; Melanie Anagnos, nonfiction editor; Marie Marandola, poetry editor. "*LUMINA*'s mission is to provide a journal where emerging and established writers and visual artists come together in exploration of the new and appreciation of the traditional. We want to see sonnets sharing space with experimental prose; we want art that pushes boundaries and bends rules with eloquence." All rights revert to author upon publication. Sample copy: $12. Guidelines online.

**MAGAZINES NEEDS** Submit via online submissions manager. All submissions are read blind; do not include personal information on submission documents. Length: up to 60 lines/poem.

## LUNGFULL!MAGAZINE

316 23rd St., Brooklyn NY 11215. **E-mail:** customerservice@lungfull.org. **Website:** lungfull.org. **Contact:** Brendan Lorber, editor/publisher. "*LUNGFULL! Magazine* World Headquarters in Brooklyn is home to a team of daredevils who make it their job to bring you only the finest in typos, misspellings, and awkward phrases. That's because *LUNGFULL!magazine* is the only literary and art journal in America that prints the rough drafts of people's work so you can see the creative process as it happens." Responds in 1 year to mss. Submit by postal mail. Include SASE. If sending by e-mail (not preferred) do NOT send attachments and put "Submission by [Your Name]" in the subject line.

○ *LUNGFULL!* was the recipient of a grant from the New York State Council for the Arts.

**MAGAZINES NEEDS** Submit up to 8 poems. Include cover letter.

## THE LUTHERAN DIGEST

The Lutheran Digest, Inc., 6160 Carmen Ave., Inver Grove Heights MN 55076. (651)451-9945. **E-mail:** editor@lutherandigest.com. **Website:** www.lutherandigest.com. **Contact:** Nick Skapyak, editor. Articles frequently reflect a Lutheran Christian perspective but are not intended to be sermonettes. Popular stories show how God has intervened in a person's life to help solve a problem. Buys first rights, second serial (reprint) rights. Pays on publication. Publishes ms an average of 6 months after acceptance. Responds in 4 months to mss. No response to e-mailed mss unless selected for publication. Editorial lead time 9 months. Sample copy: $3.50. Subscription: $16/year, $22 for 2 years. Guidelines online.

○ *The Lutheran Digest* is 64 pages, digest-sized, offset-printed, saddle-stapled, with 4-color paper cover, includes local ads. Press run is 20,000-30,000; most distributed free to Lutheran churches.

**MAGAZINES NEEDS** Submit up to 3 poems at a time. Prefers e-mail submissions but also accepts mailed submissions. Cover letter is preferred. Include SASE only if return is desired. Poems are selected by editor and reviewed by publication panel. Length: up to 25 lines/poem. Pays 1 contributor copy.

**TIPS** "Reading our writers' guidelines and sample articles online is encouraged and is the best way to get a feel for the type of material we publish."

## ⑤ LYRICAL PASSION POETRY E-ZINE

P.O. Box 17331, Arlington VA 22216. **E-mail:** lpezine-submissions@gmail.com. **Website:** lyricalpassionpoetry.yolasite.com. **Contact:** Raquel D. Bailey, founding editor. Founded by award-winning poet Raquel D. Bailey, *Lyrical Passion Poetry E-Zine* is an attractive monthly online literary magazine specializing in Japanese short-form poetry. Publishes quality artwork, well-crafted short fiction, and poetry in English by emerging and established writers. Literature of lasting literary value will be considered. Welcomes the traditional to the experimental. Poetry works written in German will be considered if accompanied by translations. Offers annual short fiction and poetry contests. Acquires first-time rights, electronic rights (must be the first literary venue to publish online or in any electronic format). Rights revert to poets upon publication. Publishes ms 1 month after acceptance.

Responds in 1-2 months. Guidelines and upcoming themes available on website.

**MAGAZINES NEEDS** Multiple submissions are permitted, but no more than 3 submissions in a 6-month period. Does not want dark, cliché, limerick, erotica, extremely explicit, violent, or depressing literature. Length: 1-40 lines (free verse).

## THE LYRIC

The Lyric Literary Arts, Inc., P.O. Box 110, Jericho Corners VT 05465. **E-mail:** themuse@thelyricmagazine.com. **Website:** www.thelyricmagazine.com. *The Lyric*, published quarterly, is the oldest magazine in North America in continuous publication devoted to traditional poetry. Responds in 3 months ("average; inquire after 6 months"). Sample: $5, available in Europe through the Rome office for 18 euros/year sent to Nancy M Mellichamp-Savo, Via Lola Montez, #14, Rome, Italy 00135. Subscription: $15/year, $28/2 years, $38/3 years (U.S.), $17/year for Canada and other countries (in U.S. funds only). Guidelines available for SASE or by e-mail.

○ *The Lyric* is 32 pages, digest-sized, professionally printed with varied typography, with matte card cover. Receives about 3,000 submissions/year, accepts 5%.

**MAGAZINES NEEDS** Submit by postal service; out-of-country poems may be submitted by e-mail. Considers simultaneous submissions (although not preferred); no previously published poems. Cover letter is often helpful, but not required. Has published poetry by Michael Burch, Gail White, Constance Rowell Mastores, Ruth Harrison, Barbara Loots, Tom Riley, Catherine Chandler, and Glenna Holloway. "Our themes are varied, ranging from religious ecstasy to humor to raw grief, but we feel no compulsion to shock, embitter, or confound our readers. We also avoid poems about contemporary political or social problems—'grief but not grievances,' as Frost put it. Frost is helpful in other ways: If yours is more than a lover's quarrel with life, we are not your best market. And most of our poems are accessible on first or second reading." Length: up to 40 lines. Pays 1 contributor copy.

**CONTEST/AWARD OFFERINGS** 5 yearly prizes ($400), 4 quarterly prizes ($50/issue).

**TIPS** All contributors are eligible for quarterly and annual prizes totaling $650. Also offers *The Lyric* College Contest, open to undergraduate students in the U.S. Awards prize of $500; 2nd Place: $100. **Deadline:** December 1. Send entries by e-mail September 1-December 1: tanycim@aol.com, or to Tanya Cimonetti, 1393 Spear St., S, Burlington, VT 05403. "Our *raison d'etre* has been the encouragement of form, music, rhyme, and accessibility in poetry. As we witness the growing tide of appreciation for traditional/lyric poetry, we are proud to have stayed the course for 94 years, helping keep the roots of poetry alive."

## ○⊙ MANOA: A PACIFIC JOURNAL OF INTERNATIONAL WRITING

English Department, University of Hawaii, Honolulu HI 96822. (808)956-3070. **Fax:** (808)956-3083. **E-mail:** mjournal-l@lists.hawaii.edu. **Website:** manoajournal.hawaii.edu. **Contact:** Frank Stewart, editor. *Mānoa* is seeking "high-quality literary fiction, poetry, essays, and translations. In general, each issue is devoted to new work from Pacific and Asian areas. Our audience is international. US writing need not be confined to Pacific settings or subjects. Please note that we seldom publish unsolicited work; you may query us at our website." Buys first North American serial rights, buys nonexclusive, one-time print rights. Pays on publication. Responds in 3 weeks to queries. Editorial lead time 9 months. Sample: $15 (US). Guidelines online.

○ *Mānoa* has received numerous awards, and work published in the magazine has been selected for prize anthologies. See website for recently published issues.

**MAGAZINES NEEDS** No light verse. Pays $25/poem.

**TIPS** "Not accepting unsolicited mss at this time because of commitments to special projects. Please query before sending mss as e-mail attachments."

## THE MACGUFFIN

Schoolcraft College, 18600 Haggerty Rd., Livonia MI 48152, United States. (734)462-4400, ext 5327. **E-mail:** macguffin@schoolcraft.edu. **Website:** http://www.schoolcraft.edu/macguffin. **Contact:** Steven A. Dolgin, editor; Gordon Krupsky, managing editor;. "Our purpose is to encourage, support and enhance the literary arts in the Schoolcraft College community, the region, the state, and the nation. We also sponsor annual literary events and give voice to deserving new writers as well as established writers." Acquires first rights. Once published, rights revert back to author. 3-4 months Responds to submissions in 2-4 months. $6. Use the order form on our website. Guidelines online.

**MAGAZINES NEEDS** Poetry should be typed, single-spaced, only one poem per page. 400 Pays 2 contributor copies.

**HOW TO CONTACT** For mail submissions, do not staple work. Include name, email, address and the page no. on each page. Include SASE for reply only. For email, submit each work (single story or five-poem submission) as a Word .doc attachment.

**CONTEST/AWARD OFFERINGS** We also sponsor a yearly Poet Hunt Contest from April-June. See contest rules online.

### THE MADISON REVIEW

University of Wisconsin, 600 N. Park St., 6193 Helen C. White Hall, Madison WI 53706. **E-mail:** madisonrevw@gmail.com. **Website:** www.english.wisc.edu/madisonreview. **Contact:** Will Conley and Sam Zisser, fiction editors; Mckenna Kohlenberg and Cody Dunn, poetry editors. *The Madison Review* is a student-run literary magazine that looks to publish the best available fiction and poetry. Buys one-time rights. Publishes ms an average of 9 months after acceptance. Responds in 4 weeks to queries; in 6 months to mss. Editorial lead time 6 months. Sample copy: $3. Guidelines online.

Does not publish unsolicited interviews or genre fiction. Send all submissions through online submissions manager.

**MAGAZINES NEEDS** Cover letter is preferred. Does not want religious or patriotic dogma and light verse. Pays 2 contributor copies.

**TIPS** "Our editors have very eclectic tastes, so don't specifically try to cater to us. Above all, we look for original, high-quality work."

### THE MAGAZINE OF FANTASY & SCIENCE FICTION

P.O. Box 3447, Hoboken NJ 07030. (201) 876-2551. **E-mail:** fandsf@aol.com. **Website:** www.fandsf.com; submissions.ccfinlay.com/fsf. **Contact:** C.C. Finlay, editor. "*The Magazine of Fantasy and Science Fiction* publishes various types of science fiction and fantasy short stories and novellas, making up about 80% of each issue. The balance of each issue is devoted to articles about science fiction, a science column, book and film reviews, cartoons, and competitions." Bimonthly.

Buys first North American serial rights, buys foreign serial rights. Pays on acceptance. Publishes ms an average of 9-12 months after acceptance. Responds in 2 months to queries. Sample: $7 US, $15.00 international. Guidelines for SASE, by e-mail, or on website at www.sfsite.com/fsf/glines.htm.

*The Magazine of Fantasy and Science Fiction* won a Nebula Award for Best Novelet for *A Guide to the Fruits of Hawai'i* by Alaya Dawn Johnson in 2015. Many other works published by *F&SF* received award nominations and reprints in various "Best of the Year" anthologies.

**MAGAZINES NEEDS** Wants only poetry that deals with the fantastic or the science fictional. Has published poetry by Rebecca Kavaler, Elizabeth Bear, Sophie M. White, and Robert Frazier. Pays $50/poem and 2 contributor copies.

**TIPS** "Good storytelling makes a submission stand out. Regarding mss, a well-prepared ms (i.e., one that follows the traditional format, like that described here: www.sfwa.org/writing/vonda/vonda.htm) stands out more than any gimmicks. Read an issue of the magazine before submitting. New writers should keep their submissions under 15,000 words—we rarely publish novellas by new writers."

### MAGMA POETRY

23 Pine Walk, Carshalton Surrey SM5 4ES, United Kingdom. **E-mail:** contributions@magmapoetry.com; info@magmapoetry.com. **Website:** www.magmapoetry.com. **Contact:** Laurie Smith. *Magma* appears 3 times/year and contains modern poetry, reviews and interviews with poets. Wants poetry that is modern in idiom and shortish (2 pages maximum). Nothing sentimental or old fashioned. Has published poetry by Thomas Lynch, Thom Gunn, Michael Donaghy, John Burnside, Vicki Feaver, and Roddy Lumsden. Guidelines online.

Only accepts contributions from the UK. *Magma* is 64 pages, 8×8, photocopied and stapled, includes b&w illustrations. Receives about 3,000 poems/year, accepts 4-5%. Press run is about 500. Single copy: £5.70 UK and Ireland, £6.15 rest of Europe, £7.50 airmail ROW. Subscription: £14.50 UK and Ireland, £18 rest of Europe, £20.50 airmail ROW. Make checks payable to *Magma*. For subscriptions, contact Helen Nicholson, distribution secretary, Flat 2, 86 St. James's Dr., London SW17 7RR England.

**MAGAZINES NEEDS** Accepts submissions by post (with SAE and IRCs) and online submissions manager. Cover letter is preferred. Deadlines for submissions: end of January, May, and September. Poems are considered for one issue only. Each issue has an editor who submits his/her selections to a board for final approval. Editor's selection very rarely changed. Occasionally publishes theme issues. Pays 1 contributor copy.

**ALSO OFFERS** "We hold a public reading in London three times/year, to coincide with each new issue, and poets in the issue are invited to read."

**TIPS** "See 'About Magma' and the contents of our website to gain an idea of the type of work we accept." Keep up with the latest news and comment from *Magma Poetry* by receiving free updates via e-mail. Sign up online to receive the Magma Blog and/or the *Magma* newsletter.

## ◯ THE MAGNOLIA QUARTERLY

P.O. Box 10294, Gulfport MS 39505. **E-mail:** writerpllevin@gmail.com. **Website:** www.gcwriters.org. **Contact:** Phil Levin, editor. *The Magnolia Quarterly* publishes poetry, fiction, nonfiction, and reviews. **For members of GCWA only.** Returns rights to author upon publication. Time between acceptance and publication varies. Single copy: $3; subscription: included in $30 GCWA annual dues. Make checks payable to Gulf Coast Writers Association. Guidelines available in magazine or on website.

◗ *The Magnolia Quarterly* is 40 pages, pocket-sized, stapled, with glossy cover, includes ads. Editing service offered on all prose.

**MAGAZINES NEEDS** Submit 1-3 poems at a time. Prefers e-mail submissions. Reads submissions year round. Has published poetry by Leonard Cirino, Catharine Savage Brosman, Angela Ball, Jack Bedell, and Larry Johnson. Will consider all styles of poetry. Does not want "pornography, racial or sexist bigotry, far-left or far-right political poems." Length: up to 40 lines/poem. No payment.

**ALSO OFFERS** Holds the "Let's Write" contest, with cash prizes for poetry and prose. Additional information available on website.

## THE MAIN STREET RAG

P.O. Box 690100, Charlotte NC 28227-7001. (704)573-2516. **E-mail:** editor@mainstreetrag.com. **Website:** www.mainstreetrag.com. **Contact:** M. Scott Douglass, editor/publisher. *The Main Street Rag*, published quarterly, prints "poetry, short fiction, essays, interviews, reviews, photos, and art. We like publishing good material from people who are interested in more than notching another publishing credit, people who support small independent publishers like ourselves." Will consider "almost anything," but prefers "writing with an edge—either gritty or bitingly humorous. Contributors are advised to visit our website prior to submission to confirm current needs." Acquires first North American print rights. Time between acceptance and publication is up to 1 year. Responds in 6 weeks. Single copy: $8. Subscription: $24/year, $45 for 2 years. E-mail submissions only. Detailed guidelines and current needs available on website.

◗ *The Main Street Rag* receives about 5,000 submissions/year; publishes 50+ poems and 3-5 short stories per issue, a featured interview, photos, and an occasional nonfiction piece. Press run is about 500 (250 subscribers, 15 libraries).

**MAGAZINES NEEDS** Submit 6 pages of poetry at a time; no more than 1 poem per page. E-mail submissions only. Cover letter is preferred. "No bios or credits—let the work speak for itself." Pays 1 contributor copy.

## ◷◑◉ THE MALAHAT REVIEW

The University of Victoria, P.O. Box 1700, STN CSC, Victoria BC V8W 2Y2, Canada. (250)721-8524. **E-mail:** malahat@uvic.ca (for queries only). **Website:** www.malahatreview.ca. **Contact:** John Barton, editor. Quarterly magazine covering poetry, fiction, creative nonfiction, and reviews. "We try to achieve a balance of views and styles in each issue. We strive for a mix of the best writing by both established and new writers." Buys first world rights. Pays on acceptance. Publishes ms an average of 6 months after acceptance. Responds in 2 weeks to queries; in 3-10 months to mss. Sample: $16.95 (US). Guidelines online.

**MAGAZINES NEEDS** Submit 3-5 poems via online submissions manager: malahatreview.ca/submission_guidelines.html#submittable. Length: up to 6 pages. Pays $50/magazine page.

**CONTEST/AWARD OFFERINGS** Presents the P.K. Page Founders' Award for Poetry, a $1,000 prize to the author of the best poem or sequence of poems to be published in *The Malahat Review*'s quarterly issues during the previous calendar year. Also offers the Open Season Awards, biennial Long Poem Prize, biennial Novella Prize, Constance Rooke Creative Nonfiction Prize, the biennial Far Horizons Award for Short Fiction, and the biennial Far Horizons Award for Poetry.

**TIPS** "Please do not send more than 1 submission at a time: 3-5 poems, 1 piece of creative nonfiction, or 1 short story (do not mix poetry and prose in the same submission). See *The Malahat Review*'s Open Season Awards for poetry and short fiction, creative nonfiction, long poem, and novella contests in the Awards section of our website."

## THE MANHATTAN REVIEW

440 Riverside Dr., #38, New York NY 10027. **E-mail:** phfried@gmail.com. **Website:** themanhattanreview. com. **Contact:** Philip Fried. *The Manhattan Review* publishes only poetry, reviews of poetry books, and poetry-related essays. The editor reads unsolicited submissions year round but requests that you observe the guidelines. Acquires first North American serial rights. Responds in 3 months if possible. Guidelines online.

**MAGAZINES NEEDS** Send 3-5 poems with SASE and brief bio. Read magazine before submitting. Pays contributor copies.

## ⓄⓈ THE MASSACHUSETTS REVIEW

University of Massachusetts, Photo Lab 309, Amherst MA 01003. (413)545-2689. **E-mail:** massrev@external. umass.edu. **Website:** www.massreview.org. **Contact:** Emily Wojcik, managing editor. Seeks a balance between established writers and promising new ones. Interested in material of variety and vitality relevant to the intellectual and aesthetic questions of our time. Aspire to have a broad appeal. Buys first North American serial rights. Pays on publication. Publishes ms an average of 18 months after acceptance. Responds in 2-6 months to mss. Sample copy: $8 for back issue, $10 for current issue. Guidelines online.

Ⓠ  Does not respond to mss without SASE.

**MAGAZINES NEEDS** Has published poetry by Catherine Barnett, Billy Collins, and Dara Wier. Include your name and contact on every page. Length: There are no restrictions for length, but generally poems are less than 100 lines. Pays $50/publication and 2 contributor copies.

**TIPS** "No manuscripts are considered May-September. Electronic submission process can be found on website. No fax or e-mail submissions. Shorter rather than longer stories preferred (up to 28-30 pages)."

Looks for works that "stop us in our tracks." Manuscripts that stand out use "unexpected language, idiosyncrasy of outlook, and are the opposite of ordinary."

## MEASURE: A REVIEW OF FORMAL POETRY

526 S. Lincoln Park Dr., Evansville IN 47714. (812)488-2963. **E-mail:** editors@measurepress.com. **Website:** www.measurepress.com/measure. *Measure*, an international journal of formal poetry, began in 2005 in conjunction with the University of Evansville. Measure Press is a new enterprise by editors Rob Griffith and Paul Bone. The goal is to continue bringing readers the best new poetry from both established and emerging writers through the biannual journal. *Measure* has a mission not only to publish the best new poetry from both established and emerging writers but also to reprint a small sampling of poems from books of metrical poetry published the previous year. Likewise, each issue includes interviews with some of the most important contemporary poets and also offers short critical essays on the poetry that has helped to shape the craft. Responds in 3 months. Guidelines online at website.

**MAGAZINES NEEDS** Send no more than 3 to 5 poems at a time. Poems must be metrical. Include poet's name and phone number. Submit electronically on website.

## MENSBOOK JOURNAL

Strategen, P.O. Box 418, Sturbridge MA 01566. **Fax:** (508)470-6477. **E-mail:** features@mensbook.com. **Website:** www.mensbook.com. **Contact:** Payson Fitch, editor/publisher. Gay-owned and operated company with arms in publishing and advertising. Two days max. Response time varies between 5 minutes and 1 month. There is no specific lead time; we are an online journal. Online journal, except for end-of-year *Mensbook* "best of" anthology printed and distributed to book stores. Do not mail—e-mail only. Do not call. Guidelines online at www.mensbook.com/ writersguidelines.htm.

**TIPS** "Be a tight writer with a cogent, potent message. Structure your work with well-organized progressive sequencing. Edit everything down before you send it over so we know it is the best you can do, and we'll work together from there."

## MERIDIAN

University of Virginia, P.O. Box 400145, Charlottesville VA 22904-4145. **E-mail:** meridianuva@gmail. com; meridianpoetry@gmail.com; meridianfiction@gmail.com. **Website:** www.readmeridian.org. *Meridian*, published semiannually, prints poetry, fiction, nonfiction, interviews, and reviews. "*Meridian* is interested in writing that is vibrant, moving, and alive, and welcomes contributions from a variety of aesthetic approaches. Has published such poets as Alexandra Teague, Gregory Pardlo, Sandra Meek, and Bob Hicok, and such fiction writers as Matt Bell, Kate Milliken, and Ron Carlson. Has recently interviewed C. Michael Curtis, Ann Beatty, and Claire Messud, among other luminaries. Also publishes a recurring feature called 'Lost Classic,' which resurrects previously unpublished work by celebrated writers and which has included illustrations from the mss of Jorge Luis Borges, letters written by Elizabeth Bishop, Stephen Crane's deleted chapter from *The Red Badge of Courage*, and a letter written by Flannery O'Connor about her novel *Wise Blood*." Publishes ms 1-2 months after acceptance. Seldom comments on rejected poems and mss. Responds in 1-4 months. Always sends prepublication galleys and author contracts. Sample copy: $6 (back issue). Single print copy: $7. Print subscription: $12 for 1 year; $22 for 2 years. Single digital copy: $3. Digital subscription: $4 for 1 year; $7 for 2 years. Buy subscriptions online via credit card, or mail an order form with a check made out to *Meridian*. Guidelines online.

○ *Meridian* is 130 pages, digest-sized, offset-printed, perfect-bound, with color cover. Receives about 2,500 poems/year, accepts about 40 (less than 1%). Press run is 1,000 (750 subscribers, 15 libraries, 200 shelf sales); 150 distributed free to writing programs. Work published in *Meridian* has appeared in *The Best American Poetry* and *The Pushcart Prize Anthology*.

**MAGAZINES NEEDS** Submit up to 5 poems via online submissions manager. Length: up to 10 pages total. Pays 2 contributor copies (additional copies available at discount).

**ALSO OFFERS** *Meridian* Editors' Prize Contest offers annual $1,000 award. Submit online only; see website for formatting details. **Entry fee:** $8.50, includes one-year subscription to *Meridian* for all U.S. entries or 1 copy of the prize issue for all international entries. **Deadline:** December or January; see website for current deadline.

**◉ MICHIGAN QUARTERLY REVIEW**

0576 Rackham Bldg., 915 E. Washington, Ann Arbor MI 48109-1070. (734)764-9265. **E-mail:** mqr@umich.edu. **Website:** www.michiganquarterlyreview.com. **Contact:** Jonathan Freedman, editor; Vicki Lawrence, managing editor. *Michigan Quarterly Review* is an eclectic interdisciplinary journal of arts and culture that seeks to combine the best of poetry, fiction, and creative nonfiction with outstanding critical essays on literary, cultural, social, and political matters. The flagship journal of the University of Michigan, *MQR* draws on lively minds here and elsewhere, seeking to present accessible work of all varieties for sophisticated readers from within and without the academy. Buys first serial rights. Pays on publication. Publishes ms an average of 1 year after acceptance. Responds in 2 months to queries and mss. Sample: $4. Guidelines online.

○ The Laurence Goldstein Award is a $500 annual award to the best poem published in *MQR* during the previous year. The Lawrence Foundation Award is a $1,000 annual award to the best short story published in *MQR* during the previous year. The Page Davidson Clayton Award for Emerging Poets is a $500 annual award given to the best poet appearing in *MQR* during the previous year who has not yet published a book.

**MAGAZINES NEEDS** No previously published poems. No e-mail submissions. Cover letter is preferred. "It puts a human face on the ms. A few sentences of biography is all I want, nothing lengthy or defensive." Prefers typed mss. Reviews books of poetry. "All reviews are commissioned." Length: should not exceed 8-12 pages. Pays $8-12/published page.

**TIPS** "Read the journal and assess the range of contents and the level of writing. We have no guidelines to offer or set expectations; every ms is judged on its unique qualities. On essays, query with a very thorough description of the argument and a copy of the first page. Watch for announcements of special issues, which are usually expanded issues and draw upon a lot of freelance writing. Be aware that this is a university quarterly that publishes a limited amount of fiction and poetry and that it is directed at an educated audience, one that has done a great deal of reading in all types of literature."

## MID-AMERICAN REVIEW

Bowling Green State University, Dept. of English, Bowling Green OH 43403. (419)372-2725. **E-mail:** mar@bgsu.edu; marsubmissions.bgsu.edu. **Website:** www.bgsu.edu/midamericanreview. **Contact:** Abigail Cloud, editor in chief; Lydia Munnell, fiction editor. "We aim to put the best possible work in front of the biggest possible audience. We publish contemporary fiction, poetry, creative nonfiction, translations, and book reviews." Buys first North American serial rights. Publishes mss an average of 6 months after acceptance. Responds in 5 months to mss. Sample copy: $9 (current issue), $5 (back issue), $10 (rare back issues). Guidelines online.

Contests: The Fineline Competition for Prose Poems, Short Shorts, and Everything In Between (June 1 deadline, $10 per 3 pieces, limit 500 words each); The Sherwood Anderson Fiction Award (November 1 deadline, $10 per piece); and the James Wright Poetry Award (November 1 deadline, $10 per 3 pieces).

**MAGAZINES NEEDS** Submit by mail with SASE or with online submission manager. Publishes poems with "textured, evocative images, an awareness of how words sound and mean, and a definite sense of voice. Each line should help carry the poem, and an individual vision must be evident." Recently published work by Mary Ann Samyn, G.C. Waldrep, and Daniel Bourne.

**TIPS** "We are seeking translations of contemporary authors from all languages into English; submissions must include the original and proof of permission to translate. We would also like to see more creative nonfiction."

## MIDWAY JOURNAL

77 Liberty Avenue #10, Somerville MA 02144. (763)516-7463. **E-mail:** editors@midwayjournal.com. **Website:** www.midwayjournal.com. See website for specific genre contacts and e-mails.. **Contact:** Christopher Lowe, nonfiction editor; Ralph Pennel, fiction editor; Paige Riehl, poetry editor. "Just off of I-94 and on the border between St. Paul and Minneapolis, the Midway, like any other state fairgrounds, is alive with a mix of energies and people. Its position as mid-way, as a place of boundary crossing, also reflects our vision for this journal. The work here complicates and questions the boundaries of genre, binary, and aesthetic. It offers surprises and ways of re-seeing,

re-thinking, and re-feeling: a veritable banquet of literary fare. Which is why, in each new issue, we are honored to present work by both new and established writers alike." Responds in 6-9 months. Sample copy online. Guidelines online.

**MAGAZINES NEEDS** Submit 3-5 poems, no more than 10 pages in a single document, via online submissions manager. No line-length limits.

**TIPS** "An interesting story with engaging writing, both in terms of style and voice, make a ms stand out. Round characters are a must. Writers who take chances either with content or with form grab an editor's immediate attention. Spend time with the words on the page. Spend time with the language. The language and voice are not vehicles; they, too, are tools."

## THE MIDWEST QUARTERLY

406A Russ Hall, Pittsburg State University, Pittsburg KS 66762. (620)235-4369 or (620)235-4037. **E-mail:** midwestq@pittstate.edu; lkmartin@pittstate.edu. **Website:** www.pittstate.edu/department/english/midwest-quarterly. **Contact:** Dr. Casie Hermansson, editor; Lori Baker Martin, poetry editor. *The Midwest Quarterly* publishes "articles on any subject of contemporary interest, particularly literary criticism, political science, philosophy, education, biography, and sociology. Each issue contains a section of poetry usually 12 poems in length. We seek discussions of an analytical and speculative nature and well-crafted poems." For publication in *MQ* and eligibility for the annual Emmett Memorial Prize competition, the editors invite submission of articles on any literary topic but preferably on Victorian or Modern British Literature, Literary Criticism, or the Teaching of Literature. The winner receives an honorarium and invitation to deliver the annual Emmett Memorial Lecture. Contact Dr. Stephen Meats, English Department, Pittsburg State University, Pittsburg, KS 66762. Acquires first serial rights. Responds in 2 months to mss. Sample: $5. Subscription: $15 US; $25 foreign. Guidelines available on website.

*The Midwest Quarterly* is 130 pages, digest-sized, professionally printed, flat-spined, with matte cover. Press run is 650 (600 subscribers, 500 are libraries).

**MAGAZINES NEEDS** Submit up to 10 poems at a time. Will accept e-mail submissions. "Mss should be typed with poet's name on each page. Include e-mail address for notification of decision. SASE only for return of poem." Submissions are also accepted on website: www.pittstate.edu/info/midwestq/submit.dot. Comments on rejected poems "if the poet or poem seems particularly promising." Occasionally publishes theme issues or issues devoted to the work of a single poet. Receives about 3,500-4,000 poems/year, accepts about 50. Has published poetry by Peter Cooley, Lyn Lifshin, Judith Skillman, Naomi Shihab Nye, Jonathan Holden, and Ted Kooser. "Both traditional forms and free verse are accepted. Whatever the form, however, we want poems that are fresh, that move us, have strong imagery, and which use language in a surprising, musical, and interesting way." Length: up to 80 lines/poem ("occasionally longer if exceptional"). Pays 2 contributor copies.

## MILLER'S POND

**E-mail:** mail@handhpress.com (C.J. Houghtaling); mpwebeditor@yahoo.com (Julie Damerell). **E-mail:** mpwebeditor@yahoo.com. **Website:** www. millerspondpoetry.com. **Contact:** C.J. Houghtaling, publisher; Julie Damerell, editor. *miller's pond* is exclusively an e-zine and does not publish in hard copy format. Web version is published 3 times/year. Submissions accepted year round but read in late December, over the school spring break, and late August. Writers are encouraged to submit near the reading dates to avoid long waits. Responses sent only in late December/early January, April, and late August. "Current guidelines, updates, and changes are always available on our website. Check there first before submitting anything."

○ Submissions that do not indicate the poet has read the guidelines are deleted without comment.

**MAGAZINES NEEDS** Submit poems to Julie Damerell, editor. All submissions must be sent in the body of an e-mail. Mail sent through the post office will be discarded. No payment for accepted poems or reviews.

**TIPS** "Follow submission guidelines on the website. Submissions that do not fulfill the guidelines are deleted without comment. Read the pages on the website to see the range of poetry I like."

## MINAS TIRITH EVENING-STAR: JOURNAL OF THE AMERICAN TOLKIEN SOCIETY

American Tolkien Society, P.O. Box 97, Highland MI 48357-0097. **E-mail:** editor@americantolkiensociety. org; americantolkiensociety@yahoo.com. **Website:** www.americantolkiensociety.org. **Contact:** Amalie A. Helms, editor. *Minas Tirith Evening-Star: Journal of the American Tolkien Society*, published quarterly, publishes poetry, book reviews, essays, and fan fiction. *Minas Tirith Evening-Star* is digest-sized, off-set-printed from typescript, with cartoon-like b&w graphics. Press run is 400. Single copy: $3.50; subscription: $12.50. Sample: $3. Make checks payable to American Tolkien Society. Responds in 2 weeks. Guidelines online.

**MAGAZINES NEEDS** Uses poetry of fantasy about Middle-earth and Tolkien. Considers poetry by children and teens. Has published poetry by Thomas M. Egan, Anne Etkin, Nancy Pope, and Martha Benedict. Submit by mail or e-mail. Reviews related books of poetry; length depends on the volume ("a sentence to several pages"). Send materials for review consideration. Pays 1 contributor copy.

**ALSO OFFERS** Membership in the American Tolkien Society is open to all, regardless of country of residence, and entitles one to receive the quarterly journal. Dues are $12.50/year to addresses in U.S., Canada, and Mexico, and $15 elsewhere. Sometimes sponsors contests.

## THE MINNESOTA REVIEW

Virginia Tech, ASPECT, 202 Major Williams Hall (0192), Blacksburg VA 24061. **E-mail:** editors@theminnesotareview.org. **Website:** minnesotareview. wordpress.com. **Contact:** Janell Watson, editor. *The Minnesota Review*, published biannually, is a journal featuring creative and critical work from writers on the rise or who are already established. Each issue is about 200 pages, digest-sized, flat-spined, with glossy card cover. Press run is 1,000 (400 subscribers). Also online. Subscription: $30/2 years for individuals, $60/year for institutions. Sample: $15. Guidelines online.

○ Open to submissions August 1-November 1 and January 1-April 1. Accepts submissions via online submissions manager.

**MAGAZINES NEEDS** Submit up to 5 poems every 3 months online. Pays 2 contributor copies.

## M.I.P. COMPANY

P.O. Box 27484, Minneapolis MN 55427. **Website:** www.mipco.com. **Contact:** Michael Peltsman, editor. The publisher of controversial Russian literature (erotic prose and poetry). Responds in 1 month to queries. Seldom comments on rejected poems.

**MAGAZINES NEEDS** Considers simultaneous submissions; no previously published poems.

## MISSISSIPPI REVIEW

University of Southern Mississippi, 118 College Dr., #5144, Hattiesburg MS 39406-0001. (601)266-4321. **Fax:** (601)266-5757. **E-mail:** msreview@usm.edu. **Website:** www.usm.edu/mississippi-review. **Contact:** Andrew Malan Milward, editor in chief; Caleb Tankersley and Allison Campbell, associate editors. *Mississippi Review* "is one of the most respected literary journals in the country. Raymond Carver, an early contributor to the magazine, once said that *Mississippi Review* 'is one of the most remarkable and indispensable literary journals of our time.' Well-known and established writers have appeared in the pages of the magazine, including Pulitzer and Nobel Prize winners, as well as new and emerging writers who have gone on to publish books and to receive awards." Buys first North American serial rights. Sample copy for $10. "We do not accept unsolicited manuscripts except under the rules and guidelines of the *Mississippi Review* Prize Competition. See website for guidelines."

Publishes 25-30 new writers/year. Annual fiction and poetry competition: $1,000 awarded in each category, plus publication of all winners and finalists. Fiction entries: 8,000 words or less. Poetry entries: 1-5 poems; page limit is 10. $15 entry fee includes copy of prize issue. No limit on number of entries. Deadline December 1. No mss returned.

## THE MISSOURI REVIEW

357 McReynolds Hall, University of Missouri, Columbia MO 65211. (573)882-4474. **Fax:** (573)884-4671. **E-mail:** mutmrquestion@moreview.com. **Website:** www.missourireview.com. **Contact:** Speer Morgan, editor; Kate McIntyre, managing editor, Evelyn Somers, associate editor; Chun Ye, poetry editor. Publishes contemporary fiction, poetry, interviews, personal essays, cartoons, special features—such as History as Literature series, Found Text series, and Curio Cabinet art features—for the literary and the general reader interested in a wide range of subjects. Offers signed contract. Responds in 2 weeks to queries; in 10-12 weeks to mss. Editorial lead time 4-6 months. Sample copy: $10 or online. Guidelines online.

**MAGAZINES NEEDS** *TMR* publishes poetry features only—6-14 pages of poems by each of 3-5 poets per issue. Keep in mind the length of features when submitting poems. Typically, successful submissions include 8-20 pages of unpublished poetry. (Note: Do not send complete mss—published or unpublished—for consideration.) No inspirational verse. Pays $40/printed page and 3 contributor copies.

**ADDITIONAL INFORMATION** The Tom McAfee Discovery Feature is awarded at least once/year to showcase an outstanding young poet who has not yet published a book; poets are selected from regular submissions at the discretion of the editors.

**TIPS** "Send your best work."

## MOBIUS

505 Christianson St., Madison WI 53714. **E-mail:** fmschep@charter.net. **Website:** www.mobiusmagazine. com. **Contact:** Fred Schepartz, publisher and executive editor. *Mobius: The Journal of Social Change* is online-only journal, published quarterly in March, June, September, and December. "At *Mobius* we believe that writing is power and good writing empowers both the reader and the writer. We feel strongly that alternatives are needed to an increasingly corporate literary scene. *Mobius* strives to provide an outlet for writers disenfranchised by a bottom-line marketplace, and challenging writing for those who feel that today's literary standards are killing us in a slow, mind-numbing fashion." Publishes ms 3-6 months after acceptance. Responds in 1 month. Guidelines online.

**MAGAZINES NEEDS** Submit poetry dealing with themes of social change. Accepts e-mailed poetry submissions only. "We have a marked distate for prosaic didacticism (but a weakness for prose poems)." Do not submit poems by postal mail.

**TIPS** "We like high impact. We like plot- and character-driven stories that function like theater of the mind. We look first and foremost for good writing. Prose must be crisp and polished; the story must pique my interest and make me care due to a certain intellectual, emotional aspect. *Mobius* is about social change. We want stories that make some statement about the society we live in, either on a macro or micro level. Not that your story needs to preach from a soapbox (actually, we prefer that it doesn't), but your story needs to have something to say."

## THE MOCCASIN

The League of Minnesota Poets, 427 N. Gorman St., Blue Earth MN 56013. (507)526-5321. **Website:** www. mnpoets.com. **Contact:** Meredith R. Cook, editor. *The Moccasin*, published annually in October, is the literary magazine of The League of Minnesota Poets. Membership is required to submit work.

○ *The Moccasin* is 40 pages, digest-sized, offset-printed, stapled, with 80 lb. linen-finish text cover with drawing and poem. Receives about 190 poems/year, accepts about 170. Press run is 200. Single copy: $6.25; subscription: free with LOMP membership.

**MAGAZINES NEEDS** Send submissions by mid-July each year. Looking for all forms of poetry. Prefer strong short poems. Considers poetry by children and teens who are student members of The League of Minnesota Poets (write grade level on poems submitted). Has published poetry by Diane Glancy, Laurel Winter, Susan Stevens Chambers, Doris Stengel, Jeanette Hinds, and Charmaine Donovan. Does not want profanity or obscenity. Do not use inversions or archaic language. Length: 24 lines max.

**TIPS** To become a member of The League of Minnesota Poets, send $20 ($10 if high school student or younger) to Angela Foster, LOMP Treasurer, 30036 St. Croix Rd, Pine City MN 55063. Make checks payable to LOMP. You do not have to live in Minnesota to become a member of LOMP. "Membership in LOMP automatically makes you a member of the National Federation of State Poetry Societies, which makes you eligible to enter its contests at a cheaper (members') rate."

## THE MOCHILA REVIEW

Missouri Western State University, 525 Downs Dr., St. Joseph MO 64507. **E-mail:** mochila@missouriwestern.edu. **Website:** www.missouriwestern.edu/orgs/mochila/homepage.htm. **Contact:** Marianne Kunkel, editor. "We are looking for writing that has a respect for the sound of language. We value poems that have to be read aloud so your mouth can feel the shape of the words. Send us writing that conveys a sense of urgency, writing that the writer can't *not* write. We crave fresh and daring work." Responds in 3-4 months to mss. Guidelines online.

**MAGAZINES NEEDS** Submit no more than 5 poems at a time by postal mail. Include cover letter, contact information, SASE. Pays in contributor copies.

**TIPS** "Manuscripts with fresh language, energy, passion, and intelligence stand out. Study the craft and be entertaining and engaging."

## ❸ MODERN HAIKU

P.O. Box 930, Portsmouth RI 02871. **E-mail:** modernhaiku@gmail.com. **Website:** modernhaiku.org. **Contact:** Paul Miller, editor. *Modern Haiku* is the foremost international journal of English-language haiku and criticism and publishes high-quality material only. Haiku and related genres, articles on haiku, haiku book reviews, and translations comprise its contents. It has an international circulation; subscribers include many university, school, and public libraries. Acquires first North American serial rights, first international serial rights. Publishes ms an average of 6 months after acceptance. Responds in 1 week to queries; in 6-8 weeks to mss. Editorial lead time 4 months. Sample copy: $15 in North America, $16 in Canada, $20 in Mexico, $22 overseas. Subscription: $35 ppd by regular mail in the U.S. Payment possible by PayPal on the *Modern Haiku* website. Guidelines available for SASE or on website.

○ *Modern Haiku* is 140 pages (average), digest-sized, printed on heavy-quality stock, with full-color cover illustrations, 4-page full-color art sections. Receives about 15,000 submissions/year, accepts about 1,000. Press run is 700.

**MAGAZINES NEEDS** Postal submissions: "Send 5-15 haiku on 1 or 2 letter-sized sheets. Put name and address at the top of each sheet. Include SASE." E-mail submissions: "May be attachments (recommended) or pasted in body of message. Subject line must read: MH Submission. Adhere to guidelines on the website." Publishes 750 poems/year. Has published haiku by Roberta Beary, Billy Collins, Lawrence Ferlinghetti, Carolyn Hall, Sharon Olds, Gary Snyder, John Stevenson, George Swede, and Cor van den Heuvel. Does not want "general poetry, tanka, renku, linked-verse forms. No special consideration given to work by children and teens." Offers no payment.

**ALSO OFFERS** Reviews of books of haiku by staff and freelancers by invitation in 350-1,000 words, usually single-book format. Send materials for review consideration with complete ordering information. Sponsors the annual Robert Spiess Memorial Haiku Competition. Guidelines available for SASE or on website.

**TIPS** "Study the history of haiku, read books about haiku, learn the aesthetics of haiku and methods of composition. Write about your sense perceptions of the suchness of entities; avoid ego-centered interpretations. Be sure the work you send us conforms to the definitions on our website."

## ○ MUDFISH

Box Turtle Press, Inc., Box Turtle Press, 184 Franklin St., Ground Floor, New York NY 10013. (212)219-9278. **E-mail:** mudfishmag@aol.com. **Website:** www.mudfish.org. **Contact:** Jill Hoffman, editor. *Mudfish*, a journal of art and poetry (and some fiction), takes its title from the storyteller's stool in Nigerian art. The poems each tell a story. They are resonant and visceral, encapsulating the unique human experience. There is a wide range to the subject matter and style, but the poems all have breath and life, a living voice. *Mudfish* has featured work from the best established and emerging artists and poets—including John Ashbery, Charles Simic, and Frank Stella—since it burst onto the poetry scene. Responds in 3 months, or ASAP.

**MAGAZINES NEEDS** Wants free verse with energy, intensity, and originality of voice, mastery of style, the presence of passion. Submit 5-6 poems at a time. No e-mail submissions; postal submissions only. Pays 1 contributor copy.

**CONTEST/AWARD OFFERINGS** Sponsors the Mudfish Poetry Prize Award of $1,000. **Entry fee:** $15 for up to 3 poems, $3 for each additional poem. **Deadline:** varies. Guidelines available for SASE.

## ◐ MUDLARK: AN ELECTRONIC JOURNAL OF POETRY & POETICS

Department of English, University of North Florida, Jacksonville FL 32224-2645. (904)620-2273. **E-mail:** mudlark@unf.edu. **Website:** www.unf.edu/mudlark. **Contact:** William Slaughter, editor and publisher. *Mudlark: An Electronic Journal of Poetry & Poetics*, published online "irregularly, but frequently," offers 3 formats: Issues of *Mudlark* "are the electronic equivalent of print chapbooks; posters are the electronic equivalent of print broadsides; and flash poems are poems that have news in them, poems that feel like current events. The poem is the thing at *Mudlark*, and the essay about it. As our full name suggests, we will consider accomplished work that locates itself anywhere on the spectrum of contemporary practice. We want poems, of course, but we want essays, too, that make us read poems (and write them?) differently somehow. Although we are not innocent, we do imagine ourselves capable of surprise. The work of hobbyists is not for *Mudlark*. As for representative authors: No naming names here. If we are, as we imagine ourselves, capable of surprise, then there is no such thing as a 'representative author' in the *Mudlark* archive, which is 'never in and never out of print.' The *Mudlark* archive, going back to 1995, is as wide as it is deep, as rich and various as it is full." *Mudlark* is archived and permanently on view at www.unf.edu/mudlark. Acquires one-time rights. No payment; however, "one of the things we can do at *Mudlark* to 'pay' our authors for their work is point to it here and there. We can tell our readers how to find it, how to subscribe to it, and how to buy it—if it is for sale. Toward that end, we maintain A-Notes on the authors we publish. We call attention to their work." Publishes ms no more than 3 months after acceptance. Responds in "1 day to 1 month, depending." Guidelines for SASE, by e-mail, or on website.

**MAGAZINES NEEDS** Submit any number of poems at a time. "Prefers not to receive simultaneous submissions but will consider them if informed of the fact, up front, and if notified immediately when poems are accepted elsewhere. Considers previously published work only as part of a *Mudlark* issue, the electronic equivalent of a print chapbook, and only if the previous publication is acknowledged in a note that covers the submission. Only poems that have not been previously published will be considered for *Mudlark* posters, the electronic equivalent of print broadsides, or for *Mudlark* flashes." Accepts e-mail or USPS submissions with SASE; no fax submissions. Cover letter is optional. Seldom comments on rejected poems. Always sends prepublication galleys "in the form of inviting the author to proof the work on a private website that *Mudlark* maintains for that purpose."

## ⑤ MYTHIC DELIRIUM

3514 Signal Hill Ave. NW, Roanoke VA 24017-5148. **E-mail:** mythicdelirium@gmail.com. **Website:** www.mythicdelirium.com. **Contact:** Mike Allen, editor. "*Mythic Delirium* is an online and e-book venue for fiction and poetry that ranges through science fiction, fantasy, horror, interstitial, and cross-genre territory—we love blurred boundaries and tropes turned on their heads. We are interested in work that demonstrates ambition, that defies traditional approaches to genre, that introduces readers to the legends of other cultures, that re-evaluates the myths of old from a modern perspective, that twists reality in unexpected ways. We are committed to diversity and are open to and encourage submissions from people of every race, gender, nationality, sexual orientation, political affiliation and religious belief. We publish 12 short stories and 24 poems a year. Our quarterly ebooks in PDF, EPUB, and MOBI formats, published in July, October, January, and April, will each contain 3 stories and 6 poems. We will also publish 1 story and 2 poems on our website each month." Reading period: August 1-October 1 annually. Responds in 2 months. Accepts electronic submissions only to mythicdelirium@gmail.com.

**MAGAZINES NEEDS** "No unsolicited reprints. Please use the words 'poetry submission' in the e-mail subject line. Poems may be included in the e-mail as RTF or DOC attachments." Length: open. Pays $5 flat fee.

**TIPS** "*Mythic Delirium* isn't easy to get into, but we publish newcomers in every issue. Show us how ambitious you can be, and don't give up."

## ⬤ NARRATIVE MAGAZINE

2443 Fillmore St. #214, San Francisco CA 94115. **E-mail:** contact@narrativemagazine.com. **Website:** www.narrativemagazine.com. **Contact:** Michael Croft, senior editor; Mimi Kusch, managing editor; Michael Wiegers, poetry editor. "*Narrative* publishes high-quality contemporary literature in a full range of styles, forms, and lengths. Submit poetry, fiction, and nonfiction, including stories, short shorts, novels, novel excerpts, novellas, personal essays, humor, sketches, memoirs, literary biographies, commentary, reportage, interviews, and short audio recordings of short-short stories and poems. We welcome submissions of previously unpublished mss of all lengths, ranging from short-short stories to complete book-length works for serialization. In addition to submissions for issues of *Narrative* itself, we also encourage submissions for our Story of the Week, literary contests, and Readers' Narratives. Please read our Submission Guidelines for all information on mss formatting, word lengths, author payment, and other policies. We accept submissions only through our electronic submission system. We do not accept submissions through postal services or e-mail. You may send us mss for the following submission categories: General Submissions, Narrative Prize, Story

of the Week, Readers' Narrative, iPoem, iStory, Six-Word Story, or a specific Contest. Your ms must be in one of the following file forms: .doc, .rtf, .pdf, .docx, .txt, .wpd, .odf, .mp3, .mp4, .mov, or .flv." Buys exclusive first North American serial rights in English for 90 days, and thereafter, for nonexclusive rights "to maintain the work in our online library." Responds in 4-14 weeks to queries. Guidelines online. Charges $23 reading fee except for 2 weeks in April.

**TIPS** "Log on and study our magazine online. Narrative fiction, graphic art, and multimedia are selected, first and foremost, for quality."

## ⬤ THE NASSAU REVIEW

Nassau Community College, Nassau Community College, English Dept., 1 Education Dr., Garden City NY 11530. **E-mail:** nassaureview@ncc.edu. **Website:** www.ncc.edu/nassaureview. **Contact:** Christina M. Rau, editor in chief. *The Nassau Review* welcomes submissions of many genres, preferring work that is "innovative, captivating, well-crafted, and unique, work that crosses boundaries of genre and tradition. You may be serious. You may be humorous. You may be somewhere in between. We are looking simply for quality. New and seasoned writers are welcome." Acquires first North American serial rights "and the right to archive your work online for an indefinite period of time." Responds in three months at most. Submit via online submissions system only. Please read all guidelines and details on the website: www.ncc.edu/nassaureview.

⬤     All open submissions are under consideration for the Writer Awards.

**MAGAZINES NEEDS** Accepts simultaneous submissions: "Please let us know they are simultaneous when you submit them." Submit via online submissions manager. Include title and bio of up to 100 words. Length: 50 lines/poem. Pays 1 contributor copy.

## THE NATIONAL POETRY REVIEW

P.O. Box 2080, Aptos CA 95001-2080. **E-mail:** editor@nationalpoetryreview.com; nationalpoetryreview@yahoo.com. **Website:** www.nationalpoetryreview.com. **Contact:** C.J. Sage, editor. *The National Poetry Review* seeks "distinction, innovation, and *joie de vivre*. We agree with Frost about delight and wisdom. We believe in rich sound. We believe in the beautiful—even if that beauty is not in the situation of the poem but simply the sounds of the poem, the images, or (and, ideally) the way the poem stays in the reader's mind long after it's been read." *TNPR* considers both experimental and 'mainstream' work." Does not want "overly self-centered or confessional poetry." Acquires first rights. Time between acceptance and publication is no more than 1 year. "The editor makes all publishing decisions." Sometimes comments on rejected poems. Usually responds in about 3-4 months. Guidelines available on website.

○ *The National Poetry Review* is an annual online journal that accepts less than 1% of submissions received. Poetry appearing in *The National Poetry Review* has also appeared in *The Pushcart Prize*. Has published poetry by Bob Hicok, Jennifer Michael Hecht, Larissa Szplorluk, Martha Zweig, Nance Van Winkel, William Waltz, and Ted Kooser.

**MAGAZINES NEEDS** "Our reading period is January 1-April 1 annually. Please submit all poems in one file. Include a brief bio with previous publications."

## ⓢ THE NATION

33 Irving Place, 8th Floor, New York NY 10003. E-mail: submissions@thenation.com. **Website:** www.thenation.com. Steven Brower, art director. **Contact:** Roane Carey, managing editory; Ange Mlinko, poetry editor. *The Nation*, published weekly, is a journal of left/liberal opinion, with arts coverage that includes poetry. The only requirement for poetry is excellence. Guidelines online.

○ Poetry published by *The Nation* has been included in *The Best American Poetry*. Has published poetry by W.S. Merwin, Maxine Kumin, James Merrill, May Swenson, Edward Hirsch, and Charles Simic.

**MAGAZINES NEEDS** "Please email poems in a single PDF attachment to PoemNationSubmit@gmail.com. Submissions are not accepted from June 1-September 15."

## NATURAL BRIDGE

Dept. of English, University of Missouri-St. Louis, One University Blvd., St. Louis MO 63121. (314)516-7327. **E-mail:** natural@umsl.edu. **Website:** www.umsl.edu/~natural. *Natural Bridge*, published biannually in May and December, invites submissions of poetry, fiction, personal essays, and translations. Acquires first North American rights. Publishes ms 9 months after acceptance. Responds in 4-8 months. Guidelines online at website.

○ No longer accepts submissions via e-mail. Accepts submissions through online submission form and postal mail only.

**MAGAZINES NEEDS** Seeks "fresh, innovative poetry, both free and formal, on any subject. We want poems that work on first and subsequent readings—poems that entertain and resonate and challenge our readers." Submit 4-6 poems at a time. "Submissions should be typewritten, with name and address on each page. Do not staple manuscripts. Send SASE." Submit year round; however, "we do not read May 1-August 1. Work is read and selected by the guest-editor and editor, along with editorial assistants made up of graduate students in our MFA program. We publish work by both established and new writers." Length: no limit. Pays 2 contributor copies and 1-year subscription.

## NAUGATUCK RIVER REVIEW

P.O. Box 368, Westfield MA 01085. **E-mail:** naugatuckriver@aol.com. **Website:** naugatuckriverreview.wordpress.com. **Contact:** Lori Desrosiers, publisher. *Naugatuck River Review*, published semiannually (summer issue online, winter issue is print), "is a literary journal for great narrative poetry looking for narrative poetry of high caliber, where the narrative is compressed with a strong emotional core." Acquires first North American serial rights. Responds in 1-4 months. Always sends prepublication galleys. Guidelines available in magazine and on website.

○ Accepts submissions through online submission form only.

**MAGAZINES NEEDS** Submit up to 3 poems. Prefers unpublished poems. Accepts online submissions through submission manager only; no e-mail, fax, or disk submissions. Include brief bio and mailing information. Reads submissions January 1-March 1 and July 1-September 1 for contest. Length: up to 50 lines.

**CONTEST/AWARD OFFERINGS** The July 1-Sept. 1 submission period is a contest. $1,350 in prizes (3 prizes).

**TIPS** "What is narrative poetry? What *NRR* is looking for are poems that tell a story or have a strong sense of story. They can be stories of a moment or an experience and can be personal or historical. A good narrative poem that would work for our journal has a compressed narrative, and we prefer poems that take up 2 pages or less of the journal (50 lines max). We are looking above all for poems that are well crafted, have an excellent lyric quality, and contain a strong emotional core. Any style of poem is considered, including prose poems. Poems with very long lines don't fit well in the 6x9 format."

## NEBO

Arkansas Tech University, Department of English, Russellville AR 72801. **E-mail:** nebo@atu.edu. **Website:** www.atu.edu/worldlanguages/Nebo.php **Contact:** Editor. *Nebo*, published in the spring and fall, publishes fiction, poetry, creative nonfiction, drama, comics, and art from Arkansas Tech students and unpublished writers as well as nationally known writers. Acquires one-time rights. Publishes mss 3-6 months after acceptance. Responds in 2 weeks-4 months to mss. Occasionally comments on rejected mss. Sample copy: $6. Subscriptions: $10. Guidelines available on website.

Reads submissions August 15-January 31.

**MAGAZINES NEEDS** Accepts all forms of poetry. Submit up to 5 poems by e-mail or postal mail.

**TIPS** "Avoid pretentiousness. Write something you genuinely care about. Please edit your work for spelling, grammar, cohesiveness, and overall purpose. Many of the mss we receive should be publishable with a little polishing. Mss should never be submitted handwritten or on 'onion skin' or colored paper."

## NEON MAGAZINE

**E-mail:** info@neonmagazine.co.uk. **Website:** www.neonmagazine.co.uk. **Contact:** Krishan Coupland. Quarterly website and print magazine covering alternative work of any form of poetry and prose, short stories, flash fiction, artwork and reviews. "Genre work is welcome. Experimentation is encouraged. We like stark poetry and weird prose. We seek work that is beautiful, shocking, intense, and memorable. Darker pieces are generally favored over humorous ones." Buys one-time rights. "After publication all rights revert back to you." Responds in 2 months. Query if you have received no reply after 10 weeks. Guidelines online.

*Neon* was previously published as *FourVolts Magazine*.

**MAGAZINES NEEDS** "No nonsensical poetry; we are not appreciative of sentimentality. Rhyming poetry is discouraged." No word limit. Pays royalties.

**TIPS** "Send several poems, 1 or 2 pieces of prose or several images via form e-mail. Include the word 'submission' in your subject line. Include a short biographical note (up to 100 words). Read submission guidelines before submitting your work."

## NEW AMERICAN WRITING

369 Molino Ave., Mill Valley CA 94941. **Website:** www.newamericanwriting.com. **Contact:** Maxine Chernoff and Paul Hoover, editors. New American Writing is a literary magazine emphasizing contemporary American poetry. The magazine is distinctive for publishing a range of contemporary innovative poetry. Sample copies available for $15. Guidelines online.

**MAGAZINES NEEDS** Reading period September 1 to January 15. Submit via postal mail. Response time varies between 2 weeks to 6 months.

## THE NEW CRITERION

900 Broadway, Suite 602, New York NY 10003. **Website:** www.newcriterion.com. Poetry Editor: David Yezzi.. **Contact:** Roger Kimball, editor and publisher. "A monthly review of the arts and intellectual life, *The New Criterion* began as an experiment in critical audacity—a publication devoted to engaging, in Matthew Arnold's famous phrase, with 'the best that has been thought and said.' This also meant engaging with those forces dedicated to traducing genuine cultural and intellectual achievement, whether through obfuscation, politicization, or a commitment to nihilistic absurdity. We are proud that *The New Criterion* has been in the forefront both of championing what is best and most humanely vital in our cultural inheritance and in exposing what is mendacious, corrosive, and spurious. Published monthly from September through June, *The New Criterion* brings together a wide range of young and established critics whose common aim is to bring you the most incisive criticism being written today."

## NEW ENGLAND REVIEW

Middlebury College, Middlebury VT 05753. (802)443-5075. **E-mail:** nereview@middlebury.edu. **Website:** www.nereview.com. **Contact:** Marcia Parlow, managing editor. *New England Review* is a prestigious, nationally distributed literary journal. Reads September 1 through May 31 (postmarked dates). Buys first North American serial rights, buys first rights, buys second serial (reprint) rights. Sends galleys to author. Pays on publication. Publishes ms an average of 6 months after acceptance. Responds in 2 weeks to queries; in 3 months to mss. Sometimes comments on rejected mss. Sample copy: $10 (add $5 for overseas). Subscription: $30. Overseas shipping fees add $25 for subscription, $12 for Canada. Guidelines online.

**MAGAZINES NEEDS** Submit up to 6 poems at a time. No previously published or simultaneous submissions for poetry. Accepts submissions by online submission manager only; accepts questions by e-mail. "Cover letters are useful." Address submissions to "Poetry Editor." Pays $20/page ($20 minimum), and 2 contributor copies.

**ALSO OFFERS** *NER* pays $50 per published online essay in their digital series "Confluences," works of 500-1,000 words. Submission details appear online.

**TIPS** "We consider short fiction, including short shorts, novellas, and self-contained extracts from novels in both traditional and experimental forms. In nonfiction, we consider a variety of general and literary but not narrowly scholarly essays; we also publish long and short poems, screenplays, graphics, translations, critical reassessments, statements by artists working in various media, testimonies, and letters from abroad. We are committed to exploration of all forms of contemporary cultural expression in the U.S. and abroad. With few exceptions, we print only work not published previously elsewhere."

## NEW LETTERS

University of Missouri-Kansas City, 5101 Rockhill Rd., Kansas City MO 64110. (816)235-1168. **Fax:** (816)235-2611. **E-mail:** newletters@umkc.edu. **Website:** www.newletters.org. **Contact:** Robert Stewart, editor in chief. *"New Letters* continues to seek the best new writing, whether from established writers or those ready and waiting to be discovered. In addition, it supports those writers, readers, and listeners who want to experience the joy of writing that can both surprise and inspire us all." Buys first North American serial rights. Pays on publication. Publishes ms an average of 6 months after acceptance. Responds in 1 month to queries; in 5 months to mss. Editorial lead time 6 months. Sample copy: $10 or sample articles on website. Guidelines online.

Submissions are not read May 1 through October 1.

**MAGAZINES NEEDS** No light verse. Length: open. Pays $10-25.

**TIPS** "We aren't interested in essays that are footnoted or essays usually described as scholarly or critical. Our preference is for creative nonfiction or personal essays. We prefer shorter stories and essays to longer ones (an average length is 3,500-4,000 words). We have no rigid preferences as to subject, style, or genre, although commercial efforts tend to put us off. Even so, our only fixed requirement is good writing."

## NEW MADRID

Journal of Contemporary Literature, Murray State University, Department of English and Philosophy, 7C Faculty Hall, Murray KY 42071-3341. (270)809-4730. **E-mail:** msu.newmadrid@murraystate.edu. **Website:** newmadridjournal.org. Jacque E. Day, managing editor. **Contact:** Ann Neelon, editor. *"New Madrid* is the national journal of the low-residency MFA program at Murray State University. It takes its name from the New Madrid seismic zone, which falls within the central Mississippi Valley and extends through western Kentucky." Acquires first North American serial rights. Publication is copyrighted. Responds within three months of close of reading period. Guidelines available on website.

See website for guidelines and upcoming themes. "We have two reading periods, one from August 15-October 15, and one from January 15-March 15." Also publishes poetry and creative nonfiction. Rarely comments on/critiques rejected mss.

**MAGAZINES NEEDS** Accepts submissions by online submissions manager only. Include brief bio, list of publications. Considers multiple submissions.

**TIPS** "Quality is the determining factor for breaking into *New Madrid*. We are looking for well-crafted, compelling writing in a range of genres, forms, and styles."

## NEW OHIO REVIEW

English Department, 360 Ellis Hall, Ohio University, Athens OH 45701. (740)597-1360. **E-mail:** noreditors@ohio.edu. **Website:** www.ohiou.edu/nor. **Contact:** David Wanczyk, editor. *New Ohio Review*, published biannually in spring and fall, publishes fiction, nonfiction, and poetry. Member CLMP. Reading period is September 15-December 15 and January 15-April 15. Responds in 2-4 months. Single copy: $9. Subscription: $16. Guidelines available on website.

**MAGAZINES NEEDS** "Please do not submit more than once every 6 months."

## ⓢ NEW ORLEANS REVIEW

Box 195, Loyola University, New Orleans LA 70118. (504)865-2295. **E-mail:** noreview@loyno.edu. **Website:** neworleansreview.org. **Contact:** Heidi Braden, managing editor. *New Orleans Review* is an annual journal of contemporary literature and culture, publishing new poetry, fiction, nonfiction, art, photography, film and book reviews. Buys first North American serial rights. Pays on publication. Responds in 4 months to mss. Sample copy: $5.

○ The journal has published an eclectic variety of work by established and emerging writers including Walker Percy, Pablo Neruda, Ellen Gilchrist, Nelson Algren, Hunter S. Thompson, John Kennedy Toole, Richard Brautigan, Barry Spacks, James Sallis, Jack Gilbert, Paul Hoover, Rodney Jones, Annie Dillard, Everette Maddox, Julio Cortazar, Gordon Lish, Robert Walser, Mark Halliday, Jack Butler, Robert Olen Butler, Michael Harper, Angela Ball, Joyce Carol Oates, Diane Wakoski, Dermot Bolger, Roddy Doyle, William Kotzwinkle, Alain Robbe-Grillet, Arnost Lustig, Raymond Queneau, Yusef Komunyakaa, Michael Martone, Tess Gallagher, Matthea Harvey, D. A. Powell, Rikki Ducornet, and Ed Skoog.

**TIPS** "We're looking for dynamic writing that demonstrates attention to the language and a sense of the medium, writing that engages, surprises, moves us. We're not looking for genre fiction or academic articles. We subscribe to the belief that in order to truly write well, one must first master the rudiments: grammar and syntax, punctuation, the sentence, the paragraph, the line, the stanza. We receive about 3,000 manuscripts a year and publish about 3% of them. Check out a recent issue, send us your best, proofread your work, be patient, be persistent."

## ⊕ⓢ THE NEW QUARTERLY

St. Jerome's University, 290 Westmount Rd. N., Waterloo ON N2L 3G3, Canada. (519)884-8111, ext. 28290. **E-mail:** editor@tnq.ca; info@tnq.ca. **Website:** www.tnq.ca. "Emphasis on emerging writers and genres, but we publish more traditional work as well if the language and narrative structure are fresh." Buys first Canadian rights. Pays on publication. Responds in early January to submissions received March 1-August 31; in early June to submissions received September 1-February 28. Editorial lead time

6 months. Sample copy: $16.95 (cover price, plus mailing). Guidelines online.

○ Open to Canadian writers only. Reading periods: March 1-August 31; September 1-February 28.

**MAGAZINES NEEDS** *Canadian work only.* Send with submission cover sheet and bio. Does not accept submissions by e-mail. Accepts simultaneoues submissions if indicated in cover letter. Pays $40/poem

**TIPS** "Reading us is the best way to get our measure. We don't have preconceived ideas about what we're looking for other than that it must be Canadian work (Canadian writers, not necessarily Canadian content). We want something that's fresh, something that will repay a second reading, something in which the language soars and the feeling is complexly rendered."

## NEW SOUTH

English Dept., Georgia State University, P.O Box 3970, Atlanta GA 30302-3970. (404)413-5874. **E-mail:** newsoutheditors@gmail.com. **Website:** www.newsouth-journal.com. Semiannual magazine dedicated to finding and publishing the best work from artists around the world. Wants original voices searching to rise above the ordinary. Seeks to publish high-quality work, regardless of genre, form, or regional ties. Acquires first North American serial rights. Time between acceptance and publication is 3-5 months. Responds in 3-5 months. Sample: $4 (back issue). Single copy: $6; subscription: $9 for 1 year. Guidelines online.

○ *New South* is 160+ pages. Press run is 2,000; 500 distributed free to students. The *New South* Annual Writing Contest offers $1,000 for the best poem and $1,000 for the best story or essay; one-year subscription to all who submit. Submissions must be unpublished. Submit up to 3 poems, 1 story, or 1 essay on any subject or in any form. Guidelines online. Competition receives 300 entries. Past judges include Sharon Olds, Jane Hirschfield, Anthony Hecht, Phillip Levine, and Jake Adam York. Winner will be announced in the Fall issue.

**MAGAZINES NEEDS** Submit up to 5 poems at a time through Submittable. Pays 2 contributor copies.

**TIPS** "We want what's new, what's fresh, and what's different—whether it comes from the Southern United States, the South of India, or the North, East or West of Anywhere."

## ◐◑ THE NEW VERSE NEWS

Tangerang , Indonesia. **E-mail:** nvneditor@gmail.com. **E-mail:** nvneditor@gmail.com. **Website:** www.newversenews.com. **Contact:** James Penha, editor. *The New Verse News*, published online and updated "every day" has "a clear liberal bias but will consider various visions and views." Acquires first rights. Rights revert to poet upon publication. "Normally, poems are published immediately upon acceptance." Responds in 1-3 weeks. Does not comment on rejected poems. Timely poems may be published immediately. Guidelines available on website.

**MAGAZINES NEEDS** Wants "previously unpublished poems, both serious and satirical, on current events and topical issues; will also consider prose poems." Accepts only e-mail submissions (pasted into body of message); use "Verse News Submission" as the subject line; no disk or postal submissions. Send brief bio. Reads submissions year round. Poems are circulated to an editorial board. Receives about 1,200 poems/year; accepts about 300. Does not want "work unrelated to the news." No length restrictions. No financial remuneration.

**TIPS** Take a look at the website to get to know the kind of poetry published.

## ◑ NEW WELSH REVIEW

P.O. Box 170, Aberystwyth, Ceredigion SY23 1 WZ, United Kingdom. 01970-626230. **E-mail:** editor@newwelshreview.com. **E-mail:** submissions@newwelshreview.com. **Website:** www.newwelshreview.com. **Contact:** Gwen Davies, editor. "*NWR*, a literary quarterly ranked in the top 5 of British literary magazines, publishes stories, poems, and critical essays. The best of Welsh writing in English, past and present, is celebrated, discussed, and debated. We seek poems, short stories, reviews, special features/articles, and commentary." Quarterly.

## ◍ THE NEW YORKER

1 World Trade Center, New York NY 10007. **E-mail:** themail@newyorker.com. **Website:** www.newyorker.com. **Contact:** David Remnick, editor in chief. A quality weekly magazine of distinct news stories, articles, essays, and poems for a literate audience. Pays on acceptance. Responds in 3 months to mss. Subscription: $59.99/year (47 issues), $29.99 for 6 months (23 issues).

*The New Yorker* receives approximately 4,000 submissions per month.

**MAGAZINES NEEDS** Submit up to 6 poems at a time by e-mail (as PDF attachment) or mail (address to Poetry Department). Pays top rates.

**TIPS** "Be lively, original, not overly literary. Write what you want to write, not what you think the editor would like."

## NIMROD: INTERNATIONAL JOURNAL OF POETRY AND PROSE

University of Tulsa, 800 S. Tucker Dr., Tulsa OK 74104-3189. (918)631-3080. **Fax:** (918)631-3033. **E-mail:** nimrod@utulsa.edu. **Website:** www.utulsa.edu/nimrod. Cassidy McCants, associate editor. **Contact:** Eilis O'Neal, editor-in-chief. "*Nimrod*'s mission is the discovery and support of new writing of vigor and quality from this country and abroad. The journal seeks new, unheralded writers; writers from other lands who become accessible to the English-speaking world through translation; and established authors who have vigorous new work to present that has not found a home within the establishment. We believe in a living literature; that it is possible to search for, recognize, and reward contemporary writing of content and vigor, without reliance on a canon." Buys first North American rights. Responds in 3 months to mss. Sample copy: $11. Subscription: $18.50/year U.S., $20 foreign. Guidelines online or for SASE.

Semiannual magazine: 200 pages; perfect-bound; 4c cover. Receives 200 unsolicited mss/month. **Publishes 10-15 new writers/year.** Reading period: January 1 through November 30. Online submissions accepted at nimrod-journal.submittable.com/submit. Does not accept submissions by e-mail unless the writer is living outside the U.S. and cannot submit using the submissions manager. Poetry published in *Nimrod* has been included in *The Best American Poetry*.

**MAGAZINES NEEDS** Submit poems by mail or through the online submissions manager. Include SASE for work submitted by mail. Pays 2 contributor copies.

**ALSO OFFERS** Sponsors the annual *Nimrod* Literary Awards, including The Pablo Neruda Prize for Poetry (see separate listing in Contests & Awards). "During the months that the *Nimrod* Literary Awards competition is being conducted, reporting time on non-contest mss will be longer."

## NINTH LETTER

Department of English, University of Illinois, 608 S. Wright St., Urbana IL 61801. (217)300-4315. **E-mail:** info@ninthletter.com; editor@ninthletter.com. **Website:** www.ninthletter.com. **Contact:** Jodee Stanley, editor. "*Ninth Letter* accepts submissions of fiction, poetry, and essays from September 1-February 28 (postmark dates). *Ninth Letter* is published semiannually at the University of Illinois, Urbana-Champaign. We are interested in prose and poetry that experiment with form, narrative, and nontraditional subject matter, as well as more traditional literary work." Buys first North American serial rights. Pays on publication.

**MAGAZINES NEEDS** Submit 3-6 poems (no more than 10 pages) at a time. "All mailed submissions must include an SASE for reply." Pays $25 per printed page and 2 contributor copies.

**ALSO OFFERS** Member: CLMP; CELJ.

## NITE-WRITER'S INTERNATIONAL LITERARY ARTS JOURNAL

158 Spencer Ave., Suite 100, Pittsburgh PA 15227. (412)882-5171. **E-mail:** nitewritersliteraryarts@gmail.com. **Website:** https://sites.google.com/site/nitewriterinternational/home. **Contact:** John Thompson. *Nite-Writer's International Literary Arts Journal* is an online literary arts journal. "We are 'dedicated to the emotional intellectual' with a creative perception of life." Retains first North American serial rights. Copyright reverts to author upon publication. Guidelines available on website. Does not pay authors but offers international exposure to the individual artist.

Journal is open to beginners as well as professionals.

**MAGAZINES NEEDS** Wants strong imagery in everything you write. Considers previously published poems and simultaneous submissions (let us know when and where your work has been published). Cover letter is preferred. "Give brief bio, state where you heard of us, state if material has been previously published and where." Receives about 1,000 poems/year, accepts about 10-15%. Has published poetry by Lyn Lifshin, Rose Marie Hunold, Peter Vetrano, Carol Frances Brown, and Richard King Perkins II. Does not want porn or violence. Open to length.

**TIPS** "Read a lot of what you write—study the market. Don't fear rejection, but use it as a learning tool to strengthen your work before resubmitting."

## THE NORMAL SCHOOL

The Press at the California State University - Fresno, 5245 North Backer Ave., M/S PB 98, Fresno CA 93740-8001. **E-mail:** editors@thenormalschool.com. **Website:** thenormalschool.com. **Contact:** Steven Church, editor. Semiannual magazine that accepts outstanding work by beginning and established writers. Acquires first North American serial rights. Publication is copyrighted. Publishes ms 3-6 months after acceptance. Responds to stories in 2 months. Sample copy available for $7 on website or via e-mail. For guidelines, send check and address or visit website.

Mss are read from September 1 to December 1 and from January 15 to April 15. Address submissions to the appropriate editor. Charges $3 fee for each online submission, due to operational costs.

**MAGAZINES NEEDS** Considers poetry of any style. Limit the number of cat poems.

## NORTH AMERICAN REVIEW

University of Northern Iowa, 1222 W. 27th St., Cedar Falls IA 50614. (319)273-6455. **Fax:** (319)273-4326. **E-mail:** nar@uni.edu. **Website:** northamericanreview.org. "The *NAR* is the oldest literary magazine in America and one of the most respected; though we have no prejudices about the subject matter of material sent to us, our first concern is quality." Buys first North American serial rights, buys first rights. Publishes ms an average of 1 year after acceptance. Responds in 3 months to queries; 4 months to mss. Sample copy: $7. Guidelines online.

This is the oldest literary magazine in the country and one of the most prestigious. Also one of the most entertaining—and a tough market for the young writer.

**MAGAZINES NEEDS** No restrictions; highest quality only.

**TIPS** "We like stories that start quickly and have a strong narrative arc. Poems that are passionate about subject, language, and image are welcome, whether they are traditional or experimental, whether in formal or free verse (closed or open form). Nonfiction should combine art and fact with the finest writing."

### 🌑 NORTH CAROLINA LITERARY REVIEW

East Carolina University, Mailstop 555 English, Greenville NC 27858-4353. (252)328-1537. **Fax:** (252)328-4889. **E-mail:** nclrsubmissions@ecu.edu; bauerm@ecu.edu. **Website:** www.nclr.ecu.edu. **Contact:** Margaret Bauer. "Articles should have a North Carolina slant. Fiction, creative nonfiction, and poetry accepted through yearly contests. First consideration is always for quality of work. Although we treat academic and scholarly subjects, we do not wish to see jargon-laden prose; our readers, we hope, are found as often in bookstores and libraries as in academia. We seek to combine the best elements of a magazine for serious readers with the best of a scholarly journal." Acquires first North American serial rights. Rights returned to writer on request. Publishes ms an average of 1 year after acceptance. Responds in 1 month to queries; in 6 months to mss. Editorial lead time 6 months. Sample copy: $5-25. Guidelines online.

🖒 Accepts submissions through Submittable.

**MAGAZINES NEEDS** Submit poetry for the James Applewhite Poetry Prize competition via Submittable. Only subscribers can submit, and all poets must have a North Carolina connection. Submit up to 3 poems with a 1-year subscription ($15) or up to 5 poems with a 2-year subscription ($25). First-place winners of contests receive a prize of $250. Other poets whose poems are selected for publication receive comp copies of the issue.

**TIPS** "By far the easiest way to break in is with special issue sections. We are especially interested in reports on conferences, readings, meetings that involve North Carolina writers, and personal essays or short narratives with a strong sense of place. See back issues for other departments. Interviews are probably the other easiest place to break in; no discussions of poetics/theory, etc., except in reader-friendly (accessible) language. Interviews should be personal, more like conversations, that explore connections between a writer's life and his/her work."

### NORTH DAKOTA QUARTERLY

University of North Dakota, 276 Centennial Dr. Stop 7209, Merrifield Hall Room 15, Grand Forks ND 58202. (701)777-3322. **Fax:** (701)777-2373. **E-mail:** ndq@und.edu. **Website:** www.ndquarterly.org. Poetry Editor: Heidi Czerwiec. Fiction Editor: Gilad Elbom. Book Reviews Editor: Sharon Carson.. **Contact:** Kate Sweney, managing editor. "*North Dakota*

*Quarterly* strives to publish the best fiction, poetry, and essays that in our estimation we can. Our tastes and interests are best reflected in what we have been recently publishing, and we suggest that you look at some current issues for guidance." Buys first North American serial rights and rights to publish electronically on website and through EBSCO. Pays only in contributors' copies. Guidelines online.

🖒 Only reads fiction and poetry between September 1-May 1. Work published in *North Dakota Quarterly* was selected for inclusion in *The O. Henry Prize Stories*, *The Pushcart Prize Series*, and *Best American Essays*.

**MAGAZINES NEEDS** Submit up to 5 poems as hard copy.

### 🌑 NOTRE DAME REVIEW

University of Notre Dame, B009C McKenna Hall, Notre Dame IN 46556. **Website:** ndreview.nd.edu. "The *Notre Dame Review* is an indepenent, noncommercial magazine of contemporary American and international fiction, poetry, criticism, and art. Especially interested in work that takes on big issues by making the invisible seen, that gives voice to the voiceless. In addition to showcasing celebrated authors like Seamus Heaney and Czelaw Milosz, the *Notre Dame Review* introduces readers to authors they may have never encountered before but who are doing innovative and important work. In conjunction with the *Notre Dame Review*, the online companion to the printed magazine, the *nd[re]view* engages readers as a community centered in literary rather than commercial concerns, a community we reach out to through critique and commentary as well as aesthetic experience." Buys first North American serial rights. Pays on publication. Publishes ms an average of 6 months after acceptance. Responds in 4 or more months to mss. Sample copy: $6. Guidelines online.

🖒 Does not accept e-mail submissions. Only reads hardcopy submissions September-November and January-March.

**MAGAZINES NEEDS** Send complete ms with cover letter. Include 4-sentence bio. Send SASE for response, return of ms, or send a disposable copy of ms.

**TIPS** "We're looking for high-quality work that takes on big issues in a literary way. Please read our back issues before submitting."

## NOW & THEN: THE APPALACHIAN MAGAZINE

East Tennessee State University, Box 70556, Johnson City TN 37614-1707. (423)439-5348. **Fax:** (423)439-6340. **E-mail:** nowandthen@etsu.edu. **E-mail:** sandersr@etsu.edu. **Website:** www.etsu.edu/cass/nowandthen. **Contact:** Randy Sanders, managing editor; Wayne Winkler, music editor; Charlie Warden, photo editor. Literary magazine published twice/year. "*Now & Then* accepts a variety of writing genres: fiction, poetry, nonfiction, essays, interviews, memoirs, and book reviews. All submissions must relate to Appalachia and to the issue's specific theme. Our readership is educated and interested in the region." Buys first North American serial rights. Rights revert back to author after publication. Responds in 5 months to queries; 5 months to mss. Sample copy: $8 plus $3 shipping. Guidelines and upcoming themes available on website.

○ *Now & Then* tells the stories of Appalachia and presents a fresh, revealing picture of life in Appalachia, past and present, with engaging articles, personal essays, fiction, poetry, and photography.

**MAGAZINES NEEDS** Submit up to 5 poems, with SASE and cover letter including "a few lines about yourself for a contributor's note and whether the work has been published or accepted elsewhere." Will consider simultaneous submissions; occasionally accepts previously published poems. Put name, address, and phone number on every poem. Deadlines: last workday in February (spring/summer issue) and August 31 (fall/winter issues). Publishes theme issues. Pays $25 for each accepted poem. Pays on publication.

**TIPS** "Keep in mind that *Now & Then* only publishes material related to the Appalachian region. Plus we only publish fiction that has some plausible connection to a specific issue's themes. We like to offer first-time publication to promising writers."

## NTH DEGREE

**E-mail:** submissions@nthzine.com. **Website:** www.nthzine.com. **Contact:** Michael D. Pederson. Free online fanzine to promote up-and-coming new science fiction and fantasy authors and artists. Also supports the world of fandom and conventions. Acquires one-time rights. Responds in 2 weeks to queries; 3 months to mss. Online e-zine; copies available upon request. Guidelines online.

○ No longer accepts hard copy submissions.

**MAGAZINES NEEDS** Submit through e-mail. Looking for poetry about science fiction, fantasy, horror, alternate history, well-crafted mystery, and humor. Pays in contributor copies.

**TIPS** "Don't submit anything that you may be ashamed of 10 years later."

## NUTHOUSE

**Website:** www.nuthousemagazine.com. *Nuthouse*, published every 3 months, uses humor of all kinds, including homespun and political. Acquires one-time rights. Publishes ms 6-12 months after acceptance. Responds in 1 month. Sample: $1.50. Make checks payable to Twin Rivers Press. Guidelines for #10 SASE.

○ *Nuthouse* is 12 pages, digest-sized, photocopied from desktop-published originals. Receives about 500 poems/year, accepts about 100. Press run is 100. Subscription: $5 for 4 issues.

**MAGAZINES NEEDS** Wants "humorous verse; virtually all genres considered." Has published poetry by Holly Day, Daveed Garstenstein-Ross, and Don Webb. Send complete ms with SASE and cover letter. Include bio (paragraph) and list of publications. No e-mail submissions. Pays 1 contributor copy per poem.

## 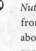 OBSIDIAN

**E-mail:** obsidianatbrown@gmail.com. **Website:** obsidian-magazine.tumblr.com. **Contact:** Maya Finoh, managing editor. *Obsidian* is a "literary and visual space to showcase the creativity and experiences of black people, specifically at Brown University, formed out of the need for a platform made for us, by us." It is "actively intersectional, safe, and open: a space especially for the stories and voices of black women, black queer and trans people, and black people with disabilities." Acquires one-time rights. Guidelines online.

**MAGAZINES NEEDS** Submit by e-mail. Include brief bio up to 3 sentences.

**TIPS** "Following proper format is essential. Your title must be intriguing and text clean. Never give up. Some of the writers we publish were rejected many times before we published them."

## OFF THE COAST

Resolute Bear Press, P.O. Box 14, Robbinston ME 04671. (207)454-8026. **E-mail:** poetrylane2@gmail.com. **Website:** www.off-the-coast.com. **Contact:** Valerie Lawson, editor/publisher. "The mission of *Off the Coast* is to become recognized around the world as

Maine's international poetry journal, a publication that prizes quality, diversity and honesty in its publications and in its dealings with poets. *Off the Coast*, a quarterly print journal, publishes poetry, artwork and reviews. Arranged much like an anthology, each issue bears a title drawn from a line or phrase from one of its poems." The rights to each individual poem and print are retained by each individual artist. Publishes mss 1-2 months after acceptance. Responds in 1-3 months. Editorial decisions are not made until after the deadline for each issue. Notifications go out the first two weeks of the month following the deadline date, e.g. early April for March 15 deadline. For samples of poetry, art and reviews, visit our website: www.off-the coast.com. Contributors receive one free copy. Additional copies of the issue their work appears in available for $5, half the cover price. Sample issue for $10. Guidelines available in magazine and online.

**MAGAZINES NEEDS** Submit 1-3 poems via online submissions manager.

**HOW TO CONTACT** "Send 1-3 previously unpublished poems, any subject or style, using our submission manager: www.offthecoast.submittable.com/submit. We accept postal submissions with SASE with sufficient postage for return. Please include contact information and brief bio with submission. We accept simultaneous submissions, but please inform us if your work is accepted elsewhere. Pays one contributor copy. "The rights to each individual poem and print are retained by each individual artist." For reviews, send a single copy of a newly published poetry book. Please send bound books only, we do not review chapbooks."

## OHIO TEACHERS WRITE

1209 Heather Run, Wilmington OH 45177. **E-mail:** ohioteacherswrite@octela.org. **Website:** www.octela.org/OTW.html. **Contact:** Eimile Máiréad Green, editor. *"Ohio Teachers Write* is a literary magazine published annually by the Ohio Council of Teachers of English Language Arts. This publication seeks to promote both poetry and prose of Ohio teachers and to provide an engaging collection of writing for our readership of educators and other like-minded adults. Invites electronic submissions from both active and retired Ohio educators for our annual literary print magazine." Guidelines online.

**MAGAZINES NEEDS** Submit up to 4 poems by e-mail. Pays 2 contributor copies.

**TIPS** Check website for yearly theme.

## ⭘ OLD RED KIMONO

Georgia Highlands College, 3175 Cedartown Highway SE, Rome GA 30161. **E-mail:** napplega@highlands.edu. **Website:** www.highlands.edu/site/ork. **Contact:** Dr. Nancy Applegate, professor of English; Thomas Dobson, literary editor. *Old Red Kimono*, published annually, prints original, high-quality poetry and fiction. Has published poetry by Walter McDonald, Peter Huggins, Ruth Moon Kempher, John Cantey Knight, Kirsten Fox, and Al Braselton. Acquires one-time rights. Responds in 3 months. Accepts e-mail submissions. Reads submissions September 1-February 15 only. Guidelines available for SASE or on website for more submission information.

⭕  *Old Red Kimono* is 72 pages, magazine-sized, professionally printed on heavy stock, with colored matte cover with art. Receives about 500 submissions/year, accepts about 60-70. Sample: $3.

**MAGAZINES NEEDS** Submit 3-5 poems at a time. Pays 2 contributor copies.

## ⭗ ON SPEC

P.O. Box 4727, Station South, Edmonton AB T6E 5G6, Canada. (780)628-7121. **E-mail:** onspec@onspec.ca. **Website:** www.onspec.ca. "We publish speculative fiction and poetry by new and established writers, with a strong preference for Canadian-authored works." Buys first North American serial rights. Pays on acceptance. Publishes ms an average of 6-18 months after acceptance. Responds in 2 weeks to queries; in 6 months after deadline to mss. Editorial lead time 6 months. Sample copy: $8. Guidelines on website.

⭕  See website guidelines for submission announcements. "Please refer to website for information regarding submissions, as we are not open year round."

**MAGAZINES NEEDS** No rhyming or religious material. Length: 4-100 lines. Pays $50 and 1 contributor copy.

**TIPS** "We want to see stories with plausible characters, a well-constructed, consistent, and vividly described setting, a strong plot, and believable emotions; characters must show us (not tell us) their emotional responses to each other and to the situation and/or challenge they face. Also: Don't send us stories written for television. We don't like media tie-ins, so don't watch

TV for inspiration! Read instead! Strong preference given to submissions by Canadians."

## ○ OPEN MINDS QUARTERLY

NISA/Northern Initiative for Social Action, Northern Initiative for Social Action, 36 Elgin St., 2nd Floor, Sudbury ON P3C 5B4, Canada. (705)222-6472 ext. 303. E-mail: openminds@nisa.on.ca. Website: www.openmindsquarterly.com. Contact: Dinah Laprairie, editor. *Open Minds Quarterly* provides a venue for individuals who have experienced mental illness to express themselves via poetry, short fiction, essays, first-person accounts of living with mental illness, and book/movie reviews. Wants unique, well-written, provocative poetry. Does not want overly graphic or sexual violence. Time between acceptance and publication is 6-16 months. Responds in up to 20 weeks. Single copy: $7 CAD, $7 USD; subscription: $24.95 CAD and USD (special rates also available). Make checks payable to NISA/Northern Initiative for Social Action. Guidelines available for SASE, by fax, e-mail, or on website.

○ *Open Minds Quarterly* is 24 pages, magazine-sized, saddle-stapled, with 100 lb. stock cover with original artwork, includes ads. Press run is 550; 150 distributed free to potential subscribers, published writers, NISA member, advertisers, and conferences and events.

**MAGAZINES NEEDS** Submit 1-4 poems at a time. Submit through website. Cover letter is required. Information in cover letter: indicate your lived experience with mental illness. Reads submissions year round. Poems are first reviewed by poetry editor, then accepted/rejected by the editor. Sometimes, submissions are passed on to a third party for input or a third opinion. Seldom comments on rejected poems. Rarely sends pre-publication galleys. Considers poetry by teens. Has published poetry by Beth Brown Preston, Sophie Soil, Ky Perraun, and Kurt Sass. Length: up to 30 lines, including stanza breaks. Pays contributor copies.

**ALSO OFFERS** The Brainstorm Poetry Contest runs in first 2 months of each year. Visit www.openmindsquarterly.com.

## ● ORBIS

17 Greenhow Ave., West Kirby Wirral CH48 5EL, United Kingdom. E-mail: carolebaldock@hotmail.com. Website: www.orbisjournal.com. Contact: Carole Baldock, editor; Noel Williams, reviews editor. "*Orbis* has long been considered one of the top 20 small-press magazines in the UK. We are interested in social inclusion projects and encouraging access to the Arts, young people, Under 20s, and 20-somethings. Subjects for discussion: 'day in the life,' technical, topical." Responds in 3 months.

○ Please see guidelines on website before submitting.

**MAGAZINES NEEDS** Readers' Award: £50 for piece receiving the most votes in each issue. Four winners selected for submissions to Forward Poetry Prize, Single Poem category. Plus £50 split between 4 or more runners-up. Feature Writer receives £50. NB, work commissioned: 3-4 poems or 1,500 words.

**TIPS** "Any publication should be read cover to cover because it's the best way to improve your chances of getting published. Enclose SAE with all correspondence. Overseas: 2 IRCs, 3 if work is to be returned."

## OSIRIS

P.O. Box 297, Deerfield MA 01342. E-mail: osirispoetry@gmail.com. Website: www.facebook.com/osiris.poetry. Contact: Andrea Moorhead, editor. *Osiris*, published semiannually, prints contemporary poetry in English, French, and Italian without translation, and in other languages with translation, including Polish, Danish, Spanish, Portuguese, and German. Responds in 1 month. Sends prepublication galleys. Sample: $10.

**MAGAZINES NEEDS** Wants poetry that is "lyrical, non-narrative, post-modern. Also looking for translations from non-Indo-European languages." Has published poetry by Abderrahmane Djelfaoui (Algeria); George Moore, Rob Cook, Simon Perchik, Ingrid Swanberg (USA); Flavio Ermini (Italy); Denise Desautels (Quebec); Yves Broussard (France); and Frances Presley (UK). Submit 4-6 poems at a time. "Poems should be sent to osirispoetry@gmail.com or by postal mail (include sase). Include short bio. Translators should include a letter of permission from the poet or publisher as well as copies of the original text." Pays 2 contributor copies.

## ● OTOLITHS

P.O. Box 531, Home Hill QLD 4806, Australia. E-mail: otolitheditor@gmail.com. Website: the-otolith.blogspot.com.au. Contact: Mark Young, editor. The intention is for *Otoliths* to appear quarterly, to contain a variety of what can be loosely described as e-things, that is, anything that can be translated (visually at this stage) to an electronic platform. "If it moves, we won't shoot at it." Sample copy online. Guidelines online.

**MAGAZINES NEEDS** *Otoliths* is open to electronic submissions of textual poetry, vispo, fiction, essays, photographs, art and any combination of the above. Text submissions should be sent as a single .doc or .rtf attachment. Please send a brief bionote with the submission.

## OVER THE TRANSOM

120 San Lorenzo Blvd., #3, Santa Cruz CA 95060. (415)678-9554. **E-mail:** jsh619@earthlink.net. **Contact:** Jonathan Hayes, editor. *Over the Transom*, published 2 times/year, is a free publication of poetry and prose. Open to all styles of poetry. "We look for the highest-quality writing that best fits the issue." Publishes ms 2-6 months after acceptance. Responds in 2 months. Sample copy: $10. Single copy: free. Make checks payable to Jonathan Hayes.

○ *Over The Transom* is 72 pages, magazine-sized, saddle-stapled, with cardstock cover. Receives about 1,000 poems/year, accepts about 5%. Press run is 200 (100 subscribers); 150 distributed free to cafés, bookstores, universities, and bars.

**MAGAZINES NEEDS** Submit up to 5 poems at a time. Accepts e-mail submissions; no disk submissions. Must include an SASE with postal submissions. Reads submissions year round. Never comments on rejected poems. Occasionally publishes theme issues. Considers poetry by children and teens. Has published poetry by Klipschutz, Normal, Garrett Caples, Michael Leong, Doug Draime, and Mel C. Thompson. Pays 1 contributor copy.

## ◐ OXFORD MAGAZINE

OxMag, Miami University, Oxford OH 45056. **Website:** www.oxfordmagazine.org. *Oxford Magazine*, published annually online in May, is open in terms of form, content, and subject matter. "Since our premiere in 1984, our magazine has received Pushcart Prizes for both fiction and poetry and has published authors such as Charles Baxter, William Stafford, Robert Pinsky, Stephen Dixon, Helena Maria Viramontes, Andre Dubus, and Stuart Dybek." Acquires first North American serial rights, one-time anthology rights, online serial rights. Responds in 6 months, starting in September.

○ Work published in *Oxford Magazine* has been included in the *Pushcart Prize* anthology. Does not read submissions June through August.

**MAGAZINES NEEDS** Submit 3-5 poems via online submissions manager.

## OYEZ REVIEW

Roosevelt University, Dept. of Literature & Languages, 430 S. Michigan Ave., Chicago IL 60605. **E-mail:** oyezreview@roosevelt.edu. **Website:** oyezreview.wordpress.com. Annual magazine of the Creative Writing Program at Roosevelt University, publishing fiction, creative nonfiction, poetry, and art. There are no restrictions on style, theme, or subject matter. Buys first North American serial rights. Publishes ms an average of 2-3 months after acceptance. Responds by mid-December each year. Sample copies available by request, or using e-book retailers. Guidelines online.

○ Reading period is August 1-October 1. Each issue has 104 pages: 92 pages of text and an 8-page spread of 1 artist's work (in color or b&w). Work by the issue's featured artist also appears on the front and back cover, totaling 10 pieces. The journal has featured work from such writers as Charles Bukowski, James McManus, Carla Panciera, Michael Onofrey, Tim Foley, John N. Miller, Gary Fincke, and Barry Silesky, and visual artists Vivian Nunley, C. Taylor, Jennifer Troyer, and Frank Spidale. Accepts queries by e-mail.

**MAGAZINES NEEDS** Send up to 5 poems via online submissions manager or postal mail. Length: up to 10 pages total.

## OYSTER BOY REVIEW

P.O. Box 1483, Pacifica CA 94044. **E-mail:** email_2015@oysterboyreview.com. **Website:** www.oysterboyreview.com. **Contact:** Damon Sauve, editor/publisher. Electronic and print magazine. *Oyster Boy Review*, published annually, is interested in "the underrated, the ignored, the misunderstood, and the varietal. We'll make some mistakes." Publishes ms 12 months after acceptance. Responds in 6 months. Guidelines by e-mail or online at website.

**MAGAZINES NEEDS** Submit by postal mail or e-mail. Pays 2 contributor copies.

**TIPS** "Keep writing, keep submitting, keep revising."

## PACIFICA LITERARY REVIEW

**E-mail:** pacificalitreview@gmail.com. **Website:** www.pacificareview.com. **Contact:** Matt Muth, editor-in-chief; Courtney Johnson, managing editor. "Pacifica Literary Review is a small literary arts magazine based in Seattle. Our print editions are published bi-annually in winter and summer and we publish year-round on the web. *PLR* is now accepting submissions of poetry, fiction, creative nonfiction, author interviews, and b&w photography. Submission period: September 15-December 15 and Jan 15-May 15." Acquires first North American rights. Rights revert to author upon publication, but we ask that Pacifica Literary Review is credited in any subsequent collections or anthologies in which the work appears. 2 copies of issue in which author was published and 1 copy of next issue 1-3 months Guidelines online.

**MAGAZINES NEEDS** Submit poems via onlline submission form.

## PACKINGTOWN REVIEW

111 S. Lincoln St., Batavia IL 60510. **E-mail:** editors@packingtownreview.com. **E-mail:** packingtownreview@gmail.com. **Website:** www.packingtownreview.com. *Packingtown Review* publishes imaginative and critical prose and poetry by emerging and established writers. Welcomes submissions of poetry, scholarly articles, drama, creative nonfiction, fiction, and literary translation, as well as genre-bending pieces. Acquires first North American serial rights. Sends galleys to author. Publication is copyrighted. Pays on publication. Publishes ms a maximum of 1 year after acceptance. Responds in 3 weeks to queries; in 3 months to mss. Single copy: $10 (back issue). Guidelines available on website.

**MAGAZINES NEEDS** Wants well-crafted poetry. Open to most styles and forms. Looking for poetry that takes risks and does so successfully. Send 3-5 poems with cover letter. Include estimated word count, brief bio, SASE. Does not want uninspired or unrevised work. Length: up to 10 pages of single-spaced verse. Pays 2 contributor copies.

**TIPS** "We are looking for well-crafted prose. We are open to most styles and forms. We are also looking for prose that takes risks and does so successfully. We will consider articles about prose."

## ⊙⑤ PAINTED BRIDE QUARTERLY

Drexel University, Department of English and Philosophy, 3141 Chestnut St., Philadelphia PA 19104. **E-mail:** pbq@drexel.edu. **Website:** pbq.drexel.edu. *Painted Bride Quarterly* seeks literary fiction (experimental and traditional), poetry, and artwork and photographs. Buys first North American serial rights. Responds in 6 months to mss. Guidelines online and by e-mail.

**MAGAZINES NEEDS** Submit via postal mail. Does not accept e-mail submissions. "We have no specifications or restrictions. We'll look at anything."

**ALSO OFFERS** Sponsors an annual poetry contest and a chapbook competition. Guidelines available for SASE or on website.

**TIPS** "We look for freshness of idea incorporated with high-quality writing. We receive an awful lot of nicely written work with worn-out plots. We want quality in whatever—we hold experimental work to as strict standards as anything else. Many of our readers write fiction; most of them enjoy a good reading. We hope to be an outlet for quality. A good story gives, first, enjoyment to the reader. We've seen a good many of them lately, and we've published the best of them."

## PANK

PANK, Department of Humanities, 1400 Townsend Dr., Houghton MI 49931-1200. **E-mail:** mbartley@pankmagazine.com. **Website:** www.pankmagazine.com. **Contact:** M. Bartley Seigel, editor. "*PANK* Magazine fosters access to emerging and experimental poetry and prose, publishing the brightest and most promising writers for the most adventurous readers. To the end of the road, up country, a far shore, the edge of things, to a place of amalgamation and unplumbed depths, where the known is made and unmade, and where unimagined futures are born, a place inhabited by contradictions, a place of quirk and startling anomaly. *PANK*, no soft pink hands allowed." Buys first North American serial rights and electronic rights. Publishes ms and average of 3-12 months after acceptance. Guidelines available on website.

**MAGAZINES NEEDS** Submit through online submissions manager. Pays $20, a one-year subscription, and a *PANK* t-shirt.

**TIPS** "To read *PANK* is to know *PANK*. Or, read a lot within the literary magazine and small press universe—there's plenty to choose from. Unfortunately, we see a lot of submissions from writers who have clearly read neither *PANK* nor much else. Serious writers are serious readers. Read. Seriously."

## ✪ PAPERPLATES

19 Kenwood Ave., Toronto ON M6C 2R8, Canada. (416)651-2551. **E-mail:** magazine@paperplates.org. **Website:** www.paperplates.org. **Contact:** Bernard Kelly, publisher. *paperplates* is a literary quarterly published in Toronto. "We make no distinction between veterans and beginners. Some of our contributors have published several books; some have never before published a single line." Acquires first North American serial rights. Responds in 6 months. Guidelines online at website.

○ No longer accepts IRCs.

**MAGAZINES NEEDS** Submit no more than 5 poems via surface mail or e-mail with short bio. Length: no more than 1,500 words.

## THE PARIS REVIEW

544 West 27th St., New York NY 10001. (212)343-1333. **E-mail:** queries@theparisreview.org. **Website:** www.theparisreview.org. **Contact:** Lorin Stein, editor; Robyn Creswell, poetry editor. *The Paris Review* publishes "fiction and poetry of superlative quality, whatever the genre, style, or mode. Our contributors include prominent, as well as less well-known and previously unpublished writers. The Writers at Work interview series includes important contemporary writers discussing their own work and the craft of writing." Buys all rights, buys first English-language rights. Pays on publication. Responds in 4 months to mss. Guidelines online.

○ Address submissions to proper department. Do not make submissions via e-mail.

**MAGAZINES NEEDS** Submit no more than 6 poems at a time. Poetry can be sent to the poetry editor (please include a self-addressed, stamped envelope). Poets receive $100/poem.

## PARNASSUS: POETRY IN REVIEW

Poetry in Review Foundation, 205 W. 89th St., No. 8F, New York NY 10024. (212)787-3569. **E-mail:** poetryinreview@gmail.com. **Website:** www.parnassus-review.com. **Contact:** Herbert Leibowitz, editor and publisher. *Parnassus: Poetry in Review* provides "a forum where poets, novelists, and critics of all persuasions can gather to review new books of poetry, including translations—international poetries have occupied center stage from our very first issue—with an amplitude and reflectiveness that Sunday book supplements and even the literary quarterlies could not afford. Our editorial philosophy is based on the assumption that reviewing is a complex art. Like a poem or a short story, a review essay requires imagination, scrupulous attention to rhythm, pacing, and supple syntax; space in which to build a persuasive, detailed argument; analytical precision and intuitive gambits; verbal play, wit, and metaphor. We welcome and vigorously seek out voices that break aesthetic molds and disturb xenophobic habits." Buys one-time rights. Pays on publication. Publishes ms an average of 12-14 months after acceptance. Responds in 2 months to mss. Sample copy: $15.

**MAGAZINES NEEDS** Accepts most types of poetry.

**TIPS** "Be certain you have read the magazine and are aware of the editor's taste. Blind submissions are a waste of everybody's time. We'd like to see more poems that display intellectual acumen and curiosity about history, science, music, etc., and fewer trivial lyrical poems about the self, or critical prose that's academic and dull. Prose should sing."

## PASSAGER

Passager Press, 1420 N. Charles St., Baltimore MD 21201. **E-mail:** editors@passagerbooks.com. **Website:** www.passagerbooks.com. "*Passager* has a special focus on older writers. Its mission is to encourage, engage, and strengthen the imagination well into old age and to give mature readers oppertunities that are sometimes closed off to them in our youth-oriented culture. We are dedicated to honoring the creativity that takes hold in later years and to making public the talents of those over the age of 50." Passager publishes 2 issues/year, an Open issue (fall/winter) and a Poetry Contest issue (spring/summer). Acquires first North American serial rights. Publication is copyrighted. Responds in 5 months to mss. Sample copy: $10. Guidelines online.

**MAGAZINES NEEDS** Publishes poetry as part of annual poetry contest. **Deadline:** April 15. Send up to 5 poems with cover letter. Include estimated word count, brief bio, list of publications. Send either SASE (or IRC) for return of ms or disposable copy of ms and #10 SASE for reply only. **Reading fee:** $20 (includes one-year subscription). Length: up to 40 lines/poem.

**TIPS** "Stereotyped images of old age will be rejected immediately. Write humorous, tongue-in-cheek essays. Read the publication, or at least visit the website."

## PASSAGES NORTH

English Department, Northern Michigan University, 1401 Presque Isle Ave., Marquette MI 49855. (906)227-1203. **E-mail:** passages@nmu.edu. **Website:** www.passagesnorth.com. **Contact:** Jennifer A. Howard, editor in chief; Matt Weinkam and Robin McCarthy, managing editors; Matthew Gavin Frank, hybrids editor; Rachel May, nonfiction editor; Patricia Killelea, poetry editor; Monica McFawn, fiction editor. *Passages North*, published annually in spring, prints poetry, short fiction, creative nonfiction, essays, and interviews. Current issue: $13; Back issues: $7. Guidelines available for SASE, by e-mail, or on website.

**MAGAZINES NEEDS** "We're looking for poems that give us pause, poems that surprise us, poems that keep us warm during long northern nights. We want them to sing and vibrate with energy. We're open to all forms and aesthetics." Submit up to 5 poems together in 1 document. Has published poetry by Moira Egan, Frannie Lindsay, Ben Lerner, Bob Hicok, Gabe Gudding, John McNally, Steve Almond, Tracy Winn, and Midege Raymond.

**TIPS** "We look for voice, energetic prose, writers who take risks. We look for an engaging story in which the author evokes an emotional response from the reader through carefully rendered scenes, complex characters, and a smart, narrative design. Revise, revise. Read what we publish."

## THE PATERSON LITERARY REVIEW

Passaic County Community College, One College Blvd., Paterson NJ 07505. (973)684-6555. **Fax:** (973)523-6085. **Website:** www.patersonliteraryreview.com/. **Contact:** Maria Mazziotti Gillan, editor/executive director. *Paterson Literary Review*, published annually, is produced by the The Poetry Center at Passaic County Community College. Wants poetry of "high quality; clear, direct, powerful work." Acquires first North American serial rights. Publishes ms 6-12 months after acceptance. Reads submissions December 1-March 31 only. Responds within 1 year. Sample cop: $13 plus $1.50 postage.

Work for *PLR* has been included in the *Pushcart Prize* anthology and *Best American Poetry*.

**MAGAZINES NEEDS** Submit up to 5 poems at a time. Has published poetry and work by Diane di Prima, Ruth Stone, Marge Piercy, Laura Boss, Robert Mooney, and Abigail Stone. Lines/poem: 100 maximum.

**ALSO OFFERS** Publishes *The New Jersey Poetry Resource Book* ($5 plus $1.50 p&h) and *The New Jersey Poetry Calendar*. The Distinguished Poets Series offers readings by poets of international, national, and regional reputation. Poetryworks/USA is a series of programs produced for UA Columbia-Cablevision. See website for details about these additional resources.

**TIPS** Looks for "clear, moving, and specific work."

## PEACE & FREEDOM

Peace & Freedom Press, 17 Farrow Rd., Whaplode Drove, Spalding, Lincs PE12 0TS, England. **Website:** pandf.booksmusicfilmstv.com/index.htm. Published semiannually; emphasizes social, humanitarian, and environmental issues. Considers submissions from subscribers only. Those new to poetry are welcome. The poetry published is pro-animal rights/welfare, anti-war, environmental; poems reflecting love; erotic, but not obscene; humorous; spiritual, humanitarian; with or without rhyme/meter. Considers poetry by children and teens. Has published poetry by Dorothy Bell-Hall, Freda Moffatt, Andrew Bruce, Bernard Shough, Mona Miller, and Andrew Savage. Responds to submissions in less than a month usually, with SAE/IRC. Submissions from subscribers only.

**MAGAZINES NEEDS** No previously published poems or simultaneous submissions. No e-mail or fax submissions. Include bio. Reads submissions year round. Publishes theme issues. Upcoming themes available in magazine, for SAE with IRC, by e-mail, or on website. "Work without correct postage will not be responded to or returned until proper postage is sent." Pays one contributor copy. Reviews books of poetry. Lines/poem: 32 max.

**CONTEST/AWARD OFFERINGS** "*Peace & Freedom* holds regular poetry contests as does one of our other publications, *Eastern Rainbow*, which is a magazine concerning 20th-century popular culture using poetry up to 32 lines." Subscription: $20 U.S., £10 UK for 6 issues. Further details of competitions and publications available for SAE with IRC or on website.

**TIPS** "Too many writers have lost the personal touch that editors generally appreciate. It can make a difference when selecting work of equal merit."

### 💲 THE PEDESTAL MAGAZINE

6815 Honors Court, Charlotte NC 28210. **E-mail:** pedmagazine@carolina.rr.com. **Website:** www.thepedestalmagazine.com. **Contact:** John Amen, editor in chief. Committed to promoting diversity and celebrating the voice of the individual. Buys first rights. All rights revert back to the author/artist upon publication. Retains the right to publish the piece in any subsequent issue or anthology without additional payment. Publishes ms 2-4 weeks after acceptance. Responds in 1-2 months to mss. Guidelines online.

**MAGAZINES NEEDS** Open to a wide variety of poetry, ranging from the highly experimental to the traditionally formal. Submit all poems in 1 form. No need to query before submitting. No length restriction.

**TIPS** "If you send us your work, please wait for a response to your first submission before you submit again."

### 🌐 PENNINE INK MAGAZINE

1 Neptune St., Burnley BB11 1SF, England. **E-mail:** sheridansdandl@yahoo.co.uk. **Website:** pennineink.weebly.com. **Contact:** Laura Sheridan, editor. *Pennine Ink*, published annually in January, prints poems and short prose pieces. Responds to submissions in 3 months. Poetry should be no longer than 40 lines, prose no longer than around 800 words. Please include your e-mail address so we can contact you, or failing that, a small SASE for our reply. Work will not be returned, so please keep a copy of everything you send.

> *Pennine Ink* is 48 pages, A5, with b&w illustrated cover. Receives about 400 poems/year, accepts about 40. Press run is 200. "Contributors wishing to purchase a copy of *Pennine Ink* should go to the Amazon website and search for Pennine Ink. More information on our website."

**MAGAZINES NEEDS** Submit up to 6 poems at a time. Accepts e-mail submissions. Seldom comments on rejected poems. Length: up to 40 lines/poem; up to 1,000 words for prose. Pays 1 contributor copy.

### PENNSYLVANIA ENGLISH

Indiana University of Pennsylvania, Department of English, Indiana University of Pennsylvania, HSS 506A, 981 Grant St., Indiana PA 15705. (724)357-2262. **E-mail:** mtwill@iup.edu. **Website:** https://paenglish.submittable.com/submit. **Contact:** Dr. Michael T. Williamson, editor (mtwill@iup.edu); Dr. Michael Cox, nonfiction and fiction editor (mwcox@pitt.edu); Dr. Anthony Vallone, poetry editor (avallone@psu.edu); Dr. John Marsden, literary criticism editor (marsden@iup.edu). *Pennsylvania English*, published annually, is "sponsored by the Pennsylvania College English Association. Our philosophy is quality. We publish literary fiction (and poetry and nonfiction). Our intended audience is literate, college-educated people." Acquires first North American serial rights. Pays upon publication. Publishes ms up to 12 months after acceptance. Responds 1-12 months to mss. Sometimes comments on rejected mss. Sample copy: $10. Guidelines available on website.

**MAGAZINES NEEDS** Submit 3 or more poems at a time via the online submission manager at https://paenglish.submittable.com/submit. "For all submissions, please include a brief bio for the contributors' page. Be sure to include your name, address, phone number, e-mail address, institutional affiliation (if you have one), the title of your poem(s), and any other relevant information. We will edit if necessary for space." Wants poetry of "any length, any style."

**TIPS** "Quality of the writing is our only measure. We're not impressed by long-winded cover letters detailing awards and publications we've never heard of. Beginners and professionals have the same chance with us. We receive stacks of competently written but boring fiction. For a story to rise from the rejection pile, it takes more than the basic competence."

### PENNSYLVANIA LITERARY JOURNAL

Anaphora Literary Press, 2419 Southdale Drive, Hephzibah GA 30815, USA. (470)289-6395. **E-mail:** director@anaphoraliterary.com. **Website:** anaphoraliterary.com. **Contact:** Anna Faktorovich, editor/director. "*Pennsylvania Literary Journal* is a printed, peer-reviewed journal that publishes critical essays, book reviews, short stories, interviews, photographs, art, and poetry. Published tri-annually, it features special issues on a wide variety of different fields from film studies to literary criticism to interviews with bestsellers. Submissions in all genres from emerging and established writers are warmly welcomed." A free pdf or print copy of the issue. A monetary payment might be offered to an A-list major award-winning author. Publishes ms an average of 2 months after acceptance. Responds on the same day to queries and manuscripts.

Sample copy: $15. Guidelines online. Accepts queries and ms submissions by e-mail at director@anaphoraliterary.com.

**MAGAZINES NEEDS** No line limit. Does not provide payment.

**TIPS** "We are just looking for great writing. Send your materials; if they are good and you don't mind working for free, we'll take it."

## PENNY DREADFUL: TALES & POEMS OF FANTASTIC TERROR

P.O. Box 719, Radio City Station, Hell's Kitchen NY 10101-0719. **E-mail:** mmpendragon@aol.com. **Website:** www.mpendragon.com/pennydreadful.html. *Penny Dreadful: Tales & Poems of Fanastic Terror*, published irregularly (about once a year), features goth-romantic poetry and prose. Publishes poetry, short stories, essays, letters, listings, reviews, and b&w artwork "which celebrate the darker aspects of Man, the World, and their Creator." Wants "literary horror in the tradition of Poe, M.R. James, Shelley, M.P. Shiel, and LeFanu—dark, disquieting tales and verses designed to challenge the reader's perception of human nature, morality, and man's place within the Darkness. Stories and poems should be set prior to 1910 and/or possess a timeless quality." Does not want "references to 20th- and 21st-century personages/events, graphic sex, strong language, excessive gore and shock elements." Acquires one-time rights. Sample: $10. Subscription: $25/3 issues. Make checks payable to Michael Pendragon. Guidelines online.

○ "Works appearing in *Penny Dreadful* have been reprinted in *The Year's Best Fantasy and Horror*." *Penny Dreadful* nominates best tales and poems for Pushcart Prizes. *Penny Dreadful* is over 100 pages, digest-sized, desktop-published, perfect-bound. Press run is 200.

**MAGAZINES NEEDS** Submit by mail or e-mail. Rhymed, metered verse preferred. Has published poetry by Nancy Bennett, Michael R. Burch, Lee Clark, Louise Webster, K.S. Hardy, and Kevin N. Roberts. Length: up to 5 pages. Pays 1 contributor copy.

**ALSO OFFERS** *Penny Dreadful* "includes market listings for, and reviews of, kindred magazines." Pendragon Publications also publishes *Songs of Innocence & Experience*.

## THE PENWOOD REVIEW

P.O. Box 862, Los Alamitos CA 90720. **E-mail:** lcameron65@verizon.net. **E-mail:** submissions@penwoodreview.com. **Website:** www.penwoodreview.com. **Contact:** Lori Cameron, editor. *The Penwood Review* has been established to embrace high-quality poetry of all kinds and to provide a forum for poets who want to write intriguing, energetic, and disciplined poetry as an expression of their faith in God. We encourage writing that elevates the sacred while exploring its mystery and meaning in our lives. Semiannual. Wants "disciplined, high-quality, well-crafted poetry on any subject. Rhyming poetry must be written in traditional forms (sonnets, tercets, villanelles, sestinas, etc.)." Acquires one-time and electronic rights. Publishes ms 6-12 months after acceptance. Responds in up to 3 months. Sample copy: $6. Single copy: $8. Subscription: $16.

○ *The Penwood Review* is about 40 pages, magazine-sized, saddle-stapled, with heavy card cover. Press run is 50-100.

**MAGAZINES NEEDS** Submit 3-5 poems at a time. Prefers e-mail submissions (pasted into body of message). Cover letter is optional. One poem to a page with the author's full name, address, and phone number in the upper right corner. "Submissions are circulated among an editorial staff for evaluations." Never comments on rejected poems. Has published poetry by Kathleen Spivack, Anne Babson, Hugh Fox, Anselm Brocki, Nina Tassi, and Gary Guinn. Does not want "light verse, doggerel, or greeting card-style poetry. Also, nothing racist, sexist, pornographic, homophobic, or blasphemous." Length: less than 2 pages preferred. Pays with subscription discount of $12 and, with subscription, 1 additional contributor copy.

## PEREGRINE

Amherst Writers & Artists Press, P.O. Box 1076, Amherst MA 01004. (413)253-3307. **Fax:** (413)253-7764. **E-mail:** peregrine@amherstwriters.com. **Website:** www.amherstwriters.com. **Contact:** Jan Haag, editor. *Peregrine*, published annually, features poetry and fiction. "*Peregrine* has provided a forum for national and international writers since 1983 and is committed to finding excellent work by emerging as well as established writers. We welcome work reflecting diversity of voice. We like to be surprised. We look for writing that is honest, unpretentious, and memorable. All decisions are made by the editors." Acquires first rights. Sample copy: $12. Guidelines online.

**MAGAZINES NEEDS** Submit 3 single-spaced, one-page poems. "We seek poems that inform and surprise us. We appreciate fresh and specific imagery and layered metaphors, but not excessive verbiage, abstractions, or clichés." "We will not consider inspirational poetry, greeting-card verse, religious tirades, or nostalgia." Length: up to 40 lines and spaces/poem. Pays in contributor copies.

**TIPS** "Check guidelines before submitting your work. Familiarize yourself with *Peregrine*. We look for heart and soul as well as technical expertise. Trust your own voice."

## PERMAFROST: A LITERARY JOURNAL

c/o English Dept., Univ. of Alaska Fairbanks, P.O. Box 755720, Fairbanks AK 99775. **E-mail:** editor@ permafrostmag.com. **Website:** permafrostmag.com. *Permafrost Magazine*, a literary journal, contains poems, short stories, creative nonfiction, b&w drawings, photographs, and prints. We print both new and established writers, hoping and expecting to see the best work out there. We have published work by E. Ethelbert Miller, W. Loran Smith, Peter Orlovsky, Jim Wayne Miller, Allen Ginsberg, and Andy Warhol. Responds in 3 to 6 months. Back issues: $5. Subscription: $10 for 1 year, $18 for 2 years. Guidelines available on website. Reads submissions May 1 through November 30 for print edition, December 1 through April 30 for summer online edition.

○ *Permafrost* is about 200 pages, digest-sized, professionally printed, flat-spined. Also publishes summer online edition.

**MAGAZINES NEEDS** We publish any style of poetry provided it is conceived, written, and revised with care. We also welcome poems about anywhere, from anywhere. Submit up to 5 poems via online submissions manager at permafrostmag.submittable. com; "e-mail submissions will not be read." Sometimes comments on poems. Pays 1 contributor copy. Reduced contributor rate of $5 on additional copies.

## PERSPECTIVES

c/o Jason Lief, Dordt College, 498 4th Ave. NE, Sioux Center, Sioux Center IA 51250. **E-mail:** submissions@ perspectivesjournal.org. **Website:** perspectivesjournal.org. Malcolm McBryde. **Contact:** Jason Lief. "*Perspectives* is a journal of theology in the broad Reformed tradition. We seek to express the Reformed faith theologically; to engage issues that Reformed Christians meet in personal, ecclesiastical, and societal life; and thus to contribute to the mission of the church of Jesus Christ. The editors are interested in submissions that contribute to a contemporary Reformed theological discussion. Our readers tend to be affiliated with the Presbyterian Church (USA), the Reformed Church in America, and the Christian Reformed Church. Some of our subscribers are academics or pastors, but we also gear our articles to thoughtful, literate laypeople who want to engage in Reformed theological reflection on faith and culture." Acquires first rights. Time between acceptance and publication is 3-12 months. Responds in 3-6 months. Sample: $3.50. Subscription: $20.

○ *Perspectives* is 24 pages, magazine-sized, Web offset-printed, saddle-stapled, with paper cover containing b&w illustration. Receives about 300 poems/year, accepts 6-20. Press run is 3,300.

**MAGAZINES NEEDS** Wants "poems excellent in craft and significant in subject, both traditional and free in form. We publish 1-2 poems every other issue." Has published poetry by Ann Hostetler, Paul Willis, and Priscilla Atkins. Submit poems via e-mail. Pays 5 contributor copies.

## PHILADELPHIA STORIES

Fiction/Art/Poetry of the Delaware Valley, 93 Old York Rd., Suite 1/#1-753, Jenkintown PA 19046. **E-mail:** christine@philadelphiastories.org; info@philadelphiastories.org. **Website:** www.philadelphiastories.org. Carla Spataro, editorial director/co-publisher. **Contact:** Christine Weiser, executive director/co-publisher. *Philadelphia Stories*, published quarterly, publishes "fiction, poetry, essays, and art written by authors living in, or originally from, Pennsylvania, Delaware, or New Jersey. *Philadelphia Stories* also hosts 2 national writing contests: The Marguerite McGlinn Short Story Contest ($2,000 first-place prize; $500 second-place prize; $250 third-place prize) and the Sandy Crimmins National Poetry Contest ($1,000 first-place prize, 3 $100 runner-up prizes). Visit our website for details." *Philadelphia Stories* also launched a "junior" version in 2012 for Philadelphia-area writers ages 12 and younger and a "teen" version for writers aged 13-18. Visit www.philadelphiastories.org/junior for details. Acquires one-time rights. Publication is copyrighted. Publishes ms 1-2 months after acceptance. Responds in 6 months. Rarely comments on/ critiques rejected mss. Sample copy: $5 and on website. Guidelines available on website. Send complete ms with cover letter via online submission form only. Include estimated word count, list of publications, and affiliation to the Philadelphia area.

**MAGAZINES NEEDS** Submit 3 poems at a time. No previously published poems. Cover letter is preferred. Reads submissions year round. "Each poem is reviewed by a preliminary board that decides on a final list; the entire board discusses this list and chooses the mutual favorites for print and Web. We send a layout proof to check for print poems." Receives about 600 poems/year, accepts about 15%. Considers poetry by teens. Has published poetry by Daniel Abdal-Hayy Moore, Scott Edward Anderson, Sandy Crimmins, Liz Dolan, Alison Hicks, and Margaret A. Robinson. Wants "polished, well-crafted poems." Does not want "first drafts." Length: 36 lines/poem.

**TIPS** "We look for exceptional, polished prose, a controlled voice, strong characters and place, and interesting subjects. Follow guidelines. We cannot stress this enough. Read every guideline carefully and thoroughly before sending anything out. Send out only polished material. We reject many quality pieces for various reasons; try not to take rejection personally. Just because your piece isn't right for one publication doesn't mean it's bad. Selection is an extremely subjective process."

### PHOEBE: A JOURNAL OF LITERATURE AND ART

MSN 2C5, George Mason University, 400 University Dr., Fairfax VA 22030. **Website:** www.phoebejournal.com. Publishes poetry, fiction, nonfiction, and visual art. "*Phoebe* prides itself on supporting up-and-coming writers, whose style, form, voice, and subject matter demonstrate a vigorous appeal to the senses, intellect, and emotions of our readers." Responds in 4-6 months. Guidelines available on website.

**MAGAZINES NEEDS** Submit 3-5 poems via online submission manager. Pays 2 contributor copies and $500 for winner.

### PILGRIMAGE MAGAZINE

Colorado State University-Pueblo, Dept. of English, 2200 Bonforte Blvd., Pueblo CO 81001. **E-mail:** info@pilgrimagepress.org. **Website:** www.pilgrimagepress.org. **Contact:** Juan Morales, editor. Serves an eclectic fellowship of readers, writers, artists, naturalists, contemplatives, activists, seekers, adventurers, and other kindred spirits. Guidelines online. Submit via online submissions manager (https://pilgrimagemagazine.submittable.com/submit) or snail mail (with SASE for reply only).

**MAGAZINES NEEDS** Fit poetry on 1 page.

**TIPS** "Our interests include wildness in all its forms; inward and outward explorations; home ground, the open road, service, witness, peace, and justice; symbols, story, and myth in contemporary culture; struggle and resilience; insight and transformation; wisdom wherever it is found; and the great mystery of it all. We like good storytellers and a good sense of humor. No e-mail submissions, please."

### THE PINCH

English Department, University of Memphis, Memphis TN 38152. (901)678-4591. **E-mail:** editor@pinchjournal.com. **Website:** www.pinchjournal.com. **Contact:** Tim Johnston, editor in chief; Derek Moseley, managing editor. Semiannual literary magazine. "We publish fiction, creative nonfiction, poetry, and art of literary quality by both established and emerging artists." Acquires first North American serial rights. Publication is copyrighted. Responds in 3 months to mss. Sample copy: $5. Guidelines online.

○ "The Pinch Literary Awards in Fiction, Poetry, and Nonfiction offer a $1,000 prize and publication. Check our website for details."

**MAGAZINES NEEDS** "We do not accept submissions via e-mail. Submissions sent via e-mail will not receive a response. To submit, see guidelines." Submit through mail or via online submissions manager.

**ALSO OFFERS** Offers an annual award in poetry. 1st Prize: $1,000 and publication; 2nd and 3rd Prize poems may also be published. Any previously unpublished poem of up to 2 pages is eligible. No simultaneous submissions. Poems should be typed and accompanied by a cover letter. Author's name should not appear anywhere on ms. Mss will not be returned. Guidelines available for SASE, by e-mail, or on website. **Entry fee:** $20 for up to 3 poems (includes one-year subscription). **Deadline:** March 15 (inclusive postmark dates). Winners will be notified in July and published in subsequent issue.

**TIPS** "We have a new look and a new edge. We're soliciting work from writers with a national or international reputation as well as strong, interesting work from emerging writers."

### THE PINK CHAMELEON

**E-mail:** dpfreda@juno.com. **Website:** www.thepink-chameleon.com. **Contact:** Dorothy Paula Freda, editor/publisher. *The Pink Chameleon*, published annually online, contains "family-oriented, upbeat poetry, stories, essays, and articles, any genre in good taste that gives hope for the future." Acquires one-time rights for 1 year. Time between acceptance and publication is up to 1 year, depending on date of acceptance. Responds in 1 month to ms. Sometimes comments on rejected mss. Sample copy and writer's guidelines online.

○ Reading period is January 1 through April 30 and September 1 through October 31.

**MAGAZINES NEEDS** Also considers poetry by children and teens. Submit 1-4 poems at a time. Accepts e-mail submissions only (pasted into body of message; no attachments.) Use plain text and include a brief bio. Often comments on rejected poems. Receives about 50 poems/year, accepts about 50%. Does not want "pornography, cursing, swearing; nothing evoking despair." Length: 6-24 lines. No payment.

**TIPS** Wants "simple, honest, evocative emotion; upbeat fiction and nonfiction submissions that give hope for the future; well-paced plots; stories, poetry, articles, essays that speak from the heart. Read guidelines carefully. Use a good, but not ostentatious, opening hook. Stories should have a beginning, middle, and end that make the reader feel the story was worth his or her time. This also applies to articles and essays. In the latter 2, wrap your comments and conclusions in a neatly packaged final paragraph. Turnoffs include violence and bad language. Simple, genuine, and sensitive work does not need to shock with vulgarity to be interesting and enjoyable."

### PINYON POETRY

Mesa State College, Languages, Literature and Mass Communications, Mesa State College, Grand Junction CO 81502. **E-mail:** rphillis@mesa5.mesa.colorado.edu. **Website:** http://org.coloradomesa.edu/~rphillis/. **Contact:** Randy Phillis, editor. *Pinyon Poetry*, published annually in June, prints "the best available contemporary American poetry. No restrictions other than excellence. We appreciate a strong voice." Subscription: $8/year. Sample: $5. Make checks payable to Pinyon Poetry. Guidelines for SASE or online.

**MAGAZINES NEEDS** Does not want "inspirational, light verse, or sing-song poetry." Has published poetry by Mark Cox, Barry Spacks, Wendy Bishop, and Anne Ohman Youngs. Receives about 4,000 poems/year, accepts 2%. Submit 3-5 poems at a time. Cover letter is preferred. "Name, address, e-mail, and phone number on each page. SASE required." Reads submissions August 1-December 1. "Three groups of assistant editors, led by an associate editor, make recommendations to the editor." Seldom comments on rejected poems. Pays 2 contributor copies.

**TIPS** "Ask yourself if the work is something you would like to read in a publication."

### PIRENE'S FOUNTAIN

Glass Lyre Press, P.O. Box 2693, Glenview Illinois 60025. **E-mail:** pirenesfountain@gmail.com. **Website:** pirenesfountain.com. **Contact:** Elizabeth Nichols, submission and review editor. *Pirene's Fountain* is published annually in November. Reading period: May 1-August 1. Poets retain copyright to their own work; rights revert to poets upon publication. Publishes the following year after acceptance. Responds in 1-4 months. Guidelines online.

○ Receives about 400 poems/year, accepts about 10%.

**MAGAZINES NEEDS** Submit 3-8 poems at a time. Poems are circulated to an editorial board. No comments on rejected poems. Sometimes publishes theme issues. A 50-100 word bio note is required with submissions. Has published work by Lisel Mueller, Linda Pastan, J.P. Dancing Bear, Dorianne Laux, Rebecca Seiferle, Joseph Millar, Kim Addonizio, Jane Hirshfeld, and Jim Moore, among others. Does not want "anything obscene, pornographic, or discriminatory in nature."

**ALSO OFFERS** "Poets whose work has been selected for publication in our journal during the past calendar year (with the exception of staff /featured poets) are automatically entered for the annual Liakoura Poetry award. Our editors will each choose 1 poem from all of the selections. The 5 nominated poems will be sent "blind" to an outside editor/publisher for the final decision. The winning poet will be awarded a certificate and a $100 Amazon gift card via e-mail. Pushcart and Best of the Net nominations: Editors select the best work published by PF during the year. This is open to all submitting and featured poets. Only previously unpublished poems will be considered; please indicate that in your submission. Nominated poets are notified after selections have been sent in."

**TIPS** "Please read submission guidelines carefully and send in at least 3 poems. We offer a poetry discussion group on Facebook, titled Pirene's Fountain Poetry."

## PISGAH REVIEW

Division of Humanities, Brevard College, 1 Brevard College Dr., Brevard NC 28712. (828)577-8324. **E-mail:** tinerjj@brevard.edu. **Website:** www.pisgahreview.com. **Contact:** Jubal Tiner, editor. "*Pisgah Review* publishes primarily literary short fiction, creative nonfiction, and poetry. Our only criteria is quality of work; we look for the best." Acquires first North American serial rights. Publication is copyrighted. Pays on publication. Sends galleys to author. Publishes mss 6-9 months after acceptance. Responds to mss in 4-6 months. Sometimes comments on/critiques rejected mss. Sample copy: $7. Guidelines available on website.

Has published Ron Rash, Thomas Rain Crowe, Joan Conner, Gary Fincke, Steve Almond, and Fred Bahnson.

**MAGAZINES NEEDS** "Send complete ms to our submission manager on our website."

**TIPS** "We select work of only the highest quality. Grab us from the beginning and follow through. Engage us with your language and characters. A clean ms goes a long way toward acceptance. Stay true to the vision of your work, revise tirelessly, and submit persistently."

## PLAINSONGS

Hastings College Press, Department of Languages & Literatures, Hastings NE 68901. **E-mail:** plainsongs@hastings.edu. **Website:** www.hastings.edu/hastings-college-press/plainsongs. **Contact:** Eric R. Tucker, editor. *Plainsongs*, published 3 times/year, considers poems on any subject, in any style, but free verse predominates. *Plainsongs*' title suggests not only its location on the great plains, but its preference for the living language, whether in free or formal verse. Acquires first rights. Responds 2 months after deadline. Sample: $5. Subscription: $15 for 3 issues.

**MAGAZINES NEEDS** Submit up to 5 poems at a time. Please use online submission form. Reads submissions according to the following deadlines: August 15 for winter issue; November 15 for spring issue;

March 15 for fall issue. Pays 2 contributor copies and one-year subscription.

**CONTEST/AWARD OFFERINGS** Three poems in each issue receive a $25 prize. "A short essay in appreciation accompanies each award poem."

## PLANET-THE WELSH INTERNATIONALIST

P.O. Box 44, Aberystwyth Ceredigion SY23 3ZZ, United Kingdom. **E-mail:** submissions@planetmagazine.org.uk. **Website:** www.planetmagazine.org.uk. **Contact:** Emily Trahair, editor. A literary/cultural/political journal centered on Welsh affairs but with a strong interest in minority cultures in Europe and elsewhere. *Planet: The Welsh Internationalist*, published quarterly, is a cultural magazine "centered on Wales, but with broader interests in arts, sociology, politics, history, and science." Publishes ms 4-6 months after acceptance. Responds in 3 months. Single copy: £6.75; subscription: £22 (£40 overseas). Sample copy: £5. Guidelines online.

*Planet* is 128 pages, A5, professionally printed, perfect-bound, with glossy color card cover. Receives about 500 submissions/year, accepts about 5%. Press run is 1,550 (1,500 subscribers, about 10% libraries, 200 shelf sales).

**MAGAZINES NEEDS** Wants "good poetry in a wide variety of styles. No limitations as to subject matter; length can be a problem." Has published poetry by Nigel Jenkins, Anne Stevenson, and Les Murray. Submit 4-6 poems via mail or e-mail (with attachment). For postal submissions, no submissions returned unless accompanied by an SASE. Writers submitting from abroad should send at least 3 IRCs for return of typescript; 1 IRC for reply only. Pays £30/poem.

**TIPS** "We do not look for fiction that necessarily has a 'Welsh' connection, which some writers assume from our title. We try to publish a broad range of fiction, and our main criterion is quality. Try to read copies of any magazine you submit to. Don't write out of the blue to a magazine which might be completely inappropriate for your work. Recognize that you are likely to have a high rejection rate, as magazines tend to favor writers from their own countries."

## PLEIADES

Pleiades Press, Department of English, University of Central Missouri, Dept. of English, Martin 336, Warrensburg MO 64093. (660)543-4268. **Website:** www.

ucmo.edu/pleiades. **Contact:** Phong Nguyen and Jenny Molberg, co-editor. "We publish contemporary fiction, poetry, interviews, literary essays, special-interest personal essays, and reviews for a general and literary audience from authors from around the world." Reads August 15-May 15. Buys first North American serial rights, buys second serial (reprint) rights. Occasionally requests rights for TV, radio reading, website. Pays on publication. Publishes ms an average of 9 months after acceptance. Responds in 2 months to queries. Responds in 1-4 months to mss. Editorial lead time 9 months. Sample copy for $5 (back issue); $6 (current issue) Guidelines online.

**MAGAZINES NEEDS** Submit 3-5 poems at a time via online submission manager. "Nothing didactic, pretentious, or overly sentimental." Pays $3/poem, and contributor copies.

**ALSO OFFERS** "Also sponsors the Lena-Miles Wever Todd Poetry Series competition, a contest for the best book ms by an American poet. The winner receives $2,000, publication by Pleiades Press (1,000 copies), and distribution by Louisiana State University Press. Check website for deadline and details."

**TIPS** "Submit only 1 genre at a time to appropriate editors. Show care for your material and your readers—submit quality work in a professional format. Include cover letter with brief bio and list of publications. Include SASE. Cover art is solicited directly from artists. We accept queries for book reviews."

**⑤ PLOUGHSHARES**

Emerson College, 120 Boylston St., Boston MA 02116. (617)824-3757. **E-mail:** pshares@pshares.org. **Website:** www.pshares.org. **Contact:** Ladette Randolph, editor-in-chief/executive director; Ellen Duffer, managing editor. *Ploughshares*, published 3 times/year, is "a journal of new writing guest-edited by prominent poets and writers to reflect different and contrasting points of view. Translations are welcome if permission has been granted. Our mission is to present dynamic, contrasting views on what is valid and important in contemporary literature and to discover and advance significant literary talent. Each issue is guest-edited by a different writer. We no longer structure issues around preconceived themes." Editors have included Carolyn Forché, Gerald Stern, Rita Dove, Chase Twichell, and Marilyn Hacker. "We do accept electronic submissions—there is a $3 fee per submission, which is waived if you are a subscriber."

Buys first North American serial rights. Pays on publication. Publishes ms an average of 6 months after acceptance. Responds in 3-5 months to mss. Sample copy: $14 current issue, $7 back issue; please inquire for shipping rates. Subscription: $30 domestic, $30 plus shipping (see website) foreign. Guidelines online.

○ *Ploughshares* is 200 pages, digest-sized. Receives about 11,000 poetry, fiction, and essay submissions/year. Reads submissions June 1-January 15 (postmark); mss submitted January 16-May 31 will be returned unread.

**MAGAZINES NEEDS** Submit up to 5 poems via online submissions form or by mail. Has published poetry by Donald Hall, Li-Young Lee, Robert Pinsky, Brenda Hillman, and Thylias Moss. Pays $25/printed page ($50 minimum, $250 maximum); 2 contributor copies; and one-year subscription.

**PMS POEMMEMOIRSTORY**

University of Alabama at Birmingham, HB 217, 1530 Third Ave. S., Birmingham AL 35294. (205)934-2641. **Fax:** (205)975-8125. **E-mail:** poemmemoirstory@gmail.com. **Website:** pms-journal.org. **Contact:** Kerry Madden, editor in chief. "*PMS poemmemoirstory* appears once a year. We accept unpublished, original submissions of poetry, memoir, and short fiction during our January 1-March 31 reading period. We accept simultaneous submissions; however, we ask that you please contact us immediately if your piece is published elsewhere so we may free up space for other authors. While *PMS* is a journal of exclusively women's writing, the subject field is wide open." Copyright returns to author after publication, but work published elsewhere should acknowledge first publication in *PMS poemmemoirstory*. Sample copy: $10. Subscription: $10 for 1 year, $15 for 2 years, $18 for 3 years. Guidelines online.

○ "*PMS* has gone all-digital on Submittable. There is now a $3 fee, which covers costs associated with our online submissions system. Please send all submissions to poemmemoirstory.submittable.com/submit."

**MAGAZINES NEEDS** Submit up to 5 poems through online submissions manager. Pays 2 contributor copies.

**TIPS** "We strongly encourage you to familiarize yourself with *PMS* before submitting. You can find links to some examples of what we publish in the pages of *PMS 8* and *PMS 9*. We look forward to reading your work."

## ⊙❸ POCKETS

The Upper Room, P.O. Box 340004, Nashville TN 37203. (615)340-7333. **E-mail:** pockets@upperroom. org. **Website:** pockets.upperroom.org. **Contact:** Lynn W. Gilliam, editor. Magazine published 11 times/ year. "*Pockets* is a Christian devotional magazine for children ages 6-12. All submissions should address the broad theme of the magazine. Each issue is built around a theme with material which can be used by children in a variety of ways. Scripture stories, fiction, poetry, prayers, art, graphics, puzzles and activities are included. Submissions do not need to be overtly religious. They should help children experience a Christian lifestyle that is not always a neatly wrapped moral package but is open to the continuing revelation of God's will. Seasonal material, both secular and liturgical, is desired." Buys first North American serial rights. Pays on acceptance. Publishes ms an average of 1 year after acceptance. Responds in 8 weeks to mss. Each issue reflects a specific theme. Guidelines online.

◯ Does not accept e-mail or fax submissions.

**MAGAZINES NEEDS** Both seasonal and theme poems needed. Considers poetry by children. Length: up to 20 lines. Pays $25 minimum.

**TIPS** "Theme stories, role models, and retold scripture stories are most open to freelancers. Poetry is also open. It is very helpful if writers read our writers' guidelines and themes on our website."

## POEM

Huntsville Literary Association, Huntsville Literary Association, P.O. Box 2006, Huntsville AL 35804. **E-mail:** poem@hlahsv.org. **Website:** www.hlahsv.org/POEM. **Contact:** Rebecca Harbor, editor; Harry V. Moore and James Miller Robinson, assistant editors. *Poem*, published twice/year in the spring and fall, consists entirely of poetry. Welcomes submissions from established poets as well as from less-known and beginning poets. Acquires first serial rights. Responds in 1-3 months. Sample copy: $7 (back issue). Single copy: $10. Subscription: $20.

◯ *Poem* is 90 pages, digest-sized, flat-spined, printed on good stock paper, with a clean design and a matte cover. Prints more than 60 poems/issue, generally features 1 per page. Press run is 500.

**MAGAZINES NEEDS** Wants poems characterized by compression, rich vocabulary, significant content, and evidence of a tuned ear and a practiced pen.

Wants coherent work that moves through the particulars of the poem to make a point. Submit poems with a cover letter. Place name, address, telephone number, and e-mail address on cover letter and on each poem. Include SASE with sufficient postage. Submissions are read year round. Has published poetry by Ronald Wallace, Bill Brown, and Margaret Holley. Does not want translations, greeting card verse, or "proselytizing or didactic poems." Pays 2 contributor copies.

## ❶ POEMELEON: A JOURNAL OF POETRY

**E-mail:** editor@poemeleon.org. **Website:** www.poemeleon.org. **Contact:** Cati Porter, editor. Each issue of *Poemeleon* is devoted to a specific kind of poetry. Previous emphases include: poetry of place, ekphrastic poetry, poems in form, prose poems, persona poems, humor, gender, and collaboration. Acquires one-time, non-exclusive rights. Responds in 1-3 months after close of submissions. Guidelines online.

**MAGAZINES NEEDS** Submit 1-5 poems using online submission manager. Include a brief third-person bio in cover letter.

## POESY MAGAZINE

P.O. Box 458, Santa Cruz CA 95061. **E-mail:** info@poesy.org; submissions@poesy.org. **Website:** www.poesy.org. **Contact:** Brian Morrisey, editor in chief. *POESY Magazine*, published biannually, is "an anthology of American poetry. *POESY*'s main concentrations are Boston, Massachusetts, and Santa Cruz, California, 2 thriving homesteads for poets, beats, and artists of nature. Our goal is to unite the 2 scenes, updating poets on what's happening across the country." Wants to see "original poems that express observational impacts with clear and concise imagery. Acceptence is based on creativity, composition, and relation to the format of *POESY*." Does not want "poetry with excessive profanity. We would like to endorse creativity beyond the likes of everyday babble." Has published poetry by Lawrence Ferlinghetti, Jack Hirschman, Edward Sanders, Todd Moore, Diane Di Prima, and Julia Vinograd. Acquires first rights. Publishes ms 1 month after acceptance. Responds in 4-6 weeks. Guidelines online.

◯ *POESY* is 16 pages, magazine-sized, newsprint, glued/folded, includes ads. Receives about 1,000 poems/year, accepts about 10%. Press run is 1,000; most distributed free to local venues.

**MAGAZINES NEEDS** Submit up to 5 poems by e-mail or postal mail. Cover letter is preferred. Reads submissions year round. Indicate if you want your poems returned, and include SASE. "We encourage poems .. that create an image, stop moments in time, and leave your reader with a lasting impression. Please no poems about dogs, cats, angels, or the food you ate recently." Length: up to 32 lines/poem. Pays 3 contributor copies.

**TIPS** "Our main focus is on Santa Cruz and Boston poetry, but we also accept submissions across the country. We see the poem as something to immerse the reader into a welcomed world of arresting images that jerks the eyes onto the page and leaves the reels of the mind turning long after the poem is finished. We see the poem as a work of art; save the narrative voice for the enlightenment of prose. We see the poem as a camera documenting a moment in time seen before the lens, rather than from the eyes of its beholder behind the lens. To accomplish this goal, we have to be very precise that everything we publish falls within our portrayal of the poem."

## POETALK

Bay Area Poets Coalition, 1791 Solano Ave. #A11, Berkeley CA 94707-2209. **E-mail:** poetalk@aol.com. **Website:** www.bayareapoetscoalition.org. **Contact:** John Rowe, acquisitions. *POETALK*, currently published 1-2 issues/year, is the poetry journal of the Bay Area Poets Coalition (BAPC) and publishes 60-plus poets in each issue. "*POETALK* is open to all. No particular genre. Rhyme must be well done." All rights revert to author upon publication. Usually responds in up to 6 months. Guidelines available early summer for SASE, by e-mail, or see posting on website.

- *POETALK* is 36 pages, digest-sized, photocopied, saddle-stapled, with heavy card cover. Press run is 400. Subscription: $6/2 issues. Sample copy: $2. Submissions are read year-round.

**MAGAZINES NEEDS** In general, poets may submit 3-5 poems at a time, no more than twice/year. Lines/poem: under 35 preferred; longer poems of "outstanding quality" considered. Considers previously published poems and simultaneous submissions, but must be noted. Cover letter is preferred. Include SASE. Mss should be clearly typed, single-spaced, and include author's name and mailing address on every page. Provide an e-mail address. Pays 1 contributor copy.

**CONTEST/AWARD OFFERINGS** Sponsors yearly contest.

**TIPS** "If you don't want suggested revisions, you need to say so clearly in your cover letter or indicate on each poem submitted." Bay Area Poets Coalition holds monthly readings (in Berkeley, CA). BAPC has 150 members; membership is $15/year (includes subscription to *POETALK* and other privileges); extra outside U.S.

## POETICA MAGAZINE, CONTEMPORARY JEWISH WRITING

P.O. Box 11014, Norfolk VA 23517. **E-mail:** poetica-publishing@aol.com. **Website:** www.poeticamagazine.com. *Poetica Magazine, Contemporary Jewish Writing*, published in print 3 times/year, offers "an outlet for the many writers who draw from their Jewish background and experiences to create poetry/prose/short stories, giving both emerging and recognized writers the opportunity to share their work with the larger community." Poets retain all rights. Publishes ms 4 months after acceptance. Responds in 1 month. Contact the editor if reply not received. Single copy: $10. We have many opportunities. Please visit the website for the latest projects.

- *Poetica* is 70 pages, perfect-bound, full-color cover. Receives about 500 poems/year, accepts about 60%. Press run is 350.

**MAGAZINES NEEDS** Submit ms through online submissions manager. Include e-mail, bio, and mailing address. Pays 1 contributor copy.

**CONTEST/AWARD OFFERINGS** Anna Davidson Rosenberg Annual Poetry Awards for Individual Works.

**TIPS** "We publish original, unpublished works by Jewish and non-Jewish writers alike. We are interested in works that have the courage to acknowledge, challenge, and celebrate modern Jewish life beyond distinctions of secular and sacred. We like accessible works that find fresh meaning in old traditions that recognize the challenges of our generation. We evaluate works on several levels, including its skillful use of craft, its ability to hold interest, and layers of meaning."

## POET LORE

The Writer's Center, 4508 Walsh St., Bethesda MD 20815. E-mail: genevieve.deleon@writer.org. Website: poetlore.com; www.writer.org. Contact: Genevieve DeLeon, managing editor; Jody Bolz, editor; E. Ethelbert Miller, editor. *Poet Lore*, published semiannually, is dedicated to the best in American and world poetry as well as timely reviews and commentary. Wants fresh uses of traditional forms and devices. Has published poetry by Ai, Denise Duhamel, Jefferey Harrison, Eve Jones, Carl Phillips, and Ronald Wallace. Responds in 3 months. Guidelines for SASE or online at website.

○ *Poet Lore* is 144 pages, digest-sized, professionally printed, perfect-bound, with glossy card cover. Receives about 4,200 poems/year, accepts 125. Press run is at least 800. Single copy: $8; subscription: $18/nonmember, $12/member. "Add $1/single copy for shipping; add $5 postage for subscriptions outside U.S."

**MAGAZINES NEEDS** Considers simultaneous submissions with notification in cover letter. No e-mail or disk submissions. Submit typed poems, with author's name and address on each page; SASE is required. Pays 2 contributor copies and a one-year subscription.

## ● POETRY

The Poetry Foundation, 61 W. Superior St., Chicago IL 60654. (312)787-7070. Fax: (312)787-6650. E-mail: editors@poetrymagazine.org. Website: www.poetrymagazine.org. Don Share, editor. Contact: Don Share, editor. *Poetry*, published monthly by The Poetry Foundation (see separate listing in Organizations), "has no special ms needs and no special requirements as to form: We examine in turn all work received and accept that which seems best." Has published poetry by the major voices of our time as well as new talent. Buys first serial rights. Pays on publication. Publishes ms an average of 9 months after acceptance. Responds in 2 months to mss and queries. Guidelines online.

○ *Poetry*'s website offers featured poems, letters, reviews, interviews, essays, and web-exclusive features. *Poetry* is elegantly printed, flat-spined. Receives 100,000 submissions/year, accepts about 300-350. Press run is 16,000.

**MAGAZINES NEEDS** Accepts all styles and subject matter. Submit up to 4 poems via online submissions manager. Reviews books of poetry in multibook formats of varying lengths. Does not accept unsolicited reviews. Length: up to 10 pages total. Pays $10 line (minimum payment of $300).

**ALSO OFFERS** Offers 8 prizes (Bess Hokin Prize, Levinson Prize, Frederick Bock Prize, J. Howard and Barbara M.J. Wood Prize, John Frederick Nims Memorial Prize for Translation, Friends of Literature Prize, Editors Prize for Feature Article, Editors Prize for Reviewing) ranging from $500-5,000 are awarded annually to poets whose work has appeared in the magazine that year. Only work already published in *Poetry* is eligible for consideration; no formal application is necessary.

## ● POETRYBAY

P.O. Box 114, Northport NY 11768. (631)427-1950. E-mail: poetrybay@aol.com. E-mail: info@poetrybay.com. Website: www.poetrybay.com. Contact: George Wallace, editor. *Poetrybay*, published semiannually online, seeks "to add to the body of great contemporary American poetry by presenting the work of established and emerging writers. Also, we consider essays and reviews." Has published poetry by Robert Bly, Yevgeny Yevtushenko, Marvin Bell, Diane Wakoski, Cornelius Eady, and William Heyen. Guidelines online.

**MAGAZINES NEEDS** Open to format, length, and style. Works previously published in magazine or online publications will not be considered. Submit 3-5 poems in the body of an e-mail, with name, a brief bio, and address. Or submit poems via snail mail with a cover letter and SASE for reply.

## POETRY INTERNATIONAL

San Diego State University, 5500 Campanile Dr., San Diego CA 92182-6020. (619)594-1522. Fax: (619)594-4998. E-mail: poetryintl@gmail.com. Website: poetryinternational.sdsu.edu. Contact: Jenny Minniti-Shippey, managing editor. *Poetry International*, published annually in November, is "an eclectic poetry magazine intended to reflect a wide range of poetry being written today." Wants "a wide range of styles and subject matter. We're particularly interested in translations." Does not want "cliché-ridden, derivative, or obscure poetry." Has published poetry by Adrienne Rich, Robert Bly, Hayden Carruth, Kim Addonizio, Maxine Kumin, and Gary Soto. "We intend to continue to publish poetry that makes a difference in people's lives, and startles us anew with the endless capacity of language to awaken our senses and expand our awareness." Responds in 6-8 months to mss. Subscription: $19.95/1 year. Sample: $15.

○ *Poetry International* is 200 pages, perfectbound, with coated cardstock cover. Features the Poetry International Prize ($1,000) for best original poem. Submit up to 3 poems with a $15 entry fee.

**MAGAZINES NEEDS** Features the poetry of a different nation of the world as a special section in each issue. Submit via online submissions manager only. Pays in contributor copies.

**TIPS** "Seeks a wide range of styles and subject matter. We read unsolicited mss only between September 1-December 31 of each year. Manuscripts received any other time will be returned unread."

### POETRY KANTO

Kanto Gakuin University, 3-22-1 Kamariya-Minami Kanazawa-ku, Yokohama 236-8502, Japan. **E-mail:** botsfordalan@gmail.com. **Website:** poetrykanto.com. **Contact:** Alan Botsford, editor. *Poetry Kanto*, published annually in November by the Kanto Gakuin University, is a journal bridging east and west, featuring (as *Mythic Imagination Magazine* wrote) "outstanding poetry that navigates the divide of ocean and language from around the world." They seek exciting, well-crafted contemporary poetry in English and also encourage and publish high-quality English translations of modern and emerging Japanese poets. All translations must be accompanied by the original poems. Guidelines available on website.

○ After 35 years as a print publication, *Poetry Kanto* is now an online digital publication available worldwide. See website for sample poems.

**MAGAZINES NEEDS** Submit 3 to 5 poems at a time. Queries welcome. Send e-mail submissions (as attachment in Word). Cover letter is required. Include brief bio. Reads submissions December through June. Has published poetry by Jane Hirshfield, Ilya Kaminsky, Beth Ann Fennelly, Vijay Seshadri, Michael S. Collins, Mari L'Esperance, Michael Sowder, Alicia Ostriker, and Sarah Arvio.

### POETRY NORTHWEST

Everett Community College, 2000 Tower St., Everett WA 98201. (425) 388-9395. **E-mail:** editors@poetrynw.org; pnw@poetrynw.org. **Website:** www.poetrynw.org. **Contact:** Aaron Barrell and Erin Malone, editors. *Poetry Northwest* is published semiannually in June and December. "The mission of *Poetry Northwest* is to publish poetry with a vibrant sense of language at play in the world and a strong presense of the physical world in language. We publish new, emerging, and established writers. In the words of founding editor Carolyn Kizer, we aim to 'encourage the young and the inexperienced, the neglected mature, and the rough major talents and the fragile minor ones.' All styles and aesthetics will find consideration." Acquires all rights. Returns rights to poets upon publication. Pays 2 contributor copies. Time between acceptance and publication is 3-12 months. Sometimes comments on rejected poems. Responds in 8-12 weeks. Single copy: $10. Sample: $10. Make checks payable to *Poetry Northwest*. Guidelines available on website. Submission accepted online only, via Submittable; no e-mail or disk submissions. Cover letter is helpful.

○ Has published poetry by Theodore Roethke, Czeslaw Milosz, Anne Sexton, Harold Pinter, Thom Gunn, Philip Larkin, Heather McHugh, and Richard Kenney. *Poetry Northwest* is 40+ pages, magazine-sized, Web press-printed, saddle-stapled, with 4-color cover, includes ads. Receives about 10,000 poems/year; accepts about 1%. Press run is 1,500.

**MAGAZINES NEEDS** Submit 3-5 poems at a time once per submission period. Sometimes publishes theme issues. Upcoming themes available in magazine or on website. Reading period is September 15 through March 15. Mss sent outside reading period will be returned unread. Always sends prepublication galleys. Reviews books of poetry in single- and multibook format.

### POETRY SALZBURG REVIEW

University of Salzburg, Department of English and American Studies, Unipark Nonntal, Erzabt-Klotz-Strasse 1, Salzburg A-5020, Austria. (43)(662)8044-4424. **Fax:** (43)(662)8044-167. **E-mail:** editor@poetrysalzburg.com. **Website:** www.poetrysalzburg.com. **Contact:** Dr. Wolfgang Goertschacher and Mag. Andreas Schachermayr, editors. *Poetry Salzburg Review*, published twice/year, contains "articles on poetry, mainly contemporary, and 70% poetry. Also includes long poems, sequences of poems, essays on poetics, review-essays, interviews, artwork, and translations. We tend to publish selections by authors who have not been taken up by the big poetry publishers. Nothing of poor quality." Acquires first rights. Time between acceptance and publication is 3-6 months. Responds in 2-3 months. Single copy: $13; subscription: $25 (cash preferred; subscribers can also pay with Pay-Pal). Published on our website

O *Poetry Salzburg Review* is about 200 pages, A5, professionally printed, perfect-bound, with illustrated card cover. Receives about 10,000 poems/year; accepts 3%. Press run is 500.

**MAGAZINES NEEDS** Accepts e-mail submissions (as attachment). Seldom comments on rejected poems. Has published poetry by Brian W. Aldiss, Rae Armantrout, Paul Muldoon, Alice Notley, Samuel Menashe, Jerome Rothenberg, Michael Heller, and Nathaniel Tarn. No length restriction. Pays one contributor copy.

**ALSO OFFERS** Reviews books/chapbooks of poetry as well as books on poetics. Send materials for review consideration.

**TIPS** "No requirements, but it's a good idea to subscribe to *Poetry Salzburg Review*."

## POETS AND ARTISTS (O&S)

**Website:** www.poetsandartists.com. **Contact:** Didi Menendez, publisher. Reviews books of poetry, chapbooks of poetry, and other magazines/journals. Reads poetry submissions year round. Sometimes upcoming themes are online at website. Authors published include Denise Duhamel, Bob Hicok, Billy Collins, Ron Androla, Blake Butler, and Matthew Hittinger. "We are a multi-interactive publication focusing on art; figurative, representational, portraits, and poetry. We interview art collectors, poets, artists, gallery owners and art dealers to keep our readers in the know." Rights revert to poets upon publication. Time between acceptance and publication is 1 month. Sample copy for $25.

O Prefers submissions from skilled, experienced poets; will consider work from beginning poets.

**MAGAZINES NEEDS** Paste submissions into body of e-mail message. Cover letter is unnecessary. Does not like "weird" formats.

**TIPS** Publisher also publishes *MiPOesias Magazine*, which has been featured in Best American Poetry, and OCHO, which has received Pushcart Prize and has been featured in *Best American Poetry*.

## THE POET'S HAVEN

**Website:** www.poetshaven.com. **Contact:** Vertigo Xavier, publisher. *The Poet's Haven* publishes poetry, artwork, stories, essays, and more. Acquires rights to publish on the website permanently. Poet retains rights to have poems published elsewhere, "provided the other publishers do not require first-time or exclusive rights." Time between acceptance and publication is about 2 weeks. Never comments on rejected poems. Guidelines available on website.

O Work published in *The Poet's Haven* online galleries is left on the website permanently. Receives about 1,000 poems/year, accepts about 50%.

**MAGAZINES NEEDS** Accepts submissions through online form only. Wants work that is "emotional, personal, and intimate with the author or subject. Topics can cover just about anything." Has published poetry by Mark Sebastian Jordan, Lori Ann Kusterbeck, Kenneth Pobo, Jennifer Polhemus, and AKeemjamal Rollins. Does not publish religious material. No payment for online publication.

**ALSO OFFERS** Also publishes chapbooks, anthologies, and audio podcasts. Check website for themed calls and submission information.

## POINTED CIRCLE

Portland Community College, Cascade Campus, SC 206, 705 N. Killingsworth Street, Portland OR 97217. **Website:** http://www.pcc.edu/about/literary-magazines/pointed-circle. **Contact:** Wendy Bourgeois, faculty advisor. Publishes "anything of interest to educationally/culturally mixed audience. We will read whatever is sent, but we encourage writers to remember we are a quality literary/arts magazine intended to promote the arts in the community. No pornography, nothing trite. Be mindful of deadlines and length limits." Accepts submissions by e-mail, mail; artwork in high-resolution digital form. Acquires one-time rights.

O Reading period: October 1-February 7. Magazine: 80 pages; b&w illustrations; photos.

**MAGAZINES NEEDS** Submit up to 6 pages of poetry. Submitted materials will not be returned; SASE for notification only. Accepts multiple submissions. No pornography, nothing trite. Pays 2 contributor copies.

## POLYPHONY H.S.

An International Student-Run Literary Magazine for High School Writers and Editors, Polyphony High School, 1514 Elmwood Ave., Suite 2, Evanston IL 60201. (847)910-3221. **E-mail:** info@polyphonyhs.com. **Website:** www.polyphonyhs.com. **Contact:** Billy

Lombardo, co-founder and managing editor. "Our mission is to create a high-quality literary magazine written, edited, and published by high school students. We believe that when young writers put precise and powerful language to their lives it helps them better understand their value as human beings. We believe the development of that creative voice depends upon close, careful, and compassionate attention. Helping young editors become proficient at providing thoughtful and informed attention to the work of their peers is essential to our mission. We believe this important exchange between young writers and editors provides each with a better understanding of craft, of the writing process, and of the value of putting words to their own lives while preparing them for participation in the broader literary community. We strive to build respectful, mutually beneficial writer-editor relationships that form a community devoted to improving students' literary skills in the areas of poetry, fiction, and creative nonfiction." Acquires first rights. Pays on publication. Responds in 2-3 months. No query letters. Sample copy: $10. Digital copies also available (see website for details). Guidelines online.

○ Does not accept hard-copy entries; submit only through online submissions form.

**MAGAZINES NEEDS** Submit poetry via online submissions form. "Avoid clichés. Please." Length: up to 80 lines/poem. Pays 1 contributor copy.

**TIPS** "We manage the Claudia Ann Seaman Awards for Young Writers; cash awards for the best poem, best story, best essay. See website for details."

### ◐ PORTLAND REVIEW

Portland State University, P.O. Box 751, Portland OR 97207. **Website:** portlandreview.org. **Contact:** Alex Dannemiller, editor-in-chief. Portland Review has been publishing exceptional writing and artwork by local and international artists since 1956. Buys first North American serial rights. Publishes ms an average of 3-6 months after acceptance. Responds in 2-4 months to mss. Single copy: $12; subscription: $30/year, $54/2 years. Guidelines online: portlandreview.submittable.com/submit.

**MAGAZINES NEEDS** Guidelines online: portlandreview.submittable.com/submit.

**TIPS** Please visit portlandreview.org for access to our submission manager and for more information.

### THE POTOMAC

2020 Pennsylvania Ave., NW, Suite 443, Washington DC 20006. **E-mail:** potomac-politics@webdelsol.com. **E-mail:** rammelkampjc@gmail.com. **Website:** http://thepotomacjournal.com. **Contact:** Charles Rammelkamp, editor; Michael Neff, publisher. *The Potomac*, published semiannually online, features political commentary, cutting-edge poetry, flash fiction, and reviews. Open to all forms of poetry by new and established writers. Acquires one-time rights. Time between acceptance and publication is 3 months. Responds in 2 months. Often comments on rejected poems. Sometimes sends prepublication galleys. Sample copy free online. Guidelines available on website.

○ Accepts submissions year round. Receives a variable number of poems/year, accepts about 30-40. Has published poetry and fiction by Robert Cooperman, Michael Salcman, Joanne Lowery, Roger Netzer, Pamela Painter, and L.D. Brodsky.

**MAGAZINES NEEDS** Submit any number of poems at a time. Considers simultaneous submissions; no previously published poems. Accepts e-mail submissions (as attachment) only; no postal or disk submissions. Cover letter is preferred. Reads submissions year round. Reviews books/chapbooks of poetry and other magazines/journals in up to 2,000 words, single- and multi-book format. Send materials for review consideration. No payment.

### POTOMAC REVIEW: A JOURNAL OF ARTS & HUMANITIES

Montgomery College, 51 Mannakee St., MT/212, Rockville MD 20850. (240)567-4100. **E-mail:** PotomacReviewEditor@montgomerycollege.edu. **E-mail:** potomacreview.submittable.com. **Website:** blogs.montgomerycollege.edu/potomacreview/. **Contact:** Julie Wakeman-Linn, editor-in-chief; Kathleen Smith, poetry editor; John W. Wang, fiction editor; J. Howard, technology editor. *Potomac Review: A Journal of Arts & Humanities*, published semiannually in August and February, welcomes poetry and fiction from across the spectrum, both traditional and nontraditional poetry, free verse and in-form (translations accepted). We like traditional fiction and experimental or meta fiction and flash fiction. Essays and creative nonfiction are also welcome. Publishes ms in the next issue. Responds in 3-6 months. Sample: $10. Subscription: $24/year (includes 2 issues). Guidelines available on website.

○ Reading period: Year round, although slower in the summer. Has published work by David Wagoner, Jacob Appel, Sandra Beasley, Marilyn Kallet, Katie Cortese, and Amy Holman.

**MAGAZINES NEEDS** Submit up to 3 poems (5 pages maximum) at a time, electronically through website. Receives about 2,000 poems a year, accepts 1.5%. Poems are read "in house" and then sent to poetry editor for comments and dialogue. Does not publish theme issues. Pays 2 contributor copies and offers 40% discount on additional copies.

**CONTEST/AWARD OFFERINGS** Sponsors an annual poetry contest and annual fiction contest. Guidelines available in magazine (fall/winter issue) for SASE.

## ○ⓈTHE PRAIRIE JOURNAL

P.O. Box 68073, 28 Crowfoot Terrace NW, Calgary AB Y3G 3N8, Canada. **E-mail:** editor@prairiejournal.org (queries only); prairiejournal@yahoo.com. **Website:** www.prairiejournal.org. **Contact:** A.E. Burke, literary editor. "The audience is literary, university, library, scholarly, and creative readers/writers." Buys first North American serial rights or buys electronic rights. In Canada, author retains copyright and owns permission to republish (with acknowledgement appreciated). Pays on publication. Publishes ms an average of 4-6 months after acceptance. Responds in 2 weeks to queries; 2-6 months to mss. Editorial lead time 2-6 months. Sample copy: $5. Guidelines online.

○ "Use our mailing address for submissions and queries with samples or for clippings."

**MAGAZINES NEEDS** Seeks poetry "of any length; free verse, contemporary themes (feminist, nature, urban, nonpolitical), aesthetic value, a poet's poetry." Does not want to see "most rhymed verse, sentimentality, egotistical ravings. No cowboys or sage brush." Has published poetry by Liliane Welch, Cornelia Hoogland, Sheila Hyland, Zoe Lendale, and Chad Norman. Receives about 1,000 poems/year, accepts 10%. No heroic couplets or greeting card verse. Length: 3-50 lines. Pays $5-50.

**TIPS** "We publish many, many new writers and are always open to unsolicited submissions because we are 100% freelance. Do not send U.S. stamps; always use IRCs. We have poems, interviews, stories, and reviews online (query first)."

## PRAIRIE SCHOONER

The University of Nebraska Press, Prairie Schooner, 110 Andrews Hall, University of Nebraska, Lincoln NE 68588. (402)472-0911. **E-mail:** prairieschooner@unl.edu. **Website:** prairieschooner.unl.edu. **Contact:** Ashley Strosnider, managing editor. "We look for the best fiction, poetry, and nonfiction available to publish, and our readers expect to read stories, poems, and essays of extremely high quality. We try to publish a variety of styles, topics, themes, points of view, and writers with a variety of backgrounds in all stages of their careers. We like work that is compelling—intellectually or emotionally—either in form, language, or content." Buys all rights, which are returned to the author upon request after publication. Pays on publication. Publishes ms an average of 1 year after acceptance. Responds in 1 week to queries; in 3-4 months to mss. Editorial lead time 6 months. Sample copy: $6. Guidelines for #10 SASE.

○ Submissions must be received between September 1 and May 1. Poetry published in *Prairie Schooner* has been selected for inclusion in *The Best American Poetry* and *The Pushcart Prize*.

**MAGAZINES NEEDS** Wants "poems that fulfill the expectations they set up." No specifications as to form, length, style, subject matter, or purpose. Has published poetry by Alicia Ostriker, Marilyn Hacker, D.A. Powell, Stephen Dunn, and David Ignatow. Pays 3 copies of the issue in which the writer's work is published.

**CONTEST/AWARD OFFERINGS** "All manuscripts published in *Prairie Schooner* will automatically be considered for our annual prizes." These include The Strousse Award for Poetry ($500), the Bernice Slote Prize for Beginning Writers ($500), the Hugh J. Luke Award ($250), the Edward Stanley Award for Poetry ($1,000), the Virginia Faulkner Award for Excellence in Writing ($1,000), the Glenna Luschei Prize for Excellence ($1,500), and the Jane Geske Award ($250). Also, each year 10 Glenna Luschei Awards ($250 each) are given for poetry, fiction, and nonfiction. All contests are open only to those writers whose work was published in the magazine the previous year. Editors serve as judges. Also sponsors The *Prairie Schooner* Book Prize.

**TIPS** "Send us your best, most carefully crafted work, and be persistent. Submit again and again. Constantly work on improving your writing. Read widely in literary fiction, nonfiction, and poetry. Read *Prairie Schooner* to know what we publish."

## ○ ❶ ⑤ PRISM INTERNATIONAL

Dept. of Creative Writing, Buch E462, 1866 Main Mall, University of British Columbia, Vancouver British Columbia V6T 1Z1, Canada. (604)822-2514. **Fax:** (604)822-3616. **E-mail:** prismcirculation@gmail.com. **Website:** www.prismmagazine.ca. A quarterly international journal of contemporary writing—fiction, poetry, drama, creative nonfiction and translation. *PRISM international* is 80 pages, digest-sized, elegantly printed, flat-spined, with original color artwork on a glossy card cover. Readership: public and university libraries, individual subscriptions, bookstores—a world-wide audience concerned with the contemporary in literature. "We have no thematic or stylistic allegiances: Excellence is our main criterion for acceptance of manuscripts." Receives 1,000 submissions/year, accepts about 80. Circulation is for 1,200 subscribers. Subscription: $35/year for Canadian subscriptions, $40/year for US subscriptions, $45/year for international. Sample: $13. Buys first North American serial rights. Pays on publication. Publishes ms an average of 4 months after acceptance. Responds in 4 months to queries. Responds in 3-6 months to mss. Sample copy for $13, more info online. Guidelines online.

**MAGAZINES NEEDS** Wants "fresh, distinctive poetry that shows an awareness of traditions old and new. We read everything." Considers poetry by children and teens. "Excellence is the only criterion." Has published poetry by Margaret Avison, Elizabeth Bachinsky, John Pass, Warren Heiti, Don McKay, Bill Bissett, and Stephanie Bolster. Pays $40/printed page, and 2 copies of issue.

**HOW TO CONTACT** Submit up to 6 poems at a time. No previously published poems or simultaneous submissions. No e-mail submissions. Cover letter is required. Include brief introduction and list of previous publications. Poems must be typed or computer-generated (font and point size open). Include SASE (or SAE with IRCs). "Note: American stamps are not valid postage in Canada. No SASEs with U.S. postage will be returned. Translations must be accompanied by a copy of the original." Guidelines available for SASE (or SAE with IRCs), by e-mail, or on website. Responds in up to 6 months. Editors sometimes comment on rejected poems. Acquires first North American serial rights.

**ADDITIONAL INFORMATION** Sponsors annual Earle Birney Prize for Poetry. Prize awarded by the outgoing poetry editor to an outstanding poetry contributor published in *PRISM international*. Enter by regular submission only: no fee required. $500 prize.

**CONTEST/AWARD OFFERINGS** Annual Poetry Contest. First prize: $2,000; second prize: $300; third prize: $200. Entry fee: $35 for 3 poems; $5 per additional poem. Entry fee includes one-year subscription. Deadline: see website.

**TIPS** "We are looking for new and exciting fiction. Excellence is still our No. 1 criterion. As well as poetry, imaginative nonfiction and fiction, we are especially open to translations of all kinds, very short fiction pieces and drama which work well on the page. Translations must come with a copy of the original language work."

## A PUBLIC SPACE

323 Dean St., Brooklyn NY 11217. (718)858-8067. **E-mail:** general@apublicspace.org. **Website:** www.apublicspace.org. **Contact:** Brigid Hughes, founding editor; Anne McPeak, managing editor. *A Public Space*, published quarterly, is an independent magazine of literature and culture. "In an era that has relegated literature to the margins, we plan to make fiction and poetry the stars of a new conversation. We believe that stories are how we make sense of our lives and how we learn about other lives. We believe that stories matter." Single copy: $15; subscription: $36/year or $60/2 years.

◔    Accepts unsolicited submissions from September 15-April 15. Submissions accepted through Submittable or by mail (with SASE).

**MAGAZINES NEEDS** Submit via online submissions manager. No limit on line length.

## PUDDING MAGAZINE: THE INTERNATIONAL JOURNAL OF APPLIED POETRY

81 Shadymere Ln., 805 Proprietors Rd., #301, Worthington OH 43085. (614)361-3161. **E-mail:** connie@puddingmagazine.com. **Website:** www.puddingmagazine.com. **Contact:** Connie Willett Everett, editor/publisher. Senior editing staff: Susan Hendrickson, Kathleen S. Burgess, and Rose Smith.. *Pudding Magazine: The International Journal of Applied Poetry*, published twice a year, with occasional special issues.

Looking for excellent poetry of all types. Occasionally publish short-short fiction, reviews, and critical literary essays. Acquires first serial rights only. Pays in free copy and discount on extras for authors Mss published 3-6 months after acceptance. Responds in 4-6 months. Sample copy: $10. Subscription: $29.95 for 4 issues. Guidelines online.

**MAGAZINES NEEDS** Previously published submissions "respected, but include credits"; Cover letter is preferred ("cultivates great relationships with writers"). Submit poems by e-mail only. No set limit. Long poems are less successful with us. Pays 1 contributor copy; discount on additional copies.

**TIPS** "Our website will be undergoing a revamp in the coming year. You may order books and subscribe, find guidelines and more at the site now. We are broad and inclusive in our interests. If it concerns quality of life and is treated with respect, we will take a look."

## PUERTO DEL SOL

New Mexico State University, English Dept., P.O. Box 30001, MSC 3E, Las Cruces NM 88003. (575)646-3931. **E-mail:** puertodelsoljournal@gmail.com. **Website:** www.puertodelsol.org. **Contact:** Evan Lavender-Smith, editor in chief; Carmen Gimenez Smith, poetry editor; Lily Hoang, prose editor. Publishes innovative work from emerging and established writers and artists. Wants poetry, fiction, nonfiction, drama, theory, artwork, interviews, reviews, and interesting combinations thereof. Acquires one-time print and electronic rights and anthology rights. Rights revert to author after publication. Responds in 3-6 months to mss. Single copy: $10. Subscriptions: $12 for 1 year, $20 for 2 years, $34 for 3 years. Guidelines online.

> *Puerto del Sol* is 150 pages, digest-sized, professionally printed, flat-spined, with matte card cover with art. Press run is 1,250 (300 subscribers, 25-30 libraries). Reading period is September 15 through December 1 and January 1 through March 1.

**MAGAZINES NEEDS** Wants top-quality poetry, any style, from anywhere; excellent poetry of any kind, any form. Submit 3-5 poems at a time through online submission manager. Brief cover letter is welcome. Do not send publication vitae. One poem/page. Sometimes sends prepublication galleys. Has published poetry by Richard Blanco, Maria Ercilla, Pamela Gemin, John Repp, and Lee Ann Roripaugh. Pays 2 contributor copies.

**TIPS** "We are especially pleased to publish emerging writers who work to push their art form or field of study in new directions."

## PULSAR POETRY MAGAZINE

Ligden Publishers, 34 Lineacre, Grange Park, Swindon, Wiltshire SN5 6DA, United Kingdom. **E-mail:** pulsar.ed@btinternet.com. **Website:** www.pulsarpoetry.com. **Contact:** David Pike, editor. Acquires first rights. "Originators retain copyright of their poems." Publishes ms 1 year after acceptance. Responds in 1 month. Guidelines available for SASE (or SAE and IRC) or on website.

**MAGAZINES NEEDS** "We will publish poems on the *Pulsar* web on a quarterly basis, i.e. March, June, September, and December. The selection process for poems will not alter, and we will continue to publish on a merit basis only; be warned, the editor is very picky! See poem submission guidelines online. We encourage the writing of poetry from all walks of life." Wants "hard-hitting, thought-provoking work; interesting and stimulating poetry." Does not want "racist material. Not keen on religious poetry." Has published poetry by Ann Egan, Mark Rutter, David Sapp, Julia Stothard, Stephen Komarnyckyi, Donna Pucciani, Sam Silva, Ian C. Smith, B. Diehl, Richard Dinges Jr., and Michael Jannings. Pays 1 contributor copy.

**TIPS** "Give explanatory notes if poems are open to interpretation. Be patient, and enjoy what you are doing. Check grammar, spelling, etc. (should be obvious). Note: We are a nonprofit society."

## PURPOSE

718 N. Main St., Newton KS 67114. **E-mail:** PurposeEditor@MennoMedia.org. **Website:** www.mennomedia.org/purpose. *Purpose* is published monthly by Mennomedia, the publisher for Mennonite Church Canada and Mennonite Church USA. It is a faith-based adult monthly magazine that focuses on discipleship-living, simplicity, and the Christian faith. Buys one-time rights. Pays upon publication. Guidelines online at www.mennomedia.org/purpose.

**MAGAZINES NEEDS** Poetry must address monthly themes. Length: 12 lines maximum. Pays $10-20/poem.

**TIPS** "We seek true stories that follow monthly themes. Be sure to look at the website for the theme list and deadlines, as we only consider stories that are tied to the themes. Follow the writer guidelines on the website for the latest submission information."

## QUANTUM FAIRY TALES

**E-mail:** editor@quantumfairytales.com. **Website:** quantumfairytales.com. **Contact:** The Gnomies. Quantum Fairy Tales is a nonprofit, all-volunteer, all-donation, quarterly e-zine showcasing art and literature with elements of science fiction, fantasy, and the supernatural, with weekly website articles and author/artist highlights. "The best part about QFT is that real, live gnomies reply with feedback to every submission." Guidelines online.

**MAGAZINES NEEDS** E-mail poetry submission with title, type of submission, and word count in submission line. Poetry submissions should be 50 lines or less and should fit into a speculative fiction category, such as: scifi, horror, fantasy, steampunk, etc.

**TIPS** "Your writing and art work must fall in the category of speculative fiction for us to consider it. Every submission gets a free critique whether published or not. If you do not hear from us within three months, please give us a nudge. Thank you!"

## QUARTER AFTER EIGHT

Ohio University, 360 Ellis Hall, Athens OH 45701. **Website:** www.quarteraftereight.org. **Contact:** Patrick Swaney and Claire Eder, editors. "Quarter After Eight is an annual literary journal devoted to the exploration of innovative writing. We celebrate work that directly challenges the conventions of language, style, voice, or idea in literary forms. In its aesthetic commitment to diverse forms, QAE remains a unique publication among contemporary literary magazines." Reading period: October 15-April 15. Acquires first North American serial rights. Rights revert to author upon publication. Publishes ms 6-12 months after acceptance. Responds in 3-5 months. Sample copy: $10. Subscriptions: one-year subscription (1 volume): $10; two-year subscription (2 volumes): $18; three-year subscription (3 volumes): $25. Guidelines online at website.

- Holds annual short prose (any genre) contest with grand prize of $1,000. Deadline is November 30.

**MAGAZINES NEEDS** Submit through online submissions manager.

**TIPS** "We look for prose and poetry that is innovative, exploratory, and—most importantly—well writ-

ten. Please subscribe to our journal and read what is published to get acquainted with the QAE aesthetic."

## QUARTERLY WEST

University of Utah, 255 S. Central Campus Dr., Room 3500, Salt Lake City UT 84112. **E-mail:** quarterlywest@gmail.com. **Website:** www.quarterlywest.com. **Contact:** Claire Wahmanholm and Sara Eliza Johnson, editors. "We publish fiction, poetry, nonfiction, and new media in long and short formats, and will consider experimental as well as traditional works." Buys first North American serial rights; buys all rights. Publishes ms an average of 6 months after acceptance. Responds in 3-4 months to mss. Guidelines online.

- Quarterly West was awarded first place for Editorial Content from the American Literary Magazine Awards. Work published in the magazine has been selected for inclusion in the Pushcart Prize anthology, the Best of the Net anthology, and The Best American Short Stories anthology.

**MAGAZINES NEEDS** Submit 3-5 poems at a time using online submissions manager only.

**TIPS** "We publish a special section of short shorts every issue, and we also sponsor an annual novella contest. We are open to experimental work—potential contributors should read the magazine! Don't send more than 1 story per submission. Novella competition guidelines online. We prefer work with interesting language and detail—plot or narrative are less important. We don't do religious work."

## QUEEN'S QUARTERLY

144 Barrie St., Queen's University, Kingston ON K7L 3N6, Canada. (613)533-2667. **E-mail:** queens.quarterly@queensu.ca. **Website:** www.queensu.ca/quarterly. **Contact:** Joan Harcourt, literary editor (fiction and poetry); Boris Castel, nonfiction editor (articles, essays and reviews). Queen's Quarterly is "a general interest intellectual review featuring articles on science, politics, humanities, arts and letters, extensive book reviews, and some poetry and fiction." Requires first North American serial rights. Pays on publication. Sends galleys to author. Publishes ms on average 6-12 months after acceptance. Responds in 2-3 months to queries; 1-2 months to ms. Sample copy: $6.50. U.S. Subscription: $20 for Canada, $25 for U.S. and foreign subscribers. Guidelines available on website.

○ Has published work by Gail Anderson-Dargatz, Tim Bowling, Emma Donohue, Viktor Carr, Mark Jarman, Rick Bowers, and Dennis Bock. **MAGAZINES NEEDS** Receives about 400 submissions of poetry/year, accepts 40. Submissions can be sent on hard copy with a SASE (no replies/returns for foreign submissions unless accompanied by an IRC) or by e-mail and will be responded to by same. "We are especially interested in poetry by Canadian writers. Shorter poems preferred." Has published poetry by Evelyn Lau, Sue Nevill, and Raymond Souster. Each issue contains about 12 pages of poetry. Usually pays $50 (Canadian)/poem (but it varies), plus 2 copies.

## QUIDDITY INTERNATIONAL LITERARY JOURNAL AND PUBLIC-RADIO PROGRAM

Benedictine University at Springfield, 1500 N. 5th St., Springfield IL 62702. **E-mail:** quidditylit@gmail.com. **Website:** www.quidditylit.com. **Contact:** Joanna Beth Tweedy, founding editor; John McCarthy, managing editor. *Quiddity*, published semi-annually, is a print journal and public-radio program featuring poetry, prose, and artwork by new, emerging, and established contributors from around the world. Has published work by J.O.J. Nwachukwu-Agbada, Kevin Stein, Karen An-Hwei Lee, and Haider Al-Kabi. Publishes ms 6 months to 2 years after acceptance. Responds in 6 months. Guidelines online.

**MAGAZINES NEEDS** Submit up to 5 poems (no more than 10 pages total) through snail mail (hard copy) or through submissions manager. Considers simultaneous submissions; no previously published poems (previously published includes work posted on a public website/blog/forum and on private, password-protected forums). Cover letter is preferred. Address to poetry editor, SASE required (except international). See website for reading dates. Pays 1 contributor copy.

## RADIX MAGAZINE

Radix Magazine, Inc., P.O. Box 4307, Berkeley CA 94704. (510)548-5329. **E-mail:** radixmag@aol.com. **Website:** www.radixmagazine.com. **Contact:** Sharon Gallagher, editor. *Radix Magazine*, published quarterly, is named for the Latin word for "root" and "has its roots both in the 'real world' and in the truth of Christ's teachings." Wants poems that reflect a Christian world-view, but aren't preachy. Has published poetry by John Leax, Czeslaw Milosz, Madeleine L'Engle, and Luci Shaw. Interested in first North American

serial rights. Publishes ms 3 months to 3 years after acceptance. Responds in 2 months to queries and to mss. Editorial lead time 6 months. Sample copy for $5. Guidelines available by e-mail.

○ *Radix* is 32 pages, magazine-sized, offset-printed, saddle-stapled, with 60-lb. self cover. Receives about 120 poems/year, accepts about 10%. Press run varies. Subscription: $15. Sample: $5. Make checks payable to *Radix Magazine*."

**MAGAZINES NEEDS** Submit 1-4 poems at a time. Length: 4-20 lines. Pays 2 contributor copies.

**TIPS** "We accept very few unsolicited manuscripts. We do not accept fiction. All articles and poems should be based on a Christian world view. Freelancers should have some sense of the magazine's tone and purpose."

## THE RAG

P.O. Box 17463, Portland OR 97217. **E-mail:** submissions@raglitmag.com. **Website:** raglitmag.com. **Contact:** Seth Porter, editor; Dan Reilly, editor. *The Rag* focuses on the grittier genres that tend to fall by the wayside at more traditional literary magazines. *The Rag*'s ultimate goal is to put the literary magazine back into the entertainment market while rekindling the social and cultural value short fiction once held in North American literature. Purchases first rights only. Pays prior to publication. Responds in 1 month or less for queries; in 1-2 months for mss. Editorial lead time 1-2 months. Guidelines online.

○ Fee to submit online ($3) is waived if you subscribe or purchase a single issue.

**TIPS** "We like gritty material: material that is psychologically believable and that has some humor in it, dark or otherwise. We like subtle themes, original characters, and sharp wit."

## THE RAINTOWN REVIEW

Central Ave. Press, 5390 Fallriver Row Court, Columbia MD 21044. **E-mail:** theraintownreview@gmail. com. **Website:** www.theraintownreview.com. **Contact:** John Oelfke, publisher; Anna Evans, editor in chief; Quincy R. Lehr, associate editor. *The Raintown Review*, published 2 times/year in Winter and Summer, contains poetry, reviews, and belletristic critical prose. Wants well-crafted poems. Primarily a venue for formal/metrical poetry. Has published poetry by Julie Kane, Alexandra Oliver, Rick Mullin, Annie Finch, Kevin Higgins, David Mason, A.E. Stallings,

Richard Wilbur, and many others. Responds in 10-12 weeks. One can also subscribe online via our website preferred method. Guidelines online.

○ *The Raintown Review* is 120 pages, perfect-bound. Receives about 2,500 poems/year, accepts roughly 5%. Press run is approximately 500. Subscription: $24/year, $45 for 2 years, $65 for 3 years. Sample: $12. Make checks/money orders payable to Central Ave Press.

**MAGAZINES NEEDS** Submit 3-5 poems at a time. Accepts e-mail submissions only (pasted into body of message); no postal submissions. Guidelines available on website. Strong bias toward formal/metrical poetry. No restrictions on length. Pays 1 contributor copy.

## RALEIGH REVIEW LITERARY & ARTS MAGAZINE

Box 6725, Raleigh NC 27628-6725. **E-mail:** info@raleighreview.org. **Website:** www.raleighreview.org. Rob Greene, editor. **Contact:** Rob Greene, editor; Landon Houle, fiction editor; Bryce Emley, poetry editor. "*Raleigh Review* is a national nonprofit magazine of poetry, short fiction (including flash), and art. We believe that great literature inspires empathy by allowing us to see the world through the eyes of our neighbors, whether across the street or across the globe. Our mission is to foster the creation and availability of accessible yet provocative contemporary literature. We look for work that is emotionally and intellectually complex. Buys first North American serial rights. Publication is copyrighted. Pays on publication. Publishes ms 3-6 months after acceptance. Responds typically in 1-3 months, though sometimes up to 3-6 months. "Poetry and fiction submissions through Tell It Slant online system; no prior query required." Sample copy: $13.50 hardcopy or $4.95 on Kindle. "Sample work also online at website." Guidelines online at www.raleighreview.org.

**MAGAZINES NEEDS** Submit up to 5 poems. "If you think your poems will make a perfect stranger's toes tingle, heart leap, or brain sizzle, then send them our way. We typically do not publish avant garde, experimental, or language poetry. We *do* like a poem that causes—for a wide audience—a visceral reaction to intellectually and emotionally rich material." Length: open. Pays $10 maximum.

**TIPS** "Please be sure to read the guidelines and look at sample work on our website. Every piece is read for its intrinsic value, so new/emerging voices are often published alongside nationally recognized, award-winning authors."

## $ RATTAPALLAX

Rattapallax Press, 217 Thompson St., Suite 353, New York NY 10012. **E-mail:** devineni@rattapallax.com. **Website:** www.rattapallax.com. **Contact:** Ram Devineni, founder & president; Flávia Rocha, editor in chief. *Rattapallax*, published semiannually, is named for "Wallace Stevens's word for the sound of thunder. The magazine includes a DVD featuring poetry films and audio files. *Rattapallax* is looking for the extraordinary in modern poetry and prose that reflect the diversity of world cultures. Our goals are to create international dialogue using literature and focus on what is relevant to our society." Buys first North American serial rights, South American rights. Pays on publication. Publishes ms an average of 6 months after acceptance. Responds in 3 months to queries; in 3 months to mss. Editorial lead time 6 months. Sample copy: $7.95. Make checks payable to *Rattapallax*. Guidelines online.

○ *Rattapallax* is 112 pages, magazine-sized, off-set-printed, perfect-bound, with 12-pt. CS1 cover; some illustrations; photos. Press run is 2,000 (100 subscribers, 50 libraries, 1,200 shelf sales); 200 distributed free to contributors, reviews, and promos.

**MAGAZINES NEEDS** Submit via online submission manager at rattapallax.submittable.com/submit. Often comments on rejected poems. Length: 1 page per poem. Pays 2 contributor copies.

## RATTLE

12411 Ventura Blvd., Studio City CA 91604. (818)505-6777. **E-mail:** tim@rattle.com. **Website:** www.rattle.com. **Contact:** Timothy Green, editor. *RATTLE* "includes poems, essays, and interviews with poets, and tribute features dedicated to a specific ethnic or vocational group." Responds in 1-3 months. Guidelines online.

**MAGAZINES NEEDS** Wants "meaningful poetry in any form." Submit up to 5 poems at a time. Accepts e-mail submissions (pasted into body of message). Cover letter is required (with e-mail address, if possible). Pays $100/poem and a 1-year subscription for print contributors; $50/poem for online contributors.

**ALSO OFFERS** "All submissions are automatically considered for the Neil Postman Award for Metaphor, an annual $1,000 prize for the best use of metaphor as judged by the editors. No entry fee or special formatting is required; simply follow the regular guidelines." Also holds the *RATTLE* Poetry Prize (see separate listing in Contests & Awards). Also considers poetry by children and teens under the age of 16 for a separate annual anthology, *Rattle Young Poets Anthology*. Parents must submit through an online portal. See www.rattle.com/poetry/children for more information.

## RATTLING WALL

c/o PEN USA, 269 S. Beverly Dr. #1163, Beverly Hills CA 90212. **E-mail:** therattlingwall@penusa.org. **Website:** therattlingwall.com. **Contact:** Michelle Meyering, editor. Acquires first rights. Rights revert to author upon publication. Pays on publication. Publishes ms 2 months after acceptance. Responds in 6 months. Sample copy for $18.95. Guidelines online.

**MAGAZINES NEEDS** Submit 3-5 poems at a time. Does not want sentimental love poetry or religious verse. Does not consider poetry by children or teens. Pays 2 contributor copies.

## 🟢 THE RAVEN CHRONICLES

A Journal of Art, Literature, & the Spoken Word, 15528 12th Ave. NE, Shoreline WA 98155. (206)941-2955. **E-mail:** editors@ravenchronicles.org. **Website:** www.ravenchronicles.org. "*The Raven Chronicles* publishes work which reflects the cultural diversity of the Pacific Northwest, Canada, and other areas of America. We promote art, literature and the spoken word for an audience that is hip, literate, funny, informed, and lives in a society that has a multicultural sensibility. We publish fiction, talk art/spoken word, poetry, essays, reflective articles, reviews, interviews, and contemporary art. We look for work that reflects the author's experiences, perceptions, and insights." Responds in 3 months. Guidelines online.

**MAGAZINES NEEDS** Send a maximum of 3 poems at a time via online submissions manager. Focus is on content that melds with form—whether traditional or experimental.

## 🐢 THE READER

The Reader Organisation, Calderstones Mansion, Calderstones Park, Liverpool L18 3JB, United Kingdom. **E-mail:** magazine@thereader.org.uk; info@thereader.org.uk. **Website:** www.thereader.org.uk. **Contact:** Philip Davis, editor. "*The Reader* is a quarterly literary magazine aimed at the intelligent 'common reader'—from those just beginning to explore serious literary reading to professional teachers, academics, and writers. As well as publishing short fiction and poetry by new writers and established names, the magazine features articles on all aspects of literature, language, and reading; regular features, including a literary quiz and a section on the Reading Revolution, reporting on The Reader Organisation's outreach work; reviews; and readers' recommendations of books that have made a difference to them. *The Reader* is unique among literary magazines in its focus on reading as a creative, important, and pleasurable activity, and in its combination of high-quality material and presentation with a genuine commitment to ordinary but dedicated readers." Also publishes literary essays, literary criticism, poetry. Pays on publication. Publishes ms 16 months after acceptance. Responds to queries and mss in 2 months. Guidelines for SASE and online.

**MAGAZINES NEEDS** Submit up to 6 poems. No e-mail submissions. Send complete ms with cover letter. Include estimated word count, brief bio, list of publications.

**TIPS** "The style or polish of the writing is less important than the deep structure of the story (though, of course, it matters that it's well written). The main persuasive element is whether the story moves us—and that's quite hard to quantify. It's something to do with the force of the idea and the genuine nature of enquiry within the story. When fiction is the writer's natural means of thinking things through, that'll get us. "

## REAL: REGARDING ARTS & LETTERS

Stephen F. Austin State University, P.O. Box 13007, SFA Station, Nacogdoches TX 75962-3007. **E-mail:** brininsta@sfasu.edu. **Website:** regardingartsandletters.wordpress.com. **Contact:** Andrew Brininstool, editor. "*REAL: Regarding Arts & Letters* was founded in 1968 as an academic journal which occasionally published poetry. Now, it is an international creative magazine dedicated to publishing the best contemporary fiction, poetry, and nonfiction." Features both established and emerging writers. Responds in 3 months, though response time is slower in summer months.

Magazine: semiannual, 120 pages, perfect-bound.

**MAGAZINES NEEDS** Submit up to 5 poems at a time via online submissions manager. Include cover letter addressed to Dr. Christine Butterworth-Mc-Dermott. Pays contributor copies.

**TIPS** "We are looking for the best work, whether you are established or not."

## REALPOETIK

**E-mail:** realpoetikblog@gmail.com. **Website:** www.realpoetik.club. **Contact:** Thibault Raoult, editor. *RealPoetik* publishes innovative work. Poems are published online and also sent to subscribers via e-mail. "We provide a club/poem atmosphere." Publishes poetry 2-4 months after acceptance. Responds in 1 month to queries. Sometimes comments on rejected mss. Sample copy online.

◘    Publishes 20-30 new poets/year.

**MAGAZINES NEEDS** Query first via e-mail with short bio, project description (if applicable), and any assertions/questions you might have.

## REDACTIONS: POETRY & POETICS

604 N. 31st Ave., Apt. D-2, Hattiesburg MS 39401. **E-mail:** redactionspoetry@yahoo.com. **E-mail:** redactionspoetry@yahoo.com. **Website:** www.redactions.com. **Contact:** Tom Holmes. *Redactions*, released every 9 months, covers poems, reviews of new books of poems, translations, manifestos, interviews, essays concerning poetry, poetics, poetry movements, or concerning a specific poet or a group of poets; and anything dealing with poetry. All rights revert back to the author. Responds in 3 months.

**MAGAZINES NEEDS** "Anything dealing with poetry." Pays contributor copy.

**TIPS** "We only accept submissions by e-mail. We read submissions throughout the year. E-mail submission as an attach in one Word, Wordpad, Notepad, .rtf, or .txt document, or place in the body of an e-mail. Include brief bio and your snail-mail address. E-mails that have no subject line or have nothing written in the body of the email will be deleted. We do not accept blank e-mails with only an attachment. Query after 90 days if you haven't heard from us. See website (redactions.com/submission-and-ordering.asp) for full guidelines, including for cover artwork."

## REDHEADED STEPCHILD

**E-mail:** redheadedstepchildmag@gmail.com. **Website:** www.redheadedmag.com/poetry. **Contact:** Malaika King Albrecht. "*Redheaded Stepchild* only accepts poems that have been rejected by other magazines. We publish biannually, and we accept submissions in the months of August and February only. We do not accept previously published work. We do, however, accept simultaneous submissions, but please inform us immediately if your work is accepted somewhere else. We are open to a wide variety of poetry and hold no allegiance to any particular style or school. If your poem is currently displayed online on your blog or website or wherever, please do not send it to us before taking it down, at least temporarily." Acquires first rights. Rights revert to poets upon publication. Time between acceptance and publication is 3 months. Poems are circulated to an editorial board. Sometimes comments on rejected poems. Responds in 3 months. Guidelines on website.

◘    Wants a wide variety of poetic styles.

**MAGAZINES NEEDS** "Submit 3-5 poems that have been rejected elsewhere with the names of the magazines that rejected the poems. We do not want multiple submissions, so please wait for a response to your first submission before you submit again. As is standard after publication, rights revert back to the author, but we request that you credit *Redheaded Stepchild* in subsequent republications. We do not accept e-mail attachments; therefore, in the body of your e-mail, please include the following: a brief bio, 3-5 poems, and the publication(s) that rejected the poems." Has published poetry by Kathryn Stripling Byer, Alex Grant, Amy King, Diane Lockward, Susan Yount, and Howie Good.

## REDIVIDER

Department of Writing, Literature, and Publishing, Emerson College, 120 Boylston St., Boston MA 02116. **E-mail:** editor@redividerjournal.org. **Website:** www.redividerjournal.org. *Redivider*, a journal of literature and art, is published twice a year by graduate students in the Writing, Literature, and Publishing Department of Emerson College. Prints new art, fiction, nonfiction, and poetry from new, emerging, and established artists and writers. Responds in 3-6 months. Sample copy: $8. One-year subscription: $15; two-year subscription: $25. Make checks payable to *Redivider* at Emerson College. Guidelines online at website.

◘    Every spring, *Redivider* hosts the Beacon Street Prize Writing Contest, awarding a cash prize and publication to the winning submission in fiction, poetry, and nonfiction categories. Hosts the Blurred Genre Contest each fall, awarding cash prizes and publication for flash fiction, flash nonfiction, and prose poetry. See www.redividerjournal.org for details.

**MAGAZINES NEEDS** Pays 2 contributor copies.

**TIPS** To get a sense of what we publish, pick up an issue!

## 🟢 THE RED MOON ANTHOLOGY OF ENGLISH LANGUAGE HAIKU

P.O. Box 2461, Winchester VA 22604-1661. **E-mail:** jim.kacian@redmoonpress.com. **Website:** www.redmoonpress.com. **Contact:** Jim Kacian, editor/publisher. *The Red Moon Anthology of English Language Haiku*, published annually in February, is "a collection of the best haiku published in English around the world." Acquires North American serial rights. Sample available for SASE or by e-mail. Subscription: $17 plus $5 p&h. Guidelines available for SASE or by e-mail.

💬 *The Red Moon Anthology of English Language Haiku* is 160 pages, digest-sized, offset-printed on quality paper, with 4-color heavy-stock cover. Receives several thousand submissions/year; accepts less than 2%. Print run is 1,000 for subscribers and commercial distribution. Considers poetry by children and teens.

**MAGAZINES NEEDS** "We do not accept direct submissions to the *Red Moon Anthology*. Rather, we employ an editorial board who are assigned journals and books from which they cull and nominate. Nominated poems are placed on a roster and judged anonymously by the entire editorial board twice a year." Has published haiku and related forms by Susan Diridoni, Dietmar Tauchner, Mike Dillon, and Fay Aoyagi.

## 🟢 RED RIVER REVIEW

**E-mail:** info@redriverreview.com. **Website:** www.redriverreview.com. **Contact:** Michelle Hartman, editor. "Our editorial philosophy is simple: It is the duty of the writer to accurately chronicle our times and to reflect honestly on how these events affect us. Poetry which strikes a truth, which artfully conveys the human condition, is most likely to be selected. Vulgarity and coarseness are part of our daily life and are thus valid. Life isn't always pretty. However, vulgarity and coarseness just for the sake of the exercise doesn't generally benefit anyone. *Red River Review* is open to all styles of writing. Abstract, beat, confessional, free verse, synthetic, formal—we will publish just about anything that has the authenticity and realism we're seeking. With this said, however, rhymed poetry of any nature is rarely accepted." Acquires first North

American electronic rights and possible future anthology electronic rights. Rights revert to poets upon publication. Time between acceptance and publication is 2 weeks. Responds in 2 weeks to poems. Sometimes comments on rejected poems. **Charges criticism fee. Handled on individual basis.** Guidelines available on website.

💬 "We are associated with the Dallas Poets Community and therefore recommend their workshops and events to poets in the North Texas area."

**MAGAZINES NEEDS** Submit 1 poem per page, up to 5 poems at a time via online submissions manager; no e-mail submissions. Receives about 2,000 poems/year. Does not consider previously published poems (poetry posted on a public website, blog, or forum). "Please be very sure you have entered your e-mail address correctly. If an acceptance comes back as bad mail, we pull the poem. Please include a serious bio. If you do not respect your work, why should we?" Has published poetry by Naomi Shihab Nye, Larry Thomas, Rob Walker, Alan Gann, Jerry Bradley, and Ann Howells. Rarely takes rhyming or form poems, "although we love a good sonnet every now and then."

## RED ROCK REVIEW

College of Southern Nevada, CSN Department of English, J2A, 3200 E. Cheyenne Ave., North Las Vegas NV 89030. (702)651-4094. **Fax:** (702)651-4455. **E-mail:** redrockreview@csn.edu. **Website:** sites.csn.edu/english/redrockreview. **Contact:** Erica Vital-Lazare, senior editor; Jacob Elison, associate editor. Dedicated to the publication of fine contemporary literature. Buys first North American serial rights. All other rights revert to the authors and artists upon publication. Sample: $6.50. Subscriptions: $9.50/year. No longer accepting snail-mail submissions. Send all submissions as Word, RTF, or PDF file attachments. Guidelines online. Occasionally comments on rejections.

💬 *Red Rock Review* is about 130 pages, magazine-sized, professionally printed, perfect-bound, with 10-pt. CS1 cover. Accepts about 15% of poems received/year. We accept fine poetry and short fiction year-round via electronic submission at redrockreview@csn.edu.

**MAGAZINES NEEDS** Looking for the very best literature. Poems need to be tightly crafted, characterised by expert use of language. Submit 2-3 poems at a time. Length: up to 80 lines/poem. Pays 2 contributor copies.

**TIPS** "Open to short fiction and poetry submissions from year-round. See guidelines online."

### RED WHEELBARROW

De Anza College, 21250 Stevens Creek Blvd., Cupertino CA 95014. **Website:** www.deanza.edu/redwheelbarrow. Buys first North American serial rights. Publishes ms an average of 2-4 months after acceptance. Responds in 2 weeks to queries; in 2-4 months to mss. Sample copy: $10 ($2.50 for back issues). Guidelines online.

🔾 "We seek to publish a diverse range of styles and voices from around the country and the world." Publishes a student edition and a national edition.

**MAGAZINES NEEDS** Send up to 5 poems by mail (include SASE) or e-mail with brief bio. Does not want excessively abstract or excessively sentimental poetry.

**TIPS** "Write freely, rewrite carefully. Resist clichés and stereotypes. We are not affiliated with Red Wheelbarrow Press or any similarly named publication."

### REED MAGAZINE

San Jose State University, Dept. of English, One Washington Square, San Jose CA 95192. **E-mail:** mail@reedmag.org; cathleen.miller@sjsu.edu. **Website:** www.reedmag.org. **Contact:** Cathleen Miller, editor in chief. *Reed Magazine* is the oldest literary journal west of the Mississippi. We publish works of short fiction, nonfiction, poetry, and art, and offer cash prizes in each category. Buys first North American rights. Pays award winners, nearly $4000 in cash prizes. Publishes ms an average of 5 months after acceptance. Responds annually in December. Guidelines available on website and through Submittable.

🔾 Accepts electronic submissions only.

**MAGAZINES NEEDS** Submit 1 poem per attachment via online submissions manager. Contest contributors receive 1 free copy; additional copies: $10.

**TIPS** Well-writen, original, clean grammatical prose is essential. We are interested in established authors as well as fresh new voices. Keep submitting!

### RENDITIONS: A CHINESE-ENGLISH TRANSLATION MAGAZINE

Research Centre for Translation, Chinese University of Hong Kong, Shatin, N.T. , Hong Kong. (852)3943-7399. **Fax:** (852)2603-5110. **E-mail:** renditions@cuhk.edu.hk; rct@cuhk.edu.hk. **Website:** www.cuhk.edu.hk/rct/renditions/index.html. *Renditions: A Chinese-English Translation Magazine*, published 2/year in May and November, uses "exclusively translations from Chinese, ancient and modern." Poems are printed with Chinese and English texts side by side. Has published translations of the poetry of Yang Lian, Gu Cheng, Shu Ting, Mang Ke, and Bei Dao. *Renditions* is about 132 pages, magazine-sized, elegantly printed, perfect-bound, with glossy card cover. Single copy: $21.90; subscription: $33.90/year, $59.90/2 years, $79.90/3 years. Responds in 2 months. Guidelines on website.

**MAGAZINES NEEDS** Submissions should be accompanied by Chinese originals. Accepts e-mail and fax submissions. "Submissions by postal mail should include two copies. Use British spelling." Sometimes comments on rejected translations. Publishes theme issues.

**ADDITIONAL INFORMATION** Also publishes a hardback series (Renditions Books) and a paperback series (Renditions Paperbacks) of Chinese literature in English translation. Will consider book mss; query with sample translations.

### RHINO

The Poetry Forum, Inc., P.O. Box 591, Evanston IL 60204. **E-mail:** editors@rhinopoetry.org. **Website:** rhinopoetry.org. "This independent, eclectic annual journal of 40 years accepts poetry, flash fiction (500 words max), and poetry-in-translation that experiments, provokes, compels. Emerging and established poets are showcased." Accepts general submissions April 1-August 31 and Founders' Prize submissions September 1-October 31. Buys first North American serial rights. Response time: 3-6 months. Single copy: $16. Back issues: $6 plus $3 s/h. Guidelines online.

**MAGAZINES NEEDS** Wants "work that reflects passion, originality, engagement with contemporary culture, and a love affair with language. We welcome free verse, formal poetry, innovation, humor, and risk-taking. All entries considered for the Editors' Prize." Submit no more than 5 poems (1 poem per page) or 5 pages maximum via online submissions manager (preferred) or by postal mail. Include cover letter. Accepted poems are published in our annual print journal and online within a year of publication. Accepted poems may include audio component on our website. Pays one contributor copy and offers contributor discounts for additional copies.

**TIPS** "Our diverse group of editors looks for the very best in contemporary writing, and we have created a dynamic process of soliciting and reading new work by local, national, and international writers. We are open to all styles and look for idiosyncratic, rigorous, well-crafted, lively, and passionate work."

### ●⑤ THE RIALTO

P.O. Box 309, Alysham, Norwich NR11 6LN, England. **E-mail:** info@therialto.co.uk. **Website:** www.therialto.co.uk. **Contact:** Michael Mackmin, editor. *The Rialto*, published 3 times/year, seeks to publish the best new poems by established and beginning poets. Seeks excellence and originality. Has published poetry by Alice Fulton, Jenny Joseph, Les Murray, George Szirtes, Philip Gross, and Ruth Padel. Copyright remains with poets. Payment on publication. Publishes ms 5 months after acceptance. Responds in 3-4 months. Submission guidelines can be found on the website. We now accept online submissions via Submittable. Details on website. Postal submissions still very welcome. We respond by e-mail to postal submissions from outside of the UK.

○ *The Rialto* is 64 pages, A4, with full-color cover. Receives about 12,000 poems/year, accepts about 1%. Press run is 1,500. Single copy: £8.50; subscription: £24 (prices listed are UK: for U.S. and Canada add £12 Shipping Charge). Make checks payable to *The Rialto*. Checks in sterling only. Online payment also available on website.

**MAGAZINES NEEDS** Submit up to 6 poems at a time with a SASE. E-mail submissions via Submittable now welcome, details on website. Pays £20/poem on publication.

**TIPS** *The Rialto* also publishes occasional books and pamphlets. Please do not send book-length manuscripts. Query first. Details available in magazine and on website. Before submitting, "you will probably have read many poems by many poets, both living and dead. You will probably have put aside each poem you write for at least 3 weeks before considering it afresh. You will have asked yourself, 'Does it work techni-

cally?'; checked the rhythm, the rhymes (if used), and checked that each word is fresh and meaningful in its context, not jaded and tired. You will hopefully have read *The Rialto*."

### RIBBONS: TANKA SOCIETY OF AMERICA JOURNAL

1470 Keoncrest Dr., Berkley CA 94702. **E-mail:** drice2@comcast.net. **Website:** https://sites.google.com/site/tankasocietyofamerica/home. **Contact:** David Rice, editor. Published three times per year, seeks and regularly prints the best tanka poetry being written in English, together with reviews, critical and historical essays, commentaries, and translations. Wants poetry that exemplifies the very best in English-language tanka, having a significant contribution to make to the short poem in English. All schools and approaches are welcome. Tanka should reflect contemporary life, issues, values, and experience, in descriptive, narrative, and lyrical modes. Does not want work that merely imitates the Japanese masters. Considers poetry by children and teens. Has published poetry by Cherie Hunter Day, Marianne Bluger, Sanford Goldstein, Larry Kimmel, John Stevenson, and George Swede. Publishes ms 2 months after acceptance. Respond in 1-2 months.

**MAGAZINES NEEDS** No previously published poems or simultaneous submissions. Prefers e-mail submissions (pasted into body of message); no disk submissions. Postal submissions must include SASE. Reads submissions year-round. See the publication or contact the editor for specific deadlines for each issue. Deadlines: April 30 (spring/summer issue), August 31 (fall issue), and December 31 (winter issue). Length: 5 lines. Sequences of up to 50 total lines considered.

**TIPS** "Work by beginning as well as established English-language tanka poets is welcome; first-time contributors are encouraged to study the tanka form and contemporary examples before submitting. No particular school or style of tanka is preferred over another; our publications seek to showcase the full range of English-language tanka expression and subject matter through the work of new and established poets in the genre from around the world."

### ⑤ RIVER STYX MAGAZINE

Big River Association, 3139A Grand Blvd., Suite 203, St. Louis MO 63118. (314)533-4541. **E-mail:** bigriver@riverstyx.org. **Website:** www.riverstyx.org. **Contact:** Richard Newman, editor. "*River Styx* publishes the highest-quality fiction, poetry, interviews, essays, and visual art. We are an internationally distributed multicultural literary magazine. Mss read May-November." Buys first North American serial rights, buys one-time rights. Pays on publication. Publishes ms an average of 6 months after acceptance. Responds in 6 months to mss. Sample copy: $9. Guidelines online.

◯ Work published in *River Styx* has been selected for inclusion in past volumes of *New Stories from the South, The Best American Poetry, Best New Poets, New Poetry from the Midwest*, and *The Pushcart Prize Anthology.*

**MAGAZINES NEEDS** Wants "excellent poetry—original, energetic, musical, and accessible." Does not want "chopped prose or opaque poetry that isn't about anything." Has published poetry by Jennifer Perrine, Dorianne Laux, Ted Kooser, Louis Simpson, Molly Peacock, Marilyn Hacker, Yusef Komunyakaa, Andrew Hudgins, and Catie Rosemurgy. Include SASE. No religious poetry. Pays 2 contributor copies, plus one-year subscription. Cash payment as funds permit.

**ALSO OFFERS** Sponsors an annual poetry contest. Past judges include Terrance Hayes, Maxine Kumin, Stephen Dunn, Kim Addonizio, Alan Shapiro, Dorianne Laux, Ellen Bryant Voigt, Philip Levine, and Naomi Shihab Nye. Guidelines available for SASE or on website.

### THE ROAD NOT TAKEN: A JOURNAL OF FORMAL POETRY

**E-mail:** kathryn.jacobs@tamuc.edu. **E-mail:** roadnottaken@tamuc.edu. **Website:** www.journalformalpoetry.com. **Contact:** Dr. Kathryn Jacobs, editor. *The Road Not Taken: A Journal of Formal Poetry*, published 3 times/year online. "Poetry should be metrical; rhyme is welcome but optional. *The Road Not Taken* aims for a modern metrical style written in contemporary idiom on contemporary subjects. Please make only sparing use of end-stopped lines; this is the 21st century, not the 18th. Likewise, strive for flexible rhymes. In short, explore tradition but make it new." Responds in up to 4 months; "please wait until the next issue appears before querying." Sometimes comments on rejected poems.

**MAGAZINES NEEDS** Submit 3-5 poems by e-mail only. "Simultaneous submissions are acceptable, but contact me promptly if a poem is accepted elsewhere."

### ⑤ ROANOKE REVIEW

221 College Lane, Salem VA 24153. **E-mail:** review@roanoke.edu. **Website:** http://roanoke-review.squarespace.com/. "The *Roanoke Review* is an online literary journal that is dedicated to publishing accessible fiction, nonfiction, and poetry that is smartly written. Humor is encouraged; humility as well." Pays on publication for one-time rights. Publishes ms 6-9 months after acceptance. Responds in 1 month to queries; 6 months to mss; 3-6 months to poetry. Sometimes comments on rejected mss. Guidelines available on website.

◯ Has published work by Siobhan Fallon, Jacob M. Appel, and JoeAnn Hart.

**MAGAZINES NEEDS** Submit original typed mss; no photocopies. Pays "cash when budget allows."

**TIPS** "Pay attention to sentence-level writing—verbs, metaphors, concrete images. Don't forget, though, that plot and character keep us reading. We're looking for stuff that breaks the MFA story style. Be real. Know rhythm. Concentrate on strong images."

### THE ROCKFORD REVIEW

The Rockford Writers Guild, P.O. Box 858, Rockford IL 61105. **E-mail:** rwg@rockfordwritersguild.com; editor@rockfordwritersguild.com. **Website:** www.rockfordwritersguild.com. **Contact:** Connie Kluntz. "Published twice/year. Members only edition in summer-fall and winter-spring edition which is open to all writers. Open season to submit for the winter-spring edition of the Rock Review is August. If pubished in the winter-spring edition of the Rockford Review, payment is one copy of magazine and $5 per published piece. Credit line given. Check website for frequent updates. We are also on Facebook under Rockford Writers' Guild." Buys first North American serial rights. Pays on publication. Sample copy available for $12. Guidelines available on website.

◯ Poetry 50 lines or less, prose 1,300 words or less.

**MAGAZINES NEEDS** Wants eclectic poetry. Length: up to 50 lines. If published in the winterspring edition of the *Rockford Review*, payment is one copy of magazine and $5 per published piece. Pays on publication.

**TIPS** "We're wide open to new and established writers alike—particularly short satire."

## ☼◐⑤ ROOM

West Coast Feminist Literary Magazine Society, P.O. Box 46160, Station D, Vancouver BC V6J 5G5, Canada. **E-mail:** contactus@roommagazine.com. **Website:** www.roommagazine.com. *"Room* is Canada's oldest feminist literary journal. Published quarterly by a collective based in Vancouver, *Room* showcases fiction, poetry, reviews, art work, interviews, and profiles by writers and artists who identify as women or genderqueer. Many of our contributors are at the beginning of their writing careers, looking for an opportunity to get published for the first time. Some later go on to great acclaim. *Room* is a space where women can speak, connect, and showcase their creativity. Each quarter we publish original, thought-provoking works that reflect women's strength, sensuality, vulnerability, and wit." Buys first rights. Pays on publication. Responds in 6 months. Sample copy: $12 or online at website.

○ *Room* is digest-sized; illustrations, photos. Press run is 1,600 (900 subscribers, 50-100 libraries, 100-350 shelf sales).

**MAGAZINES NEEDS** *Room* uses "poetry by women, including trans* and genderqueer writers, written from a feminist perspective. Nothing simplistic, clichéd. We prefer to receive up to 5 poems at a time, so we can select a pair or group." Submit via online submissions manager. Pays $50-120 (Canadian), 2 contributor copies, and a one-year subscription.

## ROSEBUD

N3310 Asje Rd., Cambridge WI 53523. (608)423-9780. **Website:** www.rsbd.net. **Contact:** Roderick Clark, publisher/managing editor; John Lehman, founder/editor-at-large. *Rosebud*, published 3 times/year in April, August, and December, has presented many of the most prominent voices in the nation and has been listed as among the very best markets for writers. Responds in 45 days. Sample copy: $7.95. Subscription: $20 for 3 issues, $35 for 6 issues.

○ *Rosebud* is elegantly printed with full-color cover. Press run is 10,000.

**MAGAZINES NEEDS** Wants poetry that avoids "excessive or well-worn abstractions, not to mention clichés. Present a unique and convincing world (you can do this in a few words!) by means of fresh and exact imagery, and by interesting use of syntax. Explore the deep reaches of metaphor. But don't forget to be playful and have fun with words." E-mail up to

3 poetry submissions to poetry editor John Smelcer at: jesmelcer@aol.com.

**ALSO OFFERS** Sponsors The William Stafford Poetry Award and the X.J. Kennedy Award for Creative Nonfiction. Guidelines for both available on website.

**TIPS** "Each issue has 6 or 7 flexible departments (selected from a total of 16 departments that rotate). We are seeking stories; articles; profiles; and poems of love, alienation, travel, humor, nostalgia and unexpected revelation. Something has to 'happen' in the pieces we choose, but what happens inside characters is much more interesting to us than plot manipulation. We like good storytelling, real emotion, and authentic voice."

## SACRED CITY PRODUCTIONS

Sacred City Productions, Ltd., 5781 Springwood Ct., Mentor on the Lake OH 44060. (440)290-9325. **E-mail:** info@sacredcityproductions.com. **E-mail:** info@sacredcityproductions.com. **Website:** sacredcityproductions.com. **Contact:** Erin Garlock, editor/owner. Sacred City Productions is dedicated to creative endeavors that promote the ideals of a positive faith life. "We ask people to think about what they believe and to take action on those beliefs. Our own actions reflect our Christian beliefs as we reach out in ministry to extend an uplifting hand to those around us." Buys first print rights for 2 months. After that period, author is free to republish the story elsewhere. Please allow 2 weeks to review work. If you haven't heard back in that time, a single inquiry letter will suffice. Sacred City Productions guarantees a response of acceptance, rejection, or under consideration. Guidelines online.

**MAGAZINES NEEDS** Submit 1-5 sample poems. Sacred City Productions tends to favor poetry with a formal structure (rhyme, meter, etc.) or poetry whose artistic visual layout is relevant to the piece. Poetry will be sparingly used with fiction anthologies.

**TIPS** "We are very interested in submissions from first-time authors and authors with a very limited record."

## ST. ANTHONY MESSENGER

Franciscan Media, 28 W. Liberty St., Cincinnati OH 45202-6498. (513)241-5615. **Fax:** (513)241-0399. **E-mail:** magazineeditors@franciscanmedia.org. **Website:** www.stanthonymessenger.org. **Contact:** John Feister, editor-in-chief. *St. Anthony Messenger* is a Catholic family magazine which aims to help its readers lead more fully human and Christian lives. "We publish articles that report on a changing church and world, opinion pieces written from the perspective of Christian faith and values, personality profiles, and fiction which entertains and informs." Buys first North American serial rights, buys electronic rights, buys first worldwide serial rights. Pays on acceptance. Publishes ms within an average of 1 year after acceptance. Responds in 3 weeks to queries. Responds in 2 months to mss. Sample copy for 9x12 SAE with 4 first-class stamps. Please study writer's guidelines at StAnthonyMessenger.org.

**MAGAZINES NEEDS** Submit a few poems at a time. "Please include your phone number and a SASE with your submission. Do not send us your entire collection of poetry. Poems must be original." Submit seasonal poems several months in advance. "Our poetry needs are very limited." Length: up to 20-25 lines; "the shorter, the better." Pays $2/line; $20 minimum.

**TIPS** "The freelancer should consider why his or her proposed article would be appropriate for us, rather than for *Redbook* or *Saturday Review*. We treat human problems of all kinds, but from a religious perspective. Articles should reflect Catholic theology, spirituality, and employ a Catholic terminology and vocabulary. We need more articles on prayer, scripture, Catholic worship. Get authoritative information (not merely library research); we want interviews with experts. Write in popular style; use lots of examples, stories, and personal quotes. Word length is an important consideration."

### ● SALMAGUNDI

Skidmore College, 815 North Broadway, Saratoga Springs NY 12866. **Fax:** (518)580-5188. **E-mail:** salmagun@skidmore.edu. **E-mail:** Only accepting hard copy submissions with SASE from now on.. **Website:** cms.skidmore.edu/salmagundi. "*Salmagundi* publishes an eclectic variety of materials, ranging from short-short fiction to novellas from the surreal to the realistic. Authors include J.M Coerzee, Russell Banks, Steven Millhauser, Marilynne Robinson, Orlando Patterson, Gordon Lish, Anthony Appiah, Clark Blaise, Henri Cole, Mary Gordon, Frank Bidart, Lousie Gluck, Robert Pinsky, Joyce Carol Oates, Mary Gaiteskill, Amy Hempel and Cynthia Ozick. Our audience is a generally literate population of people who read for pleasure." Acquires first rights, electronic rights. Publishes ms up to 2 years after acceptance.

Responds in 2 months to mss. "If you do not hear back from us within 2 months, it means we did not find a space for your work in our magazine." Sample copy: $5. Guidelines on website.

**MAGAZINES NEEDS** Submit up to 6 poems in hard copy, via snail mail only with SASE. Pays 6-10 contributor copies and one-year subscription.

**TIPS** "I look for excellence and a very unpredictable ability to appeal to the interests and tastes of the editors. Be brave. Don't be discouraged by rejection. Keep stories in circulation. Of course, it goes without saying: Work hard on the writing. Revise tirelessly. Study other magazines as well as this one and send only to those whose sensibility matches yours."

### SALT HILL JOURNAL

Creative Writing Program, Syracuse University, English Deptartment, 401 Hall of Languages, Syracuse University, Syracuse NY 13244. **Website:** salthilljournal.net. **Contact:** Emma DeMilta and Jessica Poli, editors. "*Salt Hill* is published through Syracuse University's Creative Writing MFA program. We strive to publish a mix of the best contemporary and emerging talent in poetry, fiction, and nonfiction. Your work, if accepted, would appear in a long tradition of exceptional contributors, including Steve Almond, Mary Caponegro, Kim Chinquee, Edwidge Danticat, Denise Duhamel, Brian Evenson, B.H. Fairchild, Mary Gaitskill, Terrance Hayes, Bob Hicok, Laura Kasischke, Etgar Keret, Phil Lamarche, Dorianne Laux, Maurice Manning, Karyna McGlynn, Ander Monson, David Ohle, Lucia Perillo, Tomaž Šalamun, Zachary Schomburg, Christine Schutt, David Shields, Charles Simic, Patricia Smith, Dara Wier, and Raúl Zurita among many others." Guidelines online.

Only accepts submissions by online submission form; does not accept unsolicited e-mail submissions.

**MAGAZINES NEEDS** Submit up to 5 poems via online submissions manager; contact poetry editor via e-mail for retractions and queries only.

### THE SAME

P.O. Box 494, Mount Union PA 17066. **E-mail:** editors@thesamepress.com. **E-mail:** submissions@ thesamepress.com. **Website:** www.thesamepress.com. **Contact:** Nancy Eldredge, managing editor. *The Same*, published biannually, prints nonfiction (essays, reviews, literary criticism), poetry, and short fiction. Publishes ms 11 months after acceptance. Responds within 6 months. Single copy: $6; subscription: $12 for 2 issues, $20 for 4 issues.

○ *The Same* is 50-100 pages, desktop-published, and perfect-bound.

**MAGAZINES NEEDS** "We want eclectic poetry (formal to free verse, 'mainstream' to experimental, all subject matter.)" Submit 3-5 poems at a time. No previously published poems or simultaneous submissions without query. Prefers e-mail submissions as attachments. Cover letter is optional. Include SASE if you want a snail mail response. "If you don't want your manuscript returned, you may omit the SASE if we can respond by e-mail. Please query before submitting fiction and nonfiction. Submissions are read year round. Length: up to 120 lines/poem. Pays 1 contributor copy.

○ **SAMSARA: THE MAGAZINE OF SUFFERING**

P.O. Box 467, Ashburn VA 20147. **E-mail:** rdfsamsara@gmail.com. **Website:** www.samsaramagazine.net. **Contact:** R. David Fulcher, editor. *Samsara: The Magazine of Suffering*, published biannually, prints poetry and fiction dealing with suffering and healing. Acquires first rights. Publishes ms 3 months after acceptance. Responds in 2 months. Single copy: $5.50. Subscription: $10. Make checks payable to R. David Fulcher. Guidelines for SASE or on website.

○ *Samsara* is 80 pages, magazine-sized, desktop-published, with color cardstock cover. Receives about 200 poems/year, accepts about 15%. Press run is 300 (200 subscribers).

**MAGAZINES NEEDS** "Both metered-verse and free-verse poetry are welcome if dealing with the theme of suffering/healing." Has published poetry by Michael Foster, Nicole Provencher, and Jeff Parsley. Submit up to 5 poems at a time. Considers simultaneous submissions "if noted as such"; no previously published poems. Cover letter is preferred. Accepts e-mail submissions. Length: 3-100 lines/poem. Pays 1 contributor copy.

**THE SANDY RIVER REVIEW**

University of Maine at Farmington, 114 Prescott St., Farmington ME 04938. **E-mail:** srreview@gmail.com. **E-mail:** submissions@sandyriverreview.com. **Website:** sandyriverreview.com. **Contact:** Nicole Byrne, editor. "*The Sandy River Review* seeks prose, poetry, and art submissions twice a year for our Spring and Fall issues. Prose submissions may be either fiction

or creative nonfiction and should be a maximum of 3,500 words in length, 12-point, Times New Roman font, and double-spaced. Most of our art is published in b&w and must be submitted as 300-dpi quality, CMYK color mode, and saved as a TIFF file. We publish a wide variety of work from students as well as professional, established writers. Your submission should be polished and imaginative with strongly drawn characters and an interesting, original narrative. The review is the face of the University of Maine at Farmington's venerable BFA Creative Writing program, and we strive for the highest quality prose and poetry standard." Rights for the work return to the writer once published. Pays on publication. Publishes ms 2 months after acceptance. Guidelines online.

**MAGAZINES NEEDS** Submit via e-mail.

**TIPS** "We recommend that you take time with your piece. As with all submissions to a literary journal, submissions should be fully completed, polished final drafts that require minimal to no revision once accepted. Double-check your prose pieces for basic grammatical errors before submitting."

○ **SANSKRIT LITERARY ARTS MAGAZINE**

UNC Charlotte, 9201 University City Blvd., Student Union Room 045, Charlotte NC 28223. (704)687-7141. **E-mail:** editor@sanskritmagazine.com. **Website:** sanskrit.uncc.edu; www.facebook.com/SanskritLitArtMagazine. **Contact:** Joshua Wood, editor in chief. *Sanskrit* is a collection of poems, short stories, and art from people all around the world, including students. All of the work goes through a selection process that includes staff and university professors. Finally, each year, the magazine has a theme. This theme is completely independent from the work and is chosen by the editor as a design element to unify the magazine. The theme is kept secret until the return of the magazine in April. Responds to mss and poems by February. Never comments on rejected mss. Guidelines online.

○ Submissions deadline: first Friday in November.

**MAGAZINES NEEDS** Submit up to 15 poems at a time. Considers simultaneous submissions. Accepts e-mail submissions. Cover letter is required. Include 30- to 70-word third-person bio. Do not list previous publications as a bio. Pays 1 contributor copy.

## SANTA CLARA REVIEW

Santa Clara Review, Santa Clara University, 500 El Camino Real, Box 3212, Santa Clara CA 95053-3212. (408)554-4484. **E-mail:** santaclarareview@gmail.com. **Website:** www.santaclarareview.com. "*SCR* is one of the oldest literary publications in the West. Entirely student-run by undergraduates at Santa Clara University, the magazine draws upon submissions from SCU affiliates as well as contributors from around the globe. The magazine is published in February and May each year. In addition to publishing the magazine, the Review staff organizes a writing practicum, open mic nights, and retreats for writers and artists, and hosts guest readers. Our printed magazine is also available to view free online. For contacts, queries, and general info, visit our website. *SCR* accepts submissions year round. Publishes ms an average of 2 months after acceptance. Guidelines online.

**MAGAZINES NEEDS** Submit up to 3 poems via online submissions manager or mail (include SASE for return of ms). Length: up to 10 pages.

## THE SARANAC REVIEW

Dept. of English, Champlain Valley Hall, 101 Broad St., Plattsburgh NY 12901. (518)564-2241. **Fax:** (518)564-2140. **E-mail:** saranacreview@plattsburgh.edu. **Website:** www.saranacreview.com. **Contact:** J.L. Torres, executive editor. "*The Saranac Review* is committed to dissolving boundaries of all kinds, seeking to publish a diverse array of emerging and established writers from Canada and the U.S. *The Saranac Review* aims to be a textual clearing in which a space is opened for cross-pollination between American and Canadian writers. In this way the magazine reflects the expansive, bright spirit of the etymology of its name, Saranac, meaning 'cluster of stars.'" Published annually. Purchases first North American serial rights. Pays on publication. Publishes ms 8 months to 1 year after acceptance. Responds in 4-6 months to mss. Sample copy: $4.95. Guidelines online.

"*The Saranac Review* is digest-sized, with color photo or painting on cover. Publishes both digital and print-on-demand versions. Has published Lawrence Raab, Jacob M. Appel, Marilyn Nelson, Tom Wayman, Colette Inez, Louise Warren, Brian Campbell, Gregory Pardlo, Myfanwy Collins, William Giraldi, Xu Xi, Julia Alvarez, and other fine emerging and established writers.

**MAGAZINES NEEDS** "We're open to most forms and styles. We want poetry that, to paragraph Dickinson, blows the top of your head off, and that, in Williams's view, prevents us from dying miserably every day." Submit 3-5 poems via online submissions manager. Length: up to 4 pages but typically 20-25 lines. Pays 1 contributor copy and offers discount on additional copies.

## SCIFAIKUEST

P.O. Box 782, Cedar Rapids IA 52406. **E-mail:** gatrix65@yahoo.com. **Website:** albanlake.com/scifaikuest. **Contact:** Tyree Campbell, managing editor; Teri Santitoro, editor. *Scifaikuest*, published quarterly both online and in print, features "science fiction/fantasy/horror minimalist poetry, especially scifaiku, and related forms. We also publish articles about various poetic forms and reviews of poetry collections. The online and print versions of *Scifaikuest* are different." Acquires first North American serial rights. Time between acceptance and publication is 1-2 months. Responds in 6-8 weeks. Single copy: $7; subscription: $20/year, $37 for 2 years. Make checks payable to Tyree Campbell/Alban Lake Publishing. Guidelines available on website.

*Scifaikuest* (print edition) is 32 pages, digest-sized, offset-printed, perfect-bound, with color cardstock cover, includes ads. Receives about 500 poems/year, accepts about 160 (32%). Press run is 100/issue; 5 distributed free to reviewers. Member: The Speculative Literature Foundation. *Scifaikuest* was voted #1 poetry magazine in the 2004 Preditors & Editors poll.

**MAGAZINES NEEDS** Wants "artwork, scifaiku, and speculative minimalist forms such as tanka, haibun, ghazals, senryu. Submit 10 poems at a time. Accepts e-mail submissions (pasted into body of message). No disk submissions; artwork as e-mail attachment or inserted body of e-mail. "Submission should include snail-mail address and a short (1-2 lines) bio." Reads submissions year round. "Editor Teri Santitoro makes all decisions regarding acceptances." Often comments on rejected poems. Has published poetry by Tom Brinck, Oino Sakai, Deborah P. Kolodji, Aurelio Rico Lopez III, Joanne Morcom, and John Dunphy. "No 'traditional' poetry." Length: varies, depending on poem type. Pays $1/poem, $6/review or article, and 1 contributor copy.

## SCREAMINMAMAS

Harmoni Productions, LLC, 1911 Cleveland St., Hollywood FL 33020. **E-mail:** screaminmamas@gmail.com. **Website:** www.screaminmamas.com. **Contact:** Darlene Pistocchi, editor; Lena, submissions coordinator. "We are the voice of everyday moms. We share their stories, revelations, humorous rants, photos, talent, children, ventures, etc." Acquires one-time rights. Publishes ms 1-3 months after acceptance. Responds in 3-6 weeks to queries; 1-3 months on mss. Editorial lead time: 3 months. Available for purchase by request. Sample submissions online. Guidelines online.

**MAGAZINES NEEDS** Length: 2-20 lines.

**TIPS** "Visit our submissions page and themes page on our website."

## THE SEATTLE REVIEW

Box 354330, University of Washington, Seattle WA 98195. (206)543-2302. **E-mail:** seaview@uw.edu. **Website:** www.seattlereview.org. **Contact:** Andrew Feld, editor in chief. *The Seattle Review* includes poetry, fiction, and creative nonfiction. Buys first North American serial rights. Pays on publication. Responds in 2-4 months to mss. Subscriptions: $20 for 3 issues, $32 for 5 issues. Back issue: $6. Guidelines online.

**MAGAZINES NEEDS** "We are looking for exceptional, risk-taking, intellectual, and imaginative poems between 10 and 30 pages in length." *The Seattle Review* will publish, and will only publish, long poems and novellas. The long poem can be a single long poem in its entirety, a self-contained excerpt from a book-length poem, or a unified sequence or series of poems. Accepts electronic submissions only. Pays 2 contributor copies and 1-year subscription.

**TIPS** "Know what we publish; no genre fiction. Look at our magazine and decide if your work might be appreciated. Beginners do well in our magazine if they send clean, well-written manuscripts. We've published a lot of 'first stories' from all over the country and take pleasure in discovery."

## THE SECRET PLACE

P.O. Box 851, Valley Forge PA 19482. (610)768-2434. **Fax:** (610)768-2441. **E-mail:** thesecretplace@abc-usa.org. **Website:** www.judsonpress.com/catalog_secretplace.cfm. Buys first rights. Pays on acceptance. Editorial lead time 1 year. Guidelines online.

**MAGAZINES NEEDS** Submit up to 6 poems by mail or e-mail. E-mail preferred. Length: 4-30 lines/poem. Pays $20.

**TIPS** "Prefers submissions via e-mail."

## SEEMS

P.O. Box 359, Lakeland College, Sheboygan WI 53082-0359. (920)565-1000 ext. 2295 or (920)565-3871. **E-mail:** elderk@lakeland.edu. **Website:** www.seems.lakeland.edu. *SEEMS*, published irregularly, prints poetry, fiction, and essays. Focuses on work that integrates economy of language, "the musical phrase," forms of resemblance, and the sentient. Will consider unpublished poetry, fiction, and creative nonfiction. See the editor's website at www.karlelder.com. "Links to my work and an interview may provide insight for the potential contributor." Acquires first North American serial rights and permission to publish online. Returns rights upon publication. Responds in 4 months (slower in the summer). Guidelines online.

**MAGAZINES NEEDS** Submit via mail only. Cover letter is optional. Include biographical information, SASE. Reads submissions year round. There is a one- to two-year backlog. "People may call or fax with virtually any question, understanding that the editor may have no answer." Guidelines available on website. Length: open. Pays 1 contributor copy.

## SENECA REVIEW

Hobart and William Smith Colleges, Geneva NY 14456. (315)781-3392. **Fax:** (315)781-3348. **E-mail:** senecareview@hws.edu. **Website:** www.hws.edu/academics/senecareview/index.aspx. The editors have special interest in translations of contemporary poetry from around the world. Publisher of numerous laureates and award-winning poets, *Seneca Review* also publishes emerging writers and is always open to new, innovative work. Poems from *SR* are regularly honored by inclusion in *The Best American Poetry* and *Pushcart Prize* anthologies. Distributed internationally. Accepts queries by mail or via Submittable. Responds in 3 months. Guidelines online. E-mail questions to senecareview@hws.edu.

Reading period is September 1-May 1.

## SEQUESTRUM

**E-mail:** sequr.info@gmail.com. **Website:** www.sequestrum.org. **Contact:** R.M. Cooper, managing editor. All publications are paired with a unique visual component. Regularly holds contests and features well-known authors, as well as promising new and emerging voices. Buys first North American serial rights and electronic rights. Pays on acceptance. Publishes ms 2-6 months after acceptance. Editorial lead time: 3 months. Sample copy available for free online. Guidelines available for free online.

**MAGAZINES NEEDS** Length: 35 lines max. Pays $10/set of poems.

**TIPS** "Reading a past issue goes a long way; there's little excuse not to: Our entire archive is online to preview and subscription rates are variable. Send your best, most interesting work. General submissions are open, and we regularly hold contests and offer awards which are themed."

### THE SEWANEE REVIEW

University of the South, 735 University Ave., Sewanee TN 37383-1000. (931)598-1000. **E-mail:** sreview@sewanee.edu. **Website:** review.sewanee.edu. **Contact:** George Core, editor. *The Sewanee Review* is America's oldest continuously published literary quarterly. Publishes original fiction, poetry, essays on literary and related subjects, and book reviews for well-educated readers who appreciate good American and English literature. Only erudite work representing depth of knowledge and skill of expression is published. Buys first North American serial rights, buys second serial (reprint) rights. Pays on publication. Responds in 6-8 weeks to mss. Sample copy: $8.50 ($9.50 outside U.S.). Guidelines online. Submit complete ms by mail; no electronic submissions. Queries accepted but not preferred. Rarely accepts unsolicited reviews.

○ Does not read mss June 1-August 31.

**MAGAZINES NEEDS** Submit up to 6 poems by postal mail. Keep in mind that for each poem published in *The Sewanee Review*, approximately 250 poems are considered. Length: up to 40 lines/poem. Pays $2.50/line, plus 2 contributor copies (and reduced price for additional copies).

### SHEARSMAN

Shearsman Books Ltd, 50 Westons Hill Drive, Emersons Green, Bristol BS16 7DF, England. 117-9572957. **E-mail:** editor@shearsman.com. **Website:** www.shearsman.com/pages/magazine/home.html. **Contact:** Tony Frazer. "We are inclined toward the more exploratory end of the current spectrum. Notwithstanding this, however, quality work of a more conservative kind will always be considered seriously, provided that the work is well written. I always look for some rigour in the work, though I will be more forgiving of failure in this regard if the writer is trying to push out the boundaries." Publishes ms an average

of 3 months after acceptance. Responds in 3 months. Guidelines online.

**MAGAZINES NEEDS** Avoid sending attachments with your e-mails unless they are in PDF format. Include SASE; no IRCs. If submitting from outside the UK, try to permit replies by e-mail. No poetry for children. No religious or devotional poetry. No limit. Pays 2 contributor copies.

**TIPS** "We no longer read through the year. Our reading window for magazines is March 1 through March 31 for the October issue and September 1 through September 30 for the April issue; this window is for magazine submissions only. See guidelines online."

### ○ SHEMOM

2486 Montgomery Ave., Cardiff CA 92007. **E-mail:** pdfrench@cox.net. **Contact:** Peggy French, editor. *Shemom*, published 3 times/year, is a zine that "showcases writers of all ages reflecting on life's varied experiences. We often feature haiku." Includes poetry, haiku, and occasional essays. Open to any style, but prefers free verse. "We like to hear from anyone who has a story to tell and will read anything you care to send our way." Acquires one-time rights. Publishes ms 3 months after acceptance. Responds in 1 month. Single copy: $4; subscription: $12/3 issues. Make checks payable to Peggy French. Guidelines for SASE.

○ *Shemom* is 20-30 pages. Receives about 200 poems/year, accepts 50%. Press run is 60 (30 subscribers).

**MAGAZINES NEEDS** Submit 3-10 poems at a time. Accepts e-mail submissions (as attachment or pasted into body of message). "Prefer e-mail submission, but not required; if material is to be returned, please include an SASE." Pays 1 contributor copy.

### SHENANDOAH

Washington and Lee University, Lexington VA 24450. (540)458-8908. **Fax:** (540)458-8461. **E-mail:** shenandoah@wlu.edu. **Website:** shenandoahliterary.org. Assistant Editor: William Wright. **Contact:** R.T. Smith, editor. For over half a century, *Shenandoah* has been publishing splendid poems, stories, essays, and reviews which display passionate understanding, formal accomplishment, and serious mischief. Buys first North American serial rights, one-time rights. Pays on publication. Publishes ms an average of 10 months after acceptance. Responds in 4-6 weeks to mss. Sample copy: $12. Guidelines online.

**MAGAZINES NEEDS** Submit 3-5 poems via online submissions manager or postal mail. No inspirational, confessional poetry. Pays $2.50/line, one-year subscription, and 1 contributor copy.

**ALSO OFFERS** Sponsors the annual James Boatwright III Prize for Poetry, a $1,000 prize awarded to the author of the best poem published in *Shenandoah* during a volume year.

## SIERRA NEVADA REVIEW

999 Tahoe Blvd., Incline Village NV 89451. **E-mail:** sncreview@sierranevada.edu. **Website:** blog.sierranevada.edu/sierranevadareview/. "*Sierra Nevada Review*, published annually in May, features poetry, short fiction, and literary nonfiction by new and established writers. Wants "writing that leans toward the unconventional, surprising, and risky." Responds in 3 months. Guidelines available on website.

O Reads submissions September 1-February 15 only.

**MAGAZINES NEEDS** Submit up to 5 poems at a time or 5 pages, whichever comes first. Pays 2 contributor copies.

## O SKIPPING STONES: A MULTICULTURAL LITERARY MAGAZINE

P.O. Box 3939, Eugene OR 97403-0939. (541)342-4956. **E-mail:** editor@skippingstones.org. **Website:** www.skippingstones.org. **Contact:** Arun Toké, editor. "*Skipping Stones* is an award-winning multicultural, nonprofit magazine designed to promote cooperation, creativity and celebration of cultural and ecological richness. We encourage submissions by children of color, minorities and under-represented populations. We want material meant for children and young adults/teenagers with multicultural or ecological awareness themes. Think, live and write as if you were a child, tween or teen. We want material that gives insight to cultural celebrations, lifestyle, customs and traditions, glimpse of daily life in other countries and cultures. Photos, songs, artwork are most welcome if they illustrate/highlight the points. Translations are invited if your submission is in a language other than English." Themes may include cultural celebrations, living abroad, challenging disability, hospitality customs of various cultures, cross-cultural understanding, African, Asian and Latin American cultures, humor, international understanding, turning points and magical moments in life, caring for the earth, spirituality, and multicultural awareness. *Skipping Stones* is

magazine-sized, saddle-stapled, printed on recycled paper. Published quarterly during the school year (4 issues). Buys first North American serial rights, non-exclusive reprint, and electronic rights. sends comp. contributor copies upon publication Publishes ms an average of 4-8 months after acceptance. Responds only if interested. Send nonreturnable samples. Editorial lead time 3-4 months. Sample: $7. Subscription. $25. Guidelines online or for SASE.

**MAGAZINES NEEDS** Submit up to 5 poems at a time. Considers simultaneous submissions; no previously published poems. Accepts e-mail submissions. Cover letter is preferred. "Include your cultural background, experiences, and the inspiration behind your creation." Time between acceptance and publication is 6-9 months. "A piece is chosen for publication when most of the editorial staff feel good about it." Seldom comments on rejected poems. Publishes multi-theme issues. Responds in up to 4 months. Length: 30 lines maximum. Pays 2 contributor copies, offers 40% discount for more copies and subscription, if desired.

**CONTEST/AWARD OFFERINGS** Sponsors annual youth honor awards for 7- to 17-year-olds. Theme is "multicultural, social, international, and nature awareness." Guidelines available for SASE or on website. Entry fee: $5 (entitles entrant to a free issue featuring the 10 winners). Deadline: June 25.

**TIPS** "Be original and innovative. Use multicultural, nature, or cross-cultural themes. Multilingual submissions are welcome."

## SLANT: A JOURNAL OF POETRY

University of Central Arkansas, P.O. Box 5063, Conway AR 72035-5000. (501)450-5107. **E-mail:** jamesf@uca.edu. **Website:** uca.edu/english/slant-a-journal-of-poetry. **Contact:** James Fowler, editor. *Slant: A Journal of Poetry*, published annually in May, aims "to publish a journal of fine poetry from all regions of the U.S. and beyond." Rights revert to poet after publication. On average, 6 months. Responds in 3 months from November 15 deadline. Sample: $10. Guidelines available in magazine, for SASE, or on website.

O *Slant* is 112 pages, professionally printed on quality linen stock, flat-spined, with matte card cover. Receives about 925 poems/year, accepts 70-75. Press run is 170 (65-70 subscribers). Accepts submissions September 1-November 15.

**MAGAZINES NEEDS** Wants "traditional and 'modern' poetry, even experimental; moderate length, any subject on approval of Board of Readers." Doesn't want "haiku, translations." Submit up to 5 poems at a time. Submissions should be typed; include SASE. "Put name, address (including e-mail if available), and phone number at the top of each page." Comments on rejected poems "on occasion." Has published poetry by Richard Broderick, Linda Casebeer, Marc Jampole, Sandra Kohler, Charles Harper Webb, and Ellen Roberts Young. Poems should be of moderate length. Pays 1 contributor copy.

## SLIPSTREAM

P.O. Box 2071, Dept. W-1, Niagara Falls NY 14301. **E-mail:** editors@slipstreampress.org. **Website:** www.slipstreampress.org/index.html. **Contact:** Dan Sicoli, co-editor. Guidelines online.

◐ Does not accept e-mail submissions.

**MAGAZINES NEEDS** Submit poetry via mail or online submission manager, Submittable. Prefers contemporary urban themes—writing from the grit that is not afraid to bark or bite. Shies away from pastoral, religious, and rhyming verse. Chapbook Contest prize is $1,000 plus 50 professionally printed copies of your chapbook.

## SLOW TRAINS LITERARY JOURNAL

**E-mail:** editor@slowtrains.com. **Website:** www.slowtrains.com. **Contact:** Susannah Grace Indigo, editor. Looking for fiction, essays, and poetry that reflect the spirit of adventure, the exploration of the soul, the energies of imagination, and the experience of Big Fun. Music, travel, sex, humor, love, loss, art, spirituality, childhood/coming of age, baseball, and dreams, but most of all, *Slow Trains* wants to read about the things you are passionate about. Requests one-time electronic rights with optional archiving. Responds in 2 months. Guidelines online.

**MAGAZINES NEEDS** Also publishes online poetry chapbooks. Query with samples of poetry before submitting an entire chapbook. Review current issue before submitting. Submit via e-mail only. Length: up to 200 lines/poem.

## SNREVIEW

197 Fairchild Ave., Fairfield CT 06825-4856. (203)366-5991. **E-mail:** editor@snreview.org. **Website:** www.snreview.org. **Contact:** Joseph Conlin, editor. "We search for material that not only has strong characters and plot but also a devotion to imagery." Quarterly. Acquires first electronic and print rights. Publishes ms 3 months after acceptance. Responds in 1 year to mss. Sample copy and guidelines online.

◐ Also publishes literary essays, poetry. Print and Kindle edition is now available from an on-demand printer.

**MAGAZINES NEEDS** Submit via e-mail; label the e-mail "SUB: Poetry." Copy and paste work into the body of the e-mail. Don't send attachments. Include 100-word bio and list of publications. Length: up to 200 words/poem.

## THE SOCIETY OF CLASSICAL POETS JOURNAL

The Society of Classical Poets, 11 Heather Lane, Mount Hope NY 10940. **E-mail:** submissions@classicalpoets.org. **Website:** www.classicalpoets.org. **Contact:** Evan Mantyk, president. Annual literary magazine, published in a book format, that features poetry, essays, and artwork. Interested in poetry with rhyme and meter (or syllable counting). Believes in reviving classical poetry and classical arts. Purchases electronic and reprint rights. Publishes ms an average of 6 months after acceptance. Responds in 1 weeks to queries and 1 month to mss. Editorial lead time is 2 months. Guidelines available for SASE.

**MAGAZINES NEEDS** Some type of meter, such as iambic pentameter, (or syllable counting) is preferred but not absolutely required. If you want feedback on your submission, indicate it on the submission. Accepts poetry only on 5 themes (generally): beauty (in human nature, culture, the natural world, classical art forms, and the divine), great culture (good figures, stories, and other elements from classical history and literature), persecution of Falun Dafa practitioners in China (and plight of Chinese people under communism in general), and humor (clean humor only, includes riddles), and translations. Also will consider short stories, essays, art, news, and videos on the above themes. Does not want love poetry, free verse, or any dark poetry. Does not offer payment.

## SONG OF THE SAN JOAQUIN

P.O. Box 1161, Modesto CA 95353. **E-mail:** song.poet@sbcglobal.net. **E-mail:** song.poet@sbcglobal.net. **Contact:** Jim Shuman, editor. *Song of the San Joaquin*, published quarterly, features "subjects about or pertinent to the San Joaquin Valley of Central California. This is defined geographically as the region from Fresno to Stockton, and from the foothills on the west to those on the east." Acquires one-time rights. Publishes ms 3-6 months after acceptance. Responds in up to 3 months. Guidelines available for SASE or by e-mail.

〇 Reads submissions "periodically throughout the year." Considers poetry by children and teens.

**MAGAZINES NEEDS** This is a quarterly; please keep in mind the seasons of the year. E-mail submissions are preferred; no disk submissions. Cover letter is preferred. "SASE required. All submissions must be typed on 1 side of the page only. Proofread submissions carefully. Name, address, phone number, and e-mail address should appear on all pages. Cover letter should include any awards, honors, and previous publications for each poem and a biographical sketch of 75 words or less." Has published poetry by Robert Cooperman, Taylor Graham, Dan Williams, Jennifer Fenn, and Charles Rammelkamp. Length: up to 40 lines. Pays 1 contributor copy.

## SONORA REVIEW

University of Arizona's Creative Writing MFA Program, University of Arizona, Dept. of English, Tucson AZ 85721. **E-mail:** sonorareview2@gmail.com. **Website:** sonorareview.com/. We look for the highest quality poetry, fiction, and nonfiction, with an emphasis on emerging writers. Our magazine has a long-standing tradition of publishing the best new literature and writers. Check out our website for a sample of what we publish and our submission guidelines. Buys first North American serial rights, buys one-time rights, buys electronic rights. Publishes ms an average of 3-4 months after acceptance. Responds in 2-5 weeks to queries. Responds in 3 months to mss. Sample copy: $6. Guidelines online.

**MAGAZINES NEEDS** All poetry welcome.

**TIPS** "We have no length requirements, but we usually do not consider poems, stories, or essays that are over 20 pages in length because of space. We publish mostly poems, short stories, and literary nonfiction. We do not read during June or July."

## SO TO SPEAK

George Mason University, 4400 University Dr., MSN 2C5, Fairfax VA 22030-4444. **E-mail:** sotospeak@so-tospeakjournal.org. **Website:** sotospeakjournal.org. *So to Speak*, published semiannually, prints "high-quality work relating to feminism, including poetry, fiction, nonfiction (including book reviews and interviews), photography, artwork, collaborations, lyrical essays, and other genre-questioning texts." Wants "work that addresses issues of significance to women's lives and movements for women's equality. Especially interested in pieces that explore issues of race, class, and sexuality in relation to gender." Reads submissions August 20-October 25 for Spring issue and January 1-March 15 for Fall issue. Acquires first North American serial rights. Publishes ms 6-8 months after acceptance. Responds in 6 months to mss. Sample copy: $7; subscription: $12.

〇 *So to Speak* is 100-128 pages, digest-sized, photo-offset-printed, perfect-bound, with glossy cover; includes ads. Press run is 1,000 (75 subscribers, 100 shelf sales); 500 distributed free to students/contributors.

**MAGAZINES NEEDS** Receives about 800 poems/year; accepts 10%. Accepts submissions only via submissions manager on website. No e-mail or paper submissions. "Please submit poems as you wish to see them in print. Be sure to include a cover letter with full contact info, publication credits, and awards received." Poetry submitted during the August 20-October 25 reading period will be considered for our Spring annual poetry contest and must be accompanied by a $15 reading fee. Pays 2 contributor copies.

**TIPS** "Every writer has something they do exceptionally well; do that and it will shine through in the work. We look for quality prose with a definite appeal to a feminist audience. We are trying to move away from strict genre lines. We want high-quality fiction, nonfiction, poetry, art, innovative and risk-taking work."

## SOUL FOUNTAIN

**Website:** www.antarcticajournal.com. **Contact:** Tone Bellizzi, editor. *Soul Fountain* is produced by The Antarctica Journal, a not-for-profit arts project of the Hope for the Children Foundation, committed to empowering young and emerging artists of all disciplines at all levels to develop and share their talents through performance, collaboration, and networking. Digitally publishes poetry, art, photography, short fiction, and essays on the antarcticajournal.com website. Open to all. Publishes quality submitted work, and specializes in emerging voices. Favors visionary, challenging, and consciousness-expanding material. Guidelines online.

**MAGAZINES NEEDS** Submit 2-3 poems by e-mail. No cover letters, please. Does not want poems about pets, nature, romantic love, or the occult. Sex and violence themes not welcome. Welcomes poetry by teens.

## SOUTH DAKOTA REVIEW

The University of South Dakota, Dept. of English, 414 E. Clark St., Vermillion SD 57069. (605)677-5184. E-mail: sdreview@usd.edu. **Website:** www.usd.edu/sdreview. **Contact:** Lee Ann Roripaugh, editor in chief. "*South Dakota Review,* published quarterly, is committed to cultural and aesthetic diversity. First and foremost, we seek to publish exciting and compelling work that reflects the full spectrum of the contemporary literary arts. Since its inception in 1963, *South Dakota Review* has maintained a tradition of supporting work by contemporary writers writing from or about the American West. We hope to retain this unique flavor through particularly welcoming works by American Indian writers, writers addressing the complexities and contradictions of the 'New West,' and writers exploring themes of landscape, place, and/or eco-criticism in surprising and innovative ways. At the same time, we'd like to set these ideas and themes in dialogue with and within the context of larger global literary communities. Single copy: $12; subscription: $40/year, $65/2 years. Sample: $8. Acquires first, second serial (reprint) rights. Publishes ms 1-6 months after acceptance. Responds in 10-12 weeks. Sample copy: $8.

⊘    Writing from *South Dakota Review* has appeared in *Pushcart* and *Best American Essays* anthologies. Press run is 500-600 (more than 500 subscribers, many of them libraries).

**MAGAZINES NEEDS** Submit up to 5 poems via online submissions manager. Include cover letter. *SDR* contributors include Norman Dubie, Tarfia Faizullah, Carol Guess and Daniela Olszewska, Megan Kaminski, Ted Kooser, Adrian C. Louis, Joseph Massey, Tiffany Midge, Ira Sukrungruang, Ocean Vuong, and Martha Zweig. Pays 2 contributor copies.

## THE SOUTHEAST REVIEW

Department of English, Florida State University, Tallahassee FL 32306. **Website:** southeastreview.org. **Contact:** Erin Hoover, editor. "The mission of *The Southeast Review* is to present emerging writers on the same stage as well-established ones. In each semiannual issue, we publish literary fiction, creative nonfiction, poetry, interviews, book reviews, and art.

With nearly 60 members on our editorial staff who come from throughout the country and the world, we strive to publish work that is representative of our diverse interests and aesthetics, and we celebrate the eclectic mix this produces. We receive approximately 400 submissions per month, and we accept less than 1-2% of them." Acquires first North America serial rights, which then revert to the author. Publishes ms 2-6 months after acceptance. Responds in 2-6 months.

⊘    Publishes 4-6 new (not previously published) writers/year. Has published work by A. A. Balaskovits, Hannah Gamble, Michael Homolka, Brandon Lingle, and Colleen Morrissey.

**MAGAZINES NEEDS** Submit 3-5 poems at a time through online manager. Reviews books and chapbooks of poetry. Please query the book review editor before submitting a book review. Pays 2 contributor copies.

**ALSO OFFERS** Sponsors an annual poetry, nonfiction, and short fiction contest. Winner receives $500 and publication; 2-5 finalists will also be published in each category. **Entry fee:** $16 for 3 poems, 3 short stories, or 1 piece of narrative nonfiction. **Deadline:** March. Guidelines available on website.

**TIPS** "*The Southeast Review* accepts regular submissions for publication consideration year-round exclusively through the online submission manager. **Except in the case of contests, paper submissions sent through regular postal mail will not be read or returned**. Avoid trendy experimentation for its own sake (present-tense narration, observation that isn't also revelation). Fresh stories; moving, interesting characters; and a sensitivity to language are still fiction mainstays. We also publish the winner and runners-up of the World's Best Short Story Contest, Poetry Contest, and Creative Nonfiction Contest."

## SOUTHERN HUMANITIES REVIEW

Auburn University, 9088 Haley Center, Auburn University AL 36849. (334)844-9088. **Fax:** (334)844-9027. **E-mail:** shr@auburn.edu. **Website:** www.southernhumanitiesreview.com. **Contact:** Aaron Alford, managing editor. *Southern Humanities Review* publishes fiction, nonfiction, and poetry. Acquires first American serial rights. Copyright reverts to author after publication. Sample copy: $5 U.S., $8 international. Guidelines online.

**ALSO OFFERS** Sponsors the Theodore Christian Hoepfner Award, a $50 prize for the best poem published in a given volume of *Southern Humanities Review*.

## SOUTHERN POETRY REVIEW

Dept. of LLP, Armstrong State University, 11935 Abercorn St., Savannah GA 31419. (912) 344-3196. **E-mail:** james.smith@armstrong.edu. **Website:** www.southernpoetryreview.org. **Contact:** James Smith, Editor. *Southern Poetry Review*, published twice a year, is one of the oldest poetry journals in America. Acquires one-time rights. Publishes ms 6 months after acceptance. Responds within 3 months. Single copy: $8.00. Guidelines available in journal, by SASE, by e-mail, or on website.

○ Work appearing in *Southern Poetry Review* received 2005 and 2013 Pushcart Prizes. Often has poems selected for Poetry Daily (poems.com) and VerseDaily.org. Member: CLMP. *Southern Poetry Review* is 65-75 pages, digest-sized, perfect-bound, with 80 lb. matte card stock cover and b&w photography. Includes ads.

**MAGAZINES NEEDS** Wants "poetry eclectically representative of the genre; no restrictions on form, style, or content." Has published poetry by Claudia Emerson, Carl Dennis, Robert Morgan, Linda Pastan, A.E. Stallings, R.T. Smith, and David Wagoner. Considers simultaneous submissions (with notification in cover letter); no previously published poems ("previously published" includes poems published or posted online). No e-mail submissions. Cover letter is preferred. "Include SASE for reply; ms returned only if sufficient postage is included. No international mail coupons. U.S. stamps only." Reads submissions year round. Sometimes comments on rejected poems. Sends pre-publication galleys. Also accepts online submissions at website. Does not want fiction, essays, reviews, or interviews. Pays 1-2 contributor copies.

**CONTEST/AWARD OFFERINGS** Sponsors annual Guy Owen Contest. See website for guidelines. Deadline May 15.

## THE SOUTHERN REVIEW

338 Johnston Hall, Louisiana State University, Baton Rouge LA 70803. (225)578-5104. **Fax:** (225)578-6461. **E-mail:** southernreview@lsu.edu. **Website:** thesouthernreview.org. **Contact:** Jessica Faust, co-editor and poetry editor; Emily Nemens, co-editor and prose editor. "*The Southern Review* is one of the nation's premiere literary journals. Hailed by *Time* as 'superior to any other journal in the English language,' we have made literary history since our founding in 1935. We publish a diverse array of fiction, nonfiction, and poetry by the country's—and the world's—most respected contemporary writers." Reading period: September 1 through December 1 (prose); September 1 through February 1 (poetry). All mss submitted during outside the reading period will be recycled. Buys first worldwide English-language serial rights. Pays on publication. Publishes ms an average of 6 months after acceptance. Responds in 6 months. Sample copy: $12. Guidelines online at thesouthernreview.org/submissions.

**MAGAZINES NEEDS** Has published poetry by Aimee Baker, Wendy Barker, David Bottoms, Nick Courtright, Robert Dana, Oliver de la Paz, Ed Falco, Piotr Florczyk, Rigoberto Gonzalez, Ava Leavell Haymon, and Philip Schultz. Submit poems by mail. Pays $25/printed page (max $200); 2 contributor copies, and 1-year subscription.

**TIPS** "Careful attention to craftsmanship and technique combined with a developed sense of the creation of story will always make us pay attention."

## ● SOUTH POETRY MAGAZINE

P.O. Box 4228, Bracknell RG42 9PX, United Kingdom. **E-mail:** south@southpoetry.org. **Website:** www.southpoetry.org. *SOUTH Poetry Magazine*, published biannually in Spring and Autumn, is based in the southern counties of England. Poets from or poems about the South region are particularly welcome, but poets from all over the world are encouraged to submit work on all subjects. Has published poetry by Ian Caws, Stella Davis, Lyn Moir, Elsa Corbluth, Paul Hyland, and Sean Street. Publishes ms 2 months after acceptance. Guidelines online.

○ *SOUTH* is 68 pages, digest-sized, litho-printed, saddle-stapled, with gloss-laminated duotone cover. Receives about 1,500 poems/year, accepts about 120. Press run is 350 (250 subscribers). Single copy: £5.80; subscription: £10/year, £18/2 years. Make cheques (in sterling) payable to *SOUTH Poetry Magazine*.

**MAGAZINES NEEDS** Send two copies of each poem submitted. Print submission form on website and submit via postal mail. Selection does not begin prior to the deadline and may take up to 8 weeks or more from that date. Deadlines are May 31 for the autumn issue and November 30 for the spring issue.

**TIPS** "Buy the magazine and read it. That way you will see the sort of work we publish, and whether your work is likely to fit in. You'll also be contributing to its continued success."

## SOUTHWESTERN AMERICAN LITERATURE

Center for the Study of the Southwest, Texas State University, Brazos Hall, 601 University Dr., San Marcos TX 78666-4616. (512)245-2224. **Fax:** (512)245-7462. **E-mail:** wj13@txstate.edu. **E-mail:** swpublications@txstate.edu. **Website:** www.txstate.edu/cssw/publications/sal.html. **Contact:** William Jensen, editor. *Southwestern American Literature* is a biannual scholarly journal that includes literary criticism, fiction, poetry, and book & film reviews concerning the Greater Southwest. Responds in 3-6 months. "Please feel free to e-mail the editors after 6 months to check on the status of your work." Sample copy: $11. Guidelines online.

**MAGAZINES NEEDS** Generally speaking, we seek material covering the Greater Southwest. Length: no more than 100 lines. Pays 2 contributor copies.

**TIPS Fiction and poetry must deal with the greater Southwest.** We look for crisp language, an interesting approach to material. Read widely, write often, revise carefully. We seek stories that, as William Faulkner noted in his Nobel Prize acceptance speech, treat subjects central to good literature—the old verities of the human heart, such as honor and courage and pity and suffering, fear and humor, love and sorrow.

## SOUTHWEST REVIEW

P.O. Box 750374, Dallas TX 75275-0374. (214)768-1037. **Fax:** (214)768-1408. **E-mail:** swr@smu.edu. **Website:** www.smu.edu/southwestreview. **Contact:** Willard Spiegelman, editor-in-chief. The majority of readers are well-read adults who wish to stay abreast of the latest and best in contemporary fiction, poetry, and essays in all but the most specialized disciplines. Published quarterly. Acquires first North American serial rights. Sends galleys to author. Publishes ms 6-12 months after acceptance. Responds in 1-4 months to mss. Occasionally comments on rejected mss. Sample copy: $6. Guidelines available for SASE or online.

Has published work by Alice Hoffman, Sabina Murray, Alix Ohlin. The Elizabeth Matchett Stover Memorial Award presents $250 to the author of the best poem or groups of poems (chosen by editors) published in the preceding year. Also offers The Morton Marr Poetry Prize and the David Nathan Meyerson Prize for Fiction.

**MAGAZINES NEEDS** Demands very high quality in poems. Accepts both traditional and experimental writing. Submissions accepted online for a $2 fee. No fee for submissions sent by mail. Reading period: September 1-May 31. No arbitrary limits on length. Accepted pieces receive nominal payment upon publication and copies of the issue.

**TIPS** "Despite the title, we are not a regional magazine. Before you submit your work, it's a good idea to take a look at recent issues to familiarize yourself with the magazine. We strongly advise all writers to include a cover letter. Keep your cover letter professional and concise, and don't include extraneous personal information, a story synopsis, or a résumé. When authors ask what we look for in a strong story submission, the answer is simple regardless of graduate degrees in creative writing, workshops, or whom you know: We look for good writing, period."

## SOU'WESTER

Department of English, Box 1438, Southern Illinois University Edwardsville, Edwardsville IL 62026. **Website:** http://souwester.org. **Contact:** Joshua Kryah, poetry editor; Geoff Schmidt, prose editor. *Sou'wester* appears biannually in spring and fall. Leans toward poetry with strong imagery, successful association of images, and skillful use of figurative language. Has published poetry by Robert Wrigley, Beckian Fritz Goldberg, Eric Pankey, Betsy Sholl, and Angie Estes. Returns rights. Responds in 3 months. Sample: $8.

Uses online submission form. Open to submissions in mid-August for fall and spring issues. Close submissions in winter and early spring. *Sou'wester* has 30-40 pages of poetry in each digest-sized, 100-page issue. *Sou'wester* is professionally printed, flat-spined, with textured matte card cover, press run is 300 for 500 subscribers of which 50 are libraries. Receives 3,000 poems (from 600 poets) each year, accepts 36-40, has a 6-month backlog. Subscription: $15/2 issues.

**MAGAZINES NEEDS** Submit up to 5 poems. Editor comments on rejected poems "usually, in the case of those that we almost accept." Pays 2 contributor copies and a 1-year subscription.

## THE SOW'S EAR POETRY REVIEW

308 Greenfield Ave., Winchester VA 22602. **E-mail:** sowsearpoetry@yahoo.com; nancywhitepoetry@gmail.com. **Website:** www.sows-ear.kitenet.net. **Contact:** Kristin Camitta Zimet, editor; Nancy White, associate editor. *The Sow's Ear* prints fine poetry of all styles and lengths, complemented by b&w art. Also welcomes reviews, interviews, and essays related to poetry. Open to group submissions. "Crossover" section features poetry married to any other art form, including prose, music, and visual media. Acquires first publication rights. Publishes ms an average of 1-6 months after acceptance. Responds in 2 weeks to queries. Responds in 3 months to mss. Editorial lead time 1-6 months. Sample copy for $8. Guidelines available for SASE, by e-mail, or on website.

**MAGAZINES NEEDS** Considers simultaneous submissions "if you tell us promptly when work is accepted elsewhere"; no previously published poems, although will consider poems from chapbooks if they were never published in a magazine. Previously published poems may be included in Crossover if rights are cleared. No e-mail submissions, except for poets outside the US; postal submissions only. Include brief bio and SASE. Pays 2 contributor copies. Inquire about reviews, interviews, and essays. Contest/Award offerings: *The Sow's Ear* Poetry Competition and *The Sow's Ear* Chapbook Contest. Open to any style or length. No limits on line length.

**TIPS** "We like work that is carefully crafted, keenly felt, and freshly perceived. We respond to poems with voice, a sense of place, delight in language, and a meaning that unfolds. We look for prose that opens new dimensions to appreciating poetry."

## ⑤ SPACE AND TIME

458 Elizabeth Ave., Somerset NJ 08873. **Website:** www.spaceandtimemagazine.com. **Contact:** Hildy Silverman, publisher. *Space and Time* is the longest continually published small-press genre fiction magazine still in print. We pride ourselves in having published the first stories of some of the great writers in science fiction, fantasy, and horror. Acquires first North American serial rights and one-time rights; includes electronic rights. All rights revert to author after publication. Pays on publication. Publishes stories/poems 6-12 months after acceptance. Sample copy: $6. Guidelines available only on website. Only opens periodically—announcements of open reading periods appear on Facebook page and website. No fiction or poetry considered outside of open reading periods.

○ We love stories that blend elements—horror and science fiction, fantasy with science fiction elements, etc. We challenge writers to try something new and send us their hard to classify works—what other publications reject because the work doesn't fit in their "pigeonholes."

**MAGAZINES NEEDS** "Multiple submissions are okay within reason (no more than 3 at a time). Submit embedded in an e-mail, a Word doc, or .rtf attachment. Only submit during open poetry reading periods, which are announced via the Facebook page and on the website. All other poetry submitted outside these reading periods will be rejected out of hand." Poetry without any sort of genre or speculative element. No longer than a single standard page. Pays $5/poem.

## ○⑤ SPIDER

70 E. Lake St., Suite 800, Chicago IL 60601. **E-mail:** spider@spidermagkids.com. **Website:** www.cricketmag.com/spider; www.spidermagkids.com. **Contact:** Submissions editor. *SPIDER* is full-color, 8×10, 34 pages with a 4-page activity pullout for children ages 6-9. Features the world's best children's authors.

**MAGAZINES NEEDS** Poems should be succinct, imaginative, and accessible; tend to avoid long narrative poems. Length: no more than 20 lines. Pays up to $3/line, $25 minimum.

## SPILLWAY

P.O. Box 7887, Huntington Beach CA 92615. (415)652-6161. **Website:** www.spillway.org/index.html. **Contact:** Mifanwy Kaiser, publisher; Susan Terris, editor. Published annually in June, *Spillway* celebrates "writing's diversity and power to affect our lives." Open to all voices, schools, and tendencies. Acquires one-time rights. Responds in up to 6 months. Single copy: $13.50, including shipping and handling. Subscription: $23 for 1 year including shipping and handling, $40 for 2 years including shipping and handling. To order, visit the website and use PayPal. Submissions open February 1-March 31 only.

○ *Spillway* is about 125 pages, digest-sized, attractively printed, perfect-bound, with full color card cover. Press run is 2,000. "We recommend ordering a sample copy before you submit, though acceptance does not depend upon purchasing a sample copy."

**MAGAZINES NEEDS** Submit 3-5 poems at a time (in a single document). No fiction. For more complete information about upcoming themes and submission periods, check our website. E-mail submissions only to spillway2@spillway.org (Word attachment); no disk or fax submissions. Cover letter is required. Include brief bio. Responds in up to 6 months. Pays 1 contributor copy.

### SPINNING JENNY

**E-mail:** editor@spinning-jenny.com. **Website:** www.spinning-jenny.com. **Contact:** C.E. Harrison, editor. *Spinning Jenny* has published poetry by Abraham Smith, Cynthia Cruz, Michael Morse, and Joyelle McSweeney, among others. Authors retain rights. We are not currently accepting submissions. Please check our website for updates. Single copy: $10; subscription: $20 for 2 issues. Guidelines available on website. Please note that we are not currently accepting submissions.

○ *Spinning Jenny* is 96 pages, digest-sized, perfect-bound, with heavy card cover. "We accept less than 5% of unsolicited submissions." Press run is 1,000.

**MAGAZINES NEEDS** "*Spinning Jenny* is an open forum for poetry. We are pleased to consider experimental writing and work by unpublished authors. However, writers are strongly encouraged to review a recent issue of the magazine before submitting their work." Please note that we are not currently accepting submissions. Please check our website for updates. Pays in contributor copies.

### SPITBALL: THE LITERARY BASEBALL MAGAZINE

5560 Fox Rd., Cincinnati OH 45239. **E-mail:** spitball5@hotmail.com. **Website:** www.spitballmag.com. **Contact:** Mike Shannon, editor in chief. *Spitball: The Literary Baseball Magazine*, published semiannually, is a unique magazine devoted to poetry, fiction, and book reviews exclusively about baseball. Newcomers are very welcome, but they must know the subject. "Perhaps a good place to start for beginners is one's personal reactions to the game, a game, a player, etc., and take it from there." Writers submitting to *Spitball* for the first time must buy a sample copy (waived for subscribers). "This is a one-time-only fee, which we regret, but economic reality dictates that we insist those who wish to be published in *Spitball* help sup-

port it, at least at this minimum level." Guidelines online.

○ *Spitball* is 96 pages, digest-sized, computer-typeset, perfect-bound. Receives about 1,000 submissions/year, accepts about 40. Press run is 1,000. Subscription: $12. Sample: $6.

**MAGAZINES NEEDS** Submit a "batch" of poems at a time ("we prefer to use several of same poet in an issue rather than a single poem"). Lines/poem: open. Cover letter is required. Include brif bio and SASE. "Many times we are able to publish accepted work almost immediately." All material published in *Spitball* will be automatically considered for inclusion in the next *Best of Spitball* anthology. Poems submitted to *Spitball* will be considered automatically for Poem of the Month, to appear on the website. "We sponsor the Casey Award (for best baseball book of the year) and hold the Casey Awards Banquet in late February or early March. Any chapbook of baseball poetry should be sent to us for consideration for the 'Casey' plaque that we award to the winner each year." Pays 2 contributor copies.

**TIPS** "Take the subject seriously. We do. In other words, get a clue (if you don't already have one) about the subject and about the poetry that has already been done and published about baseball. Learn from it—think about what you can add to the canon that is original and fresh—and don't assume that just anybody with the feeblest of efforts can write a baseball poem worthy of publication. And most importantly, stick with it. Genius seldom happens on the first try."

### SPOUT MAGAZINE

P.O. Box 581067, Minneapolis MN 55458. **E-mail:** editors@spoutpress.org. **Website:** www.spoutpress.org. **Contact:** Michelle Filkins. As the counterpart to Spout Press, *Spout Magazine* features poetry, art, fiction, and thought pieces with diverse voices and styles. Publishes ms 2-3 months after acceptance. Responds in 4 months. Guidelines online at website.

**MAGAZINES NEEDS** Submit up to 5 poems at a time. Considers previously published poems and simultaneous submissions. Cover letter is preferred. "Poems are reviewed by 2 of 3 editors; those selected for final review are read again by all 3."

## SPRING: THE JOURNAL OF THE E.E. CUMMINGS SOCIETY

129 Lake Huron Hall, Grand Valley State University, Allendale MI 49401. **E-mail:** websterm@gvsu.edu. **Website:** faculty.gvsu.edu/websterm/cummings. **Contact:** Michael Webster, editor. *Spring: The Journal of the E.E. Cummings Society*, published annually (usually in the fall), is designed "to broaden the audience for E.E. Cummings and to explore various facets of his life and art." **Contributors are required to subscribe.** Reads May through August. Responds in 6 months.

**MAGAZINES NEEDS** Wants poems in the spirit of Cummings, primarily poems of 1 page or less. Submit as e-mail attachment. Include cover letter. Does not want "amateurish" work.

## SRPR (SPOON RIVER POETRY REVIEW)

4241 Department of English, Illinois State University, Normal IL 61790. **E-mail:** editors@srpr.org; contact@srpr.org. **Website:** srpr.org. **Contact:** Kirstin Hotelling Zona, editor. *SRPR (Spoon River Poetry Review)*, published biannually, is "one of the nation's oldest continuously published poetry journals. We seek to publish the best of all poetic genres, experimental as well as mainstream, and are proud of our commitment to regional as well as international poets and readers. *SRPR* includes, alongside poems from emerging and established poets, a chapbook-length selection of poetry by our featured *SRPR* poet, a substantial interview with the featured poet, and a long review-essay on books of recently published poetry written by established poet-critics. The Summer/Fall issue also spotlights the winner and runners-up of our highly competitive editor's prize contest." Acquires first North American serial rights. Responds in 2-6 months. Guidelines available in magazine or on website.

○ Accepts submissions from September 15-February 15 (postmarked).

**MAGAZINES NEEDS** "We publish the best of all poetic genres, including translations, and are proud of our commitment to regional as well as international poets. At *SRPR*, both innovative and mainstream poems are welcome, though all poetry we publish must be as intellectually and emotionally ambitious as it is formally attentive." Submit 3-5 poems at a time. Submit using online submission form or by postal mail

with SASE. Pays 2 contributor copies and a 1-year subscription.

## ◐ STAND MAGAZINE

School of English, Leeds LS2 9JT, United Kingdom. (44)(113)233-4794. **E-mail:** stand@leeds.ac.uk. **Website:** www.standmagazine.org. North American submissions: David Latané, Stand Magazine, Dept. of English, Virginia Commonwealth University, Richmond VA 23284.. **Contact:** Jon Glover, managing editor. *Stand Magazine* is concerned with what happens when cultures and literatures meet, with translation in its many guises, with the mechanics of language, with the processes by which the policy receives or disables its cultural makers. *Stand* promotes debate of issues that are of radical concern to the intellectual community worldwide. U.S. submissions can be made through the Virginia office (see separate listing). Publishes ms an average of 1 year to 18 months after acceptance. Guidelines online.

○ Does not accept e-mail submissions.

**MAGAZINES NEEDS** Submit through postal mail only. Include SASE.

## ⑤ STAR*LINE

Science Fiction Poetry Association, W5679 State Rd. 60, Poynette WI 53955. **E-mail:** starlineeditor@gmail.com. **Website:** www.sfpoetry.com. **Contact:** F.J. Bergmann, editor. *Star*Line*, published quarterly in print and .pdf format by the Science Fiction Poetry Association (see separate listing in Organizations), is a speculative poetry magazine. "Open to all forms as long as your poetry uses speculative motifs: science fiction, fantasy, or horror." Buys first North American serial rights. Responds in 3 days. Guidelines online.

**MAGAZINES NEEDS** Submit 3-5 poems at a time. Accepts e-mail submissions (preferred; pasted into body of message, no attachments). Pays 3¢/word rounded to the next dollar; minimum $3, maximum $25.

**ALSO OFFERS** The Association also publishes *The Rhysling Anthology*, a yearly collection of nominations from the membership "for the best long and short speculative poetry of the preceding year, and *Dwarf Stars*, an annual collection of micro-poetry (10 lines or fewer)."

## STEPPING STONES MAGAZINE

P.O. Box 902, Norristown PA 19404-0902. **E-mail:** info@ssmalmia.com. **Website:** ssmalmia.com. **Contact:** Trinae Ross, publisher. "*Stepping Stones Magazine* is a not-for-profit organization dedicated to presenting awesome writing and art created by people from all lifestyles." Publishes fiction, nonfiction, and poetry." Acquires first electronic rights, one-time rights, reprint rights. Responds in 2 months. Guidelines available for SASE, by e-mail, or on website.

Has published poetry by Richard Fenwick, Karlanna Lewis, and Stephanie Kaylor. Receives about 600 poems/year, accepts about 10-15%.

**MAGAZINES NEEDS** Send up to 5 poems via postal mail, e-mail (poetry@ssmalmia.com), or online submissions manager. Include brief bio. Length: up to 100 lines/poem.

## STILL CRAZY

(614)746-0859. **E-mail:** editor@crazylitmag.com. **Website:** www.crazylitmag.com. **Contact:** Barbara Kussow, editor. *Still Crazy*, published biannually in January and July, features poetry, short stories, and essays written by or about people over age 50. The editor is particularly interested in material that challenges the stereotypes of older people and that portrays older people's inner lives as rich and rewarding. Wants writing by people over age 50 and writing by people of any age if the topic is about people over 50. Acquires one-time rights. Rights revert to author upon publication. Time between acceptance and publication is up to 1 year. Simultaneous submissions OK, but notify editor as soon as possible if work is accepted elsewhere. Previously published submissions are OK, but "author must make previous publication known at time of submission. We do not want materials that have appeared online elsewhere." Responds in 6 months to mss. Sometimes sends prepublication galleys. Sometimes comments on/critiques rejected mss. Single paper copy: $10. Subscriptions: $18 (2 issues per year). Downloads: $4. Sometimes publishes theme issues. Guidelines on website. Submit via submissions manager on website.

Accepts 3-4 short stories per issue; 5-7 essays; 12-14 poems. Reads submissions year round.

**MAGAZINES NEEDS** Poems that convey a story; accessible, but with compelling images and language. The editor is particularly interested in material that challenges the stereotypes of older people and that portrays older people's inner lives as rich and rewarding. Seldom publish "rhyming poetry; do not want poetry that is too sentimental." Lines/poem: up to 50. Pays 1 contributor copy.

**TIPS** Looking for interesting characters and interesting situations that might interest readers of all ages. Humor and lightness welcomed.

## STIRRING: A LITERARY COLLECTION

Sundress Publications, **E-mail:** stirring@sundress-publications.com. **E-mail:** stirring.fiction@gmail.com; stirring.poetry@gmail.com; stirring.nonfiction@gmail.com. **Website:** www.sundresspublications.com/stirring. **Contact:** Luci Brown, Managing Editor; Andrew Koch, Managing Editor; Sarah Einstein, Managing Editor. "*Stirring* is one of the oldest continually-published literary journals on the web. *Stirring* is a monthly literary magazine that publishes poetry, short fiction, creative nonfiction, and photography by established and emerging writers." Acquires first North American serial rights. Publishes ms 1-2 weeks after acceptance. Responds in 3-6 months. Visit our website for guidelines.

**MAGAZINES NEEDS** Wants free verse, formal poetry, etc. Doesn't want religious verse or children's verse. Has published poetry by Dorianne Laux, Sharon Olds, Patricia Smith, Chad Davidson. Receives about 1,500 poems/year, accepts 60. Submit up to 5 poems by e-mail to stirring.poetry@gmail.com. Length: 1-6 pages (most often accepts half- to full-page poems).

## STONE SOUP

Children's Art Foundation, P.O. Box 83, Santa Cruz CA 95063-0083. (831)426-5557. **E-mail:** editor@stonesoup.com. **Website:** http://stonesoup.com. **Contact:** Ms. Gerry Mandel, editor. *Stone Soup* is 48 pages, 7x10, professionally printed in color on heavy stock, saddle-stapled, with coated cover with full-color illustration. Receives 5,000 poetry submissions/year, accepts about 12. Press run is 15,000. Subscription: $37/year (U.S.). "We have a preference for writing and art based on real-life experiences; no formula stories or poems. We only publish writing by children ages 8 to 13. We do not publish writing by adults." Buys all rights. Pays on publication. Publishes ms an average of 4 months after acceptance. View a PDF sample copy at www.stonesoup.com.

"Stories and poems from past issues are online."

**MAGAZINES NEEDS** Wants free verse poetry. Does not want rhyming poetry, haiku, or cinquain. Pays $40/poem, a certificate, and 2 contributor copies, plus discounts.

**TIPS** "All writing we publish is by young people ages 13 and under. We do not publish any writing by adults. We can't emphasize enough how important it is to read a couple of issues of the magazine. You can read stories and poems from past issues online. We have a strong preference for writing on subjects that mean a lot to the author. If you feel strongly about something that happened to you or something you observed, use that feeling as the basis for your story or poem. Stories should have good descriptions, realistic dialogue, and a point to make. In a poem, each word must be chosen carefully. Your poem should present a view of your subject, and a way of using words that are special and all your own."

## STORYSOUTH

**E-mail:** terry@storysouth.com. **Website:** www.storysouth.com. **Contact:** Terry Kennedy, editor; Cynthia Nearman, creative nonfiction editor; Drew Perry, fiction editor; Luke Johnson, poetry editor. "*storySouth* accepts unsolicited submissions of fiction, poetry, and creative nonfiction during 2 submission periods annually: May 15-July 1 and November 15-January 1. Long pieces are encouraged. Please make only 1 submission in a single genre per reading period." Acquires first serial rights. Publishes ms 1 month after acceptance. Responds in 2-6 months to mss. Guidelines online.

**MAGAZINES NEEDS** Submit 3-5 poems via online submissions manager. No word/line limit.

**TIPS** "What really makes a story stand out is a strong voice and a sense of urgency—a need for the reader to keep reading the story and not put it down until it is finished."

## THE STORYTELLER

65 Highway 328 West, Maynard AR 72444. (870)647-2137. **E-mail:** storytellermag1@yahoo.com. **Website:** www.thestorytellermagazine.com. **Contact:** Regina Riney (Williams), editor. "We are here to help writers however we can and to help start them on their publishing career. Proofread! Make sure you know what we take and what we don't and also make sure you know the word count." Buys first North American rights. Publishes ms an average of 1-12 months after acceptance. Responds in 1 week to queries; in 2 weeks to mss. Editorial lead time 6 months. Guidelines online.

**MAGAZINES NEEDS** Submit up to 3 poems with SASE. Does not want long rambling. Length: up to 40 lines/poem.

**ALSO OFFERS** Sponsors a quarterly contest. "Readers vote on their favorite poems. Winners receive a copy of the magazine and a certificate. We also nominate for the Pushcart Prize." See website for yearly contest announcements and winners.

**TIPS** "*The Storyteller* is one of the best places you will find to submit your work, especially new writers. Our best advice, be professional. You have one chance to make a good impression. Don't blow it by being unprofessional."

## STRANGE HORIZONS

**E-mail:** editor@strangehorizons.com. **Website:** strangehorizons.com. **Contact:** Niall Harrison, editor-in-chief. "*Strange Horizons* is a magazine of and about speculative fiction and related nonfiction. Speculative fiction includes science fiction, fantasy, horror, slipstream, and other flavors of fantastica." For nonfiction: buys exclusive online publication rights for 6 months and requests ongoing nonexclusive rights to display the work in archive. For fiction and poetry: buys first world exclusive English-language rights (including audio rights) for 2 months. Responds in 1-3 month to mss. Only responds if interested.

Work published in *Strange Horizons* has been shortlisted for or won Hugo, Nebula, Rhysling, Theodore Sturgeon, James Tiptree Jr., and World Fantasy Awards.

**MAGAZINES NEEDS** "We're looking for high-quality SF, fantasy, horror, and slipstream poetry. We're looking for modern, exciting poems that explore the possible and impossible: stories about human and nonhuman experiences, dreams and reality, past and future, the here-and-now and otherwhere-and-elsewhen. We want poems from imaginative and unconventional writers; we want voices from diverse perspectives and backgrounds." Submit up to 6 poems within 2 calendar months via e-mail; 1 poem per e-mail. Include "POETRY SUB: Your Poem Title" in subject line. Pays $30 per poem.

## STRAYLIGHT

UW-Parkside, English Department, University of Wisconsin-Parkside, 900 Wood Rd., Kenosha WI 53141. **E-mail:** submissions@straylightmag.com.

**Website:** www.straylightmag.com. *Straylight*, published biannually, seeks fiction and "poetry of almost any style as long as it's inventive." Acquires first North American serial rights. Publication is copyrighted. Pays on publication. Publishes ms 6 months after acceptance. Responds in 3 weeks to queries; in 3 months to mss. Rarely comments on/critiques rejected mss. Sample copy: $10; subscription: $18. Guidelines online.

**MAGAZINES NEEDS** Submit 3-6 poems at a time. Send poems with cover letter. Accepts submissions by online submission manager or mail (send either SASE or IRC for return of ms, or disposable copy of ms and #10 SASE for reply only). Include brief bio, list of publications. Pays 2 contributor copies.

**TIPS** "We tend to publish character-based and inventive fiction with cutting-edge prose. We are unimpressed with works based on strict plot twists or novelties. Read a sample copy to get a feel for what we publish."

## STRIDE MAGAZINE

Stride Publications, 4b Tremayne Close, Devoran, Cornwall TR3 6QE, United Kingdom. **E-mail:** editor@stridemagazine.co.uk. **E-mail:** submissions@stridemagazine.co.uk. **Website:** www.stridemagazine.co.uk. **Contact:** Rupert Loydell, editor. *Stride Magazine*, published online, is "a gathering of new poetry, prose poems and reviews. *Stride* is regularly updated with new contributions."

**MAGAZINES NEEDS** Submit 4-5 poems at a time. Accepts e-mail submissions only (pasted into body of message; no attachments).

## STRUGGLE: A MAGAZINE OF PROLETARIAN REVOLUTIONARY LITERATURE

P.O. Box 28536, Detroit MI 48228. (313)273-9039. **E-mail:** timhall11@yahoo.com. **Website:** www.strugglemagazine.net. **Contact:** Tim Hall, editor. "A quarterly magazine featuring African American, Latino, and other writers of color; prisoners; disgruntled workers; activists in the anti-war, anti-racist, and other mass movements; and many writers discontented with Obama and with the Republicans, their joint austerity campaign against the workers and the poor, and their continuing aggressive wars and drone murders abroad. While we urge literature in the direction of revolutionary working-class politics and a vision of socialism as embodying a genuine workers' power, in distinction to the state-capitalist regimes of the former Soviet Union, present-day China, North Korea, Cuba, etc., we accept a broader range of rebellious viewpoints in order to encourage creativity and dialogue." No rights acquired. Responds in 3-4 months to queries. Sample copy: $5. Subscription: $10 for 4 issues; make checks payable to Tim Hall, Special Account, not to *Struggle*.

**MAGAZINES NEEDS** Submit up to 8 poems at a time. Accepts e-mail submissions (pasted into body of message, no attachments), but prefers postal mail. "Writers must include SASE. Name and address must appear on the opening page of each poem."

## STUDIO, A JOURNAL OF CHRISTIANS WRITING

727 Peel St., Albury NSW 2640, Australia. (61)(2)6021-1135. **E-mail:** studio00@bigpond.net.au. **Contact:** Paul Grover, publisher. *Studio, A Journal of Christians Writing*, published three times a year, prints poetry and prose of literary merit, offering a venue for previously published, new, and aspiring writers and seeking to create a sense of community among Christians writing. Also publishes occasional articles as well as news and reviews of writing, writers, and events of interest to members. People who send material should be comfortable being published under this banner: *Studio, A Journal of Christians Writing*. Rights remain with the author Time between acceptance and publication is 6-9 months. Responds in 2 months to poems; in 1 week to queries and mss. Editorial lead time is 1 month. Sample copy: $10 (AUD; airmail to U.S.). Subscription: $60 AUD for overseas subscribers. Guidelines available via e-mail: studio00@bigpond.net.au.

*Studio* is 60-80 pages, digest-sized, professionally printed on high-quality paper, saddle-stapled, with matte card cover. Press run is 300 (all subscriptions).

**MAGAZINES NEEDS** Wants shorter pieces (of poetry) but with no specification as to form or length (necessarily less than 200 lines), subject matter, style, or purpose. Cover letter is required in e-mail submission. E-mail submissions preferred. Include brief details of previous publishing history, if any. SAE with IRC required if sent via regular post: submissions via post must be typed and double-spaced on 1 side of A4 white paper. Name and address must appear on the reverse side of each page submitted via postal service. Has published poetry by John Foulcher, Andrew Lansdown, Geoff Page, Les Murray, and other Australian and American poets. Length: less than 200 lines/poem. Pays 1 contributor copy.

**ALSO OFFERS** Reviews books of poetry in 250 words, single-book format. Send materials for review consideration. Conducts a biannual poetry and short story contest.

## STUDIO ONE

Murray Hall 170, College of St. Benedict, 37 S. College Ave., St. Joseph MN 56374. **E-mail:** studio1@csbsju.edu. **Website:** digitalcommons.csbsju.edu/studio_one/. **Contact:** William Harren, Lucas Giese, editors in chief. *Studio One* is a literary and visual arts magazine published each spring by the College of Saint Benedict/Saint John's University. Its mission is to give new and established writers alike a forum in which to present their works. The magazine's focus is poetry, short fiction, essays, and all forms of reproducible visual art works. *Studio One* is student-run, and the student editors change yearly. Submissions are open to all students on either Saint John's or Saint Benedict's campuses and to the general public regardless of regional, national, or international location. Sample copy can be obtained by sending a self-addressed, stamped manila envelope and $6.

◐ Reading period: September through February.

**MAGAZINES NEEDS** Considers simultaneous submissions; no previously published poems. Accepts e-mail submissions (pasted into body of message); "clearly show page breaks and indentations." Seldom comments on rejected poems. Lines/poem: "poetry no more than 2 pages stands a better chance of publication."

## ⟳☉ SUBTERRAIN

Strong Words for a Polite Nation, P.O. Box 3008, MPO, Vancouver BC V6B 3X5, Canada. (604)876-8710. **Fax:** (604)879-2667. **E-mail:** subter@portal.ca. **Website:** www.subterrain.ca. Natasha Sanders-Kay, managing editor. **Contact:** Brian Kaufman, editor in chief. "*subTerrain* magazine is published 3 times/year from modest offices just off of Main Street in Vancouver, BC. We strive to produce a stimulating fusion of fiction, poetry, photography, and graphic illustration from uprising Canadian, U.S., and international writers and artists." Pays on publication for first North American serial rights. Publishes ms 4-9 months after acceptance. Responds in 6-9 months to

mss. Rarely comments on rejected mss. Sample copy: $5 (subterrain.ca/subscriptions). Writer's guidelines online (subterrain.ca/about/35/sub-terrain-writer-s-guidelines).

**MAGAZINES NEEDS** "We accept poetry, but we no longer accept unsolicited submissions, except when related to 1 of our theme issues." "We no longer accept unsolicited poetry submissions (unless specifically related to one of our theme issues)." Poems unrelated to any theme issues may be submitted to the annual "General" issue (usually the summer/fall issue). Pays $50/poem.

**TIPS** "Read the magazine first. Get to know what kind of work we publish."

## ☉ SUBTROPICS

University of Florida, P.O. Box 112075, 4008 Turlington Hall, Gainesville FL 32611-2075. **E-mail:** subtropics@english.ufl.edu. **Website:** www.english.ufl.edu/subtropics. **Contact:** David Leavitt, editor. *Subtropics* seeks to publish the best literary fiction, essays, and poetry being written today, both by established and emerging authors. Will consider works of fiction of any length, from short shorts to novellas and self-contained novel excerpts. Gives the same latitude to essays. Appreciates work in translation and, from time to time, republishes important and compelling stories, essays, and poems that have lapsed out of print by writers no longer living. Member: CLMP. Buys first North American serial rights. Pays on acceptance for prose; pays on publication of the issue preceding the issue in which the author's work will appear for poetry. Publishes ms an average of 6 months after acceptance. Responds in 1 month to queries and mss. Rarely comments on/critiques rejected mss Sample copy: $12.95. Guidelines online.

**MAGAZINES NEEDS** Submit up to 4 poems via online submissions manager. Pays $100 per poem.

**TIPS** "We publish longer works of fiction, including novellas and excerpts from forthcoming novels. Each issue includes a short-short story of about 250 words on the back cover. We are also interested in publishing works in translation for the magazine's English-speaking audience."

## THE SUN

107 N. Roberson St., Chapel Hill NC 27516. (919)942-5282. **Fax:** (919)932-3101. **Website:** www.thesunmagazine.org. **Contact:** Sy Safransky, editor. *The Sun* publishes essays, interviews, fiction, and poetry. "We are

open to all kinds of writing, though we favor work of a personal nature." Buys first rights, buys one-time rights. Pays on publication. Publishes ms an average of 6-12 months after acceptance. Responds in 3-6 months to queries and mss. Sample copy online. Guidelines online.

**MAGAZINES NEEDS** Submit up to 6 poems at a time. Considers previously published poems but strongly prefers unpublished work. "Poems should be typed and accompanied by a cover letter and SASE." Recently published poems by Tony Hoagland, Ellen Bass, Steve Kowit, Brian Doyle, and Alison Luterman. Rarely publishes poems that rhyme. Pays $100-200 and 1-year subscription.

**TIPS** "Do not send queries except for interviews. We're open to unusual work. Read the magazine to get a sense of what we're about. Our submission rate is extremely high. Please be patient after sending us your work and include return postage."

## SUNSTONE

343 N. Third W., Salt Lake City UT 84103-1215. (801)355-5926. **E-mail:** info@sunstonemagazine. com. **Website:** www.sunstonemagazine.com. *Sunstone*, published 6 times/year, prints scholarly articles of interest to an open, Mormon audience; personal essays; fiction (selected only through contests), and poetry. Has published poetry by Susan Howe, Anita Tanner, Robert Parham, Ryan G. Van Cleave, Robert Rees, and Virgil Suárez. Acquires first North American serial rights. Publishes ms 2 years after acceptance. Responds in 3 months. Sample copy: $10 postpaid. Subscription: $45 for 6 issues. Guidelines online.

○ *Sunstone* is 64 pages, magazine-sized, professionally printed, saddle-stapled, with semi-glossy paper cover. Receives more than 500 poems/year, accepts 40-50. Press run is 3,000.

**MAGAZINES NEEDS** Wants both lyric and narrative poetry that engages the reader with fresh, strong images; skillful use of language; and a strong sense of voice and/or place. Short poems, including haiku, limericks, couplets, and one liners, are welcome. Does not want didactic poetry, sing-song rhymes, or in-process work. Submit by mail or e-mail. Include name, address, and e-mail on each poem. Seldom comments on rejected poems. Length: up to 40 lines/poem. Pays 5 contributor copies.

## SYCAMORE REVIEW

Purdue University Department of English, 500 Oval Dr., West Lafayette IN 47907. (765) 494-3783. **Fax:** (765) 494-3780. **E-mail:** sycamore@purdue.edu. **Website:** www.sycamorereview.com. **Contact:** Anthony Sutton, editor in chief; Bess Cooley, managing editor. *Sycamore Review* is Purdue University's internationally acclaimed literary journal, affiliated with Purdue's College of Liberal Arts and the Dept. of English. Strives to publish the best writing by new and established writers. Looks for well-crafted and engaging work, works that illuminate our lives in the collective human search for meaning. Would like to publish more work that takes a reflective look at national identity and how we are perceived by the world. Looks for diversity of voice, pluralistic worldviews, and political and social context. Buys first North American serial rights.

○ Reading period: September 1-March 31.

**MAGAZINES NEEDS** Submi via online submissions manager. Does not publish creative work by any student currently attending Purdue University. Former students should wait 1 year before submitting. Pays $25/poem.

**TIPS** "We look for originality, brevity, significance, strong dialogue, and vivid detail. We sponsor the Wabash Prize for Poetry (deadline: December 1) and Fiction (deadline: April 17), $1,000 award for each. All contest submissions will be considered for regular inclusion in the *Sycamore Review*."

## ◐ TAB: THE JOURNAL OF POETRY & POETICS

Chapman University, *TAB: The Journal of Poetry & Poetics*, Dept. of English, One University Dr., Orange CA 92866. (714)628-7389. **E-mail:** poetry@chapman. edu; leahy@chapman.edu. **Website:** journals.chapman.edu/ojs/index.php/TAB-journal. **Contact:** Anna Leahy, editor; Claudine Jaenichen, creative director. *TAB: A Journal of Poetry & Poetics* is a national and international journal of creative and critical writing. This literary journal's mission is to discover, support, and publish the contemporary poetry and writing about poetry; to provide a forum in which the poetic tradition is practiced, extended, challenged, and discussed by emerging and established voices; and to encourage wide appreciation of poetry and expand the audience for poems and writing about poetry. Welcomes submissions of poems from established and emerging poets as well as critical essays, creative nonfiction, interviews, and reviews. *TAB* will reach audience of poets, poetry readers and appreciators, poetry scholars and critics, and students of poetry. Buys first North American serial rights. Pays on publication. Publishes ms 2-6 months after acceptance. Response time varies. Sample copy for $4 s&h or online at website. Guidelines online.

**MAGAZINES NEEDS** No greeting card poetry. No work by writers under 18 years of age. No work by students, faculty, or staff of Chapman University. No length restrictions.

**TIPS** "Read poetry and read it widely. Take a look at the range we publish. Work hard and revise."

### 🌐❸ TAKAHE

P.O. Box 13-335, Christchurch 8141, New Zealand. **E-mail:** admin@takahe.org.nz. **Website:** www.takahe. org.nz. The Takahē Collective Trust is a nonprofit organization that aims to support emerging and published writers, poets, artists, and cultural commentators. Acquires worldwide first publication rights. Pays on publication. Responds in 4 months. Guidelines online at www.takahe.org.nz.

○ *Takahē* magazine is a New Zealand-based literary and arts magazine that appears 3 times/ year with a mix of print and online issues. It publishes short stories, poetry, and art by established and emerging writers and artists as well as essays, interviews, and book reviews (by invitation) in these related areas.

**MAGAZINES NEEDS** Email submissions preferred (poetry@takahe.org.nz). Overseas submissions are only accepted by e-mail. Accepts a maximum of 6 poems per submission and no more than 3 submissions a year. "Please be aware that we publish only a handful of overseas poets each year." Long work (multiple pages) is unlikely to be accepted. Pays small honorarium to New Zealand authors, or one-year subscription to overseas writers.

**TIPS** "Editorials, book reviews, artwork, and literary commentaries are by invitation only."

### ◑ TALKING RIVER

Division of Literature and Languages, 500 8th Ave., Lewiston ID 83501. (208)792-2189. **Fax:** (208)792-2324. **E-mail:** talkingriver@lcmail.lcsc.edu. **Website:** www.lcsc.edu/talking-river. **Contact:** Kevin Goodan, editorial advisor. "We look for new voices with something to say to a discerning general audience." Wants

more well-written, character-driven stories that surprise and delight the reader with fresh, arresting yet unself-conscious language, imagery, metaphor, revelation. Reads mss September 1-May 1 only. Recently published work by Chris Dombrowski, Sherwin Bitsui, and Lia Purpura, Jim Harrison, David James Duncan, Dan Gerber, Alison Hawthorne Deming. Acquires one-time rights. Publishes ms 1-2 years after acceptance. Responds in 6 months to mss. Sample copy: $6. Writer's guidelines for #10 SASE.

○ Submission period runs August 1-April 1.

**MAGAZINES NEEDS** Submit via postal mail. Send SASE for reply and return of ms, or send disposable copy of ms. Pays contributor copies; additional copies $6.

**TIPS** "We look for the strong, the unique; we reject clichéd images and predictable climaxes."

### ◐ TARPAULIN SKY

P.O. Box 189, Grafton VT 05146. **E-mail:** editors@tarpaulinsky.com. **E-mail:** submissions@tarpaulinsky.com. **Website:** www.tarpaulinsky.com. **Contact:** Resh Daily, managing editor. *Tarpaulin Sky*, published biannually in print and online, features the highest-quality poetry, prose, cross-genre work, art, photography, interviews, and reviews. Open to all styles and forms, providing the forms appear inevitable and/or inextricable from the poems. Especially fond of inventive/experimental and cross-/trans-genre work. The best indication of aesthetic is found in the journal: Read it before submitting. Also, hardcopy submissions may be received by different editors at different times; check guidelines before submitting. Acquires first rights. Publishes ms 2-6 months after acceptance. Responds in 1-4 months.

**MAGAZINES NEEDS** Submit 4-6 poems at a time. Considers simultaneous submissions; no previously published poems. Accepts e-mail submissions ("best received as attachments in .rtf or .pdf formats"); no disk submissions. Cover letter is preferred. Reads submissions year round. Poems are read by all editors. Rarely comments on rejected poems. Guidelines available for SASE, by e-mail, or on website. Has published poetry by Jenny Boully, Matthea Harvey, Bin Ramke, Eleni Sikelianos, Juliana Spahr, and Joshua Marie Wilkinson. Receives about 3,000 poems/year. Pays in contributor copies and by waiving readings fees for Tarpaulin Sky Press Open Reading Periods.

## TAR RIVER POETRY

113 Erwin Hall, East Carolina University, East Fifth St., Greenville NC 27858. **E-mail:** TarRiverPoetry@ gmail.com. **Website:** www.tarriverpoetry.com. **Contact:** Luke Whisnant, editor. *Tar River Poetry*, published twice/year, is an all-poetry magazine that publishes 40-50 poems/issue, providing the talented beginner and experienced writer with a forum that features all styles and forms of verse. Wants skillful use of figurative language and poems that appeal to the senses. Does not want sentimental, flat-statement poetry. Acquires first rights and reassigns reprint rights after publication. Responds in 6 weeks. Rarely comments on rejections due to volume of submissions. Sample: $7, postage paid. Subscription: $12 for 1 year; $20 for 2 years. Guidelines available for SASE or on website.

Only considers submissions 2 months of the year—usually September and February; check website for reading periods before submitting. Work submitted at other times will not be considered. *Tar River Poetry* is 64 pages, 9x5, professionally printed with color cover. Receives 6,000-8,000 submissions/year, accepts 60-80. Press run is 900 (500 subscribers, 125 libraries).

**MAGAZINES NEEDS** Accepts e-mail submissions only; no print submissions; print submissions will be returned unread. Detailed submission instructions appear on the website along with writer's guidelines. Has published poetry by William Stafford, Sharon Olds, Carolyn Kizer, A.R. Ammons, and Claudia Emerson. Has also published many other well-known poets, as well as numerous new and emerging poets. Pays 2 contributor copies.

**ALSO OFFERS** Reviews books of poetry in 4,000 words maximum, single- or multibook format. Query for reviews.

**TIPS** "We are usually not interested in obscure or abstract poetry, concrete poetry, or prose poems. We favor image-based narrative and lyric poetry that is accessible and meaningful without being simplistic, sophisticated without being pretentious. We publish both free verse and formal poems; for samples, see our website. Writers of poetry should first be readers of poetry. Subscribers receive expedited editorial decisions on their submissions."

## TEARS IN THE FENCE

Portman Lodge, Durweston, Blandford Forum, Dorset DT11 0QA, England. **E-mail:** tearsinthefence@ gmail.com. **Website:** tearsinthefence.com. *Tears in the Fence*, published 2 times/year, is a "small-press magazine of poetry, fiction, interviews, essays, and reviews. We are open to a wide variety of poetic styles and work that shows social and poetic awareness whilst prompting close and divergent readings. However, we like to publish a variety of work." Time between acceptance and publication is 3 months. Sample copy: $13. Subscription: $60/3 (£40/3) issues.

*Tears in the Fence* is 176 pages, A5, digitally printed on 110-gms. paper, perfect-bound, with matte card cover. Press run is 600.

**MAGAZINES NEEDS** Send books for review to Ian Brinton, Brescia House, 2 Capel Road, Faversham, Kent, ME13 8RL, England. Submit poetry via e-mail as attachment. Has published Aidan Semmens, Hannah Silva, Jennifer K. Dick, Pansy Maurer-Alvarez, Carrie Etter, Nathaniel Tarn, Chris McCabe, Sheila E. Murphy, Robert Vas Dias, and Sarah Crewe. Length: open. Pays 1 contributor copy.

**ALSO OFFERS** The magazine runs a regular series of readings in Dorset and an annual international literary festival.

## TERRAIN.ORG: A JOURNAL OF THE BUILT + NATURAL ENVIROMENTS

Terrain.org, P.O. Box 19161, Tucson AZ 85731-9161. **E-mail:** contact2@terrain.org. **Website:** www.terrain. org. Reviews Editor address: P.O. Box 51332, Irvine CA 92619-1332.. **Contact:** Simmons B. Buntin, editor in chief. *Terrain.org* is based on, and thus welcomes quality submissions from, new and experienced authors and artists alike. Our online journal accepts only the finest poetry, essays, fiction, articles, artwork, and other contributions' material that reaches deep into the earth's fiery core, or humanity's incalculable core, and brings forth new insights and wisdom. *Terrain.org* is searching for that interface—the integration among the built and natural environments, that might be called the soul of place. The works contained within *Terrain.org* ultimately examine the physical realm around us and how those environments influence us and each other physically, mentally, emotionally, and spiritually." Acquires one-time rights. Sends galleys to author. Publication is copyrighted. Publishes mss 5 weeks-18 months after acceptance. Responds in 2 weeks to queries; in 4 months to mss. Sometimes comments on/critiques rejected mss. Guidelines online.

**MAGAZINES NEEDS** Accepts submissions online at sub.terrain.org. Include brief bio. Send complete ms with cover letter. No erotica. Length: open.

**TIPS** "We have 3 primary criteria in reviewing fiction: (1) The story is compelling and well crafted. (2) The story provides some element of surprise; whether in content, form, or delivery we are unexpectedly delighted in what we've read. (3) The story meets an upcoming theme, even if only peripherally. Read fiction in the current issue and perhaps some archived work, and if you like what you read—and our overall enviromental slant—then send us your best work. Make sure you follow our submission guidelines (including cover note with bio), and that your mss is as error-free as possible."

## TEXAS POETRY CALENDAR

Dos Gatos Press, 6452 Kola Ct. NW, Albuquerque NM 87120-4285. (505)433-4437. **E-mail:** editors@dosgatospress.org; managingeditor@dosgatospress.org. **E-mail:** dosgatospress.submittable.com/submit. **Website:** www.dosgatospress.org. **Contact:** Scott Wiggerman and David Meischen, publishers. *Texas Poetry Calendar*, published annually in July, features a "week-by-week calendar side-by-side with poems with a Texas connection." Wants "a wide variety of styles, voices, and forms, including rhyme, though a Texas connection is preferred. Humor is welcome! Poetry only!" Does not want "children's poetry, erotic poetry, profanity, obscure poems, previously published work, or poems over 35 lines." Publishes 1-2 months after acceptance. Sample copy: $14.95 plus $3 shipping. Make checks payable to Dos Gatos Press.

○ *Texas Poetry Calendar* is about 144 pages, digest-sized, offset-printed, spiral-bound, with full-color cardstock cover. Receives about 600 poems/year, accepts about 80-85. Press run is 1,000; 80-85 distributed free to contributors. Reads submissions January-May.

**MAGAZINES NEEDS** Submit 3 poems through Submittable: dosgatospress.submittable.com/submit. No fax, e-mail, or snail mail submissions; only electronic submissions via Submittable. Cover letter is required. "Include a short bio (100-200 words) and poem titles in cover letter. Also include e-mail address and phone number. Do not include poet's name on

the poems themselves!" Never comments on rejected poems, but nominates poems for Pushcart Prizes each year. Deadline: January 15 (postmark). Length: up to 35 lines/poem, "including spaces and title."

## ○ TEXAS REVIEW

Texas Review Press, Department of English, Sam Houston State University, Box 2146, Huntsville TX 77341-2146. (936)294 1992. **Fax:** (936)294-3070. **E-mail:** eng_pdr@shsu.edu; cww006@shsu.edu. **Website:** www.shsu.edu/~www_trp. **Contact:** Dr. Paul Ruffin, editor/director; Greg Bottoms, essay editor; Eric Miles Williamson, fiction editor; Nick Lantz, poetry editor. "We publish top-quality poetry, fiction, articles, interviews, and reviews for a general audience." Semiannual. Pays on publication for first North American serial, one-time rights. Sends galleys to author. Publishes ms 6-12 months after acceptance. Responds in 2 weeks to queries; 3-6 months to mss. Sometimes comments on rejected mss. Sample copy: $5. Guidelines available on website: texasreview.submittable.com/submit.

**MAGAZINES NEEDS** No previously published poems or simultaneous submissions. Include SASE. Reads submissions September 1-April 30 only. Seldom comments on rejected poems. Pays one-year subscription and 1 contributor copy (may request more).

**ALSO OFFERS** Sponsors the X.J. Kennedy Poetry Prize (for best full-length book of poetry), the Robert Phillips Poetry Chapbook Prize (for best poetry chapbook), the George Garrett Fiction Prize (for best book of stories or short novel), and the Clay Reynolds Novella Prize (for best novella.) Publication of winning mss and 50 copies of book. **Entry fee:** $20.

## ○ ⊘ THEMA

Thema Literary Society, P.O. Box 8747, Metairie LA 70011-8747. **E-mail:** thema@cox.net. **Website:** http://themaliterarysociety.com. **Contact:** Gail Howard, poetry editor. "*THEMA* is designed to stimulate creative thinking by challenging writers with unusual themes, such as 'Golden Isn't Silent' and 'Lost in the Zoo.' Appeals to writers, teachers of creative writing, and general reading audience." Acquires one-time rights. Pays on acceptance. Publishes ms, on average, within 6 months after acceptance. Responds in 1 week to queries. Responds in 5 months to mss. Sample $15 U.S./$25 foreign. Upcoming themes and guidelines available in magazine, for SASE, by e-mail, or on website.

○ *THEMA* is 100 pages, digest-sized professionally printed, with glossy card cover. Receives about 400 poems/year, accepts about 8%. Press run is 400 (230 subscribers, 30 libraries). Subscription: $30 U.S./$40 foreign. Has published poetry by Beverly Boyd, John Grey, James Penha and Matthew J. Spireng.

**MAGAZINES NEEDS** All poems must relate to one of *THEMA*'s upcoming themes (**indicate the target theme on submission of manuscript**). See website for themes. Submit up to 3 poems at a time. Include SASE. "All submissions should be typewritten on standard $8\frac{1}{2}$x11 paper. Submissions are accepted all year, but evaluated after specified deadlines." Specify target theme. Editor comments on submissions. "Each issue is based on an unusual premise. Please send SASE for guidelines before submitting poetry to find out the upcoming themes." Does not want "scatologic language, explicit love poetry." 1 - 3 pages Pays $10/poem and 1 contributor copy.

## ◐○ THICK WITH CONVICTION

**E-mail:** twczine@gmail.com. **Website:** twczine.blogspot.com/. **Contact:** Danielle Masters, Sara Blanton-Allison, Kristina Marie Blanton. *Thick With Conviction*, published biannually online, is "looking for fresh and exciting voices in poetry. I don't want to take a nap while I'm reading, so grab my attention, make me sit up and catch my breath." Wants all genres of poetry, "poems that make me exhale a deep sigh after reading them. Basically, if I can't feel the words in front of me, I'm not going to be happy. I'd like to see new and cutting-edge poets who think outside the box, but still know how to keep things from getting too strange and inaccessible." Does not want "teen angst poems, religious poems, or greeting card tripe." Has published poetry by Kendall A. Bell, April Michelle Bratten, Kristina Marie Darling, James H. Duncan, Paul Hostovsky, and Kelsey Upward. Receives about 300 poems/year, accepts about 15%. Never comments on rejected poems. Acquires one-time rights. Rights revert to poet upon publication. Publishes ms 3 months after acceptance. Responds in "roughly 2-3 months." Guidelines available on website.

**MAGAZINES NEEDS** Submit 3-5 poems at a time. Lines/poem: no limit. Considers previously published poems; no simultaneous submissions. Accepts e-mail submissions (pasted into body of message; "any attachments will be deleted"); no disk submissions.

Cover letter and bio is required. Reads submissions year round.

## ◑ THINK JOURNAL

Western State Colorado University, Taylor Hall 222B Western State Colorado University, 600 N Adams St., Gunnison CO 81231. (970)943-2058. **E-mail:** drothman@western.edu; susandelaneyspear@msn.com. **Website:** www.western.edu/academics/graduate-programs/master-fine-arts-creative-writing/think-journal. **Contact:** Susan Spear, managing editor. *Think Journal*, established in 2008 by Christine Yurick, was acquired by the Graduate Program in Creative Writing at Western State Colorado University in 2013. *Think* publishes twice yearly and focuses metered, rhymed poems, in received or nonce forms, or free verse with a clear organizing principle. The language we admire in poetry and in prose is both intellectually precise and emotionally rich. We welcome work from both established and emerging poets. Responds in 2-4 weeks to queries. Editorial lead time 6 months. Yearly subscription: $15. Contact the webpage on Western's site at www.western.edu. Direct any questions to Susan Spear, managing editor, at susandelaneyspear@msn.com.

**MAGAZINES NEEDS** Submit up to 5 poems on think-journal.submittable.com/submit. Pays 1 contributor copy.

## THIRD COAST

Western Michigan University, English Dept., 1903 W. Michigan Ave., Kalamazoo MI 49008-5331. **Website:** www.thirdcoastmagazine.com. David Greendonner. **Contact:** S.Marie LaFata-Clay, editor in chief. "*Third Coast* publishes poetry, fiction (including traditional and experimental fiction, shorts, and novel excerpts, but not genre fiction), creative nonfiction (including reportage, essay, memoir, and fragments), drama, and translations." Acquires first North American serial rights. Publishes ms an average of 6 months after acceptance. Responds in 4 months to queries and mss. Sample copy: $6 (back issue). Make checks payable to *Third Coast*. Guidelines online at www.thirdcoastmagazine.com/submit.*Third Coast* only accepts submissions submitted to its online submission manager. All hard copy submissions will be returned unread.

○ *Third Coast* is 176 pages, digest-sized, professionally printed, perfect-bound, with 4-color cover with art. Reads mss from September through December of each year.

**MAGAZINES NEEDS** Has published poetry by Marianne Boruch, Terence Hayes, Alex Lemon, Philip Levine, David Shumate, Tomz Salamun, and Jean Valentine. Submit up to 5 poems via online submissions manager. No simple narratives or any simplistic poetry. Pays 2 contributor copies and 1-year subscription.

**ALSO OFFERS** Sponsors an annual poetry contest. First Prize: $1,000 and publication. Guidelines available on website. **Entry fee:** $16, includes 1-year subscription to *Third Coast*.

**TIPS** "We will consider many different types of fiction and favor those exhibiting a freshness of vision and approach."

## THE THREEPENNY REVIEW

P.O. Box 9131, Berkeley CA 94709. (510)849-4545. **E-mail:** wlesser@threepennyreview.com. **Website:** www.threepennyreview.com. **Contact:** Wendy Lesser, editor. "We are a general-interest, national literary magazine with coverage of politics, the visual arts, and the performing arts." Reading period: January 1-June 30. Buys first North American serial rights. Pays on acceptance. Publishes ms an average of 1 year after acceptance. Responds in 1 month to queries; in 2 months to mss. Sample copy: $12, or online. Guidelines online.

**MAGAZINES NEEDS** No poems without capital letters or poems without a discernible subject. Length: up to 100 lines/poem. Pays $200.

**TIPS** Nonfiction (political articles, memoirs, reviews) is most open to freelancers.

## TIMBER JOURNAL

**E-mail:** timberjournal@gmail.com. **Website:** www.timberjournal.com. *Timber* is a literary journal, run by students in the MFA program at the University of Colorado Boulder, dedicated to the promotion of innovative literature. Publishes work that explores the boundaries of poetry, fiction, creative nonfiction, and digital literatures. Produces both an online journal that explores the potentials of the digital medium and an annual print anthology. Responds in 2-3 months to mss. Guidelines online.

○ Reading period: August-March (submit just once during this time). Staff changes regularly; see website for current staff members.

**MAGAZINES NEEDS** Submit up to 6 poems in single document via online submissions manager. Include 30-50 word bio. Pays 1 contributor copy.

**TIPS** "We are looking for innovative poetry, fiction, creative nonfiction, and digital lit (screenwriting, digital poetry, multimedia lit, etc.)."

## TIME OF SINGING: A JOURNAL OF CHRISTIAN POETRY

Wind & Water Press, P.O. Box 5276, Conneaut Lake PA 16316. **E-mail:** timesing@zoominternet.net. **E-mail:** timesing@zoominternet.net. **Website:** www.timeofsinging.com. **Contact:** Lora Homan Zill, editor. "*Time of Singing* publishes Christian poetry in the widest sense but prefers literary type. Welcomes forms, fresh rhyme, well-crafted free verse. Likes writers who take chances, who have the courage to wrestle with faith and spiritual issues and not have to provide answers or tie everything up neatly. Especially appreciate writers who stay away from religious jargon and trite imagery. Acquires first North American serial rights, one-time rights, second serial (reprint) rights. Publishes ms within 1 year of acceptance. Responds in 3 months to mss. Editorial lead time 6 months. Sample copy: $4 each or 2 for $7 (postage paid). Subscription: $18 U.S., $21 Canada, $30 overseas. Guidelines for SASE or on website.

○ *TOS* is 44 pages, digest-sized, digitally printed. Receives more than 800 submissions/year, accepts about 175. Press run is 250 (150 subscribers).

**MAGAZINES NEEDS** Wants free verse and well-crafted rhyme; would like to see more forms. Accepts e-mail submissions (pasted into body of message or as attachment). Poems should be single-spaced. Comments "with suggestions for improvement if close to publication." *TOS* has published poets from the U.S., Canada, England, South Africa, Mexico, New Zealand, Scotland, Russia, Australia, Germany, Slovakia, Albania, and Ireland. Has published poetry by John Grey, Luci Shaw, Bob Hostetler, Tony Cosier, Barbara Crooker, and Charles Waugaman. Does not want "collections of uneven lines, sermons that rhyme, greeting card type poetry, unstructured 'prayers,' and trite sing-song rhymes." Length: 3-60 lines. Pays 1 contributor copy and the opportunity to purchase more at the contributor's rate.

**ALSO OFFERS** Sponsors theme contests for specific issues. Guidelines available for SASE, by e-mail, or on website.

**TIPS** "Read widely and study the craft. You need more than feelings and religious jargon to make it into *TOS*.

It's helpful to get honest critiques of your work. A cover letter is not necessary. Your poems speak for themselves."

## TIN HOUSE

McCormack Communications, P.O. Box 10500, Portland OR 97296. (503)219-0622. **E-mail:** info@tinhouse.com. **Website:** www.tinhouse.com. **Contact:** Cheston Knapp, managing editor; Holly MacArthur, founding editor. "We are a general-interest literary quarterly. Our watchword is quality. Our audience includes people interested in literature in all its aspects, from the mundane to the exalted." Buys first North American serial rights, anthology rights. Pays on publication. Publishes ms an average of 6 months after acceptance. Responds in 6 weeks to queries; in 4 months to mss. Editorial lead time 6 months. Sample copy: $15. Guidelines online.

 Reading period: September 1-May 31.

**MAGAZINES NEEDS** Submit via online submissions manager or postal mail. Include cover letter. Pays $50-150.

## TOASTED CHEESE

**E-mail:** editors@toasted-cheese.com. **E-mail:** submit@toasted-cheese.com. **Website:** www.toasted-cheese.com. *Toasted Cheese* accepts submissions of previously unpublished fiction, flash fiction, creative nonfiction, poetry, and book reviews. See site for book review requirements and guidelines. "Our focus is on quality of work, not quantity. Some issues will therefore contain fewer or more pieces than previous issues. We don't restrict publication based on subject matter. We encourage submissions from innovative writers in all genres and actively seek diverse voices." Acquires electronic rights. Final acceptances are sent quarterly, approximately one month before each issue publishes. Responds in 4 months or less. Sample copy online. Follow submission guidelines at our website; see site for submission guidelines and samples of what Toasted Cheese publishes

 No simultaneous submissions. Be mindful that final notification of acceptance or rejection may take four months. No chapters or excerpts unless they read as a stand-alone story. No first drafts.

**MAGAZINES NEEDS** See site for submission guidelines and samples of what Toasted Cheese publishes. We don't publish poetry that is rhyming, sen-

timental, or non-specific. Toasted Cheese is a non-paying market.

**TIPS** "We are looking for clean, professional work from writers and poets of any experience level. Accepted stories and poems will be concise and compelling with a strong voice. We're looking for writers who are serious about the craft: tomorrow's literary stars before they're famous. Take your submission seriously, yet remember that levity is appreciated. See site for submission guidelines and samples of what Toasted Cheese publishes."

## TORCH LITERARY ARTS

TORCH: Creative Writing by Black Women, 3720 Gattis School Rd., Suite 800, Round Rock TX 78664. **E-mail:** torchliteraryarts@gmail.com. **E-mail:** torchliteraryarts@gmail.com. **Website:** www.torchliteraryarts.org. **Contact:** Amanda Johnston, founder/editor. *TORCH: Creative Writing by Black Women* , published semiannually online, provides "a place to publish contemporary poetry, prose, and short stories by experienced and emerging writers alike. We prefer our contributors to take risks, and offer a diverse body of work that examines and challenges preconceived notions regarding race, ethnicity, gender roles, and identity." Has published poetry by Sharon Bridgforth, Patricia Smith, Crystal Wilkinson, Tayari Jones, and Natasha Trethewey. Reads submissions April 15-August 31 only. Sometimes comments on rejected poems. Always sends prepublication galleys. No payment. "Within *TORCH*, we offer a special section called Flame that features an interview, biography, and work sample by an established writer as well as an introduction to their Spark—an emerging writer who inspires them and adds to the boundless voice of creative writing by Black women." A free online newsletter is available; see website. Acquires rights to publish accepted work in online issue and in archives. Rights revert to authors upon publication. Publishes ms 2-7 months after acceptance. Guidelines available on website.

## TRANSFERENCE

Department of World Languages and Literatures at Western Michigan University, 1903 West Michigan Ave., Kalamazoo MI 49008-5338. **E-mail:** lang-transference@wmich.edu. **E-mail:** molly.lynde-recchia@wmich.edu; david.kutzko@wmich.edu. **Website:** scholarworks.wmich.edu/transference. David Kutzko, Jenaba D. Waggy. **Contact:** Molly Lynde-Recchia and David Kutzko, editors. Annual literary magazine. Publishes poetry from Arabic, Chinese, French and Old French, German, Classical Greek and Latin, Japanese, and Russian into English, along with short reflections on the art of translation and the choices and challenges involved with the process. Retains first North American serial rights and electronic rights. Does not offer payment. Publishes ms 4-8 months after acceptance. Responds in 3-8 months to mss; 1 month to queries. Editorial lead time is 6 months. Sample copy online, or send SASE and $10. Guidelines online.

**MAGAZINES NEEDS** Poetry must be a translation from another language into English. No minimum or maximum line length. Does not pay.

**TIPS** "Submitting poets should have a good knowledge of the source language of their poetry and should include a short discussion of their translation approach. Authors are responsible for obtaining permission to publish their translation from the original poem's author. Please see previous issues for an understanding of what we publish."

## TRIQUARTERLY

School of Professional Studies, Northwestern University, 339 E. Chicago Ave., Chicago IL 60611. **E-mail:** triquarterly@northwestern.edu. **Website:** www.triquarterly.org. **Contact:** Adrienne Gunn, managing editor. *TriQuarterly*, the literary magazine of Northwestern University, welcomes submissions of fiction, creative nonfiction, poetry, short drama, and hybrid work. "We also welcome short-short prose pieces." Reading period: October 15-May 1.

**MAGAZINES NEEDS** Submit up to 6 poems via online submissions manager. Pays honoraria.

**TIPS** "We are especially interested in work that embraces the world and continues, however subtly, the ongoing global conversation about culture and society that *TriQuarterly* pursued from its beginning in 1964."

## TULANE REVIEW

Tulane University, Suite G08A Lavin-Bernick Center, Tulane University, New Orleans LA 70118. **E-mail:** litsoc@tulane.edu. **Website:** www.tulane.edu/~litsoc/index.html. *Tulane Review*, published biannually, is a national literary journal seeking quality submissions of prose, poetry, and art. Acquires first North American serial rights, second serial rights. Single copy: $8; subscription: $15. Make checks payable to *Tulane Review*. Guidelines online.

**MAGAZINES NEEDS** Considers all types of poetry. Wants imaginative poems with bold, inventive images. Receives about 1,200 poems/year, accepts about 50 per issue. Has published poetry by Tom Chandler, Ace Boggess, Carol Hamilton, and Brady Rhoades. Submit up to 5 poems via online submissions manager. No longer accepts paper and e-mail submissions. Pays 2 contributor copies.

## TULE REVIEW

P.O. Box 160406, Sacramento CA 95816. (916)451-5569. **E-mail:** info@sacpoetrycenter@gmail.com. **Website:** www.tulereview.com. **Contact:** Frank Dixon Graham, editor in chief; Linda Collins, associate editor; Connie Gutowsky, associate editor. *Tule Review*, published 1-2 times/year, uses "poetry, book reviews, and essays concerning contemporary poetry" Acquires first North American serial rights. Publishes ms 1-6 months after acceptance. Responds in 3-4 monts. Guidelines and upcoming themes available by e-mail or on website.

○ *Tule Review* accepts poetry and cover art submissions on a rolling basis, from May 1 to April 30. All material should be submitted through Submittable.com.

**MAGAZINES NEEDS** Submit up to 3 poems at a time using online submission form. Provide short, 5 line bio. Reads submissions year round. Wants "all styles and forms of poetry." Primarily publishes poets living in the greater Sacramento area, but accepts work from anywhere. Length: 96 lines maximum. Pays 1 contributor copy.

## ☻ URTHONA MAGAZINE

Old Abbey House, Abbey Rd., Cambridge CB5 8HQ, UK. +44 (0) 774 499384. **E-mail:** urthonamag@gmail.com. **Website:** www.urthona.com. **Contact:** Ambrose Gilson. *Urthona*, published anually, explores the arts and Western culture from a Buddhist perspective. Wants "poetry rousing the imagination." Does not want "undigested autobiography, political, or New Age-y poems." Acquires one-time rights. Publishes ms 8 months after acceptance. Responds in 6 months. Sample copy (including guidelines): $7.99 USD, $8.99 CAD. "See website for current subscription rates."

○ *Urthona* is 60 pages, A4, offset-printed, saddle-stapled, with 4-color glossy cover; includes ads. Receives about 300 poems/year, accepts about 40. Press run is 1,200 (200 subscribers, plus shelf sales in Australia and America).

**MAGAZINES NEEDS** Submit up to 6 poems at a time. Accepts e-mail submissions (as attachment). Cover letter is preferred. Poems are circulated to an editorial board and are read and selected by poetry editor. Other editors have right of veto. Has published poetry by Peter Abbs, Robert Bly, and Peter Redgrove. Pays 1 contributor copy.

**ALSO OFFERS** Reviews books/chapbooks of poetry and other magazines in 600 words. Send materials for review consideration.

## U.S. 1 WORKSHEETS

U.S. 1 Poets' Cooperative, U.S. 1 Worksheets, P.O. Box 127, Kingston NJ 08528. **E-mail:** us1poets@gmail.com. **Website:** www.us1poets.com. "*U.S. 1 Worksheets*, published annually, uses high-quality poetry and prose poems. We prefer complex, well-written work." Responds in 3-6 months to mss. Guidelines online.

**MAGAZINES NEEDS** Submit up to 5 poems at a time, no more than 7 pages total. Considers simultaneous submissions if indicated; no previously published poems. "We are looking for well-crafted poetry with a focused point of view."

**ADDITIONAL INFORMATION** The U.S. 1 Poets' Cooperative co-sponsors (with the Delaware Valley Poets) a series of monthly poetry readings at the Princeton Public Library. "The group is open to poets who want to share their original work and receive feedback."

**TIPS** "Mss are accepted from April 15-June 30 and are read by rotating editors from the cooperative. Send us something unusual, something we haven't read before, but make sure it's poetry. Proofread carefully."

## U.S. CATHOLIC

Claretian Publications, 205 W. Monroe St., Chicago IL 60606. (312)236-7782. **Fax:** (312)236-8207. **E-mail:** literaryeditor@uscatholic.org. **E-mail:** submissions@uscatholic.org. **Website:** www.uscatholic.org. "*U.S. Catholic* puts faith in the context of everyday life. With a strong focus on social justice, we offer a fresh and balanced take on the issues that matter most in our world, adding a faith perspective to such challenges as poverty, education, family life, the environment, and even pop culture." Buys all rights. Pays on acceptance. Publishes ms an average of 6 months after acceptance. Responds in 1 month to queries; in 2 months to mss. Editorial lead time 8 months. Guidelines on website.

Please include SASE with written ms.

**MAGAZINES NEEDS** Submit 3-5 poems at a time. Accepts e-mail submissions (pasted into body of message or as attachments). Cover letter is preferred. No light verse. Length: up to 50 lines/poem. Pays $75.

## VALLUM: CONTEMPORARY POETRY

5038 Sherbrooke West, P.O. Box 23077, CP Vendome, Montreal Quebec H4A 1T0, Canada. **E-mail:** info@vallummag.com; editors@vallummag.com. **Website:** www.vallummag.com. **Contact:** Joshua Auerbach and Eleni Zisimatos, editors. Poetry/fine arts magazine published twice/year. Publishes exciting interplay of poets and artists. Content for magazine is selected according to themes listed on website. Material is not filed but is returned upon request by SASE. E-mail response is preferred. Seeking exciting, unpublished, traditional or avant-garde poetry that reflects contemporary experience. Buys first North American serial rights. Copyright remains with the author. Pays on publication. Sample copy online. Guidelines available on website.

**MAGAZINES NEEDS** Pays honorarium for accepted poems.

**ADDITIONAL INFORMATION** "The Vallum Chapbook Series publishes 2-3 chapbooks by both well-known and emerging poets. Past editions include *Gospel of X* by George Elliott Clarke, *The Art of Fugue* by Jan Zwicky and *Address* by Franz Wright. *Vallum* does not currently accept unsolicited mss for this project."

**CONTEST/AWARD OFFERINGS** "Sponsors annual contest. First Prize: $750, Second Prize: $250 and publication in an issue of *Vallum*. Honourable mentions may be selected but are not eligible for cash prizes. Submit 3 poems. Entry fee: $25 U.S. / CAD (includes subscription to *Vallum*). Deadline: July 15. Guidelines available in magazine, by e-mail, and on website. Poems may be submitted in any style or on any subject; max. 3 poems, up to 60 lines per poem. Entries should be labelled 'Vallum Contest' and submitted online or by regular mail. Submissions are not returned. Winners will be notified via e-mail."

## VALPARAISO POETRY REVIEW

Valparaiso Poetry Review, Department of English, Valparaiso University, Valparaiso IN 46383-6493. (219)464-5278. **Fax:** (219)464-5511. **E-mail:** vpr@valpo.edu. **Website:** www.valpo.edu/vpr. **Contact:** Edward Byrne, editor. *Valparaiso Poetry Review: Contemporary Poetry and Poetics*, published semiannually online, accepts "submissions of unpublished poetry, book reviews, author interviews, and essays on poetry or poetics that have not yet appeared online and for which the rights belong to the author. Query for anything else." Acquires one-time rights. "All rights remain with author." Publishes ms 6-12 months after acceptance. Responds in 6 weeks. Guidelines online.

**MAGAZINES NEEDS** Wants poetry of any length or style, free verse, or traditional forms. Submit 3-5 poems at a time. Accepts e-mail submissions only. Reads submissions year round. Seldom comments on rejected poems. Receives about 9,000 poems/year, accepts about 1%. Has published poetry by Charles Wright, Cornelius Eady, Dorianne Laux, Dave Smith, Claudia Emerson, Billy Collins, Brian Turner, Daisy Fried, Stanley Plumly, and Annie Finch.

**ALSO OFFERS** Reviews books of poetry in single- and multibook formats. Send materials for review consideration.

### 🟣 VAN GOGH'S EAR: BEST WORLD POETRY & PROSE

French Connection Press, 12 Rue Lamartine, Paris 75009, France. (33)(1)4016-1147. **E-mail:** tinafayeayres@gmail.com. **Website:** www.frenchcx.com/press; theoriginalvangoghsearanthology.com. *Van Gogh's Ear*, published annually in April, is an anthology series "devoted to publishing powerful poetry and prose in English and English translations by major voices and innovative new talents from around the globe." Acquires one-time rights. Time between acceptance and publication is 1 year. Responds in 9 months. Seldom comments on rejections. Always sends prepublication galleys. Single copy: $19; subscription: $36 for 2 years. Guidelines available in anthology or on website. "Every submission is closely read by all members of the editorial board and voted upon. Our continued existence, and continued ability to read your work, depends mainly on subscriptions/donations. Therefore, we must ask that you at least purchase a sample copy before submitting work."

🖥 *Van Gogh's Ear* is 280 pages, digest-sized, offset-printed, perfect-bound, with 4-color matte cover with commissioned artwork. Poetry published in *Van Gogh's Ear* has appeared in *The Best American Poetry.*

**MAGAZINES NEEDS** Receives about 1,000 poems/year, accepts about 30%. Press run is 2,000 (105 subscribers, 25 libraries, 1,750 shelf/online sales); 120 distributed free to contributors and reviewers. Has published poetry by Tony Curtis, Yoko Ono, James Dean, Xaviera Hollander, and Charles Manson. Submit up to 6 poems by e-mail. Cover letter is preferred, along with a brief bio of up to 120 words. Length: up to 165 lines/poem. Pays 1 contributor copy.

**TIPS** "As a 501(c)(3) nonprofit enterprise, *Van Gogh's Ear* needs the support of individual poets, writers, and readers to survive. Any donation, large or small, will help *Van Gogh's Ear* continue to publish the best cross-section of contemporary poetry and prose. Because of being an anglophone publication based in France, *Van Gogh's Ear* is unable to get any grants or funding. Your contribution will be tax-deductible. Make donation checks payable to Committee on Poetry-VGE, and mail them (donations **only**) to the Allen Ginsberg Trust, P.O. Box 582, Stuyvesant Station, New York NY 10009."

### 🟣💲 VANILLEROTICA LITERARY EZINE

Cleveland OH 44102. (216)799-9775. **E-mail:** talentdripseroticpublishing@yahoo.com. **Website:** eroticatalentdrips.wordpress.com. **Contact:** Kimberly Steele, founder. *Vanillerotica*, published monthly online, focuses solely on showcasing new erotic fiction. Acquires electronic rights only. Rights revert to authors and poets upon publication. Work archived on the site for 2 months. Time between acceptance and publication is 2 months. Responds to general and submission queries within a week. Guidelines available on website.

**MAGAZINES NEEDS** Submit by e-mail to talentdripseroticpublishing@yahoo.com. Accepts e-mail pasted into body of message. Reads submissions during publication months only. Length: up to 30 lines/poem. Pays $10 for each accepted poem.

**CONTEST/AWARD OFFERINGS** *Vanillerotica Literary EZine* Poet of the Year Contest is held annually. **Prizes:** $75 1st place, $50 2nd place, and certificate. **Deadline:** November 25. Guidelines on website.

**TIPS** "Please read our take on the difference between *erotica* and *pornography*; it's on the website. *Vanillerotica* does not accept pornography. And please keep poetry 30 lines or less."

### VEGETARIAN JOURNAL

P.O. Box 1463, Baltimore MD 21203-1463. (410)366-8343. **E-mail:** vrg@vrg.org. **Website:** www.vrg.org. **Contact:** Debra Wasserman, editor. Quarterly nonprofit vegetarian magazine that examines the health, ecological and ethical aspects of vegetarianism. "Highly-educated audience including health professionals." Sample copy: $4.

○ *Vegetarian Journal* is 36 pages, magazine-sized, professionally printed, saddle-stapled, with glossy card cover. Press run is 20,000.

**MAGAZINES NEEDS** "Please, no submissions of poetry from adults; 18 and under only."

**CONTEST/AWARD OFFERINGS** The Vegetarian Resource Group offers an annual contest for ages 18 and under: $50 prize in 3 age categories for the best contribution on any aspect of vegetarianism. "Most entries are essay, but we would accept poetry with enthusiasm." **Deadline:** May 1 (postmark). Details available at website: http://www.vrg.org/essay/

**TIPS** Areas most open to freelancers are recipe section and feature articles. "Review magazine first to learn our style. Send query letter with photocopy sample of line drawings of food."

### ●○ VERANDAH LITERARY & ART JOURNAL

Faculty of Arts, Deakin University, 221 Burwood Hwy., Burwood, Victoria 3125, Australia. (61)(3)9251-7134. E-mail: verandah@deakin.edu.au. **Website:** verandahjournal.wordpress.com/. *Verandah*, published annually in August, is a high-quality literary journal edited by professional writing students. It aims to give voice to new and innovative writers and artists. Acquires first Australian publishing rights. Sample: $20 AUD. Guidelines available on website.

○ Submission period: February 1 through June 5. Has published work by Christos Tsiolka, Dorothy Porter, Seamus Heaney, Les Murray, Ed Burger, and John Muk Muk Burke. *Verandah* is 120 pages, professionally printed on glossy stock, flat-spined, with full-color glossy card cover.

**MAGAZINES NEEDS** Submit by mail or e-mail. However, electronic version of work must be available if accepted by *Verandah*. Do not submit work without the required submission form (available for download on website). Reads submissions by June 5 deadline (postmark). Length: 100 lines maximum. Pays 1 contributor copy, "with prizes awarded accordingly."

### VERSE

English Department, University of Richmond, Richmond VA 23173. **Website:** versemag.blogspot.com. **Contact:** Brian Henry, co-editor; Andrew Zawacki,

co-editor. *Verse*, published 3 times/year, is an international poetry journal which also publishes interviews with poets, essays on poetry, and book reviews. Wants no specific kind; looks for high-quality, innovative poetry. Focus is not only on American poetry, but on all poetry written in English, as well as translations. Has published poetry by James Tate, John Ashbery, Barbara Guest, Gustaf Sobin, and Rae Armantrout. Guidelines online.

○ *Verse* is 128-416 pages, digest-sized, professionally printed, perfect-bound, with card cover. Receives about 5,000 poems/year, accepts 10%. Press run is 1,000. Single copy: $10; subscription: $15 for individuals, $39 for institutions. Sample: $6. *Verse* has a $10 reading fee for the print edition. Note that *Verse* will sometimes publish individual pieces on the website if they decide not to publish the entire body of work.

**MAGAZINES NEEDS** Submissions should be chapbook-length (20-40 pages). Pays $10/page, $250 minimum.

**TIPS** "Read widely and deeply. Avoid inundating a magazine with submissions; constant exposure will not increase your chances of getting accepted."

### ⑤ VINE LEAVES PRESS

E-mail: vineleaves.editors@gmail.com. **Website:** www.vineleavespress.com. **Contact:** Jessica Bell, publisher; Dawn Ius, senior editor. In late 2011, Australian award-winning author, poet, and singer/songwriter Jessica Bell and author/screenwriter Dawn Ius founded *Vine Leaves Literary Journal* to offer the vignette, a forgotten literary form, the exposure and credit it deserves. Submissions are open on a rolling basis year round and they accept unsolicited manuscripts. Rights remain with the author for *Vine Leaves Literary Journal* publications. Print and e-Book rights are acquired for book publications with Vine Leaves Press. See website for more details. Publishes 3-12 months after acceptance. Responds in 1-6 months. Editorial lead time 3 months. Sample copy and guidelines online. See website for payment rates. See website.

○ Visit the website for submission guidelines as guidelines are different for the journal and the press.

**MAGAZINES NEEDS** Length: up to 40 lines.

**TIPS** Please see guidelines on websites: www.vineleavespress.com, www.vineleavesliteraryjournal.com.

## 💲 THE VIRGINIA QUARTERLY REVIEW

VQR, P.O. Box 400223, Charlottesville VA 22904. E-mail: editors@vqronline.org. **Website:** www.vqronline.org. **Contact:** Allison Wright, managing editor. "*VQR*'s primary mission has been to sustain and strengthen Jefferson's bulwark, long describing itself as 'A National Journal of Literature and Discussion.' And for good reason. From its inception in prohibition, through depression and war, in prosperity and peace, *The Virginia Quarterly Review* has been a haven—and home—for the best essayists, fiction writers, and poets, seeking contributors from every section of the United States and abroad. It has not limited itself to any special field. No topic has been alien: literary, public affairs, the arts, history, the economy. If it could be approached through essay or discussion, poetry or prose, *VQR* has covered it." Press run is 4,000. Buys first North American print and digital magazine rights, nonexclusive online rights, and other limited rights. Responds in 3 months to mss. Guidelines available on website.

**MAGAZINES NEEDS** Sponsors the Emily Clark Balch Prize for Poetry, an annual award of $1,000 given to the best poem or group of poems published in the *Review* during the year. *The Virginia Quarterly Review* prints approximately 12 pages of poetry in each issue. No length or subject restrictions. Issues have largely included lyric and narrative free verse, most of which features a strong message or powerful voice. Accepts online submissions only at virginiaquarterlyreview.submittable.com/submit. Pays $200/poem.

## VISIONS-INTERNATIONAL

Black Buzzard Press, 3503 Ferguson Lane, Austin TX 78754. **E-mail:** vias.poetry@gmail.com. **Website:** visions2010.wordpress.com. Buys first North American serial rights. Pays on publication. Publishes ms an average of 6 months after acceptance. Responds in 3 weeks to queries. Responds in 2 months to mss. Editorial lead time 1 month. Sample copy: $5.50. Guidelines online.

○ "We publish well crafted exciting poetry and translations from modern poets, everywhere. Particularly interested in translations from less well-known languages. For example we've published work from Albanian, Armenian, Bulgarian, Faroese, Kurdish, Icelandic, Urdu, just to name a few."

**MAGAZINES NEEDS** "Send 3-5 unpublished poems not sent elsewhere. Please no self-centered workshop ramblings; no perfect form without meaningful content; no questionable language used purely for shock value." Length: 2-120 lines.

**TIPS** "Know your craft. We are not a magazine for amateurs. We also are interested in translation from modern poets writing in any language into English."

## 💲 VOICES ISRAEL

P.O. Box 21, Metulla 10292, Israel. **E-mail:** voicesisraelpoetryanthology@gmail.com. **Website:** www.voicesisrael.com. **Contact:** Dina Yehuda, editor. *Voices Israel*, published annually by The Voices Israel Group of Poets, is "an anthology of poetry in English, with worldwide contributions. We consider all kinds of poetry." Poems must be in English; translations must be accompanied by the original poem. Single copy: $25 for nonmembers. Sample: $15 (back issue). "Members receive the anthology with annual dues ($35)."

○ *Voices Israel* is about 300 pages, digest-sized, offset from laser output on ordinary paper, flat-spined, with varying cover. Press run is 350.

**MAGAZINES NEEDS** Submit up to 3 poems/year via online submissions manager. "We do not guarantee publication of any poem. In poems we publish, we reserve the right to correct obviously unintentional errors in spelling, punctuation, etc." Length: 40 lines or 400 words maximum.

**ALSO OFFERS** The annual International Reuben Rose Memorial Poetry Competition offers 1st Prize: $500; 2nd Prize $200; 3rd Prize $100; and Honorable Mentions. Winning poems are published and distributed together with the *Voices Israel* anthology.

## THE WALLACE STEVENS JOURNAL

University of Antwerp, Prinsstraat 13, 2000 Antwerp, Belgium. **E-mail:** bart.eeckhout@uantwerp.be; jforjames@aol.com. **Website:** www.press.jhu.edu/journals/wallace_stevens_journal. **Contact:** Bart Eeckhout, editor; James Finnegan, poetry editor. *The Wallace Stevens Journal*, published semiannually by the Wallace Stevens Society, welcomes submissions on all aspects of Wallace Stevens's poetry and life. Subscription: $30 (includes membership in the Wallace Stevens Society).

○ *The Wallace Stevens Journal* is 100-160 pages, digest-sized, typeset, flat-spined, with glossy cover with art. Receives 200 poems/year, accepts 15-20. Press run is 400+ institutional subscriptions through Project Muse (Johns Hopkins University Press).

**MAGAZINES NEEDS** Has published poetry by David Athey, Jacqueline Marcus, Charles Wright, X.J. Kennedy, A.M. Juster, and Robert Creeley. Submit poems to James Finnegan at jforjames@aol.com.

### THE WAR CRY

The Salvation Army, 615 Slaters Lane, Alexandria VA 22314. (703)684-4128. **Fax:** (703)684-5539. **E-mail:** war.cry@usn.salvationarmy.org. **Website:** publications.salvationarmyusa.org. "Inspirational magazine with evangelical emphasis and portrayals that express the mission of the Salvation Army. Twelve issues published per year, including special Easter and Christmas issues." Buys first rights, buys one-time rights. Pays on acceptance. Publishes ms an average of 2 months to 1 year after acceptance. Responds in 3-4 weeks to mss. Editorial lead time 2 months before issue date; Christmas and Easter issues 6 months before issue date. Sample copy, theme list, and writer's guidelines free with #10 SASE or online.

◯   Word limit for mss 800-1,500 words.

**MAGAZINES NEEDS** Purchases limited poetry (10 per year maximum).

### ◯ WATERWAYS: POETRY IN THE MAINSTREAM

Ten Penny Players, Inc., Ten Penny Players, 393 Saint Pauls Ave., Staten Island NY 10304-2127. (718)442-7429. **E-mail:** tenpennyplayers@si.rr.com. **Website:** www.tenpennyplayers.org/mags.html. **Contact:** Barbara Fisher and Richard Spiegel, poetry editors. *Waterways: Poetry in the Mainstream*, published 11 times/year, prints work by adult poets. "We publish theme issues and are trying to increase an audience for poetry and the printed and performed word. While we do 'themes,' sometimes an idea for a future magazine is inspired by a submission, so we try to remain open to poets' inspirations. Poets should be guided, however, by the fact that we are disability, children's, and animal rights advocates and are a NYC press. We are open to reading material from people we have never published, writing in traditional and experimental poetry forms." Acquires one-time rights. Responds in less than 1 month. Sometimes comments on rejected poems. Sample: $5. Subscription: $45. Guidelines available for SASE or on website.

**MAGAZINES NEEDS** Submit less than 10 poems at a time (for first submission). Accepts e-mail (pasted into body of message) and postal mail submissions (include SASE). Pays 1 contributor copy.

**ALSO OFFERS** Ten Penny Players publishes chapbooks "by children and young adults only—not by submission. They come through our workshops in the library and schools. Adult poets are published through our Bard Press imprint, **by invitation only**. Books evolve from the relationship we develop with writers we publish in *Waterways* and to whom we would like to give more exposure."

**TIPS** "Send for our theme sheet and a sample issue, or view online. Mss that arrive without a return envelope are not sent back."

### ⑤ WEBER: THE CONTEMPORARY WEST

Weber State University, 1395 Edvalson St., Dept. 1405, Ogden UT 84408-1405. **Website:** www.weber.edu/weberjournal. *Weber: The Contemporary West*, published 2 times/year, "spotlights personal narrative, commentary, fiction, nonfiction, and poetry that speaks to the environment and culture of the American West and beyond." Acquires all rights. Copyright reverts to author after first printing. Publishes ms 15 months after acceptance. Responds in 6 months. Sample: $10 (back issue). Subscription: $20 ($30 for institutions); $40 for outside the U.S. Themes and guidelines available in magazine, for SASE, by e-mail, or on website.

◯   Poetry published in *Weber* has appeared in *The Best American Poetry*. *Weber* is 150 pages, offset-printed on acid-free paper, perfect-bound, with color cover. Receives about 250-300 poems/year, accepts 30-40. Press run is 1,000; 80% libraries.

**MAGAZINES NEEDS** Submit 3-4 poems at a time, 2 copies of each (one without name). "We publish multiple poems from a poet." Cover letter is preferred. Poems are selected by anonymous (blind) evaluation. Always sends prepublication galleys. Has published poetry by Naomi Shihab Nye, Carolyn Forche, Stephen Dunn, Billy Collins, William Kloefkorn, David Lee, Gary Gildner, and Robert Dana. Does not want "poems that are flippant, prurient, sing-song, or preachy." Pays 2 contributor copies, one-year subscription, and a small honorarium ($100-300) depending on fluctuating grant monies.

**ALSO OFFERS** The Dr. Sherwin W. Howard Poetry Award, a $500 cash prize, is awarded annually to the author of the best set of poems published in *Weber* during the previous year. The competition is announced each year in the Spring/Summer issue.

## WEST BRANCH

Stadler Center for Poetry, Bucknell University, Lewisburg PA 17837-2029. (570)577-1853. **Fax:** (570)577-1885. **E-mail:** westbranch@bucknell.edu. **Website:** www.bucknell.edu/westbranch. **Contact:** G.C. Waldrep, editor. *West Branch* publishes poetry, fiction, and nonfiction in both traditional and innovative styles. Buys first North American serial rights. Pays on publication. Sample copy for $3. Guidelines online.

○ Reading period: August 15 through April 1. No more than 3 submissions from a single contributor in a given reading period.

**MAGAZINES NEEDS** Pays $50/submission.

**TIPS** "All submissions must be sent via our online submission manager. Please see website for guidelines. We recommend that you acquaint yourself with the magazine before submitting."

## ● ● WESTERLY

University of Western Australia, The Westerly Centre (M202), Crawley WA 6009, Australia. (61)(8)6488-3403. **Fax:** (61)(8)6488-1030. **E-mail:** westerly@uwa.edu.au. **Website:** westerlymag.com.au. **Contact:** Catherine Noske, editor. *Westerly*, published in July and November, prints quality short fiction, poetry, literary criticism, socio-historical articles, and book reviews with special attention given to Australia, Asia, and the Indian Ocean region. "We assume a reasonably well-read, intelligent audience. Past issues of *Westerly* provide the best guides. Not consciously an academic magazine." Acquires first publication rights; requests acknowledgment on reprints. Time between acceptance and publication may be up to 1 year, depending on when work is submitted. "Please wait for a response before forwarding any additional submissions for consideration."

○ *Westerly* is about 200 pages, digest-sized, "electronically printed." Press run is 1,200. Subscription information available on website. Deadline for July edition: March 31; deadline for November edition: August 31.

**MAGAZINES NEEDS** "We don't dictate to writers on rhyme, style, experimentation, or anything else. We are willing to publish short or long poems." Submit up to 3 poems by mail, e-mail, or online submissions form. Pays $75 for 1 page or 1 poem, or $100 for 2 or more pages/poems, and contributor copies.

**ALSO OFFERS** The Patricia Hackett Prize (value approximately $750 AUD) is awarded annually for the best contribution published in the previous year's issue of *Westerly*.

## WESTERN HUMANITIES REVIEW

University of Utah, English Department, 255 S. Central Campus Dr., Salt Lake City UT 84112-0494. (801)581-6070. **Fax:** (801)585-5167. **E-mail:** whr@mail.hum.utah.edu. **Website:** ourworld.info/whrweb/. **Contact:** Barry Weller, editor; Nate Liederbach, managing editor. *Western Humanities Review* is a journal of contemporary literature and culture housed in the University of Utah English Department. Publishes poetry, fiction, nonfiction essays, artwork, and work that resists categorization. Buys one-time rights. Pays in contributor copies. Publishes ms an average of 1 year after acceptance. Responds in 3-5 months. Sample copy: $10. Guidelines online.

○ Reading period: September 1 through April 15. All submissions must be sent through online submissions manager.

**MAGAZINES NEEDS** Considers simultaneous submissions but no more than 5 poems or 25 pages per reading period. No fax or e-mail submissions. Reads submissions October 1 through April 1 only. Wants quality poetry of any form, including translations. Has published poetry by Charles Simic, Olena Kalytiak Davis, Ravi Shankar, Karen Volkman, Dan Beachy-Quick, Lucie Brock-Broido, Christine Hume, and Dan Chiasson. Innovative prose poems may be submitted as fiction or nonfiction to the appropriate editor. Pays 2 contributor copies.

**CONTEST/AWARD OFFERINGS** Sponsors an annual contest for Utah writers.

**TIPS** "Because of changes in our editorial staff, we urge familiarity with recent issues of the magazine. We do not publish writer's guidelines because we think that the magazine itself conveys an accurate picture of our requirements. Please, no e-mail submissions."

## WESTVIEW: A JOURNAL OF WESTERN OKLAHOMA

Southwestern Oklahoma State University, 100 Campus Dr., Weatherford OK 73096. **E-mail:** westview@swosu.edu. **Website:** www.swosu.edu/academics/

langarts/westview/. **Contact:** Amanda Smith, editor; Kevin Collins, managing editor. *Westview: A Journal of Western Oklahoma* is published semiannually by the Language Arts Department of Southwestern Oklahoma State University. Publications include previously unpublished fiction, poetry, prose poems, drama, nonfiction, book reviews, literary criticism, and artwork. *Westview* holds only first rights for all works published. Sample: $6.

- Has published poetry by Carolynne Wright, Miller Williams, Walter McDonald, Robert Cooperman, Alicia Ostriker, and James Whitehead. *Westview* is 64 pages, magazine-sized, perfect-bound, with full-color glossy card cover. Receives about 500 poems/year; accepts 7%. Press run is 600 (250 subscribers; about 25 libraries). Subscription: $15/2 years; $25/2 years international.

## ○ WESTWARD QUARTERLY: THE MAGAZINE OF FAMILY READING

Laudemont Press, P.O. Box 369, Hamilton IL 62341. (800)440-4043. **E-mail:** editor@wwquarterly.com. **Website:** www.wwquarterly.com. **Contact:** Shirley Anne Leonard, editor. *WestWard Quarterly: The Magazine of Family Reading* prints poetry. Acquires one-time rights. Responds in "weeks." Often comments on rejected poems. Single copy: $4 ($6 foreign); subscription: $15/year ($18 foreign). Contributors to an issue may order extra copies at a discounted price. Make checks payable to Laudemont Press. Guidelines available for SASE, by e-mail, or on website.

- Every issue includes a "Featured Writer" and a piece on improving writing skills or writing different forms of poetry. *WestWard Quarterly* is 32 pages, digest-sized, laser-printed, saddle-stapled, with inkjet color cover with scenic photos, includes ads. Receives about 1,500 poems/year, accepts about 12%. Press run is 150 (60 subscribers).

**MAGAZINES NEEDS** Wants "all forms, including rhyme—we welcome inspirational, positive, reflective, humorous material promoting nobility, compassion, and courage." Does not want "experimental or avant-garde forms, offensive language, depressing or negative poetry." Submit up to 5 poems at a time. Prefers e-mail submissions (pasted into body of message); no disk submissions. Reads submissions year round. Considers poetry by children and teens. Has

published poetry by Wynne Alexander, Leland Jamieson, Joyce I. Johnson, Michael Keshigian, Richard Luftig, Arlene Mandell, Dennis Ross, J. Alvin Speers, Jane Stuart, and Charles Waugaman. Length: up to 40 lines/poem. Pays 1 contributor copy.

## WHISKEY ISLAND MAGAZINE

English Dept., Cleveland State University, 2121 Euclid Ave., Cleveland OH 44115. (216)687-3951. **E-mail:** whiskeyisland@csuohio.edu. **Website:** whiskeyislandmagazine.com. "*Whiskey Island* is a nonprofit literary magazine that has been published in one form or another by students of Cleveland State University for over 30 years." Responds in 3 months to mss. Sample copy: $6.

- Reading periods: August 15 through November 15 and January 15 through April 15. Paper and e-mail submissions are not accepted. No multiple submissions.

**MAGAZINES NEEDS** "Submit 3-5 poems via online submissions manager. Please combine all the poems you wish to submit into one document." Pays 2 contributor copies.

## ○ WHITE WALL REVIEW

Department of English, Ryerson University, 10th Floor, Jorgenson Hall, 350 Victoria St., Toronto ON M5B 2K3, Canada. **E-mail:** wwr@arts.ryerson.ca. **Website:** www.ryerson.ca/wwr/. *White Wall Review*, published annually in August, focuses on printing "clearly expressed, innovative poetry and prose. No style is unacceptable." Has published poetry by Vernon Mooers and David Sidjak. *White Wall Review* is 90-144 pages, digest-sized, professionally printed, perfect-bound, with glossy card cover. Press run is 500. Subscription: $10 plus GST.

**MAGAZINES NEEDS** Submit up to 5 poems at a time by mail only. Length: 5 pages/piece maximum. Cover letter is required. Include short bio. Guidelines available in magazine, for SASE. Responds "as soon as possible." Pays 1 contributor copy.

**TIPS** "Innovative work is especially appreciated."

## WICKED ALICE

**E-mail:** wickedalicepoetry@yahoo.com. **Website:** www.sundresspublications.com/wickedalice. **Contact:** Kristy Bowen, editor. "*Wicked Alice* is a women-centered online journal dedicated to publishing quality work by both sexes, depicting and exploring the female experience." Wants "work that has a strong sense of image and music. Work that is interesting and surprising, with innovative, sometimes unusual, use of language. We love humor when done well, strangeness, wackiness. Hybridity, collage, intertexuality." Acquires one-time rights. Responds in 1-6 months. Guidelines online.

**MAGAZINES NEEDS** Submit 3-5 poems via e-mail. Has published poetry by Daniela Olszewska, Rebecca Loudon, Robyn Art, Simone Muench, Brandi Homan, and Karyna McGlynn. Receives about 500 poems/year, accepts about 8%. Does not want greeting card verse. Length: open.

## ⊙⊙ WILD GOOSE POETRY REVIEW

Hickory NC 28235-5009. **E-mail:** asowens1@yahoo.com. **Website:** www.wildgoosepoetryreview.com. *Wild Goose Poetry Review* is "looking for good contemporary poetry. No particular biases. We enjoy humor, strong imagery, strong lines, narrative, lyric, etc. Not a fan of abstraction, cliché, form for the sake of form, shock for the sake of shock. As in any good poem, everything should be purposeful." Author retains all rights. Time between acceptance and publication is up to 3 months. Usually responds to mss within 1 month.

◯   Receives more than 1,000 poems/year, accepts less than 10%. Reviews books/chapbooks of poetry. Send materials for review consideration to Scott Owens. Has published poetry by Anthony Abbott, Karen Douglass, and Lisa Zaran.

**MAGAZINES NEEDS** Accepts e-mail submissions only, pasted into body of e-mail; no attachments; no disk submissions. Cover letter is preferred; include bio. Reads submissions year round.

## WILD VIOLET

P.O. Box 39706, Philadelphia PA 19106. **E-mail:** wildvioletmagazine@yahoo.com. **Website:** www.wildviolet.net. **Contact:** Alyce Wilson, editor. *Wild Violet*, published weekly online, aims "to make the arts more accessible, to make a place for the arts in modern life, and to serve as a creative forum for writers and artists. Our audience includes English-speaking readers from all over the world who are interested in both 'high art' and pop culture." Requests limited electronic rights for online publication and archival only. Time between acceptance and publication is 6 months. "Decisions on acceptance or rejection are made by the editor." Responds in 1 week to queries; 3-6 months to mss. Guidelines online by e-mail or on website.

**MAGAZINES NEEDS** Wants "poetry that is well crafted, that engages thought, that challenges or uplifts the reader. We have published free verse, haiku, blank verse, and other forms. If the form suits the poem, we will consider any form." Does not want "abstract, self-involved poetry; poorly managed form; excessive rhyming; self-referential poems that do not show why the speaker is sad, happy, or in love." Has published poetry by Lyn Lifshin, Kimberly Gladman, Andrew H. Oerke, Simon Perchik, John Grey, Joanna Weston, and Amy Barone. Accepts about 15% of work submitted. Submit 3-5 poems at a time. Accepts e-mail submissions (pasted into body of message, or as text or Word attachment) and postal mail submissions; no disk submissions. Cover letter is preferred. Reads submissions year round. Seldom comments on rejected poems, unless requested. Occasionally publishes theme issues.

**ALSO OFFERS** Reviews books/chapbooks of poetry in 250 words, single-book format. Query for review consideration. Sponsors an annual poetry contest, offering 1st Prize: $100 and publication in *Wild Violet*; 2 Honorable Mentions will also be published. Guidelines available by e-mail or on website. **Entry fee:** $5/poem. Judged by independent judges.

**TIPS** "We look for stories that are well-paced and show character and plot development. Even short shorts should do more than simply paint a picture. Manuscripts stand out when the author's voice is fresh and engaging. Avoid muddying your story with too many characters, and don't attempt to shock the reader with an ending you have not earned. Experiment with styles and structures, but don't resort to experimentation for its own sake."

## WILLARD & MAPLE

163 S. Willard St., Box #3636, Burlington VT 05401. (802)860-2700 ext.2462. **E-mail:** willardandmaple@champlain.edu. **Website:** willardandmaple.com. *Willard & Maple*, published annually in spring, is a student-run literary magazine from Champlain College's Professional Writing Program that considers short fiction, essays, reviews, fine art, and poetry by adults, children, and teens. Wants creative work of the highest quality. Acquires one-time rights. Time between acceptance and publication is less than 1 year. Responds in 6 months to queries; in 6 months to mss.

Single copy: $12. Contact Lulu Press for contributor copy. Writer's guidelines for SASE or send e-mail.

○ *Willard & Maple* is 200 pages, digest-sized, digitally printed, perfect-bound. Receives about 500 poems/year, accepts about 20%. Press run is 600 (80 subscribers, 4 libraries); 200 are distributed free to the Champlain College writing community.

**MAGAZINES NEEDS** Send up to 5 poems via e-mail or postal mail. Send SASE for return of ms or send disposable copy of mss and #10 SASE for reply only. Length: up to 100 lines/poem. Pays 2 contributor copies.

**TIPS** "The power of imagination makes us infinite."

## WILLOW REVIEW

College of Lake County Publications, College of Lake County, 19351 W. Washington St., Grayslake IL 60030-1198. (847)543-2956. **E-mail:** com426@clcillinois.edu. **Website:** www.clcillinois.edu/community/willowreview.asp. **Contact:** Michael Latza, editor. *Willow Review*, published annually, is interested in poetry, creative nonfiction, and fiction of high quality. "We have no preferences as to form, style, or subject, as long as each piece stands on its own as art and communicates ideas." All rights revert to author upon publication. Responds in 3-4 months to mss. Sample: $5 (back issue). Subscription: $18/3 issues, $30/6 issues. International: add $5 per issue. Guidelines available on website.

○ The editors award prizes for best poetry and prose in the issue. Prize awards vary contingent on the current year's budget but normally range from $100-400. There is no reading fee or separate application for these prizes. All accepted mss are eligible."*Willow Review* can be found on EBSCOhost databases, assuring a broader targeted audience for our authors' work. *Willow Review* is a nonprofit journal partially supported by a grant from the Illinois Arts Council (a state agency), College of Lake County Publications, private contributions, and sales."

**MAGAZINES NEEDS** Considers simultaneous submissions "if indicated in the cover letter." No e-mail submissions; postal submissions only. Include SASE; mss will not be returned unless requested. Reads submissions September through May. Has published poetry by Lisel Mueller, Lucien Stryk, Da-

vid Ray, Louis Rodriguez, John Dickson, and Patricia Smith. Pays 2 contributor copies.

**ALSO OFFERS** Prizes totaling $400 are awarded to the best poetry and short fiction/creative nonfiction in each issue. The College of Lake County Reading Series (4-7 readings/academic year) has included Thomas Lux, Isabel Allende, Donald Justice, Galway Kinnell, Lisel Mueller, Amiri Baraka, and others. One reading is for contributors to *Willow Review*. Readings, usually held on Thursday evenings and widely publicized in Chicago and suburban newspapers, are presented to audiences of about 150 students and faculty of the College of Lake County and other area colleges, as well as residents of local communities.

## WINDFALL: A JOURNAL OF POETRY OF PLACE

Windfall Press, P.O. Box 19007, Portland OR 97280-0007. **E-mail:** bsiverly@comcast.net. **Website:** www.windfalljournal.com. **Contact:** Bill Siverly and Michael McDowell, co-editors. *Windfall: A Journal of Poetry of Place*, published semiannually in March and September, is "looking for poems of place, specifically places in the Pacific Northwest (the broad bioregion extending from the North Slope of Alaska to the San Francisco Bay Area, and from the Rocky Mountains to the Pacific Coast). 'Place' can be named or unnamed, but if unnamed, then location should be clearly implied or suggested by observed detail. The poet does not have to be living in the Pacific Northwest, but the poem does. We favor poetry based on imagery derived from sensory observation. *Windfall* also favors poetry that occurs in lines and stanzas." Does not want "language poetry, metapoetry, surrealism, 'Internet poetry' (constructed from search engine information rather than experience), abstract, or self-centered poetry of any kind." Acquires first North American serial rights. "Poem may appear in sample pages on *Windfall* website." Rights revert to poet upon publication. Publishes ms 2 months after acceptance. Responds within 6 months ("depends on when poems are submitted in the biannual cycle"). Single copy: $7; subscription: $14/year. Make checks payable to Windfall Press. Guidelines available in magazine or on website.

○ Has published poetry by Judith Barrington, Gloria Bird, Barbara Drake, Clem Starck, Tom Wayman, and Robert Wrigley. *Windfall* is 52 pages, digest-sized, stapled, with art on covers ("all are drawings or prints by Portland artist Sharon Bronzan"). Receives about 160 poems/year, accepts about 60. Press run is 250.

**MAGAZINES NEEDS** Submit 5 poems at a time. Accepts e-mail submissions (as attachment) or postal mail. Cover letter is preferred. "SASE required for submissions by U.S. mail." Reads submissions after the deadlines for each issue: February 1 for spring and August 1 for fall. Length: up to 50 lines/poem.

## ○ WINDHOVER

A Journal of Christian Literature, P.O. Box 8008, 900 College St., Belton TX 76513. (254)295-4563. **E-mail:** windhover@umhb.edu. **Website:** undergrad.umhb.edu/english/windhover-journal. **Contact:** Dr. Nathaniel Hansen, editor. "*Windhover* is devoted to promoting writers and literature with Christian perspectives and with a broad definition of those perspectives. We accept poetry, short fiction, nonfiction, and creative nonfiction." Publishes ms 1 year after acceptance. Sample copy: $5. Writer's guidelines available at undergrad.umhb.edu/english/windhover-journal. Accepts electronic submissions only through online submission manager; no e-mailed submissions. Include estimated word count, brief bio, and list of publications.

○ Reading period is February 1 through August 1.

**MAGAZINES NEEDS** Pays 1 contributor copy.

**TIPS** "We are looking for writing that avoids the didactic, the melodramatic, the trite, the obvious. Eschew tricks and gimmicks. We want writing that invites rereading."

## WISCONSIN REVIEW

University of Wisconsin Oshkosh, 800 Algoma Blvd., Oshkosh WI 54901. (920)424-2267. **E-mail:** wisconsinreview@uwosh.edu. **Website:** www.uwosh.edu/wisconsinreview. *Wisconsin Review*, published biannually, is a "contemporary poetry, prose, and art magazine run by students at the University of Wisconsin Oshkosh." Acquires first North American serial rights. Time between acceptance and publication is 4-6 months. Responds in 6-9 months. Sometimes comments on rejected poems. Single copy: $10; subscription: $15 plus $3 extra per issue for shipments outside the U.S. Guidelines available in magazine, for SASE, by e-mail, and on website.

○ *Wisconsin Review* is around 100 pages, digest-sized, perfect-bound, with 4-color glossy coverstock. Receives about 400 poetry submissions/year, accepts about 50; Press run is

1,000. Reading period: May through October for Spring issue; November through April for Fall issue.

**MAGAZINES NEEDS** Wants all forms and styles of poetry. Considers poetry by children and teens. "Minors may submit material by including a written letter of permission from a parent or guardian." Submit via postal mail or online submission manager. Type 1 poem/page, single-spaced, with name and address of writer on each page. Cover letter is required. Include 3-5 sentence bio and SASE if submitting by mail. There is a $2 reading fee for online submissions. Does not want "poetry that is racist, sexist, or unnecessarily vulgar." Pays 2 contributor copies.

**TIPS** "We are open to any poetic form and style, and look for outstanding imagery, new themes, and fresh voices—poetry that induces emotions."

## ● THE WOLF

**E-mail:** thewolfpoetry@hotmail.com. **Website:** www.wolfmagazine.co.uk. **Contact:** James Byrne, editor. *The Wolf*, published 3 times/year, publishes international translations, critical prose, and interviews with leading contemporary poets, which are frequently mentioned as distinguishing characteristics of the magazine. The poetry, however, comes purely through work submitted. There is no special treatment with regard to the consideration of any poet or poem. Since January 2008, *The Wolf* has benefited from Arts Council funding. Since receiving its grant the magazine has increased its content by a third and is perfect bound. Responds in 6 months. Sample copy on website. Single issue: $12, including postage and packing. Subscription: $35. Accepts PayPal. Guidelines online.

**MAGAZINES NEEDS** Submit up to 5 poems at a time. Accepts any poetry of various styles or theme. Advisible to read a few issues of the magazine to see what is accepted. The editor prefers poems to hold a modernist aesthetic over the postmodern, experimental over mainstream, serious over light verse. It's worth seeing how this fits in with recent publications of *The Wolf*. Pays 1 contributor copy.

**ALSO OFFERS** Also accepts critical essays on any poetry subject between 2,000-3,000 words. Welcomes artwork or photographs.

## THE WORCESTER REVIEW

1 Ekman St., Worcester MA 01607. (508)797-4770. **E-mail:** twr.diane@gmail.com. **Website:** www.theworcesterreview.org. **Contact:** Diane Vanaskie

Mulligan, managing editor. *The Worcester Review*, published annually by the Worcester County Poetry Association, encourages "critical work with a New England connection; no geographic limitation on poetry and fiction." Wants "work that is crafted, intuitively honest and empathetic. We like high-quality, creative poetry, artwork, and fiction. Critical articles should be connected to New England." Acquires one-time rights. Publishes ms within 1 year of acceptance. Responds in 4-8 months to mss. Sometimes comments on rejected mss. Sample copy: $8. Subscription: $30 (includes membership in WCPA). Guidelines available for SASE or on website.

◐ *The Worcester Review* is 160 pages, digest-sized, professionally printed in dark type on quality stock, perfect-bound, with matte card cover. Press run is 600.

**MAGAZINES NEEDS** Submit up to 5 poems at a time via online submission manager. Cover letter is optional. Has published poetry by Kurt Brown, Cleopatra Mathis, and Theodore Deppe. Pays 2 contributor copies plus small honorarium.

**TIPS** "We generally look for creative work with a blend of craftsmanship, insight, and empathy. This does not exclude humor. We won't print work that is shoddy in any of these areas."

## WORD RIOT

P.O. Box 414, Middletown NJ 07748-3143. (732)706-1272. **Fax:** (732)706-5856. **E-mail:** wr.submissions@gmail.com. **Website:** www.wordriot.org. **Contact:** Jackie Corley, publisher; Kevin O'Cuinn, fiction editor; Doug Paul Case, poetry editor; Antonia Crane, creative nonfiction editor. "*Word Riot* publishes the forceful voices of up-and-coming writers and poets. We like edgy. We like challenging. We like unique voices. Each month we provide readers with book reviews, author interviews, and, most importantly, writing from some of the best and brightest making waves on the literary scene." Acquires electronic rights. Not copyrighted. Publishes ms 1-2 months after acceptance. Responds in 4-6 weeks to ms.

◐ Online magazine. Member CLMP.

**MAGAZINES NEEDS** Submit via online submissions manager at wordriot.submittable.com/submit. Do not send submissions by mail.

**TIPS** "We're always looking for something edgy or quirky. We like writers who take risks."

## 🌐 WORKERS WRITE!

Blue Cubicle Press, LLC, P.O. Box 250382, Plano TX 75025. **E-mail:** info@workerswritejournal.com. **Website:** www.workerswritejournal.com. **Contact:** David LaBounty, managing editor. "*Workers Write!* is an annual print journal published by Blue Cubicle Press, an independent publisher dedicated to giving voice to writers trapped in the daily grind. Each issue focuses on a particular workplace; check website for details. Submit your stories via e-mail or send a hard copy." Buys first North American serial rights, electronic rights, one-time rights, second serial (reprint) rights. Pays on acceptance. Publishes mss 6 months after acceptance. Responds in 1 week to queries; in 3 months to mss. Sample copy available on website. Writer's guidelines free for #10 SASE and on website.

**MAGAZINES NEEDS** Pays $5-10.

## WRITER'S BLOC

MSC 162, Fore Hall Rm. 110, 700 University Blvd., Texas A&M University-Kingsville, Kingsville TX 78363. (361)593-2516. **E-mail:** octavio.quintanilla@tamuk.edu. **E-mail:** WritersBlocLitMag@hotmail.com. **Website:** www.tamuk.edu/artsci/langlit/writers_bloc.html. **Contact:** Dr. Octavio Quintanilla. *Writer's Bloc*, published annually, prints poetry, short fiction, flash fiction, one-act plays, interviews, and essays. "About half of our pages are devoted to the works of Texas A&M University-Kingsville students and half to the works of writers and artists from all over the world." Wants quality poetry; no restrictions on content or form. Sample copy: $7. Guidelines online or in magazine.

◐ *Writer's Bloc* is 96 pages, digest-sized. Press run is 300. Reading period: February through May.

**MAGAZINES NEEDS** Submit via e-mail or postal mail. Include cover letter with contact info, short bio. "Prose poems okay. Submissions should be typed, double-spaced; SASE required for reply. Mss are published upon recommendation by a staff of students and faculty." Seldom comments on rejected poems. Length: no more than 50 lines. Pays 1 contributor copy.

## WRITER'S DIGEST

F+W Media, Inc., 10151 Carver Rd., Suite #200, Blue Ash OH 45242. (513)531-2690. **E-mail:** wdsubmissions@fwmedia.com. **Website:** www.writersdigest.com. *Writer's Digest*, the No. 1 magazine for writers, celebrates the writing life and what it means to be a writer in today's publishing environment. Buys first

North American print and perpetual world digital rights. Pays 25% print reprint fee. Pays on acceptance. Publishes ms an average of 4 months after acceptance. Responds in 1-4 months to queries and mss. Guidelines and editorial calendar online (writersdigest.com/submission-guidelines).

○ The magazine does not accept or read e-queries with attachments.

**TIPS** "*InkWell* is the best place for new writers to break in. We recommend you consult our editorial calendar before pitching feature-length articles. Check our writer's guidelines for more details."

### THE WRITING DISORDER

P.O. Box 93613, Los Angeles CA 90093. (323)336-5822. **E-mail:** submit@thewritingdisorder.com. **Website:** www.writingdisorder.com. **Contact:** C.E. Lukather, editor; Paul Garson, managing editor; Julianna Woodhead, poetry editor; Pamela Ramos Langley, fiction editor; C.E. Lukather, nonfiction editor. "*The Writing Disorder* is an online literary magazine devoted to literature, art, and culture. The mission of the magazine is to showcase new and emerging writers—particularly those in writing programs—as well as established ones. The magazine also features original artwork, photography, and comic art. Although we strive to publish original and experimental work, *The Writing Disorder* remains rooted in the classic art of storytelling." Acquires first North American serial rights. Pays on publication. Publishes ms an average of 3-6 months after acceptance. Responds in 6-12 weeks to queries; 3-6 months to ms. Editorial lead time 3 months. Sample copy online. Guidelines online.

**MAGAZINES NEEDS** Query. Annual print anthology of best work published online. Pays a contributor copy of anthology to writers whose work has been selected for inclusion.

**TIPS** "We are looking for work from new writers, writers in writing programs, and students and faculty of all ages."

### XAVIER REVIEW

Xavier University of Louisiana, 1 Drexel Dr., Box 89, New Orleans LA 70125-1098. **Website:** www.xula.edu/review. **Contact:** Ralph Adamo, editor. "*Xavier Review* accepts poetry, fiction, translations, creative nonfiction, and critical essays. Content focuses on African American, Caribbean, and Southern literature, as well as works that touch on issues of religion and spirituality. We do, however, accept quality work on all themes. (Please note: This is not a religious publication.)" Guidelines online.

**MAGAZINES NEEDS** Submit 3-5 poems at a time via postal mail. Include 2-3 sentence bio and SASE. "Overseas authors only may submit by e-mail attachment." Pays 2 contributor copies; offers 40% discount on additional copies.

### THE YALE REVIEW

Yale University, P.O. Box 208243, New Haven CT 06520-8243. (203)432-0499. **Fax:** (203)432-0510. **Website:** www.yale.edu/yalereview. **Contact:** J.D. McClatchy, editor. "Like Yale's schools of music, drama, and architecture, like its libraries and art galleries, *The Yale Review* has helped give the University its leading place in American education. In a land of quick fixes and short view and in a time of increasingly commercial publishing, the journal has an authority that derives from its commitment to bold established writers and promising newcomers, to both challenging literary work and a range of essays and reviews that can explore the connections between academic disciplines and the broader movements in American society, thought, and culture. With independence and boldness, with a concern for issues and ideas, with a respect for the mind's capacity to be surprised by speculation and delighted by elegance, *The Yale Review* proudly continues into its third century." Buys one-time rights. Pays prior to publication. Publishes ms an average of 6 months after acceptance. Responds in 1-3 months to mss. Sample copy online. Guidelines online.

**MAGAZINES NEEDS** Submit with SASE. All submissions should be sent to the editorial office. Pays $100-250.

### THE YALOBUSHA REVIEW

**E-mail:** yreditors@gmail.com. **Website:** yr.olemiss.edu. **Contact:** Maggie Woodward and Marty Cain, senior editors. Acquires first North American serial rights. Responds in 2-4 months to mss.

**MAGAZINES NEEDS** Submit 3-5 poems via online submissions manager.

### YEMASSEE

University of South Carolina, Department of English, Columbia SC 29208. **E-mail:** editor@yemasseejournal.com. **Website:** yemasseejournal.com. "*Yemassee* is the University of South Carolina's literary journal. Our readers are interested in high-quality fiction, poetry, and creative nonfiction. We have no editorial slant; quality of work is our only concern. We publish in the fall and spring, printing 5-7 stories, 2-3 essays, and 12-15 poems per issue. We tend to solicit reviews, essays, and interviews but welcome unsolicited queries. We do not favor any particular aesthetic or school of writing." Buys first North American serial rights; buys electronic rights. Publishes ms an average of 4-6 months after acceptance. Responds in 1-4 months to queries and mss. Editorial lead time 3 months. Sample copy: $5. Guidelines online.

**MAGAZINES NEEDS** Submit 3-5 poems combined into a single document. "Submissions for all genres should include a cover letter that lists the titles of the pieces included, along with your contact information (including author's name, address, e-mail address, and phone number)." Does not want workshop poems, unpolished drafts, generic/unoriginal themes, or bad Hemingway. Does not want "poems of such a highly personal nature that their primary relevance is to the author; bad Ginsberg." Length: 1-120 lines. Pays 2 contributor copies.

**CONTEST/AWARD OFFERINGS** Yemassee Poetry Contest: $100 award. Check website for deadline.

## ZEEK: A JEWISH JOURNAL OF THOUGHT AND CULTURE

125 Maiden Ln., 8th Floor, New York NY 10038. (212)453-9435. **E-mail:** zeek@zeek.net. **Website:** www.zeek.net. **Contact:** Erica Brody, editor in chief. *ZEEK* "relaunched in late February 2013 as a hub for the domestic Jewish social justice movement, one that showcases the people, ideas, and conversations driving an inclusive and diverse progressive Jewish community. At the same time, we've reaffirmed our commitment to building on *ZEEK*'s reputation for original, ahead-of-the-curve Jewish writing and arts, culture and spirituality content, incubating emerging voices and artists, as well as established ones." *ZEEK* seeks "great writing in a variety of styles and voices, original thinking, and accessible content. That means we're interested in hearing your ideas for first-person essays, reflections and commentary, reporting, profiles, Q&As, analysis, infographics, and more. For the near future, *ZEEK* will focus on domestic issues. Our discourse will be civil." Responds in 6 weeks to queries.

**MAGAZINES NEEDS** "Pitches should be sent to zeek@zeek.net, with 'submission' or 'pitch' in the subject line. And please include a little bit about yourself and why you think your pitch is a good fit for *ZEEK*."

## ZYLOPHONE POETRY JOURNAL

95/31 Moo 10 Classic Village, T. Nongphure A. Banglamung, Chonburi Chonburi 20150, Thailand. +6689-432-1389. **E-mail:** rogerbarrow52@yahoo.com. **Website:** www.poetezines.4mg.com. **Contact:** J. Rogers Barrow. *Zylophone* is published semiannually in print and online. Wants all common formats. Has published poetry by Edward W. Cousins, Daisy Whitmore, and David Barger. Publishes ms 6 weeks after acceptance. Sample copy: $6. Guidelines available by e-mail.

*Zylophone* is 16 pages, tabloid-sized, staple-bound with line-drawing artwork. Receives about 60 poems/year; accepts about 12. Press run is 20.

**MAGAZINES NEEDS** Submit up to 3 poems at a time by e-mail. Cover letter is preferred. Reads submissions year round. Length: 4-16 lines/poem. Pays 1 contributor copy.

## ZYZZYVA

57 Post St., Suite 604, San Francisco CA 94104. (415)757-0465. **E-mail:** editor@zyzzyva.org. **Website:** www.zyzzyva.org. **Contact:** Laura Cogan, editor; Oscar Villalon, managing editor. "Every issue is a vibrant mix of established talents and new voices, providing an elegantly curated overview of contemporary arts and letters with a distinctly San Francisco perspective." Buys first North American serial and one-time anthology rights. Pays on acceptance. Publishes ms an average of 3 months after acceptance. Responds in 1 week to queries; in 1 month to mss. Sample copy: $12. Guidelines online.

Accepts submissions January 1-May 31 and August 1-November 30. Does not accept online submissions.

**MAGAZINES NEEDS** Submit by mail. Include SASE and contact information. Length: no limit. Pays $50.

**TIPS** "We are not currently seeking work about any particular theme or topic; that said, reading recent issues is perhaps the best way to develop a sense for the length and quality we are looking for in submissions."

# BOOK/CHAPBOOK PUBLISHERS

Every poet dreams of publishing a collection of his or her work. However, it's surprising how many poets still envision putting out a thick, hardbound volume containing hundreds of poems. In reality, poetry books are usually slim, often paperback, with varying levels of production quality, depending on the publisher.

More common than full-length poetry books (i.e., 50-150 pages by modern standards) are poetry *chapbooks*, small editions of approximately 24-32 pages. They may be printed on quality paper with beautiful cover art on heavy stock; or they may be photocopied sheets of plain printer paper, folded and stapled or hand-sewn along the spine.

In this section you'll find a variety of presses and publishers of poetry books and chapbooks. However, it's a reflection of how poetry publishing works in the early 21st century that many book/chapbook publishing opportunities appear in the Contest & Awards section instead.

## GETTING STARTED, FINDING A PUBLISHER

If you don't have a publisher in mind, read randomly through the listings, making notes as you go. (Don't hesitate to write in the margins, underline, use highlighters; it also helps to flag markets that interest you with Post-It Notes). Browsing the listings is an effective way to familiarize yourself with the kind of information presented and the publishing opportunities that are available at various skill levels. If you're thinking of a specific publisher by name, however, begin with the General Index. Here all *Poet's Market* listings are alphabetized.

## AHSAHTA PRESS

MFA Program in Creative Writing, Boise State University, 1910 University Dr., MS 1525, Boise ID 83725. (208)426-3414. **E-mail:** ahsahta@boisestate.edu. **Website:** ahsahtapress.org. **Contact:** Janet Holmes, director. Publishes trade paperback originals. Pays 8% royalty on retail price for first 1,000 sold; 10% thereafter. Publishes ms 2 years after acceptance. Responds in 3 months to mss. Book catalog online. Guidelines online; submit through submissions manager.

**NEEDS** "We hold an open submissions period in May as well as the Sawtooth Poetry Prize competition, from which we publish 2-3 mss per year."

**HOW TO CONTACT** Submit complete ms. The press publishes runners-up as well as winners of the Sawtooth Poetry Prize. Forthcoming, new, and backlist titles available on website. Most backlist titles: $9.95; most current titles: $18.

**TIPS** "Ahsahta's motto is that poetry is art, so our readers tend to come to us for the unexpected—poetry that makes them think, reflect, and even do something they haven't done before."

## ANHINGA PRESS

P.O. Box 3665, Tallahassee FL 32315. Phone/Fax: (850)577-0745. **E-mail:** info@anhinga.org. **Website:** www.anhinga.org. **Contact:** Kristine Snodgrass, co-director. Publishes only full-length collections of poetry (60-80 pages). No individual poems or chapbooks. Publishes hardcover and trade paperback originals. Pays 10% royalty on retail price. Responds in 3 months. Guidelines online.

**NEEDS** Not accepting any unsolicited submissions at this time. Enter Robert Dana-Anhinga Prize for Poetry.

## ANVIL PRESS

P.O. Box 3008 MPO, Vancouver BC V6B 3X5, Canada. (604)876-8710. **Fax:** (604)879-2667. **E-mail:** info@anvilpress.com. **Website:** www.anvilpress.com. "Anvil Press publishes contemporary adult fiction, poetry, and drama, giving voice to up-and-coming Canadian writers, exploring all literary genres, discovering, nurturing, and promoting new Canadian literary talent. Currently emphasizing urban/suburban themed fiction and poetry; de-emphasizing historical novels." Canadian authors only. No e-mail submissions. Publishes trade paperback originals. Pays advance. Average advance is $500-2,000, depending on the genre. Publishes book 8 months after acceptance of ms. Re-

sponds in 2 months to queries; 6 months to mss. Book catalog for 9×12 SAE with 2 first-class stamps. Guidelines online.

**NEEDS** "Get our catalog, look at our poetry. We do very little poetry-maybe 1-2 titles per year."

**HOW TO CONTACT** Query with 8-12 poems and SASE.

**TIPS** "Audience is informed, educated, aware, with an opinion, culturally active (films, books, the performing arts). No U.S. authors. Research the appropriate publisher for your work."

## ARC PUBLICATIONS

Nanholme Mill, Shaw Wood Rd., Todmorden, Lancashire OL14 6DA, United Kingdom. **E-mail:** info@arcpublications.co.uk. **E-mail:** international-editor@arcpublications.co.uk. **Website:** www.arcpublications.co.uk. **Contact:** John W. Clarke, domestic editor; James Byrne, international editor (outside Ireland/England). Responds in 6 weeks.

**NEEDS** Publishes "contemporary poetry from new and established writers from the UK and abroad, specializing in the work of world poets writing in English, and the work of overseas poets in translation."

**HOW TO CONTACT** Send 16-24 pages of poetry and short cover letter.

## ARTE PUBLICO PRESS

University of Houston, 4902 Gulf Fwy, Bldg 19, Rm 100, Houston TX 77204-2004. **Fax:** (713)743-2847. **E-mail:** submapp@uh.edu. **Website:** artepublicopress.com. **Contact:** Nicolas Kanellos, editor. Arte Publico Press is the oldest and largest publisher of Hispanic literature for children and adults in the United States. "We are a showcase for Hispanic literary creativity, arts and culture. Our endeavor is to provide a national forum for U.S.-Hispanic literature." Publishes hardcover originals, trade paperback originals and reprints. Pays 10% royalty on wholesale price. Provides 20 author's copies; 40% discount on subsequent copies. Pays $1,000-3,000 advance. Publishes book 2 years after acceptance of ms. Responds in 1 month to queries and proposals; 4 months to mss. Book catalog available free. Guidelines online.

**HOW TO CONTACT** Submissions made through online submission form.

**TIPS** "Include cover letter in which you 'sell' your book—why should we publish the book, who will want to read it, why does it matter, etc. Use our ms submission online form. Format files accepted are: Word, plain/text, rich/text files. Other formats will not be accepted. Manuscript files cannot be larger than 5MB. Once editors review your ms, you will receive an e-mail with the decision. Revision process could take up to 4 months."

## ASHLAND POETRY PRESS

401 College Ave., Ashland OH 44805. (419)289-5098. **E-mail:** app@ashland.edu. **Website:** www.ashlandpoetrypress.com. **Contact:** Cassandra Brown, managing editor. Publishes trade paperback originals. Makes outright purchase of $500-1,000. Publishes book 10 months after acceptance. Responds in 1 month to queries; 6 months to mss. Book catalog online. Guidelines online.

**NEEDS** "We accept unsolicited manuscripts through the Snyder Prize competition each spring-the deadline is April 1. Judges are mindful of dedication to craftsmanship and thematic integrity."

**TIPS** "We rarely publish a title submitted off the transom outside of our Snyder Prize competition."

## AUTUMN HOUSE PRESS

87½ Westwood St., Pittsburgh PA 15211. (412)381-4261. **E-mail:** info@autumnhouse.org. **Website:** www.autumnhouse.org. Alison Taverna, Managing Editor. **Contact:** Christine Stroud, Senior Editor. "We are a non-profit literary press specializing in high-quality poetry, fiction, and nonfiction. Our editions are beautifully designed and printed, and they are distributed nationally. Approximately one-third of our sales are to college literature and creative writing classes." Member CLMP and Academy of American Poets. "We distribute our own titles. We do extensive national promotion through ads, web-marketing, reading tours, book fairs and conferences. We are open to all genres. The quality of writing concerns us, not the genre." You can also learn about our annual Fiction Prize, Poetry Prize, Nonfiction Prize, and Chapbook Award competitions, as well as our online journal, *Coal Hill Review*. (Please note that Autumn House accepts unsolicited mss *only* through these competitions.) Publishes hardcover, trade paperback, and electronic originals. Format: acid-free paper; offset printing; perfect and casebound (cloth) bound; sometimes contains illustrations. Average print order: 1,000. Debut novel print order: 1,000. Pays 7% royalty on wholesale price. Pays $0-2,500 advance. Publishes 9 months after acceptance. Responds in 1-3 days on

queries and proposals; 3 months on mss Catalog online. Guidelines online.

**NEEDS** "We ask that all submissions from authors new to Autumn House come through one of our annual contests." All finalists will be considered for publication.

**HOW TO CONTACT** Submit only through our annual contest. See guidelines online.

**TIPS** "The competition to publish with Autumn House is very tough. Submit only your best work."

## THE BACKWATERS PRESS

1124 PACIFIC ST, #8392, Omaha NE 68108. **E-mail:** thebackwaterspress@gmail.com. **Website:** www.thebackwaterspress.org. Greg Kosmicki, Editor Emeritus. **Contact:** James Cihlar, editor. Poetry in English Pays in copies, publication. Contest winner receives $1,000 and copies. Does not pay advance. Publishes ms 6-12 months after acceptance. Contest: 2-3 months. All others, up to 6 months. Catalog online. Guidelines online.

**NEEDS** Only considers submissions to Backwaters Prize. More details on website. Open to all styles and forms.

**HOW TO CONTACT** Postal mail to above address; e-mail to the press.

**TIPS** "Send your best work."

## BEAR STAR PRESS

185 Hollow Oak Dr., Cohasset CA 95973. (530)891-0360. **Website:** www.bearstarpress.com. **Contact:** Beth Spencer, publisher/editor. "Bear Star is committed to publishing the best poetry it can attract. Each year it sponsors the Dorothy Brunsman contest, open to poets from Western and Pacific states. From time to time we add to our list other poets from our target area whose work we admire." Publishes trade paperback originals. Pays $1,000, and 25 copies to winner of annual Dorothy Brunsman contest. Publishes book 9 months after acceptance. Responds in 2 weeks to queries. Guidelines online.

**NEEDS** Wants well-crafted poems. No restrictions as to form, subject matter, style, or purpose. "Poets should enter our annual book competition. Other books are occasionally solicited by publisher, sometimes from among contestants who didn't win."

**HOW TO CONTACT** Online submissions strongly preferred.

**TIPS** "Send your best work, consider its arrangement. A 'wow' poem early keeps me reading."

## BIRCH BOOK PRESS

Birch Brook Impressions, P.O. Box 81, Delhi NY 13753. **Fax:** (607)746-7453. **E-mail:** birchbrook@copper.net. **Website:** www.birchbrookpress.info. **Contact:** Tom Tolnay, editor/publisher; Leigh Eckmair, art & research editor; Joyce Tolnay, account services. Birch Brook Press "is a book printer/typesetter/designer that uses monies from these activities to publish several titles of its own each year with cultural and literary interest." Specializes in literary work, flyfishing, baseball, outdoors, themed short fiction anthologies, and books about books. Occasionally publishes trade paperback originals. Pays modest royalty on acceptance. Publishes ms 10-18 months after acceptance. Responds in 3 to 6 months. Book catalog online.

**HOW TO CONTACT** Query first with a few sample poems or chapters, or send entire ms. No e-mail submissions; submissions by postal mail only. Must include SASE with submissions. Occasionally comments on rejected poems. Royalty on co-op contracts.

**TIPS** "Write well on subjects of interest to BBP, such as outdoors, flyfishing, baseball, music, literary stories, fine poetry, books about books."

## BKMK PRESS

University of Missouri - Kansas City, 5101 Rockhill Rd., Kansas City MO 64110-2499. (816)235-2558. **Fax:** (816)235-2611. **E-mail:** bkmk@umkc.edu. **Website:** newletters.org. "BkMk Press publishes fine literature. Reading period February-June." Publishes trade paperback originals. Responds in 4-6 months to queries. Guidelines online.

**HOW TO CONTACT** Submit 10 sample poems and SASE.

**TIPS** "We skew toward readers of literature, particularly contemporary writing. Because of our limited number of titles published per year, we discourage apprentice writers or 'scattershot' submissions."

## ⑤ BLACK LAWRENCE PRESS

326 Bigham St., Pittsburgh PA 15211. **E-mail:** editors@blacklawrencepress.com. **Website:** www.blacklawrencepress.com. **Contact:** Diane Goettel, executive editor. Black Lawrence press seeks to publish intriguing books of literature—novels, short story collections, poetry collections, chapbooks, anthologies, and creative nonfiction. Will also publish the occasional translation from German. Publishes 15-20 books/year, mostly poetry and fiction. Mss are selected through open submission and competition. Books are 20-400 pages, offset-printed or high-quality POD, perfect-bound, with 4-color cover. Pays royalties. Responds in 6 months to mss.

**HOW TO CONTACT** Submit complete ms.

## BLACK OCEAN

P.O. Box 52030, Boston MA 02205. **Fax:** (617)849-5678. **E-mail:** carrie@blackocean.org. **Website:** www.blackocean.org. **Contact:** Carrie Olivia Adams, poetry editor. Responds in 6 months to mss.

**NEEDS** Wants poetry that is well-considered, risks itself, and by its beauty and/or bravery disturbs a tiny corner of the universe. Mss are selected through open submission. Books are 60+ pages.

**HOW TO CONTACT** Book/chapbook mss may include previously published poems. "We have an open submission period in June of each year; specific guidelines are updated and posted on our website in the months preceding."

## BLAZEVOX [BOOKS]

131 Euclid Ave., Kenmore NY 14217. **E-mail:** editor@blazevox.org. **Website:** www.blazevox.org. **Contact:** Geoffrey Gatza, editor/publisher. "We are a major publishing presence specializing in innovative fictions and wide-ranging fields of innovative forms of poetry and prose. Our goal is to publish works that are challenging, creative, attractive, and yet affordable to individual readers. Articles of submission depend on many criteria, but overall items submitted must conform to one ethereal trait, your work must not suck. This put plainly, bad art should be punished; we will not promote it. However, all submissions will be reviewed and the author will receive feedback. We are human too." Pays 10% royalties on fiction and poetry books, based on net receipts. This amount may be split across multiple contributors. "We do not pay advances." Guidelines online.

**HOW TO CONTACT** Submit complete ms via e-mail.

**TIPS** "We actively contract and support authors who tour, read and perform their work, play an active part of the contemporary literary scene, and seek a readership."

## BLUE LIGHT PRESS

1563 45th Ave., San Francisco CA 94122. **E-mail:** bluelightpress@aol.com. **Website:** www.bluelightpress.com. **Contact:** Diane Frank, chief editor. "We like poems that are imagistic, emotionally honest, and push the edge—where the writer pushes through the imagery to a deeper level of insight and understanding. No rhymed poetry." Has published poetry by Stephen Dunn, Kim Addonizio, Jane Hirshfield, Rustin Larson, Mary Kay Rummel, Daniel J. Langton, and K.B. Ballentine. "Books are elegantly designed and artistic. Our books are professionally printed, with original cover art, and we publish full-length books of poetry and chapbooks." Catalog online.

**NEEDS** "We have an online poetry workshop with a wonderful group of American and international poets—open to new members 3 times/year. Send an e-mail for info." No rhymed poetry.

**HOW TO CONTACT** Send an e-mail for guidelines. Does not accept e-mail submissions. Deadlines: January 30 for full-sized mss. and June 15 for chapbooks. "Read our guidelines before sending your ms."

**TIPS** "To see more than 100 poets we love, get a copy of *River of Earth and Sky: Poems for the Twenty-First Century*. It is full of examples of the kinds of poems we like to publish."

## BLUE MOUNTAIN PRESS

Blue Mountain Arts, Inc., P.O. Box 4219, Boulder CO 80306. (800)525-0642. **E-mail:** bmpbooks@sps.com. **Website:** www.sps.com. **Contact:** Patti Wayant, Director. *"Please note: We are not accepting works of fiction, rhyming poetry, children's books, chapbooks, or memoirs."* Publishes hardcover originals, trade paperback originals, electronic originals. Pays royalty on wholesale price. Publishes ms 12-16 months after acceptance. Responds in 2-4 months. Guidelines by e-mail.

**NEEDS** "We publish poetry appropriate for gift books, self-help books, and personal growth books. We do not publish chapbooks or literary poetry."

**HOW TO CONTACT** Query. Submit 10+ sample poems.

## BOA EDITIONS, LTD.

P.O. Box 30971, Rochester NY 14603. (585)546-3410. **Fax:** (585)546-3913. **E-mail:** contact@boaeditions.org. **Website:** www.boaeditions.org. Melissa Hall, Director of Development and Operations. **Contact:** Jenna Fisher, Director of Marketing and Production; Peter Conners, Publisher. BOA Editions, Ltd., a not-for-profit publisher of poetry, short fiction, and poetry-in-translation, fosters readership and appreciation of contemporary literature. By identifying, cultivating, and publishing both new and established poets

and selecting authors of unique literary talent, BOA brings high quality literature to the public. Publishes hardcover, trade paperback, and digital e-book originals. Negotiates royalties. Pays variable advance. Publishes ms 18 months after acceptance. Responds in 1 week to queries; 5 months to mss. Book catalog online. Guidelines online.

**NEEDS** Readers who, like Whitman, expect the poet to 'indicate more than the beauty and dignity which always attach to dumb real objects .. They expect him to indicate the path between reality and their souls,' are the audience of BOA's books. BOA Editions, a Pulitzer Prize and National Book Award-winning not-for-profit publishing house, acclaimed for its work, reads poetry mss for the American Poets Continuum Series (new poetry by distinguished poets in mid-to-late career), the Lannan Translations Selection Series (publication of 2 new collections of contemporary international poetry annually, supported by the Lannan Foundation of Santa Fe, NM), the New Poets of America Series (publication of a poet's first book, selected through the A. Poulin, Jr. Poetry Prize), and the America Reader Series (short fiction and prose on poetics).

**HOW TO CONTACT** Check BOA's website for reading periods for the American Poets Continuum Series and the Lannan Translation Selection Series. Please adhere to the general submission guidelines for each series. Guidelines online.

## BOTTOM DOG PRESS, INC.

P.O. Box 425, Huron OH 44839. (419)433-3573. **E-mail:** lsmithdog@smithdocs.net. **Website:** smithdocs.net. **Contact:** Larry Smith, director; Susanna Sharp-Schwacke, associate editor. Bottom Dog Press, Inc., "is a nonprofit literary and educational organization dedicated to publishing the best writing and art from the Midwest and Appalachia." Pays 10 copies and 15% royalty. Does not pay advance. Publishes ms 4 months after acceptance.

○ "Query via e-mail first."

## BOYDS MILLS PRESS

Highlights for Children, Inc., 815 Church St., Honesdale PA 18431. (570)253-1164. **Website:** www.boydsmillspress.com. Boyds Mills Press publishes picture books, nonfiction, activity books, and paperback reprints. Their titles have been named notable books by the International Reading Association, the American Library Association, and the National Council of Teachers of English. They've earned numerous awards, including the National Jewish Book Award, the Christopher Medal, the NCTE Orbis Pictus Honor, and the Golden Kite Honor. Boyds Mills Press welcomes unsolicited submissions from published and unpublished writers and artists. Submit a ms with a cover letter of relevant information, including experience with writing and publishing. Label the package "Manuscript Submission" and include an SASE. For art samples, label the package "Art Sample Submission." All submissions will be evaluated for all imprints. Responds to mss within 3 months. Catalog online. Guidelines online.

**HOW TO CONTACT** Send a book-length collection of poems. Do not send an initial query. Keep in mind that the strongest collections demonstrate a facility with multiple poetic forms.

### ✪ BRICK BOOKS

Box 20081, 431 Boler Rd., London ON N6K 4G6, Canada. (519)657-8579. **E-mail:** brick.books@sympatico.ca. **Website:** www.brickbooks.ca. **Contact:** Kitty Lewis, General Manager. Brick Books has a reading period of January 1-April 30. Mss received outside that period will be returned. No multiple submissions. Pays 10% royalty in book copies only. Publishes trade paperback originals. Publishes ms 2 years after acceptance. Responds in 3-4 months to queries. Book catalog free or online. Guidelines online.

◖ "We publish only poetry."

**HOW TO CONTACT** Submit only poetry.

**TIPS** "Writers without previous publications in literary journals or magazines are rarely considered by Brick Books for publication."

### BRICK ROAD POETRY PRESS, INC.

513 Broadway, Columbus GA 31901. (706)649-3080. **Fax:** (706)649-3094. **E-mail:** kbadowski@brickroadpoetrypress.com. **Website:** www.brickroadpoetrypress.com. **Contact:** Ron Self and Keith Badowski, co-editors/founders. The mission of Brick Road Poetry Press is to publish and promote poetry that entertains, amuses, edifies, and surprises a wide audience of appreciative readers. "We are not qualified to judge who deserves to be published, so we concentrate on publishing what we enjoy. Our preference is for poetry geared toward dramatizing the human experience in language rich with sensory image and metaphor, recognizing that poetry can be, at one and the same time, both familiar as the perspiration of daily labor and as

outrageous as a carnival sideshow. We prefer poetry that offers a coherent human voice, a sense of humor, attentiveness to words and language, narratives with surprise twists, persona poems, and/or philosophical or spiritual themes explored through the concrete scenes and images." Does not want overemphasis on rhyme, intentional obscurity or riddling, highfalutin vocabulary, greeting card verse, overt religious statements of faith and/or praise, and/or abstractions.

**HOW TO CONTACT** Publishes poetry only: books (single author collections) "We accept .doc, .rtf, or .pdf file formats. We prefer electronic submissions but will reluctantly consider hard copy submissions by mail if USPS Flat Rate Mailing Envelope is used and with the stipulation that, should the author's work be chosen for publication, an electronic version (.doc or .rtf) must be prepared in a timely manner and at the poet's expense." Please include cover letter with poetry publication/recognition highlights and something intriguing about your life story or ongoing pursuits. "We would like to develop a connection with the poet as well as the poetry." Please include the collection title in the cover letter. "We want to publish poets who are engaged in the literary community, including regular submission of work to various publications and participation in poetry readings, workshops, and writers' groups. That said, we would never rule out an emerging poet who demonstrates ability and motivation to move in that direction."

**CONTEST/AWARD OFFERINGS** Brick Road Poetry Press Book Contest, $1,000 prize and publication. Annually accepts entries August 1-November 1. See www.brickroadpoetrypress.com for submission guidelines.

**TIPS** "The best way to discover all that poetry can be and to expand the limits of your own poetry is to read expansively. We recommend the following poets: Kim Addonizio, Ken Babstock, Coleman Barks, Billy Collins, Morri Creech, Cynthia Cruz, Alice Friman, John Glenday, Beth A. Gylys, Jane Hirshfield, Jane Kenyon, Ted Kooser, Stanley Kunitz, Thomas Lux, Barry Marks, Michael Meyerhofer, Linda Pastan, Mark Strand, and Natasha D. Trethewey."

### BRONZE MAN BOOKS

Millikin University, 1184 W. Main, Decatur IL 62522. (217)424-6264. **E-mail:** rbrooks@millikin.edu. **Website:** www.bronzemanbooks.com. **Contact:** Dr. Randy Brooks, editorial board; Edwin Walker, editorial board. A student-owned and operated press located on Millikin University's campus in Decatur, Ill., Bronze Man Books is dedicated to integrating quality design and meaningful content. The company exposes undergraduate students to the process of publishing by combining the theory of writing, publishing, editing and designing with the practice of running a book publishing company. This emphasis on performance learning is a hallmark of Millikin's brand of education. Publishes hardcover, trade paperback, literary chapbooks and mass market paperback originals. Outright purchase based on wholesale value of 10% of a press run. Publishes book 6-12 months after acceptance. Responds in 1-3 months.

**HOW TO CONTACT** Submit completed ms.

**TIPS** "The art books are intended for serious collectors and scholars of contemporary art, especially of artists from the Midwestern US. These books are published in conjunction with art exhibitions at Millikin University or the Decatur Area Arts Council. The children's books have our broadest audience, and the literary chapbooks are intended for readers of contemporary fiction, drama, and poetry."

## ⊘ CALAMARI PRESS

Via Titta Scarpetta #28, Rome 00153, Italy. **E-mail:** derek@calamaripress.net. **Website:** www.calamaripress.com. Calamari Press publishes books of literary text and art. Mss are selected by invitation. Occasionally has open submission period—check website. Helps to be published in *SleepingFish* first. Publishes paperback originals. Pays in author's copies. Ms published 2-6 months after acceptance. Responds to mss in 2 weeks. Guidelines online.

## CARCANET PRESS

Alliance House, 4th Floor, 30 Cross St., Manchester England M2 7AQ, United Kingdom. 44(0)161 834 8730. **Fax:** 44(0)161 832 0084. **E-mail:** info@carcanet.co.uk. **Website:** www.carcanet.co.uk. **Contact:** Michael Schmidt, editorial and managing director. "Carcanet Press is one of Britain's leading poetry publishers. It provides a comprehensive and diverse list of modern and classic poetry in English and in translation. It now incorpprates Anvil Press Poetry and represents Northern House." Publishes hardcover and trade paperback originals.

**NEEDS** Familiarize yourself with our books, and then submit between 6 and 10 pages or work (poetry or translations) and SASE. Replies are usually sent within 6 weeks. Writers wishing to propose other projects should send a full synopsis and cover letter, with sample pages, having first ascertained that the kind of book proposed is suitable for our programme. Do not call in person.

## CARNEGIE MELLON UNIVERSITY PRESS

5032 Forbes Ave., Pittsburgh PA 15289-1021. (412)268-2861. **Fax:** (412)268-8706. **E-mail:** carnegiemellonuniversitypress@gmail.com. **Website:** www.cmu.edu/universitypress/. Publishes hardcover and trade paperback originals. Book catalog and guidelines online.

**NEEDS** Holds annual reading period. "This reading period is only for poets who have not previously been published by CMP."

**HOW TO CONTACT** Submit complete ms. **Requires reading fee of $15.**

## CAROLINA WREN PRESS

120 Morris St., Durham NC 27701. (919)560-2738. **E-mail:** carolinawrenpress@earthlink.net. **Website:** www.carolinawrenpress.org. **Contact:** Andrea Selch, president. "We publish poetry, fiction, and memoirs by, and/or about people of color, women, gay/lesbian issues, and work by writers from, living in, or writing about the U.S. South." Publishes ms 2 year after acceptance. Responds in 3 months to queries; 6 months to mss. Guidelines online.

Accepts simultaneous submissions, but "let us know if work has been accepted elsewhere."

**NEEDS** Publishes 2 poetry books/year, "usually through the Carolina Wren Press Poetry Series Contest. Otherwise we primarily publish women, minorities, and authors from, living in, or writing about the U.S. South." Not accepting unsolicited submissions except through Poetry Series Contest.

**HOW TO CONTACT** Accepts e-mail queries, but send only letter and description of work, no large files. Carolina Wren Press Poetry Contest for a First or Second Book takes submissions, electronically, from January to March of odd-numbered years.

**TIPS** "Best way to get read is to submit to a contest."

## CHRONICLE BOOKS

680 Second St., San Francisco CA 94107. **E-mail:** submissions@chroniclebooks.com. **Website:** www.chroniclebooks.com. "We publish an exciting range of books, stationery, kits, calendars, and novelty formats. Our list includes children's books and interac-

tive formats; young adult books; cookbooks; fine art, design, and photography; pop culture; craft, fashion, beauty, and home decor; relationships, mind-body-spirit; innovative formats such as interactive journals, kits, decks, and stationery; and much, much more." Generally pays authors in royalties based on retail price, "though we do occasionally work on a flat fee basis." Advance varies. Illustrators paid royalty based on retail price or flat fee. Publishes a book 1-3 years after acceptance. Responds to queries in 1 month. Book catalog for 9×12 SAE and 8 first-class stamps. Ms guidelines for #10 SASE.

**HOW TO CONTACT** Submit via mail only. Children's submissions only. Submit proposal (guidelines online) and allow up to 3 months for editors to review. If submitting by mail, do not include SASE since our staff will not return materials.

**ADDITIONAL INFORMATION** Generally pays authors in royalties based on retail price, "though we do occasionally work on a flat fee basis." Advance varies. Illustrators paid royalty based on retail price or flat fee.

## CITY LIGHTS BOOKS

261 Columbus Ave., San Francisco CA 94133. (415)362-8193. **Fax:** (415)362-4921. **Website:** www.citylights.com.

**NEEDS** City Lights Books is the legendary paperback house that achieved prominence with the publication of Allen Ginsberg's *Howl* and other poetry of the "Beat" school. Publishes "poetry, fiction, philosophy, political and social history."

**HOW TO CONTACT** Does not accept unsolicted mss. No inquiries or submissions by e-mail. "Before sending a book proposal, we urge you to look at our catalog to familiarize yourself with our publication. If you feel certain that your work is appropriate to our list, then please send a query letter that includes your reésumeé (with a list of previous publications and a sample of no more than 10 pages." Include SASE for response. Responds in 3 months. Guidelines available on website.

## CLEVELAND STATE UNIVERSITY POETRY CENTER

2121 Euclid Ave., RT 1841, Cleveland OH 44115. (216)687-3986. **Fax:** (216)687-6943. **E-mail:** poetrycenter@csuohio.edu. **Website:** www.csupoetrycenter.com. **Contact:** Amber Allen, managing editor. The Cleveland State University Poetry Center was established in 1962 at the former Fenn College of Engineering to promote poetry through readings and community outreach. In 1971, it expanded its mission to become a national non-profit independent press under the auspices of the Cleveland State University Department of English, and has since published nearly 200 rangy, joyful, profound, astonishing, complicated, surprising, and aesthetically diverse collections of contemporary poetry and prose by established and emerging authors. The Cleveland State University Poetry Center publishes between three and five collections of contemporary poetry and prose a year, with a national distribution and reach. The Poetry Center currently acquires manuscripts through three annual contests (one dedicated to publishing and promoting first books of poetry, one to supporting an established poet's career, and one to publishing collections of literary essays). Pays $1,000 for competition winners. Publishes ms 1-2 years after acceptance. Responds in less than a year. Catalog online. Guidelines online.

**HOW TO CONTACT** Most mss are accepted through the competitions. All mss sent for competitions are considered for publication. Outside of competitions, mss are accepted by solicitation only.

## ◎ COACH HOUSE BOOKS

80 bpNichol Ln., Toronto ON M5S 3J4, Canada. (416)979-2217. **Fax:** (416)977-1158. **E-mail:** editor@chbooks.com. **Website:** www.chbooks.com. **Contact:** Alana Wilcox, editorial director. Publishes trade paperback originals by Canadian authors. Pays 10% royalty on retail price. Publishes ms 1 year after acceptance. Responds in 6-8 months to queries. Guidelines online.

**TIPS** "We are not a general publisher, and publish only Canadian poetry, fiction, select nonfiction and drama. We are interested primarily in innovative or experimental writing."

## COFFEE HOUSE PRESS

79 13th NE, Suite 110, Minneapolis MN 55413. (612)338-0125. **Fax:** (612)338-4004. **E-mail:** info@coffeehousepress.org. **Website:** www.coffeehousepress.org. **Contact:** Molly Fuller, production editor. This successful nonprofit small press has received numerous grants from various organizations including the NEA, the McKnight Foundation and Target. Books published by Coffee House Press have won numerous honors and awards. Example: *The Book of Medicines*, by Linda Hogan won the Colorado Book Award for Poetry and the Lannan Foundation Literary Fellow-

ship. Publishes hardcover and trade paperback originals. Responds in 4-6 weeks to queries; up to 6 months to mss. Book catalog and ms guidelines online.

**HOW TO CONTACT** Coffee House Press will not accept unsolicited poetry submissions. Please check our web page periodically for future updates to this policy.

**TIPS** "Look for our books at stores and libraries to get a feel for what we like to publish. No phone calls, e-mails, or faxes."

## COPPER CANYON PRESS

P.O. Box 271, Port Townsend WA 98368. (360)385-4925. **Fax:** (360)385-4985. **E-mail:** poetry@coppercanyonpress.org. **Website:** www.coppercanyonpress.org. Managing Editor: Tonaya Craft. **Contact:** Joseph Bednarik and George Knotek, co-publishers. Copper Canyon Press is a nonprofit publisher that believes poetry is vital to language and living. Since 1972, the press has published poetry exclusively and has established an international reputation for its commitment to authors, editorial acumen, and dedication to the poetry audience. Catalog online. Guidelines online.

**NEEDS** Has open submission periods throughout the year; see website for details. Charges $35 fee for each submission, which entitles poets to select 2 Copper Canyon Press titles from a list.

**HOW TO CONTACT** Submit complete ms via Submittable.

**TIPS** "Please familiarize yourself with our mission, catalog, and submissions FAQ before submitting a manuscript."

## COTEAU BOOKS

Thunder Creek Publishing Co-operative Ltd., 2517 Victoria Ave., Regina SK S4P 0T2, Canada. (306)777-0170. **Fax:** (306)522-5152. **E-mail:** coteau@coteaubooks.com. **Website:** www.coteaubooks.com. **Contact:** Geoffrey Ursell, publisher. "Our mission is to publish the finest in Canadian fiction, nonfiction, poetry, drama, and children's literature, with an emphasis on Saskatchewan and prairie writers. De-emphasizing science fiction, picture books." Publishes chapter books for young readers aged 9-12 and novels for older kids ages 13-15 and for ages 15 and up. Publishes trade paperback originals and reprints. Pays 10% royalty on retail price. Publishes book 1 year after acceptance. Responds in 3 months. Book catalog available free. Guidelines online.

**HOW TO CONTACT** Submit 20-25 sample poems.

**TIPS** "Look at past publications to get an idea of our editorial program. We do not publish romance, horror, or picture books but are interested in juvenile and teen fiction from Canadian authors. Submissions, even queries, must be made in hard copy only. We do not accept simultaneous/multiple submissions. Check our website for new submission timing guidelines."

## CRESCENT MOON PUBLISHING

P.O. Box 1312, Maidstone Kent ME14 5XU, United Kingdom. (44)(162)272-9593. **E-mail:** cresmopub@yahoo.co.uk. **Website:** www.crmoon.com. **Contact:** Jeremy Robinson, director (arts, media, cinema, literature); Cassidy Hughes (visual arts). "Our mission is to publish the best in contemporary work, in poetry, fiction, and critical studies, and selections from the great writers. Currently emphasizing nonfiction (media, film, music, painting). De-emphasizing children's books." Publishes hardcover and trade paperback originals. Pays royalty. Pays negotiable advance. Publishes ms 18 months after acceptance. Responds in 2 months to queries; 4 months to proposals and mss. Book catalog and ms guidelines free.

**NEEDS** "We prefer a small selection of the poet's very best work at first. We prefer free verse or non-rhyming poetry. Do not send too much material."

**HOW TO CONTACT** Query and submit 6 sample poems.

**TIPS** "Our audience is interested in new contemporary writing."

## CROSS-CULTURAL COMMUNICATIONS

Cross-Cultural Literary Editions, Cross-Cultural Communications, 239 Wynsum Ave., Merrick NY 11566-4725. (516)869-5635. **Fax:** (516)379-1901. **E-mail:** info@cross-culturalcommunications.com; cccpoetry@aol.com. **Website:** www.cross-cultural-communications.com. **Contact:** Stanley H. Barkan; Bebe Barkan. Publishes hardcover and trade paperback originals. Publishes book 1 year after acceptance. Responds in 1 month to proposals; 2 months to mss. Book catalog (sample flyers) for #10 SASE.

**HOW TO CONTACT** For bilingual poetry submit 3-6 short poems in original language with English translation, a brief (3-5 lines) bio of the author and translator(s).

**TIPS** "Best chance: poetry from a translation."

## DIAL BOOKS FOR YOUNG READERS

Imprint of Penguin Group (USA), 345 Hudson St., New York NY 10014. (212)366-2000. **Website:** www.penguin.com/children. "Dial Books for Young Readers publishes quality picture books for ages 18 months-6 years; lively, believable novels for middle readers and young adults; and occasional nonfiction for middle readers and young adults." Publishes hardcover originals. Pays royalty. Pays varies advance. Responds in 4-6 months to queries. Book catalog and guidelines online.

**TIPS** "Our readers are anywhere from preschool age to teenage. Picture books must have strong plots, lots of action, unusual premises, or universal themes treated with freshness and originality. Humor works well in these books. A very well-thought-out and intelligently presented book has the best chance of being taken on. Genre isn't as much of a factor as presentation."

## DINK PRESS

**E-mail:** dink@dinkpress.com. **Website:** dinkpress. com. **Contact:** Kristopher D. Taylor, founder/publisher/editor. Dink Press has released a number of chapbooks of contemporary poetry and a lit mag called Dink Mag. Dink's primary mission is to help revitalize the poetry culture with cheaper volumes of unique and powerful work. Responds in 3 months. Catalog online. Guidelines online.

**NEEDS** At this time, we are only accepting chapbook and full-length manuscript submissions.

**HOW TO CONTACT** Submit complete ms.

**TIPS** "Feel free to include any ideas you may have for the cover of the collection, we would love to hear from you."

## DUFOUR EDITIONS

P.O. Box 7, 124 Byers Rd., Chester Springs PA 19425. (610)458-5005. **Fax:** (610)458-7103. **Website:** www. dufoureditions.com. "We publish literary fiction by good writers which is well received and achieves modest sales. De-emphsazing poetry and nonfiction." Publishes hardcover originals, trade paperback originals and reprints. Pays $100-500 advance. Publishes ms 18 months after acceptance. Responds in 3-6 months. Book catalog available free.

**HOW TO CONTACT** Query.

## THE ECCO PRESS

195 Broadway, New York NY 10007. (212)207-7000. **Fax:** (212)702-2460. **Website:** www.harpercollins. com. Publishes hardcover and trade paperback originals and reprints. Pays royalty. Pays negotiable advance. Publishes ms 1 year after acceptance.

## ÉDITIONS DU NOROÎT

4609 D'Iberville, Bureau 202, Montreal QC H2H 2L9, Canada. (514)727-0005. **Fax:** (514)723-6660. **E-mail:** lenoroit@lenoroit.com. **Website:** www.lenoroit. com. **Contact:** Paul Belanger, director. "Editions du Noiroît publishes poetry and essays on poetry." Publishes trade paperback originals and reprints. Pays 10% royalty on retail price. Publishes ms 1 year after acceptance. Responds in 4 months to mss.

**HOW TO CONTACT** Submit 40 sample poems.

## EYEWEAR PUBLISHING

United Kingdom. **E-mail:** info@eyewearpublishing. com. **Website:** store.eyewearpublishing.com. Senior Poetry Editor: Kelly Davio. **Contact:** Dr. Todd Swift, director/editor. Eyewear Publishing is a new independent press, passionate about producing beautifully designed, fascinating books that remain affordable. "Based in London, we celebrate the best writing in English from the UK and overseas. Guidelines online.

**NEEDS** As a small independent press Eyewear understands the importance of an open door policy, especially at a time when so few presses accept unsolicited manuscripts.

## FARRAR, STRAUS & GIROUX

18 W. 18th St., New York NY 10011. (646)307-5151. **Website:** us.macmillan.com/fsg. **Contact:** Editorial Department. "We publish original and well-written material for all ages." Publishes hardcover originals and trade paperback reprints. Pays 2-6% royalty on retail price for paperbacks, 3-10% for hardcovers. Pays $3,000-25,000 advance. Publishes ms 18 months after acceptance. Responds in 2-3 months. Catalog available by request. Guidelines online.

**HOW TO CONTACT** Send cover letter describing submission with 3-4 poems. By mail only.

## FARRAR, STRAUS & GIROUX FOR YOUNG READERS

Macmillan Children's Publishing Group, 175 Fifth Ave., New York NY 10010. (212)741-6900. **Fax:** (212)633-2427. **E-mail:** childrens.editorial@fsgbooks.

com. **Website:** www.fsgkidsbooks.com. Book catalog available by request. Ms guidelines online.

**HOW TO CONTACT** Submit cover letter, 3-4 poems by mail only.

**TIPS** "Study our catalog before submitting. We will see illustrators' portfolios by appointment. Don't ask for criticism and/or advice—due to the volume of submissions we receive, it's just not possible. Never send originals. Always enclose SASE."

## FENCE BOOKS

Science Library 320, Univ. of Albany, 1400 Washington Ave., Albany NY 12222. (518)591-8162. **E-mail:** fencesubmissions@gmail.com. **Website:** www.fenceportal.org. **Contact:** Submissions Manager. "Fence Books publishes poetry, fiction, and critical texts and anthologies, and prioritizes sustained support for its authors, many of whom come to us through our book contests and then go on to publish second, third, fourth books." Publishes hardcover originals. Guidelines online.

**HOW TO CONTACT** Submit via contests and occasional open reading periods.

## FINISHING LINE PRESS

P.O. Box 1626, Georgetown KY 40324. (859)514-8966. **E-mail:** FinishingBooks@aol.com. **Website:** www. finishinglinepress.com. **Contact:** Leah Maines, director. Finishing Line Press seeks to "discover new talent" and hopes to publish chapbooks by both men and women poets who have not previously published a book or chapbook of poetry. Has published *Parables and Revelations* by T. Crunk, *Family Business* by Paula Sergi, *Putting in a Window* by John Brantingham, and *Dusting the Piano* by Abigail Gramig. Publishes 50-60 poetry chapbooks/year. Chapbooks are usually 25-30 pages, digest-sized, laser-printed, saddle-stapled, with card covers with textured matte wrappers. Submit up to 26 pages of poetry with cover letter, bio, acknowledgments, and **$12 reading fee**. Responds to queries and mss in up to 1 month. Pay varies; pays in author's copies. "Sales profits, if any, go to publish the next new poet." Sample chapbooks available by sending $6 to Finishing Line Press or through website. See The Finishing Line Press Open Chapbook Competition and the New Women's Voices Chapbook Competition.

**NEEDS** Finishing Line Press seeks to "discover new talent" and hopes to publish chapbooks by both men and women poets who have not previously published a book or chapbook of poetry. Has published *Parables and Revelations* by T. Crunk, *Family Business* by Paula Sergi, *Putting in a Window* by John Brantingham, and *Dusting the Piano* by Abigail Gramig. Publishes 50-60 poetry chapbooks/year. Chapbooks are usually 25-30 pages, digest-sized, laser-printed, saddle-stapled, with card covers with textured matte wrappers.

**HOW TO CONTACT** Submit up to 26 pages of poetry with cover letter, bio, acknowledgments, and **$12 reading fee**. Responds to queries and mss in up to 1 month. Pay varies; pays in author's copies. "Sales profits, if any, go to publish the next new poet." Sample chapbooks available by sending $6 to Finishing Line Press or through website.

**CONTEST/AWARD OFFERINGS** The Finishing Line Press Open Chapbook Competition and the New Women's Voices Chapbook Competition.

## FLOATING BRIDGE PRESS

909 NE 43rd St., #205, Seattle WA 98105. **E-mail:** floatingbridgepress@yahoo.com. **Website:** www. floatingbridgepress.org.

Floating Bridge Press publishes the work of poets residing in Washington State.

**NEEDS** Floating Bridge Press publishes chapbooks and anthologies by Washington State poets, selected through an annual competition.

## FOLDED WORD

79 Tracy Way, Meredith NH 03253. **Website:** www. foldedword.com. Editor-in-Chief: J.S. Graustein. Poetry Editor: Rose Auslander. Fiction Editor: Casey Tingle. **Contact:** Barbara Flaherty, Submissions Editor. Folded Word is a literary micro-press that explores the world, one voice at a time. "Our list includes globally-distributed work by authors from four continents. We give individualized attention to the editing and design of each title." Pays royalty. Advance only in rare cases with solicited books. Publishes ms 2 years after acceptance. Responds in 60 days for queries. If a full ms is requested, it may take 6 months for a final decision. Catalog online. Guidelines online.

**NEEDS** "We enjoy narrative poetry that has a strong sense of place and/or time, especially the exploration of unfamiliar place/time. We enjoy mind-bending images and creative spacing on the page. We are also looking for poetry that is ecologically and culturally aware. We enjoy humor, word-play, and voices that take a chance. Please, surprise us."

**HOW TO CONTACT** "We are especially seeking regional poetry (any region), haiku (and other Japanese-form poetry), and bilingual chapbooks of poetry in translation."

**TIPS** "Please be sure you have read some of our titles prior to submitting; our ebooks are reasonably priced to make exploring our list easier."

## FOUR WAY BOOKS

Box 535, Village Station, New York NY 10014. **E-mail:** editors@fourwaybooks.com. **Website:** www.fourwaybooks.com. **Contact:** Martha Rhodes, director. "Four Way Books is a not-for-profit literary press dedicated to publishing poetry and short fiction by emerging and established writers. Each year, Four Way Books publishes the winners of its national poetry competitions, as well as collections accepted through general submission, panel selection, and solicitation by the editors."

**NEEDS** Four Way Books publishes poetry and short fiction. Considers full-length poetry mss only. Books are about 70 pages, offset-printed digitally, perfect-bound, with paperback binding, art/graphics on covers. Does not want individual poems or poetry intended for children/young readers.

**HOW TO CONTACT** See website for complete submission guidelines and open reading period in June. Book mss may include previously published poems. Responds to submissions in 4 months. Payment varies. Order sample books from Four Way Books online or through bookstores.

## FUTURECYCLE PRESS

**Website:** www.futurecycle.org. **Contact:** Diane Kistner, director/editor-in-chief. Publishes English-language poetry books, chapbooks, and anthologies in print-on-demand and digital editions. Awards the FutureCycle Poetry Book Prize and honorarium for the best full-length book the press publishes each year. Pays in deeply discounted author copies (no purchase required). Responds in 3 months. Guidelines, sample contract, and detailed *Guide for Authors* online.

**NEEDS** Wants "poetry from imaginative, highly skilled poets, whether well known or emerging. We abhor the myopic, self-absorbed, and sloppy, but otherwise are eclectic in our tastes." Does not want concrete or visual poetry. Publishes 15+ poetry books/year and 5+ chapbooks/year. Ms. selected through open submission. Books average 62-110 pages; chapbooks 30-42 pages; anthologies 100+ pages.

**HOW TO CONTACT** Submit complete ms. No need to query.

## GERTRUDE PRESS

P.O. Box 28281, Portland OR 97228. (503)515-8252. **E-mail:** editor@gertrudepress.org. **Website:** www.gertrudepress.org. "Gertrude Press is a nonprofit organization developing and showcasing the creative talents of lesbian, gay, bisexual, trans, queer-identified and allied individuals. We publish limited-edition fiction and poetry chapbooks plus the biannual literary journal, *Gertrude*." Reads chapbook mss only through contests.

**TIPS** Sponsors poetry and fiction chapbook contest. Prize is $175 and 50 contributor's copies. Submission guidelines and fee information on website. "Read the journal and sample published work. We are not impressed by pages of publications; your work should speak for itself."

## GIVAL PRESS

Gival Press, LLC, P.O. Box 3812, Arlington VA 22203. (703)351-0079. **E-mail:** givalpress@yahoo.com. **Website:** www.givalpress.com. **Contact:** Robert L. Giron, editor-in-chief (area of interest: literary). "We publish literary works: fiction, nonfiction (essays, academic), and poetry in English, Spanish, and French." Publishes trade paperback, electronic originals, and reprints. Pays royalty. Publishes ms 12 months after acceptance. Responds in 3-5 months. Book catalog online. Guidelines online.

**HOW TO CONTACT** Query via e-mail; provide description, bio, etc.; submit 5-6 sample poems via e-mail.

**TIPS** "Our audience is those who read literary works with depth to the work. Visit our website—there is much to be read/learned from the numerous pages."

## ⊘ DAVID R. GODINE, PUBLISHER

15 Court Square, Suite 320, Boston MA 02108. (617)451-9600. **Fax:** (617)350-0250. **E-mail:** info@godine.com. **Website:** www.godine.com. "We publish books that matter for people who care." This publisher is no longer considering unsolicited mss of any type. Only interested in agented material.

## GOLD WAKE PRESS

**E-mail:** gwakepress@gmail.com. **Website:** goldwake.com. **Contact:** Nick Courtright and Kyle McCord. Gold Wake Press is an independent literary house founded in the suburbs of Boston by Jared Michael

Wahlgren, who ran the press until 2014. Guidelines online.

**NEEDS** Check website for open submission periods.

**TIPS** "The press seeks to bring voices to the spotlight who combine daring content with meticulous attention to form."

## GOOSE LANE EDITIONS

500 Beaverbrook Ct., Suite 330, Fredericton NB E3B 5X4, Canada. (506)450-4251. **Fax:** (506)459-4991. **E-mail:** submissions@gooselane.com. **Website:** www.gooselane.com. **Contact:** Angela Williams, publishing assistant. "Goose Lane publishes literary fiction and nonfiction from well-read and highly skilled Canadian authors." Publishes hardcover and paperback originals and occasional reprints. Pays 8-10% royalty on retail price. Pays $500-3,000, negotiable advance. Responds in 6 months to queries.

**NEEDS** Considers mss by Canadian poets only.

**HOW TO CONTACT** Submit cover letter, list of publications, synopsis, entire ms, SASE.

**TIPS** "Writers should send us outlines and samples of books that show a very well-read author with highly developed literary skills. Our books are almost all by Canadians living in Canada; we seldom consider submissions from outside Canada. We consider submissions from outside Canada only when the author is Canadian and the book is of extraordinary interest to Canadian readers. We do not publish books for children or for the young adult market."

## GRAYWOLF PRESS

250 Third Ave. N., Suite 600, Minneapolis MN 55401. (651)641-0077. **Fax:** (651)641-0036. **Website:** www.graywolfpress.org. "Graywolf Press is an independent, nonprofit publisher dedicated to the creation and promotion of thoughtful and imaginative contemporary literature essential to a vital and diverse culture." Publishes trade cloth and paperback originals. Pays royalty on retail price. Pays $1,000-25,000 advance. Publishes 18 months after acceptance. Responds in 3 months to queries. Book catalog free. Guidelines online.

**NEEDS** "We are interested in linguistically challenging work."

**HOW TO CONTACT** Agented submissions only.

## GROVE/ATLANTIC, INC.

154 W. 14th St., 12th Floor, New York NY 10011. **E-mail:** info@groveatlantic.com. **Website:** www.grove-atlantic.com. "Due to limited resources of time and staffing, Grove/Atlantic cannot accept manuscripts that do not come through a literary agent. In today's publishing world, agents are more important than ever, helping writers shape their work and navigate the main publishing houses to find the most appropriate outlet for a project." Publishes hardcover and trade paperback originals, and reprints. Pays 7 ½-12 ½% royalty. Makes outright purchase of $5-500,000. Book published 9 months after acceptance of ms. Responds in 1 month to queries; 2 months to proposals; 4 months to mss. Book catalog available online.

**HOW TO CONTACT** Agented submissions only.

## GUERNICA EDITIONS

1569 Heritage Way, Oakville Ontario L6M 2Z7, Canada. (905)599-5304. **Fax:** (416)981-7606. **E-mail:** michaelmirolla@guernicaeditions.com. **Website:** www.guernicaeditions.com. **Contact:** Michael Mirolla, editor/publisher (poetry, nonfiction, short stories, novels). Guernica Editions is a literary press that produces works of poetry, fiction and nonfiction often by writers who are ignored by the mainstream. Publishes trade paperback originals and reprints. Pays 8-10% royalty on retail price, or makes outright purchase of $200-5,000. Pays $450-750 advance. Publishes 24-36 months after acceptance. Responds in 1 month to queries. Responds in 6 months to proposals. Responds in 1 year to manuscripts Book catalog available online. Queries and submissions accepted via e-mail.

**NEEDS** Feminist, gay/lesbian, literary, multicultural, poetry in translation. We wish to have writers in translation. Any writer who has translated Italian poetry is welcomed. Full books only. No single poems by different authors, unless modern, and used as an anthology.

**HOW TO CONTACT** Query.

## HARPERCOLLINS

195 Broadway, New York NY 10007. (212)207-7000. **Website:** www.harpercollins.com. HarperCollins, one of the largest English language publishers in the world, is a broad-based publisher with strengths in academic, business and professional, children's, educational, general interest, and religious and spiritual books, as well as multimedia titles. Publishes hardcover and paperback originals and paperback reprints. Pays royalty. Pays negotiable advance.

**TIPS** "We do not accept any unsolicited material."

## HARPER PERENNIAL

10 E. 53rd St., New York NY 10022. **E-mail:** harper-perennial@harpercollins.com. **Website:** harperperennial.tumblr.com. Harper Perennial is one of the paperback imprints of HarperCollins. "We publish paperback originals and reprints of authors like Ann Patchett, Justin Taylor, Barbara Kingsolver, and Blake Butler."

## HIGH PLAINS PRESS

P.O. Box 123, 403 Cassa Rd., Glendo WY 82213. (307)735-4370. **Fax:** (307)735-4590. **E-mail:** editor@highplainspress.com. **Website:** www.highplainspress.com. **Contact:** Nancy Curtis, publisher. High Plains Press is a regional book publishing company specializing in books about the American West, with special interest in things relating to Wyoming. Publishes hardcover and trade paperback originals. Pays 10% royalty on wholesale price. Pays $200-2000 advance. Publishes book 2 years after acceptance of ms. Responds in 1 month to queries and proposals; 6 months on mss. Book catalog and guidelines online.

**NEEDS** "We publish 1 poetry volume a year. Sometimes we skip a year. Require connection to West. Consider poetry in August."

**HOW TO CONTACT** Submit 5 sample poems.

**TIPS** "Our audience comprises general readers interested in history and culture of the Rockies."

## 🐷 HIPPOPOTAMUS PRESS

22 Whitewell Rd., Frome Somerset BA11 4EL, United Kingdom. (44)(173)466-6653. **E-mail:** rjhippopress@aol.com. **Contact:** R. John, editor; M. Pargitter (poetry); Anna Martin (translation). "Hippopotamus Press publishes first, full collections of verse by those well represented in the mainstream poetry magazines of the English-speaking world." Publishes hardcover and trade paperback originals. Pays 7½-10% royalty on retail price. Pays advance. Publishes book 10 months after acceptance. Responds in 1 month to queries. Book catalog available free.

**NEEDS** "Read one of our authors—poets often make the mistake of submitting poetry without knowing the type of verse we publish."

**HOW TO CONTACT** Query and submit complete ms.

**TIPS** "We publish books for a literate audience. We have a strong link to the Modernist tradition. Read what we publish."

## ⬤⊘ HOUSE OF ANANSI PRESS

128 Sterling Rd., Lower Level, Toronto ON M6R 2B7, Canada. (416)363-4343. **Fax:** (416)363-1017. **Website:** www.anansi.ca. House of Anansi publishes literary fiction and poetry by Canadian and international writers. Pays 8-10% royalties. Pays $750 advance and 10 author's copies. Responds to queries within 1 year; to mss (if invited) within 4 months.

**NEEDS** "We seek to balance the list between well-known and emerging writers, with an interest in writing by Canadians of all backgrounds. We publish Canadian poetry only, and poets must have a substantial publication record—if not in books, then definitely in journals and magazines of repute." Does not want "children's poetry or poetry by previously unpublished poets."

**HOW TO CONTACT** Canadian poets should query first with 10 sample poems (typed double-spaced) and a cover letter with brief bio and publication credits. Considers simultaneous submissions. Poems are circulated to an editorial board. Often comments on rejected poems.

## IBEX PUBLISHERS

P.O. Box 30087, Bethesda MD 20824. (301)718-8188. **Fax:** (301)907-8707. **E-mail:** info@ibexpub.com. **Website:** www.ibexpublishers.com. "IBEX publishes books about Iran and the Middle East and about Persian culture and literature." Publishes hardcover and trade paperback originals and reprints. Payment varies. Book catalog available free.

**NEEDS** "Translations of Persian poets will be considered."

## ILIUM PRESS

2407 S. Sonora Dr., Spokane WA 99037. (509)701-8866. **E-mail:** iliumpress@outlook.com. **E-mail:** iliumpress@outlook.com. **Contact:** John Lemon, owner/editor. "Ilium is a small, 1-man press that I run in my spare time that was created to cultivate and promote the relevance of epic poetry in today's world. I am very selective about my projects, but I provide extensive editorial care to those I take on." Publishes trade paperback originals and reprints, electronic originals and reprints. Pays 20-50% royalties on receipts. Does not pay advance. Publishes ms up to 1 year after acceptance. Responds in 6 months.

**NEEDS** Ilium Press specializes in original, book-length narrative epic poems written in blank or sprung (non-rhyming) metered verse in contemporary language. "I'm looking for original work that shows how epic poetry is still relevant in today's world. Please query via e-mail if you have questions."

**HOW TO CONTACT** Submit via e-mail (preferred) or via mail with first 20 pages.

## ⊙ INSOMNIAC PRESS

520 Princess Ave., London ON N6B 2B8, Canada. (416)504-6270. **E-mail:** mike@insomniacpress.com. **Website:** www.insomniacpress.com. **Contact:** Mike O'Connor, publisher. Publishes trade paperback originals and reprints, mass market paperback originals, and electronic originals and reprints. Pays 10-15% royalty on retail price. Pays $500-1,000 advance. Publishes ms 6 months after acceptance. Guidelines online.

**NEEDS** "Our poetry publishing is limited to 2-4 books per year and we are often booked up a year or two in advance."

**HOW TO CONTACT** Submit complete ms.

**TIPS** "We envision a mixed readership that appreciates up-and-coming literary fiction and poetry as well as solidly researched and provocative nonfiction. Peruse our website and familiarize yourself with what we've published in the past."

## ITALICA PRESS

595 Main St., Suite 605, New York NY 10044-0047. (917)371-0563. **E-mail:** inquiries@italicapress.com. **Website:** www.italicapress.com. **Contact:** Ronald G. Musto and Eileen Gardiner, publishers. "Italica Press publishes English translations of modern Italian fiction and medieval and Renaissance nonfiction." Publishes hardcover and trade paperback originals. Pays 7-15% royalty on wholesale price; author's copies. Publishes ms 1 year after acceptance. Responds in 1 month to queries; 4 months to mss. Book catalog and guidelines online.

**NEEDS** Poetry titles are always translations and generally dual language.

**HOW TO CONTACT** Query with 10 sample translations of medieval and Renaissance Italian poets. Include cover letter, bio, and list of publications.

**TIPS** "We are interested in considering a wide variety of medieval and Renaissance topics (not historical fiction), and for modern works we are only interested in translations from Italian fiction by well-known Italian authors. *Only* fiction that has been previously published in Italian. A *brief* e-mail saves a lot of time. 90% of proposals we receive are completely off base—but we are very interested in things that are right on target."

## ALICE JAMES BOOKS

114 Prescott St., Farmington ME 04938. (207)778-7071. **Fax:** (207)778-7766. **E-mail:** info@alicejamesbooks.org. **Website:** www.alicejamesbooks.org. **Contact:** Carey Salerno, executive director. "Alice James Books is a nonprofit cooperative poetry press. The founders' objectives were to give women access to publishing and to involve authors in the publishing process. The cooperative selects mss for publication through both regional and national competitions." Publishes trade paperback originals. Pays through competition awards. Publishes ms 1 year after acceptance. Responds promptly to queries; 4 months to mss. Book catalog online. Guidelines online.

**NEEDS** Does not want children's poetry or light verse.

**TIPS** "Send SASE for contest guidelines or check website. Do not send work without consulting current guidelines."

## THE JOHNS HOPKINS UNIVERSITY PRESS

2715 N. Charles St., Baltimore MD 21218. (410)516-6900. **Fax:** (410)516-6968. **Website:** www.press.jhu.edu. **Contact:** Jacqueline C. Wehmueller, executive editor (consumer health, psychology and psychiatry, and history of medicine; jcw@press.jhu.edu); Matthew McAdam, editor (mxm@jhu.press.edu); Robert J. Brugger, senior acquisitions editor (American history; rjb@press.jhu.edu); Vincent J. Burke, exec. editor (biology; vjb@press.jhu.edu). Publishes hardcover originals and reprints, and trade paperback reprints. Pays royalty. Publishes ms 1 year after acceptance.

**NEEDS** "One of the largest American university presses, Johns Hopkins publishes primarily scholarly books and journals. We do, however, publish short fiction and poetry in the series Johns Hopkins: Poetry and Fiction, edited by John Irwin."

## KAYA PRESS

c/o USC ASE, 3620 S. Vermont Ave. KAP 462, Los Angeles CA 90089. (213) 740-2285. **E-mail:** info@kaya.com. **Website:** www.kaya.com. **Contact:** Sunyoung Lee, editor. Kaya is an independent literary press dedicated to the publication of innovative literature from the Asian Pacific diaspora. Publishes hardcover originals and trade paperback originals and reprints. Responds in 6 months to mss. Book catalog available free. Guidelines online.

**HOW TO CONTACT** Submit complete ms.

**TIPS** "Audience is people interested in a high standard of literature and who are interested in breaking down easy approaches to multicultural literature."

### KELSEY STREET PRESS

Poetry by Women, 2824 Kelsey St., Berkeley CA 94705. **E-mail:** info@kelseyst.com. **Website:** www.kelseyst. com. "A Berkeley, California press publishing collaborations between women poets and artists. Many of the press's collaborations focus on a central theme or conceit, like the sprawl and spectacle of New York in *Arcade* by Erica Hunt and Alison Saar." Hardcover and trade paperback originals and electronic originals.

**HOW TO CONTACT** Query.

### KNOPF

Imprint of Random House, 1745 Broadway, New York NY 10019. **Fax:** (212)940-7390. **Website:** knopfdoubleday.com/imprint/knopf. Publishes hardcover and paperback originals. Royalties vary. Offers advance. Publishes ms 1 year after acceptance. Responds in 2-6 months to queries.

### ⬤◎ LAPWING PUBLICATIONS

1 Ballysillan Dr., Belfast BT14 8HQ, Northern Ireland. (44)2890-500-796. **Fax:** (44)2890-295-800. **E-mail:** lapwing.poetry@ntlworld.com. **Website:** www.lapwingpoetry.com. **Contact:** Dennis Greig, editor. Pays 20 author's copies, no royalties. Responds to queries in 1 month; mss in 2 months.

⬤ Lapwing will produce work only if and when resources to do so are available.

**NEEDS** Lapwing publishes "emerging Irish poets and poets domiciled in Ireland, plus the new work of a suitable size by established Irish writers. Non-Irish poets are also published. Poets based in continental Europe have become a major feature. Emphasis on first collections preferably not larger than 80 pages.

**HOW TO CONTACT** "Submit 6 poems in the first instance; depending on these, an invitation to submit more may follow." Considers simultaneous submissions. Accepts e-mail submissions in body of message or in DOC format. Cover letter is required. "All submissions receive a first reading. If these poems have minor errors or faults, the writer is advised. Those which appeal at first reading are retained, and a con-

ditional offer is sent." Often comments on rejected poems. "After initial publication, irrespective of the quantity, the work will be permanently available using 'print-on-demand' production; such publications may not always be printed exactly as the original, although the content will remain the same."

**TIPS** "We are unable to accept new work from beyond mainland Europe and the British Isles due to delivery costs."

### LEAPFROG PRESS

Box 505, Fredonia NY 14063. (508)274-2710. **E-mail:** leapfrog@leapfrogpress.com. **E-mail:** acquisitions@leapfrogpress.com. **Website:** www.leapfrogpress.com. **Contact:** Rebecca Schwab, acquisitions editor; Layla Al-Bedawi, publicity. Pays 10% royalty on net receipts. Average advance: negotiable. Publishes ms approximately 1 year after acceptance. Response time varies. Guidelines online.

**TIPS** "We like anything that is superbly written and genuinely original. We like the idiosyncratic and the peculiar. We rarely publish nonfiction. Send only your best work, and send only completed work that is ready. That means the completed ms has already been through extensive editing and is ready to be judged. We consider submissions from both previously published and unpublished writers. We are uninterested in an impressive author bio if the work is poor; if the work is excellent, the author bio is equally unimportant."

### LEE & LOW BOOKS

95 Madison Ave., #1205, New York NY 10016. (212)779-4400. **E-mail:** general@leeandlow.com. **Website:** www.leeandlow.com. "Our goals are to meet a growing need for books that address children of color, and to present literature that all children can identify with. We only consider multicultural children's books. Sponsors a yearly New Voices Award for first-time picture book authors of color. Contest rules online at website or for SASE." Publishes hardcover originals and trade paperback reprints. Pays net royalty. Pays authors advances against royalty. Pays illustrators advance against royalty. Photographers paid advance against royalty. Publishes book 2 years after acceptance. Responds in 6 months to mss if interested. Book catalog available online. Guidelines available online or by written request with SASE.

**HOW TO CONTACT** Submit complete ms.

**TIPS** "Check our website to see the kinds of books we publish. Do not send mss that don't fit our mission."

## LES FIGUES PRESS

P.O. Box 7736, Los Angeles CA 90007. **E-mail:** info@lesfigues.com. **Website:** www.lesfigues.com. **Contact:** Teresa Carmody, director. Les Figues Press is an independent, nonprofit publisher of poetry, prose, visual art, conceptual writing, and translation. With a mission is to create aesthetic conversations between readers, writers, and artists, Les Figues Press favors projects which push the boundaries of genre, form, and general acceptability. Submissions are only reviewed through its annual NOS Book Contest.

## LETHE PRESS

118 Heritage Ave., Maple Shade NJ 08052. (609)410-7391. **E-mail:** lethepress@aol.com. **Website:** www.lethepressbooks.com. "Welcomes submissions from authors of any sexual or gender identity." Guidelines online.

**NEEDS** "Lethe Press is a small press seeking gay and lesbian themed poetry collections." Lethe Books are distributed by Ingram Publications and Bookazine, and are available at all major bookstores, as well as the major online retailers.

**HOW TO CONTACT** Query with 7-10 poems, list of publications.

## LOST HORSE PRESS

105 Lost Horse Ln., Sandpoint ID 83864. (208)255-4410. **E-mail:** losthorsepress@mindspring.com. **Website:** www.losthorsepress.org. **Contact:** Christine Holbert, publisher. Distributed by University of Washington Press. Publishes hardcover and paperback originals. Publishes ms 3-9 months after acceptance.

 "*Does not accept unsolicited mss.* However, we welcome submissions for the Idaho Prize for Poetry, a national competition offering $1,000 prize money plus publication for a book-length ms. Please check the submission guidelines for the Idaho Prize for Poetry online."

## LSU PRESS

338 Johnston Hall, Baton Rouge LA 70803. (225)578-6294. **Website:** lsupress.org. **Contact:** MaryKatherine Callaway, director poetry. LSU Press has established itself as one of the nation's outstanding scholarly presses and garners national and international accolades, including 4 Pulitzer Prizes. Responds in 4-6 months. Catalog online. Guidelines online.

**NEEDS** Poetry proposals should include a cover letter, 4-5 sample pages from the ms, and a current resume.

## LUNA BISONTE PRODS

137 Leland Ave., Columbus OH 43214-7505. **E-mail:** bennettjohnm@gmail.com. **Website:** www.johnmbennett.net. **Contact:** John M. Bennett, editor/publisher. Pays copy or copies of book; further copies at cost. Does not pay advance.

**NEEDS** "Interested in avant-garde and highly experimental work only." Has published poetry by Jim Leftwich, Sheila E. Murphy, Al Ackerman, Richard Kostelanetz, Carla Bertola, Olchar Lindsann, and many others.

**HOW TO CONTACT** Query first, with a few sample poems and cover letter with brief bio and publication credits. "Keep it brief. Chapbook publishing usually depends on grants or other subsidies, and is usually by solicitation. **Will also consider subsidy arrangements on negotiable terms.**" A sampling of various Luna Bisonte Prods products is available for $20.

## MAGE PUBLISHERS, INC.

1780 Crossroads Dr., Odenton MD 21113. (202)342-1642. **Fax:** (202)342-9269. **E-mail:** as@mage.com. **Website:** www.mage.com. Mage publishes books relating to Persian/Iranian culture. Publishes hardcover originals and reprints, trade paperback originals. Pays royalty. Responds in 1 month to queries. Book catalog available free. Guidelines online.

**NEEDS** Must relate to Persian/Iranian culture.

**HOW TO CONTACT** Query.

**TIPS** "Audience is the Iranian-American community in America and Americans interested in Persian culture."

## MANOR HOUSE PUBLISHING, INC.

452 Cottingham Crescent, Ancaster ON L9G 3V6, Canada. **E-mail:** mbdavie@manor-house.biz. **E-mail:** mbdavie@manor-house.biz. **Website:** www.manor-house.biz. **Contact:** Mike Davie, president (novels and nonfiction). Publishes hardcover, trade paperback, and mass market paperback originals reprints. Pays 10% royalty on retail price. Publishes book 1 year after acceptance. Queries and mss to be sent by e-mail only. "We will respond in 30 days if interested-if not, there is no response. Do not follow up unless asked to do so." Book catalog online. Guidelines available via e-mail.

**NEEDS** Poetry should engage, provoke, involve the reader.

**TIPS** "Our audience includes everyone-the general public/mass audience. Self-edit your work first, make sure it is well written with strong Canadian content."

## ⊘ MARINER BOOKS

222 Berkeley St., Boston MA 02116. (617)351-5000. **Website:** www.hmco.com.

**NEEDS** Has published poetry by Thomas Lux, Linda Gregerson, and Keith Leonard.

**HOW TO CONTACT** Agented submissions only.

## MAVERICK DUCK PRESS

**E-mail:** maverickduckpress@yahoo.com. **Website:** www.maverickduckpress.com. Assistant Editors: Kayla Marie Middlebrook and Brielle Kelton. **Contact:** Kendall A. Bell, editor. Maverick Duck Press is a "publisher of chapbooks from undiscovered talent. We are looking for fresh and powerful work that shows a sense of innovation or a new take on passion or emotion. Previous publication in print or online journals could increase your chances of us accepting your manuscript." Does not want "unedited work." Pays 20 author's copies.

**HOW TO CONTACT** Send ms in Microsoft Word format with a cover letter with brief bio and publication credits. Chapbook mss may include previously published poems. "Previous publication is always a plus, as we may be more familiar with your work. Chapbook mss should have 16-24 poems, but no more than 24 poems."

## ✪ MCCLELLAND & STEWART, LTD.

The Canadian Publishers, 320 Front St. W., Suite 1400, Toronto ON M5V 3B6, Canada. (416)364-4449. **Fax:** (416)598-7764. **Website:** www.mcclelland.com. Publishes hardcover, trade paperback, and mass market paperback originals and reprints. Pays 10-15% royalty on retail price (hardcover rates). Pays advance. Publishes ms 1 year after acceptance. Responds in 3 months to proposals.

**NEEDS** Only Canadian poets should apply. We publish only 4 titles each year. Query. *No unsolicited mss.*

## MCSWEENEY'S POETRY SERIES

San Francisco CA **E-mail:** poetry@mcsweeneys.net. **Website:** mcsweeneys.net. McSweeney's regularly publishes poetry collections, as part of the McSweeney's Poetry Series. Catalog online. Guidelines online.

**NEEDS** The McSweeney's Poetry Series publishes new collections of poetry. "We are open to all styles.

**HOW TO CONTACT** Book-length mss should be sent as PDF to poetry@mcsweeneys.net. In the cover letter, include your name, phone number, and e-mail address.

**TIPS** "We're a very small operation, and we may not be able to get back to you about the manuscript. We will do our very best."

## MERRIAM PRESS

133 Elm St., Suite 3R, Bennington VT 05201. (802)447-0313. **E-mail:** ray@merriam-press.com. **Website:** www.merriam-press.com. "Merriam Press specializes in military history, particularly World War II history. We are also branching out into other genres, including fiction, historical fiction, poetry, children." Publishes hardcover and softcover trade paperback originals and reprints. Many titles are also made available in PDF and eBook editions. Pays 10% royalty on actual selling price. Does not pay advance. Publishes ms 6 months or less after acceptance. Responds quickly (e-mail preferred) to queries. Book catalog and guidelines online.

**NEEDS** Especially but not limited to military topics.

**HOW TO CONTACT** Query with SASE or by e-mail first.

**TIPS** "Our military history books are geared for military historians, collectors, model kit builders, wargamers, veterans, general enthusiasts. We now publish some historical fiction and poetry and will consider well-written books on a variety of non-military topics."

## ⊘ MIAMI UNIVERSITY PRESS

356 Bachelor Hall, Miami University, Oxford OH 45056. **E-mail:** mupress@miamioh.edu. **Website:** www.miamioh.edu/mupress. **Contact:** Keith Tuma, editor; Amy Toland, managing editor. Publishes 1-2 books of poetry/year and 1 novella, in paperback editions.

**HOW TO CONTACT** Miami University Press is unable to respond to unsolicited mss and queries.

## MICHIGAN STATE UNIVERSITY PRESS

1405 S. Harrison Rd., Suite 25, East Lansing MI 48823. (517)355-9543. **Fax:** (517)432-2611. **E-mail:** mspress@msu.edu. **Website:** msupress.org. **Contact:** Alex Schwartz and Julie Loehr, acquisitions. Michigan State University Press has notably represented both scholarly publishing and the mission of Michigan State University with the publication of numerous award-winning books and scholarly journals. In addition, they publish nonfiction that addresses, in a more contemporary way, social concerns, such as diversity and civil rights. They also publish literary fiction and poetry. Publishes hardcover and softcover originals. Pays variable royalty. Book catalog and ms guidelines online.

**NEEDS** Publishes poetry collections.

**HOW TO CONTACT** Submit proposal with sample poems.

## MILKWEED EDITIONS

1011 Washington Ave. S., Suite 300, Minneapolis MN 55415. (612)332-3192. **Fax:** (612)215-2550. **Website:** www.milkweed.org. **Contact:** Patrick Thomas, managing editor. "Milkweed Editions publishes with the intention of making a humane impact on society, in the belief that literature is a transformative art uniquely able to convey the essential experiences of the human heart and spirit. To that end, Milkweed Editions publishes distinctive voices of literary merit in handsomely designed, visually dynamic books, exploring the ethical, cultural, and esthetic issues that free societies need continually to address." Publishes hardcover, trade paperback, and electronic originals; trade paperback and electronic reprints. Pays authors variable royalty based on retail price. Offers advance against royalties. Pays varied advance from $500-10,000. Publishes book in 18 months. Responds in 6 months. Book catalog online. Only accepts submissions during open submission periods. See website for guidelines.

**NEEDS** Milkweed Editions is "looking for poetry manuscripts of high quality that embody humane values and contribute to cultural understanding." Not limited in subject matter. Open to writers with previously published books of poetry or a minimum of 6 poems published in nationally distributed commercial or literary journals. Considers translations and bilingual mss.

**HOW TO CONTACT** Query with SASE; submit completed ms.

**TIPS** "We are looking for excellent writing with the intent of making a humane impact on society. Please read submission guidelines before submitting and acquaint yourself with our books in terms of style and quality before submitting. Many factors influence our selection process, so don't get discouraged. Nonfiction is focused on literary writing about the natural world, including living well in urban environments."

## MOVING PARTS PRESS

10699 Empire Grade, Santa Cruz CA 95060. (831)427-2271. **E-mail:** frice@movingpartspress.com. **Website:** www.movingpartspress.com. **Contact:** Felicia Rice, poetry editor. Moving Part Press publishes handsome, innovative books, broadsides, and prints that "explore the relationship of word and image, typography and the visual arts, the fine arts and popular culture."

**HOW TO CONTACT** *Does not accept unsolicited mss.*

## NEW DIRECTIONS

80 Eighth Ave., New York NY 10011. **Fax:** (212)255-0231. **E-mail:** editorial@ndbooks.com. **Website:** www.ndbooks.com. **Contact:** Editorial Assistant. "Currently, New Directions focuses primarily on fiction in translation, avant garde American fiction, and experimental poetry by American and foreign authors. If your work does not fall into one of those categories, you would probably do best to submit your work elsewhere." Hardcover and trade paperback originals. Responds in 3-4 months to queries. Book catalog and guidelines online.

**HOW TO CONTACT** Query.

**TIPS** "Our books serve the academic community."

## NEWEST PUBLISHERS LTD.

201, 8540-109 St., Edmonton AB T6G 1E6, Canada. (780)432-9427. **Fax:** (780)433-3179. **E-mail:** info@newestpress.com. **E-mail:** submissions@newestpress.com. **Website:** www.newestpress.com. NeWest publishes Western Canadian fiction, nonfiction, poetry, and drama. Publishes trade paperback originals. Pays 10% royalty. Publishes ms 2-3 years after acceptance. Responds in 6-8 months to queries. Book catalog for 9×12 SASE. Guidelines online.

## NEW ISSUES POETRY & PROSE

Western Michigan University, 1903 W. Michigan Ave., Kalamazoo MI 49008-5463. (269)387-8185. **Fax:** (269)387-2562. **E-mail:** new-issues@wmich.edu. **Website:** wmich.edu/newissues. **Contact:** Managing Editor. Publishes 18 months after acceptance. Guidelines online.

**NEEDS** New Issues Poetry & Prose offers two contests annually. The Green Rose Prize is awarded to an author who has previously published at least one full-length book of poems. The New Issues Poetry Prize, an award for a first book of poems, is chosen by a guest judge. Past judges have included Philip Levine, C.K. Williams, C.D. Wright, and Campbell McGrath. New Issues does not read mss outside our contests. Graduate students in the Ph.D. and M.F.A. programs of Western Michigan Univ. often volunteer their time reading mss. Finalists are chosen by the editors. New Issues often publishes up to 2 additional mss selected from the finalists.

### NEW RIVERS PRESS

1104 Seventh Ave. S., Moorhead MN 56563. **Website:** www.newriverspress.com. **Contact:** Nayt Rundquist, managing editor. New Rivers Press publishes collections of poetry, novels, nonfiction, translations of contemporary literature, and collections of short fiction and nonfiction. "We continue to publish books regularly by new and emerging writers, but we also welcome the opportunity to read work of every character and to publish the best literature available nationwide. Each fall through the Many Voices Project competition, we choose 2 books: 1 poetry and 1 prose."

**NEEDS** The Many Voices Project awards $1,000, a standard book contract, publication of a book-length ms by New Rivers Press, and national distribution. All previously published poems must be acknowledged. "We will consider simultaneous submissions if noted as such. If your manuscript is accepted elsewhere during the judging, you must notify New Rivers Press immediately. If you do not give such notification and your manuscript is selected, your entry gives New Rivers Press permission to go ahead with publication."

**HOW TO CONTACT** Guidelines online.

### NIGHTBOAT BOOKS

P.O. Box 10, Callicoon NY 12723. **Fax:** (603)448-9429. **E-mail:** info@nightboat.org. **Website:** nightboat.org. Managing Editor: Lindsey Boldt. Nightboat Books, a nonprofit organization, seeks to develop audiences for writers whose work resists convention and transcends boundaries, by publishing books rich with poignancy, intelligence and risk. Catalog online. Guidelines online.

**NEEDS** Considers poetry submitted to its poetry prize. More information online.

**TIPS** "The name Nightboat signifies travel, passage, and possibility—of mind and body, and of language. The night boat maneuvers in darkness at the mercy of changing currents and weather, always immersed in forces beyond itself."

### NINETY-SIX PRESS

Special Collections, James B. Duke Library, 3300 Poinsett Hwy., Greenville SC 29613. (864)294-2194. **E-mail:** specialcollections@furman.edu. **Website:** library.furman.edu/specialcollections/96Press/index.htm. **Contact:** Jeffrey Makala, Special Collections Librarian and University Archivist. For a sample, send $10.

**TIPS** "Between 1991 and 2015, the Ninety-Six Press published only poetry by South Carolina authors. The Press is not considering new publishing projects at this time. Check our website for up-to-date information."

### W.W. NORTON & COMPANY, INC.

500 Fifth Ave., New York NY 10110. (212)354-5500. **Fax:** (212)869-0856. **Website:** www.wwnorton.com. "W. W. Norton & Company, the oldest and largest publishing house owned wholly by its employees, strives to carry out the imperative of its founder to 'publish books not for a single season, but for the years' in fiction, nonfiction, poetry, college textbooks, cookbooks, art books and professional books. Due to the workload of our editorial staff and the large volume of materials we receive, *Norton is no longer able to accept unsolicited submissions.* If you are seeking publication, we suggest working with a literary agent who will represent you to the house."

### OBERLIN COLLEGE PRESS

50 N. Professor St., Oberlin OH 44074. (440)775-8408. **Fax:** (440)775-8124. **E-mail:** oc.press@oberlin.edu. **Website:** www.oberlin.edu/ocpress. **Contact:** Marco Wilkinson, managing editor. Publishes hardcover and trade paperback originals. Pays 7½-10% royalty. Responds promptly to queries; 2 months to mss.

**NEEDS** *FIELD Magazine*—submit 2-6 poems through website "submissions" tab; FIELD Translation Series—query with SASE and sample poems; FIELD Poetry Series—*no unsolicited mss.* Enter mss in FIELD Poetry Prize ($1,000 and a standard royalty contract) held annually in May.

**HOW TO CONTACT** Submit complete ms.

**TIPS** "Queries for the FIELD Translation Series: send sample poems and letter describing project. Winner of the annual FIELD poetry prize determines publication. Do not send unsolicited manuscripts."

## OHIO STATE UNIVERSITY PRESS

1070 Carmack Rd., 180 Pressey Hall, Columbus OH 43210-1002. (614)292-6930. **Fax:** (614)292-2065. **E-mail:** eugene@osupress.org. **E-mail:** lindsay@osu-press.org. **Website:** www.ohiostatepress.org. **Contact:** Eugene O'Connor, acquisitions editor (medieval studies and classics); Lindsay Martin, acquisitions editor (literary studies). The Ohio State University Press publishes scholarly nonfiction, and offers short fiction and short poetry prizes. Currently emphasizing history, literary studies, political science, women's health, classics, Victoria studies. Pays royalty. Pays advance. Responds in 3 months to queries. Guidelines online.

**NEEDS** Offers poetry competition through *The Journal.*

## ⚙ OOLICHAN BOOKS

P.O. Box 2278, Lantzville BC V0R 1M0, Canada. (250)390-4839. **Fax:** (866)299-0026. **E-mail:** info@oolichan.com. **Website:** www.oolichan.com. Publisher: Randal Macnair. Publishes hardcover and trade paperback originals and reprints. Pays royalty on retail price. Publishes ms 6-12 months after acceptance. Responds in 1-3 months. Book catalog online. Guidelines online.

◐    Only publishes Canadian authors.

**NEEDS** "We are one of the few small literary presses in Canada that still publishes poetry. We try to include 2-3 poetry titles each year. We attempt to balance our list between emerging and established poets. Our poetry titles have won or been shortlisted for major national awards, including the Governor General's Award, the BC Book Prizes, and the Alberta Awards."

**HOW TO CONTACT** Submit 10 sample poems.

**TIPS** "Our audience is adult readers who love good books and good literature. Our audience is regional and national, as well as international. Follow our submission guidelines. Check out some of our titles at your local library or bookstore to get an idea of what we publish. Don't send us the only copy of your manuscript. Let us know if your submission is simultaneous, and inform us if it is accepted elsewhere. Above all, keep writing!"

## OOLIGAN PRESS

369 Neuberger Hall, 724 SW Harrison St., Portland OR 97201. (503)725-9410. **E-mail:** acquisitions@ooliganpress.pdx.edu. **Website:** ooligan.pdx.edu. **Contact:** Acquisitions Co-Managers. "We seek to publish regionally significant works of literary, histori-cal, and social value. We define the Pacific Northwest as Northern California, Oregon, Idaho, Washington, British Columbia, and Alaska. We recognize the importance of diversity, particularly within the publishing industry, and are committed to building a literary community that includes traditionally underrepresented voices; therefore, we are interested in works originating from, or focusing on, marginalized communities of the Pacific Northwest." Publishes trade paperbacks, electronic originals, and reprints. Pays negotiable royalty on retail price. Publishes ms 12-18 months after acceptance. Responds in 2 weeks for queries; 3 months for proposals. Catalog online. Guidelines online.

**NEEDS** Ooligan is a not-for-profit general trade press that publishes books honoring the cultural and natural diversity of the Pacific Northwest. "We are limited in the number of poetry titles that we publish as poetry represents only a small percentage of our overall acquisitions. We are open to all forms of style and verse; however, we give special preference to prose poetry and traditional verse. Although spoken word, slam, and rap poetry are of interest to the press, we will consider such work if it does not translate well to the written page. Ooligan does not publish chapbooks."

**HOW TO CONTACT** Query first through e-mail or Submittable.

**TIPS** "Search the blog for tips."

## ⊘ ORCHARD BOOKS (US)

557 Broadway, New York NY 10012. **Website:** www.scholastic.com. *Orchard is not accepting unsolicited mss.* Most commonly offers an advance against list royalties.

## ⊘ ORCHISES PRESS

P.O. Box 320533, Alexandria VA 22320. (703)683-1243. **E-mail:** lathbury@gmu.edu. **Website:** mason.gmu.edu/~lathbury. **Contact:** Roger Lathbury, editor-in-chief. Orchises Press is a general literary publisher specializing in poetry with selected reprints and textbooks. No new fiction or children's books. Publishes hardcover and trade paperback originals and reprints. Pays 36% of receipts after Orchises has recouped its costs. Publishes book 1 year after acceptance. Responds in 3 months to queries. Guidelines online.

**NEEDS** Poetry must have been published in respected literary journals. *Orchises Press no longer reads un-*

*solicited mss.* Publishes free verse, but has strong formalist preferences.

## PALETTES & QUILLS

1935 Penfield Rd., Penfield NY 14526. (585)383-0812. **E-mail:** palettesnquills@gmail.com. **Website:** www.palettesnquills.com. **Contact:** Donna M. Marbach, publisher/owner. Palettes & Quills is devoted to the celebration and expansion of the literary and visual arts, offering both commissioned and consulting services. It works to support beginning and emerging writers and artists to expand their knowledge, improve their skills, and connect to other resources in the community. Further, Palettes & Quills seeks to increase the public's awareness and appreciation of these arts through education, advocacy, hands-on program assistance, and functioning as a small literary press. "We publish a chapbook every other year in a contest judged by a well-known poet. We also publish a monthly e-newsletter, and chapbooks/anthologies/ and broadsides on an irregular schedule. Reprints accepted only for our e-newsletter." Publishes chapbooks, broadsides, e-newsletter. Contest winner gets $200 and 50 books. Others are paid copies. Response time varies. "We try to respond as quick as we can." Guidelines online.

**NEEDS** Palettes & Quills "is at this point is only considering chapbooks that are poetry, creative nonfiction, or fiction, a poetry press only, and produces only a handful of publications each year, specializing in anthologies, individual chapbooks, and broadsides." Wants "work that should appeal to a wide audience." Does not want "poems that are sold blocks of text, long-lined and without stanza breaks. Wildly elaborate free-verse would be difficult and in all likelihood fight with art background, amateurish rhyming poem, overly sentimental poems, poems that use excessive profanity, or which denigrate other people, or political and religious diatribes."

**HOW TO CONTACT** Query first with 3-5 poems and a cover letter with brief bio and publication credits for individual unsolicited chapbooks. May include previously published poems. Chapbook poets would get 20 copies of a run; broadside poets and artists get 5-10 copies and occasionally paid $10 for reproduction rights. Anthology poets get 1 copy of the anthology. All poets and artists get a discount on purchases that include their work.

**TIPS** "We are very small and the best bet with us with our monthly e-newsletter Pencil Marks."

## PANKHEARST

**Website:** pankhearst.wordpress.com. Pankhearst is a collective of independent writers. "We exist to develop and promote new writers, and to learn while doing. We have published 4 spiffing full-length collections of fiction, 2 novels, and more than a dozen Kindle 'singles' to date. We've also published 2 collections of poetry and flash fiction." Guidelines online.

**TIPS** "Pankhearst welcomes everybody, regardless of age, color, disability, familial or parental status, gender identity, marital status, national origin, race, religion, sex, sexual orientation, and anything else you or we can think of."

## PAYCOCK PRESS

3819 N. 13th St., Arlington VA 22201. (703)525-9296. **E-mail:** rchrdpeabody9@gmail.com. **Website:** www.gargoylemagazine.com. **Contact:** Richard Peabody. "Too academic for the underground, too outlaw for the academic world. We tend to be edgy and look for ultra-literary work." Publishes paperback originals. Books: POD printing. Average print order: 500. Averages 1 total title/year. Member CLMP. Distributes through Amazon and website. Publishes ms 1 year after acceptance. Responds to queries in 1 month; mss in 4 months.

**NEEDS** Considers experimental, edgy poetry collections.

**HOW TO CONTACT** Accepts unsolicited mss. Accepts queries by e-mail. Include brief bio. Send SASE for return of ms or send a disposable ms and SASE for reply only.

**TIPS** "Check out our website. Two of our favorite writers are Paul Bowles and Jeanette Winterson."

## PELICAN PUBLISHING COMPANY

1000 Burmaster St., Gretna LA 70053. (504)368-1175. **Fax:** (504)368-1195. **E-mail:** editorial@pelicanpub.com. **Website:** www.pelicanpub.com. "We believe ideas have consequences. One of the consequences is that they lead to a best-selling book. We publish books to improve and uplift the reader. Currently emphasizing business and history titles." Publishes 20 young readers/year; 1 middle reader/year. "Our children's books (illustrated and otherwise) include history, biography, holiday, and regional. Pelican's mission is to publish books of quality and permanence that enrich the lives of those who read them." Publishes hardcover, trade paperback and mass market paperback originals and reprints. Pays authors in royalties; buys ms outright "rarely." Illustrators paid by "various arrangements." Advance considered. Publishes a book 9-18 months after acceptance. Responds in 1 month to queries; 3 months to mss. Requires exclusive submission. Book catalog and ms guidelines online.

**NEEDS** Considers poetry for "hardcover children's books only (1,100 words maximum), preferably with a regional focus. However, our needs for this are very limited; we publish 20 juvenile titles per year, and most of these are prose, not poetry." Books are 32 pages, magazine-sized, include illustrations.

**TIPS** "We do extremely well with cookbooks, popular histories, and business. We will continue to build in these areas. The writer must have a clear sense of the market and knowledge of the competition. A query letter should describe the project briefly, give the author's writing and professional credentials, and promotional ideas."

## PENGUIN POETS

375 Hudson St., New York NY 10014. **Website:** www.penguinrandomhouse.com. Agented submissions only. Catalog online.

## ⊘ PENGUIN RANDOM HOUSE, LLC

Division of Bertelsmann Book Group, 1745 Broadway, New York NY 10019. (212)782-9000. **Website:** www.penguinrandomhouse.com. Penguin Random House LLC is the world's largest English-language general trade book publisher. *Agented submissions only. No unsolicited mss.*

## PERSEA BOOKS

277 Broadway, Suite 708, New York NY 10007. (212)260-9256. **Fax:** (212)267-3165. **E-mail:** info@perseabooks.com. **Website:** www.perseabooks.com. The aim of Persea is to publish works that endure by meeting high standards of literary merit and relevance. "We have often taken on important books other publishers have overlooked, or have made significant discoveries and rediscoveries, whether of a single work or writer's entire oeuvre. Our books cover a wide range of themes, styles, and genres. We have published poetry, fiction, essays, memoir, biography, titles of Jewish and Middle Eastern interest, women's studies, American Indian folklore, and revived classics, as well as a notable selection of works in transla-

tion." Responds in 8 weeks to proposals; 10 weeks to mss. Guidelines online.

**NEEDS** "We have a longstanding commitment to publishing extraordinary contemporary poetry and maintain an active poetry program. At this time, due to our commitment to the poets we already publish, we are limited in our ability to add new collections."

**HOW TO CONTACT** Send an e-mail to poetry@perseabooks.com describing current project and publication history, attaching a pdf or Word document with up to 12 sample pages of poetry. "If the timing is right and we are interested in seeing more work, we will contact you."

## ⊘ PERUGIA PRESS

P.O. Box 60364, Florence MA 01062. **Website:** www.perugiapress.com. **Contact:** Susan Kan, director. The best new women poets, for 20 years. "Contact us through our website."

## PIÑATA BOOKS

Imprint of Arte Publico Press, University of Houston, 4902 Gulf Fwy., Bldg. 19, Room 100, Houston TX 77204-2004. (713)743-2845. **Fax:** (713)743-3080. **E-mail:** submapp@uh.edu. **Website:** www.artepublicopress.com. "Piñata Books is dedicated to the publication of children's and young adult literature focusing on U.S. Hispanic culture by U.S. Hispanic authors. Arte Publico's mission is the publication, promotion and dissemination of Latino literature for a variety of national and regional audiences, from early childhood to adult, through the complete gamut of delivery systems, including personal performance as well as print and electronic media." Publishes hardcover and trade paperback originals. Pays 10% royalty on wholesale price. Pays $1,000-3,000 advance. Publishes book 2 years after acceptance. Responds in 2-3 months to queries; 4-6 months to mss. Book catalog and guidelines online.

**NEEDS** Appropriate to Hispanic theme.

**HOW TO CONTACT** Submissions made through online submission form.

**TIPS** "Include cover letter with submission explaining why your manuscript is unique and important, why we should publish it, who will buy it, etc."

## ⊘ PLAN B PRESS

2714 Jefferson Dr., Alexandria VA 22303. (215)732-2663. **E-mail:** planbpress@gmail.com. **Website:** www.planbpress.com. **Contact:** Steven Allen May, president. Plan B Press is a "small publishing company with an international feel. Our intention is to have Plan B Press be part of the conversation about the direction and depth of literary movements and genres. Plan B Press's new direction is to seek out authors rarely-to-never published, sharing new voices that might not otherwise be heard. Plan B Press is determined to merge text with image, writing with art." Publishes poetry and short fiction. Wants "experimental poetry, concrete/visual work." Pays author's copies. Responds to queries in 1 month; mss in 3 months.

**NEEDS** Wants to see: experimental, concrete, visual poetry. Does not want "sonnets, political or religious poems, work in the style of Ogden Nash."

## PRESA PRESS

P.O. Box 792, 8590 Belding Rd. NE, Rockford MI 49341. **E-mail:** presapress@aol.com. **Website:** www.presapress.com. **Contact:** Roseanne Ritzema, editor. Presa Press publishes perfect-bound paperbacks of poetry. Wants "imagistic poetry where form is an extension of content, surreal, experimental, and personal poetry." Does not want "overtly political or didactic material." Pays 10-25 author/quotes copies. Time between acceptance and publication is 8-12 weeks. Responds to queries in 2-4 weeks; to mss in 8-12 weeks

**NEEDS** Acquires first North American serial rights and the right to reprint in anthologies. Rights include e-book publishing rights. Rights revert to poets upon publication. Accepts postal submissions only. Cover letter is preferred. Reads submissions year round. Poems are circulated to an editorial board. Send materials for review consideration to Roseanne Ritzema.

**HOW TO CONTACT** Query first, with a few sample poems and a cover letter with brief bio and publication credits. Book/chapbook mss may include previously published poems.

## PRESS 53

560 N. Trade St., Suite 103, Winston-Salem NC 27101. (336)770-5353. **E-mail:** kevin@press53.com. **Website:** www.press53.com. **Contact:** Kevin Morgan Watson, publisher.. "Press 53 was founded in October 2005 and quickly began earning a reputation as a quality publishing house of short fiction and poetry collections." Poetry and short fiction collections only. Catalog online. Guidelines online.

**NEEDS** "We love working with poets who have been widely published and are active in the poetry community. We publish roughly 6-8 full-length poetry collections of around 70 pages or more each year, plus the winner of our Press 53 Award for Poetry." Prefers that at least 30-40% of the poems in the collection be previously published. Experimental. Does not want overtly political or religious.

**HOW TO CONTACT** Finds mss through contest and referrals.

**TIPS** "We are looking for writers who are actively involved in the writing community, writers who are submitting their work to journals, magazines and contests, and who are getting published, building readership, and earning a reputation for their work."

## PRESS HERE

22230 NE 28th Place, Sammamish WA 98074-6408. **Website:** www.gracecuts.com/press-here. Press Here publishes award-winning books of haiku, tanka, and related poetry by the leading poets of these genres, as well as essays, criticism, and interviews about these genres. "We publish work only by those poets who are already frequently published in the leading haiku and tanka journals." Publishes 1-2 poetry books/year, plus occasional books of essays or interviews. Mss are selected through open submission. Pays a negotiated percentage of author's copies (out of a press run of 200-1,000). Responds to queries in up to 1 month; to mss in up to 2 months. Catalog available for #10 SASE.

⚲ Press Here publications have won the 1st-place Merit Book Award and other awards from the Haiku Society of America.

**NEEDS** Does not want any poetry other than haiku, tanka, and related genres. Has published poetry by Lee Gurga, paul m., Paul O. Williams, Adele Kenny, Pat Shelley, Cor van den Heuvel, and William J. Higginson.

**HOW TO CONTACT** Query first, with a few sample poems and a cover letter with brief bio and publication credits. Book mss may include previously published poems ("previous publication strongly preferred"). "All proposals must be by well-established haiku or tanka poets, and must be for haiku or tanka poetry, or criticism/discussion of these genres. If the editor does not already know your work well from leading haiku and tanka publications, then he is not likely to be interested in your manuscript."

## PRINCETON UNIVERSITY PRESS

41 William St., Princeton NJ 08540. (609)258-4900. **Fax:** (609)258-6305. **Website:** press.princeton.edu.

"The Lockert Library of Poetry in Translation embraces a wide geographic and temporal range, from Scandinavia to Latin America to the subcontinent of India, from the Tang Dynasty to Europe of the modern day. It especially emphasizes poets who are established in their native lands and who are being introduced to an English-speaking audience. Manuscripts are judged with several criteria in mind: the ability of the translation to stand on its own as poetry in English; fidelity to the tone and spirit of the original, rather than literal accuracy; and the importance of the translated poet to the literature of his or her time and country." Responds in 3-4 months. Guidelines online.

**NEEDS** Submit hard copy of proposal with sample poems or full ms. Cover letter is required. Reads submissions year round. Mss will not be returned. Comments on finalists only.

## RAGGED SKY PRESS

P.O. Box 312, Annandale NJ 08801. **E-mail:** raggedskyanthology@gmail.com. **Website:** www.raggedsky.com. **Contact:** Ellen Foos, publisher; Vasiliki Katsarou, managing editor; Arlene Weiner, editor. Produces poetry anthologies and single-author poetry collections along with occasional inspired prose. Ragged Sky is a small, highly selective cooperative press. "We work with our authors closely." Individual poetry collections currently by invitation only. Learn more online.

## ⊘❸ RATTAPALLAX PRESS

217 Thompson St., Suite 353, New York NY 10012. **E-mail:** devineni@rattapallax.com. **Website:** www.rattapallax.com. **Contact:** Ram Devineni, founder/president; Flavia Rocha, editor-in-chief. Rattapallax Press publishes "contemporary poets and writers with unique, powerful voices." Publishes 5 paperbacks and 3 chapbooks/year. Books are usually 64 pages, digest-sized, offset-printed, perfect-bound, with 12-pt. CS1 covers.

**HOW TO CONTACT** Query first, with a few sample poems and cover letter with brief bio and publication credits. Include SASE. Requires authors to first be published in *Rattapallax*. Responds to queries in 1 month; to mss in 2 months. Pays royalties of 10-25%. Order sample books from website.

## RED HEN PRESS

P.O. Box 40820, Pasadena CA 91114. (626)356-4760. **Fax:** (626)356-9974. **Website:** www.redhen.org. Managing Editor: Kate Gale. **Contact:** Mark E. Cull, publisher/executive director. "At this time, the best opportunity to be published by Red Hen is by entering one of our contests. Please find more information in our award submission guidelines." Publishes trade paperback originals. Publishes ms 1 year after acceptance. Responds in 1-2 months. Book catalog available free. Guidelines online.

**HOW TO CONTACT** Submit to Benjamin Saltman Poetry Award.

**TIPS** "Audience reads poetry, literary fiction, intelligent nonfiction. If you have an agent, we may be too small since we don't pay advances. Write well. Send queries first. Be willing to help promote your own book."

## ⊘ RED MOON PRESS

P.O. Box 2461, Winchester VA 22604. (540)722-2156. **E-mail:** jim.kacian@redmoonpress.com. **Website:** www.redmoonpress.com. **Contact:** Jim Kacian, editor/publisher. Red Moon Press "is the largest and most prestigious publisher of English-language haiku and related work in the world." Publishes 8-10 volumes/year, usually 2-3 anthologies, 4-5 individual collections of English-language haiku, and 1-3 books of essays, translations, or criticism of haiku. Under other imprints, the press also publishes chapbooks of various sizes and formats. English-language haiku, contemporary haiku in other languages in English translation, haiku anthologies, books of haiku theory and criticism, books on related genres (tanka, haibun, haiga, renga, renku, etc.). Every book is a separate consideration. Publishes ms 1 month after acceptance. Catalog online. Guidelines available.

**HOW TO CONTACT** Query first with book concept (not just "I've written a few haiku . ."); if interested we'll ask for samples. "Each contract separately negotiated."

## ☯ RONSDALE PRESS

3350 W. 21st Ave., Vancouver BC V6S 1G7, Canada. (604)738-4688. **Fax:** (604)731-4548. **E-mail:** ronsdale@shaw.ca. **Website:** ronsdalepress.com. **Contact:** Ronald B. Hatch (fiction, poetry, nonfiction, social commentary); Veronica Hatch (YA novels and short stories). "Ronsdale Press is a Canadian literary publishing house that publishes 12 books each year, four of which are young adult titles. Of particular interest are books involving children exploring and discovering new aspects of Canadian history." Publishes trade paperback originals. Pays 10% royalty on retail price.

Publishes book 1 year after acceptance. Responds to queries in 2 weeks; mss in 2 months. Book catalog for #10 SASE. Guidelines online.

**NEEDS** Poets should have published some poems in magazines/journals and should be well-read in contemporary masters.

**HOW TO CONTACT** Submit complete ms.

**TIPS** "Ronsdale Press is a literary publishing house, based in Vancouver, and dedicated to publishing books from across Canada, books that give Canadians new insights into themselves and their country. We aim to publish the best Canadian writers."

### ROSE ALLEY PRESS

4203 Brooklyn Ave. NE, #103A, Seattle WA 98105-5911. (206)633-2725. **E-mail:** rosealleypress@juno.com. **Website:** www.rosealleypress.com. **Contact:** David D. Horowitz. "Rose Alley Press primarily publishes books featuring rhymed metrical poetry and an annually updated booklet about writing and publication. We do not read or consider unsolicited manuscripts."

### SAKURA PUBLISHING & TECHNOLOGIES

(330)360-5131. **E-mail:** skpublishing124@gmail.com. **Website:** www.sakura-publishing.com. **Contact:** Derek Vasconi, submissions coordinator. Mss that don't follow guidelines will not be considered. Sakura Publishing is a traditional, independent book publishing company that focuses on fiction, Asian culture-related books, nonfiction, and horror books. Publishes hardcover, trade paperback, mass market paperback and electronic originals and reprints. Currently accepts only the following genres: Asian fiction, Japanese fiction (in English), Nonfiction, and horror. Please do not send queries for any other genres. Royalty payments on paperback, e-book, wholesale, and merchandise Does not pay advance. Publishes ms 6 months after acceptance. Responds in 1 week. Book catalog available for #10 SASE. Guidelines online.

**HOW TO CONTACT** Follow guidelines online.

**TIPS** "Please make sure you visit our submissions page at our website and follow all instructions exactly as written. Also, Sakura Publishing has a preference for fiction/nonfiction books specializing in Asian culture."

### SALINA BOOKSHELF

1120 W. University Ave., Suite 102, Flagstaff AZ 86001. (877)527-0070. **Fax:** (928)526-0386. **Website:** www. salinabookshelf.com. Publishes trade paperback originals and reprints. Pays varying royalty. Pays advance. Publishes ms 1 year after acceptance. Responds in 3 months to queries.

**NEEDS** "We accept poetry in English/Southwest language for children."

**HOW TO CONTACT** Submit 3 sample poems.

### SALMON POETRY

Knockeven, Cliffs of Moher, County Clare, Ireland. 353(0)852318909. **E-mail:** info@salmonpoetry.com. **E-mail:** jessie@salmonpoetry.com. **Website:** www.salmonpoetry.com. **Contact:** Jessie Lendennie, editor. Publishes contemporary poetry and literary nonfiction Pays advance. Publishes ms 2 years after acceptance. Responds in 3 months. Guidelines available.

**NEEDS** "Salmon Press is one of the most important publishers in the Irish literary world; specializing in the promotion of new poets, particularly women. Established in 1981 as an alternative voice in Irish literature, Salmon is known for its international list and over the years has developed a cross-cultural literary dialog, broadening Irish Literature and urging new perspectives on established traditions."

**HOW TO CONTACT** E-mail query with short biographical note and 5-10 sample poems.

**TIPS** "Read as much poetry as you can, and always research the publisher before submitting!"

### SARABANDE BOOKS, INC.

2234 Dundee Rd., Suite 200, Louisville KY 40205. (502)458-4028. **Fax:** (502)458-4065. **E-mail:** info@sarabandebooks.org. **Website:** www.sarabandebooks.org. **Contact:** Sarah Gorham, Editor-in-Chief. "Sarabande Books was founded to publish poetry, short fiction, and creative nonfiction. We look for works of lasting literary value. Please see our titles to get an idea of our taste. Accepts submissions through contests and open submissions." Publishes trade paperback originals. Pays royalty. 10% on actual income received. Also pays in author's copies. Pays $500-1,000 advance. Publishes ms 18 months after acceptance. Book catalog available free. Contest guidelines for #10 SASE or on website.

Charges $15 handling fee with alternative option of purchase of book from website (e-mail confirmation of sale must be included with submission).

**NEEDS** Poetry of superior artistic quality; otherwise no restraints or specifications. Sarabande Books publishes books of poetry of 48 pages minimum. Wants "poetry that offers originality of voice and subject matter, uniqueness of vision, and a language that startles because of the careful attention paid to it—language that goes beyond the merely competent or functional."

**HOW TO CONTACT** Mss selected through literary contests, invitation, and recommendation by a well-established writer.

**TIPS** "Sarabande publishes for a general literary audience. Know your market. Read-and buy-books of literature. Sponsors contests for poetry and fiction. Make sure you're not writing in a vacuum, that you've read and are conscious of contemporary literature. Have someone read your manuscript, checking it for ordering, coherence. Better a lean, consistently strong manuscript than one that is long and uneven. We like a story to have good narrative, and we like to be engaged by language."

## SATURNALIA BOOKS

105 Woodside Rd., Ardmore PA 19003. (267)278-9541. **E-mail:** info@saturnaliabooks.com. **Website:** www. saturnaliabooks.org. **Contact:** Henry Israeli, publisher. "We do not accept unsolicited submissions. We hold a contest, the Saturnalia Books Poetry Prize, annually in which 1 anonymously submitted title is chosen by a poet with a national reputation for publication. Submissions are accepted during the month of March. The submission fee is $30, and the prize is $2,000 and 20 copies of the book. See website for details." Publishes trade paperback originals and digital versions for e-readers. Pays authors 4-6% royalty on retail price. Pays $400-2,000 advance. Responds in 4 months on mss. Catalog online. No unsolicited submissions. Contest guidelines online.

**HOW TO CONTACT** "Saturnalia Books has no bias against any school of poetry, but we do tend to publish writers who take chances and push against convention in some way, whether it's in form, language, content, or musicality." Submit complete ms to contest only.

**CONTEST/AWARD OFFERINGS** Saturnalia Books Poetry Prize. Contest is open during the month of March.

**TIPS** "Our audience tend to be young avid readers of contemporary poetry. Read a few sample books first."

## SHEARSMAN BOOKS, LTD

50 Westons Hills Dr., Emersons Green Bristol BS16 7DF, United Kingdom. **E-mail:** editor@shearsman. com. **Website:** www.shearsman.com. **Contact:** Tony Frazer, editor. Publishes trade paperback originals. Pays 10% royalty on retail price after 150 copies have sold; authors also receive 10 free copies of their books. Does not pay advance. Publishes ms 9-12 months after acceptance. Responds in 3 months to mss. Book catalog online. Guidelines online.

**NEEDS** "Shearsman only publishes poetry, poetry collections, and poetry in translation (from any language but with an emphasis on work in Spanish & in German). Some critical work on poetry and also memoirs and essays by poets. Mainly poetry by British, Irish, North American, and Australian poets." No children's books. No devotional or religious verse.

**TIPS** "Book ms submission: most of the ms must have already appeared in the UK or USA magazines of some repute, and it has to fill 70-72 pages of half letter or A5 pages. You must have sufficient return postage. Submissions can also be made by email. It is unlikely that a poet with no track record will be accepted for publication as there is no obvious audience for the work. Try to develop some exposure to UK and US magazines and try to assemble a MS only later."

## SHIPWRECKT BOOKS PUBLISHING COMPANY LLC

309 W. Stevens Ave., Rushford MN 55971. (507)458-8190. **E-mail:** editor@shipwrecktbooks.com. **E-mail:** contact@shipwrecktbooks.com. **Website:** www.shipwrecktbooks.com. **Contact:** Tom Driscoll, managing editor. Publishes trade paperback originals, mass market paperback originals, and electronic originals. Authors receive a maximum of 35% royalties. Average length of time between acceptance of a book-length ms and publication is 6 months. Responds to queries within 6 months. Catalog and guidelines online.

**HOW TO CONTACT** Submit 3 sample poems by e-mail.

**CONTEST/AWARD OFFERINGS** Midwest Independent Publishing Assn. Silver medal poetry 2015.

**TIPS** "Quality writing. Query first. Development and full editorial services available."

## SIBLING RIVALRY PRESS

P.O. Box 26147, Little Rock AR 72221. **E-mail:** info@siblingrivalrypress.com. **Website:** siblingrivalrypress.

com. **Contact:** Bryan Borland, publisher; Seth Pennington, editor. "While we champion our LGBTIQ authors and artists, and while we've been very fortunate in our successes in LGBTIQ publishing, we are an inclusive publishing house and welcome all authors, artists, and readers regardless of sexual orientation or identity. We publish work we love. Merit trumps category." Catalog online. Guidelines online.

**NEEDS** Opening reading period: March 1-June 1.

**HOW TO CONTACT** Submit complete ms.

## SILVERFISH REVIEW PRESS

P.O. Box 3541, Eugene OR 97403. (541)344-5060. **E-mail:** sfrpress@earthlink.net. **Website:** www.silverfishreviewpress.com. "Sponsors the Gerald Cable Book Award. This prize is awarded annually to a book length manuscript of original poetry by an author who has not yet published a full-length collection. There are no restrictions on the kind of poetry or subject matter; translations are not acceptable. Winners will receive $1,000, publication, and 25 copies of the book. Entries must be postmarked by October 15. Entries may be submitted by e-mail. See website for instructions." Publishes trade paperback originals. Guidelines online.

**TIPS** "Read recent Silverfish titles."

## SOUTHERN ILLINOIS UNIVERSITY PRESS

1915 University Press Dr., SIUC Mail Code 6806, Carbondale IL 62901. (618)453-6613. **Fax:** (618)453-1221. **E-mail:** kageff@siu.edu. **Website:** www.siupress.com. **Contact:** Karl Kageff, editor-in-chief. Scholarly press specializes in theater studies, rhetoric and composition studies, American history, Civil War, regional and nonfiction trade, poetry. No fiction. Currently emphasizing theater and American history, especially Civil War. Publishes hardcover and trade paperback originals and reprints. Pays 5-10% royalty on wholesale price. Rarely offers advance. Publishes ms 1 year after acceptance. Responds in 2 months to queries. Book catalog and ms guidelines free.

**NEEDS** Crab Orchard Series in Poetry.

**HOW TO CONTACT** Guidelines online.

**CONTEST/AWARD OFFERINGS** Crab Orchard Series in Poetry Open Competition and First Book Award.

## STEEL TOE BOOKS

Department of English, Western Kentucky University, 1906 College Heights Blvd. #11086, Bowling Green KY 42101. (270)745-5769. **E-mail:** tom.hunley@wku.edu. **Website:** www.steeltoebooks.com. **Contact:** Dr. Tom C. Hunley, director. Steel Toe Books publishes "full-length, single-author poetry collections. Our books are professionally designed and printed. We look for workmanship (economical use of language, high-energy verbs, precise literal descriptions, original figurative language, poems carefully arranged as a book); a unique style and/or a distinctive voice; clarity; emotional impact; humor (word plays, hyperbole, comic timing); performability (a Steel Toe poet is at home on the stage as well as on the page)." Does not want "dry verse, purposely obscure language, poetry by people who are so wary of being called 'sentimental' they steer away from any recognizable human emotions, poetry that takes itself so seriously that it's unintentionally funny." Has published poetry by Allison Joseph, Susan Browne, James Doyle, Martha Silano, Mary Biddinger, John Guzlowski, Jeannine Hall Gailey, and others. Publishes 1-3 poetry books/year. Mss are normally selected through open submission.

**HOW TO CONTACT** "Check the website for news about our next open reading period." Book mss may include previously published poems. Responds to mss in 3 months. Pays $500 advance on 10% royalties and 10 author's copies. Order sample books by sending $12 to Steel Toe Books. *Must purchase a ms in order to submit.* See website for submission guidelines.

## SUBITO PRESS

University of Colorado at Boulder, Dept. of English, 226 UCB, Boulder CO 80309-0226. **E-mail:** subitopressucb@gmail.com. **Website:** www.subitopress.org. Subito Press is a non-profit publisher of literary works. Each year Subito publishes one work of fiction and one work of poetry through its contest. Publishes trade paperback originals. Guidelines online.

**HOW TO CONTACT** Submit complete ms to contest.

**TIPS** "We publish 2 books of innovative writing a year through our poetry and fiction contests. All entries are also considered for publication with the press."

## SUNBURY PRESS, INC.

105 S Market St., Mechanicsburg PA 17055. **E-mail:** info@sunburypress.com. **E-mail:** proposals@sunburypress.com. **Website:** www.sunburypress.com. Sunbury Press, Inc., headquartered in Mechanicsburg, PA is a publisher of trade paperback, hard cover and digital books featuring established and emerg-

ing authors in many fiction and non-fiction categories. Sunbury's books are printed in the USA and sold through leading booksellers worldwide. "Please use our online submission form." Publishes trade paperback and hardcover originals and reprints; electronic originals and reprints. Pays 10% royalty on wholesale price. Publishes ms 6 months after acceptance. Responds in 3 months. Catalog and guidelines online.

**HOW TO CONTACT** Submit complete ms.

**TIPS** "Our books appeal to very diverse audiences. We are building our list in many categories, focusing on many demographics. We are not like traditional publishers—we are digitally adept and very creative. Don't be surprised if we move quicker than you are accustomed to!"

## SWAN ISLE PRESS

P.O. Box 408790, Chicago IL 60640. (773)728-3780. **E-mail:** info@swanislepress.com. **Website:** www.swanislepress.com. *"We do not accept unsolicited mss."* Publishes hardcover and trade paperback originals. Pays 7-10% royalty on wholesale price. Publishes book 18 months after acceptance. Responds in 6-12 months. Book catalog online. Guidelines online.

**HOW TO CONTACT** Query with SASE.

## SWAN SCYTHE PRESS

1468 Mallard Way, Sunnyvale CA 94087. **E-mail:** robert.pesich@gmail.com. **Website:** www.swanscythe.com. **Contact:** Robert Pesich, editor.

**NEEDS** "After publishing 25 chapbooks, a few full-sized poetry collections, and 1 anthology, then taking a short break from publishing, Swan Scythe Press is now re-launching its efforts with some new books, under a new editorship. We have also begun a new series of books, called Poetas/Puentes, from emerging poets writing in Spanish, translated into English. We will also consider mss in indigenous languages from North, Central and South America, translated into English."

**HOW TO CONTACT** Query first before submitting a ms via e-mail or through website.

## TARPAULIN SKY PRESS

P.O. Box 189, Grafton VT 05146. **Website:** www.tarpaulinsky.com. **Contact:** Resh Daily, managing editor. Tarpaulin Sky Press publishes cross- and trans-genre works as well as innovative poetry and prose. Produces full-length books and chapbooks, hand-bound books and trade paperbacks, and offers both hand-bound and perfect-bound paperback editions of full-length books. "We're a small, author-centered press endeavoring to create books that, as objects, please our authors as much their texts please us."

**HOW TO CONTACT** Writers whose work has appeared in or been accepted for publication in *Tarpaulin Sky* may submit chapbook or full-length mss at any time, with no reading fee. Tarpaulin Sky Press also considers chapbook and full-length mss from writers whose work has not appeared in the journal, but **asks for a $20 reading fee**. Make checks/money orders to Tarpaulin Sky Press. Cover letter is preferred. Reading periods may be found on the website.

## TEBOT BACH

P.O. Box 7887, Huntington Beach CA 92615. (714)968-0905. **Fax:** 714-968-0905. **E-mail:** info@tebotbach.org. **Website:** www.tebotbach.org. **Contact:** Mifanwy Kaiser, editor/publisher. Publishes mss 6 months-1 years after acceptance. Responds in 3 months.

**NEEDS** Offers 2 contests per year. The Patricia Bibby First Book Contest and The Clockwise Chapbook contest. Go online for more information.

**HOW TO CONTACT** Query first via e-mail, with a few sample poems and cover letter with brief bio.

## TEXAS TECH UNIVERSITY PRESS

1120 Main St., Second Floor, Box 41037, Lubbock TX 79415. (806)742-2982. **Fax:** (806)742-2979. **E-mail:** ttup@ttu.edu. **Website:** www.ttupress.org. Texas Tech University Press, the book publishing office of the university since 1971 and an AAUP member since 1986, publishes nonfiction titles in the areas of natural history and the natural sciences; 18th century and Joseph Conrad studies; studies of modern Southeast Asia, particularly the Vietnam War; costume and textile history; Latin American literature and culture; and all aspects of the Great Plains and the American West, especially history, biography, memoir, sports history, and travel. In addition, the Press publishes several scholarly journals, acclaimed series for young readers, an annual invited poetry collection, and literary fiction of Texas and the West. Guidelines online.

**NEEDS** "TTUP publishes an annual invited first-book poetry manuscript (please note that we cannot entertain unsolicited poetry submissions)."

## ✪ THISTLEDOWN PRESS LTD.

410 2nd Ave., Saskatoon SK S7K 2C3, Canada. (306)244-1722. **Fax:** (306)244-1762. **E-mail:** edito-

rial@thistledownpress.com. **Website:** www.thistle-downpress.com. **Contact:** Allan Forrie, publisher. "Thistledown originates books by Canadian authors only, although we have co-published titles by authors outside Canada. We do not publish children's picture books." Pays authors royalty of 10-12% based on net dollar sales. Pays illustrators and photographers by the project (range: $250-750). Publishes book 1 year after acceptance. Responds to queries in 6 months. Book catalog on website.

**NEEDS** "We do not publish cowboy poetry, inspirational poetry, or poetry for children."

**TIPS** "Send cover letter including publishing history and SASE."

### TIA CHUCHA PRESS

13197 Gladstone Ave., Unit A, Sylmar CA 91342. (818)939-3433. **Fax:** (818)367-5600. **E-mail:** info@tiachucha.com. **Website:** www.tiachucha.com. **Contact:** Luis Rodriguez, director. Tia Chucha's Centro Cultural is a nonprofit learning and cultural arts center. "We support and promote the continued growth, development and holistic learning of our community through the many powerful means of the arts. Tia Centra provides a positive space for people to activate what we all share as humans: the capacity to create, to imagine and to express ourselves in an effort to improve the quality of life for our community." Publishes hardcover and trade paperback originals. Pays 10% royalty on wholesale price. Publishes ms 1 year after acceptance. Responds in 9 months to mss. Guidelines online.

**NEEDS** No restrictions as to style or content. "We only publish poetry at this time. We do cross-cultural and performance-oriented poetry. It has to work on the page, however."

**HOW TO CONTACT** Query and submit complete ms.

**TIPS** "We will cultivate the practice. Audience is those interested."

### TIGHTROPE BOOKS

#207-2 College St., Toronto ON M5G 1K3, Canada. (416)928-6666. **E-mail:** tightropeasst@gmail.com. **Website:** www.tightropebooks.com. **Contact:** Jim Nason, publisher. Publishes trade paperback originals. Pays 5-15% royalty on retail price. Pays advance of $200-300. Publishes book 1-2 years after acceptance. Responds if interested. Catalog and guidelines online.

Accepting submissions for literary fiction, nonfiction and poetry from Canadian citizens and permanent Canadian residents only.

**TIPS** "Audience is urban, literary, educated, unconventional."

### TITAN PRESS

PMB 17897, Encino CA 91416. **E-mail:** titan91416@yahoo.com. **Website:** https://www.facebook.com/RV-Clef. **Contact:** Romana V. Clef, editor. Little literary publisher. Publishes hardcover and paperback originals. Pays 20-40% royalty. Publishes ms 1 year after acceptance. Responds to queries in 3 months.

**NEEDS** Literary, not MFA banality.

**TIPS** "Look, act, sound, and *be* professional."

### TORREY HOUSE PRESS, LLC

2806 Melony Dr., Salt Lake City UT 84124. **E-mail:** anne@torreyhouse.com. **Website:** torreyhouse.com. **Contact:** Anne Terashima. Torrey House Press is an independent nonprofit publisher promoting environmental conservation through literature. Publishes hardcover, trade paperback, and electronic originals. Pays 5-15% royalty on retail price. Publishes ms 12-18 months after acceptance. Responds in 3 months. Catalog online. Guidelines online.

**HOW TO CONTACT** Query; submit complete ms.

**TIPS** "Include writing experience (none okay)."

### TRADEWIND BOOKS

202-1807 Maritime Mews, Granville Island, Vancouver BC V6H 3W7, Canada. (604)662-4405. **Website:** www.tradewindbooks.com. "Tradewind Books publishes juvenile picture books and young adult novels. Requires that submissions include evidence that author has read at least 3 titles published by Tradewind Books." Publishes hardcover and trade paperback originals. Pays 7% royalty on retail price. Pays variable advance. Publishes book 3 years after acceptance. Responds to mss in 2 months. Book catalog and ms guidelines online.

**HOW TO CONTACT** Please send a book-length collection only.

### TRUMAN STATE UNIVERSITY PRESS

100 E. Normal Ave., Kirksville MO 63501. (660)785-7336. **Fax:** (660)785-4480. **E-mail:** tsup@truman.edu. **E-mail:** bsm@truman.edu. **Website:** tsup.truman.edu. **Contact:** Barbara Smith-Mandell, editor-in-chief. Truman State University Press (TSUP) pub-

lishes peer-reviewed research in the humanities for
the scholarly community and the broader public, and
publishes creative literary works. Guidelines online.
**NEEDS** Not accepting unsolicited mss. Submit to
annual T.S. Eliot Prize for Poetry.

## TUPELO PRESS

P.O. Box 1767, North Adams MA 01247. (413)664-
9611. **E-mail:** publisher@tupelopress.org. **Website:**
www.tupelopress.org. **Contact:** Jeffrey Levine, pub-
lish/editor-in-chief; Jim Schley, managing editor.
"We're an independent nonprofit literary press. We
accept book-length poetry, poetry collections (48+
pages), short story collections, novellas, literary non-
fiction/memoirs and up to 80 pages of a novel." Guidelines online.

**NEEDS** "Our mission is to publish thrilling, visually and emotionally and intellectually stimulating
books of the highest quality, inside and out. We want
contemporary poetry, etc. by the most diverse list of
emerging and established writers in the U.S."

**HOW TO CONTACT** Submit complete ms. **Charges
$28 reading fee.**

## TURNING POINT

WordTech Communications LLC, P.O. Box 541106,
Cincinnati OH 45254. **E-mail:** connect@wordtech-
communications.com. **Website:** www.turningpoint-
books.com. Pays in royalties. Catalog and guidelines
online.

**NEEDS** "Dedicated to the art of story in poetry. We
seek to publish collections of narrative poetry that tell
the essential human stories of our times."

**HOW TO CONTACT** No e-mail submissions. No
calls for book-length poetry right now.

## ☺ TURNSTONE PRESS

Artspace Building, 206-100 Arthur St., Winnipeg
MB R3B 1H3, Canada. (204)947-1555. **Fax:** (204)942-
1555. **Website:** www.turnstonepress.com. **Contact:**
Submissions Assistant. "Turnstone Press is a literary
publisher, not a general publisher, and therefore we
are only interested in literary fiction, literary nonfiction—including literary criticism—and poetry. We do
publish literary mysteries, thrillers, and noir under
our Ravenstone imprint. We publish only Canadian
authors or landed immigrants, we strive to publish a
significant number of new writers, to publish in a variety of genres, and to have 50% of each year's list be
Manitoba writers and/or books with Manitoba con-

tent." Publishes ms 2 years after acceptance. Responds
in 4-7 months. Guidelines online.

**HOW TO CONTACT** Poetry mss should be a minimum 70 pages. Submit complete ms. Include cover
letter.

**TIPS** "As a Canadian literary press, we have a man-
date to publish Canadian writers only. Do some
homework before submitting works to make sure
your subject matter/genre/writing style falls within
the publishers area of interest."

## TWO SYLVIAS PRESS

P.O. Box 1524, Kingston WA 98346. **E-mail:** twosyl-
viaspress@gmail.com. **Website:** twosylviaspress.com.
**Contact:** Kelli Russell Agodon and Annette Spauld-
ing-Convy. Two Sylvias Press draws its inspiration
from the poetic literary talent of Sylvia Plath and the
editorial business sense of Sylvia Beach. Catalog online. Sign up for updates on submission periods.

**TIPS** "Created with the belief that great writing is
good for the world, Two Sylvias Press mixes modern
technology, classic style, and literary intellect with an
eco-friendly heart."

## THE UNIVERSITY OF AKRON PRESS

120 E. Mill St., Suite 415, Akron OH 44325. **E-mail:**
uapress@uakron.edu. **Website:** www.uakron.edu/
uapress. **Contact:** Jon Miller, transitional director
and acquisitions. "The University of Akron Press is
the publishing arm of The University of Akron and
is dedicated to the dissemination of scholarly, professional, and regional books and other content." Publishes hardcover and paperback originals and reissues.
Pays 7-15% royalty. Publishes book 9-12 months after
acceptance. Responds in 2 weeks to queries/proposals;
3-4 months to solicited mss. Query prior to submitting. Guidelines online.

**NEEDS** Follow the guidelines and submit mss only
for the contest: www.uakron.edu/uapress/poetry.
html. "We publish two books of poetry annually, one
of which is the winner of The Akron Poetry prize. We
also are interested in literary collections based around
one theme, especially collections of translated works."

**HOW TO CONTACT** If you are interested in publishing with The University of Akron Press, please fill
out form online.

## THE UNIVERSITY OF ARKANSAS PRESS

McIlroy House, 105 N. McIlroy Ave., Fayetteville AR
72701. (479)575-3246. **Fax:** (479)575-6044. **E-mail:**

mbieker@uark.edu. **Website:** uapress.com. **Contact:** Mike Bieker, director. "The University of Arkansas Press publishes series on Ozark studies, the Civil War in the West, poetry and poetics, food studies, and sport and society." Publishes hardcover and trade paperback originals and reprints. Publishes book 1 year after acceptance. Responds in 3 months to proposals. Book catalog and ms guidelines online.

**HOW TO CONTACT** University of Arkansas Press publishes 4 poetry books per year through the Miller Williams Poetry Prize.

## ⊘ THE UNIVERSITY OF CHICAGO PRESS

1427 East 60th St., Chicago IL 60637. (773)702-7700. **Fax:** (773)702-9756. **Website:** www.press.uchicago. edu. **Contact:** Randolph Petilos, Poetry and Medieval Studies Editor. "The University of Chicago Press has been publishing scholarly books and journals since 1891. Annually, we publish an average of 4 books in our Phoenix Poets series and 2 books of poetry in translation. Occasionally, we may publish a book of poetry outside Phoenix Poets, or as a paperback reprint from another publisher."

## UNIVERSITY OF IOWA PRESS

100 Kuhl House, 119 W. Park Rd., Iowa City IA 52242. (319)335-2000. **Fax:** (319)335-2055. **E-mail:** james-mccoy@uiowa.edu; elisabeth-chretien@uiowa.edu; cath-campbell@uiowa.edu. **Website:** www.uiowapress.org. **Contact:** James McCoy, director (short fiction, poetry, general trade); Elisabeth Chretien, acquisitions editor (literary criticism, literary and general nonfiction, military and veterans' studies); Catherine Cocks, acquisitions editor (book arts, fan studies, food studies, Midwestern history and culture, theater history and culture). The University of Iowa Press publishes both trade and academic work in a variety of fields. Publishes hardcover and paperback originals. Book catalog available free. Guidelines online.

**NEEDS** Currently publishes winners of the Iowa Poetry Prize Competition and Kuhl House Poets (by invitation only). Competition guidelines available on website.

## UNIVERSITY OF NORTH TEXAS PRESS

1155 Union Circle, #311336, Denton TX 76203. (940)565-2142. **Fax:** (940)565-4590. **E-mail:** bonnie. stufflebeam@unt.edu. **Website:** untpress.unt.edu. **Contact:** Ronald Chrisman, director; Karen De Vinney, assistant director; Amy Pierce, administrative assistant; Bonnie Stufflebeam, Marketing Manager. "We are dedicated to producing the highest quality scholarly, academic, and general interest books. We are committed to serving all peoples by publishing stories of their cultures and experiences that have been overlooked. Currently emphasizing military history, Texas history, music, Mexican-American studies." Publishes hardcover and trade paperback originals and reprints. Publishes ms 1-2 years after acceptance. Responds in 1 month to queries. Book catalog for 8½×11 SASE. Guidelines online.

**NEEDS** "The only poetry we publish is the winner of the Vassar Miller Prize in Poetry, an annual, national competition with a $1,000 prize and publication of the winning ms each Spring."

**HOW TO CONTACT** Query.

**TIPS** "We publish series called War and the Southwest; Texas Folklore Society Publications; the Western Life Series; Practical Guide Series; Al-Filo: Mexican-American studies; North Texas Crime and Criminal Justice; Katherine Anne Porter Prize in Short Fiction; and the North Texas Lives of Musicians Series."

## UNIVERSITY OF PITTSBURGH PRESS

7500 Thomas Blvd., Pittsburgh PA 15260. (412)383-2456. **Fax:** (412)383-2466. **E-mail:** info@upress.pitt. edu. **Website:** www.upress.pitt.edu. **Contact:** Sandy Crooms, editorial director. The University of Pittsburgh Press is a scholarly publisher with distinguished books in several academic areas and in poetry and short fiction, as well as books about Pittsburgh and western Pennsylvania for general readers, scholars, and students. "Our mission is to extend the reach and reputation of the university through the publication of scholarly, artistic, and educational books that advance learning and knowledge and through the publication of regional books that contribute to an understanding of and are of special benefit to western Pennsylvania and the Upper Ohio Valley region. Book catalog online. Guidelines online.

**NEEDS** Publishes at least 4 books by poets who have previously published full-length collections of poetry.

**HOW TO CONTACT** Submit complete ms in September and October only.

**TIPS** "We pride ourselves on the eclectic nature of our list. We are not tied to any particular style or school of writing, but we do demand that any book we publish be of exceptional merit."

## UNIVERSITY OF SOUTH CAROLINA PRESS

1600 Hampton St., 5th Floor, Columbia SC 29208. (803)777-5243. **Fax:** (803)777-0160. **Website:** www.

sc.edu/uscpress. **Contact:** Jonathan Haupt, director. "We focus on scholarly monographs and regional trade books of lasting merit." Publishes hardcover originals, trade paperback originals and reprints. Publishes ms 1 year after acceptance. Responds in 3 months to mss. Book catalog available free. Guidelines online.

**NEEDS** Palmetto Poetry Series, a South Carolina-based original poetry series edited by Nikky Finney. Director: Jonathan Haupt, director (jhaupt@mailbox. sc.edu).

## UNIVERSITY OF TAMPA PRESS

University of Tampa, 401 W. Kennedy Blvd., Tampa FL 33606. (813)253-6266. **Fax:** (813)258-7593. **E-mail:** utpress@ut.edu. **Website:** www.ut.edu/tampapress. **Contact:** Richard Mathews, editor. "We are a small university press publishing a limited number of titles each year, primarily in the areas of local and regional history and printing history." Publishes hardcover originals and reprints; trade paperback originals and reprints. Does not pay advance. Publishes ms 6 months-2 years after acceptance. Responds in 3-4 months to queries. Book catalog online. "We do not accept unsolicited book manuscripts except for poetry manuscripts submitted through the annual Tampa Review Prize for Poetry."

**NEEDS** "We consider original poetry collections through the annual Tampa Review Prize for Poetry competition, with a December 31 deadline each year."

**CONTEST/AWARD OFFERINGS** Tampa Review Prize for Poetry: $2,000 plus book publication

## UNIVERSITY OF WISCONSIN PRESS

1930 Monroe St., 3rd Floor, Madison WI 53711. (608)263-1110. **Fax:** (608)263-1132. **E-mail:** gcwalker@wisc.edu. **E-mail:** kadushin@wisc.edu. **Website:** uwpress.wisc.edu. **Contact:** Raphael Kadushin, senior acquisitions editor; Gwen Walker, acquisitions editor. Publishes hardcover originals, paperback originals, and paperback reprints. Pays royalty. Publishes ms 9-18 months after acceptance. Responds in 2 weeks to queries; 8 weeks to mss. Rarely comments on rejected mss. Guidelines online.

**NEEDS** The University of Wisconsin Press awards the Brittingham Prize in Poetry and Felix Pollack Prize in Poetry. More details online.

## ✪ VÉHICULE PRESS

P.O.B. 42094 BP Roy, Montreal QC H2W 2T3, Canada. (514)844-6073. **Fax:** (514)844-7543. **E-mail:** sd@vehiculepress.com. **E-mail:** admin@vehiculepress.

com. **Website:** www.vehiculepress.com. **Contact:** Simon Dardick, nonfiction; Carmine Starnino, poetry; Dimitri Nasrallah, fiction. "Montreal's Véhicule Press has published the best of Canadian and Quebec literature-fiction, poetry, essays, translations, and social history." Publishes trade paperback originals by Canadian authors mostly. Pays 10-15% royalty on retail price. Pays $200-500 advance. Publishes ms 1 year after acceptance. Responds in 4 months to queries.

**NEEDS** Vehicle Press is a "literary press with a poetry series, Signal Editions, publishing the work of Canadian poets only." Publishes flat-spined paperbacks. Publishes Canadian poetry that is "first-rate, original, content-conscious."

**TIPS** "Quality in almost any style is acceptable. We believe in the editing process."

## ✪ WAKE FOREST UNIVERSITY PRESS

P.O. Box 7333, Winston-Salem NC 27109. (336)758-5448. **Fax:** (336)758-5636. **E-mail:** wfupress@wfu. edu. **Website:** wfupress.wfu.edu. **Contact:** Jefferson Holdridge, director/poetry editor; Dillon Johnston, advisory editor. "We publish only poetry from Ireland. I am able to consider only poetry written by native Irish poets. I must return, unread, poetry from American poets." Query with 4-5 samples and cover letter. Sometimes sends prepublication galleys. Buys North American or U.S. rights. Pays on 8% list royalty contract, plus 6-8 author's copies. Negotiable advance. Responds to queries in 1-2 weeks; to submissions (*if invited*) in 2-3 months.

## WASHINGTON WRITERS' PUBLISHING HOUSE

P.O. Box 15271, Washington DC 20003. **E-mail:** wwphpress@gmail.com. **Website:** www.washingtonwriters.org. Offers $1,000 and 50 copies of published book plus additional copies for publicity use. Guidelines online.

**NEEDS** Washington Writers' Publishing House considers book-length mss for publication by poets living within 75 driving miles of the U.S. Capitol (Baltimore area included) through competition only. Publishes 1-2 poetry books/year.

**HOW TO CONTACT** "No specific criteria, except literary excellence."

## WAVE BOOKS

1938 Fairview Ave. E., Suite 201, Seattle WA 98102. (206)676-5337. **E-mail:** info@wavepoetry.com. **Website:** www.wavepoetry.com. "Wave Books is an independent poetry press based in Seattle, Washington, dedicated to publishing the best in contemporary American poetry, poetry in translation, and writing by poets. The Press was founded in 2005, merging with established publisher Verse Press. By publishing strong innovative work in finely crafted trade editions and handmade ephemera, we hope to continue to challenge the values and practices of readers and add to the collective sense of what's possible in contemporary poetry." Publishes hardcover and trade paperback originals. Catalog online.

**HOW TO CONTACT** "Please no unsolicited mss or queries. We will post calls for submissions on our website."

### THE WAYWISER PRESS

P.O. Box 6205, Baltimore MD 21206. **E-mail:** waywiserpress@aol.com. **Website:** waywiser-press.com. The Waywiser Press is a small independent company, with its main office in the UK, and a subsidiary in the USA. Guidelines online.

**NEEDS** Poets who've published 1 or fewer collections should submit to the Anthony Hecht Poetry Prize.

**HOW TO CONTACT** Submit complete ms by post (if prospective author published 2 or more collections).

**TIPS** "We are keen to promote the work of new as well as established authors, and would like to rescue still others from undeserved neglect."

### ⊘ WESLEYAN UNIVERSITY PRESS

215 Long Ln., Middletown CT 06459. (860)685-7711. **Fax:** (860)685-7712. **E-mail:** stamminen@wesleyan. edu. **Website:** www.wesleyan.edu/wespress. **Contact:** Suzanna Tamminen, director and editor-in-chief. "Wesleyan University Press is a scholarly press with a focus on poetry, music, dance and cultural studies." Wesleyan University Press is one of the major publishers of poetry in the nation. Poetry publications from Wesleyan tend to get widely (and respectfully) reviewed. **"We are accepting manuscripts by invitation only until further notice."** Publishes hardcover originals and paperbacks. Pays royalties, plus 10 author's copies. Responds to queries in 2 months; to mss in 4 months. Book catalog available free. Guidelines online. *Does not accept unsolicited mss.*

### ⊘ WHITE PINE PRESS

P.O. Box 236, Buffalo NY 14201. (716)627-4665. **Fax:** (716)627-4665. **E-mail:** wpine@whitepine.org. Web-

site: www.whitepine.org. **Contact:** Dennis Maloney, editor. Publishes trade paperback originals. Pays contributor's copies. Publishes ms 18 months after acceptance. Responds in 1 month to queries and proposals; 4 months to mss. Catalog online. Guidelines online.

**NEEDS** "Only considering submissions for our annual poetry contest."

### ⊘ WORDSONG

815 Church St., Honesdale PA 18431. **Fax:** (570)253-0179. **Website:** www.wordsongpoetry.com. "We publish fresh voices in contemporary poetry." Pays authors royalty or work purchased outright. Responds to mss in 3 months.

**HOW TO CONTACT** *Agented submissions only.*

**TIPS** "Collections of original poetry, not anthologies, are our biggest need at this time. Keep in mind that the strongest collections demonstrate a facility with multiple poetic forms and offer fresh images and insights. Check to see what's already on the market and on our website before submitting."

### WRITE BLOODY PUBLISHING

Austin TX **E-mail:** writebloody@gmail.com. **Website:** writebloody.com. **Contact:** Derrick Brown, president. We publish and promote great books of poetry every year. We are a small press with a snappy look, dedicated to quality literature that is proud to be printed in the USA. We are not a printer. We are a sweet publishing house located on the outskirts of Austin, Texas. Catalog online. Guidelines online.

**NEEDS** Reading period August 1-31. Check online for details.

**TIPS** "You must tour if you are part of our family. At least 20 shows a year. Just like a band."

### YALE UNIVERSITY PRESS

P.O. Box 209040, New Haven CT 06520. (203)432-0960. **Fax:** (203)432-0948. **E-mail:** chris.rogers@ yale.edu. **Website:** yalebooks.com. **Contact:** Christopher Rogers, executive editor for history and current events. "Yale University Press publishes scholarly and general interest books." Publishes hardcover and trade paperback originals. Book catalog and ms guidelines online. Submit to Yale Series of Younger Poets Competition. Guidelines online.

**TIPS** "Audience is scholars, students and general readers."

# CONTESTS & AWARDS

///////////////////////////////////////////////////////////////////////////////////////////

This section contains a wide array of poetry competitions and literary awards. These range from state poetry society contests (with a number of modest monetary prizes) to prestigious honors bestowed by private foundations, elite publishers and renowned university programs. Because these listings reflect such a variety of skill levels and degrees of competitiveness, it's important to read each carefully and note its unique requirements. *Never* enter a contest without consulting the guidelines and following directions to the letter (including manuscript formatting, number of lines or pages of poetry accepted, amount of entry fee, entry forms needed and other details).

**IMPORTANT NOTE:** As we gathered information for this edition of *Poet's Market*, we found that some competitions hadn't yet established their 2017 fees and deadlines. In such cases, we list the most recent information available as a general guide. Always consult current guidelines for updates before entering any competition.

## WHAT ABOUT ENTRY FEES?

Most contests charge entry fees, and these are usually quite legitimate. The funds are used to cover expenses such as paying the judges, putting up prize monies, printing prize editions of magazines and journals, and promoting the contest through mailings and ads. If you're concerned about a poetry contest or other publishing opportunity, see "Is It a 'Con'?" for advice on some of the more questionable practices in the poetry world.

## 49TH PARALLEL AWARD FOR POETRY

Western Washington University, Mail Stop 9053, Bellingham WA 98225. (360)650-4863. **E-mail:** bellingham.review@wwu.edu. **Website:** www.bhreview.org. **Contact:** Susanne Paola Antonetta, editor-in-chief; Louis McLaughlin, managing editor. Annual poetry contest, supported by the *Bellingham Review,* given for a poem or group of poems of any style or length. Deadline: March 15. Submissions period begins December 1. Prize: $1,000.

## ✪ J.M. ABRAHAM POETRY PRIZE

Writers' Federation of Nova Scotia, 1113 Marginal Rd., Halifax NS B3H 4P7, Canada. (902)423-8116. **Fax:** (902)422-0881. **E-mail:** director@writers.ns.ca. **Website:** www.writers.ns.ca. The J.M. Abraham Poetry Prize is an annual award designed to honor the best book of poetry by a resident of Atlantic Canada. Formerly known as the Atlantic Poetry Prize. Deadline: First Friday in December. Prize: Valued at $2,000 for the winning title.

## AKRON POETRY PRIZE

**E-mail:** uapress@uakron.edu. **Website:** www.uakron.edu/uapress/akron-poetry-prize/. **Contact:** Mary Biddinger, editor/award director. Submissions must be unpublished. Considers simultaneous submissions (with notification of acceptance elsewhere). Submit at least 48 pages and no longer than 90 pages, typed, single-spaced. See website for complete guidelines. Manuscripts will be accepted via Submittable.com between April 15 and June 15 each year. Competition receives 500+ entries. 2015 winner was Sandra Simonds for *Further Problems With Pleasure.* Winner posted on website by September 30. Deadline: April 15-June 15. Prize: $1,500, plus publication of a book-length ms.

○ Mss must include a cover page (with author's name, mailing address, phone number, email address, and ms title), a title page (with no identifying information), and an acknowledgments page listing poems previously published in periodicals (if applicable). Please do not submit mss that have the author's name on each page. Mss will go to the final judge blind.

## MARIE ALEXANDER POETRY SERIES

English Department, 2801 S. University Ave., Little Rock AR 72204. **E-mail:** editor@mariealexanderseries.com. **Website:** mariealexanderseries.com. **Contact:** Nickole Brown. Annual contest for a collection of previously unpublished prose poems or flash fiction by a U.S. writer. Deadline: July 31. Open to submissions on July 1. Prize: $1,000, plus publication.

## AGHA SHAHID ALI PRIZE IN POETRY

University of Utah Press, J. Willard Marriott Lib., Ste 5400, 295 S. 1500 East, Salt Lake City UT 84112. (801)581-6771. **Fax:** (801)581-3365. **Website:** www.uofupress.com/ali-poetry-prize.php. Honoring the memory of a celebrated poet and a beloved teacher, the Agha Shahid Ali Prize in Poetry is awarded annually and is sponsored by The University of Utah Press and The University of Utah Department of English. Deadline: March 31. Open to submissions on February 1. Prize: $1,000.

## ALLIGATOR JUNIPER AWARD

*Alligator Juniper*/Prescott College, 220 Grove Ave., Prescott AZ 86301. (928)350-2012. **Fax:** (928)776-5102. **E-mail:** alligatorjuniper@prescott.edu. **Website:** www.prescott.edu/alligatorjuniper/national-contest/index.html. **Contact:** Skye Anicca, managing editor. Annual contest for unpublished fiction, creative nonfiction, and poetry. Open to all age levels. Each entrant receives a personal letter from staff regarding the status of their submission, as well as minor feedback on the piece. Deadline: October 1. Prize: $1,000 plus publication in all three categories. Finalists in each genre are recognized as such, published, and paid in copies. Judged by the distinguished writers in each genre and Prescott College writing students enrolled in the Literary Journal Practicum course.

## AMERICAN LITERARY REVIEW CONTESTS

*American Literary Review,* P.O. Box 311307, University of North Texas, Denton TX 76203-1307. (940)565-2755. **E-mail:** americanliteraryreview@gmail.com. **Website:** www.americanliteraryreview.com. Contest to award excellence in short fiction, creative nonfiction, and poetry. Multiple entries are acceptable, but each entry must be accompanied with a reading fee. Do not put any identifying information in the file itself; include the author's name, title(s), address, e-mail address, and phone number in the boxes provided in the online submissions manager. Short fiction: Limit 8,000 words per work. Creative nonfiction: Limit 6,500 words per work. Deadline: October 1. Submission period begins June 1. Prize: $1,000 prize for each category, along with publication in the Spring online issue of the *American Literary Review.*

## THE AMERICAN POETRY JOURNAL BOOK PRIZE

P.O. Box 2080, Aptos CA 95001-2080. **E-mail:** dreamhorsepress@yahoo.com. **Website:** www.dreamhorsepress.com. Deadline: Last day in February for snail mail postmarks, five days later for electronic submissions. Prize: $1,000, publication and 20 copies. All entries will be considered for publication.

## THE AMERICAN POETRY REVIEW/ HONICKMAN FIRST BOOK PRIZE

320 S. Broad St., Hamilton 313, Philadelphia PA 19102. 215 717 6800. **E-mail:** escanlon@aprweb.org. **Website:** www.aprweb.org. **Contact:** Elizabeth Scanlon, editor. The prize is open to poets who have not published a book-length collection of poems with a registered ISBN. Translations are not eligible nor are works written by multiple authors. 2016 guest judge is Gabrielle Calvocoressi. Reading period: August 1-October 31. Prize: $3,000, plus publication and reading at the University of the Arts Visiting Writers Series in 2018.

## AMERICAN-SCANDINAVIAN FOUNDATION TRANSLATION PRIZE

The American-Scandinavian Foundation, 58 Park Ave., New York NY 10016. (212)779-3587. **E-mail:** grants@amscan.org; info@amscan.org. **Website:** www.amscan.org. **Contact:** Matthew Walters, director of fellowships & grants. The annual ASF translation competition is awarded for the most outstanding translations of poetry, fiction, drama, or literary prose written by a Scandinavian author born after 1800. Deadline: June 1. Prize: The Nadia Christensen Prize includes a $2,500 award, publication of an excerpt in *Scandinavian Review*, and a commemorative bronze medallion; The Leif and Inger Sjöberg Award, given to an individual whose literature translations have not previously been published, includes a $2,000 award, publication of an excerpt in *Scandinavian Review*, and a commemorative bronze medallion.

## THE AMY AWARD FOR POETRY

Poets & Writers, 90 Broad St., Suite 2100, New York NY 10004. **E-mail:** admin@pw.org. **E-mail:** amyaward@pw.org. **Website:** www.pw.org/about-us/amy_award. **Contact:** Elliot Figman, executive director. The Amy Award celebrates promising young women poets from the New York City Area. Deadline: June 1. Prize: An invitation to read at the awards presentation and reception in New York City in autumn 2013, an honorarium, and a one-year subscription to *Poets & Writers* magazine and a selection of poetry books. Up to three winners will be selected.

## ANABIOSIS PRESS CHAPBOOK CONTEST

2 South New St., Bradford MA 01835. (978)469-7085. **E-mail:** rsmyth@anabiosispress.org. **Website:** www.anabiosispress.org. **Contact:** Richard Smyth, editor. Deadline: June 30 (postmarked). Prize: $100, plus publication of the winning chapbook, and 100 copies of the first run.

## THE ANHINGA PRESS-ROBERT DANA PRIZE FOR POETRY

Anhinga Press, P.O. Box 3665, Tallahassee FL 32315. **E-mail:** info@anhinga.org. **Website:** www.anhinga.org. **Contact:** Kristine Snodgrass, poetry editor. Offered annually for a book-length collection of poetry by an author writing in English. Guidelines on website. Past winners include Frank X. Gaspar, Earl S. Braggs, Julia Levine, Keith Ratzlaff, Lynn Aarti Chandhok, and Rhett Iseman Trull. Deadline: Submissions will be accepted from February 15-May 15. Prize: $2,000, a reading tour of selected Florida colleges and universities, and the winning ms will be published. Past judges include Jan Beatty, Richard Blaco, Denise Duhamel, Donald Hall, Joy Harjo, Robert Dana, Mark Jarman, and Tony Hoagland.

## ANNUAL GIVAL PRESS OSCAR WILDE AWARD

Gival Press, LLC, P.O. Box 3812, Arlington VA 22203. (703)351-0079. **E-mail:** givalpress@yahoo.com. **Website:** www.givalpress.com. **Contact:** Robert L. Giron. Award given to the best previously unpublished original poem—written in English of any length, in any style, typed, double-spaced on 1 side only—which best relates gay/lesbian/bisexual/transgendered (GLBTQ) life, by a poet who is 18 years or older. Deadline: June 27 (postmarked). Prize: $100 and the poem, along with information about the poet, will be published on the Gival Press website. Judged by the previous winner, who reads the poems anonymously.

## ANNUAL WORLD HAIKU COMPETITION & ANNUAL WORLD TANKA CONTEST

P.O. Box 17331, Arlington VA 22216. **E-mail:** LPEzineSubmissions@gmail.com. **Website:** http://lyricalpassionpoetry.yolasite.com. **Contact:** Raquel D. Bailey. Contest is now closed. Promotes Japanese short form poetry. Deadline: See website for details. Prize: Monetary compensation and publication. Judged by experienced editors and award-winning writers from the contemporary writing community.

## ARIZONA LITERARY CONTEST & BOOK AWARDS

Arizona Authors' Association, 6939 East Chaparral Road, Paradise Valley AZ 85253-7000. (602) 554-8101. **E-mail:** AzAuthors@gmail.com. **Website:** www.azauthors.com. **Contact:** Lisa Aquilina, President. Arizona Authors' Association sponsors annual literary competition in poetry, short story, essay, unpublished novels, and published books (fiction, nonfiction, and children's literature) and Arizona Book of the Year. Cash prizes awarded ($500 Book of the Year) from Green Pieces Press and 1st, 2nd, and 3rd place in seven categories ($150, $75 and $30, respectively) from Vignetta Syndicate LLC. New category in 2016, New Drama Writing, with a grand prize of $250. All category winners are published in the *Arizona Literary Magazine*. Deadline: July 1. Begins accepting submissions January 1. Finalists notified by Labor Day weekend. Prizes: Grand Prize, Arizona Book of the Year Award: $500. All categories except new drama writing: 1st Prize: $150 and publication; 2nd Prize: $75 and publication; 3rd Prize: $30 and publication. New drama writing grand prize $250 and publication. Features in *Arizona Literary Magazine* can be taken instead of money and publication. 1st and 2nd prize winners in poetry, essay, and short story are nominated for the Pushcart Prize. Judged by nationwide published authors, editors, literary agents, and reviewers. Winners announced at an awards dinner and ceremony held the first Saturday in November.

## ARIZONA STATE POETRY SOCIETY ANNUAL CONTEST

P.O. Box 16125, Phoenix AZ 85011. (480)575-1222. **Website:** azpoetry.webs.com. **Contact:** Carol Hogan, contest chair. Deadline: September 30. Prize: Offers a variety of cash prizes in several categories ranging from $10-125; 1st, 2nd, and 3rd Prize winners are published in Sandcutters, ASPS's quarterly publication, which also lists names of Honorable Mention winners.

## ARROWHEAD REGIONAL ARTS COUNCIL INDIVIDUAL ARTIST CAREER DEVELOPMENT GRANT

Arrowhead Regional Arts Council, 600 E Superior St., Suite 404, Duluth MN 55802. (218)722-0952 or (800)569-8134. **E-mail:** info@aracouncil.org. **Website:** www.aracouncil.org. Award is to provide financial support to regional artists wishing to take advantage of impending, concrete opportunities that will advance their work or careers. Deadline: October and April. Grant awards of up to $3,000. Candidates are reviewed by a panel of ARAC Board Members and Community Artists.

## ART AFFAIR POETRY CONTEST

Art Affair Annual Literary Contests, P.O. Box 54302, Oklahoma City OK 73154. **E-mail:** okpoets@aol.com. **Website:** www.shadetreecreations.com. **Contact:** Barbara Shepherd, contest chair. The annual Art Affair Poetry Contest is open to any poet. Multiple entries accepted with entry fee for each and may be mailed in the same packet. Guidelines available on website. Winners' list will be published on the Art Affair website in December. Deadline: October 1. Prizes: 1st Prize: $40 and certificate; 2nd Prize: $25 and certificate; and 3rd Prize: $15 and certificate. Honorable Mention certificates will be awarded at the discretion of the judges.

Does not publish contest entries, which allows poets to publish their award-winning poems in major publications and enter them in other contests.

## ARTS & LETTERS PRIZES

*Arts & Letters Journal of Contemporary Culture*, Campus Box 89, GC&SU, Milledgeville GA 31061. (478)445-1289. **E-mail:** al.journal@gcsu.edu. **Website:** al.gcsu.edu. **Contact:** The Editors. Offered annually for unpublished work. Deadline: March 31. Prize: $1,000 prize for each of the four major genres. Fiction, poetry, and creative nonfiction winners are published in Fall or Spring issue. The prize-winning one-act play is produced at the Georgia College campus (usually in March). Judged by the editors (initial screening); see website for final judges and further details about submitting work.

## ATLANTIC WRITING COMPETITION FOR UNPUBLISHED MANUSCRIPTS

Writers' Federation of Nova Scotia, 1113 Marginal Rd., Halifax NS B3H 4P7. (902)423-8116. **Fax:** (902)422-0881. **E-mail:** programs@writers.ns.ca. **Website:** www.writers.ns.ca. **Contact:** Robin Spittal, communications and development officer. Annual program designed to honor work by unpublished writers in all 4 Atlantic Provinces. Entry is open to writers unpublished in the category of writing they wish to enter. Prizes are presented in the fall of each year. Categories include: novel, writing for children, poetry, short story, juvenile/young adult novel, creative non-fiction, and play. Judges return written comments when competition is concluded. Deadline: January 7. Prizes vary based on categories. See website for details.

## ATLANTIS AWARD

The Poet's Billow, 245 N. Collingwood, Syracuse NY 13206. **E-mail:** thepoetsbillow@gmail.com. **Website:** http://thepoetsbillow.org. **Contact:** Robert Evory. Annual award open to any writer to recognize one outstanding poem from its entries. Finalists with strong work will also be published. Submissions must be previously unpublished. Deadline: October 1. Submissions open July 1. Prize: $200 and winning poet will be featured in an interview on The Poet's Billow website. Poem will be published and displayed in The Poet's Billow Literary Art Gallery and nominated for a Pushcart Prize. If the poet qualifies, the poem will also be submitted to The Best New Poets anthology. Judged by the editors, and, occasionally, a guest judge.

## AUTUMN HOUSE POETRY, FICTION, AND NONFICTION PRIZES

P.O. Box 60100, Pittsburgh PA 15211. (412)381-4261. **E-mail:** gcerto@autumhouse.org; info@autumn-house.org. **E-mail:** https://autumnhousepress.sub-mittable.com/submit. **Website:** http://autumnhouse.org. **Contact:** Christine Stroud, senior editor. Offers annual prize and publication of book-length ms with national promotion. Submission must be unpublished as a collection, but individual poems, stories, and essays may have been previously published elsewhere. Considers simultaneous submissions. "Autumn House is a nonprofit corporation with the mission of publishing and promoting poetry and other fine literature. We have published books by Chana Bloch, Ellery Akers, Gerald Stern, Ruth L. Schwartz, Ed Ochester, Andrea Hollander, George Bilgere, Ada Limon, and many others." Deadline: June 30. Prize: The winner (in each of three categories) will receive book publication, $1,000 advance against royalties, and a $1,500 travel/publicity grant to promote his or her book. Judged by David St. John(poetry), William Lychack (fiction), and Michael Martone (nonfiction). **TIPS** "Include only your best work."

## AWP AWARD SERIES

Association of Writers & Writing Programs, George Mason University, 4400 University Drive, MSN 1E3, Fairfax VA 22030. **E-mail:** supriya@awpwriter.org.

**Website:** www.awpwriter.org. **Contact:** Supriya Bhatnagar, director of publications. AWP sponsors the Award Series, an annual competition for the publication of excellent new book-length works. The competition is open to all authors writing in English regardless of nationality or residence, and is available to published and unpublished authors alike. Offered annually to foster new literary talent. Deadline: Postmarked between January 1 and February 28. Prize: AWP Prize for the Novel: $2,500 and publication by New Issues Press; Donald Hall Prize for Poetry: $5,500 and publication by the University of Pittsburgh Press; Grace Paley Prize in Short Fiction: $5,500 and publication by the University of Massachusetts Press; and AWP Prize for Creative Nonfiction: $2,500 and publication by the University of Georgia Press.

## THE MURIEL CRAFT BAILEY MEMORIAL AWARD

4956 St. John Dr., Syracuse NY 13215. (315)488-8077. **E-mail:** poetry@comstockreview.org. **Website:** www.comstockreview.org. Annual contest for best previously unpublished poem. 2016 final judge: Marge Piercy. Submission period: April 1-July 1.

## THE BALTIMORE REVIEW CONTESTS

*The Baltimore Review,* 6514 Maplewood Rd., Baltimore MD 21212. **E-mail:** editor@baltimorereview.org. **Website:** www.baltimorereview.org. **Contact:** Barbara Westwood Diehl, senior editor. Each summer and winter issue includes a contest theme (see submissions guidelines for theme). Prizes are awarded for first, second, and third place among all categories—poetry, short stories, and creative nonfiction. All entries are considered for publication. Deadline: May 31 and November 30. Prize: 1st Place: $500; 2nd Place: $200; 3rd Place: $100. All entries are considered for publication. Provides a small compensation to all contributors. Judged by the editors of *The Baltimore Review* and a guest, final judge.

## THE WILLIS BARNSTONE TRANSLATION PRIZE

The Evansville Review, Dept. of Creative Writing, University of Evansville, 1800 Lincoln Ave., Evansville IN 47722. (812)488-1042. **E-mail:** evansvillereview@evansville.edu. **Website:** english.evansville.edu/EvansvilleReview.htm. The competition welcomes submissions of unpublished poetry translations from any language and time period (ancient to contemporary). The length limit for each translation is 200 lines. Deadline: December 1.

## BARROW STREET PRESS BOOK CONTEST

P.O. Box 1558, Kingston RI 02881. **Website:** www.barrowstreet.org. The Barrow Street Press Book Contest award will be given for the best previously unpublished ms of poetry in English. Deadline: June 30. Prize: $1,000. Judged by Denise Duhamel.

## THE BASKERVILLE PUBLISHERS POETRY AWARD & THE BETSY COLQUITT POETRY AWARD

*descant*, Texas Christian University's literary journal, TCU, Box 297270, Fort Worth TX 76129. **Fax:** (817)257-6239. **Website:** www.descant.tcu.edu. **Contact:** Matthew Pitt, editor. Annual award for an outstanding poem published in the latest issue of *descant*. Deadline: September-April. Prize: $250 for Baskerville Award; $500 for Betsy Colquitt Award. Publication retains copyright, but will transfer it to the author upon request.

## ELINOR BENEDICT POETRY PRIZE

*Passages North*, Northern Michigan University, 1401 Presque Isle Ave., Marquette MI 49855. **E-mail:** passages@nmu.edu. **Website:** passagesnorth.com/contests/. **Contact:** Jennifer A. Howard, Editor-in-Chief. Prize given biennially for a poem or a group of poems. Deadline: April 15. Submission period begins February 15. Prize: $1,000 and publication for winner; 2 honorable mentions are also published; all entrants receive a copy of *Passages North*.

## GEORGE BENNETT FELLOWSHIP

Phillips Exeter Academy, 20 Main Street, Exeter NH 03833. **E-mail:** teaching_opportunities@exeter.edu. **Website:** www.exeter.edu/bennettfellowship. Annual award for fellow and family to provide time and freedom from material considerations to a person seriously contemplating or pursuing a career as a writer. Applicants should have a ms in progress which they intend to complete during the fellowship period. Ms should be fiction, nonfiction, novel, short stories, or poetry. Duties: To be in residency at the Academy for the academic year; to make oneself available informally to students interested in writing. Committee favors writers who have not yet published a book with a major publisher. Deadline: November 30. A choice will be made, and all entrants notified in mid-April. Prize: Cash stipend (currently $14,933), room

and board. Judged by committee of the English department.

## BERMUDA TRIANGLE PRIZE

The Poet's Billow, 6135 Avon St., Portage MI 49024. **E-mail:** thepoetsbillow@gmail.com. **Website:** http://thepoetsbillow.org. **Contact:** Robert Evory. Annual award open to any writer to recognize three poems that address a theme set by the editors. Finalists with strong work will also be published. Submissions must be previously unpublished. Please submit online. Deadline: March 15. Submission period begins November 15. Prize: $50 each to three poems. The winning poems will be published and displayed in The Poet's Billow Literary Art Gallery and nominated for a Pushcart Prize. If the poet qualifies, the poem will also be submitted to The Best New Poets anthology. Judged by the editors, and, occasionally, a guest judge.

## THE PATRICIA BIBBY FIRST BOOK AWARD

Patricia Bibby Award, Tebot Bach, P.O. Box 7887, Huntington Beach CA 92615-7887. **E-mail:** mifanwy@tebotbach.org; info@tebotbach.org. **Website:** www.tebotbach.org. **Contact:** Mifanwy Kaiser. Annual competition open to all poets writing in English who have not committed to publishing collections of poetry of 36 poems or more in editions of over 400 copies. Offers award and publication of a book-length poetry ms by Tebot Bach. Deadline: November 30. Prize: $500 and book publication. Judges for each year's competition announced online.

## BINGHAMTON UNIVERSITY MILT KESSLER POETRY BOOK AWARD

Binghamton University Creative Writing Program, Department of English, General Literature, and Rhetoric, Library North Room 1149, Vestal Parkway East, P.O. Box 6000, Binghamton NY 13902-6000. (607)777-2713. **Fax:** (607)777-2408. **E-mail:** cwpro@binghamton.edu. **Website:** www2.binghamton.edu/english/creative-writing/binghamton-center-for-writers. **Contact:** Maria Mazziotti Gillan, creative writing program director. Annual award for a book of poems written in English, 48 pages or more in length, selected by judges as the strongest collection of poems published in that year. Deadline: March 1. Prize: $1,000.

## THE BITTER OLEANDER PRESS LIBRARY OF POETRY AWARD

The Bitter Oleander Press, 4983 Tall Oaks Dr., Fayetteville NY 13066-9776. (315)637-3047. **E-mail:** info@

bitteroleander.com. **Website:** www.bitteroleander.com. **Contact:** Paul B. Roth. The Bitter Oleander Press Library of Poetry Book Award replaces the 15-year long run of the Frances Locke Memorial Poetry Award. Guidelines available on website. Deadline: June 15 (postmarked). Open to submissions on May 1. Early or late entries will be disqualified. Prize: $1,000, plus book publication of the winning ms.

## THE BLACK RIVER CHAPBOOK COMPETITION

Black Lawrence Press, 326 Bingham St., Pittsburgh PA 15211. **E-mail:** editors@blacklawrencepress.com. **Website:** www.blacklawrence.com. **Contact:** Kit Frick, senior editor. Twice each year Black Lawrence Press will run the Black River Chapbook Competition for an unpublished chapbook of poems or short fiction between 16-36 pages in length. Spring deadline: May 31. Fall deadline: October 31. Prize: $500, publication, and 10 copies. Judged by a revolving panel of judges, in addition to the Chapbook Editor and other members of the *BLP* editorial staff.

## BLUE LIGHT POETRY PRIZE AND CHAPBOOK CONTEST

1563 - 45th Avenue, San Francisco CA 94122. **E-mail:** bluelightpress@aol.com. **E-mail:** bluelightpress@aol.com. **Website:** www.bluelightpress.com. **Contact:** Diane Frank, Chief Editor. The Blue Light Poetry Prize and Chapbook Contest offers a cash prize and publication by Blue Light Press (see separate listing in Book/Chapbook Publishers). Deadline: June 15. The winner will be published by Blue Light Press, with 20 copies the author's book. We have a group of poets who read manuscripts. Some years, we publish more than one winner.

**TIPS** "Our new anthology, *River of Earth and Sky: Poems for the Twenty-First Century,* has more than 100 poets whose work we deeply admire. It will show you the kind of poetry we love to publish."

## BLUE MOUNTAIN ARTS/SPS STUDIOS POETRY CARD CONTEST

P.O. Box 1007, Boulder CO 80306. (303)449-0536. **Fax:** (303)447-0939. **E-mail:** poetrycontest@sps.com; editorial@sps.com. **Website:** www.sps.com. **Contact:** Becky Milanski. Biannual poetry card contest. All entries must be the original creation of the submitting author. Looking for original poetry that's non-rhyming, although rhyming poetry may be considered. Poems may also be considered for possible publication on greeting cards or in book anthologies. Guidelines available online. Deadline: December 31 and June 30. Prize: 1st Place: $300; 2nd Place: $150; 3rd Place: $50. Judged by the Blue Mountain Arts editorial staff.

**TIPS** "We suggest that you write about real emotions and feelings and that you have some special person or occasion in mind as you write."

## THE BOARDMAN TASKER PRIZE FOR MOUNTAIN LITERATURE

The Boardman Tasker Charitable Trust, 8 Bank View Rd., Darley Abbey Derby DE22 1EJ, UK. 01332 342246. **E-mail:** steve@people-matter.co.uk. **Website:** www.boardmantasker.com. **Contact:** Steve Dean. Offered annually to reward a work with a mountain theme, whether fiction, nonfiction, drama, or poetry, written in the English language (initially or in translation). Subject must be concerned with a mountain environment. Previous winners have been books on expeditions, climbing experiences, a biography of a mountaineer, novels. Guidelines available in January by e-mail or on website. Entries must be previously published. Open to any writer. The award is to honor Peter Boardman and Joe Tasker, who disappeared on Everest in 1982. Deadline: August 1. Prize: £3,000 Judged by a panel of 3 judges elected by trustees.

## THE FREDERICK BOCK PRIZE

*Poetry*, 61 W. Superior St., Chicago IL 60654. (312)787-7070. **Fax:** (312)787-6650. **E-mail:** editors@poetry-magazine.org. **Website:** www.poetryfoundation.org. Several prizes are awarded annually for the best work printed in *Poetry* during the preceding year. Only poems already published in the magazine are eligible for consideration, and no formal application is necessary. The winners are announced in the November issue. Upon acceptance, *Poetry* licenses exclusive worldwide first serial rights, including electronic rights, for publication, as well as non-exclusive rights to reprint, reuse, and archive the work, in any format, in perpetuity. Copyright reverts to author upon first publication. Any writer may submit poems to *Poetry*. Prize: $500.

## BOSTON GLOBE-HORN BOOK AWARDS

*The Boston Globe*, Horn Book, Inc., 300 The Fenway, Palace Road Building, Suite P-311, Boston MA 02115. (617)278-0225. **Fax:** (617)278-6062. **E-mail:** info@hbook.com; khedeen@hbook.com. **Website:** hbook.com/bghb/. **Contact:** Katrina Hedeen. Offered annually for excellence in literature for children and young adults (published June 1-May 31). Categories: picture book, fiction and poetry, nonfiction. Judges may also name up to 2 honor books in each category. Books must be published in the US, but may be written or illustrated by citizens of any country. The Horn Book Magazine publishes speeches given at awards ceremonies. Guidelines for SASE or online. Deadline: May 15. Prize: $500 and an engraved silver bowl; honor book recipients receive an engraved silver plate. Judged by a panel of 3 judges selected each year.

## THE BOSTON REVIEW ANNUAL POETRY CONTEST

Poetry Contest, Boston Review, P.O. Box 425786, Cambridge MA 02142. (617)324-1360. **Fax:** (617)452-3356. **E-mail:** review@bostonreview.net. **Website:** www.bostonreview.net. Offers $1,500 and publication in *Boston Review* (see separate listing in Magazines/Journals). Deadline: June 1. Winner announced in early November on website. Prize: $1,500 and publication.

## BOULEVARD POETRY CONTEST FOR EMERGING POETS

PMB 325, 6614 Clayton Rd., Richmond Heights MO 63117. **E-mail:** editors@boulevardmagazine.org. **Website:** www.boulevardmagazine.org. **Contact:** Jessica Rogen, editor. Annual Emerging Poets Contest offers $1,000 and publication in *Boulevard* (see separate listing in Magazines/Journals) for the best group of 3 poems by a poet who has not yet published a book of poetry with a nationally distributed press. All entries will be considered for publication and payment at regular rates. Deadline: June 1. Prize: $1,000 and publication.

## BARBARA BRADLEY PRIZE

New England Poetry Club, 376 School St., Watertown MA 02472. **E-mail:** contests@nepoetryclub.org. **Website:** www.nepoetryclub.org. **Contact:** Audrey Kalajin. For a lyric poem under 20 lines, written by a woman. Deadline: May 31. Prize: $200. Judged by well-known poets and sometimes winners of previous NEPC contests.

## THE BRIAR CLIFF REVIEW FICTION, POETRY, AND CREATIVE NONFICTION COMPETITION

*The Briar Cliff Review*, Briar Cliff University, 3303 Rebecca St., Sioux City IA 51104-0100. **E-mail:** tricia. currans-sheehan@briarcliff.edu (editor); jeanne.emmons@briarcliff.edu (poetry). **Website:** www.bcreview.org. **Contact:** Tricia Currans-Sheehan, editor.

*The Briar Cliff Review* sponsors an annual contest offering $1,000 and publication to each 1st Prize winner in fiction, poetry, and creative nonfiction. Previous year's winner and former students of editors ineligible. Winning pieces accepted for publication on the basis of first-time rights. Considers simultaneous submissions, "but notify us immediately upon acceptance elsewhere. We guarantee a considerate reading." No mss returned. Award to reward good writers and showcase quality writing. Deadline: November 1. Prize: $1,000 and publication to each 1st Prize winner in fiction, poetry, and creative nonfiction. Judged by *Briar Cliff Review* editors.

## BRICK ROAD POETRY BOOK CONTEST

Brick Road Poetry Press, Inc., 513 Broadway, Columbus GA 31901. (706) 649-3080. **Fax:** (706) 649-3094. **E-mail:** kbadowski@brickroadpoetrypress.com. **Website:** www.brickroadpoetrypress.com. **Contact:** Ron Self and Keith Badowski, co-editors/founders. Annual competition for an original collection of 50-100 pages of poetry. Deadline: November 1. Submission period begins August 1. Prize: $1,000, publication in both print and e-book formats, and 25 copies of the book. May also offer publication contracts to the top finalists. Judged by Keith Badowski & Ron Self, Brick Road poetry editors.

**TIPS** "The best way to discover all that poetry can be and to expand the limits of your own poetry is to read expansively."

## ◑ THE BRIDPORT PRIZE

P.O. Box 6910, Dorset DT6 9QB, United Kingdom. **E-mail:** info@bridportprize.org.uk; kate@bridportprize.org.uk. **Website:** www.bridportprize.org.uk. **Contact:** Kate Wilson, Bridport Prize administrator. Award to promote literary excellence, discover new talent. Categories: Short stories, poetry, flash fiction, first novel. Deadline: May 31 each year. Open for submissions starting November 15. Prize: £5,000; £1,000; £500; various runners-up prizes and publication of approximately 13 best stories and 13 best poems in anthology; plus 6 best flash fiction stories. 1st Prize of £1,000 for the best short, short story of under 250 words. £1,000 plus up to a year's mentoring for winner of Peggy Chapman-Andrews Award for a first novel. Judged by 1 judge for short stories (in 2016, Tessa Hadley), 1 judge for poetry (in 2016, Patience Agbabi ) and 1 judge for flash fiction (in 2016, Tim Stevenson). The Novel award is judged by a group comprising representatives from

The Literary Consultancy, A.M. Heath Literary Agents, and (in 2016) judge Kerry Young.

## BRIGHT HILL PRESS POETRY BOOK AWARD

94 Church St., Treadwell NY 13846. **Website:** www.brighthillpress.org. Competition to publish a full-length poetry collection (48-64 pages).

## BRIGHT HILL PRESS POETRY CHAPBOOK COMPETITION

Bright Press Hill & Literary Center, 94 Church St., Treadwell NY 13846. (607)829-5055. **E-mail:** brighthillpress@stny.rr.com; wordthur@stny.rr.com. **Website:** www.brighthillpress.org. The annual Bright Hill Press Chapbook Award recognizes an outstanding collection of poetry. Guidelines available for SASE, by e-mail, or on website. Deadline: November 30. Prize: A publication contract with Bright Hill Press and $1,000, publication in print format, and 30 copies of the printed book. Judged by a nationally-known poet. **TIPS** "Publish your poems in literary magazines before trying to get a whole ms published. Publishing individual poems is the best way to hone your complete ms."

## BRITTINGHAM PRIZE IN POETRY

University of Wisconsin Press, 1930 Monroe Street, 3rd Floor, Madison WI 5311-2059. (608)263-1110. **Fax:** (608)263-1132. **E-mail:** rwallace@wisc.edu. **E-mail:** uwiscpress@uwpress.wisc.edu. **Website:** www.wisc.edu/wisconsinpress/poetryguide.html. **Contact:** Ronald Wallace, contest director. The annual Brittingham Prize in Poetry is 1 of 2 prizes awarded by The University of Wisconsin Press (see separate listing for the Felix Pollak Prize in Poetry in this section). The Brittingham Prize in Poetry is awarded annually to the best book-length manuscript of original poetry submitted in an open competition. The award is administered by the University of Wisconsin–Madison English Department, and the winner is chosen by a nationally recognized poet. The resulting book is published by the University of Wisconsin Press. Deadline: Submit August 15-September 15. Prize: Offers $1,000, plus publication. Judged by a distinguished poet who will remain anonymous until the winners are announced in mid-February.

## ☼ THE RBC BRONWEN WALLACE AWARD FOR EMERGING WRITERS

The Writers' Trust of Canada, 460 Richmond St. W., Suite 600, Toronto ON M5C 1P1, Canada. (416)504-8222. **Fax:** (416)504-9090. **E-mail:** info@writerstrust.com. **Website:** www.writerstrust.com. **Contact:** Amanda Hopkins. Presented annually to a Canadian writer under the age of 35 who is not yet published in book form. The award, which alternates each year between poetry and short fiction, was established in memory of Bronwen Wallace. Deadline: March 7. Prize: $5,000. Two finalists receive $1,000 each.

## BURNING BUSH POETRY PRIZE

P.O. Box 4658, Santa Rosa CA 95402. **Website:** www.bbbooks.com. Purpose of contest to reward a poet whose writing inspires others to value human life and natural world instead of values based on short-term economic advantage; speaks for community-centered values, democratic processes, especially those whose voices are seldom heard; demonstrates poetic excellence; and educates readers of the relevance of the past to the present and future. Deadline: June 1.

## BURNSIDE REVIEW CHAPBOOK COMPETITION

P.O. Box 1782, Portland OR 97207. **E-mail:** sid@burnsidereview.org. **Website:** www.burnsidereview.org. **Contact:** Sid Miller, editor. Deadline: June 30. Competition begins March 15. Prize: $200 and 10 copies of the chapbook printed by Burnside Review Press. Judged by Jennifer L. Knox in 2015.

## BOB BUSH MEMORIAL AWARD FOR FIRST BOOK OF POETRY

**E-mail:** tilsecretary@yahoo.com. **Website:** www.texasinstituteofletters.org. Offered annually for best first book of poetry published in previous year. Writer must have been born in Texas, have lived in the state at least 2 consecutive years at some time, or the subject matter should be associated with the state. Deadline: See website for exact date. Prize: $1,000.

## ☼ CAA POETRY AWARD

Canadian Authors Association, 74 Mississaga Street E., Orillia ON L3V 1V5, Canada. **Website:** canadianauthors.org/national. Contest for full-length English-language book of poems for adults by a Canadian writer. Deadline: January.

## GERALD CABLE BOOK AWARD

Silverfish Review Press, P.O. Box 3541, Eugene OR 97403. (541)344-5060. **E-mail:** sfrpress@earthlink.net. **Website:** www.silverfishreviewpress.com. **Contact:** Rodger Moody, editor. Awarded annually to a book-length ms of original poetry by an author who has not yet published a full-length collection. There are no restrictions on the kind of poetry or subject matter; translations are not acceptable. Deadline: October 15. Prize: $1,000, publication, and 25 copies of the book. The winner will be announced in March.

### CAKETRAIN COMPETITION

P.O. Box 82588, Pittsburgh PA 15218. **E-mail:** editors@caketrain.org. **Website:** www.caketrain.org. **Contact:** Amanda Raczkowski, editor; Joseph Reed, editor. Annual contest for full length works of fiction and poetry chapbooks sponsored by *Caketrain* literary journal. Can submit by mail with SASE or by e-mail. See website for guidelines. Deadline: October 1. Prize: $250 cash and 25 copies of their book.

### CALIFORNIA BOOK AWARDS

Commonwealth Club of California, 555 Post St., San Francisco CA 94102. (415) 597-6700. **Fax:** (415 )597-6729. **E-mail:** bookawards@commonwealthclub.org. **Website:** www.commonwealthclub.org/. **Contact:** Renee Miguel. Offered annually to recognize California's best writers and illuminate the wealth and diversity of California-based literature. Award is for published submissions appearing in print during the previous calendar year. Can be nominated by publisher or author. Open to California residents (or residents at time of publication). Deadline: December 22. Prize: Medals and cash prizes to be awarded at publicized event. Judged by 12-15 California professionals with a diverse range of views, backgrounds, and literary experience.

### ✪ CANADIAN AUTHORS ASSOCIATION AWARD FOR POETRY

6 West St. N, Suite 203, Orillia ON L3V 5B8, Canada. (705)325-3926. **E-mail:** admin@canadianauthors.org. **Website:** www.canadianauthors.org. **Contact:** Anita Purcell, executive director. Offered annually for a full-length English-language book of poems for adults, by a Canadian writer. Deadline: January 15. Prize: $1,000 and a silver medal. Judging: Each year a trustee for each award appointed by the Canadian Authors Association selects up to 3 judges. Identities of the trustee and judges are confidential.

### CAROLINA WREN PRESS POETRY SERIES CONTEST

120 Morris St., Durham NC 27701. (919)560-2738. **Fax:** (919)560-2759. **E-mail:** carolinawrenpress@earthlink.net. **Website:** www.carolinawrenpress.org.

**Contact:** Andrea Selch, Poetry Editor. Carolina Wren Press is a nonprofit organization whose mission is to publish quality writing, especially by writers historically neglected by mainstream publishing, and to develop diverse and vital audiences through publishing, outreach, and educational programs. Deadline: June 15 of odd-numbered years. Prize: $1,000 and publication.

### JAMIE CAT CALLAN HUMOR PRIZE

Category in the Soul-Making Keats Literary Competition, The Webhallow House, 1544 Sweetwood Dr., Broadmoor Village CA 94015-2029. **E-mail:** SoulKeats@mail.com. **Website:** www.soulmakingcontest.us. **Contact:** Eileen Malone. Deadline: November 30. Prize: First Place: $100; Second Place: $50; Third Place: $25. Judged by Jamie Cat Callan. **TIPS** "Make me laugh out loud."

### CAVE CANEM POETRY PRIZE

Cave Canem Foundation, Inc., 20 Jay St., Suite 310-A, Brooklyn NY 11201. (718)858-0000. **Website:** www.cavecanempoets.org. This 1st book award is dedicated to the discovery of exceptional mss by black poets of African descent. Deadline: March 15.

### THE CENTER FOR BOOK ARTS POETRY CHAPBOOK COMPETITION

The Center for Book Arts, 28 W. 27th St., 3rd Floor, New York NY 10001. (212)481-0295. **Fax:** (866)708-8994. **E-mail:** info@centerforbookarts.org. **Website:** http://centerforbookarts.org/opportunities/for-writers/. Annual competition for unpublished collections of poetry. Individual poems may have been previously published. Collection must not exceed 500 lines or 24 pages (does not include cover page, title pages, table of contents, or acknowledgements pages). Copies of winning chapbooks available through website. Deadline: December 15. Prize: $500 award, $500 honorarium for a reading, publication, and 10 copies of chapbook.

### JOHN CIARDI PRIZE FOR POETRY

BkMk Press, University of Missouri-Kansas City, 5101 Rockhill Rd., Kansas City MO 64110. (816)235-2558. **E-mail:** bkmk@umkc.edu. **Website:** www.newletters.org. Offered annually for the best book-length collection (unpublished) of poetry in English by a living author. Translations are not eligible. Guidelines for SASE, by e-mail, or on website. Deadline: January 15. Prize: $1,000, plus book publication by BkMk Press.

Judged by a network of published writers. Final judging is done by a writer of national reputation.

## CIDER PRESS REVIEW BOOK AWARD

P.O. Box 33384, San Diego CA 92163. **E-mail:** editor@ciderpressreview.com. **Website:** http://ciderpressreview.com/. Annual award from *Cider Press Review*. Deadline: November 30. Open to submissions on September 1. Prize: $1,500, publication, and 25 author's copies of a book length collection of poetry. Author receives a standard publishing contract. Initial print run is not less than 1,000 copies. CPR acquires first publication rights. Judged by Jeffrey Harrison in 2014. Previous judge was Charles Harper Webb.

## ◯ THE CITY OF VANCOUVER BOOK AWARD

Cultural Services Dept., Woodward's Heritage Building, 111 W. Hastings St., Suite 501, Vancouver BC V6B 1H4, Canada. (604) 829-2007. **Fax:** (604)871-6005. **E-mail:** marnie.rice@vancouver.ca; culture@vancouver.ca. **Website:** https://vancouver.ca/people-programs/city-of-vancouver-book-award.aspx. The annual City of Vancouver Book Award recognizes authors of excellence of any genre who contribute to the appreciation and understanding of Vancouver's history, unique character, or the achievements of its residents. The book must exhibit excellence in one or more of the following areas: content, illustration, design, format. Deadline: May 18. Prize: $3,000. Judged by an independent jury.

## CLEVELAND STATE UNIVERSITY POETRY CENTER FIRST BOOK

Dept. of English, 2121 Euclid Ave., Cleveland OH 44115-2214. (216)687-2000. **E-mail:** poetrycenter@csuohio.edu. **Website:** www.csuohio.edu/poetrycenter/. **Contact:** Caryl Pagel, Director. The CSU Poetry Center publishes collections of contemporary poetry and prose by established and emerging authors. The Poetry Center is committed to acquiring, through first book, open book, and essay collection competitions, stylistically distinctive and skillfully crafted writing from an aesthetically diverse range of authors. Offered for the best full-length volumes of original poetry in English. Deadline: March 31. Prize: $1,000 and publication in the CSU Poetry Series.

## CLEVELAND STATE UNIVERSITY POETRY CENTER OPEN BOOK POETRY COMPETITION

Dept. of English, 2121 Euclid Ave., Cleveland OH 44115-2214. (216)687-2000. **E-mail:** poetrycenter@csuohio.edu. **Website:** www.csupoetrycenter.com/open-book-poetry. **Contact:** Frank Giampietro, Interim Director. For the best full-length volume of original poetry by a poet who has published at least one full-length collection of poetry in a book of 48 pages or more with a press run of 500. Deadline: March 13. Submission period begins November 1. Prize: $1,000 and publication in the CSU Poetry Series. Judged by a panel of previous CSU authors.

## CLOCKWISE CHAPBOOK COMPETITION

Tebot Bach, Tebot Bach, Clockwise, P.O. Box 7887, Huntington Beach CA 92615. (714)968-0905. **Fax:** (714)968-4677. **E-mail:** mifanwy@tebotbach.org. **Website:** www.tebotbach.org/clockwise.html. Annual competition for a collection of poetry. Submit 24-32 pages of original poetry in English. Deadline: July 15. Prize: $500 and a book publication in Perfect Bound Editions. Winner announced in September with publication January. Judged by Gail Wronsky.

## CLOUDBANK JOURNAL CONTEST

P.O. Box 610, Corvallis OR 97339. (541)752-0075. **E-mail:** michael@cloudbankbooks.com. **Website:** www.cloudbankbooks.com. **Contact:** Michael Malan. Deadline: April 30, 2016 Prize: $200 and publication, plus an extra copy of the issue in which the winning poem appears. Two contributors' copies will be sent to writers whose work appears in the magazine. Judged by Michael Malan and Peter Sears.

◯ Submissions for contests are accepted via Submittable and by mail. Complete guidelines are available at website. Accept both poetry and flash fiction.

## ◐ TOM COLLINS POETRY PRIZE

Fellowship of Australian Writers (WA), P.O. Box 6180, Swanbourne WA 6910, Australia. (61)(8)9384-4771. **Fax:** (61)(8)9384-4854. **E-mail:** fellowshipaustralianwriterswa@gmail.com. **Website:** www.fawwa.org. Annual contest for unpublished poems, maximum 60 lines. Reserves the right to publish entries in a FAW-WA publication or on its website. Guidelines online or for SASE. Deadline: December 15. Submission period begins September 1. Prize: 1st Place: $1,000; 2nd Place; $400; 4 Highly Commended: $150 each.

## COLORADO BOOK AWARDS

(303)894-7951. **Fax:** (303)864-9361. **E-mail:** lansdown@coloradohumanities.org. **Website:** www.coloradohumanities.org. **Contact:** Marnie Lansdown. An annual program that celebrates the accomplishments of Colorado's outstanding authors, editors, illustrators, and photographers. Awards are presented in at least ten categories including anthology/collection, biography, children's, creative nonfiction, fiction, history, nonfiction, pictorial, poetry, and young adult. Deadline: January 8.

## THE COLORADO PRIZE FOR POETRY

*Colorado Review*/Center for Literary Publishing, Department of English, Colorado State University, 9105 Campus Delivery, Ft. Collins CO 80523. (970)491-5449. **E-mail:** creview@colostate.edu. **Website:** http://coloradoprize.colostate.edu. **Contact:** Stephanie G'schwind, editor. Submission must be unpublished as a collection, but individual poems may have been published elsewhere. Submit mss of 48-100 pages of poetry on any subject, in any form, double- or single-spaced. Include 2 titles pages: 1 with ms title only, the other with ms title and poet's name, address, and phone number. Enclose SASP for notification of receipt and SASE for results; mss will not be returned. Guidelines available for SASE or by e-mail. Guidelines available for SASE or online at website. Poets can also submit online via online submission manager through website. Deadline: January 14. Prize: $2,000 and publication of a book-length ms. Judged by Tyrone Williams in 2016 (final round).

## CONCRETE WOLF POETRY CHAPBOOK CONTEST

P.O. Box 1808, Kingston WA 98346. **E-mail:** concretewolf@yahoo.com. **Website:** http://concretewolf.com. Prefers chapbooks that have a theme, either obvious (i.e., chapbook about a divorce) or understated (i.e., all the poems mention the color blue). Likes a collection that feels more like a whole than a sampling of work. No preference as to formal or free verse. Slightly favors lyric and narrative poetry to language and concrete, but excellent examples of any style will grab their attention. Considers simultaneous submissions if notified of acceptance elsewhere. Deadline: November 30. Prize: Publication and 100 author copies of a perfectly-bound chapbook.

## THE CONNECTICUT RIVER REVIEW POETRY CONTEST

P.O. Box 270554, W. Hartford CT 06127. **E-mail:** conpoetry@comcast.net. **Website:** ctpoetry.net. Deadline: September 30. Open to submissions on August 1. 1st Place: $400; 2nd Place: $100; 3rd Place: $50.

## CPR EDITOR'S PRIZE

P.O. Box 33384, San Diego CA 92163. **E-mail:** editor@ciderpressreview.com. **Website:** http://ciderpressreview.com/bookaward. Annual award from *Cider Press Review*. Deadline: submit between April 1-June 30. Prize: $1,000, publication, and 25 author's copies of a book length collection of poetry. Author receives a standard publishing contract. Initial print run is not less than 1,000 copies. CPR acquires first publication rights. Judged by *Cider Press Review* editors.

## CRAB ORCHARD SERIES IN POETRY FIRST BOOK AWARD

First Book Award, Dept. of English, Mail Code 4503, Southern Illinois University Carbondale, 1000 Faner Drive, Carbondale IL 62901. (618)453-6833. **Fax:** (618)453-8224. **E-mail:** jtribble@siu.edu. **Website:** www.craborchardreview.siu.edu. **Contact:** Jon Tribble, series editor. Annual award that selects a first book of poems for publication from an open competition of manuscripts, in English, by a U.S. citizen, permanent resident, or person who has DACA/TPS status who has neither published, who has neither published, nor committed to publish, a volume of poetry 48 pages or more in length in an edition of over 500 copies (individual poems may have been previously published; for the purposes of the Crab Orchard Series in Poetry, a ms which was in whole or in part submitted as a thesis or dissertation as a requirement for the completion of a degree is considered unpublished and is eligible). Current or former students, colleagues, and close friends of the final judge, and current and former students and employees of Southern Illinois University Carbondale and authors who have published a book with Southern Illinois University Press or have a book under contract with Southern Illinois University Press are not eligible. Deadline: July 8. Submission period begins May 15. Prize: The winner will be awarded a publication contract with Southern Illinois University Press, a $2,500 prize, and a $1,500 as an honorarium for a reading at Southern Illinois University Carbondale. The reading will follow the publication of the poet's collection. Judged by a published poet. Check website for current judge.

**TIPS** "Carefully read directions for entering and follow them exactly. Note that simultaneous submissions are accepted for this book prize, but the winning entry must not be accepted elsewhere. All submissions should be made through Submittable: https://craborchardseriesinpoetry.submittable.com/submit ."

## CRAB ORCHARD SERIES IN POETRY OPEN COMPETITION AWARDS

Department of English, Mail Code 4503, Faner Hall 2380, Southern Illinois University Carbondale, Carbondale IL 62901. (618)453-6833. **Fax:** (618)453-8224. **E-mail:** jtribble@siu.edu. **Website:** www.craborchardreview.siu.edu. **Contact:** Jon Tribble, series editor. Annual competition to award unpublished, original collections of poems written in English by United States citizens, permanent residents, or persons who have DACA/TPS status (individual poems may have been previously published; for the purposes of the Crab Orchard Series in Poetry, a ms which was in whole or in part submitted as a thesis or dissertation as a requirement for the completion of a degree is considered unpublished and is eligible). Two volumes of poems will be selected from the open competition of mss. Current or former students, colleagues, and close friends of the final judge, and current and former students and employees of Southern Illinois University Carbondale and authors who have published a book with Southern Illinois University Press or have a book under contract with Southern Illinois University Press are not eligible. Deadline: November 22. Submission period begins October 1. Prize: Both winners will be awarded a publication contract with Southern Illinois University Press, a $2,500 prize, and a $1,500 as an honorarium for a reading at Southern Illinois University Carbondale. Both readings will follow the publication of the poets' collections. Judged by a published poet. Check website for current judge.

## LOIS CRANSTON MEMORIAL POETRY PRIZE

CALYX, Inc., P.O. Box B, Corvallis OR 97339. **E-mail:** calyx@proaxis.com. **Website:** www.calyxpress.org/LoisPrize.html. This poetry prize in Lois Cranston's name honors the memory of her commitment to the creative work of women from all walks of life. Deadline: June 30 (submission period begins on March 1).

Prize: $300, publication, and one-volume subscription. Judged by Willa Schneberg in 2015.

## THE CRAZYHORSE PRIZE IN POETRY

Crazyhorse, Department of English, College of Charleston, 66 George St., Charleston SC 29424. (843)953-4470. **E-mail:** crazyhorse@cofc.edu. **Website:** http://crazyhorse.cofc.edu. **Contact:** Prize Director. The *Crazyhorse* Prize in Poetry is for a single poem. All entries will be considered for publication. Submissions must be unpublished. Deadline: January 31. Submissions period begins January 1. Prize: $2,000 and publication in *Crazyhorse*. Judged by genre judges for first round, guest judge for second round. Judges change on a yearly basis.

## THE CUTBANK CHAPBOOK CONTEST

*CutBank* Literary Magazine, *CutBank*, University of Montana, English Dept., LA 133, Missoula MT 59812. **E-mail:** editor.cutbank@gmail.com. **Website:** www.cutbankonline.org. **Contact:** Allison Linville, editor-in-chief. This competition is open to original English language mss in the genres of poetry, fiction, and creative nonfiction. While previously published standalone pieces or excerpts may be included in a ms, the ms as a whole must be an unpublished work. Looking for startling, compelling, and beautiful original work. "We're looking for a fresh, powerful manuscript. Maybe it will overtake us quietly; gracefully defy genres; satisfyingly subvert our expectations; punch us in the mouth page in and page out. We're interested in both prose and poetry—and particularly work that straddles the lines between genres." Deadline: March 31. Submissions period begins January1. Prize: $1,000 and 25 contributor copies. Judged by a guest judge each year.

## CWW ANNUAL WISCONSIN WRITERS AWARDS

Council for Wisconsin Writers, 6973 Heron Way, De Forest WI 53532. **E-mail:** karlahuston@gmail.com. **Website:** www.wiswriters.org. **Contact:** Geoff Gilpin, president and annual awards co-chair; Karla Huston, secretary and annual awards co-chair; Jennifer Morales, annual awards co-chair; Edward Schultz, annual awards co-chair. Offered annually for work published by Wisconsin writers during the previous calendar year. Nine awards: Major Achievement (presented in alternate years); short fiction; short nonfiction; nonfiction book; poetry book; fiction book; children's literature; Lorine Niedecker Poetry Award;

Christopher Latham Sholes Award for Outstanding Service to Wisconsin Writers p(resented in alternate years); Essay Award for Young Writers. Open to Wisconsin residents. Deadline: February 1. Submissions open on November 1. Prizes: First place prizes: $500. Honorable mentions: $50.

## DANA AWARDS IN THE NOVEL, SHORT FICTION, AND POETRY

200 Fosseway Dr., Greensboro NC 27445. (336)644-8028. **E-mail:** danaawards@gmail.com. **Website:** www.danaawards.com. **Contact:** Mary Elizabeth Parker, chair. Three awards offered annually for unpublished work written in English. Works previously published online are not eligible. The Dana Awards are re-vamping. The Novel Award is now increased to $2,000, based on a new partnership with Blue Mary Books: Blue Mary has agreed to consider for possible publication not only the Novel Award winning manuscript, but the top 9 other Novel finalists, as well as the 30 top Novel semifinalists. The Short Fiction and Poetry Awards offer the traditional $1,000 awards each and do not offer a publishing option (currently, Blue Mary publishes only novels). See website for further updates. Purpose is monetary award for work that has not been previously published or received monetary award, but will accept work published simply for friends and family. Deadline: October 31 (postmarked). Prizes: $2,000 for the Novel Award; $1,000 each for the Short Fiction and Poetry awards awards.

○ The Dana Awards and Blue Mary Books are separate entities. Blue Mary has no part in the reading and judging of manuscripts to determine the Novel Award and the Dana Awards does not advise Blue Mary on publishing. The Dana Awards gives its monetary award only; then, as a further courtesy, will put winner, finalists and semifinalists in touch with Blue Mary. All further agreements and contracts are solely between the authors and Blue Mary.

## DANCING POETRY CONTEST

AEI Contest Chair, Judy Cheung, 704 Brigham Ave., Santa Rosa CA 95404-5245. (707)528-0912. **E-mail:** jhcheung@comcast.net. **Website:** www.dancingpoetry.com. **Contact:** Judy Cheung, contest chair. Deadline: May 15. Prizes: Three Grand Prizes will receive $100 each plus the poems will be danced and videotaped at this year's Dancing Poetry Festival; six First Prizes will receive $50 each; twelve Second Prizes will

receive $25 each; and thirty Third Prizes will receive $10 each.

**TIPS** "We always look for something new and different including new twists to old themes, different looks at common situations, inovative concepts for dynamic, thought provoking entertainment."

## DELAWARE DIVISION OF THE ARTS

820 N. French St., Wilmington DE 19801. (302)577-8278. **Fax:** (302)577-6561. **E-mail:** Roxanne.stanulis@state.de.us. **Website:** www.artsdel.org. **Contact:** Roxanne Stanulis. Award to help further careers of emerging and established professional artists. For Delaware residents only. Guidelines available after May 1 on website. Accepts inquiries by e-mail, phone. Results announced in December. Winners notified by mail. Results available on website. Deadline: August 1. Prize: $10,000 for masters; $6,000 for established professionals; $3,000 for emerging professionals. Judged by out-of-state, nationally recognized professionals in each artistic discipline.

**TIPS** "Follow all instructions and choose your best work sample."

## DER-HOVANESSIAN PRIZE

New England Poetry Club, 376 School St., Watertown MA 02472. **E-mail:** contests@nepoetryclub.org. **Website:** www.nepoetryclub.org. **Contact:** Audrey Kalajin. For a translation from any language into English. Send a copy of the original. Funded by John Mahtesian. Deadline: May 31 Prize: $200. Judges are well-known poets and sometimes winners of previous NEPC contests.

## DIAGRAM/NEW MICHIGAN PRESS CHAPBOOK CONTEST

New Michigan Press, P.O. Box 210067, English, ML 424, University of Arizona, Tucson AZ 85721. **E-mail:** nmp@thediagram.com. **Website:** www.thediagram.com. **Contact:** Ander Monson, editor. The annual *DIAGRAM*/New Michigan Press Chapbook Contest offers $1,000, plus publication and author's copies, with discount on additional copies. Deadline: April 29. Prize: $1,000, plus publication. Finalist chapbooks also considered for publication.

## JAMES DICKEY PRIZE FOR POETRY

Georgia State University, P.O. Box 3999, Atlanta GA 30302-3999. **Website:** fivepoints.gsu.edu. The James Dickey Prize for Poetry is for the best previously unpublished poem. Submission period: September 1-December 1.

## DOBIE PAISANO WRITER'S FELLOWSHIP

The Graduate School, The University of Texas at Austin, Attn: Dobie Paisano Program, 110 Inner Campus Drive Stop G0400, Austin TX 78712-0531. (512)232-3609. **Fax:** (512)471-7620. **E-mail:** gbarton@austin. utexas.edu. **Website:** www.utexas.edu/ogs/Paisano. **Contact:** Gwen Barton. Sponsored by the Graduate School at The University of Texas at Austin and the Texas Institute of Letters, the Dobie Paisano Fellowship Program provides solitude, time, and a comfortable place for Texas writers or writers who have written significantly about Texas through fiction, nonfiction, poetry, plays, or other mediums. The Dobie Paisano Ranch is a very rural and rustic setting, and applicants should read the guidelines closely to insure their ability to reside in this secluded environment. Deadline: January 15. Applications are accepted beginning December 1 and must be post-marked no later than January 15. The Ralph A. Johnston memorial Fellowship is for a period of 4 months with a stipend of $6,250 per month. It is aimed at writers who have already demonstrated some publishing and critical success. The Jesse H. Jones Writing Fellowship is for a period of approximately 6 months with a stipend of $3,000 per month. It is aimed at, but not limited to, writers who are early in their careers.

**TIPS** "Three sets of each complete application must be submitted. Electronic submissions are not allowed. Guidelines and application forms are on the website (http://www.utexas.edu/ogs/Paisano/info.html) or may be requested by sending a SASE (3-ounce postage) to the above address, attention of 'Dobie Paisano Fellowship Project.'"

## DREAM HORSE PRESS NATIONAL POETRY CHAPBOOK PRIZE

P.O. Box 2080, Aptos CA 95001-2080. **E-mail:** dreamhorsepress@yahoo.com. **Website:** www.dreamhorsepress.com. **Contact:** J.P. Dancing Bear, Editor/Publisher. Deadline: June 30. Prize: $500, publication, and 25 copies of a handsomely printed chapbook. Judged by C.J. Sage.

## T.S. ELIOT PRIZE

Poetry Book Society, Unit G07, Screenworks, 22 Highbury Grove, London N4 2EF, United Kingdom. **E-mail:** editor@poetrybooks.co.uk. **Website:** www. poetrybooks.co.uk. Offers annual award for the best poetry collection published in the UK/Republic of Ireland each year. Deadline: early August. Prize: £20,000 will be awarded to the best collection of new verse in English. Shortlisted poets will also receive a cheque for £1,500.

## T.S. ELIOT PRIZE FOR POETRY

Truman State University Press, 100 E. Normal Ave., Kirksville MO 63501. (660)785-7336. **Fax:** (660)785-4480. **E-mail:** tsup@truman.edu. **Website:** tsup.truman.edu. **Contact:** Barbara Smith-Mandell, Editor-in-Chief. The ms may include individual poems previously published in journals or anthologies, but may not include more than 1/3 of the total poems from a published chapbook or self-published book. Deadline: October 31. Prize: $2,000 and publication. Judge announced after close of competition.

## EMERGING VOICES

P.O. Box 6037, Beverly Hills CA 90212. (323)424-4939. **Fax:** (323)424-4944. **E-mail:** pen@penusa.org; ev@penusa.org. **Website:** www.penusa.org. Emerging Voices is a literary fellowship program that aims to provide new writers, who lack access, with the tools they will need to launch a professional writing career. During the eight month fellowship, each Emerging Voices fellow participates in a professional mentorship, hosted Q & A evenings with prominent local authors, a series of master classes focused on genre, a voice class, a volunteer project, and several public readings. Deadline: September 5. Accepting applications starting March 30. Offers a $1,000 stipend.

## ERSKINE J. POETRY PRIZE

P.O. Box 22161, Baltimore MD 21203. **E-mail:** smartishpace@gmail.com. **Website:** www.smartishpace. com. **Contact:** Stephen Reichert, editor. Deadline: October 15. Prize: Winning poet receives $200. Top three poets and all finalists (usually about 10) are published in *Smartish Place*.

## ⊘ FAR HORIZONS AWARD FOR POETRY

The Malahat Review, University of Victoria, P.O. Box 1700, Stn CSC, Victoria BC V8W 2Y2, Canada. (250)721-8524. **Fax:** (250)472-5051. **E-mail:** malahat@uvic.ca. **Website:** www.malahatreview.ca. **Contact:** John Barton, editor. The biennial Far Horizons Award for Poetry offers $1,000 CAD and publication in *The Malahat Review* (see separate listing in Magazines/Journals). 2010 winner: Darren Bifford; 2012 winner: Kayla Czaga. 2014 winner: Laura Ritland. Winner and finalists contacted by e-mail. Winner published in fall in *The Malahat Review* and announced on website, Facebook page, and in quarterly e-newsletter, *Malahat lite*. Open to "emerging poets from Canada, the United States, and elsewhere" who have not yet published a full-length book (48 pages or more). Deadline: May 1 (even-numbered years). Prize: $1,000. Judged by Steven Heighton in 2016.

## JANICE FARRELL POETRY PRIZE CATEGORY

Soul-Making Keats Literary Competition, The Webhallow House, 1544 Sweetwood Dr., Broadmoor Village CA 94015. **E-mail:** SoulKeats@mail.com. **Website:** www.soulmakingcontest.us. **Contact:** Eileen Malone. Deadline: November 30. Prizes: First: $100, Second: $50, Third: $25. Judged by a local San Francisco Bay Area successfully published poet.

## THE WILLIAM FAULKNER-WILLIAM WISDOM CREATIVE WRITING COMPETITION

Pirate's Alley Faulkner Society, Inc., 624 Pirate's Alley, New Orleans LA 70116-3233. (504)586-1609. **E-mail:** faulkhouse@aol.com. **Website:** www.wordsandmusic.org. **Contact:** Rosemary James, award director. general craft See guidelines posted at www.wordsandmusic.org. Deadline: May 15. Prizes: $750-7,500 depending on category. Judged by established authors, literary agents, and acquiring editors.

## THE JEAN FELDMAN POETRY PRIZE

**E-mail:** wwphpress@gmail.com. **Website:** www.washingtonwriters.org. **Contact:** Holly Karapetkova. Poets living within 75 miles of the Capitol are invited to submit a ms of either a novel or a collection of short stories. Ms should be 50-70 pages, single spaced. Deadline: November 1. Submission period begins July 1. Prize: $1,000 and 50 copies of the book.

## FIELD POETRY PRIZE

Oberlin College Press/FIELD, 50 N. Professor St., Oberlin OH 44074-1095. (440)775-8408. **Fax:** (440)775-8124. **E-mail:** oc.press@oberlin.edu. **Website:** www.oberlin.edu/ocpress/prize.htm. **Contact:** Marco Wilkinson, managing editor. Offered annually for an unpublished book-length collection of poetry (mss of 50-80 pages). Contest seeks to encourage the finest in contemporary poetry writing. Open to any writer. Deadline: Submit in May only. Prize: $1,000 and a standard royalty contract.

## FINELINE COMPETITION FOR PROSE POEMS, SHORT SHORTS, AND ANYTHING IN BETWEEN

*Mid-American Review*, Dept. of English, Bowling Green State University, Bowling Green OH 43403. (419)372-2725. **E-mail:** mar@bgsu.edu. **Website:** www.bgsu.edu/midamericanreview. **Contact:** Abigail Cloud, editor-in-chief. Offered annually for previously unpublished submissions. Contest open to all writers not associated with current judge or *Mid-American Review*. Deadline: June 1. Prize: $1,000, plus publication in fall issue of *Mid-American Review*; 10 finalists receive notation plus possible publication. 2015 judge: Michael Czyzniejewski.

## THE FINISHING LINE PRESS OPEN CHAPBOOK COMPETITION

P.O. Box 1626, Georgetown KY 40324. (859)514-8966. **E-mail:** finishingbooks@aol.com. **Website:** www.finishinglinepress.com. **Contact:** Leah Maines, director. Annual competition for previously unpublished poetry chapbook.

## FIRST BOOK AWARD FOR POETRY

*Zone 3*, Austin Peay State University, Austin Peay State University, PO Box 4565, Clarksville TN 37044. (931)221-7031. **Fax:** (931)221-7149. **E-mail:** zone3@apsu.edu. **Website:** www.apsu.edu/zone3/. **Contact:** Andrea Spofford, poetry editor; Susan Wallace, managing editor. Annual poetry award for anyone who has not published a full-length collection of poems (48 pages or more). Deadline: April 1. Prize: $1,000 and publication.

## FISH POETRY PRIZE

Durrus, Bantry Co. Cork, Ireland. **E-mail:** info@fishpublishing.com. **Website:** www.fishpublishing.com. For poems up to 300 words. Age Range: Adult. The best 10 will be published in the Fish Anthology, launched in July at the West Cork Literary Festival. Entries must not have been published before. Enter online or by post. See website for full details of competitions, and information on the Fish Editorial and Critique Services, and the Fish Online Writing Courses. The aim of the competition is to discover and publish new writers. Deadline: March 31. Prize: $1,000. Results announced May 15. Judged by Dave Lordan in 2016.

## FIVE POINTS JAMES DICKEY PRIZE FOR POETRY

Five Points, Georgia State University, P.O. Box 3999, Atlanta GA 30302-3999. (404)413-5812. **Website:** five-points.gsu.edu. Offered annually for unpublished poetry. Deadline: December 1. Prize: $1,000, plus publication.

## FOLEY POETRY CONTEST

106 W. 56th St., New York NY 10019. (212)581-4640. **Fax:** (212)399-3596. **Website:** www.americamagazine.org. *America*, the national Catholic weekly by the Jesuits of North America, sponsors the annual Foley Poetry Contest. Offers $1,000 and 2 contributor's copies for the winning poem. Winner will be announced in the mid-June issue of America and on the website. Runners-up will have their poems printed in subsequent issues of *America*. Submissions must be unpublished and may not be entered in other contests. "Submit 1 poem per person, not to exceed 30 lines of verse, in any form. Name, address, telephone number, and e-mail address (if applicable) should be appended to the bottom of the page. Poems will not be returned, and e-mailed submissions are not accepted." Guidelines available in magazine, for SASE, or on website. Competition receives more than 1,000 entries/year. Deadline: January 1-March 31.

## THE FOUR WAY BOOKS INTRO PRIZE IN POETRY

Four Way Books, Box 535, Village Station, New York NY 10014. (212)334-5430. **Fax:** (212)334-5435. **E-mail:** editors@fourwaybooks.com. **Website:** www.fourwaybooks.com. **Contact:** Ryan Murphy, Assoc. Director. The Four Way Books Intro Prize in Poetry, offered biennially in even-numbered years, offers publication by Four Way Books (see separate listing in Book Publishers), honorarium, and a reading at one or more participating series In New York City. Open to any poet writing in English who has not published a book-length collection of poetry. Entry form and guidelines available on website at www.fourwaybooks.com. Deadline: March 31 (postmark or online submission). Winner announced by e-mail and on website. Prize: Publication and $1,000. Copies of winning books available through Four Way Books online and at bookstores.

## FREEFALL SHORT PROSE AND POETRY CONTEST

Freefall Literary Society of Calgary, 922 9th Ave. SE, Calgary AB T2G 0S4, Canada. **E-mail:** editors@freefallmagazine.ca. **Website:** www.freefallmagazine.ca. **Contact:** Ryan Stromquist, managing editor. Offered annually for unpublished work in the categories of poetry (5 poems/entry) and prose (3,000 words or less). Recognizes writers and offers publication credits in a literary magazine format. Contest rules and entry form online. Acquires first Canadian serial rights; ownership reverts to author after one-time publication. Deadline: December 31. Prize: 1st Place: $500 (CAD); 2nd Place: $250 (CAD); 3rd Place: $75; Honorable Mention: $25. All prizes include publication in the spring edition of *FreeFall Magazine*. Winners will also be invited to read at the launch of that issue, if such a launch takes place. Honorable mentions in each category will be published and may be asked to read. Travel expenses not included. Judged by current guest editor for issue (who are also published authors in Canada).

## THE ROBERT FROST FOUNDATION ANNUAL POETRY AWARD

Lawrence Library, 51 Lawrence St., Lawrence MA 01841. (978)725-8828. **E-mail:** frostfoundation@gmail.com. **E-mail:** rffpoetrycontest@gmail.com. **Website:** www.frostfoundation.org. Established 1997. Offers $100 award in three categories: couplets (2-line); quatrains (4-line); and sonnets (14-line), all forms which Frost used. Guidelines online.

## GERTRUDE PRESS POETRY CHAPBOOK CONTEST

P.O. Box 28281, Portland OR 97228. **E-mail:** editor@gertrudepress.org; poetry@gertrudepress.org. **Website:** www.gertrudepress.org. Annual chapbook contest for 25-30 pages of poetry. Deadline: May 15. Submission period begins September 15. Prize: $175, publication, 50 complimentary copies of the chapbook, and 2 e-book files.

## ALLEN GINSBERG POETRY AWARDS

The Poetry Center at Passaic County Community College, One College Blvd., Paterson NJ 07505. (973)684-6555. **Fax:** (973)523-6085. **E-mail:** mgillan@pccc.edu. **Website:** www.pccc.edu/poetry. **Contact:** Maria Mazziotti Gillan, executive director. All winning poems, honorable mentions, and editor's choice poems will be published in *The Paterson Literary Review*. Winners will be asked to participate in a reading that will be held in the Paterson Historic District. Submissions must be unpublished. Deadline: April 1 (postmark). Prize: 1st Prize: $1,000; 2nd Prize: $200; 3rd Prize: $100.

## GIVAL PRESS POETRY AWARD

Gival Press, LLC, P.O. Box 3812, Arlington VA 22203. (703)351-0079. **E-mail:** givalpress@yahoo.com. **Website:** www.givalpress.submittable.com. **Contact:** Robert L. Giron, editor. Offered annually for a previously unpublished poetry collection as a complete ms, which may include previously published poems; previously published poems must be acknowledged, and poet must hold rights. Guidelines for SASE, by e-mail, or online. Open to any writer, as long as the work is original, not a translation, and is written in English. The copyright remains in the author's name; certain rights fall to the publisher per the contract. The competition seeks to award well-written, origional poetry in English on any topic, in any style. Deadline: December 15 (postmarked). Prize: $1,000, publication, and 20 copies of the publication. The editor narrows entries to the top 10; previous winner selects top 5 and chooses the winner—all done anonymously.

## PATRICIA GOEDICKE PRIZE IN POETRY

*CutBank* Literary Magazine, *CutBank*, University of Montana, English Dept., LA 133, Missoula MT 59812. **E-mail:** editor.cutbank@gmail.com. **Website:** www.cutbankonline.org. **Contact:** Billy Wallace, editor-in-chief. The Patricia Goedicke Prize in Poetry seeks to highlight work that showcases an authentic voice, a boldness of form, and a rejection of functional fixedness. Deadline: January 15. Submissions period begins November 1. Prize: $500 and featured in the magazine. Judged by a guest judge each year.

## GOLDEN ROSE AWARD

New England Poetry Club, 654 Green St., No. 2, Cambridge MA 02139. **E-mail:** contests@nepoetryclub.org; info@nepoetryclub.org. **Website:** www.nepoetryclub.org. **Contact:** NEPC contest coordinator. Given annually to the poet, who by their poetry and inspiration to and encouragement of other writers, has made a significant mark on American poetry. Traditionally given to a poet with some ties to New England so that a public reading may take place. Deadline: May 31. Judged by well-known poets and sometimes winners of previous NEPC contests.

## ☼ GOVERNOR GENERAL'S LITERARY AWARDS

Canada Council for the Arts, 150 Elgin St., P.O. Box 1047, Ottawa ON K1P 5V8, Canada. 1-800-263-5588, ext. 5573. **Website:** www.canadacouncil.ca. The Canada Council for the Arts provides a wide range of grants and services to professional Canadian artists and art organizations in dance, media arts, music, theatre, writing, publishing, and the visual arts. The Governor General's Literary Awards are given annually for the best English-language and French-language work in each of 7 categories, including fiction, non-fiction, poetry, drama, children's literature (text), children's literature (illustrated books), and translation. Deadline: Depends on the book's publication date. See website for details. Prize: Each GG winner receives $25,000. Non-winning finalists receive $1,000. Publishers of the winning titles receive a $3,000 grant for promotional purposes. Evaluated by fellow authors, translators, and illustrators. For each category, a jury makes the final selection.

## GREAT LAKES COLLEGES ASSOCIATION NEW WRITERS AWARD

The Great Lakes Colleges Association, 535 W. William, Suite 301, Ann Arbor MI 48103. (734)661-2350. **Fax:** (734)661-2349. **E-mail:** wegner@glca.org. **Website:** www.glca.org. **Contact:** Gregory R. Wegner, Director of Program Development. The Great Lakes Colleges Association (GLCA) is a consortium of 13 independent liberal arts colleges in Ohio, Michigan, Indiana, and Pennsylvania. Deadline: July 25. Prize: Honorarium of at least $500 for winning writers who are invited to give a reading at a member college campus. Each award winner receives invitations from several of the 13 colleges of the GLCA to visit campus. At these campus events an author will give readings, meet students and faculty, and occasionally lead discussions or classes. In addition to an honorarium for each campus visit, travel costs to colleges are paid by GLCA and its member colleges. Judged by professors of literature and writers in residence at GLCA colleges.

## THE GREEN ROSE PRIZE IN POETRY

*New Issues Poetry & Prose*, Deptartment of English, Western Michigan University, 1903 W. Michigan Ave., Kalamazoo MI 49008-5463. **E-mail:** new-issues@wmich.edu. **Website:** www.wmich.edu/newissues. Offered annually for unpublished poetry. The university will publish a book of poems by a poet writing in English who has published 1 or more full-length collections of poetry. *New Issues* may publish as many as 3 additional mss from this competition. Guidelines for SASE or online. *New Issues Poetry & Prose* obtains rights for first publication. Book is copyrighted in the author's name. Deadline: Submit May 1-September 30. Winner is announced in January or February on website. Prize: $2,000 and publication of a book of poems.

## GREG GRUMMER POETRY AWARD

*Phoebe*, MSN 2C5, George Mason University, 4400 University Dr., Fairfax VA 22030. **E-mail:** phoebe@gmu.edu. **Website:** www.phoebejournal.com. **Contact:** Q Wang & Doug Luman, poetry editors. Offered annually for unpublished work. Submit up to 4 poems, no more than 10 pages total. Guidelines online. Requests first serial rights, if work is to be published, and $500 first prize. Judge will be Jericho Brown. The purpose of the award is to recognize new and exciting poetry. Deadline: March 31. Prize: $500 and publication in the *Phoebe*. Judged by poet Jericho Brown.

## GUGGENHEIM FELLOWSHIPS

John Simon Guggenheim Memorial Foundation, 90 Park Ave., New York NY 10016. (212)687-4470. **E-mail:** fellowships@gf.org. **Website:** www.gf.org. Often characterized as "midcareer" awards, Guggenheim Fellowships are intended for men and women who have already demonstrated exceptional capacity for productive scholarship or exceptional creative ability in the arts. Fellowships are awarded through two annual competitions: one open to citizens and permanent residents of the United States and Canada, and the other open to citizens and permanent residents of Latin America and the Caribbean. Candidates must apply to the Guggenheim Foundation in order to be considered in either of these competitions. The Foundation receives between 3,500 and 4,000 applications each year. Although no one who applies is guaranteed success in the competition, there is no prescreening: all applications are reviewed. Approximately 200 Fellowships are awarded each year. Deadline: September 15.

## HACKNEY LITERARY AWARDS

4650 Old Looney Mill Rd, Birmingham AL 35243. **E-mail:** info@hackneyliteraryawards.org. **Website:** www.hackneyliteraryawards.org. **Contact:** Myra Crawford, PhD, executive director. Offered annually for unpublished novels, short stories (maximum 5,000 words), and poetry (50 line limit). Guidelines on website. Deadline: September 30 (novels), November 30 (short stories and poetry). Prize: $5,000 in annual prizes for poetry and short fiction ($2,500 national and $2,500 state level). 1st Place: $600; 2nd Place: $400; 3rd Place: $250; plus $5,000 for an unpublished novel. Competition winners will be announced on the website each March.

## THE DONALD HALL PRIZE IN POETRY

AWP, Carty House, Mail Stop 1E3, George Mason University, Fairfax VA 22030-4444. **E-mail:** chronicle@awpwriter.org. **Website:** www.awpwriter.org. The Donald Hall Prize for Poetry offers an award of $5,500, supported by Amazon.com, and publication by the University of Pittsburgh Press. 2016 judge: Vijay Seshadri. Submission period: January 1-February 28.

## JAMES HEARST POETRY PRIZE

North American Review, University of Northern Iowa, 1222 W. 27th St., Cedar Falls IA 50614-0516. (319)273-3026. **Fax:** (319)273-4326. **E-mail:** nar@uni.edu. **Website:** www.northamericanreview.org. Contest to find the best previously unpublished poem. 2017 judge: Major Jackson. Deadline: October 31. 1st place: $1,000; 2nd place: $100; 3rd place: $50.

**TIPS** "We have noticed that long poems rarely do well—too much can go wrong in a large space. Poems that have reached the finalist stage in our competition in the past are typically 1 to 2 pages (often much shorter). Winning poems always balance interesting subject matter and consummate poetic craft. We value both free verse and formal poems."

## THE HILARY THAM CAPITAL COLLECTION

The Word Works, Nancy White, c/o SUNY Adiorndack, 640 Bay Rd., Queensbury NY 12804. **E-mail:** editor@wordworksbooks.org. **Website:** www.wordworksbooks.org. **Contact:** Nancy White, editor. The Hilary Tham Capital Collection publishes only poets who volunteer for literary nonprofits. Every nominated poet is invited to submit; authors have until May 1 to send their ms via online submissions at website, or to Nancy White. Deadline: April 15 to send nomination. Judged by Eduardo Corral in 2016. Past judges include Denise Duhamel, Kimiko Hahn, and Michael Klein.

## ⬤ THE HODDER FELLOWSHIP

Lewis Center for the Arts, 185 Nassau St., Princeton NJ 08544. (609)258-6926. **E-mail:** ysabelg@princeton.edu. **Website:** arts.princeton.edu. **Contact:** Ysabel Gonzalez, fellowships assistant. The Hodder Fellowship will be given to writers of exceptional promise to pursue independent projects at Princeton University during the current academic year. Typically the fellows are poets, playwrights, novelists, creative nonfiction writers and translators who have published one highly acclaimed work and are undertaking a significant new project that might not be possible without the "studious leisure" afforded by the fellowship. Deadline: October 1. Open to applications in July. Prize: $75,000 stipend.

## ERIC HOFFER AWARD

Hopewell Publications, LLC, P.O. Box 11, Titusville NJ 08560-0011. **Fax:** (609)964-1718. **E-mail:** info@hopepubs.com. **Website:** www.hofferaward.com. **Contact:** Christopher Klim, chair. Annual contest for previously published books. Recognizes excellence in independent publishing in many unique categories: Art (titles capture the experience, execution, or demonstration of the arts); Poetry (all styles); General Fiction (nongenre-specific fiction); Commercial Fiction (genre-specific fiction); Children (titles for young children); Young Adult (titles aimed at the juvenile and teen markets); Culture (titles demonstrating the human or world experience); Memoir (titles relating to personal experience); Business (titles with application to today's business environment and emerging trends); Reference (titles from traditional and emerging reference areas); Home (titles with practical applications to home or home-related issues, including family); Health (titles promoting physical, mental, and emotional well-being); Self-help (titles involving new and emerging topics in self-help); Spiritual (titles involving the mind and spirit, including relgion); Legacy (titles over 2 years of age that hold particular relevance to any subject matter or form). Open to any writer of published work within the last 2 years, including categores for older books. This contest recognizes excellence in independent publishing in many unique categories. Also awards the Montaigne Medal for most though-provoking book, the Da Vinci Eye for best cover, and the First Horizon Award for best new authors. Results published in the US Review of Books. Deadline: January 21. 1st place: $2,000.

## THE BESS HOKIN PRIZE

*Poetry*, 61 W. Superior St., Chicago IL 60654. (312)787-7070. **Fax:** (312)787-6650. **E-mail:** editors@poetry-magazine.org. **Website:** www.poetrymagazine.org. Offered annually for poems published in *Poetry* during the preceding year (October-September). Upon acceptance, *Poetry* licenses exclusive worldwide first serial rights, including electronic rights, for publication, as well as non-exclusive rights to reprint, reuse, and archive the work, in any format, in perpetuity. Copyright reverts to author upon first publication. "Established in 1947 through the generosity of our late friend and guarantor, Mrs. David Hokin, and is given annually in her memory." Prize: $1,000.

## FIRMAN HOUGHTON PRIZE

New England Poetry Club, 53 Regent St., Cambridge MA 02140. **E-mail:** info@nepoetryclug.org. **Website:** www.nepoetryclub.org. **Contact:** Mary Buchinger, co-president NEPC. For a lyric poem in honor of the former president of NEPC. Deadline: May 31. Prize: $200. Judged by well-known poets and sometimes winners of previous NEPC contests.

## THE JULIA WARD HOWE/BOSTON AUTHORS AWARD

The Boston Authors Club, The Boston Authors Club, 36 Sunhill Lane, Newton Center MA 02459. **E-mail:** bostonauthors@aol.com;. **Website:** www.bostonauthorsclub.org. **Contact:** Alan Lawson. This annual award honors Julia Ward Howe and her literary friends who founded the Boston Authors Club in 1900. It also honors the membership over 110 years, consisting of novelists, biographers, historians, governors, senators, philosophers, poets, playwrights, and other luminaries. There are 2 categories: trade books and books for young readers (beginning with chapter books through young adult books). Deadline: January 15. Prize: $1,000. Judged by the members.

## HENRY HOYNS & POE/FAULKNER FELLOWSHIPS

Creative Writing Program, 219 Bryan Hall, P.O. Box 400121, University of Virginia, Charlottesville VA 22904-4121. (434)924-6675. **Fax:** (434)924-1478. **E-mail:** creativewriting@virginia.edu. **Website:** creativewriting.virginia.edu. **Contact:** Jeb Livingood, associate director. Two-year MFA program in poetry and fiction; all students receive fellowships and teaching stipends that total $18,000 in both years of study. Sample poems/prose required with application. Deadline: December 15.

## ILLINOIS STATE POETRY SOCIETY ANNUAL CONTEST

Illinois State Poetry Society, 543 E. Squirrel Trail Dr., Tucson AZ 85704. **E-mail:** oasis@alharris.com. **Website:** www.illinoispoets.org. **Contact:** Alan Harris. Annual contest to encourage the crafting of excellent poetry. Guidelines and entry forms available for SASE. Deadline: September 30. Cash prizes of $50, $30, and $10. Three Honorable Mentions. Poet retains all rights. Judged by out-of-state professionals.

## INDIANA REVIEW ½ K PRIZE

*Indiana Review*, Ballantine Hall 465, 1020 E. Kirkwood Ave., Indiana University, Bloomington IN 47405-7103. (812)855-3439. **Fax:** (812)855-9535. **E-mail:** inreview@indiana.edu. **Website:** http://indianareview.org. **Contact:** Katie Moulton, consulting editor. Offered annually for unpublished work. Maximum story/poem length is 500 words. Guidelines available in March for SASE, by phone, e-mail, on website, or in publication. Deadline: August 15. Submission period begins July 1. Prize: $1,000, plus publication, contributor's copies, and a year's subscription to *Indiana Review*.

## INDIANA REVIEW POETRY CONTEST

Ballantine Hall 465, Indiana University, 1020 E. Kirkwood Ave., Bloomington IN 47405-7103. **E-mail:** inreview@indiana.edu. **Website:** http://indianareview. org. **Contact:** Peter Kispert, editor. Contest for poetry in any style and on any subject. Open to any writer. Deadline: April 1. Submission period begins February 15. Prize: $1,000, publication in the *Indiana Review* and contributor's copies. Judged by Camille Rankine.

**TIPS** "We look for a command of language and structure, as well as a facility with compelling and unusual subject matter. It's a good idea to obtain copies of issues featuring past winners to get a more concrete idea of what we are looking for."

## INDIANA REVIEW POETRY PRIZE

*Indiana Review*, Poetry Prize, Indiana Review, Ballantine Hall 529, 1020 E. Kirkwood Ave., Bloomington IN 47405-7103. **E-mail:** inreview@indiana.edu. **Website:** www.indianareview.org. Offered annually for unpublished work. Open to any writer. Guidelines available on website. All entries are considered for publication. Deadline: April 1. Submission period begins February 1. Prize: $1,000 and publication. Judged by Camille Rankine in 2016. Different judge every year.

## IOWA POETRY PRIZE

University of Iowa Press, 119 West Park Rd., 100 Kuhl House, Iowa City IA 52242. (319)335-2000. **Fax:** (319)335-2055. **E-mail:** uipress@uiowa.edu. **Website:** www.uiowapress.org. Offered annually to encourage poets and their work. Submissions must be postmarked during the month of April; put name on title page only. This page will be removed before ms is judged. Open to writers of English (US citizens or not). Mss will not be returned. Previous winners are not eligible. Deadline: April 30. Prize: Publication under standard royalty agreement.

## THE IOWA REVIEW AWARD IN POETRY, FICTION, AND NONFICTION

308 EPB, University of Iowa, Iowa City IA 52242. **E-mail:** iowa-review@uiowa.edu. **Website:** www.iowareview.org. *The Iowa Review* Award in Poetry, Fiction, and Nonfiction presents $1,500 to each winner in each genre and $750 to runners-up. Winners and runners-up published in *The Iowa Review*. Deadline: January 31. Submission period begins January 1. Judged by Brenda Shaughnessy, Kelly Link, and Eula Biss in 2016.

## ALICE JAMES AWARD

Alice James Books, 114 Prescott Street, Farmington ME 04938. (207)778-7071. **Fax:** (207)778-7766. **E-mail:** ajb@alicejamesbooks.org. **Website:** www.alicejamesbooks.org. **Contact:** Alyssa Neptune, Managing Editor. For complete contest guidelines, visit website or send a SASE. Offered annually for unpublished, full-length poetry collection. Deadline: October 1. Prize: $2,000 and publication.

## ALICE JAMES AWARD

Alice James Books, University of Maine at Farmington, 114 Prescott St., Farmington ME 04938. (207)778-7071. **Fax:** (207)778-7766. **E-mail:** ajb@alicejamesbooks.org; info@alicejamesbooks.org. **Website:** www.alicejamesbooks.org. **Contact:** Alyssa Neptune, managing editor. Offered annually for unpublished, full-length poetry collections. Emerging and established poets are welcome. Deadline: October 1. Prize: $2,000, publication, and distribution through Consortium.

## JAPAN-U.S. FRIENDSHIP COMMISSION PRIZE FOR THE TRANSLATION OF JAPANESE LITERATURE

**Website:** http://www.keenecenter.org/. **Contact:** Yoshiko Niiya, Program Coordinator. The Donald Keene Center of Japanese Culture at Columbia University annually awards Japan-U.S. Friendship Commission Prizes for the Translation of Japanese Literature. A prize is given for the best translation of a modern work or a classical work, or the prize is divided between equally distinguished translations. Deadline: June 1. Prize: $6,000.

○ Translations must be book-length Japanese literary works: novels, collections of short stories, manga, literary essays, memoirs, drama, or poetry. Works may be unpublished manuscripts, works in press, or books published during the two years prior to the prize year.

## RANDALL JARRELL POETRY COMPETITION

North Carolina Writers' Network, Terry L. Kennedy, MFA Writing Program, 3302 MHRA Building, UNC Greensboro, Greensboro NC 27402-6170. **E-mail:** tlkenned@uncg.edu. **Website:** www.ncwriters.org. **Contact:** Terry L. Kennedy, associate director. Offered annually for unpublished work to honor Randall Jarrell and his life at UNC Greensboro, by recognizing the best poetry submitted. Deadline: March 1. Prize: $200 and publication at *storySouth* (www.storysouth.com).

## JUNIPER PRIZE FOR POETRY

University of Massachusetts Press, East Experiment Station, 671 North Pleasant St., Amherst MA 01003. (413)545-2217. **Fax:** (413)545-1226. **E-mail:** info@umpress.umass.edu; kfisk@umpress.umass.edu; poetry@umpress.umass.edu. **Website:** www.umass.edu/umpress. **Contact:** Karen Fisk, competition coordinator. The University of Massachusetts Press offers the annual Juniper Prize for Poetry, awarded in alternate years for the first and subsequent books. Deadline: September 30. Submissions period begins August 1. Winners announced online in April on the press website. Prize: Publication and $1,000 in addition to royalties.

○ In even-numbered years, only subsequent books will be considered—mss whose authors have had at least 1 full-length book or chapbook (of at least 30 pages) of poetry published or accepted for publication. Self-published work is not considered to lie within this books and chapbooks category. In odd-numbered years, only first books will be considered—mss by writers whose poems may have appeared in literary journals and/or anthologies but have

not been published or accepted for publication in book form.

## BARBARA MANDIGO KELLY PEACE POETRY AWARDS

Nuclear Age Peace Foundation, PMB 121, 1187 Coast Village Rd., Suite 1, Santa Barbara CA 93108-2794. (805)965-3443. **Fax:** (805)568-0466. **E-mail:** cwarner@napf.org. **Website:** www.wagingpeace.org; www.peacecontests.org. **Contact:** Carol Warner, poetry award coordinator. The Barbara Mandigo Kelly Peace Poetry Contest was created to encourage poets to explore and illuminate positive visions of peace and the human spirit. The annual contest honors the late Barbara Kelly, a Santa Barbara poet and longtime supporter of peace issues. Awards are given in 3 categories: adult (over 18 years), youth between 12 and 18 years, and youth under 12. All submitted poems should be unpublished. Deadline: April 1 (postmarked) or e-mailed (cwarner@napf.org). Prize: Adult: $1,000; Youth (13-18): $200; Youth (12 and under): $200. Honorable Mentions may also be awarded. Judged by a committee of poets selected by the Nuclear Age Peace Foundation. The foundation reserves the right to publish and distribute the award-winning poems, including honorable mentions.

## MILTON KESSLER MEMORIAL PRIZE FOR POETRY

Dept. of English, Binghamton University, Library North Room 1149, Vestal Parkway E., P.O. Box 6000, Binghamton NY 13902-6000. **Website:** www.binghamton.edu/english/creative-writing/binghamton-center-for-writers/binghamton-book-awards/kessler-poetry-awards.html. **Contact:** Maria Mazziotti Gillan, director. Annual award for best previously published book (previous year). Deadline: March 1. 1st place: $1,000.

## HAROLD MORTON LANDON TRANSLATION AWARD

The Academy of American Poets, The Academy of American Poets, 75 Maiden Lane, Suite 901, New York NY 10038. (212)274-0343 ext. 13. **E-mail:** awards@poets.org. **Website:** www.poets.org. **Contact:** Patricia Guzman, Programs Assistant. Recognizes a published translation of poetry from any language into English. Deadline: February 15. Open to submissions on September 15. Prize: $1,000. Judged by a noted translator.

## THE JAMES LAUGHLIN AWARD

The Academy of American Poets, 584 Broadway, Suite 604, New York NY 10012. **Website:** www.poets.org. Offered since 1954, the James Laughlin Award is given to recognize and support a second book of poetry forthcoming in the next calendar year. It is named for the poet and publisher James Laughlin, who founded New Directions in 1936. The winner receives a prize of $5,000, an all-expenses-paid weeklong residency at The Betsy Hotel in Miami Beach, FL, and distribution of the winning book to approximately 1,000 Academy of American Poets members. Deadline: May 16.

## ◯ THE STEPHEN LEACOCK MEMORIAL MEDAL FOR HUMOUR

149 Peter St. N., Orillia ON L3V 4Z4, Canada. (705)326-9286. **E-mail:** bettewalkerca@gmail.com. **Website:** www.leacock.ca. **Contact:** Bette Walker, award committee, Stephen Leacock Associates. The Leacock Associates awards the prestigious Leacock Medal for the best book of literary humor written by a Canadian and published in the current year. The winning author also receives a cash prize of $15,000 thanks to the generous support of the TD Financial Group. 2 runners-up are each awarded a cash prize of $1,500. Entry fee: $200. Deadline: December 31.

## LEAGUE OF UTAH WRITERS CONTEST

The League of Utah Writers, The League of Utah Writers, P.O. Box 64, Lewiston UT 84320. (435)755-7609. **E-mail:** luwcontest@gmail.com; luwriters@gmail.com. **Website:** www.luwriters.org. Open to any writer, the LUW Contest provides authors an opportunity to get their work read and critiqued. Multiple categories are offered; see website for details. Entries must be the original and unpublished work of the author. Winners are announced at the Annual Writers Round-Up in September. Those not present will be notified by e-mail. Deadline: June 15. Submissions period begins March 15. Prize: Cash prizes are awarded. Judged by professional authors and editors from outside the League.

## LES FIGUES PRESS NOS BOOK CONTEST

P.O. Box 7736, Los Angeles CA 90007. (323)734-4732. **E-mail:** info@lesfigues.com. **Website:** www.lesfigues.com. **Contact:** Teresa Carmody, director. Les Figues Press creates aesthetic conversations between writers/artists and readers, especially those interested in innovative/experimental/avant-garde work. The Press intends in the most premeditated fashion to champi-

on the trinity of Beauty, Belief, and Bawdry. Deadline: September 15. Prize: $1,000, plus publication by Les Figues Press. Each entry receives LFP book.

## LET'S WRITE LITERARY CONTEST

The Gulf Coast Writers Association, P.O. Box 4808, Biloxi MS 39535. **E-mail:** writerpllevin@gmail.com. **Website:** www.gcwriters.org. **Contact:** Philip Levin. The Gulf Coast Writers Association sponsors this nationally recognized contest, which accepts unpublished poems and short stories from authors all around the US. This is an annual event which has been held for over 26 years. Deadline: July 31. 1st Prize: $100; 2nd Prize: $60; 3rd Prize: $25.

## LEVIS READING PRIZE

Virginia Commonwealth University, Department of English, Levis Reading Prize, VCU Department of English, 900 Park Avenue, Hibbs Hall, Room 306, P.O. Box 842005, Richmond VA 23284-2005. (804)828-1329. **Fax:** (804)828-8684. **E-mail:** bloomquistjmp@mymail.vcu.edu. **Website:** www.english.vcu.edu/mfa/levis. **Contact:** John-Michael Bloomquist. Offered annually for books of poetry published in the previous year to encourage poets early in their careers. The entry must be the writer's first or second published book of poetry. Previously published books in other genres, or previously published chapbooks or self-published material, do not count as books for this purpose. Deadline: February 1. Prize: $5,000 and an expense-paid trip to Richmond to present a public reading.

## THE RUTH LILLY POETRY PRIZE

*Poetry*, 61 W. Superior St., Chicago IL 60654. (312)787-7070. **Fax:** (312)787-6650. **E-mail:** editors@poetrymagazine.org. **Website:** www.poetrymagazine.org. Awarded annually, the $100,000 Ruth Lilly Poetry Prize honors a living U.S. poet whose lifetime accomplishments warrant extraordinary recognition. Established in 1986 by Ruth Lilly, the Prize is one of the most prestigious awards given to American poets and is one of the largest literary honors for work in the English language. Deadline: No submissions or nominations considered. Prize: $100,000.

## LITERAL LATTÉ POETRY AWARD

*Literal Latté*, 200 E. 10th St., Suite 240, New York NY 10003. (212)260-5532. **E-mail:** LitLatte@aol.com. **Website:** www.literal-latte.com. **Contact:** Jenine Gordon Bockman, editor. Offered annually to any writer for unpublished poetry (maximum 2,000 words per poem). All styles welcome. Winners published in *Literal Latté*. Deadline: Postmark by July 15. Prizes: 1st Place: $1,000; 2nd Place: $300; 3rd Place: $200. Judged by the editors.

### THE HUGH J. LUKE AWARD

*Prairie Schooner*, 123 Andrews Hall, University of Nebraska-Lincoln, Lincoln NE 68588-0334. (402)472-0911. **Fax:** (402)472-1817. **E-mail:** prairieschooner@unl.edu. **Website:** www.prairieschooner.unl.edu. **Contact:** Kwame Dawes. Offered annually for work published in *Prairie Schooner* in the previous year. Results announced in the Spring issue. Winners notified by mail in February or March. Prize: $250. Judged by editorial staff of *Prairie Schooner*.

### LUMINA POETRY CONTEST

**Website:** www.luminajournal.com. Annual poetry competition held by the Sarah Lawrence College's graduate literary journal. Deadline: October 15. Prize: 1st Place: $500 and publication; 2nd Place: $250 and publication; 3rd Place: $100 and online publication.

### THE MACGUFFIN'S NATIONAL POET HUNT CONTEST

*The MacGuffin*, The MacGuffin, Schoolcraft College, 18600 Haggerty Rd., Livonia MI 48152. (734)462-4400, ext. 5327. **Fax:** (734)462-4679. **E-mail:** macguffin@schoolcraft.edu. **E-mail:** macguffin@schoolcraft.edu. **Website:** www.schoolcraft.edu/a-z-index/the-macguffin. **Contact:** Gordon Krupsky, managing editor. *The MacGuffin* is a national literary magazine from Schoolcraft College in Livonia, Michigan. The mission of *The MacGuffin* is to encourage, support, and enhance the literary arts in the Schoolcraft College community, the region, the state, and the nation. Deadline: June 3. Submissions period begins April 1. Prize: $500. Judged by Li-Young Lee.

### NAOMI LONG MADGETT POETRY AWARD

Lotus Press, Inc., 8300 East Jefferson Ave., #504, Detroit MI 48214. (313)736-5338. **E-mail:** broadsidelotus@gmail.com. **Website:** www.lotuspress.org. **Contact:** Gloria House. Offered annually to recognize an unpublished book-length poetry ms by an African American. Guidelines available online. Deadline: March 1. Submission period begins January 2. Prize: $500 and publication by Lotus Press.

### MAIN STREET RAG'S ANNUAL POETRY BOOK AWARD

Main Street Rag Publishing Company, P.O. Box 690100, Charlotte NC 28227-7001. (704)573-2516. **E-mail:** editor@mainstreetrag.com. **Website:** www.mainstreetrag.com. **Contact:** M. Scott Douglass, publisher/managing editor. The purpose of this contest is to select manuscripts for publication and offer prize money to the manuscript we feel best represents our label. Deadline: January 31. Prize: 1st Place: $1,200 and 50 copies of book; runners-up are also be offered publication. Judged by 1 panel that consists of *MSR* editors, associated editors and college-level instructors, and previous contest winners.

### ✪ THE MALAHAT REVIEW LONG POEM PRIZE

*The Malahat Review*, Box 1700 STN CSC, Victoria BC V8W 2Y2, Canada. **E-mail:** malahat@uvic.ca. **Website:** www.malahatreview.ca. **Contact:** John Barton, editor. Long Poem Prize offered in alternate years with the Novella Contest. Open to any writer. Offers 2 awards of $1,000 CAD each for a long poem or cycle (10-20 printed pages). Includes publication in *The Malahat Review* and a 1-year subscription. Open to entries from Canadian, American, and overseas authors. Obtains first world rights. Publication rights after revert to the author. Deadline: February 1 (odd-numbered years). Prize: Two $1,000 prizes. Winners published in the summer issue of *The Malahat Review*, announced in summer on website, Facebook page, and in quarterly e-newsletter *Malahat lite*. Judged by 3 recognized poets. Preliminary readings by editorial board.

### THE MORTON MARR POETRY PRIZE

Southwest Review, Southern Methodist University, P.O. Box 750374, Dallas TX 75275-0374. (214)768-1037. **Fax:** (214)768-1408. **E-mail:** swr@mail.smu.edu. **Website:** www.smu.edu/southwestreview. **Contact:** Prize coordinator. Annual award for poem(s) by a writer who has not yet published a book of poetry. Submit no more than 6 poems in a "traditional" form (e.g., sonnet, sestine, villanelle, rhymed stanzas, blank verse, et al.). Submissions will not be returned. All entrants will receive a copy of the issue in which the winning poems appear. Deadline: September 30. Prizes: $1,000 for 1st place; $500 for 2nd place; plus publication in the *Southwest Review*.

## THE LENORE MARSHALL POETRY PRIZE

The Academy of American Poets, 584 Broadway, Suite 604, New York NY 10012. (212)274-0343. **Fax:** (212)274-9427. **E-mail:** awards@poets.org. **Website:** www.poets.org. Established in 1975, this $25,000 award recognizes the most outstanding book of poetry published in the United States in the previous calendar year. The prize includes distribution of the winning book hundreds of Academy of American Poets members. Deadline: May 16. Charges $75 entry fee.

## MARSH HAWK PRESS POETRY PRIZE

Marsh Hawk Press, P.O. Box 206, East Rockaway NY 11518-0206. **E-mail:** marshhawkpress1@aol.com. **Website:** www.MarshHawkPress.org. **Contact:** Prize Director. The Marsh Hawk Press Poetry Prize offers $1,000, plus publication of a book-length ms. Additionally, The Robert Creeley Poetry Prize and The Rochelle Ratner Poetry Award, both cash prizes, go to the runners-up. Deadline: April 30. Judged by Mark Doty.

## KATHLEEN MCCLUNG SONNET PRIZE CATEGORY

Soul-Making Keats Literary Competition, The Webhallow House, 1544 Sweetwood Dr., Broadmoor Village CA 94015-2029. **E-mail:** soulkeats@mail.com. **Website:** www.soulmakingcontest.us. **Contact:** Eileen Malone. Call for Shakespearean and Petrarchan sonnets on the theme of the "beloved." Deadline: November 30. Prize:1st Place: $100; 2nd Place: $50; 3rd Place: $25.

## MCKNIGHT ARTIST FELLOWSHIPS FOR WRITERS, LOFT AWARD(S) IN CHILDREN'S LITERATURE/CREATIVE PROSE/POETRY

The Loft Literary Center, 1011 Washington Ave. S., Suite 200, Open Book, Minneapolis MN 55415. (612)215-2575. **Fax:** (612)215-2576. **E-mail:** loft@loft.org. **Website:** www.loft.org. **Contact:** Bao Phi. "The Loft administers the McKnight Artists Fellowships for Writers. Five $25,000 awards are presented annually to accomplished Minnesota writers and spoken word artists. Four awards alternate annually between creative prose (fiction and creative nonfiction) and poetry/spoken word. The fifth award is presented in children's literature and alternates annually for writing for ages 8 and under and writing for children older than 8." The awards provide the writers the opportunity to focus on their craft for the course of the fellowship year. Prize: $25,000.

## MISSISSIPPI REVIEW PRIZE

*Mississippi Review*, 118 College Dr., #5144, Hattiesburg MS 39406-0001. (601)266-4321. **Fax:** (601)266-5757. **E-mail:** msreview@usm.edu. **Website:** www.mississippireview.com. Annual contest starting August 1 and running until January 1. Winners and finalists will make up next spring's print issue of the national literary magazine *Mississippi Review*. Each entrant will receive a copy of the prize issue. Deadline: January 1. Prize: $1,000 in fiction and poetry. Judged by Andrew Malan Milward in fiction, and Angela Ball in poetry.

## JENNY MCKEAN MOORE VISITING WRITER

English Department, George Washington University, Rome Hall, 801 22nd St. NW, Suite 760, Washington DC 20052. (202)994-6180. **Fax:** (202)994-7915. **E-mail:** tvmallon@gwu.edu. **Website:** http://columbian.gwu.edu/departmentsprograms/english/creativewriting/activitiesevents. **Contact:** Lisa Page, Acting Director of Creative Writing. The position is filled annually, bringing a visiting writer to The George Washington University. During each semester the Writer teaches 1 creative-writing course at the university as well as a community workshop. Seeks someone specializing in a different genre each year—fiction, poetry, creative nonfiction. Annual stipend between $50,000 and $60,000, plus reduced-rent townhouse on campus (not guaranteed). Application Deadline: December 3. Annual stipend varies, depending on endowment performance; most recently, stipend was $58,000, plus reduced-rent townhouse.

## THE KATHRYN A. MORTON PRIZE IN POETRY

Sarabande Books, Inc., 2234 Dundee Rd., Suite 200, Louisville KY 40205. (502)458-4028. **E-mail:** info@sarabandebooks.org. **Website:** www.sarabandebooks.org. **Contact:** Sarah Gorham, editor-in-chief. The Kathryn A. Morton Prize in Poetry is awarded annually to a book-length ms (at least 48 pages). All finalists are considered for publication. Competition receives approximately 1,400 entries. Deadline: April 30. Submissions period begins March 15. Prize: $2,000, publication, and a standard royalty contract.

## SHEILA MARGARET MOTTON PRIZE

New England Poetry Club, 2 Farrar St., Cambridge MA 02138. (617)744-6034. **E-mail:** info@nepoetryclub.org. **Website:** www.nepoetryclub.org. **Contact:**

Audrey Kalajin. Awarded for a book of poems published in the last 2 years. Deadline: May 31. Prize: $500. Judged by well-known poets and sometimes winners of previous NEPC contests.

### ERIKA MUMFORD PRIZE

New England Poetry Club, 376 School St., Watertown MA 02472. **E-mail:** contests@nepoetryclub.org. **Website:** www.nepoetryclub.org/contests.htm. **Contact:** Audrey Kalajin. Offered annually for a poem in any form about foreign culture or travel. Funded by Erika Mumford's family and friends. Deadline: May 31. Prize: $250. Judged by well-known poets and sometimes winners of previous NEPC contests.

### NATIONAL BOOK AWARDS

The National Book Foundation, 90 Broad St., Suite 604, New York NY 10004. (212)685-0261. **E-mail:** nationalbook@nationalbook.org; agall@nationalbook.org. **Website:** www.nationalbook.org. **Contact:** Amy Gall. The National Book Foundation and the National Book Awards celebrate the best of American literature, expand its audience, and enhance the cultural value of great writing in America. The contest offers prizes in 4 categories: fiction, nonfiction, poetry, and young people's literature. Books should be published between December 1 and November 30 of the past year. Deadline: Submit entry form, payment, and a copy of the book by July 1. Prize: $10,000 in each category. Finalists will each receive a prize of $1,000. Judged by a category specific panel of 5 judges for each category.

### 🌑 NATIONAL POETRY COMPETITION

The Poetry Society, 22 Betterton St., London WC2H 9BX, United Kingdom. 020 7420 9880. **E-mail:** info@poetrysociety.org.uk. **Website:** www.poetrysociety.org.uk. **Contact:** Competition organizer. The Poetry Society was founded in 1909 to promote "a more general recognition and appreciation of poetry". Since then, it has grown into one of Britain's most dynamic arts organizations, representing British poetry both nationally and internationally. Today it has nearly 4000 members worldwide and publishes *The Poetry Review*. With innovative education and commissioning programs and a packed calendar of performances, readings and competitions, The Poetry Society champions poetry for all ages. Deadline: October 31. 1st Prize: £5,000; 2nd Prize: £2,000; 3rd Prize: £1,000; plus 7 commendations of £200 each. Winners will be published in *The Poetry Review*, and on the Poetry

Society website; the top 3 winners will receive a year's free membership of The Poetry Society.

### THE NATIONAL POETRY REVIEW BOOK PRIZE

*The National Poetry Review*, P.O. Box 2080, Aptos CA 95001-2080. **E-mail:** editor@nationalpoetryreview.com. **Website:** www.nationalpoetryreview.com. **Contact:** C.J. Sage, editor. Deadline: June 30 (postmark). Prize: $1,000 plus publication and 15 copies of the book.

### NATIONAL WRITERS ASSOCIATION POETRY CONTEST

The National Writers Association, 10940 S. Parker Rd. #508, Parker CO 80134. (303)841-0246. **E-mail:** natlwritersassn@hotmail.com. **Website:** www.nationalwriters.com. **Contact:** Sandy Whelchel, director. Annual contest to encourage the writing of poetry, an important form of individual expression but with a limited commercial market. Deadline: October 1. Prize: 1st Place: $100; 2nd Place: $50; 3rd Place: $25.

### THE PABLO NERUDA PRIZE FOR POETRY

*Nimrod International Journal*, 800 S. Tucker Dr., Tulsa OK 74104. (918)631-3080. **Fax:** (918)631-3033. **E-mail:** nimrod@utulsa.edu. **Website:** www.utulsa.edu/nimrod. **Contact:** Eilis O'Neal. Annual award to discover new writers of vigor and talent. Open to US residents only. Deadline: April 30. Prizes: 1st Place: $2,000 and publication; 2nd Place: $1,000 and publication. Judged by the *Nimrod* editors (finalists). A recognized author selects the winners.

### THE NEUTRINO SHORT-SHORT CONTEST

*Passages North*, Dept. of English, Northern Michigan University, 1401 Presque Isle Ave., Marquette MI 49855. (906)227-1203. **Fax:** (906)227-1096. **E-mail:** passages@nmu.edu. **Website:** www.passagesnorth.com. **Contact:** Jennifer Howard. Offered every 2 years to publish new voices in literary fiction, nonfiction, hybrid-essays and prose poems (maximum 1,000 words). Guidelines available for SASE or online. Deadline: April 15. Submission period begins February 15. Prize: $1,000, and publication for the winner; 2 honorable mentions also published; all entrants receive a copy of *Passages North*. Judged by Lindsay Hunter in 2016.

### THE NEW CRITERION POETRY PRIZE

**Website:** www.newcriterion.com. Deadline: September 30. Prize: $3,000.

## THE NEW ISSUES POETRY PRIZE

New Issues Poetry & Prose, New Issues Poetry & Prose, Department of English, Western Michigan University, 1903 W. Michigan Ave., Kalamazoo MI 49008-5331. **E-mail:** new-issues@wmich.edu. **Website:** www.wmich.edu/newissues. Offered annually for publication of a first book of poems by a poet writing in English who has not previously published a full-length collection of poems in an edition of 500 or more copies. *New Issues Poetry & Prose* obtains rights for first publication. Book is copyrighted in author's name. Guidelines for SASE or online. Additional mss will be considered from those submitted to the competition for publication. Considers simultaneous submissions, but *New Issues* must be notified of acceptance elsewhere. Deadline: November 30. Prize: $2,000, plus publication of a book-length ms. A national judge selects the prize winner and recommends other manuscripts. The editors decide on the other books considering the judge's recommendation, but are not bound by it. 2016 judge: Mary Szybist.

## NEW LETTERS LITERARY AWARDS

*New Letters*, University of Missouri-Kansas City, 5101 Rockhill Rd., Kansas City MO 64110-2499, USA. (816)235-1168. **Fax:** (816)235-2611. **Website:** http://www.newletters.org/writers-wanted/writing-contests. Award has 3 categories (fiction, poetry, and creative nonfiction) with 1 winner in each. Offered annually for previously unpublished work. For guidelines, send an SASE to *New Letters*, or visit http://www.newletters.org/writers-wanted/writing-contests. Deadline: May 18. Prize: 1st place: $1,500, plus publication. Judged by regional writers of prominence and experience. Final judging by someone of national repute. Previous judges include Maxine Kumin, Albert Goldbarth, Charles Simic, and Janet Burroway.

## NEW LETTERS PRIZE FOR POETRY

*New Letters* Awards for Writers, UMKC, University House, 5101 Rockhill Rd., Kansas City MO 64110-2499. 816-235-1168. **E-mail:** newletters@umkc.edu. **Website:** www.newletters.org. The annual New Letters Poetry Prize awards $1,500 and publication in *New Letters* (see separate listing in Magazines/Journals) to the best group of 3-6 poems. All entries will be considered for publication in *New Letters*. Deadline: May 18 (postmarked). Prize: $1,500 and publication.

## NEW MILLENNIUM AWARDS FOR FICTION, POETRY, AND NONFICTION

New Millennium Writings, 4021 Garden Dr., Knoxville TN 37918. (865)254-4880. **Website:** www.newmillenniumwritings.org. **Contact:** Alexis Williams, Editor and Publisher. No restrictions as to style, content or number of submissions. Previously published pieces acceptable if online or under 5,000 print circulation. Simultaneous and multiple submissions welcome. Deadline: Postmarked on or before January 31 for the Winter Awards and July 31 for the Summer Awards. Prize: $1,000 for Best Poem; $1,000 for Best Fiction; $1,000 for Best Nonfiction; $1,000 for Best Short-Short Fiction.

## NEW SOUTH WRITING CONTEST

English Department, Georgia State University, P.O. Box 3970, Atlanta GA 30302-3970. **E-mail:** newsouth@gsu.edu. **Website:** newsouthjournal.com/contest. **Contact:** Stephanie Devine, editor-in-chief. Offered annually to publish the most promising work of up-and-coming writers of poetry (up to 3 poems) and fiction (9,000 word limit). Rights revert to writer upon publication. Guidelines online. Deadline: April 15. Prize: 1st Place: $1,000 in each category; 2nd Place: $250; and publication to winners. Judged by Anya Silver in poetry and Matthew Salesses in prose.

**TIPS** "We look for engagement with language and characters we care about."

## NEW WOMEN'S VOICES CHAPBOOK COMPETITION

Finishing Line Press, P.O. Box 1626, Georgetown KY 40324. (859)514-8966. **E-mail:** FinishingBooks@aol.com. **Website:** www.finishinglinepress.com. **Contact:** Leah Maines, poetry editor. The New Women's Voices Chapbook Competition offers publication by Finishing Line Press for a chapbook-length ms by a woman poet who has not yet published a full-length collection (previous chapbook publication is okay). Deadline: April 15. Prize: $1,000 and print and Kindle publication.

## NFSPS POETRY CONVENTION MADNESS CONTEST

2029 103rd Ave. NW, Coon Rapids MN 55433. **E-mail:** pwilliamstein@yahoo.com; schambersmediator@yahoo.com. **Website:** www.mnpoets.com. **Contact:** Peter Stein; Sue Chambers. Enter to win your way to the NFSPS National Poetry Convention in Chaska, MN June 9th-13th. For more details about the event, visit www.nfspsconvention.com. Deadline: January 31. Prizes: 1st Place: Hotel Lodging at Oak Ridge Convention Center for four nights, June 9th-12th. 2nd Place: Meals payed for during the course of the convention. 3rd Place: Registration to the Convention. 1st-3rd Honorable Mentions: Subscription to Poem by Post for one year.

## THE NIGHTBOAT POETRY PRIZE

Nightboat Books, P.O. Box 10, Callicoon NY 12723. **E-mail:** info@nightboat.org. **Website:** www.nightboat.org. **Contact:** Stephen Motika. Annual contest for previously unpublished collection of poetry (48-90 pages). Deadline: November 15. 1st place: $1,000, plus publication and 25 copies of published book.

## JESSIE BRYCE NILES MEMORIAL CHAPBOOK AWARD

The Comstock Review, 4956 St. John Dr., Syracuse NY 13215. (315)488-8077. **E-mail:** poetry@comstockreview.org. **Website:** www.comstockreview.org. Deadline: September 30. Contest begins August 1. Prize: $1,000 and 50 copies of chapbook. Judged by Kathleen Bryce Niles. All chapbooks are screened by the editors.

## NORTH CAROLINA WRITERS' FELLOWSHIPS

North Carolina Arts Council, North Carolina Arts Council, Writers' Fellowships, Department of Cultural Resources, Raleigh NC 27699-4632. (919)807-6512. **Fax:** (919)807-6532. **E-mail:** david.potorti@ncdcr.gov. **Website:** www.ncarts.org. **Contact:** David Potorti, literature and theater director. The North Carolina Arts Council offers grants in two categories to writers, spoken-word artists, playwrights, and screenwriters: fellowships (every other year) and residency grants (every year). Offered every even year to support writers of fiction, poetry, literary nonfiction, literary translation, and spoken word. See website for guidelines and other eligibility requirements. Deadline: November 1. Prize: $10,000 grant. Reviewed by a panel of literature professionals (writers and editors).

## NORTHERN CALIFORNIA BOOK AWARDS

Northern California Book Reviewers Association, c/o Poetry Flash, 1450 Fourth St. #4, Berkeley CA 94710. (510)525-5476. **E-mail:** ncbr@poetryflash.org; editor@poetryflash.org. **Website:** www.poetryflash.org. **Contact:** Joyce Jenkins, executive director. Annual Northern California Book Award for outstanding book in literature, open to books published in the current calendar year by Northern California authors.

NCBR presents annual awards to Bay Area (northern California) authors annually in fiction, nonfiction, poetry and children's literature. Encourages writers and stimulates interest in books and reading. Deadline: December 28. Prize: $100 honorarium and award certificate. Judging by voting members of the Northern California Book Reviewers.

## NSW PREMIER'S LITERARY AWARD
## THE KENNETH SLESSOR PRIZE

**Website:** www.sl.nsw.gov.au. The NSW Premier's Literary Awards have a proud history, both in celebrating achievement by Australian writers and in helping to establish values and standards in Australian literature. The Kenneth Slessor Prize is offered to a poet for a book of collected poems or for a single poem of substantial length published in book form. A collection of poems may consist partly of work previously published in book form, but this work must be clearly identified by the nominator. In such cases the judges will assess only the new work and determine whether it is sufficient, in quantity and quality, to merit an award. The NSW Government is committed to increasing public engagement with the arts. Administered by the State Library of NSW, the NSW Premier's Literary Awards provide an opportunity to highlight the importance of literacy and to encourage everyone to enjoy and learn from the work of writers. These annual awards honor distinguished achievement by Australian writers, contribute to Australia's artistic reputation, and draw international attention to some of the best writers and to the cultural environment that nurtures them. Deadline: November 23. Prize: $30,000. Judged by an independent committee of writers, academics, critics and other sector professionals who have been appointed by the NSW Premier.

## OHIO POETRY DAY CONTESTS

Dept. of English, Heidelberg College, 310 East Market, Tiffin OH 44883. **Website:** ohiopoetryday.blogspot.com. **Contact:** Bill Reyer, Contest Chair. Several poetry categories open to poets from Ohio and out-of-state. Prizes range $5-100. Deadline: May 31.

## OPEN SEASON AWARDS

The Malahat Review, University of Victoria, P.O. Box 1700, Stn CSC, Victoria BC V8V 2Y2, Canada. (250)721-8524. **Fax:** (250)472-5051. **E-mail:** malahat@uvic.ca. **Website:** www.malahatreview.ca. **Contact:** John Barton, editor. The Open Season Awards accepts entries of poetry, fiction, and creative nonfiction.

Winners published in spring issue of *Malahat Review* announced in winter on website, facebook page, and in quarterly e-newsletter, *Malahat lite*. Deadline: November 1. Prize: $1,000 CAD and publication in *The Malahat Review* in each category.

## OREGON BOOK AWARDS

925 SW Washington St., Portland OR 97205. (503)227-2583. **Fax:** (503)241-4256. **E-mail:** la@literary-arts.org. **Website:** www.literary-arts.org. **Contact:** Susan Denning, director of programs and events. The annual Oregon Book Awards celebrate Oregon authors in the areas of poetry, fiction, nonfiction, drama and young readers' literature published between August 1 and July 31 of the previous calendar year. Awards are available for every category. See website for details. Deadline: August 29. Prize: Grant of $2,500. (Grant money could vary.) Judged by writers who are selected from outside Oregon for their expertise in a genre. Past judges include Mark Doty, Colson Whitehead and Kim Barnes.

## OREGON LITERARY FELLOWSHIPS

925 S.W. Washington, Portland OR 97205. (503)227-2583. **E-mail:** susan@literary-arts.org. **Website:** www.literary-arts.org. **Contact:** Susan Moore, Director of programs and events. Oregon Literary Fellowships are intended to help Oregon writers initiate, develop, or complete literary projects in poetry, fiction, literary nonfiction, drama, and young readers literature. Writers in the early stages of their career are encouraged to apply. The awards are merit-based. Deadline: Last Friday in June. Prize: $3,000 minimum award, for approximately 8 writers and 2 publishers. Judged by out-of-state writers

## THE ORPHIC PRIZE FOR POETRY

Dream Horse Press, P.O. Box 2080, Aptos CA 95001-2080. **E-mail:** dreamhorsepress@yahoo.com. **Website:** www.dreamhorsepress.com. **Contact:** J.P. Dancing Bear, Editor/Publisher. The Orphic Prize for Poetry is an annual award offered by Dream Horse Press. All entries will be considered for publication. Both free verse and formal verse styles are welcome. Deadline: October 31. Five day extended deadline for electronic submissions. Prize: $1,000 and publication of a book-length ms by Dream Horse Press. Judging is anonymous.

## GUY OWEN AWARD

*Southern Poetry Review*, Department of Languages, Literature, and Philosophy, Armstrong Atlantic State University, 11935 Abercorn St., Savannah GA 31419-1997. (912)344-3196. **E-mail:** editor@southernpoetryreview.org. **Website:** www.southernpoetryreview.org. **Contact:** Tony Morris, associate editor. The annual Guy Owen Prize offers $1,000 and publication in *Southern Poetry Review* to the winning poem selected by a distinguished poet. All entries will be considered for publication. Deadline: March 1-May 31 (postmarked).

## PACIFIC NORTHWEST WRITERS ASSOCIATION (PNWA) LITERARY CONTEST

PMB 2717-1420 NW Gilman Blvd., Suite 2, Issaquah WA 98027. (425)673-2665. **E-mail:** pnwa@pnwa.org. **E-mail:** https://pnwa.submittable.com/submit. **Website:** www.pnwa.org; https://pnwa.submittable.com/submit. **Contact:** Monica Malveaux. Annual literary contest open to everyone, with first, second, and third place awards, along with cash prizes. Twelve categories, from Mainstream to Mystery to Nonfiction and Poetry. For more information, visit website. Deadline: February 19. Judged by librarians, agents, editors, authors, and former contest finalists.

## PANGAEA PRIZE

The Poet's Billow, 6135 Avon St, Portage MI 49024. **E-mail:** thepoetsbillow@gmail.com. **Website:** http://thepoetsbillow.org. **Contact:** Robert Evory. Annual award open to any writer to recognize the best series of poems, ranging between two and up to seven poems in a group. Finalists with strong work will also be published. Submissions must be previously unpublished. Please submit online. Deadline: May 1. Prize: $100. The winning poem will be published and displayed in The Poet's Billow Literary Art Gallery and nominated for a Pushcart Prize. If the poet qualifies, the poem will also be submitted to The Best New Poets anthology. Judged by the editors, and, occasionally, a guest judge.

## THE PATERSON POETRY PRIZE

The Poetry Center at Passaic County Community College, One College Blvd., Paterson NJ 07505. (973)684-6555. **Fax:** (973)523-6085. **E-mail:** mgillan@pccc.edu. **Website:** www.pccc.edu/poetry. **Contact:** Maria Mazziotti Gillan, executive director. The Paterson Poetry Prize offers an annual award for the strongest book of poems (48 or more pages) published in the previous year. The winner will be asked to participate in an awards ceremony and to give a reading at The Poetry Center. Minimum press run: 500 copies.

Publishers may submit more than 1 title for prize consideration; 3 copies of each book must be submitted. Include SASE for results; books will not be returned (all entries will be donated to The Poetry Center Library). Guidelines and application form (required) available for SASE or on website. Deadline: February 1. Prize: $1,000.

## PAUMANOK POETRY AWARD

English Department, Farmingdale State College, Knapp Hall, Farmingdale State College of New York, 2350 Broadhollow Rd., Route 110, Farmingdale NY 11735. **E-mail:** brownml@farmingdale.edu. **Website:** www.farmingdale.edu. **Contact:** Margery L. Brown, director, Visiting Writers Program. "Offered annually for published or unpublished poems. Send cover letter, 1-paragraph bio, 3-5 poems (name and address on each poem). Include SASE for notification of winners. (Send photocopies only; mss will *not* be returned.)" Deadline: September 15, postmark. Prize: 1st Place: $1,500, plus expenses for a reading in series; Runners-up (2): $750, plus expenses for a reading in series.

## PAVEMENT SAW PRESS CHAPBOOK AWARD

321 Empire St., Montpelier OH 43543-1301. **E-mail:** info@pavementsaw.org. **E-mail:** editor@pavement-saw.org. **Website:** www.pavementsaw.org. **Contact:** David Baratier, editor. Pavement Saw Press has been publishing steadily since the fall of 1993. Each year since 1999, they have published at least 4 full-length paperback poetry collections, with some printed in library edition hard covers, 1 chapbook, and a yearly literary journal anthology. They specialize in finding authors who have been widely published in literary journals but have not published a chapbook or full-length book. Deadline: December 31 (postmark). Prize: Chapbook Award offers $500, publication, and 50 author copies.

## JUDITH SIEGEL PEARSON AWARD

**E-mail:** fm8146@wayne.edu. **Website:** https://wsu-writingawards.submittable.com/submit. **Contact:** Donovan Hohn. Offers an annual award for the best creative or scholarly work on a subject concerning women. The type of work accepted rotates each year: drama in 2016, poetry in 2017; nonfiction in 2018; fiction in 2019. Open to all interested writers and scholars. Only submit the appropriate genre in each year. Deadline: February 22. Prize: $500. Judged by members of the writing faculty of the Wayne State University English Department.

## JEAN PEDRICK PRIZE

New England Poetry Club, 2 Farrar St., Cambridge MA 02138. **E-mail:** contests@nepoetryclub.org. **Website:** www.nepoetryclub.org. **Contact:** Audrey Kalajin. Prize for a chapbook of poems published in the last two years. Deadline: May 31. Prize: $100. Judged by well-known poets and sometimes winners of previous NEPC contests.

## PEN AWARD FOR POETRY IN TRANSLATION

PEN America, 588 Broadway, Suite 303, New York NY 10012. **E-mail:** awards@pen.org. **Website:** www.pen.org/awards. **Contact:** Arielle Anema. This award recognizes book-length translations of poetry from any language into English, published during the current calendar year. All books must have been published in the US. Translators may be of any nationality. US residency/citizenship not required. Deadline: Submissions are accepted during the summer of each year. Visit PEN.org/awards for updated on deadline dates. Prize: $3,000. Judged by a single translator of poetry appointed by the PEN Translation Committee.

## PEN CENTER USA LITERARY AWARDS

(323)424-4939. **E-mail:** awards@penusa.org. **E-mail:** awards@penusa.org. **Website:** www.penusa.org. Offered for work published or produced in the previous calendar year. Open to writers living west of the Mississippi River. Award categories: fiction, poetry, research nonfiction, creative nonfiction, translation, children's/young adult, graphic literature, drama, screenplay, teleplay, journalism. Deadline for book categories: 4 copies must be postmarked by December 31. Deadline for non-book categories: 4 copies must be postmarked by February 28. Prize: $1,000.

## PEN/JOYCE OSTERWEIL AWARD FOR POETRY

**E-mail:** awards@pen.org. **Website:** www.pen.org/awards. **Contact:** Arielle Anema, Literary Awards Coordinator. *Candidates may only be nominated by members of PEN.* This award recognizes the high literary character of the published work to date of a new and emerging American poet of any age, and the promise of further literary achievement. Nominated writer may not have published more than 1 book of poetry. Offered in odd-numbered years and alternates with the PEN/Voelcker Award for Poetry.

Submissions will be accepted during the summer of even-numbered year. Visit PEN.org/awards for up-to-date information on deadlines. Prize: $5,000. Judged by a panel of 3 judges selected by the PEN Awards Committee.

## PENNSYLVANIA POETRY SOCIETY ANNUAL CONTEST

5 Coachmans Court, Norwalk CT 06850. **Website:** nfsps.com/pa. **Contact:** Colleen Yarusavage. Pennsylvania Poetry Society offers several categories of poetry contests with a range of prizes from $10-100. Deadline: January 15.

## PEN/VOELCKER AWARD FOR POETRY

**E-mail:** awards@pen.org. **Website:** www.pen.org/awards. **Contact:** Arielle Anema, Literary Awards Coordinator. The PEN/Voelcker Award for Poetry, established by a bequest from Hunce Voelcker, this award is given to a poet whose distinguished and growing body of work to date represents a notable and accomplished presence in American literature. The poet honored by the award is one for whom the exceptional promise seen in earlier work has been fulfilled, and who continues to mature with each successive volume of poetry. The award is given in even-numbered years and carries a stipend of $5,000. Deadline: Nominations from PEN Members will be accepted during the summer of each odd-numbered year. Visit PEN.org/awards for up-to-date information on deadlines. Prize: $5,000. Judged by a panel of 3 poets or other writers chosen by the PEN Literary Awards Committee.

## PERUGIA PRESS PRIZE

Perugia Press, P.O. Box 60364, Florence MA 01062. **Website:** www.perugiapress.com. **Contact:** Susan Kan. The Perugia Press Prize is for a first or second poetry book by a woman. Poet must have no more than 1 previously published book of poems (chapbooks don't count). Deadline: November 15. Open to submissions on August 1. Prize: $1,000 and publication. Judged by panel of Perugia authors, booksellers, scholars, etc.

## THE RICHARD PETERSON POETRY PRIZE

*Crab Orchard Review*, Dept. of English, Mail Code 4503, Faner Hall 2380, Southern Illinois University at Carbondale, 1000 Faner Drive, Carbondale IL 62901. (618)453-6833. **Fax:** (618)453-8224. **E-mail:** jtribble@siu.edu. **Website:** www.craborchardreview.siu.edu. **Contact:** Jon Tribble, managing editor. Annual

award for unpublished poetry. Entries should consist of 1 poem up to 5 pages in length. *Crab Orchard Review* acquires first North American serial rights to all submitted work. One winner and at least 2 finalists will be chosen. Deadline: April 21. Submission period begins February 21. Prize: $2,000 plus publication. At least 2 finalists will be chosen and offered $500 each plus publication. Judged by the editors of *Crab Orchard Review*.

**TIPS** "Carefully read directions for entering and follow them exactly. Send us your best work. Note that simultaneous submissions are accepted for this prize, but the winning entry must not be accepted elsewhere. All submissions should be made through Submittable: https://craborchardreview.submittable.com/submit."

## THE PINCH LITERARY AWARDS

Literary Awards, The Pinch, Department of English, The University of Memphis, Memphis TN 38152-6176. (901)678-4591. **E-mail:** editor@thepinchjournal.com. **Website:** www.thepinchjournal.com. Offered annually for unpublished short stories and prose of up to 5,000 words and 1-3 poems. Deadline: March 15. Open to submissions on December 15. Prizes: $1,000 for 1st place in each category.

## PNWA LITERARY CONTEST

Pacifc Northwest Writers Association, PMB 2717, 1420 NW Gilman Blvd., Suite 2, Issaquah WA 98027. (452)673-2665. **Fax:** (452)961-0768. **E-mail:** pnwa@pnwa.org. **Website:** www.pnwa.org. Annual literary contest with 12 different categories. See website for details and specific guidelines. Each entry receives 2 critiques. Winners announced at the PNWA Summer Conference, held annually in mid-July. Deadline: February 20. Prize: 1st Place: $600; 2nd Place: $300; 3rd Place: $100. Judged by an agent or editor attending the conference.

## THE POETRY CENTER BOOK AWARD

The Poetry Center, San Francisco State University, 1600 Holloway Ave., San Francisco CA 94132. (415)338-2227. **Fax:** (415)338-0966. **E-mail:** poetry@sfsu.edu. **Website:** www.sfsu.edu/~poetry. Offered annually for books of poetry and chapbooks, published in year of the prize. "Prize given for an extraordinary book of American poetry written in English." Please include a cover letter noting author name, book title(s), name of person issuing check, and check number. Will not consider anthologies or translations. Deadline: January 31 for books published and copywrited in the previous year. 1st place: $500 and an invitation to read in the Poetry Center Reading Series.

## POETRY SOCIETY OF AMERICA AWARDS

15 Gramercy Park, New York NY 10003. **E-mail:** psa@poetrysociety.org. **Website:** www.poetrysociety.org. Offers 7 categories of poetry prizes between $250-2,500. 5 categories are open to PSA members only. Free entry for members; $15 for non-members. Submit between October 1-December 22.

## THE POETRY SOCIETY OF VIRGINIA ADULT AND STUDENT CONTESTS

11594 Hume Road, Hume VA 22639-1806. **E-mail:** ggterr@infionline.net. **E-mail:** nancy1734@aol.com. **Website:** www.poetrysocietyofvirginia.org. **Contact:** Guy Terrell, Adult Contest Co-Chair. Deadline: January 19. Open to submissions on November 1. Multiple prizes with different prize amounts are offered. See website for details.

## POETS & PATRONS ANNUAL CHICAGOLAND POETRY CONTEST

Sponsored by Poets & Patrons of Chicago, 416 Gierz St., Downers Grove IL 60515. **E-mail:** eatonb1016@aol.com. **Website:** www.poetsandpatrons.net. **Contact:** Barbara Eaton, director. Annual contest for unpublished poetry. Guidelines available for self-addressed, stamped envelope. The purpose of the contest is to encourage the crafting of poetry. Deadline: September 1. Prize: 1st Place: $45; 2nd Place: $20; 3rd Place: $10 cash. Poet retains rights. Judged by out-of-state professionals.

## FELIX POLLAK PRIZE IN POETRY

University of Wisconsin Press, 1930 Monroe St., 3rd Floor, Madison WI 53711. (608)263-1110. **Fax:** (608)263-1120. **E-mail:** uwiscpress@wisc.edu. **Website:** uwpress.wisc.edu. The Felix Pollak Prize in Poetry is awarded annually to the best book-length ms of original poetry submitted in an open competition. The award is administered by the University of Wisconsin–Madison English department, and the winner is chosen by a nationally recognized poet. The resulting book is published by the University of Wisconsin Press. Deadline: September 15. Prize: $1,000 cash prize, plus publication.

## A. POULIN, JR. POETRY PRIZE

BOA Editions, Ltd., BOA Editions, Ltd., P.O. Box 30971, Rochester NY 14603. **E-mail:** fisher@boaeditions.org. **Website:** www.boaeditions.org. The A. Poulin, Jr. Poetry Prize is awarded to honor a poet's first book, while also honoring the late founder of BOA Editions, Ltd., a not-for-profit publishing house of poetry, poetry in translation, and short fiction. Published books in other genres do not disqualify contestants from entering this contest. Deadline: November 30. Open to submissions on August 1. Prize: Awards $1,500 honorarium and book publication in the A. Poulin, Jr. New Poets of America Series.

## PRAIRIE SCHOONER BOOK PRIZE

*Prairie Schooner* and the University of Nebraska Press, Prairie Schooner Prize Series, 123 Andrews Hall, Lincoln NE 68588-0334. (402)472-0911. **E-mail:** PSBookPrize@unl.edu. **Website:** prairieschooner.unl.edu. **Contact:** Kwame Dawes, editor. Annual competition/award for story collections. Deadline: March 15. Prize: $3,000 and publication through the University of Nebraska Press.

## PRESS 53 AWARD FOR POETRY

Press 53, 560 N. Trade St., Suite 103, Winston-Salem NC 27101. (336)770-5353. **E-mail:** kevin@press53.com. **Website:** www.press53.com. **Contact:** Kevin Morgan Watson, publisher. Awarded to an outstanding, unpublished collection of poetry. Deadline: July 31. Submission period begins April 1. Winner and finalists announced on by November 1. Publication in April. Prize: Publication of winning poetry collection as a Tom Lombardo Poetry Selection, $1,000 cash advance, 1/4-page color ad in *Poets & Writers* magazine, and 10 copies of the book. Judged by Press 53 poetry series editor Tom Lombardo.

## PRIME NUMBER MAGAZINE AWARDS

Press 53, 560 N. Trade St., Suite 103, Winston-Salem NC 27101. (336)770-5353. **Fax:** N/A. **E-mail:** kevin@press53.com. **Website:** www.press53.com. **Contact:** Kevin Morgan Watson, Publisher. Awards $1,000 in poetry and short fiction. Deadline: April 15. Submission period begins January 1. Finalists announced June 1. Winner announced on August 1. Prize: $1,000 cash. All winners receive publication in *Prime Number Magazine* online. Judged by industry professionals to be named when the contest begins.

## THE PSA NATIONAL CHAPBOOK FELLOWSHIPS

Poetry Society of America, 15 Gramercy Park, New York NY 10003. (212)254-9628. **Fax:** (212)673-2352. **Website:** www.poetrysociety.org. Open to any US citizen or anyone currently living within the US who has not published a full-length poetry collection. Charges $12 entry fee. Winner receives $1,000 and welcomed as guest for a month-long artist's residency at PLAYA and invited to teach a single class at Purchase College for $1,000 under the sponsorshp of the Royal and Shirley Durst Chair in Literature.

## THE PSA NEW YORK CHAPBOOK FELLOWSHIPS

Poetry Society of America, 15 Gramercy Park, New York NY 10003. (212)254-9628. **Fax:** (212)673-2352. **Website:** www.poetrysociety.org. **Contact:** Contest Coordinator. Open to any US citizen or anyone currently living within the US who has not published a full-length poetry collection. Deadline: December 22. Open to submissions on October 1. Prize: Offers 2 prizes of $1,000 and publication of each of winning chapbook mss, with distribution by the Poetry Society of America.

## THE PULITZER PRIZE IN LETTERS

709 Pulitzer Hall, 2950 Broadway, Columbia University, New York NY 10027. (212)854-3841. **Fax:** (212)854-3342. **E-mail:** pulitzer@pulitzer.org. **Website:** www. pulitzer.org.

## PUSHCART PRIZE

Pushcart Press, P.O. Box 380, Wainscott NY 11975. (631)324-9300. **Website:** www.pushcartprize.com. **Contact:** Bill Henderson. Published every year since 1976, The Pushcart Prize - Best of the Small Presses series "is the most honored literary project in America. Hundreds of presses and thousands of writers of short stories, poetry and essays have been represented in the pages of our annual collections." Little magazine and small book press editors (print or online) may make up to six nominations from their year's publicatoins by the deadline. The nominations may be any combination of poetry, short fiction, essays or literary whatnot. Editors may nominate self-contained portions of books — for instance, a chapter from a novel. Deadline: December 1.

## RATTLE POETRY PRIZE

12411 Ventura Blvd., Studio City CA 91604. (818) 505-6777. **E-mail:** tim@rattle.com. **Website:** www.rattle. com. **Contact:** Timothy Green, editor. *Rattle*'s mission is to promote the practice of poetry. "More than anything, our goal is to promote a community of active poets." Deadline: July 15. Prize: One $10,000 winner and ten $200 finalists will be selected in a blind review by the editors of *Rattle* and printed in the Winter issue; one $1,000 Readers' Choice Award will then be chosen from among the finalists by subscriber and entrant vote. Judged by the editors of *Rattle*.

## RHINO FOUNDERS' PRIZE

RHINO, The Poetry Forum, P.O. Box 591, Evanston IL 60204. **E-mail:** editors@rhinopoetry.org. **Website:** rhinopoetry.org. **Contact:** Editors. Send best unpublished poetry (3-5 pages). Visit website for previous winners and more information. Deadline: October 31. Open to submissions on September 1. Prize: $500, publication, featured on website, and nominated for a Pushcart Prize. Two runners-ups will receive $50, publication, and will be featured on website. Occasionally nominates runner-up for a Pushcart Prize.

**TIPS** "RHINO values original voice, musicality, fresh language, and respect for the reader."

## RHODE ISLAND ARTIST FELLOWSHIPS AND INDIVIDUAL PROJECT GRANTS

Rhode Island State Council on the Arts, State of Rhode Island, One Capitol Hill, 3rd Floor, Providence RI 02908. (401)222-3880. **Fax:** (401)222-3018. **E-mail:** Cristina.DiChiera@arts.ri.gov. **Website:** www.arts. ri.gov. **Contact:** Cristina DiChiera, director of individual artist programs. Annual fellowship competition is based upon panel review of poetry, fiction, and playwriting/screenwriting manuscripts. Project grants provide funds for community-based arts projects. Rhode Island artists who have lived in the state for at least 12 consecutive months may apply without a nonprofit sponsor. Applicants for all RSCA grant and award programs must be at least 18 years old and not currently enrolled in an arts-related degree program. Online application and guidelines can be found at www.arts.ri.gov/grants/guidelines/. Deadline: April 1 and October 1. Fellowship awards: $5,000 and $1,000. Grants range from $500-5,000, with an average of around $1,500. Judged by a rotating panel of artists.

## ROANOKE-CHOWAN POETRY AWARD

The North Carolina Literary & Historical Assoc., 4610 Mail Service Center, Raleigh NC 27699-4610. (919)807-7290. **Fax:** (919)733-8807. **E-mail:** michael. hill@ncdcr.gov. **Website:** litandhist.ncdcr.gov. **Contact:** Michael Hill, awards coordinator. Offers annual award for an original volume of poetry published during the 12 months ending June 30 of the year for which the award is given. Deadline: July 15.

## BEULLAH ROSE POETRY PRIZE

P.O. Box 22161, Baltimore MD 21203. **E-mail:** cbanks@smartishspace.com. **Website:** www.smartishspace.com. **Contact:** Clare Banks, associate editor. Purpose is to recognize exceptional poetry by women. Deadline: November 15. Prize: $200. Judged by Clare Banks and Traci O'Dea.

## LORI RUDNITSKY FIRST BOOK PRIZE

Persea Books, P.O. Box 1388, Columbia MO 65205. **Website:** www.perseabooks.com. "This annual competition sponsors the publication of a poetry collection by an American woman poet who has yet to publish a full-length book of poems." Deadline: October 31. Prize: $1,000, plus publication of book. In addition, the winner receives the option of an all-expenses-paid residency at the Civitella Ranieri Center, a renowned artists retreat housed in a 15th-century castle in Umbertide, Italy.

## VERN RUTSALA POETRY PRIZE

P.O. Box 610, Corvallis OR 97339. (541)752-0075. **E-mail:** michael@cloudbankbooks.com. **Contact:** Michael Malan. Deadline: January 2. Prize: $1,000 plus publication of full-length ms. Judged by Dennis Schmitz.

## BENJAMIN SALTMAN POETRY AWARD

Red Hen Press, P.O. Box 40820, Pasadena CA 91114. (818)831-0649. **Fax:** (818)831-6659. **E-mail:** productioncoordinator@redhen.org. **Website:** www.redhen.org. Offered annually for unpublished work to publish a winning book of poetry. Open to any writer. Deadline: August 31. 1st place: $3,000 and publication.

## ERNEST SANDEEN PRIZE IN POETRY AND THE RICHARD SULLIVAN PRIZE IN SHORT FICTION

University of Notre Dame, Dept. of English, 356 O'shaughnessy Hall, Notre Dame IN 46556-5639. (574)631-7526. **Fax:** (574)631-4795. **E-mail:** creative-writing@nd.edu. **Website:** http://english.nd.edu/creative-writing/publications/sandeen-sullivan-prizes. **Contact:** Director of Creative Writing. The Sandeen & Sullivan Prizes in Poetry and Short Fiction is awarded to the author who has published at least one volume of short fiction or one volume of poetry. Awarded biannually, but judged quadrennially. Submissions Period: May 1-September 1. Prize: $1,000, a $500 award

and a $500 advance against royalties from the Notre Dame Press.

## MAY SARTON AWARD

New England Poetry Club, 654 Green St., No. 2, Cambridge MA 02139. (617)744-6034. **E-mail:** contests@nepoetryclub.org. **Website:** www.nepoetryclub.org. **Contact:** NEPC contest coordinator. "Given intermittently to a poet whose work is an inspiration to other poets. Recipients are chosen by the board." To recognize emerging poets of exceptional promise and distinguished achievement. Established to honor the memory of longtime Academy Fellow May Sarton, a poet, novelist, and teacher who during her career encouraged the work of young poets. Deadline: May 31. Prize: $250. Judges are well-known poets and sometimes winners of previous NEPC contests.

## ☼ SASKATCHEWAN BOOK AWARDS

315-1102 Eighth Ave., Regina SK S4R 1C9, Canada. (306)569-1585. **E-mail:** director@bookawards.sk.ca. **Website:** www.bookawards.sk.ca. **Contact:** Courtney Bates-Hardy, Administrative Director. Saskatchewan Book Awards celebrates, promotes, and rewards Saskatchewan authors and publishers worthy of recognition through 14 awards, granted on an annual or semiannual basis. Awards: Fiction, Nonfiction, Poetry, Scholarly, First Book, *Prix du Livre Français*, Regina, Saskatoon, Aboriginal Peoples' Writing, Aboriginal Peoples' Publishing, Publishing in Education, Publishing, Children's Literature/Young Adult Literature, Book of the Year. Deadline: Early November. Prize: $2,000 (CAD) for all awards except Book of the Year, which is $3,000 (CAD). Juries are made up of writing and publishing professionals from outside of Saskatchewan.

○ Saskatchewan Book Awards is the only provincially focused book award program in Saskatchewan and a principal ambassador for Saskatchewan's literary community. Its solid reputation for celebrating artistic excellence in style is recognized nationally.

## THE SCARS EDITOR'S CHOICE AWARDS

**E-mail:** editor@scars.tv. **Website:** http://scars.tv. **Contact:** Janet Kuypers, editor/publisher (whom all reading fee checks need to be made out to). Award to showcase good writing in an annual book. Prize: Publication of story/essay and 1 copy of the book.

## HELEN SCHAIBLE INTERNATIONAL SONNET CONTEST

Sponsored by Poets & Patrons of Chicago, 416 Gierz St., Downers Grove IL 60515-3838. **E-mail:** eatonb1016@aol.com. **Website:** http://poetsandpatrons.net. **Contact:** Barbara Eaton. Annual poetry contest held same time each year. Poems must be in English. Guidelines and entry forms available for self-addressed, stamped envelope. The purpose of the contest is to encourage the crafting of sonnets and to honor Helen Schaible. Deadline: September 1. Prize: $50, $35, $15. Poet retains all rights. Judged by out-of-state professionals.

## THE MONA SCHREIBER PRIZE FOR HUMOROUS FICTION & NONFICTION

3940 Laurel Canyon Blvd., #566, Studio City CA 91604. **E-mail:** brad.schreiber@att.net. **Website:** www.bradschreiber.com. **Contact:** Brad Schreiber. The purpose of the contest is to award the most creative humor writing, in any form less than 750 words, in either fiction or nonfiction, including but not limited to stories, articles, essays, speeches, shopping lists, diary entries, and anything else writers dream up. Complete rules and previous winning entries on website. Deadline: December 1. Prize: 1st Place: $500; 2nd Place: $250; 3rd Place: $100. Judged by Brad Schreiber, author, journalist, consultant, and instructor.

## SCREAMINMAMAS MOTHER'S DAY POETRY CONTEST

1911 Cleveland St., Hollywood FL 33020. **E-mail:** screaminmamas@gmail.com. **Website:** www.screaminmamas.com/contests. **Contact:** Darlene Pistocchi, editor/managing director. "What does it mean to be a mom? There is so much to being a mom—get deep, get creative! We challenge you to explore different types of poetry: descriptive, reflective, narrative, lyric, sonnet, ballad, limerick.. you can even go epic!" Open only to moms. Deadline: December 31. Prize: complementary subscription to magazine, publication.

## ✪ SHORT GRAIN CONTEST

P.O. Box 3986, Regina SK S4P 3R9, Canada. (306)791-7749. **E-mail:** grainmag@skwriter.com. **Website:** www.grainmagazine.ca/short-grain-contest. **Contact:** Jordan Morris, business administrator (inquiries only). The annual Short Grain Contest includes a category for poetry of any style up to 100 lines and fiction of any style up to 2,500 words, offering 3 prizes. Deadline: April 1. Prize: $1,000, plus publication in *Grain Magazine*; 2nd Place: $750; 3rd Place: $500.

## SKIPPING STONES HONOR (BOOK) AWARDS

P.O. Box 3939, Eugene OR 97403. (541)342-4956. **Fax:** (541)342-4956. **E-mail:** editor@skippingstones.org. **Website:** www.skippingstones.org. **Contact:** Arun N. Toké. *Skipping Stones* is a well respected, multicultural literary magazine now in its 28th year. Annual award to promote multicultural and/or nature awareness through creative writings for children and teens and their educators. Seeks authentic, exceptional, child/youth friendly books that promote intercultural, international, intergenerational harmony, or understanding through creative ways. Deadline: February 29. Prize: Honor certificates; gold seals; reviews; press release/publicity. Judged by a multicultural committee of teachers, librarians, parents, students and editors.

**TIPS** "Books that come out of author's own research, experiences and cultural understanding seem to have an edge. We like authentic, educational, entertaining and exceptional books. There are three categories: International and Multicultural, Nature and Ecology, and Theaching Resources and educational DVDs."

## SKIPPING STONES YOUTH AWARDS

P.O. Box 3939, Eugene OR 97403-0939. (541)342-4956. **Fax:** (541)342-4956. **E-mail:** editor@skippingstones.org. **Website:** www.skippingstones.org. **Contact:** Arun N. Toké. Annual awards to promote creativity as well as multicultural and nature awareness in youth. Deadline: June 25. Prize: Publication in the autumn issue of *Skipping Stones*, honor certificate, subscription to magazine, plus 5 multicultural and/or nature books. Judged by editors and reviewers at *Skipping Stones* magazine.

## SLAPERING HOL PRESS CHAPBOOK COMPETITION

The Hudson Valley Writers' Center, 300 Riverside Dr., Sleepy Hollow NY 10591. (914)332-5953. **Fax:** (914)332-4825. **E-mail:** info@writerscenter.org. **Website:** www.writerscenter.org. **Contact:** Margo Stever, editor. The annual competition is open to poets who have not published a book or chapbook, though individual poems may have already appeared. Purpose is to provide publishing opportunities for emerging poets. Deadline: May 15. Prize: $1,000, publication of chapbook, 20 copies of chapbook, and a reading at The Hudson Valley Writers' Center.

## SLIPSTREAM ANNUAL POETRY CHAPBOOK CONTEST

Slipstream, Slipstream Poetry Contest, Dept. W-1, P.O. Box 2071, Niagara Falls NY 14301. **E-mail:** editors@slipstreampress.org. **Website:** www.slipstreampress.org. **Contact:** Dan Sicoli, co-editor. *Slipstream Magazine* is a yearly anthology of some of the best poetry you'll find today in the American small press. Offered annually to help promote a poet whose work is often overlooked or ignored. Open to any writer. Deadline: December 1. Prize: $1,000, plus 50 professionally-printed copies of your book.

## SLOPE EDITIONS BOOK PRIZE

4 Lynde St., Nashua NH 03064. **E-mail:** ethan@slope.org. **Website:** www.slopeeditions.org. **Contact:** Christopher Janke, senior editor and Ethan Paquin, editor-in-chief. Deadline: March 15. Prize: $1,000 plus publication.

## THE BERNICE SLOTE AWARD

*Prairie Schooner*, 123 Andrews Hall, PO Box 880334, Lincoln NE 68588-0334. (402)472-0911. **Fax:** (402)472-1817. **E-mail:** PrairieSchooner@unl.edu. **Website:** www.prairieschooner.unl.edu. **Contact:** Kwame Dawes. Offered annually for the best work by a beginning writer published in *Prairie Schooner* in the previous year. Celebrates the best and finest writing that they have published for the year. Prize: $500. Judged by editorial staff of *Prairie Schooner*.

## JEFFREY E. SMITH EDITORS' PRIZE IN FICTION, ESSAY AND POETRY

*The Missouri Review*, 357 McReynolds Hall, UMC, Columbia MO 65211. (573)882-4474. **Fax:** (573)884-4671. **E-mail:** contest_question@moreview.com. **Website:** www.missourireview.com. **Contact:** Editor. Offered annually for unpublished work in 3 categories: fiction, essay, and poetry. Guidelines online or for SASE. Deadline: October 15. Prize: $5,000 and publication for each category winner.

## HELEN C. SMITH MEMORIAL AWARD FOR BEST BOOK OF POETRY

**E-mail:** tilsecretary@yahoo.com. **Website:** http://texasinstituteofletters.org/. Offered annually for the best book of poems published January 1-December 31 of previous year. Poet must have been born in Texas, have lived in the state at some time for at least 2 con-

secutive years, or the subject matter must be associated with the state. Deadline: January 10. Prize: $1,200.

## KAY SNOW WRITING CONTEST

Willamette Writers, Willamette Writers, 2108 Buck St., West Linn OR 97068. (503)305-6729. **Fax:** (503)344-6174. **E-mail:** reg@willamettewriters.com. **Website:** www.willamettewriters.com. Willamette Writers is the largest writers' organization in Oregon and one of the largest writers' organizations in the United States. It is a non-profit, tax-exempt Oregon corporation led by volunteers. Elected officials and directors administer an active program of monthly meetings, special seminars, workshops, and an annual writing conference. Continuing with established programs and starting new ones is only made possible by strong volunteer support. The purpose of this annual writing contest, named in honor of Willamette Writer's founder, Kay Snow, is to help writers reach professional goals in writing in a broad array of categories and to encourage student writers. Deadline: April 23. Submission deadline begins January 15. Prize: One first prize of $300, one second place prize of $150, and a third place prize of $50 per winning entry in each of the six categories. Student first prize is $50, $20 for second place, $10 for third.

## THE RICHARD SNYDER MEMORIAL PUBLICATION PRIZE

Ashland Poetry Press, 401 College Ave., Ashland University, Ashland OH 44805. **E-mail:** app@ashland.edu. **Website:** www.ashlandpoetrypress.com. **Contact:** Cassandra Brown, managing editor. Submissions must be unpublished in book form. Considers simultaneous submissions. Submit 50-96 pages of poetry. Competition receives 400+ entries/year. Winners will be announced in *Writer's Chronicle* and *Poets & Writers*. Copies of winning books available from Small Press Distribution and directly from the Ashland University Bookstore online. The Ashland Poetry Press publishes 2-4 books of poetry/year. Deadline: April 1. Prize: $1,000 plus book publication. Judged by Andrew Hudgins in 2016.

## SOCIETY OF CLASSICAL POETS POETRY COMPETITION

The Society of Classical Poets, 11 Heather Ln., Mount Hope NY 10940. **E-mail:** submissions@classicalpoets.org. **Website:** www.classicalpoets.org. **Contact:** Evan Mantyk, president. Annual competition for a group of poems that address one or more of the following themes: beauty, Falun Dafa, great culture, or humor. Poems must incorporate meter and rhyme. All entries are considered for publication. Deadline: December 31. Prize: $500. Judged by Evan Mantyk, the society's president.

○ There are minor modifications to themes and the amount of money awarded from year to year, check website for details.

## SOCIETY OF MIDLAND AUTHORS AWARD

Society of Midland Authors, Society of Midland Authors, P.O. Box 10419, Chicago IL 60610-0419. **E-mail:** marlenetbrill@comcast.net. **Website:** www.midlandauthors.com. **Contact:** Marlene Targ Brill, awards chair. Since 1957, the Society has presented annual awards for the best books written by Midwestern authors. The Society of Midland Authors (SMA) Award is presented to one title in each of six categories: adult nonfiction, adult fiction, adult biography and memoir, children's nonfiction, children's fiction, and poetry. Books and entry forms must be mailed to the 3 judges in each category; for a list of judges and the entry form, visit the website. Do not mail books to the society's P.O. box. The fee can be sent to the SMA P.P. box or paid via Paypal. Deadline: January 7. Prize: $500 and a plaque that is awarded at the SMA banquet in May in Chicago. Honorary winners receive a plaque.

## SOUL-MAKING KEATS LITERARY COMPETITION

The Webhallow House, 1544 Sweetwood Dr., Broadmoor Village CA 94015-2029. **E-mail:** SoulKeats@mail.com. **Website:** www.soulmakingcontest.us. **Contact:** Eileen Malone, award director. Annual open contest offers cash prizes in each of 13 literary categories. Competition receives 600 entries/year. Names of winners and judges are posted on website. Winners announced in January by SASE and on website. Winners are invited to read at the Koret Auditorium, San Francisco. Event is televised. Deadline: November 30. Prizes: 1st Prize: $100; 2nd Prize: $50; 3rd Prize: $25.

## THE SOW'S EAR CHAPBOOK COMPETITION

*The Sow's Ear Review*, 1748 Cave Ridge Rd., Mount Jackson VA 22842. (540)955-3955. **E-mail:** sepoetryreview@gmail.com. **Website:** www.sows-ear.kite-net.net. **Contact:** Sarah Kohrs, managing editor. *The Sow's Ear Poetry Review* sponsors an annual chapbook competition. Open to adults. Deadline: May 1 (postmark). Prize: Offers $1,000, publication as the spring

issue of the magazine, 25 author's copies, and distribution to subscribers.

## THE SOW'S EAR POETRY COMPETITION

*The Sow's Ear Poetry Review*, 1748 Cave Ridge Road, Mount Jackson VA 22842. **E-mail:** rglesman@gmail.com. **Website:** www.sowsearpoetry.org. **Contact:** Sarah Kohrs, managing editor. Deadline: November 1. Prize: $1,000, publication, and the option of publication for approximately 20 finalists.

## WALLACE E. STEGNER FELLOWSHIPS

Creative Writing Program, Stanford University, Stanford CA 94305-2087. (650)723-0011. **Fax:** (650)723-3679. **E-mail:** stegnerfellowship@stanford.edu. **Website:** www.stanford.edu/group/creativewriting/stegner. Offers 5 fellowships in poetry and 5 in fiction for promising writers who can benefit from 2 years of instruction and participation in the program. Online application preferred. Deadline: December 1. Open to submissions on September 1. Prize: Fellowships of $26,000, plus tuition of over $7,000/year.

## STEVENS POETRY MANUSCRIPT CONTEST

NFSPS Stevens Poetry Manuscript Competition, 499 Falcon Ridge Way, Bolingbrook IL 60440. **E-mail:** stevens.nfsps@gmail.com. **Website:** www.nfsps.org. **Contact:** Wilda Morris, Chair. National Federation of State Poetry Societies (NFSPS) offers annual award of $1,000, publication of ms, and 50 author's copies for the winning poetry manuscript by a single author. Deadline: October 1. Submissions open September 1. Prize: $1,000, publication and 50 copies of the book.

## THE ST. LAWRENCE BOOK AWARD

**E-mail:** editors@blacklawrencepress.com. **Website:** www.blacklawrencepress.com. "Black Lawrence Press is an independent publisher of contemporary poetry, fiction, and creative nonfiction. We also publish the occasional translation from German. Founded in 2004, Black Lawrence became an imprint of Dzanc Books in 2008. In January 2014, we spread our wings and became an independent company in the state of New York. Our books are distributed nationally through Small Press Distribution to Amazon, Barnes & Noble, and various brick and mortar retailers. We also make our titles available through our website and at various conferences and book fairs. Through our annual contests and open reading periods, we seek innovative, electrifying, and thoroughly intoxicating manuscripts that ensnare themselves in our hearts and minds and won't let go." Each year Black Lawrence Press awards The St. Lawrence Book Award for an unpublished first collection of poems or short stories. The St. Lawrence Book Award is open to any writer who has not yet published a full-length collection of short stories or poems. The winner of this contest will receive book publication, a $1,000 cash award, and ten copies of the book. Prizes are awarded on publication. Deadline: August 31. Prize: Publication and $1000. Judged by the Black Lawrence Press editors.

### THE RUTH STONE POETRY PRIZE

Vermont College, 36 College St., Montpelier VT 05602. (802)828-8517. **E-mail:** hungermtn@vcfa.edu. **Website:** www.hungermtn.org. **Contact:** Samantha Kolber, managing editor. The Ruth Stone Poetry Prize is an annual poetry contest. Deadline: March 1 Prize: One first place winner receives $1,000 and publication on Hunger Mountain online. Two honorable mentions receive $100 and publication on Hunger Mountain online. Judged by Lee Upton in 2016.

### THE ELIZABETH MATCHETT STOVER MEMORIAL AWARD

*Southwest Review*, Southern Methodist University, P.O. Box 750374, Dallas TX 75275-0374. (214)768-1037. **Fax:** (214)768-1408. **E-mail:** swr@mail.smu.edu. **Website:** www.smu.edu/southwestreview. **Contact:** Jennifer Cranfill, senior editor, and Willard Spiegelman, editor-in-chief. Offered annually to the best works of poetry that have appeared in the magazine in the previous year. Please note that mss are submitted for publication, not for the prizes themselves. Guidelines for SASE and online. Prize: $300. Judged by Jennifer Cranfill and Willard Spiegelman.

**TIPS** "Not an open contest. Annual prize in which winners are chosen from published pieces during the preceding year."

### ● STROKESTOWN INTERNATIONAL POETRY COMPETITION

Strokestown International Poetry Festival, Strokestown Poetry Festival Office, Strokestown, County Roscommon, Ireland. (+353) 71 9633759. **E-mail:** director@strokestownpoetry.org. **Website:** www.strokestownpoetry.org. **Contact:** Martin Dyar, Director. This annual competition was established to promote excellence in poetry and participation in the reading and writing of it. Acquires first publication rights. Deadline: January. Prize: 1st Place: €1,500; 2nd

Place: €500; 3rd Place: €300; 3 shortlisted prizes of €100 each.

### MAY SWENSON POETRY AWARD

Utah State University Press, Merrill-Cazier Library, 3000 Old Main Hill, Logan UT 84322-3078. (435)797-1362. **Fax:** (435)797-0313. **E-mail:** michael.spooner@usu.edu; scholarlycommunications@usu.edu. **Website:** www.usupress.org. **Contact:** Michael Spooner, director. "This annual competition, named for May Swenson, honors her as one of America's most provocative and vital writers." Deadline: September 30. Prize: $1,000 and publication. Previous judges include Harold Bloom, Grace Schulman, Billy Collins, and Edward Field. See website for guidelines and the full series of Swenson volumes.

### THE TAMPA REVIEW PRIZE FOR POETRY

University of Tampa, 401 W. Kennedy Blvd., Tampa FL 33606. 813-253-6266. **E-mail:** utpress@ut.edu. **Website:** www.ut.edu/tampareview. Annual award for the best previously unpublished collection of poetry (at least 48 pages, though preferably 60-100). Deadline: December 31. Prize: $2,000, plus publication.

### THE TENTH GATE PRIZE

**E-mail:** editor@wordworksbooks.org. **Website:** www.wordworksbooks.org. **Contact:** Leslie McGrath, Series Editor; Nancy White, Editor. Publication and cash prize awarded annually by The Word Works to a full-length ms by a poet who has already published at least 2 full-length collections. Founded in honor of Jane Hirshfield, The Tenth Gate Prize supports the work of mid-career poets. Deadline: July 15. Open to submissions on June 1. Prize: $1,000 and publication. Judged by the editors.

### THE TEXAS INSTITUTE OF LETTERS LITERARY AWARDS

**E-mail:** Betwx@aol.com. **Website:** www.texasinstituteofletters.org. The Texas Institute of Letters gives annual awards for books by Texas authors and writers who have produced books about Texas, including Best Books of Poetry, Fiction, and Nonfiction. Awards are also given for best Short Story, Magazine or Newspaper Article, Essay, and best Books for Children and Young Adults. Work submitted must have been published in the year stipulated, and entries may be made by authors or by their publishers. Complete guidelines and award information is available on the Texas Institute of Letters website.

## LENA-MILES WEVER TODD POETRY SERIES BOOK COMPETITION

Pleiades Press, Lena-Miles Wever Todd Poetry Prize, Dept of English, Martin 336, University of Central Missouri, Warrensburg MO 64093. (660)543-8106. **E-mail:** pleiades@ucmo.edu. **Website:** www.ucmo.edu/pleiades/. The annual Lena-Miles Wever Todd Poetry Series Book Competition is open to all American writers, regardless of previous publication. Submission must be unpublished as a collection, but individual poems may have been previously published elsewhere. Submit at least 48 pages of poetry (one copy). Include 2 cover sheets: one with ms title, poet's name, address, and phone number; the second with ms title only. Also include acknowledgments page for previously published poems. Guidelines online. Deadline: November 15. Prize: $2,000 and the winning collection will be published in paperback and nationally distributed.

## TOM HOWARD/MARGARET REID POETRY CONTEST

Winning Writers, Winning Writers, 351 Pleasant St., PMB 222, Northampton MA 01060-3961, USA. (866)946-9748. **Fax:** (413)280-0539. **E-mail:** adam@winningwriters.com. **Website:** www.winningwriters.com. **Contact:** Adam Cohen. Winning Writers provides expert literary contest information to the public. It is one of the "101 Best Websites for Writers" (*Writer's Digest*). Deadline: September 30. Submission period begins April 15. Prizes: Two top awards of $1,500 each, with 10 Honorable Mentions of $100 each (any style). All entries that win cash prizes will be published on the Winning Writers website. Judged by Soma Mei Sheng Frazier.

Offers annual awards of Tom Howard Prize, for a poem in any style or genre, and Margaret Reid Prize, for a poem that rhymes or has a traditional style. See website for guidelines and to submit your poem. Nonexclusive right to publish submissions online, in e-mail newsletters, in e-books, and in press releases.

**TIPS** Read past winning entries and judges' remarks on website.

## TOR HOUSE PRIZE FOR POETRY

Robinson Jeffers Tor House Foundation, Poetry Prize Coordinator, Tor House Foundation, Box 223240, Carmel CA 93922. (831)624-1813. **Fax:** (831)624-3696. **E-mail:** thf@torhouse.org. **Website:** www.torhouse.

org. **Contact:** Eliot Ruchowitz-Roberts, Poetry Prize Coordinator. The annual Prize for Poetry is a living memorial to American poet Robinson Jeffers (1887-1962). Open to well-crafted poetry in all styles, ranging from experimental work to traditional forms, including short narrative poems. Poems must be original and unpublished. Deadline: March 14. Prize: $1,000 honorarium for award-winning poem; $200 Honorable Mention.

## KINGSLEY & KATE TUFTS POETRY AWARDS

Claremont Graduate University, Claremont Graduate University, 160 E. Tenth St., Harper East B7, Claremont CA 91711-6165. (909)621-8974. **E-mail:** tufts@cgu.edu. **Website:** www.cgu.edu/tufts. The $100,000 Kingsley Tufts Poetry Award was created to both honor the poet and provide the resources that allow artists to continue working towards the pinnacle of their craft; the Kingsley Tufts Awards goes to a book published by a mid-career poet. The $10,000 Kate Tufts Award is presented annually for a first book by a poet of genuine promise. "Any poet will tell you that the only thing more rare than meaningful recognition is a meaningful payday. For two outstanding poets each year, the Kingsley and Kate Tufts awards represent both." Deadline: July 1, for books published in the preceding year. Prize: $100,000 for the Kingsley Tufts Poetry Award and $10,000 for the Kate Tufts Discovery Award. Please see website for current judges.

## UTMOST CHRISTIAN POETRY CONTEST

Utmost Christian Writers Foundation, 121 Morin Maze, Edmonton Alberta T6K 1V1, Canada. (780)265-4650. **E-mail:** nnharms@telusplanet.net. **Website:** www.utmostchristianwriters.com. **Contact:** Nathan Harms, executive director. Utmost is founded on—and supported by—the dreams, interests and aspirations of individual people. Deadline: February 28. Prizes: 1st Place: $1,000; 2nd Place: $500; 10 prizes of $100 are offered for honorable mention; $300 for best rhyming poem; and $200 for an honorable mention rhyming poem. Judged by a committee of the Directors of Utmost Christian Writers Foundation (who work under the direction of Barbara Mitchell, chief judge).

**TIPS** "Besides providing numerous resources for Christian writers and poets, Utmost also provides a marketplace where Christian writers and poets can sell their work. Please follow our guidelines. We receive numerous unsuitable submissions from writers. We encourage writers to submit suitable material. The best way to do this is to read the guidelines specific to your project—poetry, book reviews, articles—and then take time to look at the material we have already published in that area. The final step is to evaluate your proposed submission in comparison to the material we have used previously. If you complete these steps and strongly feel that your material is appropriate for us, we encourage you to submit it."

### DANIEL VAROUJAN AWARD

New England Poetry Club, 376 School St., Watertown MA 02472. **E-mail:** contests@nepoetryclub.org. **Website:** www.nepoetryclub.org. **Contact:** Audrey Kalajin. For an unpublished poem (not a translation) worthy of Daniel Varoujan, a poet killed by the Turks in the genocide which destroyed three-fourths of the Armenian population. Deadline: May 31. Prize: $1,000. Judged by well-known poets and sometimes winners of previous NEPC contests.

### VASSAR MILLER PRIZE IN POETRY

University of North Texas Press, 1155 Union Circle, #311336, Denton TX 76203. (940)565-2142. **Fax:** (940)565-4590. **Website:** http://untpress.unt.edu. **Contact:** John Poch. Annual prize awarded to a collection of poetry. Deadline: Mss may be submitted between 9 A.M. on September 1 and 5 P.M. on October 31, through online submissions manager only. Prize: $1,000 and publication by University of North Texas Press. Judged by a different eminent writer selected each year. Some prefer to remain anonymous until the end of the contest.

### VENTURA COUNTY WRITERS CLUB POETRY CONTEST

Ventura County Writers Club Poetry Contest, P.O. Box 3373, Thousand Oaks CA 91362. **E-mail:** poetrycontest@venturacountywriters.com. **Website:** www.venturacountywriters.com. **Contact:** Poetry Contest Chair. Annual poetry contest for youth and adult poets. Youth division for poets under 18: Division A is open to entrants ages 13-18; and, Division B is open to poets ages 12 and under. Adult division for poets 18 and older. Club membership not required to enter and entries accepted worldwide as long as fees are paid, poem is unpublished and in English. Enter through website. Deadline: February 14. Entries accepted beginning January 1. Prize: The adult winners will be awarded $100 for first place, $75 for second

and $50 for third place. The two youth categories will receive $50 for first place, $35 for second and $25 for third place.

### MARICA AND JAN VILCEK PRIZE FOR POETRY

Bellevue Literary Review, New York University School of Medicine, OBV-A612, 550 First Ave., New York NY 10016. (212)263-3973. **E-mail:** info@BLReview.org. **Website:** www.BLReview.org. **Contact:** Stacy Bodziak. The annual Marica and Jan Vilcek Prize for Poetry recognizes outstanding writing related to themes of health, healing, illness, the mind, and the body. All entries will be considered for publication. No previously published poems (including Internet publication). Submit up to 3 poems (5 pages maximum). Electronic (online) submissions only; combine all poems into 1 document and use first poem as document title. See guidelines for additional submission details. Guidelines available for SASE or on website. Deadline: July 1. Prize: $1,000 for best poem and publication in *Bellevue Literary Review*. Previous judges include Mark Doty, Cornelius Eady, Naomi Shihab Nye, and Tony Hoagland.

### WABASH PRIZE FOR POETRY

*Sycamore Review*, Department of English, 500 Oval Dr., Purdue University, West Lafayette IN 47907. **E-mail:** sycamore@purdue.edu; sycamorepoetry@purdue.edu. **Website:** www.sycamorereview.com/contest/. **Contact:** Anthony Sutton, editor-in-chief. Annual contest for unpublished poetry. Deadline: December 1. Prize: $1,000 and publication.

### THE WASHINGTON PRIZE

The Word Works, Dearlove Hall, SUNY Adirondack, 640 Bay Rd., Queensbury NY 12804. **E-mail:** editor@wordworksbooks.org. **Website:** www.wordworksbooks.org. **Contact:** Rebecca Kutzer-Rice, Washington Prize administrator. In addition to its general poetry book publications, The Word Works runs four imprints: The Washington Prize, The Tenth Gate Prize, International Editions, and the Hilary Tham Capital Collection. Selections announced in late summer. Book publication planned for spring of the following year. The Washington Prize allows poets from all stages of their careers to compete on a level playing field for publication and national recognition. Deadline: Submit January 15-March 15 (postmark). Prize: $1,500 and publication of a book-length ms of original poetry in English by a living US or Canadian citizen.

Judged by two tiers of readers, followed by five final judges working as a panel.

○ The Washington Prize is open to all American and Canadian poets with a full-length collection ready to publish. Submissions are read blind, so the poets' past publication history is not known by the readers or judges.

## THE ROBERT WATSON LITERARY PRIZE IN FICTION AND POETRY

The Robert Watson Literary Prizes, *The Greensboro Review*, MFA Writing Program, 3302 MHRA Building, Greensboro NC 27402-6170. (336)334-5459. **E-mail:** jlclark@uncg.edu. **Website:** www.greensbororeview.org. **Contact:** Jim Clark, editor. Offered annually for fiction (up to 25 double-spaced pages) and poetry (up to 10 pages). Entries must be unpublished. Open to any writer. Deadline: September 15. Prize: $1,000 each for best short story and poem. Judged by editors of *The Greensboro Review*.

## WERGLE FLOMP HUMOR POETRY CONTEST

Winning Writers, 351 Pleasant St., PMB 222, Northampton MA 01060, USA. (866)946-9748. **Fax:** (413)280-0539. **E-mail:** adam@winningwriters.com. **Website:** www.winningwriters.com. **Contact:** Adam Cohen. Winning Writers provides expert literary contest information to the public. It is one of the "101 Best Websites for Writers" (*Writer's Digest*). Deadline: April 1 Prize: 1st prize of $1,000; 2nd prize of $250; 10 honorable mentions of $100 each. All winners of cash prizes published on website. Judged by Jendi Reiter, assisted by Lauren Singer.

○ This annual contest seeks today's best humor poems. Nonexclusive right to publish winning entries on WinningWriters.com, in e-mail newsletters, in e-books, and in press releases. Competition receives about 4,000 entries/year. Winners are announced on August 15 at WinningWriters.com. Entrants who provide a valid e-mail address will also receive notification.

## ● WESTERN AUSTRALIAN PREMIER'S BOOK AWARDS

State Library of Western Australia, Perth Cultural Centre, 25 Francis St., Perth WA 6000, Australia. (61)(8)9427-3151. **E-mail:** premiersbookawards@slwa.wa.gov.au. **Website:** pba.slwa.wa.gov.au. **Contact:** Karen de San Miguel. Annual competition for Australian citizens or permanent residents of Australia, or writers whose work has Australia as its primary focus. Categories: children's books, digital narrative, fiction, nonfiction, poetry, scripts, writing for young adults, West Australian history, and Western Australian emerging writers. Deadline: January 31. Prize: Awards $25,000 for Premier's Prize; awards $15,000 each for the Children's Books, Digital Narrative, Fiction, and Nonfiction categories; awards $10,000 each for the Poetry, Scripts, Western Australian History, Western Australian Emerging Writers, and Writing for Young Adults; awards $5,000 for People's Choice Award.

## WESTERN HERITAGE AWARDS

National Cowboy & Western Heritage Museum, 1700 NE 63rd St., Oklahoma City OK 73111-7997. (405)478-2250. **Fax:** (405)478-4714. **Website:** www.nationalcowboymuseum.org. **Contact:** Jessica Limestall. The National Cowboy & Western Heritage Museum Western Heritage Awards were established to honor and encourage the legacy of those whose works in literature, music, film, and television reflect the significant stories of the American West. Accepted categories for literary entries: western novel, nonfiction book, art book, photography book, juvenile book, magazine article, or poetry book. The WHA are presented annually to encourage the accurate and artistic telling of great stories of the West through 16 categories of western literature, television, film and music; including fiction, nonfiction, children's books and poetry. See website for details and category definitions. Deadline: November 30. Prize: Awards a Wrangler bronze sculpture designed by famed western artist, John Free. Judged by a panel of judges selected each year with distinction in various fields of western art and heritage.

## WESTMORELAND POETRY & SHORT STORY CONTEST

Westmoreland Arts & Heritage Festival, 252 Twin Lakes Road, Latrobe PA 15650-9415. (724)834-7474. **Fax:** (724)850-7474. **E-mail:** info@artsandheritage.com. **Website:** www.artsandheritage.com. **Contact:** Diane Shrader. Offered annually for unpublished work. Two categories: Poem and Short Story. Short story entries no longer than 4,000 words. Family-oriented festival and contest. Deadline: February 16. Prizes: Award: $200; 1st Place: $125; 2nd Place: $100; 3rd Place: $75.

## STAN AND TOM WICK POETRY PRIZE

Wick Poetry Center, P.O. Box 5190, Kent OH 44240. (330)672-2067. **E-mail:** wickpoetry@kent.edu. **Web-**

site: www.kent.edu/wick/stan-and-tom-wick-poetry-prize. **Contact:** David Hassler, director. Offered annually to a poet who has not previously published a full-length collection of poetry (a volume of 50 or more pages published in an edition of 500 or more copies). Deadline: May 1. Submissions period begins February 1. Prize: $2,500 and publication of full-length book of poetry by Kent State University Press.

## WILLA LITERARY AWARD

**E-mail:** Anneschroederauthor@gmail.com. **Website:** www.womenwritingthewest.org. **Contact:** Anne Schroeder. The WILLA Literary Award honors the year's best in published literature featuring women's or girls' stories set in the West. Women Writing the West (WWW), a nonprofit association of writers and other professionals writing and promoting the Women's West, underwrites and presents the nationally recognized award annually (for work published between January 1 and December 31). The award is named in honor of Pulitzer Prize winner Willa Cather, one of the country's foremost novelists. The award is given in 7 categories: historical fiction, contemporary fiction, original softcover fiction, creative nonfiction, scholarly nonfiction, poetry, and children's/young adult fiction/nonfiction. Entry forms available on the website. Deadline: November 1–February 1. Prize: $100 and a trophy. Finalist receives a plaque. Both receive digital and sticker award emblems for book covers. Notice of Winning and Finalist titles mailed to more than 4,000 booksellers, libraries, and others. Award announcement is in early August, and awards are presented to the winners and finalists at the annual WWW Fall Conference. Judged by professional librarians not affiliated with WWW.

## TENNESSEE WILLIAMS/NEW ORLEANS LITERARY FESTIVAL CONTESTS

Tennessee Williams/New Orleans Literary Festival, 938 Lafayette St., Suite 514, New Orleans LA 70113. (504)581-1144. **E-mail:** info@tennesseewilliams.net. **Website:** www.tennesseewilliams.net/contests. **Contact:** Paul J. Willis. Annual contests for: Unpublished One Act, Unpublished Short Fiction, and Unpublished Poem. "Our competitions provide playwrights an opportunity to see their work fully produced before a large audience during one of the largest literary festivals in the nation, and for the festival to showcase the undiscovered talents of poetry and fiction writers." Deadline: November 1 (One Act); November 15 (Po-

etry); December 1 (Fiction). Prize: One Act: $1,500, staged read at the next festival, full production at the festival the following year, VIP All-Access Festival pass for two years ($1,000 value), and publication in *Bayou*. Poetry: $1,500, public reading at next festival, publication in *Louisiana Cultural Vistas Magazine*. Fiction: $1,500, public reading at next festival, publication in *Louisiana Literature*. Judged by an anonymous expert panel for One Act contest. Judged by special guest judges, who change every year, for fiction and poetry.

## MILLER WILLIAMS POETRY PRIZE

University of Arkansas Press, McIlroy House, 105 N. McIlroy Avenue, Fayetteville AR 72701. (479)575-7258. **Fax:** (479)575-6044. **E-mail:** info@uapress.com; mbieker@uark.edu. **Website:** www.uapress.com. **Contact:** Billy Collins, judge and series editor; Mike Bieker, director. Each year, the University of Arkansas Press accepts submissions for the Miller Williams Poetry Series and from the books selected awards the Miller Williams Poetry Prize in the following summer. Deadline: September 30. Accepts submissions all year long. Prize: $5,000, publication, and featured reading at the University of Arkansas. Judged by Billy Collins, series editor.

## WISCONSIN INSTITUTE FOR CREATIVE WRITING FELLOWSHIP

6195B H.C. White Hall, 600 N. Park St., Madison WI 53706. **E-mail:** rfkuka@wisc.edu. **Website:** creativewriting.wisc.edu/fellowships.html. **Contact:** Sean Bishop, graduate coordinator. Fellowship provides time, space and an intellectual community for writers working on first books. Receives approximately 300 applicants a year for each genre. Judged by English Department faculty and current fellows. Candidates can have up to one published book in the genre for which they are applying. Open to any writer with either an M.F.A. or Ph.D. in creative writing. Please enclose a SASE for notification of results. Results announced on website by May 1. Deadline: Last day of February. Open to submissions on December 15. Prize: $30,000 for a 9-month appointment.

## THE J. HOWARD AND BARBARA M.J. WOOD PRIZE

*Poetry*, 61 W. Superior St., Chicago IL 60654. (312)787-7070. **Fax:** (312)787-6650. **E-mail:** editors@poetrymagazine.org. **Website:** www.poetrymagazine.org. Offered annually for poems published in *Poetry* during the preceding year (October-September). Upon acceptance, *Poetry* licenses exclusive worldwide first serial rights, including electronic rights, for publication, as well as non-exclusive rights to reprint, reuse, and archive the work, in any format, in perpetuity. Copyright reverts to author upon first publication. Prize: $5,000.

## WORKING PEOPLE'S POETRY COMPETITION

Blue Collar Review, P.O. Box 11417, Norfolk VA 23517. **E-mail:** red-ink@earthlink.net. **Website:** www.partisanpress.org. Deadline: May 15. Prize: $100, 1-year subscription to *Blue Collar Review* (see separate listing in Magazines/Journals) and 1-year posting of winning poem to website.

## WORLD'S BEST SHORT-SHORT STORY CONTEST, NARRATIVE NONFICTION CONTEST & SOUTHEAST REVIEW POETRY CONTEST

*The Southeast Review*, Florida State University, English Department, Tallahassee FL 32306. **E-mail:** southeastreview@gmail.com. **Website:** www.southeastreview.org. **Contact:** Erin Hoover, editor. Annual award for unpublished short-short stories (500 words or less), poetry, and narrative nonfiction (6,000 words or less). Visit website for details. Deadline: March 15. Prize: $500 per category. Winners and finalists will be published in *The Southeast Review*.

## JAMES WRIGHT POETRY AWARD

*Mid-American Review*, Dept. of English, Bowling Green State University, Bowling Green OH 43403. (419)372-2725. **Fax:** (419)372-4642. **E-mail:** clouda@bgsu.edu. **Website:** www.bgsu.edu/midamericanreview. **Contact:** Abigail Cloud, poetry editor. Offered annually for unpublished poetry. Open to all writers not associated with *Mid-American Review* or judge. Deadline: November 1. Prize: $1,000 and publication in spring issue of *Mid-American Review*. Judged by editors and a well known poet, i.e., Kathy Fagan, Bob Hicok, Michelle Boisseau.

## WRITER'S DIGEST ANNUAL WRITING COMPETITION

*Writer's Digest*, a publication of F+W Media, Inc., 10151 Carver Rd., Suite 200, Cincinnati OH 45242. (715)445-4612, ext. 13430. **E-mail:** writing-competition@fwmedia.com. **Website:** www.writersdigest.com. Writing contest with 10 categories: Inspirational Writing (spiritual/religious, maximum 2,500 words); Memoir/Personal Essay (maximum 2,000 words); Magazine Feature Article (maximum 2,000 words); Short Story (genre, maximum 4,000 words); Short Story (mainstream/literary, maximum 4,000 words); Rhyming Poetry (maximum 32 lines); Non-rhyming Poetry (maximum 32 lines); Stage Play (first 15 pages and 1-page synopsis); TV/Movie Script (first 15 pages and 1-page synopsis). Entries must be original, in English, unpublished/unproduced (except for Magazine Feature Articles), and not accepted by another publisher/producer at the time of submission. *Writer's Digest* retains one-time publication rights to the winning entries in each category. Deadline: May (early bird); June. Grand Prize: $3,000 and a trip to the Writer's Digest Conference to meet with editors and agents; 1st Place: $1,000 and $100 of Writer's Digest Books; 2nd Place: $500 and $100 of Writer's Digest Books; 3rd Place: $250 and $100 of Writer's Digest Books; 4th Place: $100 and $50 of *Writer's Digest* Books.

## WRITER'S DIGEST SELF-PUBLISHED BOOK AWARDS

*Writer's Digest*, 10151 Carver Road, Suite #200, Blue Ash OH 45242. (715)445-4612, ext. 13430. **E-mail:** WritersDigestSelfPublishingCompetition@fwmedia.com. **Website:** www.writersdigest.com. **Contact:** Nicole Howard. Contest open to all English-language, self-published books for which the authors have paid the full cost of publication, or the cost of printing has been paid for by a grant or as part of a prize. Categories include: Mainstream/Literary Fiction, Genre Fiction, Nonfiction, Inspirational (spiritual/new age), Life Stories (biographies/autobiographies/family histories/memoirs), Children's Books, Reference Books (directories/encyclopedias/guide books), Poetry, and Middle-Grade/Young Adult Books. Judges reserve the right to re-categorize entries. Judges reserve the right to withhold prizes in any category. All winners will be notified in October. Early bird deadline: April 1; Deadline: May 2. Prizes: Grand Prize: $8,000, a trip to the Writer's Digest Conference, promotion in *Writer's Digest*, 10 copies of the book will be sent to major review houses, and a guaranteed review in *Midwest Book Review*; 1st Place (9 winners): $1,000 and promotion in *Writer's Digest*; Honorable Mentions: $50 worth of Writer's Digest Books and promotion on writersdigest.com. All entrants will receive a brief commentary from one of the judges.

## WRITER'S DIGEST SELF-PUBLISHED E-BOOK AWARDS

*Writer's Digest*, 10151 Carver Road, Suite #200, Blue Ash OH 45242. (715)445-4612, ext. 13430. **E-mail:** WritersDigestSelfPublishingCompetition@fwmedia. com. **Website:** www.writersdigest.com. **Contact:** Nicole Howard. Contest open to all English-language, self-published e-books for which the authors have paid the full cost of publication, or the cost of publication has been paid for by a grant or as part of a prize. Categories include: Mainstream/Literary Fiction, Genre Fiction, Nonfiction (includes reference books), Inspirational (spiritual/new age), Life Stories (biographies/autobiographies/family histories/memoirs), Children's Books, Poetry, and Middle-Grade/Young Adult Books. Judges reserve the right to recategorize entries. Judges reserve the right to withhold prizes in any category. All winners will be notified by December 31. Early bird deadline: August 1; Deadline: September 19. Prizes: Grand Prize: $3,000, promotion in *Writer's Digest*, a full 250-word (minimum) editorial review, $200 worth of Writer's Digest Books, and more; 1st Place (9 winners): $1,000 and promotion in *Writer's Digest*; Honorable Mentions: $50 worth of Writer's Digest Books and promotion on writersdigest.com. All entrants will receive a brief commentary from one of the judges.

## WRITERS-EDITORS NETWORK INTERNATIONAL WRITING COMPETITION

CNW Publishing, P.O. Box A, North Stratford NH 03590-0167. **E-mail:** contestentry@writers-editors. com. **E-mail:** info@writers-editors.com. **Website:** www.writers-editors.com. **Contact:** Dana K. Cassell, executive director. Annual award to recognize publishable talent. New categories and awards for 2016: Nonfiction (unpublished or self-published; may be an article, blog post, essay/opinion piece, column, nonfiction book chapter, children's article or book chapter); fiction (unpublished or self-published; may be a short story, novel chapter, Young Adult [YA] or children's story or book chapter); poetry (unpublished or self-published; may be traditional or free verse poetry or children's verse). Guidelines available online. Deadline: March 15. Prize: 1st Place: $150 plus one year Writers-Editors membership; 2nd Place: $100; 3rd Place: $75. All winners and Honor-

able Mentions will receive certificates as warranted. Most Promising entry in each category will receive a free critique by a contest judge. Judged by editors, librarians, and writers.

**TIPS** Review full guidelines and Contest Tip Sheet at http://www.Writers-Editors.com

## ○ WRITERS' GUILD OF ALBERTA AWARDS

Writers' Guild of Alberta, Percy Page Centre, 11759 Groat Rd., Edmonton AB T5M 3K6, Canada. (780)422-8174. **Fax:** (780)422-2663. **E-mail:** mail@writersguild. ca. **Website:** writersguild.ca. **Contact:** Executive Director. Offers the following awards: Wilfrid Eggleston Award for Nonfiction; Georges Bugnet Award for Fiction; Howard O'Hagan Award for Short Story; Stephan G. Stephansson Award for Poetry; R. Ross Annett Award for Children's Literature; Gwen Pharis Ringwood Award for Drama; Jon Whyte Memorial Essay Award; James H. Gray Award for Short Nonfiction. Deadline: December 31. Prize: Winning authors receive $1,500; short piece prize winners receive $700.

## THE YALE SERIES OF YOUNGER POETS

Yale University Press, P.O. Box 209040, New Haven CT 06520-9040. **Website:** youngerpoets.yupnet.org. The Yale Series of Younger Poets champions the most promising new American poets. The Yale Younger Poets prize is the oldest annual literary award in the United States. Deadline: November 15. Submissions period begins October 1.

## THE YEMASSEE POETRY CONTEST

*Yemassee*, Department of English, University of South Carolina, Columbia SC 29208. **E-mail:** editor@yemasseejournal.com. **Website:** http://yemasseejournal.com. **Contact:** Contest Coordinator. The annual Yemassee Poetry Contest offers a $1000 prize and publication in *Yemassee*. Deadline: January 15.

## ZONE 3 FIRST BOOK AWARD FOR POETRY

*Zone 3*, Austin Peay State University, Austin Peay State University, PO Box 4565, Clarksville TN 37044. (931)221-7031. **Fax:** (931)221-7149. **E-mail:** spofforda@aspu.edu; wallacess@apsu.edu. **Website:** www.apsu.edu/zone3/. **Contact:** Andrea Spofford, poetry editor; Susan Wallace, managing editor. Offered annually for anyone who has not published a full-length collection of poems (48 pages or more). Submit a ms of 48-80 pages. Deadline: April 15. Prize: $1,000 and publication.

# GRANTS

## State & Provincial

////////////////////////////////////////////////////////////////////////////////////////////////////

Arts councils provide assistance to artists (including poets) in the form of fellowships or grants. These grants can be substantial and confer prestige upon recipients; however, only state or province residents are eligible. Check websites for guidelines.

## UNITED STATES ARTS AGENCIES

**ALABAMA STATE COUNCIL ON THE ARTS,** 201 Monroe St., Montgomery AL 36130-1800. (334)242-4076. E-mail: staff@arts.alabama.gov. Website: www.arts.state.al.us.

**ALASKA STATE COUNCIL ON THE ARTS,** 411 W. Fourth Ave., Suite 1-E, Anchorage AK 99501-2343. E-mail: aksca_info@eed.state.ak.us. Website: www.eed.state.ak.us/aksca.

**ARIZONA COMMISSION ON THE ARTS,** 417 W. Roosevelt St., Phoenix AZ 85003-1326. (602)771-6501. E-mail: info@azarts.gov. Website: www.azarts.gov.

**ARKANSAS ARTS COUNCIL,** 1500 Tower Bldg., 323 Center St., Little Rock AR 72201. (501)324-9766. E-mail: info@arkansasarts.com. Website: www.arkansasarts.com.

**CALIFORNIA ARTS COUNCIL,** 1300 I St., Suite 930, Sacramento CA 95814. (916)322-6555. E-mail: info@caartscouncil.com. Website: www.cac.ca.gov.

**COLORADO COUNCIL ON THE ARTS,** 1625 Broadway, Suite 2700, Denver CO 80202. (303)892-3802. E-mail: online form. Website: www.coloarts.state.co.us.

**COMMONWEALTH COUNCIL FOR ARTS AND CULTURE,** P.O. Box 5553, CHRB, Saipan MP 96950. E-mail: galaidi@vzpacifica.net. Website: www.geocities.com/ccacarts/ccacwebsite.html.

**CONNECTICUT COMMISSION ON CULTURE & TOURISM,** Arts Division, One Financial Plaza, 755 Main St., Hartford CT 06103. (860)256-2800. Website: www.cultureandtourism.org.

**DELAWARE DIVISION OF THE ARTS,** Carvel State Office Bldg., 4th Floor, 820 N. French St., Wilmington DE 19801. E-mail: delarts@state.de.us. Website: www.artsdel.org.

**DISTRICT OF COLUMBIA COMMISSION ON THE ARTS & HUMANITIES,** 410 Eighth St. NW, 5th Floor, Washington DC 20004. E-mail: cah@dc.gov. Website: http://dcarts.dc.gov.

**FLORIDA ARTS COUNCIL,** Division of Cultural Affairs, R.A. Gray Building, Third Floor, 500 S. Bronough St., Tallahassee FL 32399-0250. (850)245-6470. E-mail: info@florida-arts.org. Website: http://dcarts.dc.gov.

**GEORGIA COUNCIL FOR THE ARTS,** 260 14th St., Suite 401, Atlanta GA 30318. (404)685-2787. E-mail: gaarts@gaarts.org. Website: www.gaarts.org.

**GUAM COUNCIL ON THE ARTS & HUMANITIES AGENCY,** P.O. Box 2950, Hagatna GU 96932. (671)646-2781. Website: www.guam.net.

**HAWAII STATE FOUNDATION ON CULTURE & THE ARTS,** 2500 S. Hotel St., 2nd Floor, Honolulu HI 96813. (808)586-0300. E-mail: ken.hamilton@hawaii.gov. Website: http.state.hi.us/sfca.

**IDAHO COMMISSION ON THE ARTS,** 2410 N. Old Penitentiary Rd., Boise ID 83712. (208)334-2119 or (800)278-3863. E-mail: info@arts.idaho.gov. Website: www.arts.idaho.gov.

**ILLINOIS ARTS COUNCIL,** James R. Thompson Center, 100 W. Randolph, Suite 10-500, Chicago IL 60601. (312)814-6750. E-mail: iac.info@illinois.gov. Website: www.state.il.us/agency/iac.

**INDIANA ARTS COMMISSION,** 150 W. Market St., Suite 618, Indianapolis IN 46204. (317)232-1268. E-mail: IndianaArtsCommission@iac.in.gov. Website: www.in.gov/arts.

**INSTITUTE OF PUERTO RICAN CULTURE,** P.O. Box 9024184, San Juan PR 00902-4184. (787)724-0700. E-mail: www@icp.gobierno.pr. Website: www.icp.gobierno.pr.

**IOWA ARTS COUNCIL,** 600 E. Locust, Des Moines IA 50319-0290. (515)281-6412. Website: www.iowaartscouncil.org.

**KANSAS ARTS COMMISSION,** 700 SW Jackson, Suite 1004, Topeka KS 66603-3761. (785)296-3335. E-mail: KAC@arts.state.ks.us. Website: http://arts.state.ks.us.

**KENTUCKY ARTS COUNCIL,** 21st Floor, Capital Plaza Tower, 500 Mero St., Frankfort KY 40601-1987. E-mail: kyarts@ky.gov. Website: http://artscouncil.ky.gov.

**LOUISIANA DIVISION OF THE ARTS,** Capitol Annex Bldg., 1051 N. 3rd St., 4th Floor, Room #420, Baton Rouge LA 70804. (225)342-8180. Website: www.crt.state.la.us/arts.

**MAINE ARTS COMMISSION,** 193 State St., 25 State House Station, Augusta ME 04333-0025. (207)287-2724. E-mail: MaineArts.info@maine.gov. Website: www.mainearts.com.

**MARYLAND STATE ARTS COUNCIL,** 175 W. Ostend St., Suite E, Baltimore MD 21230. (410)767-6555. E-mail: msac@msac.org. Website: www.msac.org.

**MASSACHUSETTS CULTURAL COUNCIL,** 10 St. James Ave., 3rd Floor, Boston MA 02116-3803. (617)727-3668. E-mail: mcc@art.state.ma.us. Website: www.massculturalcouncil.org.

**MICHIGAN COUNCIL OF HISTORY, ARTS, AND LIBRARIES,** 702 W. Kalamazoo St., P.O. Box 30705, Lansing MI 48909-8205. (517)241-4011. E-mail: artsinfo@michigan.gov. Website: www.michigan.gov/hal/0,1607,7-160-17445_19272---,00.html.

**MINNESOTA STATE ARTS BOARD,** Park Square Court, 400 Sibley St., Suite 200, St. Paul MN 55101-1928. (651)215-1600 or (800)866-2787. E-mail: msab@arts.state.mn.us. Website: www.arts.state.mn.us.

**MISSISSIPPI ARTS COMMISSION,** 501 N. West St., Suite 701B, Woolfolk Bldg., Jackson MS 39201. (601)359-6030. Website: www.arts.state.ms.us.

**MISSOURI ARTS COUNCIL,** 815 Olive St., Suite 16, St. Louis MO 63101-1503. (314)340-6845 or (866)407-4752. E-mail: moarts@ded.mo.gov. Website: www.missouriartscouncil.org.

**MONTANA ARTS COUNCIL,** 316 N. Park Ave., Suite 252, Helena MT 59620-2201. (406)444-6430. E-mail: mac@mt.gov. Website: www.art.state.mt.us.

**NATIONAL ASSEMBLY OF STATE ARTS AGENCIES,** 1029 Vermont Ave. NW, 2nd Floor, Washington DC 20005. E-mail: nasaa@nasaa-arts.org. Website: www.nasaa-arts.org.

**NEBRASKA ARTS COUNCIL,** 1004 Farnam St., Plaza Level, Omaha NE 68102. (402)595-2122 or (800)341-4067. Website: www.nebraskaartscouncil.org.

**NEVADA ARTS COUNCIL,** 716 N. Carson St., Suite A, Carson City NV 89701. (775)687-6680. E-mail: online form. Website: http://dmla.clan.lib.nv.us/docs/arts.

**NEW HAMPSHIRE STATE COUNCIL ON THE ARTS,** 21/2 Beacon St., 2nd Floor, Concord NH 03301-4974. (603)271-2789. Website: www.nh.gov/nharts.

**NEW JERSEY STATE COUNCIL ON THE ARTS,** 225 W. State St., P.O. Box 306, Trenton NJ 08625. (609)292-6130. Website: www.njartscouncil.org.

**NEW MEXICO ARTS, DEPT. OF CULTURAL AFFAIRS,** P.O. Box 1450, Santa Fe NM 87504-1450. (505)827-6490 or (800)879-4278. Website: www.nmarts.org.

**NEW YORK STATE COUNCIL ON THE ARTS,** 175 Varick St., New York NY 10014. (212)627-4455. Website: www.nysca.org.

**NORTH CAROLINA ARTS COUNCIL,** 109 East Jones St., Cultural Resources Building, Raleigh NC 27601. (919)807-6500. E-mail: ncarts@ncmail.net. Website: www.ncarts.org.

**NORTH DAKOTA COUNCIL ON THE ARTS,** 1600 E. Century Ave., Suite 6, Bismarck ND 58503. (701)328-7590. E-mail: comserv@state.nd.us. Website: www.state.nd.us/arts.

**OHIO ARTS COUNCIL,** 727 E. Main St., Columbus OH 43205-1796. (614)466-2613. Website: www.oac.state.oh.us.

**OKLAHOMA ARTS COUNCIL,** Jim Thorpe Building, 2101 N. Lincoln Blvd., Suite 640, Oklahoma City OK 73105. (405)521-2931. E-mail: okarts@arts.ok.gov. Website: www.arts.state.ok.us.

**OREGON ARTS COMMISSION,** 775 Summer St. NE, Suite 200, Salem OR 97301-1280. E-mail: oregon.artscomm@state.or.us. Website: www.oregonartscommission.org.

**PENNSYLVANIA COUNCIL ON THE ARTS,** 216 Finance Bldg., Harrisburg PA 17120. (717)787-6883. Website: www.pacouncilonthearts.org.

**RHODE ISLAND STATE COUNCIL ON THE ARTS,** One Capitol Hill, Third Floor, Providence RI 02908. (401)222-3880. E-mail: info@arts.ri.gov. Website: www.arts.ri.gov.

**SOUTH CAROLINA ARTS COMMISSION,** 1800 Gervais St., Columbia SC 29201. (803)734-8696. E-mail: info@arts.state.sc.us. Website: www.southcarolinaarts.com.

**SOUTH DAKOTA ARTS COUNCIL,** 711 E. Wells Ave., Pierre SD 57501-3369. (605)773-3301. E-mail: sdac@state.sd.us. Website: www.artscouncil.sd.gov.

**TENNESSEE ARTS COMMISSION,** 401 Charlotte Ave., Nashville TN 37243-0780. (615)741-1701. Website: www.arts.state.tn.us.

**TEXAS COMMISSION ON THE ARTS,** E.O. Thompson Office Building, 920 Colorado, Suite 501, Austin TX 78701. (512)463-5535. E-mail: front.desk@arts.state.tx.us. Website: www.arts.state.tx.us.

**UTAH ARTS COUNCIL,** 617 E. South Temple, Salt Lake City UT 84102-1177. (801)236-7555. Website: http://arts.utah.gov.

**VERMONT ARTS COUNCIL,** 136 State St., Drawer 33, Montpelier VT 05633-6001. (802)828-3291. E-mail: online form. Website: www.vermontartscouncil.org.

**VIRGIN ISLANDS COUNCIL ON THE ARTS,** 5070 Norre Gade, St. Thomas VI 00802-6872. (340)774-5984. Website: http://vicouncilonarts.org.

**VIRGINIA COMMISSION FOR THE ARTS,** Lewis House, 223 Governor St., 2nd Floor, Richmond VA 23219. (804)225-3132. E-mail: arts@arts.virginia.gov. Website: www.arts.state.va.us.

**WASHINGTON STATE ARTS COMMISSION,** 711 Capitol Way S., Suite 600, P.O. Box 42675, Olympia WA 98504-2675. (360)753-3860. E-mail: info@arts.wa.gov. Website: www.arts.wa.gov.

**WEST VIRGINIA COMMISSION ON THE ARTS,** The Cultural Center, Capitol Complex, 1900 Kanawha Blvd. E., Charleston WV 25305-0300. (304)558-0220. Website: www.wvculture.org/arts.

**WISCONSIN ARTS BOARD,** 101 E. Wilson St., 1st Floor, Madison WI 53702. (608)266-0190. E-mail: artsboard@arts.state.wi.us. Website: www.arts.state.wi.us.

**WYOMING ARTS COUNCIL,** 2320 Capitol Ave., Cheyenne WY 82002. (307)777-7742. E-mail: ebratt@state.wy.us. Website: http://wyoarts.state.wy.us.

## CANADIAN PROVINCES ARTS AGENCIES

**ALBERTA FOUNDATION FOR THE ARTS,** 10708-105 Ave., Edmonton AB T5H 0A1. (780)427-9968. Website: www.affta.ab.ca/index.shtml.

**BRITISH COLUMBIA ARTS COUNCIL,** P.O. Box 9819, Stn. Prov. Govt., Victoria BC V8W 9W3. (250)356-1718. E-mail: BCArtsCouncil@gov.bc.ca. Website: www.bcartscouncil.ca.

**THE CANADA COUNCIL FOR THE ARTS,** 350 Albert St., P.O. Box 1047, Ottawa ON K1P 5V8. (613)566-4414 or (800)263-5588 (within Canada). Website: www.canadacouncil.ca.

**MANITOBA ARTS COUNCIL,** 525-93 Lombard Ave., Winnipeg MB R3B 3B1. (204)945-2237 or (866)994-2787 (in Manitoba). E-mail: info@artscouncil.mb.ca. Website: www.artscouncil.mb.ca.

**NEW BRUNSWICK ARTS BOARD (NBAB),** 634 Queen St., Suite 300, Fredericton NB E3B 1C2. (506)444-4444 or (866)460-2787. Website: www.artsnb.ca.

**NEWFOUNDLAND & LABRADOR ARTS COUNCIL,** P.O. Box 98, St. John's NL A1C 5H5. (709)726-2212 or (866)726-2212. E-mail: nlacmail@nfld.net. Website: www.nlac.nf.ca.

**NOVA SCOTIA DEPARTMENT OF TOURISM, CULTURE, AND HERITAGE,** Culture Division, 1800 Argyle St., Suite 601, P.O. Box 456, Halifax NS B3J 2R5. (902)424-4510. E-mail: cultaffs@gov.ns.ca. Website: www.gov.ns.ca/dtc/culture.

**ONTARIO ARTS COUNCIL,** 151 Bloor St. W., 5th Floor, Toronto ON M5S 1T6. (416)961-1660 or (800)387-0058 (in Ontario). E-mail: info@arts.on.ca. Website: www.arts.on.ca.

**PRINCE EDWARD ISLAND COUNCIL OF THE ARTS,** 115 Richmond St., Charlottetown PE C1A 1H7. (902)368-4410 or (888)734-2784. E-mail: info@peiartscouncil.com. Website: www.peiartscouncil.com.

**QUÉBEC COUNCIL FOR ARTS & LITERATURE,** 79 boul. René-Lévesque Est, 3e étage, Quebec QC G1R 5N5. (418)643-1707 or (800)897-1707. E-mail: info@calq.gouv.qc.ca. Website: www.calq.gouv.qc.ca.

**THE SASKATCHEWAN ARTS BOARD,** 2135 Broad St., Regina SK S4P 1Y6. (306)787-4056 or (800)667-7526 (Saskatchewan only). E-mail: sab@artsboard.sk.ca. Website: www.artsboard.sk.ca.

**YUKON ARTS FUNDING PROGRAM,** Cultural Services Branch, Dept. of Tourism & Culture, Government of Yukon, Box 2703 (L-3), Whitehorse YT Y1A 2C6. (867)667-8589 or (800)661-0408 (in Yukon). E-mail: arts@gov.yk.ca. Website: www.tc.gov.yk.ca/216.html.

# CONFERENCES, WORKSHOPS & FESTIVALS

There are times when we want to immerse ourselves in learning. Or perhaps we crave a change of scenery, the creative stimulation of being around other artists, or the uninterrupted productivity of time alone to work.

That's what this section of *Poet's Market* is all about, providing a selection of writing conferences and workshops, artist colonies and retreats, poetry festivals, and even a few opportunities to go traveling with your muse. These listings give the basics: contact information, a brief description of the event, lists of past presenters, and offerings of special interest to poets. Contact an event that interests you for additional information, including up-to-date costs and housing details. (Please note that most directors had not finalized their 2017 plans when we contacted them for this edition of *Poet's Market*. However, where possible, they provided us with their 2016 dates, costs, faculty names or themes to give you a better idea of what each event has to offer.)

Before you seriously consider a conference, workshop or other event, determine what you hope to get out of the experience. Would a general conference with one or two poetry workshops among many other types of sessions be acceptable? Or are you looking for something exclusively focused on poetry? Do you want to hear poets speak about poetry writing, or are you looking for a more participatory experience, such as a one-on-one critiquing session or a group workshop? Do you mind being one of hundreds of attendees, or do you prefer a more intimate setting? Are you willing to invest in the expense of traveling to a conference, or would something local better suit your budget? Keep these questions and others in mind as you read these listings, view websites and study conference brochures.

## ABROAD WRITERS CONFERENCES

17363 Sutter Creek Rd., (209)296-4052. **E-mail:** abroadwriters@yahoo.com; nancy@abroadwritersconference.com. **Website:** http://abroadwritersconference.com/. "Abroad Writers Conferences are devoted to introducing our participants to world views here in the United States and Abroad. Throughout the world we invite several authors to come join us to give readings and to participate on a panel. Our discussion groups touch upon a wide range of topics from important issues of our times to publishing abroad and in the United States. Our objective is to broaden our cultural and scientific perspectives of the world through discourse and writing." Conferences are held throughout the year in various places worldwide. See website for scheduling details. Conference duration: 7-10 days. "Instead of being lost in a crowd at a large conference, Abroad Writers Conference prides itself on holding small group meetings where participants have personal contact with everyone. Stimulating talks, interviews, readings, Q&A's, writing workshops, film screenings, private consultations and social gatherings all take place within a week to ten days. Abroad Writers' Conference promises you true networking opportunities and full detailed feedback on your writing."

**COSTS/ACCOMMODATIONS** See website for details.

**ADDITIONAL INFORMATION** Agents participate in conference. Application is online at website.

## AMERICAN CHRISTIAN WRITERS CONFERENCES

P.O. Box 110390, Nashville TN 37222-0390. (800)219-7483, (800)21-WRITE. **E-mail:** ACWriters@aol.com. **Website:** www.ACWriters.com. **Contact:** Reg Forder, director. ACW hosts a dozen annual two-day writers conferences and mentoring retreats across America taught by editors and professional freelance writers. These events provide excellent instruction, networking opportunities, and valuable one-on-one time with editors. Annual conferences promoting all forms of Christian writing (fiction, nonfiction, scriptwriting). Conferences are held between March and November during each year.

**COSTS/ACCOMMODATIONS** Special rates are available at the host hotel (usually a major chain like Holiday Inn). Costs vary based on conference. Prices also depend on whether it is a conference or a mentoring retreat.

**ADDITIONAL INFORMATION** Email or call for conference brochures

## ANAM CARA WRITER'S AND ARTIST'S RETREAT

Eyeries, Beara, Co. Cork, Ireland. (353)(027)74441. **Fax:** (353)(027)74448. **E-mail:** anamcararetreat@gmail.com. **Website:** www.anamcararetreat.com. **Contact:** Sue Booth-Forbes, director.

**COSTS/ACCOMMODATIONS** 2016 costs are available upon request. The event features editorial consulting, laundry, sauna, hot tub overlooking Coulagh Bay, 5 acres of gardens, meadows, riverbank and cascades, river island, swimming hole, and several unique working spots, such as the ruin of a stone mill and a sod-roofed beehive hut. Overflow from workshops stay in nearby B&Bs, a 10-minute walk or 2-minute drive away. Transportation provided if needed. Details regarding workshops scheduled for 2016 and their fees as well as transportation to Anam Cara are available on the website.

**ADDITIONAL INFORMATION** Requests for specific information about rates and availability can be made through the website.

## ANNUAL SPRING POETRY FESTIVAL

City College, 160 Convent Ave., New York NY 10031. (212)650-6356. **Website:** www1.ccny.cuny.edu/prospective/humanities/poetry. Writer workshops geared to all levels. **Open to students.** Annual poetry festival. 2016 dates: May 13, 2016. Write for more information. Site: Theater B of Aaron Davis Hall.

## ART WORKSHOPS IN GUATEMALA

4758 Lyndale Ave. S., Minneapolis MN 55419-5304. (612)825-0747. **E-mail:** info@artguat.org. **Website:** www.artguat.org. **Contact:** Liza Fourre, director. Art & cultural workshops held year-round. Maximim class size: 10 students per class.

**COSTS/ACCOMMODATIONS** All transportation and accommodations included in price of conference.

**ADDITIONAL INFORMATION** Conference information available. For brochure/guidelines visit website, e-mail or call. Accepts inquiries by e-mail, phone.

## ASPEN SUMMER WORDS LITERARY FESTIVAL & WRITING RETREAT

Aspen Words, 110 E. Hallam St., #116, Aspen CO 81611. (970)925-3122. **Fax:** (970)925-5700. **E-mail:** aspenwords@aspeninstitute.org. **Website:** www.aspenwords.org. **Contact:** Caroline Tory, programs coordinator. 2016 dates: June 19-24. The 40th annual Aspen Summer Words Writing Retreat and Literary Festival offers workshops in fiction, memoir, novel editing, and playwriting. The faculty includes fiction writers Ann Hood, Richard Russo, Akhil Sharma, and Hannah Tinti; memoir writers Andre Dubus III and Dani Shapiro; and playwright Sharr White. Aspen Summer Words features lectures, readings, panel discussions, and the opportunity to meet with agents and editors. Tuition for the writing workshops is $1,375, which includes some meals. Financial aid is available on a limited basis. To apply for a juried workshop, submit up to 10 pages of prose with a $30 application fee by February 26. Registration to non-juried workshops (Beginning Fiction and Playwriting) is first-come, first-served. Call, e-mail, or visit the website for an application and complete guidelines.

## ASSOCIATION OF WRITERS & WRITING PROGRAMS ANNUAL CONFERENCE

Association of Writers & Writing Programs, George Mason University, 4400 University Drive, MSN 1E3, Fairfax VA 22030-4444. (703)993-4317. **Fax:** (703)993-4302. **E-mail:** conference@awpwriter.org; events@awpwriter.org. **Website:** www.awpwriter.org/awp_conference. Each year, AWP holds its Annual Conference & Bookfair in a different city to celebrate the authors, teachers, writing programs, literary centers, and independent publishers of that region. The conference typically features hundreds of readings, lectures, panel discussions, and forums, as well as hundreds of book signings, receptions, dances, and informal gatherings. AWP's is now the largest literary conference in North America.

**ADDITIONAL INFORMATION** Upcoming conference locations include Los Angeles (March 30-April 2, 2016), and Washington, D.C. (February 8-11, 2017).

## ATLANTIC CENTER FOR THE ARTS

1414 Art Center Ave., New Smyrna Beach FL 32168. (386)427-6975. **E-mail:** program@atlanticcenterforthearts.org. **Website:** www.atlanticcenterforthearts.org. Internship and residency programs. A Florida artist-in-residence program in which artists of all disciplines work with current prominent artists in a supportive and creative environment.

**COSTS/ACCOMMODATIONS** $900; $25 nonrefundable application fee. Financial aid is available. Participants responsible for all materials, transportation, and weekend meals. Accommodations avail-

able on site. See website for application schedule and materials.

## AUSTIN INTERNATIONAL POETRY FESTIVAL

(512)777-1888. **E-mail:** mark@aipf.org; aipfest@outlook.com. **Website:** www.aipf.org. **Contact:** Mark Wendel. The 24th Austin International Poetry Festival (AIPF) will be held April 7-10, 2016. Registration is required for all poets. Nikki Giovanni was featured during the 2015 conference. This four-day citywide, all-inclusive celebration of poetry and poets has grown to become "the largest non-juried poetry festival in the U.S." The festival will include a minimum of the following: 20 readings, one youth anthology read, 10 workshops, 5 open mics, 2 music and poetry presentations, 2 anthology competitions and complete readings, 2 poetry slams, an all-night open mic and a poetry panel symposium. Additional information available online at www.aipf.org. Discount registration fees available for retired, college students, and military poets.

**COSTS/ACCOMMODATIONS** Includes anthology submission fee, program bio, scheduled reading at one of AIPF's 15 venues, participation in all events, 1 catered meal, workshop participation, and more.

**ADDITIONAL INFORMATION** Offers multiple poetry contests as part of festival. Guidelines available on website. Registration form available on website. "Largest non-juried poetry festival in the U.S."

## BREAD LOAF WRITERS' CONFERENCE

Middlebury College, Middlebury College, Middlebury VT 05753. (802)443-5286. **Fax:** (802)443-2087. **E-mail:** blwc@middlebury.edu. **Website:** www.middlebury.edu/bread-loaf-conferences/bl_writers. Annual conference held in late August. Conference duration: 10 days. Offers workshops for fiction, nonfiction, and poetry. Agents and editors will be in attendance.

**COSTS/ACCOMMODATIONS** Bread Loaf Campus in Ripton, Vermont.

**ADDITIONAL INFORMATION** 2016 Conference Dates: August 10-20. Location: Bread Loaf campus of Middlebury College in Vermont. Average attendance: 230. The application deadline for the 2016 event is March 1, 2015; there is $15 application fee.

## CAPE COD WRITERS CENTER ANNUAL CONFERENCE

P.O. Box 408, Osterville MA 02655. **E-mail:** writers@capecodwriterscenter.org. **Website:** www.capecodwriterscenter.org. **Contact:** Nancy Rubin Stuart, executive director. Duration: 3 days; held during first week in August. Offers workshops in fiction, commercial fiction, nonfiction, poetry, writing for children, memoir, pitching your book, screenwriting, digital communications, and getting published. There are ms evaluation and mentoring sessions with faculty.

**COSTS/ACCOMMODATIONS** Held at Resort and Conference Center of Hyannis, Hyannis, MA. Costs vary, depending on the number of courses selected.

## CAVE CANEM

20 Jay St., Suite 310-A, Brooklyn NY 11201. (718)858-0000. **Fax:** (718)858-0002. **E-mail:** alisonmeyers@ccpoets.org. **Website:** www.cavecanempoets.org. **Contact:** Alison Meyers, Executive Director.

**COSTS/ACCOMMODATIONS** Costs vary by workshop. Check website for updated information.

## CELEBRATION OF SOUTHERN LITERATURE

Southern Lit Alliance, 3069 S. Broad St., Suite 2, Chattanooga TN 37408-3056. (423)267-1218. **Fax:** (866)483-6831. **E-mail:** srobinson@southernlitalliance.org. **Website:** www.southernlitalliance.org. **Contact:** Susan Robinson. "The Celebration of Southern Literature stands out because of its unique collaboration with the Fellowship of Southern Writers, an organization founded by towering literary figures like Eudora Welty, Cleanth Brooks, Walker Percy, and Robert Penn Warren to recognize and encourage literature in the South. The Fellowship awards 11 literary prizes and induct new members, making this event the place to discover up-and-coming voices in Southern literature. The Southern Lit Alliance's Celebration of Southern Literature attracts more than 1,000 readers and writers from all over the U.S. It strives to maintain an informal atmosphere where conversations will thrive, inspired by a common passion for the written word. The Southern Lit Alliance (formerly The Arts & Education Council) started as 1 of 12 pilot agencies founded by a Ford Foundation grant in 1952. The Alliance is the only organization of the 12 still in existence. The Southern Lit Alliance celebrates southern writers and readers through community education and innovative literary arts experiences."

This event happens every other year in odd-numbered years.

## CHAUTAUQUA WRITERS' CENTER

P.O. Box 28, Chautauqua NY 14722. **Website:** ciweb. org/season/literary-arts/writers-center.

**COSTS/ACCOMMODATIONS** Tuition: $110/all stages workshop; $150/advanced poetry workshop. See website for accommodations options, which range from the Athenaeum Hotel to local rooming houses and condos.

## COLGATE WRITERS' CONFERENCE

Office of Summer Programs, Colgate University, 13 Oak Dr., Hamilton NY 13346. (315)228-7770. **E-mail:** writersconference@colgate.edu. **Website:** www.colgate.edu/community/summerprograms/adult-programs/colgate-writers-conference. Conferene: June 12-18. Retreat application date: May 15.

**COSTS/ACCOMMODATIONS** 2016 cost: for poetry workshop, $1,095 (tuition, room, and board); $845 for day students. Meal plan available for day students. Accommodations available on site.

**ADDITIONAL INFORMATION** Each applicant must submit a ms with his/her application. Brochure and registration form available for SASE or on website.

## THE COLRAIN POETRY MANUSCRIPT CONFERENCE

**Website:** www.colrainpoetry.com. "Colrain is the original, one-of-a-kind manuscript conference. Faculty includes nationally-renowned poet-editors and publishers. Work with the best for the best results. Our unique, realistic method of manuscript evaluation sets poets with a manuscript-in-progress on a path toward publication. Poets also get a look into the publication world and make important contacts with leading editors, teachers, and publishers."

**COSTS/ACCOMMODATIONS** The first Colrain Classic is March 11-14, 2016 in Massachusetts. The second Colarin Classic is April 29-May 12, 2016 in Maine. The third Colrain Classic is June 10-13, 2016 in New Mexico.

**ADDITIONAL INFORMATION** Details, application, and registration form available on website.

## GERALDINE R. DODGE POETRY FESTIVAL

**Website:** www.dodgepoetryfestival.org.

**COSTS/ACCOMMODATIONS** Check website for latest information. Passes can be purchased at a discount for multiple days. Audience members responsible for own lodging and meals. Information on overnight accommodations available on website.

**ADDITIONAL INFORMATION** Sign up online for mailing list.

## FINE ARTS WORK CENTER

24 Pearl St., Provincetown MA 02657. (508)487-9960, ext. 103. **Fax:** (508)487-8873. **E-mail:** workshops@fawc.org. **Website:** www.fawc.org.

**COSTS/ACCOMMODATIONS** Summer Workshop Program fees range $600-725. Limited accommodations available at the Work Center for $700 for 6 nights. Additional accommodations available locally. Cost: $600-725/week, $675/week (housing).

**ADDITIONAL INFORMATION** See website for details and an application form.

## THE FROST PLACE CONFERENCE ON POETRY

The Frost Place, P.O. Box 74, Franconia NH 03580. (603)823-5510. **E-mail:** frost@frostplace.org. **Website:** www.frostplace.org. 2016 conference: July 10-16. More information online.

## THE FROST PLACE SEMINAR ON POETRY AND TEACHING

The Frost Place, P.O. Box 74, Franconia NH 03580. (603)823-5510. **E-mail:** frost@frostplace.org. **Website:** www.frostplace.org. 2016 conference: June 25-29. More details online.

## GREAT LAKES WRITERS FESTIVAL

Lakeland College, P.O. Box 359, Sheboygan WI 53082-0359. **E-mail:** elderk@lakeland.edu. **Website:** www.greatlakeswritersfestival.org. Annual. Last conference held November 5-6, 2015. Conference duration: 2 days. "Festival celebrates the writing of poetry, fiction, and creative nonfiction." Site: "Lakeland College is a small, 4-year liberal arts college of 235 acres, a beautiful campus in a rural setting, founded in 1862." No themes or panels; just readings and workshops.

**COSTS/ACCOMMODATIONS** Does not offer overnight accommodations. Provides list of area hotels or lodging options. Free and open to the public. Participants may purchase meals and must arrange for their own lodging.

**ADDITIONAL INFORMATION** All participants who would like to have their writing considered as an object for discussion during the festival workshops should submit it to Karl Elder electronically by October 15. Participants may submit material for workshops in 1 genre only (poetry, fiction, or creative nonfiction). Sponsors contest. Contest entries must contain the writer's name and address on a separate title page, typed, and be submitted as clear, hard copy on Friday at the festival registration table. Entries may be in each of 3 genres per participant, yet only 1 poem, 1 story, and/or 1nonfiction piece may be entered. There are 2 categories—high school students on 1 hand, all others on the other—of cash awards for first place in each of the 3 genres. Information available in September. For brochure, visit website.

## HAIKU NORTH AMERICA CONFERENCE

1275 Fourth St., PMB 365, Santa Rosa CA 95404. **E-mail:** welchm@aol.com. **Website:** www.haikunorthamerica.com. **Contact:** Michael Dylan Welch. Biennial conference. 2017 dates: Sept 13-17, in Santa Fe, N.M. Haiku North America (HNA) is the largest and oldest gathering of haiku poets in the United States and Canada. There are no membership fees and HNA provides breaking news and interaction at the HNA blog. All haiku poets and interested parties are welcome. HNA is a long weekend of papers, panels, workshops, readings, performances, book sales, and much socialization with fellow poets, translators, scholars, editors, and publishers. Both established and aspiring haiku poets are welcome.

**COSTS/ACCOMMODATIONS** Accommodations at discounted hotels nearby are an additional cost. Information available on website as details are finalized closer to the conference date. Typically around $200, including a banquet and a conference anthology.

## HIGHLAND SUMMER CONFERENCE

Box 7014, Radford University, Radford VA 24142-7014. **E-mail:** tburriss@radford.edu; rbderrick@radford.edu. **Website:** tinyurl.com/q8z8ej9. **Contact:** Dr. Theresa Burriss, Ruth Derrick. 2015 dates: June 15-19. The Highland Summer Writers' Conference is a 4-day lecture-seminar workshop combination conducted by well-known guest writers. It offers the opportunity to study and practice creative and expository writing within the context of regional culture. The course is graded on Pass/Fail basis for undergraduates and letter grades for graduate students. It may be taken twice for credit. The evening readings are free and open to the public. Services at a reduced rate for continuing education credits or to simply participate.

## HOFSTRA UNIVERSITY SUMMER WRITING WORKSHOPS

University College for Continuing Education, 250 Hofstra University, Hempstead NY 11549-2500.

(516)463-7200. **Fax:** (516)463-4833. **E-mail:** ce@hofstra.edu. **Website:** www.hofstra.edu/ucce/summerwriting/. Summer Writers Program, a cooperative endeavor of the Creative Writing Program, the English Department, and Hofstra University Continuing Education (Hofstra CE), offers classes which may be taken on a noncredit or credit basis, for both graduate and undergraduate students. Led by master writers, the Summer Writing Program operates on the principle that true writing talent can be developed, nurtured and encouraged by writer-in-residence mentors. Through instruction, discussion, criticism and free exchange among the program members, writers begin to find their voice and their style. The program provides group and individual sessions for each writer. The Summer Writing Program includes a banquet, guest speakers, and exposure to authors such as Oscar Hijuelos, Robert Olen Butler (both Pulitzer Prize winners), Maurice Sendak, Cynthia Ozick, Nora Sayre, and Denise Levertov. Often agents, editors, and publishers make presentations during the conference, and authors and students read from published work and works in progress. These presentations and the conference banquet offer additional opportunities to meet informally with participants, master writers and guest speakers. Average attendance: 65. Conference offers workshops in short fiction, nonfiction, poetry, and occasionally other genres such as screenplay writing or writing for children. Site is the university campus on Long Island, 25 miles from New York City. **COSTS/ACCOMMODATIONS** Check website for current fees. Credit is available for undergraduate and graduate students.

## INDIANA UNIVERSITY WRITERS' CONFERENCE

464 Ballantine Hall, 1020 E. Kirkwood Ave., Bloomington IN 47405-7103. (812)855-1877. **E-mail:** writecon@indiana.edu. **Website:** www.indiana.edu/~writecon. Annual. Conference/workshops held in June. 2016 dates: June 4-8. Average attendance: 115. "The Indiana University Writers' Conference believes in a craft-based teaching of fiction writing. We emphasize an exploration of creativity through a variety of approaches, offering workshop-based craft discussions, classes focusing on technique, and talks about the careers and concerns of a writing life."
**COSTS/ACCOMMODATIONS** Information on accommodations available on website.

**ADDITIONAL INFORMATION** Connect on Twitter at @iuwritecon.

## IOWA SUMMER WRITING FESTIVAL

The University of Iowa, C215 Seashore Hall, University of Iowa, Iowa City IA 52242. (319)335-4160. **Fax:** (319)335-4743. **E-mail:** iswfestival@uiowa.edu. **Website:** http://www.iowasummerwritingfestival.org. Annual festival held in June and July. 2015 event had 138 workshops with 72 instructors. Conference duration: Workshops are 1 week or a weekend. Average attendance: Limited to 12 people/class, with over 1,500 participants throughout the summer. "We offer courses across the genres: novel, short story, poetry, essay, memoir, humor, travel, playwriting, screenwriting, writing for children, and women's writing. Held at the University of Iowa campus." Speakers have included Marvin Bell, Lan Samantha Chang, John Dalton, Katie Ford, Patricia Foster, Bret Anthony Johnston, Barbara Robinette Moss, among others.
**COSTS/ACCOMMODATIONS** Accommodations available at area hotels. Information on overnight accommodations available by phone or on website.

**ADDITIONAL INFORMATION** Brochures are available in February. Inquire via e-mail or on website.

## IWWG SPRING BIG APPLE CONFERENCE

917-720-6959. **E-mail:** iwwgquestions@gmail.com. **Website:** www.iwwg.wildapricot.org/events. Spring Big Apple (April 16-17) Scandinavia House, New York City.

○ Writing workshops; author panel discussing publishing trends; book fair; agent panel and one-on-one pitch sessions.

## JACKSON HOLE WRITERS CONFERENCE

PO Box 1974, Jackson WY 83001. (307)413-3332. **E-mail:** connie@blackhen.com. **Website:** jacksonholewritersconference.com. Annual conference. 2016 dates: June 23-25. Conference duration: 3-4 days. Average attendance: 110. Covers fiction, creative nonfiction, and young adult and offers ms critiques from authors, agents, and editors. Agents in attendance will take pitches from writers. Paid manuscript critique programs are available.

**ADDITIONAL INFORMATION** Held at the Center for the Arts in Jackson, Wyoming and online.

## JENTEL ARTIST RESIDENCY PROGRAM

Jentel Foundation, 130 Lower Piney Creek Rd., Banner WY 82832. (307)737-2311. **Fax:** (307)737-2305.

**E-mail:** jentel@jentelarts.org. **Website:** www.jentel-arts.org.

**COSTS/ACCOMMODATIONS** Residents are responsible for travel expenses and personal items. "Jentel provides a private accommodation in a shared living space, a comfortable private studio, and a stipend to help defray the cost of food and personal expenses. Staff takes residents grocery shopping weekly after the stipend is distributed. Staff will pick up and drop off residents at the airport and bus station in Sheridan, 20 miles from the ranch setting of Jentel." Accommodation provided in a large house with common living and dining areas; fully equipped kitchen; library with computer, printer, and Wireless Internet access; media room with television, DVD/video player, and CD player; spacious private bedroom; and separate private studio.

**ADDITIONAL INFORMATION** Brochure and application form online.

## KENTUCKY WOMEN WRITERS CONFERENCE

University of Kentucky College of Arts & Sciences, 232 E. Maxwell St., Lexington KY 40506. (859)257-2874. **E-mail:** kentuckywomenwriters@gmail.com. **Website:** kentuckywomenwriters.org. **Contact:** Julie Wrinn, director. Conference held in second or third weekend of September. The 2015 dates were Sept. 11-12. The location is the Carnegie Center for Literacy in Lexington, Kentucky. Conference duration: 2 days. Average attendance: 150-200. Conference covers poetry, fiction, creative nonfiction, playwriting. Writing workshops, panels, and readings featuring contemporary women writers. The 2014 conference featured prize-winning poet Tracy K. Smith as its keynote speaker.

**COSTS/ACCOMMODATIONS** 2015 prices are $200 for general admission and a workshop and $125 for admission with no workshop. Check website for 2017 pricing.

**ADDITIONAL INFORMATION** Sponsors prizes in poetry ($200), fiction ($200), nonfiction ($200), playwriting ($500), and spoken word ($500). Winners also invited to read during the conference. Pre-registration opens May 1.

## KENYON REVIEW WRITERS WORKSHOP

*Kenyon Review*, Kenyon College, Gambier OH 43022. (740) 427-5196. **Fax:** (740) 427-5417. **E-mail:** kenyonreview@kenyon.edu; writers@kenyonreview.org.

**Website:** www.kenyonreview.org. **Contact:** Anna Duke Reach, director. Annual 8-day workshop held in June. Participants apply in poetry, fiction, literary nonfiction, book arts, nature writing, novel writing, or the workshop for teachers and then participate in intensive daily workshops which focus on the generation and revision of significant new work. Held on the campus of Kenyon College in the rural village of Gambier, Ohio. Workshop leaders have included David Baker, Carl Phillips, Mary Szybist, Rebecca McClanahan, Dinty Moore, Caitlin Horrocks, Lee K. Abbott, and Nancy Zafris.

**COSTS/ACCOMMODATIONS** The workshop operates a shuttle to and from Gambier and the airport in Columbus, Ohio. Offers overnight accommodations. Participants are housed in Kenyon College student housing. The cost is covered in the tuition. Fiction, Literary Nonfiction, Poetry, Nature Writing: $2,295. Novel: $2,995. Art of Text: $1,595. Teachers: $1,495. All rates includes tuition, room and board.

**ADDITIONAL INFORMATION** Application includes a writing sample. Admission decisions are made on a rolling basis. Workshop information is available online at www.kenyonreview.org/workshops in November. For brochure send e-mail, visit website, call, or fax. Accepts inquiries by SASE, e-mail, phone, fax.

## KUNDIMAN POETRY RETREAT

P.O. Box 4248, Sunnyside NY 11104. **E-mail:** info@kundiman.org. **Website:** kundiman.org/retreat. **Contact:** June W. Choi, executive director. Held annually. 2016 dates: June 15-19. Held at Fordham University's Rose Hill campus. "This is a special event for Asian American poets. Renowned faculty will conduct workshops and provide one-on-one mentorship sessions with fellows. Readings and informal social gatherings will also be scheduled. Fellows selected based on sample of 6-8 poems and short essay answer.

**COSTS/ACCOMMODATIONS** Room and board is free to accepted Fellows. Tuition is $375.

**ADDITIONAL INFORMATION** Additional information, guidelines, and online application available on website.

## MONTEVALLO LITERARY FESTIVAL

Comer Hall, Station 6420, University of Montevallo, Montevallo AL 35115. (205)665-6420. **Fax:** (205) 665-6420. **E-mail:** murphyj@montevallo.edu. **Website:** http://www.montevallo.edu/arts-sciences/college-of-arts-sciences/departments/english-foreign-languag-es/student-organizations/montevallo-literary-festi-val/. **Contact:** Dr. Jim Murphy, director. "Each April, the University of Montevallo's Department of English and Foreign Languages hosts the annual Montevallo Literary Festival, a celebration of creative writing dedicated to bringing literary writers and readers together on a personal scale. Our friendly, relaxed festival runs all day into the evening featuring readings by all invited writers, book signings, a Q&A panel, social gatherings and dinner with live music."

## JENNY MCKEAN MOORE COMMUNITY WORKSHOPS

English Department, George Washington University, 801 22nd St. NW, Rome Hall, Suite 760, Washington DC 20052. (202)994-6180. **Fax:** (202)994-6637. **E-mail:** lpageinc@gwu.edu. **Website:** www.gwu.edu/~english/creative_jennymckeanmoore.html. **Contact:** Lisa Page, director of creative writing. Workshop held each semester at the university. Average attendance: 15. Concentration varies depending on professor—usually fiction or poetry. The Creative Writing department brings an established poet or novelist to campus each year to teach a writing workshop for GW students and a free community workshop for adults in the larger Washington community. Details posted on website in June, with an application deadline at the end of August or in early September. **ADDITIONAL INFORMATION** Admission is competitive and by decided by the quality of a submitted ms.

## MOUNT HERMON CHRISTIAN WRITERS CONFERENCE

PO Box 413, Mount Hermon CA 95041. **E-mail:** info@mounthermon.org. **Website:** writers.mounthermon.org. Annual professional conference. 2016 dates: March 18-22. Average attendance: 450. Sponsored by and held at the 440-acre Mount Hermon Christian Conference Center near San Jose, California in the heart of the coastal redwoods, we are a broad-ranging conference for all areas of Christian writing, including fiction, nonfiction, fantasy, children's, teen, young adult, poetry, magazines, inspirational and devotional writing. This is a working, how-to conference, with Major Morning tracks in all genres (including a track especially for teen writers), and as many as 20 optional workshops each afternoon. Faculty-to-student ratio is about 1 to 6. The bulk of our more than 70 faculty

members are editors and publisher representatives from major Christian publishing houses nationwide. Speakers have included T. Davis Bunn, Debbie Macomber, Jerry Jenkins, Bill Butterworth, Dick Foth and others.

## NAPA VALLEY WRITERS' CONFERENCE

Napa Valley College, 1088 College Ave., St. Helena CA 94574. (707)967-2900. **E-mail:** writecon@napavalley.edu. **Website:** www.napawritersconference.org. **Contact:** Andrea Bewick, managing director. Established 1981. Annual weeklong event. 2016 dates: July 24 - July 29. Location: Upper Valley Campus in the historic town of St. Helena, 25 miles north of Napa in the heart of the valley's wine growing community. Average attendance: 48 in poetry and 48 in fiction. "Serious writers of all backgrounds and experience are welcome to apply." Offers poets and fiction writers workshops, lectures, faculty readings at Napa Valley wineries, and one-on-one faculty counseling. "Poetry session provides the opportunity to work both on generating new poems and on revising previously written ones." **COSTS/ACCOMMODATIONS** $975; $25 application fee.

## THE NEW LETTERS WEEKEND WRITERS CONFERENCE

University of Missouri-Kansas City, 5101 Rockhill Rd., Kansas City MO 64110-2499. (816)235-1168. **E-mail:** newletters@umkc.edu. **Website:** http://newletters.org/writers-wanted/nl-weekend-writing-conference. **Contact:** Robert Stewart, director. Annual conference held in late June. Conference duration: 3 days. Average attendance: 75. The conference brings together talented writers in many genres for seminars, readings, workshops, and individual conferences. The emphasis is on craft and the creative process in poetry, fiction, screenwriting, playwriting, and journalism, but the program also deals with matters of psychology, publications, and marketing. The conference is appropriate for both advanced and beginning writers. The conference meets at the university's beautiful Diastole Conference Center. **COSTS/ACCOMMODATIONS** Registrants are responsible for their own transportation, but information on area accommodations is available. Participants may choose to attend as a noncredit student or they may attend for 1 hour of college credit from the University of Missouri-Kansas City. Conference registration includes Friday evening reception and keynote speaker, Saturday and Sunday continental breakfast and lunch.

**ADDITIONAL INFORMATION** Those registering for college credit are required to submit a ms in advance. Ms reading and critique are included in the credit fee. Those attending the conference for non-credit also have the option of having their ms critiqued for an additional fee. Brochures are available for a SASE after March. Accepts inquiries by e-mail and fax.

## PALM BEACH POETRY FESTIVAL

Old School Square Cultural Arts Center, 51 N. Swinton Ave., Delray Beach FL **E-mail:** coordinator@palmbeachpoetryfestival.org. **Website:** www.palmbeachpoetryfestival.org. **Contact:** Susan R. Williamson, director.

**COSTS/ACCOMMODATIONS** 2016: Accommodations available at area hotels, especially The Colony Hotel & Hyatt Place with group rates. Information available by e-mail or on website. Participants responsible for all meals except Gala Dinner.

**ADDITIONAL INFORMATION** Festival poets visit and perform in Palm Beach County High School locations and offers a Palm Beach County High School Poetry Contest. Contest Awards are presented at the festival during festival week. Guidelines available by e-mail. Brochure and registration forms available by fax, e-mail, and on website. Application deadline in November.

## PIMA WRITERS' WORKSHOP

Pima College, 2202 W. Anklam Rd., Tucson AZ 85709. (520)206-6084. **Fax:** (520)206-6020. **E-mail:** mfiles@pima.edu. **Website:** https://www.pima.edu/pressroom/news-releases/2015/201505-writers-workshop.html. **Contact:** Meg Files, director. Annual conference geared toward beginner, intermediate and advanced levels. Open to students. The conference features presentations and writing exercises on writing and publishing stories for children and young adults, among other genres. Participants may attend for college credit. Meals and accommodations not included. Features a dozen authors, editors, and agents talking about writing and publishing fiction, nonfiction, poetry, and stories for children. E-mail us for more info, or check the website.

## SAN DIEGO STATE UNIVERSITY WRITERS'

## CONFERENCE

SDSU College of Extended Studies, 5250 Campanile Dr., San Diego State University, San Diego CA 92182-1920. (619)594-3946. **Fax:** (619)594-8566. **E-mail:** sdsuwritersconference@mail.sdsu.edu. **Website:** ces.sdsu.edu/writers. Annual conference held in January. Conference duration: 2.5 days. Average attendance: 350. Covers fiction, nonfiction, scriptwriting and e-books. Held at the San Diego Marriott Mission Valley Hotel. Each year the conference offers a variety of workshops for the beginner and advanced writers. This conference allows the individual writer to choose which workshop best suits his/her needs. In addition to the workshops, editor reading appointments and agent/editor consultation appointments are provided so attendees may meet with editors and agents one-on-one to discuss specific questions. A reception is offered Saturday immediately following the workshops, offering attendees the opportunity to socialize with the faculty in a relaxed atmosphere. Previous years, approximately 60 faculty members have attended.

**COSTS/ACCOMMODATIONS** Attendees must make their own travel arrangements. A conference rate for attendees is available at the event hotel (Marriott Mission Valley Hotel). Approximately $495-549. Extra costs for consultations.

## SANTA BARBARA WRITERS CONFERENCE

27 W. Anapamu St., Suite 305, Santa Barbara CA 93101. (805)568-1516. **E-mail:** info@sbwriters.com. **Website:** www.sbwriters.com. Annual conference held in June. 2016 dates: June 5-10. Average attendance: 200. Covers fiction, nonfiction, journalism, memoir, poetry, playwriting, screenwriting, travel writing, young adult, children's literature, humor, and marketing. Speakers have included Ray Bradbury, William Styron, Eudora Welty, James Michener, Sue Grafton, Charles M. Schulz, Clive Cussler, Fannie Flagg, Elmore Leonard, and T.C. Boyle. Agents will appear on a panel; in addition, there will be an agents and editors day that allows writers to pitch their projects in one-on-one meetings.

**COSTS/ACCOMMODATIONS** Hyatt Santa Barbara. Early conference registration is $575, and regular registration is $650.

**ADDITIONAL INFORMATION** Register online or contact for brochure and registration forms.

## ✪ SASKATCHEWAN FESTIVAL OF WORDS

217 Main St. N., Moose Jaw SK S6J 0W1, Canada. **Website:** www.festivalofwords.com. Annual 4-day event, third week of July (2016 dates: July 14-17). Location: Moose Jaw Library/Art Museum complex in Crescent Park. Average attendance: about 4,000 admissions. "Canadian authors up close and personal for readers and writers of all ages in mystery, poetry, memoir, fantasy, graphic novels, history, and novel. Each summer festival includes more than 60 events within 2 blocks of historic Main Street. Audience favorite activities include workshops for writers, audience readings, drama,performance poetry, concerts, panels, and music."

**COSTS/ACCOMMODATIONS** Information available at www.templegardens.sk.ca, campgrounds, and bed and breakfast establishments. Complete information about festival presenters, events, costs, and schedule also available on website.

## ✪ THE SCHOOL FOR WRITERS FALL WORKSHOP

The Humber School for Writers, Humber Institute of Technology & Advanced Learning, 3199 Lake Shore Blvd. W., Toronto ON M8V 1K8, Canada. (416)675-6622 extension 3449. **E-mail:** antanas.sileika@humber.ca; hilary.higgins@humber.ca. **Website:** www.humber.ca/scapa/programs/school-writers. The School for Writers Workshop has moved to the fall with the International Festival of Authors. The workshop runs during the last week in October. Conference duration: 1 week. Average attendance: 60. New writers from around the world gather to study with faculty members to work on their novels, short stories, poetry, or creative nonfiction. Agents and editors participate in the conference. Include a work-in-progress with your registration. Faculty has included Martin Amis, David Mitchell, Kevin Barry, Rachel Kushner, Peter Carey, Roddy Doyle, Tim O'Brien, Andrea Levy, Edward Albee, Ha Jin, Julia Glass, Mavis Gallant, Bruce Jay Friedman, Isabel Huggan, Alistair MacLeod, Lisa Moore, Kim Moritsugu, Francine Prose, Paul Quarrington, Olive Senior, D.M. Thomas, Annabel Lyon, Mary Gaitskill, Miriam Toews, Nino Ricci, and M.G. Vassanji,

**COSTS/ACCOMMODATIONS** $850 (in 2015). Some scholarships are available.

**ADDITIONAL INFORMATION** Accepts inquiries by e-mail, phone, and fax.

## SEWANEE WRITERS' CONFERENCE

735 University Ave., 119 Gailor Hall, Stamler Center, Sewanee TN 37383-1000. (931)598-1654. **E-mail:** swc@sewanee.edu. **Website:** www.sewaneewriters.org. **Contact:** Adam Latham. Annual conference. 2016 dates: July 19-31. Average attendance: 150. "The University of the South will host the 27th session of the Sewanee Writers' Conference. Thanks to the generosity of the Walter E. Dakin Memorial Fund, supported by the estate of the late Tennessee Williams, the Conference will gather a distinguished faculty to provide instruction and criticism through workshops and craft lectures in poetry, fiction, and playwriting. During an intense 12-day period, participants will read and critique workshop manuscripts under the leadership of some of our country's finest fiction writers, poets, and playwrights. Faculty members and fellows give scheduled readings; senior faculty members offer craft lectures; open-mic readings accommodate many others. Additional writers, along with a host of writing professionals, visit to give readings, participate in panel discussions, and answer questions from the audience. Receptions and mealtimes offer ample social opportunities. This year's faculty includes includes fiction writers Richard Bausch, John Casey, Tony Earley, Randall Kenan, Jill McCorkle, Alice McDermott, Erin McGraw, Christine Schutt, Allen Wier, and Steve Yarbrough; and poets Daniel Anderson, B.H. Fairchild, Robert Hass, Mark Jarman, Maurice Manning, Marilyn Nelson, A.E. Stallings, and Sidney Wade. Naomi Iizuka and Dan O'Brien will lead the playwriting workshop. Charles Martin, A.E. Stallings, and N.S. Thompson will offer a supplemental poetry translation workshop. Adrianne Harun, Andrew Hudgins, Charles Martin, and Wyatt Prunty will read from their work."

**COSTS/ACCOMMODATIONS** Participants are housed in single rooms in university dormitories. Bathrooms are shared by small groups. $1,100 for tuition; and $800 for room, board, and activity costs.

## THE SOUTHAMPTON WRITERS CONFERENCE

Stony Brook Southampton MFA in Creative Writing Program, 239 Montauk Highway, Southampton NY 11968. (631)632-5007. **E-mail:** christian.mclean@stonybrook.edu. **Website:** www.stonybrook.edu/southampton/mfa/summer/cwl_home.html. **Contact:** Christian McLean. 2016 dates: July 6-17. Since 1976, the Southampton Writers Conference has brought together writers at all stages of their careers with world-class novelists, essayists, editors, poets and children's book authors for lectures, readings, panels and workshops. All writers are welcome to apply to the conference. Options include a 12-day Master Class with Roger Rosenblatt, 5-day and 12-day writing workshops, and a 12-day residency program. 2016 faculty includes: Melissa Bank, Billy Collins, Martín Espada, Gayle Forman, Adam Gopnik, Lauren Groff, Jane Hamilton, Matthea Harvey, Lucas Hnath, Matthew Klam, Daniel Menaker, Peter H. Reynolds, Tor Seidler, John Patrick Shanley, Frederic Tuten, and Meg Wolitzer.

**COSTS/ACCOMMODATIONS** Participants can stay on campus in air-conditioned dorms. Shared room: $35 per night (5-day conference: $140). Shared room with linen: $42 per night (5-day conference: $168). Single room: $40.55 per night (5-day conference: $162.20). Single room with linen: $47.50 per night (5-day conference: $190). 12-day Master Class: $975 (does not include afternoon faculty-led workshop). 5-day workshop only: $1,395. 5-day workshop + residency: $1,995 (12 days total). 12-day workshop: $1,995. 12-day residency: $975.

## SOUTH CAROLINA WRITERS WORKSHOP

4840 Forest Drive, Suite 6B: PMB 189, Columbia SC 29206. **E-mail:** scwwliaison@gmail.com. **Website:** www.myscww.org. Conference in October held at the Metropolitan Conference Center in Columbia, SC. Held almost every year. Conference duration: 3 days. The conference features critique sessions, open mic readings, presentations from agents and editors and more. The conference features more than 50 different workshops for writers to choose from, dealing with all subjects of writing craft, writing business, getting an agent and more. Agents will be in attendance.

## SOUTH COAST WRITERS CONFERENCE

Southwestern Oregon Community College, P.O. Box 590, 29392 Ellensburg Ave., Gold Beach OR 97444. (541) 247-2741. **Fax:** (541) 247-6247. **E-mail:** scwc@socc.edu. **Website:** www.socc.edu/scwriters. **Contact:** Karim Shumaker. Annual conference held Presidents Day weekend in February. Conference duration: 2 days. Covers fiction, poetry, children's, nature, screenwriting, songwriting, and marketing. Peter Brown Hoffmeister is the next scheduled keynote speaker, and presenters include Jason Brick, Barri Chase, Daryll Lynne Evans, Miriam Gershow, Peter Brown Hoffmeister, Anne Osterlund, Heidi Schulz, Eric Witchey and Carolyne Wright.

**COSTS/ACCOMMODATIONS** List of local motels that offer discounts to conference participants is available on request. Friday conference cost is $55.00, Saturday conference cost is $60 before January 31, and $70 after. Lunch is $12.00 and available for purchase in advance.

**ADDITIONAL INFORMATION** See website for cost and additional details.

## STEAMBOAT SPRINGS WRITERS CONFERENCE

A Day For Writers, Steamboat Springs Arts Council, Eleanor Bliss Center for the Arts at the Depot, 1001 13th St., Steamboat Springs CO 80487, U.S.. (970)879-9008. **E-mail:** info@steamboatwriters.com. **Website:** www.steamboatwriters.com. **Contact:** Barbara Sparks. Writers' workshops geared toward intermediate levels. Open to professionals and amateurs alike.

**COSTS/ACCOMMODATIONS** Check website for updated pricing.

**ADDITIONAL INFORMATION** For additional information, please consult the website.

## SUMMER WRITING PROGRAM

Naropa University, 2130 Arapahoe Ave., Boulder CO 80302. (303)245-4862. **Fax:** (303)546-5287. **E-mail:** swpr@naropa.edu. **Website:** www.naropa.edu/swp. **Contact:** Kyle Pivarnik, special projects manager. Annual event in summer. Workshop duration: 4 weeks. Average attendance: 250. Offers college credit. Accepts inquiries by e-mail, phone. With 13 workshops to choose from each of the 4 weeks of the program, students may study poetry, prose, hybrid/cross-genre writing, small press printing, or book arts. Site: All workshops, panels, lectures and readings are hosted on the Naropa University main campus. Located in downtown Boulder, the campus is within easy walking distance of restaurants, shopping, and the scenic Pearl Street Mall.

**ADDITIONAL INFORMATION** Writers can elect to take the Summer Writing Program for noncredit, graduate, or undergraduate credit. The registration procedure varies, so consider whether or not you'll be taking the SWP for academic credit. All participants can elect to take any combination of the first, second, third, and/or fourth weeks. To request a catalog of upcoming program or to find additional information, visit naropa.edu/swp. Naropa University also welcomes participants with disabilities.

## TAOS SUMMER WRITERS' CONFERENCE

Department of English Language and Literature, MSC 03 2170, 1 University of New Mexico, Albuquerque NM 87131-0001. **E-mail:** swarner@unm.edu. **Website:** taosconf.unm.edu. **Contact:** Sharon Oard Warner. Annual conference held in July. 2016 dates: July 24-31. Offers workshops and master classes in the novel, short story, poetry, creative nonfiction, memoir, prose style, screenwriting, humor writing, yoga and writing, literary translation, book proposal, the query letter and revision. Participants may also schedule a consultation with a visiting agent/editor.

**COSTS/ACCOMMODATIONS** Week-long workshop registration $700, weekend workshop registration $400, master classes between $1,350 and $1,625, publishing consultations are $175.

## UNIVERSITY OF NORTH DAKOTA WRITERS CONFERENCE

Department of English, 110 Merrifield Hall, 276 Centennial Dr., Stop 7209, Grand Forks ND 58202. (701)777-2393. **Fax:** (701)777-2373. **E-mail:** crystal.alberts@email.und.edu. **Website:** http://und.edu/orgs/writers-conference. **Contact:** Crystal Alberts, director. Annual event of 3-5 days. 2016 dates: April 6-8. Offers panels, readings, and films focused around a specific theme. Almost all events take place in the UND Memorial Union, which has a variety of small rooms and a 1,000-seat main hall. Past speakers include Art Spiegelman, Truman Capote, Sir Salman Rushdie, Allen Ginsberg, Alice Walker, and Louise Erdrich.

**COSTS/ACCOMMODATIONS** Accommodations available at area hotels. Information on overnight accommodations available on website. All events are free and open to the public. Donations accepted.

**ADDITIONAL INFORMATION** Schedule and other information available on website.

## VERMONT STUDIO CENTER

P.O. Box 613, 80 Pearl Street, Johnson VT 05656. (802)635-2727. **Fax:** (802)635-2730. **E-mail:** info@vermontstudiocenter.org. **Website:** www.vermontstudiocenter.org.. **Contact:** Gary Clark, Writing Program Director. Founded by artists in 1984, the Vermont Studio Center is the largest international artists' and writers' Residency Program in the United States, hosting 50 visual artists and writers each month from across the country and around the world. The Studio Center provides 4-12 week studio residencies on an historic 30-building campus along the Gihon River in Johnson, Vermont, a village in the heart of the northern Green Mountains.

**COSTS/ACCOMMODATIONS** "The cost of a 4-week residency is $3,950. Generous fellowship and grant assistance available. "Accommodations available on site. "Residents live in single rooms in ten modest, comfortable houses adjacent to the Red Mill Building. Rooms are simply furnished and have shared baths. Complete linen service is provided. The Studio Center is unable to accommodate guests at meals, overnight guests, spouses, children or pets."

**ADDITIONAL INFORMATION** Fellowships application deadlines are February 15, June 15 and October 1. Writers encouraged to visit website for more information. May also e-mail, call, fax.

## WESLEYAN WRITERS CONFERENCE

Wesleyan University, 294 High St., Room 207, Middletown CT 06459. (860)685-3604. **Fax:** (860)685-2441. **E-mail:** agreene@wesleyan.edu. **Website:** www.wesleyan.edu/writing/conference. Annual conference. 2016 dates: June 15-19. Average attendance: 100. Focuses on the novel, fiction techniques, short stories, poetry, screenwriting, nonfiction, literary journalism, memoir, mixed media work and publishing. The conference is held on the campus of Wesleyan University, in the hills overlooking the Connecticut River. Features a faculty of award-winning writers, seminars and readings of new fiction, poetry, nonfiction and mixed media forms - as well as guest lectures on a range of topics including publishing. Both new and experienced writers are welcome. Participants may attend seminars in all genres. Speakers have included Esmond Harmsworth (Zachary Schuster Agency), Daniel Mandel (Sanford J. Greenburger Associates), Amy Williams (ICM and Collins McCormick), and many others. Agents will be speaking and available for meetings with attendees. Participants are often successful in finding agents and publishers for their mss. Wesleyan participants are also frequently featured in the anthology *Best New American Voices*.

**COSTS/ACCOMMODATIONS** Meals are provided on campus. Lodging is available on campus or in town.

**ADDITIONAL INFORMATION** Ms critiques are available, but not required.

## WESTERN RESERVE WRITERS & FREELANCE CONFERENCE

7700 Clocktower Dr., Kirtland OH 44094. (440)525-7812. **E-mail:** deencr@aol.com. **Website:** www.deannaadams.com. **Contact:** Deanna Adams, director/conference coordinator. Annual. Last conference held September 26, 2015. Conference duration: 1 day or half-day. Average attendance: 120. "The Western Reserve Writers Conferences are designed for all writers, aspiring and professional, and offer presentations in all genres—nonfiction, fiction, poetry, essays, creative nonfiction, and the business of writing, including Web writing and successful freelance writing." Site: "Located in the main building of Lakeland Community College, the conference is easy to find and just off the I-90 freeway. The Fall 2013 conference featured top-notch presenters from newspapers and magazines, along with published authors, freelance writers, and professional editors. Presentations included 'Writing Believable Dialogue,' 'Creating a Sense of Place,' 'Writing Your Life Story,' 'First Fiction,' 'Writing and Researching Crime Stories,' as well as tips on submissions, getting books into stores, and storytelling for both fiction and nonfiction writers. Included throughout the day are one-on-one editing consults, Q&A panel, and book sale/author signings."

**COSTS/ACCOMMODATIONS** Previous costs for Fall all-day conference includes lunch: $105.

**ADDITIONAL INFORMATION** Brochures for the conferences are available by January (for spring conference) and July (for fall). Also accepts inquiries by e-mail and phone. Check Deanna Adams' website for all updates. Editors always attend the conferences. Private editing consultations are available, as well.

## WILDACRES WRITERS WORKSHOP

233 S. Elm St., Greensboro NC 27401. (336)255-8210. **E-mail:** judihill@aol.com. **Website:** www.wildacreswriters.com. **Contact:** Judi Hill, Director. 2016 summer workshop dates: July 9-16. Conference duration: 1 week. Average attendance: 100. Workshop focuses on novel, short story, flash fiction, poetry, and nonfiction. Faculty include Ron Rash, Carrie Brown, Dr. Janice Fuller, Phillip Gerard, Luke Whisnant, Dr. Joe Clark, John Gregory Brown, Dr. Phebe Davidson, Lee Zacharias, and Vicki Lane. This group also has a week-long writing retreat that is different from the workshop.

**COSTS/ACCOMMODATIONS** The current price is $830. Check the website for more info.

**ADDITIONAL INFORMATION** Include a 1-page writing sample with your registration. See the website for information.

## WRITE IT OUT

P.O. Box 704, Sarasota FL 34230-0704. (941)359-3824. **E-mail:** rmillerwio@aol.com. **Website:** www.write-itout.com. **Contact:** Ronni Miller, director. Workshops held through the year for varying lengths of time. Check the website for more information. Workshops retreats on "expressive writing and painting, fiction, poetry, memoirs. We also offer intimate, motivational, in-depth free private conferences with instructors." Past facilitators included Arturo Vivante, novelist.

**COSTS/ACCOMMODATIONS** Costs vary by workshop.

**ADDITIONAL INFORMATION** "Critiques on work are given at the workshops." Conference information available year round. For brochures/guidelines e-mail, call, or visit website. Accepts inquiries by phone, e-mail. Workshops have "small groups, option to spend time writing and not attend classes, with personal appointments with instructors."

## WRITER'S DIGEST CONFERENCES

F+W Media, Inc., 10151 Carver Rd., Suite 200, Blue Ash OH 45242. 877-436-7764 (option 2). **E-mail:** writersdigestconference@fwmedia.com. **E-mail:** phil.sexton@fwmedia.com. **Website:** www.writersdigestconference.com. **Contact:** Taylor Sferra. The Writer's Digest conferences feature an amazing line up of speakers to help writers with the craft and business of writing. Each calendar year typically features multiple conferences around the country. In 2016, the New York conference will be August 12-14 at the New York Hilton Midtown. The most popular feature of the east coast conference is the agent pitch slam, in which potential authors are given the ability to pitch their books directly to agents. For the 2016 conference, there will be more than 50 agents in attendance. For more details, see the website. Stay tuned to the website for additional conference information for the west coast event.

**COSTS/ACCOMMODATIONS** A block of rooms at the event hotel are reserved for guests. See the travel page on the website for more information. Cost varies by location and year. There are typically different pricing options for those who wish attend the pitch slam and those who just want to attend the conference education.

## WRITERS OMI AT LEDIG HOUSE

55 Fifth Ave., 15th Floor, New York NY 10003. (212)206-6114. **E-mail:** writers@artomi.org. **Website:** www.artomi.org. Residency duration: 2 weeks to 2 months. Average attendance and site: "Up to 20 writers per session—10 at a given time—live and write on the stunning 300 acre grounds and sculpture park that overlooks the Catskill Mountains." Deadline: October 20.

**COSTS/ACCOMMODATIONS** Residents provide their own transportation. Offers overnight accommodations.

**ADDITIONAL INFORMATION** "Agents and editors from the New York publishing community are invited for dinner and discussion. Bicycles, a swimming pool, and nearby tennis court are available for use."

## WRITING WORKSHOPS AT CASTLE HILL

10 Meetinghouse Rd., P.O. Box 756, Truro MA 02666. (508)349-7511. **Fax:** (508)349-7513. **E-mail:** info@castlehill.org. **Website:** www.castlehill.org/workshop-writing.html. Workshops about poetry, fiction, narrative nonfiction, memoir, and more; these writing workshops are geared toward intermediate and advanced levels. **Open to students.** The dates, courses, and instructors change each year, so check the website for individual details of upcoming events. Held at the Truro Center for the Arts at Castle Hill in Massachusetts.

## THE HELENE WURLITZER FOUNDATION

P.O. Box 1891, Taos NM 87571. (575)758-2413. **Fax:** (575)758-2559. **E-mail:** hwf@taosnet.com. **Website:** www.wurlitzerfoundation.org. **Contact:** Michael A. Knight, executive director.

**COSTS/ACCOMMODATIONS** "Provides individual housing in fully furnished studio/houses (casitas), rent and utility free. Artists are responsible for transportation to and from Taos, their meals, and materials for their work. Bicycles are provided upon request."

# ORGANIZATIONS

There are many organizations of value to poets. These groups may sponsor workshops and contests, stage readings, publish anthologies and chapbooks or spread the word about publishing opportunities. A few provide economic assistance or legal advice. The best thing organizations offer, though, is a support system to which poets can turn for a pep talk, a hard-nosed (but sympathetic) critique of a manuscript or simply the comfort of talking and sharing with others who understand the challenges, and joys, of writing poetry.

Whether national, regional or as local as your library or community center, each organization has something special to offer. The listings in this section reflect the membership opportunities available to poets with a variety of organizations. Some groups provide certain services to both members and nonmembers.

To find out more about groups in your area (including those that may not be listed in *Poet's Market*), contact your YMCA, community center, local colleges and universities, public library and bookstores (and don't forget newspapers and the Internet). If you can't find a group that suits your needs, consider starting one yourself. You might be surprised to discover there are others in your locality who would welcome the encouragement, feedback and moral support of a writer's group.

## 92ND STREET Y UNTERBERG POETRY CENTER

1395 Lexington Ave., New York NY 10128. (212)415-5500. **Website:** www.92y.org/poetry. The Unterberg Poetry Center offers "students of all ages the opportunity to hone their skills as writers and deepen their appreciation as readers." Offers annual series of readings by major literary figures (weekly readings late September through May), writing workshops, master classes in fiction and poetry, and lectures and literary seminars. Also co-sponsors the "Discovery"/Boston Review Poetry Contest.

## THE ACADEMY OF AMERICAN POETS

75 Maiden Ln., Suite 901, New York NY 10038. (212)274-0343. **Fax:** (212)274-9427. **E-mail:** academy@poets.org. **Website:** www.poets.org. The Academy of American Poets was founded to support the nation's poets at all stages of their careers and to foster the appreciation of contemporary poetry. Administers The Walt Whitman Award; The James Laughlin Award; The Harold Morton Landon Translation Award; The Lenore Marshall Poetry Prize; The Raiziss/de Palchi Translation Award; and The Wallace Stevens Award. Also awards The Fellowship of the Academy of American Poets and The University & College Poetry Prizes. Publishes *American Poet*, an informative semiannual journal sent to all Academy members. The Academy's other programs include National Poetry Month (April), the largest literary celebration in the world; the Poetry Audio Archive, a 700-volume audio library capturing the voices of contemporary American poets for generations to come; an annual series of poetry readings and special events; and Poets.org, which includes thousands of poems, hundreds of essays and interviews, lesson plans for teachers, a National Poetry Almanac, a national Calendar of Events, and the National Poetry Map.

## AMERICAN HAIKU ARCHIVES

California State Library, Library & Courts II Bldg, 900 N St., Sacramento CA 95814. **E-mail:** welchm@aol.com. **Website:** www.americanhaikuarchives.org. **Contact:** Michael Dylan Welch. The American Haiku Archives is "the world's largest public collection of haiku and related poetry books and papers outside Japan." This repository is housed at the California State Library in Sacramento, California, and is dedicated to preserving the history of North American haiku. Materials are publicly available for research purposes through the library's California History Room. The American Haiku Archives actively seeks donations of books, journals, recordings, letters, ephemera, and personal papers relating to haiku and related poetry in all languages, but especially North American languages. The American Haiku Archives also appoints an honorary curator every July for a one-year term. The intent of this appointment is to honor leading haiku poets, translators, or scholars for their accomplishments or service in support of haiku poetry as a literary art. Past honorary curators have been Ruth Yarrow, Marlene Mountain, Charles Trumbull, LeRoy Gorman, Jerry Ball, Gary Snyder, Stephen Addiss, George Swede, H. F. Noyes, Hiroaki Sato, Francine Porad, Makoto Ueda, William J. Higginson, Leroy Kanterman, Lorraine Ellis Harr, Robert Spiess, Cor van den Heuvel, Jerry Kilbride, and Elizabeth Searle Lamb. Additional information online.

## THE AMERICAN POETS' CORNER

The Cathedral Church of St. John the Divine, 1047 Amsterdam Ave., New York NY 10025. (212)316-7540. **Website:** www.stjohndivine.org. Initiated in 1984 with memorials for Emily Dickinson, Walt Whitman, and Washington Irving. Similar in concept to the British Poets' Corner in Westminster Abbey, was established and dedicated to memorialize this country's greatest writers. A board of electors chooses one deceased author each year for inclusion in The American Poets' Corner. The Cathedral is also home to the Muriel Rukeyser Poetry Wall, a public space for posting poems, which was dedicated in 1976 by Ms. Rukeyser and the Cathedral's Dean. Send poems for the Poetry Wall to the above address. Designated a National Poetry Landmark by the Academy of American Poets.

## ARIZONA AUTHORS' ASSOCIATION

6939 East Chaparral Rd., Paradise Valley AZ 85253. (602)554-8101. **E-mail:** azauthors@gmail.com. **E-mail:** lisa@greenpiecestoons.com. **Website:** www.azauthors.com. **Contact:** Lisa Aquilina, President. Since 1978, Arizona Authors' Association has served to offer professional, educational and social opportunities to writers and authors and serves as an informational and referral network for the literary community. Members must be authors, writers working toward publication, agents, publishers, publicists, printers, illustrators, etc. Az Authors' publishes a bimonthly newsletter and the renown annual *Arizona Literary Magazine*. The Association sponsors the international Arizona Literary Contest including poetry, essays, short stories, new drama writing, novels, and published books with cash prizes and awards bestowed at a Fall ceremony. Winning entries are published or advertised in the *Arizona Literary Magazine*. First and second place winners in poetry, essay and short story categories are entered in the annual Pushcart Prize. Learn more online.

## THE AUTHORS GUILD, INC.

31 E. 32nd St., 7th Floor, New York NY 10016. (212)563-5904. **Fax:** (212)564-5363. **E-mail:** staff@authorsguild.org. **Website:** www.authorsguild.org. **Contact:** Mary Rasenberger, executive director. Purpose of organization: to offer services and materials intended to help authors with the business and legal aspects of their work, including contract problems, copyright matters, freedom of expression and taxation. Guild has 8,000 members. Qualifications for membership: Must be book author published by an established American publisher within 7 years or any author who has had 3 works (fiction or nonfiction) published by a magazine or magazines of general circulation in the last 18 months. Associate membership also available. Different levels of membership include: associate membership with all rights except voting available to an author who has a firm contract offer or is currently negotiating a royalty contract from an established American publisher. "The Guild offers free contract reviews to its members. The Guild conducts several symposia each year at which experts provide information, offer advice and answer questions on subjects of interest and concern to authors. Typical subjects have been the rights of privacy and publicity, libel, wills and estates, taxation, copyright, editors and editing, the art of interviewing, standards of criticism and book reviewing. Transcripts of these symposia are published and circulated to members. The *Authors Guild Bulletin*, a quarterly journal, contains articles on matters of interest to writers, reports of Guild activities, contract surveys, advice on problem clauses in contracts, transcripts of Guild and League symposia and information on a variety of professional topics. Subscription included in the cost of the annual dues.

## BOWERY POETRY CLUB

308 Bowery St., New York NY 10012. (212)614-0505. **Fax:** (212)614-8539. **E-mail:** mail@bowerypoetry.com. **Website:** bowerypoetry.com. The Bowery Poetry Club and Cafe hosts regional open mic and poetry events. "Hosting between 20 and 30 shows a week, the Bowery Poetry Club (BPC) is proud of our place in the lineage of populist art: The Yiddish theater, burlesque, vaudeville, beat poetry, jazz, and punk that gave the Bowery its name." Offers workshops for adults and young poets. "Each Tuesday night at 6:30 pm touring Slam poets give a craft talk as part of our WordShop series." Nationally known writers give readings that are open to the public. Sponsors open mic readings for the public each Tuesday night at 7 pm as part of the Urbana Poetry Slam; format: open mic, featured poet, poetry slam. See website for more information and schedule.

## BRIGHT HILL LITERARY CENTER

94 Church St., Treadwell NY 13846. (607)829-5055. **E-mail:** wordthur@stny.rr.com. **E-mail:** brighthillpress@stny.rr.com. **Website:** www.brighthillpress.org. Bright Hill Literary Center serves residents in the Catskill Mountain region, greater New York, and throughout the U.S. Includes the Bright Hill Library and Internet Center, with "thousands of volumes of literary journals, literary prose and poetry, literary criticism and biography, theater, reference, art, and children's books available for reading and research (noncirculating, for the time being). Wireless Internet access is available." Sponsors workshops for children and adults. Learn more online.

## ✪ BURNABY WRITERS' SOCIETY

6584 Deer Lake Ave., Burnaby BC V5G 3T7, Canada. **E-mail:** info@bws.bc.ca. **Website:** burnabywritersnews.blogspot.com. **Contact:** Lara Varesi. Corresponding membership in the society, including a newsletter subscription, is open to anyone, anywhere. Currently has 130 members. Members of the society stage regular public readings of their own work. Sponsors open mic readings for the public. Sponsors a poetry contest open to British Columbia residents. Competition receives about 100-200 entries/year. Past contest winners include Mildred Tremblay, Irene Livingston, and Kate Braid. Additional information online.

## COLUMBINE POETS OF COLORADO

P.O. Box 6245, Broomfield CO 80021. (303)431-6774. **E-mail:** president@columbinepoetsofcolorado.com. **Website:** columbinepoetsofcolorado.com. **Contact:** Julie Cummings, president. Statewide organization open to anyone interested in poetry. Currently has around 100 members in 3 Chapters, now in Denver, Salida, and Loveland, CO. An affiliate of the National Federation of State Poetry Societies (NFSPS). Offerings for the Denver Foothills Chapter include weekly workshops and monthly critiques. Sponsors contests, awards for students and adults, an Annual Poetry Fest and some publications. Additional information available with SASE, by phone or e-mail.

## CONNECTICUT POETRY SOCIETY

P.O. Box 702, Manchester CT 06040. **E-mail:** connpoetry@comcast.net. **Website:** ctpoetry.net. **Contact:** Tony Fusco, president. The Connecticut Poetry Society is a nonprofit organization dedicated to the promotion and enjoyment of poetry through chapter meetings, contests, and poetry-related events. Statewide organization open to non-Connecticut residents. Currently has about 175 members. Membership benefits include automatic membership in The National Federation of State Poetry Societies (NFSPS); a free copy of *The Connecticut River Review*, a national poetry journal published by CPS; opportunity to publish in *Long River Run II*, a members-only poetry journal; quarterly CPS and NFSPS newsletters; annual April poetry celebration; and membership in any of 10 state chapters. Sponsors conferences and workshops. Sponsors The Connecticut River Review Annual Poetry Contest, The Brodinsky-Brodine Contest, The Winchell Contest, and The Lynn Decaro High School Competition. Members and nationally known writers give readings that are open to the public. Members meet monthly. Additional information online.

## COMMUNITY OF LITERARY MAGAZINES AND PRESSES (CLMP)

154 Christopher St., Suite 3C, New York NY 10014. (212)741-9110. **E-mail:** info@clmp.org. **Website:** www.clmp.org. "Dedicated to supporting and actively promoting the field of independent literary publishing." Open to publishers who are primarily literary in nature, have published at least 1 issue/title prior to applying for membership, publish at least 1 issue/title annually on an ongoing basis, have a minimum print run of 500 per issue or title, do not charge authors a fee, are not primarily self-publishing, and do not primarily publish children's/students' work. Currently has over 500 members. Levels of membership/dues: based on publishing organization's annual budget. See website for complete member application process. Benefits include free and discounted monographs, subscription to e-mail listserves and online databases, plus many valuable services. Additional information online.

## FURIOUS FLOWER POETRY CENTER

500 Cardinal Dr., MSC3802, James Madison University, Harrisonburg VA 22807. (540)568-8883. **Fax:** (540)568-8888. **E-mail:** gabbinjv@jmu.edu. **E-mail:** furiousflower@jmu.edu. **Website:** www.jmu.edu/furiousflower. **Contact:** Joanne Gabbin, executive director. The mission of the Furious Flower Poetry Center is to advance the genre of African American Poetry by providing opportunities for education, research, and publication. Furious Flower Poetry Center serves as a resource for the campus and local Harrisonburg community. The Center hosts visiting poets, sponsors poetry workshops for emerging poets, holds an annual poetry camp for children in the community, and produces scholarly texts, videos and DVDs on African American poetry. Furious Flower has sponsored two decade-defining conferences celebrating the African American poetic tradition.

## GEORGIA POETRY SOCIETY

740 Emily Place NW, Atlanta GA 30318. **E-mail:** gps@georgiapoetrysociety.org. **Website:** www.georgiapoetrysociety.org. Statewide organization open to any person who is in accord with the objectives to secure fuller public recognition of the art of poetry, stimulate an appreciation of poetry, and enhance the writing and reading of poetry. Currently has 200 members. Membership includes affiliation with NFSPS. Holds at least 1 workshop annually. Contests are sponsored throughout the year, some for members only. "Our contests have specific general rules, which should be followed to avoid the disappointment of disqualification. See the website for details." Publishes The Reach of Song, an annual anthology devoted to contest-winning poems and member works. Each quarterly meeting (open to the public) features at least 1 poet of regional prominence. Also sponsors monthly local poetry groups listed on our website. Sponsors Poetry in the Schools project. Additional information online.

## GREATER CINCINNATI WRITERS' LEAGUE

**E-mail:** ignatius@gmail.com. **Website:** www.cincinnatiwritersleague.org. **Contact:** Bucky Ignatius, president. Purpose is to "support those who write poetry in the Cincinnati area and to promote excellence in poetry writing. We believe in creative freedom, with open, constructive critique as a learning tool." Offerings include monthly meetings with critique or a workshop on a subject of interest to poets. Poems submitted by members are critiqued by guest critics (published poets who are also teachers or professors of poetry and/or creative writing). Group discussion of critiqued poems follows. Sponsors fall poetry contest with cash prizes; also sponsors a category of the annual Ohio Poetry Day contest with cash prizes. Occasionally publishes an anthology. Members occasionally give readings that are open to the public (see website for meeting time and place). Additional information online.

## HAIKU SOCIETY OF AMERICA

930 Pine St. #105, San Francisco CA 94108. **E-mail:** fay.hsa.president@gmail.com. **Website:** www.hsa-haiku.org. The Haiku Society of America is composed of haiku poets, editors, critics, publishers, and enthusiasts dedicated to "promoting the creation and appreciation of haiku and related forms (haibun, haiga, renku, senryu, sequences, and tanka) among its members and the public." Currently has over 800 members. Membership benefits include a year's subscription to the Society's journal, *Frogpond*, and to the quarterly HSA newsletter *Ripples*; the annual information sheet; an annual address/e-mail list of HSA members; and eligibility to submit work to the members' anthology. Administers the following annual awards: The Harold G. Henderson Awards for haiku, The Gerald Brady Awards for senryu, The Bernard Lionel Einbond Awards for renku, The Merit Book Awards, and The Nicholas Virgilio Haiku Awards for youth. Additional information online.

## THE HUDSON VALLEY WRITERS' CENTER

300 Riverside Dr., Sleepy Hollow NY 10591. (914)332-5953. **Fax:** (914)332-4825. **E-mail:** info@writerscenter.org. **Website:** www.writerscenter.org. **Contact:** Jewel Kinch-Thomas, executive director. "The Hudson Valley Writers' Center is a nonprofit organization devoted to furthering the literary arts in our region. Its mission is to promote the appreciation of literary excellence, to stimulate and nurture the creation of literary works in all sectors of the population, and to bring the diverse works of gifted poets and prose artists to the attention of the public." Open to all. Currently has 350 members. Offerings include public readings by established and emerging poets/writers, workshops and classes, monthly open mic nights, paid and volunteer outreach opportunities, and an annual chapbook competition with Slapering Hol Press. Additional information online.

## INTERNATIONAL READING ASSOCIATION

P.O. Box 8139, Newark DE 19714. (302)731-1600 ext. 293. **Fax:** (302)731-1057. **E-mail:** councils@reading.org. **E-mail:** mpost@reading.org. **Website:** www.reading.org. The International Reading Association seeks to promote high levels of literacy for all by improving the quality of reading instruction through studying the reading process and teaching techniques; serving as a clearinghouse for the dissemination of reading research through conferences, journals, and other publications; and actively encouraging the lifetime reading habit. Its goals include professional development, advocacy, partnerships, research, and global literacy development. Sponsors annual convention. Publishes a newsletter called "Reading Today." Sponsors a number of awards and fellowships. More information online.

## INTERNATIONAL WOMEN'S WRITING GUILD

International Women's Writing Guild, 274 Madison Ave., Suite 1202, New York NY 10016. (917)720-6959. **E-mail:** iwwgquestions@gmail.com. **Website:** www.iwwg.wildapricot.org. **Contact:** Kristin Rath, director of operations. IWWG is a network for the personal and professional empowerment of women through writing. Open to any woman connected to the written word regardless of professional portfolio. IWWG sponsors several annual conferences a year in all areas of the U.S. The major conference, held in summer, is a week-long conference attracting hundreds of women writers from across the globe.

## IOWA POETRY ASSOCIATION

2325 61st St., Des Moines IA 50322. (515)279-1106. **E-mail:** ipa@iowapoetry.com. **Website:** www.iowapoetry.com. **Contact:** Lucille Morgan Wilson, editor. Statewide organization open to "anyone interested in poetry, with a residence or valid address in the state of Iowa." Offerings include "semiannual workshops to which a poem may be sent in advance for critique; annual contest—also open to nonmembers—with no entry fee; IPA Newsletter, published 5 or 6 times/year, including a quarterly national publication listing of contest opportunities; and an annual poetry anthology, *Lyrical Iowa*, containing prize-winning and high-ranking poems from contest entries. No requirement for purchase to ensure publication." Semiannual workshops "are the only 'meetings' of the association." Additional information online.

## THE KENTUCKY STATE POETRY SOCIETY

**Website:** www.kystatepoetrysociety.org. Regional organization open to all. Member of The National Federation of State Poetry Societies (NFSPS). Currently has about 230 members. Offerings include association with other poets; information on contests and poetry happenings across the state and nation; annual state and national contests; national and state annual conventions with workshops, selected speakers, and open poetry readings. Sponsors workshops, contests, awards. Membership includes the quarterly KSPS Newsletter. Also includes a quarterly newsletter, *Strophes*, of the NFSPS; and the KSPS journal, *Pegasus*, published 3 times/year: a Spring/ Summer and Fall/ Winter issue which solicits good poetry for publication (need not be a member to submit), and a Prize Poems issue of 1st Place contest winners in over 30 categories. Members or nationally known writers give readings that are open to the public. Members meet annually. More information online.

## ✪ THE LEAGUE OF CANADIAN POETS

312-192 Spadina Ave., Toronto ON M5T 2C2, Canada. (416)504-1657. **E-mail:** admin@poets.ca. **Website:** www.poets.ca. **Contact:** Joanna Poblocka, executive director. A nonprofit national association of professional publishing and performing poets in Canada. Its purpose is "to enhance the status of poets and nurture a professional poetic community to facilitate the teaching of Canadian poetry at all levels of education and to develop the audience for poetry by encouraging publication, performance, and recognition of Canadian poetry nationally and internationally. As well as providing members and the public with many benefits and services, the League speaks for poets on many issues such as freedom of expression, Public Lending Right, CanCopy, contract advice, and grievance." Open to all Canadian citizens and landed immigrants; applications are assessed by a membership committee. Currently has 600 members. Membership benefits include a 1-year subscription to monthly e-newsletter, discount on Gift Shop purchases, listing in online members' catalog, and more (benefits increase with membership level). Sponsors The Pat Lowther Memorial Award (for a book of poetry by a Canadian woman published in the preceding year; $1,000 CAD prize) and The Gerald Lampert Memorial Award (recognizes the best first book of poetry published by a

Canadian in the preceding year; $1,000 CAD). Additional information online.

## THE LOFT LITERARY CENTER

Suite 200, Open Book, 1011 Washington Ave. S., Minneapolis MN 55415. (612)215-2575. **E-mail:** loft@loft. org. **Website:** www.loft.org. The Loft is the largest and most comprehensive literary center in the country, serving both writers and readers with a variety of readings, Spoken Word performances, educational programs, contests and grants, and writing facilities. Supporting members receive benefits including discounted tuition, admission charges, and contest fees; check-out privileges at The Loft's Rachel Anne Gaschott Resource Library; rental access to the Book Club Meeting Room and writers' studios and more. Additional information online.

## MASSACHUSETTS STATE POETRY SOCIETY

64 Harrison Ave., Lynn MA 01905. **E-mail:** msps.jc-maes@comcast.net. **Website:** mastatepoetrysociety. tripod.com. **Contact:** Jeanette C. Maes, president. Dedicated to the writing and appreciation of poetry and promoting the art form. Statewide organization open to anyone with an interest in poetry. Currently has 200 members. Member benefits include subscription to *Bay State Echo*, published 5 times/year with members' news and announcements; members-only contests; round-robin critique groups; members-only annual anthology; workshops at society meetings; and automatic membership in National Federation of State Poetry Societies (NFSPS). Sponsors contests open to all poets. Guidelines online. Members or nationally known writers give readings that are open to the public. Sponsors open mic readings for members and the public for National Poetry Day. Members meet 5 times/year. Additional information online.

## MISSISSIPPI POETRY SOCIETY, INC.

**E-mail:** poetsail5@gmail.com. **Website:** misspoetry. net. **Contact:** Michael Shelton, president. Purpose is "to foster interest in the writing of poetry through a study of poetry and poetic form; to provide an opportunity for, and give recognition to, individual creative efforts relating to poetry; and to create an audience for poetry; and suggest or otherwise make known markets and contests for poetry to its members." Statewide organization, affiliated with the National Federation of State Poetry Societies (NFSPS), consisting of 3 branches open to "anyone who writes poetry or is interested in fostering the interests of poetry." Currently has 100 members. Offerings include monthly meetings, annual contests, an annual awards banquet, and opportunities to have poems critiqued in sessions at state and branch meetings. State also holds a 1-day Mini-Festival in the fall and an annual 2-day Spring Festival; includes noted speakers and contests. Publishes bimonthly newsletter *Magnolia Muse* (members who win places in contests are published in *The Mississippi Poetry Journal*; student winners are published in *Fledglings*). Additional information online.

## MOUNTAIN WRITERS SERIES

Mountain Writers Center, 2804 S.E. 27th Ave., #2, Portland OR 97202. **E-mail:** programs@mountainwriters.org. **Website:** www.mountainwriters.org. "Mountain Writers Series is an independent nonprofit organization dedicated to supporting writers, audiences, and other sponsors by promoting literature and literacy through artistic and educational literary arts events in the Pacific Northwest." Currently has about 150 members. Mountain Writers Series offers intensive one-day and 2-day workshops, weekend master classes, 5-week, 8-week, and 10-week courses about writing. Sponsors readings that are open to the public. Nationally and internationally known writers are sponsored by the Mountain Writers Series Northwest Regional Residencies Program (reading tours) and the campus readings program (Pulitzer Prize winners, Nobel Prize winners, MacArthur Fellows, etc.). Additional information online.

## NATIONAL FEDERATION OF STATE POETRY SOCIETIES (NFSPS)

**E-mail:** paperlesspoetsonline@hotmail.com. **Website:** www.nfsps.com. "NFSPS is a nonprofit organization exclusively educational and literary. Its purpose is to recognize the importance of poetry with respect to national cultural heritage. It is dedicated solely to the furtherance of poetry on the national level and serves to unite poets in the bonds of fellowship and understanding." Currently has 7,000 members. Any poetry group located in a state not already affiliated, but interested in affiliating with NFSPS, may contact the membership chairman (see website). In a state where no valid group exists, help may also be obtained by individuals interested in organizing a poetry group for affiliation. Most reputable state poetry societies are members of the National Federation and advertise their various poetry contests through the NFSPS quarterly newsletter *Strophes*. NFSPS holds an annual 3-day convention in a different state each year with workshops, an awards banquet, and addresses by nationally known poets. Sponsors an annual 50-category national contest. Additional information online.

## NATIONAL WRITERS ASSOCIATION

10940 S. Parker Rd., #508, Parker CO 80138. (303)841-0246. **Fax:** (303)841-2607. **E-mail:** natlwritersassn@hotmail.com. **Website:** www.nationalwriters.com. Association for freelance writers. Qualifications for membership: associate membership—must be serious about writing; professional membership—must be published and paid writer (cite credentials). Sponsors workshops/conferences: TV/screenwriting workshops, NWAF Annual Conferences, Literary Clearinghouse, editing and critiquing services, local chapters, National Writer's School. Open to non-members. Publishes industry news of interest to freelance writers; how-to articles; market information; member news and networking opportunities. Sponsors poetry contest; short story contest; article contest; novel contest. Awards cash for top 3 winners; books and/or certificates for other winners; honorable mention certificate places 5-10. Contests open to nonmembers.

## NATIONAL WRITERS UNION

256 W. 38th St., Suite 703, New York NY 10018. (212)254-0279. **Fax:** (212)254-0673. **E-mail:** nwu@nwu.org. **Website:** www.nwu.org. Advocacy for freelance writers. Qualifications for membership: "Membership in the NWU is open to all qualified writers, and no one shall be barred or in any manner prejudiced within the Union on account of race, age, sex, sexual orientation, disability, national origin, religion or ideology. You are eligible for membership if you have published a book, a play, three articles, five poems, one short story or an equivalent amount of newsletter, publicity, technical, commercial, government or institutional copy. You are also eligible for membership if you have written an equal amount of unpublished material and you are actively writing and attempting to publish your work." Holds workshops throughout the country. Members only section on website offers rich resources for freelance writers. Skilled contract advice and grievance help for members.

## NEW HAMPSHIRE WRITERS' PROJECT

2500 North River Rd., Manchester NH 03106. (603)314-7980. **Fax:** (603)314-7981. **E-mail:** info@nhwritersproject.org. **Website:** www.nhwritersproject.org. Statewide organization open to writers at all levels in all genres. Currently has 600+ members. Offerings include workshops, seminars, an annual conference, and a literary calendar. Sponsors day-long workshops and 4- to 6-week intensive courses. Also sponsors the biennial New Hampshire Literary Awards for outstanding literary achievement (including The Jane Kenyon Award for Outstanding Book of Poetry). Publishes *NH Writer*, a quarterly newsletter for and about New Hampshire writers. Members and nationally known writers give readings that are open to the public. Additional information online.

## THE NORTH CAROLINA POETRY SOCIETY

NCPS, 3814 Hulon Dr., Durham NC 27705. **Website:** www.ncpoetrysociety.org. The North Carolina Poetry Society holds poetry-related contests and gives away several awards each year, for both Adults and Students (which includes 3rd Graders all the way to University Undergraduates). Statewide organization open to non-NC residents. Purpose: to encourage the reading, writing, study, and publication of poetry. NCPS brings poets together in meetings that feature workshops, presentations by noted poets and publishers, book and contest awards, and an annual anthology of award-winning poems. Currently has 350 members from NC and beyond. Sponsors annual Poetry Contest with categories for adults and students. Contests are open to anyone, with small fee for non-members. Winning poems are published in *Pinesong*, NCPS's annual anthology. A free copy is given to all winners, who are also invited to read at Awards Day. NCPS also sponsors the annual Brockman-Campbell Book Award for a book of poetry over 20 pages by a North Carolina poet (native-born or current resident for 3 years). NCPS also cosponsors the Gilbert-Chappell Distinguished Poet Series with The North Carolina Center for the Book, for the purpose of mentoring young poets across the state. Additional information online.

## NORTH CAROLINA WRITERS' NETWORK

P.O. Box 21591, Winston-Salem NC 27120. (336)293-8844. **E-mail:** ed@ncwriters.org. **Website:** www.ncwriters.org. Supports the work of writers, writers' organizations, independent bookstores, little magazines and small presses, and literary programming statewide. Currently has 1,000 members. Membership benefits include *The Writers' Network News*, a 24-page quarterly newsletter containing organizational news, trend in writing and publishing, and other literary material of interest to writers; and access to the NCWN online resources, other writers, workshops, writer's residencies, conferences, readings and competitions, and NCWN's critiquing and editing service. Annual fall conference features nationally known writers, publishers, and editors, held in a different North Carolina location each November. Sponsors competitions in short fiction, nonfiction, and poetry for North Carolina residents and NCWN members. Guidelines online.

## OHIO POETRY ASSOCIATION

**E-mail:** charles@ohiopoetryassn.org. **Website:** www.ohiopoetryassn.org. Promotes the art of poetry, and furthers the support of poets and others who support poetry. Statewide membership with additional members in several other states, Japan, and England. Affiliated with the National Federation of State Poetry Societies (NFSPS). Open to poets and writers of all ages and ability, as well as to non-writing lovers of poetry. Currently has about 215 members. Member benefits include regular contests; meeting/workshop participation; assistance with writing projects; networking; twice-yearly magazine, *Common Threads*, publishing only poems by members; quarterly Ohio Poetry Association Newsletter ; quarterly NFSPS newsletters (*Strophes*); automatic NFSPS membership; and contest information and lower entry fees for NFSPS contests. Members are automatically on the mailing list for Ohio Poetry Day contest guidelines (OPA financially supports Ohio Poetry Day). Individual chapters regularly host workshops and seminars. Members and nationally known writers give readings that are open to the public (at quarterly meetings; public is invited). Sponsors open mic readings for members and the public. Members meet quarterly (September, December, March, May). Additional information available online. "In short, OPA provides poets with opportunities to share info, critique, publish, sponsor contests, and just socialize."

## PEN AMERICAN CENTER

588 Broadway, Suite 303, New York NY 10012. (212)334-1660. **Fax:** (212)334-2181. **E-mail:** info@pen.org. **Website:** www.pen.org. "An association of writers working to advance literature, to defend free expression, and to foster international literary fellowship. PEN welcomes to its membership all writers and those belonging to the larger literary community. We

ask that writers have at least one book published or be writers with proven records as professional writers; playwrights and screenwriters should have at least one work produced in a professional setting. Others should have achieved recognition in the literary field. Editors, literary agents, literary scouts, publicists, journalists, bloggers, and other literary professionals are all invited to join as Professional Members. If you feel you do not meet these guidelines, please consider joining as an Advocate Member. Candidates for membership may be nominated by a PEN member or they may nominate themselves with the support of two references from the literary community or from a current PEN member. PEN members receive a subscription to the PEN journal, the PEN Annual Report, and have access to medical insurance at group rates. Members living in the New York metropolitan and tri-state area, or near the Branches, are invited to PEN events throughout the year. Membership in PEN American Center includes reciprocal privileges in PEN American Center branches and in foreign PEN Centers for those traveling abroad. Application forms are available online. PEN American Center is the largest of the 141 centers of PEN International, the world's oldest human rights organization and the oldest international literary organization. PEN International was founded in 1921 to dispel national, ethnic, and racial hatreds and to promote understanding among all countries. PEN American Center, founded a year later, works to advance literature, to defend free expression, and to foster international literary fellowship. The Center has a membership of 3,400 distinguished writers, editors, and translators. In addition to defending writers in prison or in danger of imprisonment for their work, PEN American Center sponsors public literary programs and forums on current issues, sends prominent authors to inner-city schools to encourage reading and writing, administers literary prizes, promotes international literature that might otherwise go unread in the United States, and offers grants and loans to writers facing financial or medical emergencies."

## PITTSBURGH POETRY EXCHANGE

P.O. Box 4279, Pittsburgh PA 15203. (412)481-POEM. **E-mail:** ppepoets@yahoo.com. **Website:** pghpoetry-exchange.pghfree.net. **Contact:** Michael Wurster, coordinator. A community-based volunteer organization for local poets, it functions as a service organization and information exchange, conducting ongoing workshops, readings, and discussions to promote poets and poetry. No dues or fees. "Any monetary contributions are voluntary, often from outside. Currently has about 30 members (with a mailing list of 400). Sponsors a monthly workshop (first Monday, 8 pm, Brentwood Public Library) a discussion of a poetry book (fourth Wed., Coffee Tree, Walnut St., 7:30 pm). Poets from out of town may contact the Exchange for assistance in setting up readings at bookstores to help sell their books. "We have been partnering with Autumn House Press in co-sponsoring events and bringing some of its authors to town." Additional information online. "Pittsburgh is a very exciting literary town."

## POETRY BOOK SOCIETY

Unit G07, Screenworks, 22 Highbury Grove, London N5 2EF, United Kingdom. (44)(207)831-7468. **E-mail:** info@poetrybooks.co.uk. **Website:** www.poetrybooks.co.uk. A book club that promotes "the best newly published contemporary poetry to as wide an audience as possible." Membership: 2,200. All members receive a subscription to the quarterly *PBS Bulletin*, 25% discount on almost all poetry books published in the UK, and advance notice of poetry events; Full Members also receive 4 PBS Choice selections free. New members receive a welcome gift. The PBS selectors also recommend other books of special merit each quarter. Sponsors the T.S. Eliot Prize for the best new single author collection published in the UK and Ireland in the calendar year. The Poetry Book Society is subsidized by the Arts Council of England. Additional information online.

## THE POETRY FOUNDATION

61 W. Superior St., Chicago IL 60654. (312)787-7070. **Fax:** (312)787-6650. **E-mail:** info@poetryfoundation.org. **Website:** poetryfoundation.org. "The Poetry Foundation is an independent literary organization committed to a vigorous presence for poetry in our culture. It exists to discover and celebrate the best poetry and to place it before the largest possible audience. Initiatives include publishing *Poetry* magazine; distributing Ted Kooser's *American Life in Poetry* newspaper project; funding and promotion of Poetry Out Loud: National Recitation Contest (in partnership with the National Endowment for the Arts and state arts associations); *Poetry Everywhere*, a series of short poetry films airing on public television and on

transportation systems across the country; *The Essential American Poets* podcast series featuring seminal recordings of major American Poets reading from their work, as selected by former Poet Laureate Donald Hall; and www.poetryfoundation.org, an award-winning comprehensive online resource for poetry featuring an archive of more than 6,500 poems by more than 600 classic and contemporary poets. The site also includes the poetry blog "Harriet," poetry-related articles, a bestseller list, video programming, a series of poetry podcasts, and reading guides about poets and poetry. The Poetry Foundation annually awards the Ruth Lilly Poetry Prize, of $100,000, and the Ruth Lilly Poetry Fellowships, 5 annual awards of $15,000 to young poets to support their further studies in poetry." More information online.

## THE POETRY SOCIETY

22 Betterton St., London WC2H 9BX, United Kingdom. (44)(207)420-9880. **E-mail:** info@poetrysociety.org.uk. **Website:** www.poetrysociety.org.uk. One of Britain's most dynamic arts organizations, with membership open to all. "The Poetry Society exists to help poets and poetry thrive in Britain today. Our members come from all over the world, and their support enables us to promote poetry on a global scale." Publishes *Poetry Review*, Britain's most prominent poetry magazine, and *Poetry News*, the Society's newsletter, as well as books and posters to support poetry in the classroom. Runs the National Poetry Competition and The Foyle Young Poets of the Year Award (for poets aged 11-17), as well as many other competitions, services, and education projects for readers and writers of poetry. More information online.

## POETRY SOCIETY OF AMERICA

15 Gramercy Park, New York NY 10003. (212)254-9628. **Fax:** (212)673-2352. **Website:** www.poetrysociety.org. The Poetry Society of America is a national nonprofit organization for poets and lovers of poetry. All paid members receive *Crossroads: The Journal of the Poetry Society of America*; additional benefits available as membership levels increase. Sponsors readings and lectures as well as the Poetry in Motion program. Provides free-to-join PSA electronic mailing list for news of upcoming events. PSA also sponsors a number of competitions for members and nonmembers.

## POETRY SOCIETY OF NEW HAMPSHIRE

170 Browns Ridge Rd., Ossipee NH 03864. **E-mail:** info@poetrysocietyofnewhampshire.org. **Website:** www.poetrysocietyofnewhampshire.org. A statewide organization for anyone interested in poetry. Currently has 200 members. Offerings include annual subscription to quarterly magazine, *The Poet's Touchstone*; critiques, contests, and workshops; public readings; and quarterly meetings with featured poets. Members and nationally known writers give readings that are open to the public. Sponsors open mic readings for members and the public. Additional information available for SASE or by e-mail. "We do sponsor a national contest four times a year. People from all over the country enter and win."

## THE POETRY SOCIETY OF SOUTH CAROLINA

P.O. Box 1090, Charleston SC 29402. **E-mail:** president@poetrysocietysc.org. **Website:** www.poetrysocietysc.org. The Poetry Society of South Carolina supports "the reading, writing, study, and enjoyment of poetry." Statewide organization open to anyone interested in poetry. Offers programs in Charleston that are free and open to the public September-May (except for members-only holiday party in December). Currently has 150 members. Membership benefits include discounts to PSSC-sponsored seminars and workshops held in various SC locations; a copy of the annual Yearbook of contest-winning poems; eligibility to read at the open mic and to enter contests without a fee; and an invitation to the annual holiday party. Sponsors a monthly Writers' Group, a January open mic reading featuring PSSC members, a Charleston Poetry Walk during Piccolo Spoleto in June, and a May Forum leading to an audience-selected poetry prize. Sponsors two yearly contests, totaling 20-25 contest categories, some with themes; some are open to all poets, others open only to SC residents or PSSC members. Guidelines available online. Also offers the Skylark Prize, a competition for SC high school students. Sometimes offers a chapbook competition. Members and nationally known writers give readings that are open to the public. Additional information online.

## POETRY SOCIETY OF TENNESSEE

18 S. Rembert, Memphis TN 38104. **Website:** poetrysocietytn.org. Purpose is "to promote writing, reading, and appreciation of poetry among members of

the society and the community; to improve poetry writing skills of members and local students." State poetry society, with some out-of-state members. Affiliate of National Federation of State Poetry Societies (NFSPS). Current membership about 70. Yearbook contains names, addresses, e-mail addresses of officers and members; winning poems by members and student members; and more. Society activities include programs with speakers; poetry contests, readings, and workshops; one meeting a year dedicated to students; plus Mid-South Poetry Festival first Saturday in October with workshop and prizes. Poetry readings about four times a year in local restaurants and bookstores.

## POETRY SOCIETY OF TEXAS

518 Grinnell Dr., Garland TX 75043. (972)270-4994. **E-mail:** catherinepoet@juno.com. **Website:** www.poetrysocietyoftexas.org. "The purpose of the society shall be to secure fuller public recognition of the art of poetry, to encourage the writing of poetry by Texans, and to kindle a finer and more intelligent appreciation of poetry, especially the work of living poets who interpret the spirit and heritage of Texas." Poetry Society of Texas is a member of the National Federation of State Poetry Societies (NFSPS). Has 18 chapters in cities throughout the state. Currently has 300 members. Offerings include annual contests with prizes in excess of $6,000 as well as monthly contests (general and humorous); 8 monthly meetings; annual awards banquet; annual summer conference in a different location each year; and Poetry in Schools with contests at state and local chapter levels. "Our monthly state meetings are held at the Preston Royal Branch of the Dallas Public Library. Our annual awards banquet is held at a nice hotel in Dallas. Our summer conference is held at a site chosen by the hosting chapter. Chapters determine their meeting sites." PST publishes *A Book of the Year*, which presents annual and monthly award-winning poems, coming contest descriptions, minutes of meetings, by-laws of the society, history, and information. Also publishes the *The Bulletin*, a monthly newsletter that features statewide news documenting contest winners, state meeting information, chapter and individual information, news from the NFSPS, and announcements of coming activities and offerings for poets. Members and nationally known writers give readings. "All of our meetings are open to the public." Additional information online.

## POETS & WRITERS, INC.

90 Broad St, Suite 2100, New York NY 10004. (212)226-3586. **Website:** www.pw.org. Poets & Writers' mission is "to foster the professional development of poets and writers, to promote communication throughout the U.S. literary community, and to help create an environment in which literature can be appreciated by the widest possible public." The largest nonprofit literary organization in the nation, P&W offers information, support, resources, and exposure to poets, fiction writers, and nonfiction writers at all stages in their careers. Sponsors the Readings/Workshops Program, through which P&W sponsors more than 1,700 literary events in New York, California, and other cities in the U.S. Sponsors the Writers Exchange Contest; the Jacobson Poetry Prize; and the Amy Award. Additional information online.

## POETS HOUSE

10 River Terrace, New York NY 10282. (212)431-7920. **Fax:** (212)431-8131. **E-mail:** info@poetshouse.org. **Website:** www.poetshouse.org. Poets House, a national poetry library and literary center, is a "home for all who read and write poetry." Resources include the 60,000-volume poetry collection, conference room, exhibition space, a programming hall, and a Children's Room. Over 200 annual public programs include panel discussions and lectures, readings, seminars and workshops, and children's events. In addition, Poets House continues its collaboration with public library systems, Poetry in The Branches, a multi-faceted program model to help libraries nationwide create a complete environment for poetry locally (see website for information). Finally, each year Poets House hosts the Poets House Showcase, a comprehensive exhibit of the year's new poetry releases from commercial, university, and independent presses across the country. "Poets House depends, in part, on tax-deductible contributions of its nationwide members." Additional information online.

## SCIENCE FICTION POETRY ASSOCIATION

P.O. Box 907, Winchester CA 92596. **E-mail:** sfpatreasurer@gmail.com. **Website:** www.sfpoetry.com. The Science Fiction Poetry Association was founded "to bring together poets and readers interested in science fiction poetry (poetry with some element of speculation, usually science fiction, fantasy, or horror)." Membership benefits include 6 issues/year of *Star*Line*, a journal filled with poetry, reviews, articles, and more; one issue of the annual Rhysling Anthology of the best science fiction poetry of the previous year; opportunity to nominate one short poem and one long poem to be printed in the anthology, and to vote for which poems should receive that year's Rhysling award; half-priced advertising on the SFPA website, with greater subject matter leeway than nonmembers; eligibility to vote for SFPA officers (or run for officer); mailings with the latest news. Additional information online.

## SCOTTISH POETRY LIBRARY

5 Crichton's Close, Edinburgh EH8 8DT, Scotland. (44)(131)557-2876. **Fax:** (44)(131)557-8393. **Website:** www.scottishpoetrylibrary.org.uk. A reference information source and free lending library; also lends by post. Arranges poetry-writing workshops throughout Scotland, mainly for young people. The library has a web-based catalog available that allows searches of all the library's resources, including books, magazines, and audio material—over 30,000 items of Scottish and international poetry. Need not be a member to borrow material; memberships available strictly to support the library's work. Benefits include semiannual newsletter, annual report, new publications listings, and book offers. The School of Poets is open to anyone; "at meetings, members divide into small groups in which each participatn reads a poem, which is then analyzed and discussed." Also offers a Critical Service in which groups of up to 6 poems, not exceeding 200 lines in all, are given critical comment by members of the School: 15 for each critique (with SAE). Additional information online.

## TANKA SOCIETY OF AMERICA

439 S. Catalina Ave., #306, Pasadena CA 91106. **Website:** www.tankasocietyofamerica.org. **Contact:** Kathabela Wilson, secretary. The Tanka Society of America, a nonprofit volunteer organization, aims to further the writing, reading, study, and appreciation of tanka poetry in English. Open to anyone interested in tanka. Membership dues for USA, Canada, and International are available online. Membership offerings include the quarterly *Ribbons: Tanka Society of America Journal* and eligibility to submit poems to annual members' anthology. The Tanka Society of American also conducts an annual international tanka competition with cash awards and publication of winning poems. Additional information online.

## THE POETRY LIBRARY

The Poetry Library, Level 5, Royal Festival Hall, London SE1 8XX, United Kingdom. (44)(207)921-0943/0664. **Fax:** (44)(207)921-0607. **E-mail:** info@poetrylibrary.org.uk. **Website:** www.poetrylibrary.org.uk. **Contact:** Chris McCabe, Poetry Librarian. A "free public library of modern poetry. It contains a comprehensive collection of all British poetry published since 1912 and an international collection of poetry from all over the world, either written in or translated into English. As the United Kingdom's national library for poetry, it offers loan and information services and a large collection of poetry magazines, cassettes, compact discs, videos, records, poem posters, and cards; also press cuttings and photographs of poets."

## UNIVERSITY OF ARIZONA POETRY CENTER

1508 E. Helen St., P.O. Box 210129, Tucson AZ 85721. (520)626-3765. **E-mail:** poetry@email.arizona.edu. **Website:** www.poetrycenter.arizona.edu. **Contact:** Tyler Meier, Executive Director. "Open to the public, the University of Arizona Poetry Center is a contemporary poetry archive and a nationally acclaimed poetry collection that includes over 70,000 items. Programs and services include a library with a noncirculating poetry collection and space for small classes; online lesson plan library; High School Bilingual Corrido Contest; K-16 field trip program; summer camps; poetry-related meetings and activities; facilities, research support, and referral information about poetry and poets for local and national communities; reading series; community creative writing classes and workshops; a summer residency offered each year to two writers (one prose, one poetry) selected by jury; and poetry awards, readings, and special events for high school, undergraduate, and graduate students. Additional information available by phone, e-mail, or website. Become a 'Friend of the Poetry Center' by making an annual contribution."

## UTAH STATE POETRY SOCIETY

**Website:** www.utahpoets.com. Purpose is to secure a wider appreciation of the poetry arts and to promote excellence in writing poetry. Statewide organization. Membership is open to all citizens of the State of Utah and to interested people from any other state in the union, without consideration of age, race, regional, religious, educational, or other backgrounds. Currently has about 200 members. Membership benefits include membership in National Federation of State Poetry Societies (NFSPS) and subscription to their newsletter *Strophes*, copy of the *Book of the Year* and other publications, and full contest privileges. Sponsors conferences, workshops, contests, awards. USPS publishes, semiannually, work of members in a chapbook anthology. Publishes *Poet Tree*, a semiannual newsletter (also available online). Publishes one winning manuscript annually. Members or nationally known writers give readings/workshops that are open to the public. Chapters meet at least once a month, with open readings, critiques, lessons. Annual Awards Festival includes open reading. Additional information online. "We welcome all potential members."

## WISCONSIN FELLOWSHIP OF POETS

**Website:** www.wfop.org. Statewide organization open to residents and former residents of Wisconsin who are interested in the aims and endeavors of the organization. Currently has 485 members. Sponsors biannual conferences, workshops, contests and awards. Publishes *Wisconsin Poets' Calendar*, poems of Wisconsin (resident) poets. Also publishes *Museletter*, a quarterly newsletter. Members or nationally known writers give readings that are open to the public. Sponsors open mic readings. Additional information online.

## WORCESTER COUNTY POETRY ASSOCIATION

1 Ekman St., Worcester MA 01607. (508)797-4770. **E-mail:** wcpaboard@yahoo.com. **Website:** worcestercountypoetry.org. **Contact:** Membership Chair. The Worcester County Poetry Association is "open to all who appreciate poetry and wish to support the vibrant Worcester poetry community." Membership benefits include annual subscription to *The Worcester Review*; all WCPA mailings, including broadsides, calendars, and *The Issue*; and fee-free submission to the WCPA Annual Poetry Contest. Additional information online.

## WORDS WITHOUT BORDERS

154 Christopher St., Suite 3C, New York NY 10014. **E-mail:** info@wordswithoutborders.org. **Website:** www.wordswithoutborders.org. "Words Without Borders opens doors to international exchange through translation, publications, and promotion of the world's best writing. Our ultimate aim is to introduce exciting international writing to the general public—travelers, teachers, students, publishers, and a new generation of eclectic readers— by presenting international literature as a portal through which to explore the world. The heart of WWB's work is its online magazine. Monthly issues feature new selections of contemporary world literature, most of which would never have been accessible to English-speaking readers without WWB. Members and international writers give readings that are open to the public. Finally, our education program WWB Campus, introduces students at both the high school and college levels to a broad spectrum of contemporary international literature. Our goal is to provide content and resources that help educators incorporate contemporary literature in their curricula."

## THE WORD WORKS

P.O. Box 42164, Washington DC 20015. **E-mail:** editor@wordworksdc.com. **Website:** www.wordworksdc.com. Word Works is "a nonprofit literary organization publishing contemporary poetry in single-author editions." Membership benefits at the basic level include choice of 2 books from The Word Works book list, newsletter, and 20% discount on additional book orders; in addition to these benefits, sustaining members are eligible for online critique of several poems via e-mail. Sponsors an ongoing poetry reading series, educational programs, and the Hilary Tham Capital Collection. Sponsors The Washington Prize, one of the older ms publishing prizes, and The Jacklyn Potter Young Poets Competition. Additional information online.

## THE WRITER'S CENTER

4508 Walsh St., Bethesda MD 20815. (301)654-8664. **E-mail:** post.master@writer.org. **Website:** www.writer.org. **Contact:** Joe Callahan, Executive Director. The Writer's Center is a nonprofit community of writers supporting each other in the creation and marketing of literary texts. Annually conducts over 300 workshops; hosts literary events, readings, and conferences; publishes *The Workshop & Event Guide*, a quarterly magazine of articles and writing news for members. Also publishes *Poet Lore*, America's oldest poetry journal. Additional information online.

## ◯ WRITERS' FEDERATION OF NOVA SCOTIA

1113 Marginal Rd., Halifax NS B3H 4P7, Canada. (902)423-8116. **Fax:** (902)422-0881. **E-mail:** director@writers.ns.ca. **Website:** www.writers.ns.ca. Purpose of organization: "to foster creative writing and the profession of writing in Nova Scotia; to provide advice and assistance to writers at all stages of their careers; and to encourage greater public recognition of Nova Scotian writers and their achievements." Regional organization open to anybody who writes. Currently has 800+ members. Offerings include resource library with over 2,500 titles, promotional services, workshop series, annual festivals, mentorship program. Publishes *Eastword*, a bimonthly newsletter containing "a plethora of information on who's doing what; markets and contests; and current writing events and issues." Members and nationally known writers give readings that are open to the public. Additional information online.

## ☺ WRITERS GUILD OF ALBERTA

11759 Groat Rd., Edmonton AB T5M 3K6, Canada. (780)422-8174. **E-mail:** mail@writersguild.ab.ca. **Website:** www.writersguild.ab.ca. Purpose of organization: to support, encourage and promote writers and writing, to safeguard the freedom to write and to read, and to advocate for the well-being of writers in Alberta. Currently has over 1,000 members. Offerings include retreats/conferences; monthly events; bimonthly magazine that includes articles on writing and a market section; weekly electronic bulletin with markets and event listings; and the Stephan G. Stephansson Award for Poetry (Alberta residents only). Holds workshops/conferences. Publishes a newsletter focusing on markets, competitions, contemporary issues related to the literary arts (writing, publishing, censorship, royalties etc.). Sponsors annual literary awards in 5 categories (novel, nonfiction, children's literature, poetry, drama). Awards include $1,500. Open to nonmembers.

## THE WRITERS ROOM

740 Broadway at Astor Place, 12th Floor, New York NY 10003. (212)254-6995. **E-mail:** writersroom@ writersroom.org. **Website:** www.writersroom.org. Provides a "home away from home" for any writer who needs space to work. Currently has about 350 members. Emerging and established writers may apply. Large loft provides desk space, Internet access, storage, and more. Call for application or download from website.

## W.B. YEATS SOCIETY OF NEW YORK

National Arts Club, 15 Gramercy Park S., New York NY 10003. **E-mail:** info@yeatssociety.org. **Website:** www.yeatssociety.org. **Contact:** Andrew McGowan, president. Founded "to promote the legacy of Irish poet and Nobel Laureate William Butler Yeats through an annual program of lectures, readings, poetry competition, and special events." National organization open to anyone. Currently has 450 members. Sponsors The W.B. Yeats Society Annual Poetry Competition. Also sponsors conferences/workshops. Each April, presents an all-day Saturday program, "A Taste of Yeats Summer School in Ireland." Nationally known writers give readings that are open to the public. Members meet approximately monthly, September to June. Additional information online.

# POETS IN EDUCATION

Whether known as PITS (Poets in the Schools), WITS (Writers in the Schools), or similar names, programs exist nationwide that coordinate residencies, classroom visits and other opportunities for experienced poets to share their craft with students. Many state arts agencies include such "arts in education" programs in their activities. Another good source is the National Assembly of State Arts Agencies, which offers an online directory of contact names and addresses for arts education programs state-by-state. The following list is a mere sampling of programs and organizations that link poets with schools.

**THE ACADEMY OF AMERICAN POETS,** 584 Broadway, Suite 604, New York NY 10012-5243. (212)274-0343. E-mail: academy@poets.org. Website: www.poets.org.

**ARKANSAS WRITERS IN THE SCHOOLS,** WITS Director, 333 Kimpel Hall, University of Arkansas, Fayetteville AR 72701. (479)575-5991. E-mail: wits@cavern.uark.edu. Website: www.uark.edu/~wits.

**CALIFORNIA POETS IN THE SCHOOLS,** 1333 Balboa St. #3, San Francisco CA 94118. (415)221-4201. E-mail: info@cpits.org. Website: www.cpits.org.

**E-POETS.NETWORK,** a collective online cultural center that promotes education through videoconferencing (i.e., "distance learning"); also includes the *Voces y Lugares* project. Website: http://learning.e-poets.net (includes online contact form).

**IDAHO WRITERS IN THE SCHOOLS,** Log Cabin Literary Center, 801 S. Capitol Blvd., Boise ID 83702. (208)331-8000. E-mail: info@thecabinidaho.org. Website: www.thecabin idaho.org.

**INDIANA WRITERS IN THE SCHOOLS,** University of Evansville, Dept. of English, 1800 Lincoln Ave., Evansville IN 47722. (812)488-2962. E-mail: rg37@evansville.edu. Website: http://english.evansville.edu/WritersintheSchools.htm.

**MICHIGAN CREATIVE WRITERS IN THE SCHOOLS,** ArtServe Michigan, 17515 W. Nine Mile Rd., Suite 1025, Southfield MI 48075. (248)557-8288. Website: www.artservemichigan.org.

**NATIONAL ASSEMBLY OF STATE ARTS AGENCIES,** 1029 Vermont Ave. NW, 2nd Floor, Washington DC 20005. (202)347-6352. E-mail: nasaa@nasaa-arts.org. Website: www.nasaa-arts.org.

**NATIONAL ASSOCIATION OF WRITERS IN EDUCATION (NAWE),** P.O. Box 1, Sheriff Hutton, York YO60 7YU England. (44)(1653)618429. Website: www.nawe.co.uk.

**OREGON WRITERS IN THE SCHOOLS,** Literary Arts, 224 NW 13th Ave., Suite 306, Portland OR 97209. (503)227-2583. E-mail: john@literary-arts.org. Website: www.literary-arts.org/wits.

**PEN IN THE CLASSROOM (PITC),** Pen Center USA, Þco Antioch University, 400 Corporate Pointe, Culver City CA 90230. (310)862-1555. E-mail: pitc@penusa.org. Website: www.penusa.org/go/classroom.

**"PICK-A-POET,"** The Humanities Project, Arlington Public Schools, 1439 N. Quincy St., Arlington VA 22207. (703)228-6299. E-mail: online form. Website: www.humanitiesproject.org.

**POTATO HILL POETRY,** 6 Pleasant St., Suite 2, South Natick MA 01760. (888)5-POETRY. E-mail: info@potatohill.com. Website: www.potatohill.com (includes online contact form).

**SEATTLE WRITERS IN THE SCHOOLS (WITS),** Seattle Arts & Lectures, 105 S. Main St., Suite 201, Seattle WA 98104. (206)621-2230. Website: www.lectures.org/wits.html.

**TEACHERS & WRITERS COLLABORATIVE,** 520 Eighth Ave., Suite 2020, New York NY 10018. (212)691-6590 or (888)BOOKS-TW (book orders). E-mail: info@twc.org. Website: www.twc.org. "A catalog of T&W books is available online, or call toll-free to request a print copy.

**TEXAS WRITERS IN THE SCHOOLS,** 1523 W. Main, Houston TX 77006. (713)523-3877. E-mail: mail@witshouston.org. Website: www.writersintheschools.org.

**WRITERS & ARTISTS IN THE SCHOOLS (WAITS),** COMPAS, Landmark Center, Suite 304, 75 Fifth St. West, St. Paul MN 55102-1496. (651)292-3254. E-mail: daniel@compas.org. Website: www.compas.org.

**YOUTH VOICES IN INK,** Badgerdog Literary Publishing, Inc., P.O. Box 301209, Austin TX 78703-0021. (512)538-1305. E-mail: info@badgerdog.org. Website: www.badgerdog.org

# GLOSSARY

////////////////////////////////////////////////////////////////////////////////////

This glossary is provided as a quick-reference only, briefly covering poetic styles and terms that may turn up in articles and listings in *Poet's Market*.

**A3, A4, A5.** Metric equivalents of 11¾×16½, 8¼×11¾, and 5⅞×8¼ respectively.

**ABSTRACT POEM.** Conveys emotion through sound, textures, rhythm and rhyme rather than through the meanings of words.

**ACKNOWLEDGMENTS PAGE.** A page in a poetry book or chapbook that lists the publications where the poems in the collection were originally published; may be presented as part of the copyright page or as a separate page on its own.

**ACROSTIC.** Initial letters of each line, read downward, form a word, phrase, or sentence.

**ALLITERATION.** Close repetition of consonant sounds, especially initial consonant sounds.

**ALPHABET POEM.** Arranges lines alphabetically according to initial letter.

**AMERICAN CINQUAIN.** Derived from Japanese haiku and tanka by Adelaide Crapsey; counted syllabic poem of 5 lines of 2-4-6-8-2 syllables, frequently in iambic feet.

**ANAPEST.** Foot consisting of 2 unstressed syllables followed by a stress.

**ANTHOLOGY.** A collection of selected writings by various authors.

**ASSONANCE.** Close repetition of vowel sounds.

**AVANT-GARDE.** Work at the forefront—cutting edge, unconventional, risk-taking.

**ATTACHMENT.** A computer file electronically "attached" to an e-mail message.

**AUD.** Abbreviation for Australian Dollar.

**B&W.** Black & white (photo or illustration).

**BALLAD.** Narrative poem often in ballad stanza (4-line stanza with 4 stresses in lines 1 and 3, 3 stresses in lines 2 and 4, which also rhyme).

**BALLADE.** 3 stanzas rhymed *ababbcbC* (*C* indicates a refrain) with envoi rhymed *bcbC*.

**BEAT POETRY.** Anti-academic school of poetry born in '50s San Francisco; fast-paced free verse resembling jazz.

**BIO.** A short biographical statement often requested with a submission.

**BLANK VERSE.** Unrhymed iambic pentameter.

**CAD.** Abbreviation for Canadian Dollar.

**CAESURA.** A deliberate rhetorical, grammatical, or rhythmic pause, break, cut, turn, division, or pivot in poetry.

**CAMERA-READY.** Poems ready for copy camera platemaking; camera-ready poems usually appear in print exactly as submitted.

**CHANT.** Poem in which one or more lines are repeated over and over.

**CHAPBOOK.** A small book of about 24-50 pages.

**CIRCULATION.** The number of subscribers to a magazine/journal.

**CINQUAIN.** Any 5-line poem or stanza; also called "quintain" or "quintet." (See also *American cinquain*.)

**CLMP.** Council of Literary Magazines and Presses; service organization for independent publishers of fiction, poetry, and prose.

**CONCRETE POETRY.** See *emblematic poem*.

**CONFESSIONAL POETRY.** Work that uses personal and private details from the poet's own life.

**CONSONANCE.** See *alliteration*.

**CONTRIBUTOR'S COPY.** Copy of book or magazine containing a poet's work, sometimes given as payment.

**COUPLET.** Stanza of 2 lines; pair of rhymed lines.

**COVER LETTER.** Brief introductory letter accompanying a poetry submission.

**COVERSTOCK.** Heavier paper used as the cover for a publication.

**DACTYL.** Foot consisting of a stress followed by 2 unstressed syllables.

**DIDACTIC POETRY.** Poetry written with the intention to instruct.

**DIGEST-SIZED.** About 5½×8½, the size of a folded sheet of conventional printer paper.

**DOWNLOAD.** To "copy" a file, such as a registration form, from a website.

**ECLECTIC.** Open to a variety of poetic styles (as in "eclectic taste").

**EKPHRASTIC POEM.** Verbally presents something originally represented in visual art, though more than mere description.

**ELECTRONIC MAGAZINE.** See *online magazine*.

**ELEGY.** Lament in verse for someone who has died, or a reflection on the tragic nature of life.

**EMBLEMATIC POEM.** Words or letters arranged to imitate a shape, often the subject of the poem.

**ENJAMBMENT.** Continuation of sense and rhythmic movement from one line to the next; also called a "run-on" line.

**ENVOI.** A brief ending (usually to a ballade or sestina) no more than 4 lines long; summary.

**EPIC POETRY.** Long narrative poem telling a story central to a society, culture, or nation.

**EPIGRAM.** Short, satirical poem or saying written to be remembered easily, like a punch-line.

**EPIGRAPH.** A short verse, note, or quotation that appears at the beginning of a poem or section; usually presents an idea or theme on which the poem elaborates, or contributes background information not reflected in the poem itself.

**EPITAPH.** Brief verse commemorating a person/group of people who died.

**EURO.** Currency unit for the 27 member countries of the European Union.

**EXPERIMENTAL POETRY.** Work that challenges conventional ideas of poetry by exploring new techniques, form, language, and visual presentation.

**FAQ.** Frequently Asked Questions.

**FIBS.** Short form based on the mathematical progression known as the Fibonacci sequence; syllable counts for each line are 1/1/2/3/5/8/13 (count for each line is derived by adding the counts for the previous two lines).

**FLARF.** A malleable term that may refer to 1) poetic and creative text pieces by the Flarflist Collective; any poetry created from search engine (such as Google) results; any intentionally bad, zany, or trivial poetry.

**FONT.** The style/design of type used in a publication; typeface.

**FOOT.** Unit of measure in a metrical line of poetry.

**FOUND POEM.** Text lifted from a non-poetic source such as an ad and presented as a poem.

**FREE VERSE.** Unmetrical verse (lines not counted for accents, syllables, etc.).

**GALLEYS.** First typeset version of a poem, magazine, or book/chapbook.

**GHAZAL.** Persian poetic form of 5-15 unconnected, independent couplets; associative jumps may be made from couplet to couplet.

**GLBT.** Gay/lesbian/bisexual/transgender (as in "GLBT themes").

**GREETING CARD POETRY.** Resembles verses in greeting cards; sing-song meter and rhyme.

**HAIBUN.** Originally, a Japanese form in which elliptical, often autobiographical prose is interspersed with haiku.

**HAIKAI NO RENGA.** See *renku*.

**HAY(NA)KU.** A 3-line form, with 1 word in line 1, 2 words in line 2, and 3 words in line 3.

**HAIKU.** Originally, a Japanese form of a single vertical line with 17 sound symbols in a 5-7-5 pattern. In English, typically a 3-line poem with fewer than 17 syllables in no set pattern, but exhibiting a 2-part juxtapositional structure, seasonal reference, imagistic immediacy, and a moment of keen perception of nature or human nature.

**HOKKU.** The starting verse of a renga or renku, in 5, 7, and then 5 sound symbols in Japanese; or in three lines, usually totaling fewer than 17 syllables, in English; the precursor for what is now called haiku. (See also *haiku*.)

**HONORARIUM.** A token payment for published work.

**IAMB.** Foot consisting of an unstressed syllable followed by a stress.

**IAMBIC PENTAMETER.** Consists of 5 iambic feet per line.

**IMAGIST POETRY.** Short, free verse lines that present images without comment or explanation; strongly influenced by haiku and other Oriental forms.

**IRC.** International Reply Coupon; a publisher can exchange IRCs for postage to return a manuscript to another country.

**JPEG.** Short for *Joint Photographic Experts Group*; an image compression format that allows digital images to be stored in relatively small files for electronic mailing and viewing on the Internet.

**KYRIELLE.** French form; 4-line stanza with 8-syllable lines, the final line a refrain.

**LANGUAGE POETRY.** Attempts to detach words from traditional meanings to produce something new and unprecedented.

**LIMERICK.** 5-line stanza rhyming *aabba*; pattern of stresses/line is traditionally 3-3-2-2-3; often bawdy or scatalogical.

**LINE.** Basic compositional unit of a poem; measured in feet if metrical.

**LINKED POETRY.** Written through the collaboration of 2 or more poets creating a single poetic work.

**LONG POEM.** Exceeds length and scope of short lyric or narrative poem; defined arbitrarily, often as more than 2 pages or 100 lines.

**LYRIC POETRY.** Expresses personal emotion; music predominates over narrative or drama.

**MAGAZINE-SIZED.** About 8½×11, the size of an unfolded sheet of conventional printer paper.

**METAPHOR.** 2 different things are likened by identifying one as the other (A=B).

**METER.** The rhythmic measure of a line.

**MINUTE.** 12-line poem consisting of 60 syllables, with a syllabic line count of 8,4,4,4,8,4,4,4, 8,4,4,4; often consists of rhyming couplets.

**MODERNIST POETRY.** Work of the early 20th century literary movement that sought to break with the past, rejecting outmoded literary traditions, diction, and form while encouraging innovation and reinvention.

**MS.** Manuscript.

**MSS.** Manuscripts.

**MULTI-BOOK REVIEW.** Several books by the same author or by several authors reviewed in one piece.

**NARRATIVE POETRY.** Poem that tells a story.

**NEW FORMALISM.** Contemporary literary movement to revive formal verse.

**NONSENSE VERSE.** Playful, with language and/or logic that defies ordinary understanding.

**OCTAVE.** Stanza of 8 lines.

**ODE.** A songlike, or lyric, poem; can be passionate, rhapsodic, and mystical, or a formal address to a person on a public or state occasion.

**OFFSET-PRINTED.** Printing method in which ink is transferred from an image-bearing plate to a "blanket" and then from blanket to paper.

**ONLINE MAGAZINE.** Publication circulated through the Internet or e-mail.

**P&H.** Postage & handling.

**P&P.** Postage & packing.

**PANTOUM.** Malayan poetic form of any length; consists of 4-line stanzas, with lines 2 and 4 of one quatrain repeated as lines 1 and 3 of the next; final stanza reverses lines 1 and 3 of the previous quatrain and uses them as lines 2 and 4; traditionally each stanza rhymes *abab*.

**"PAYS IN COPIES."** See *contributor's copy*.

**PDF.** Short for *Portable Document Format*, developed by Adobe Systems, that captures all elements of a printed document as an electronic image, allowing it to be sent by e-mail, viewed online, and printed in its original format.

**PERFECT-BOUND.** Publication with glued, flat spine; also called "flat-spined."

**PETRARCHAN SONNET.** Octave rhymes *abbaabba*; sestet may rhyme *cdcdcd*, *cdedce*, *ccdccd*, *cddcdd*, *edecde*, or *cddcee*.

**POD.** See *print-on-demand*.

**PRESS RUN.** The total number of copies of a publication printed at one time.

**PREVIOUSLY PUBLISHED.** Work that has appeared before in print, in any form, for public consumption.

**PRINT-ON-DEMAND.** Publishing method that allows copies of books to be published as they're requested, rather than all at once in a single press run.

**PROSE POEM.** Brief prose work with intensity, condensed language, poetic devices, and other poetic elements.

**PUBLISHING CREDITS.** A poet's magazine publications and book/chapbook titles.

**QUATRAIN.** Stanza of 4 lines.

**QUERY LETTER.** Letter written to an editor to raise interest in a proposed project.

**READING FEE.** A monetary amount charged by an editor or publisher to consider a poetry submission without any obligation to accept the work.

**REFRAIN.** A repeated line within a poem, similar to the chorus of a song.

**REGIONAL POETRY.** Work set in a particular locale, imbued with the look, feel, and culture of that place.

**RENGA.** Originally, a Japanese collaborative form in which 2 or more poets alternate writing 3 lines, then 2 lines for a set number of verses (such as 12, 18, 36, 100, and 1,000). There are specific rules for seasonal progression, placement of moon and flower verses, and other requirements. (See also *linked poetry*.)

**RENGAY.** An American collaborative 6-verse, thematic linked poetry form, with 3-line and 2-line verses in the following set pattern for 2 or 3 writers (letters represent poets, numbers indicate the lines in each verse): A3-B2-A3-B3-A2-B3 or A3-B2-C3-A2-B3-C2. All verses, unlike renga or renku, must develop at least one common theme.

**RENKU.** The modern term for renga, and a more popular version of the traditionally more aristocratic renga. (See also *linked poetry*.)

**RHYME.** Words that sound alike, especially words that end in the same sound.

**RHYTHM.** The beat and movement of language (rise and fall, repetition and variation, change of pitch, mix of syllables, melody of words).

**RICH TEXT FORMAT.** Carries the .rtf filename extension. A file format that allows an exchange of text files between different word processor operating systems with most of the formatting preserved.

**RIGHTS.** A poet's legal property interest in his/her literary work; an editor or publisher may acquire certain rights from the poet to reproduce that work.

**RONDEAU.** French form of usually 15 lines in 3 parts, rhyming *aabba aabR aabbaR* (*R* indicates a refrain repeating the first word or phrase of the opening line).

**ROW.** "Rest of world."

**ROYALTIES.** A percentage of the retail price paid to the author for each copy of a book sold.

**SADDLE-STAPLED.** A publication folded, then stapled along that fold; also called "saddle-stitched."

**SAE.** Self-addressed envelope.

**SASE.** Self-addressed, stamped envelope.

**SASP.** Self-addressed, stamped postcard.

**SENRYU.** Originally, a Japanese form, like haiku in form, but chiefly humorous, satirical, or ironic, and typically aimed at human foibles. (See also *haiku* and *zappai*.)

**SEQUENCE.** A group or progression of poems, often numbered as a series.

**SESTET.** Stanza of 6 lines.

**SESTINA.** Fixed form of 39 lines (6 unrhymed stanzas of 6 lines each, then an ending 3-line stanza), each stanza repeating the same 6 non-rhyming end-words in a different order; all 6 end-words appear in the final 3-line stanza.

**SHAKESPEAREAN SONNET.** Rhymes *abab cdcd efef gg.*

**SIJO.** Originally a Korean narrative or thematic lyric form. The first line introduces a situation or problem that is countered or developed in line 2, and concluded with a twist in line 3. Lines average 14-16 syllables in length.

**SIMILE.** Comparison that uses a linking word (*like, as, such as, how*) to clarify the similarities.

**SIMULTANEOUS SUBMISSION.** Submission of the same manuscript to more than one publisher at the same time.

**SONNET.** 14-line poem (traditionally an octave and sestet) rhymed in iambic pentameter; often presents an argument but may also present a description, story, or meditation.

**SPONDEE.** Foot consisting of 2 stressed syllables.

**STANZA.** Group of lines making up a single unit; like a paragraph in prose.

**STROPHE.** Often used to mean "stanza"; also a stanza of irregular line lengths.

**SUBSIDY PRESS.** Publisher who requires the poet to pay all costs, including typesetting, production, and printing; sometimes called a "vanity publisher."

**SURREALISTIC POETRY.** Of the artistic movement stressing the importance of dreams and the subconscious, nonrational thought, free associations, and startling imagery/juxtapositions.

**TABLOID-SIZED.** 11×15 or larger, the size of an ordinary newspaper folded and turned sideways.

**TANKA.** Originally, a Japanese form in one or 2 vertical lines with 31 sound symbols in a 5-7-5-7-7 pattern. In English, typically a 5-line lyrical poem with fewer than 31 syllables in no set syllable pattern, but exhibiting a caesura, turn, or pivot, and often more emotional and conversational than haiku.

**TERCET.** Stanza or poem of 3 lines.

**TERZA RIMA.** Series of 3-line stanzas with interwoven rhyme scheme (*aba*, *bcb*, *cdc* . . .).

**TEXT FILE.** A file containing only textual characters (i.e., no graphics or special formats).

**TROCHEE.** Foot consisting of a stress followed by an unstressed syllable.

**UNSOLICITED MANUSCRIPT.** A manuscript an editor did not ask specifically to receive.

**URL.** Stands for "Uniform Resource Locator," the address of an Internet resource (i.e., file).

**USD.** Abbreviation for United States Dollar.

**VILLANELLE.** French form of 19 lines (5 tercets and a quatrain); line 1 serves as one refrain (repeated in lines 6, 12, 18), line 3 as a second refrain (repeated in lines 9, 15, 19); traditionally, refrains rhyme with each other and with the opening line of each stanza.

**VISUAL POEM.** See *emblematic poem*.

**WAKA.** Literally, "Japanese poem," the precursor for what is now called tanka. (See also *tanka*.)

**WAR POETRY.** Poems written about warfare and military life; often written by past and current soldiers; may glorify war, recount exploits, or demonstrate the horrors of war.

**ZAPPAI.** Originally Japanese; an unliterary, often superficial witticism masquerading as haiku or senryu; formal term for joke haiku or other pseudo-haiko.

**ZEUGMA.** A figure of speech in which a single word (or, occasionally, a phrase) is related in one way to words that precede it, and in another way to words that follow it.

# SUBJECT INDEX

## BILINGUAL/FOREIGN LANGUAGE

## BUDDHISM

## CHRISTIAN

## COWBOY POETRY/AMERICAN WEST

## FORM/STYLE ASIAN

## GAY/LESBIAN/BISEXUAL/TRANSGENDERED

## POETRY BY CHILDREN

## POETRY BY TEENS

## RELIGIOUS VARIOUS

## SCIENCE FICTION

## SENIOR CITIZEN/AGING

## WOMEN VARIOUS

## WORKING CLASS ISSUES

# GENERAL INDEX